RONALD BROWNSTEIN

THE POWER AND THE GLITTER

Ronald Brownstein is a national political corre-
spondent for the *Los Angeles Times*. From 1983 to
1989 he was a correspondent for the *National
Journal*, covering national politics and the White
House and then the West Coast. Prior to that, he
served as chief staff writer for Ralph Nader. He
has contributed to *The New York Times*, *Esquire*,
New Republic, and the *Wall Street Journal*. Mr.
Brownstein lives in Los Angeles with his wife,
Nina Easton, and their son, Taylor.

THE
POWER
AND THE
GLITTER

THE
POWER
AND THE
GLITTER

THE HOLLYWOOD-WASHINGTON
CONNECTION

RONALD BROWNSTEIN

VINTAGE BOOKS
A DIVISION OF RANDOM HOUSE, INC.
NEW YORK

FIRST VINTAGE BOOKS EDITION, MAY 1992

Library of Congress Cataloging-in-Publication Data
Brownstein, Ronald.
The power and the glitter: the Hollywood-Washington connection /
Ronald Brownstein.
p. cm.
Originally published: New York: Pantheon Books, 1991.
Includes bibliographical references and index.
ISBN 0-679-73830-4 (pbk.)
1. United States—Politics and government—20th century.   2. Politics and
culture—United States—History—20th century.   3. Motion picture actors
and actresses—United States—Political activity—History—20th century.
4. Motion picture industry—Political aspects—United States—History—
20th century.
I. Title.
[E743.B773 1992]
973.9—dc20   91-50711
CIP

Manufactured in the United States of America
10 9 8 7 6 5 4 3 2 1

AS ALWAYS, FOR NINA

CONTENTS

CONTENTS

PART TWO: THE AGE OF TELEVISION

ACKNOWLEDGMENTS

Many people helped me untangle the long and complex history of the relationship between Hollywood and Washington. Chief among them were the 325 figures from the entertainment and political worlds who shared their ideas and memories in interviews. Without them, this book could not have been written.

My agent, Rafe Sagalyn, conceived the idea for this book, and then stood by me as I altered it. Several friends graciously put me up during the many weeks of research in distant locations: Bill Taylor and Chloe Mantel in Boston, Craig Unger in New York, Michael Duffy and Demetra Lambros and David Carmen in Washington. Though I'm sure I wore out my welcome long before I finished this project, none of them ever told me so.

My research assistant, Danny Feingold, was an indefatigable and valued partner in this effort. His doggedness at tracking facts and exploring leads enriched the book immeasurably. Gary Bailey researched the Orson Welles and Wendell Willkie collections at the Lilly Library in Indiana for relevant material. In my own research in various archives, I found especially helpful the staffs at the Herbert Hoover, Franklin Roosevelt, Dwight Eisenhower, John Kennedy, and Lyndon Johnson presidential libraries. Universally they were professional, informative, and helpful, the models of public service. The Wisconsin State Historical Society, which has an enormous collection of material related to leftist political activity in Hollywood, was equally responsive and thorough. Ned Comstock at USC was particularly responsive in helping me through their collections. At a crucial moment, Mark Litchman and Graham Huber stepped in to unravel a technical tangle that might have held up completion of the manuscript.

Friends also allowed me to benefit from their own work. Jeff Gerth made available crucial files; Bill Lambrecht provided valuable clips; Craig Unger shared interviews; Michael Duffy recounted events from the campaign trail that I had missed; Jim Roberts opened files; Joyce Miller spent many hours reading the manuscript to protect me from errors of syntax and construction; my editors at the *Los Angeles Times Magazine,* the *National Journal,* and the *New Republic* allowed me to explore some of these themes in their pages. Patti Zohn, Derek Shearer, Mark Green, Herbert Alexander, Mark Mellman, and others who prefer not to be named all provided valuable comments and insights on portions of the manuscript. Gary Ross proved a dependable lunch partner—and provided the title for the book. At Pantheon, Sara Bershtel saw the book through to its final stages, and then Jonathan Segal at Knopf found time in his busy schedule to take it to completion. I owe much to both of them.

My parents encouraged me throughout, and I'm sorry my father wasn't able to see the book finally completed. Last, I have to thank my wife, Nina, who not only read and edited the manuscript, provided interviews from her own reportage on the film industry, and sustained me through the difficult process of writing this book, but also gave me a good reason to finish: so I could have more time to spend with her. And now with the little guy, too.

APRIL 1990

THE

POWER

AND THE

GLITTER

INTRODUCTION:
THE CAPITAL OF GLAMOUR
AND THE CAPITAL OF POWER

On the evening of October 12, 1989, the huge downstairs foyer of the Century Plaza Hotel in Los Angeles crackled with the excitement of an exclusive Hollywood opening night. Enough wealth and fame had gathered in the hall to occupy Robin Leach for a month. Near the entrance stood Michael D. Eisner, board chairman and chief executive officer of The Walt Disney Company, who chatted with friends and fingered his garish Mickey Mouse tie; a few feet to his left, producer Norman Lear, the iconoclastic father of "All in the Family" and another of the industry's wealthiest men, bantered with an associate over the din. Just behind Lear, Frederick W. (Ted) Field, the reclusive heir to the immense Marshall Field fortune, and more recently the producer of such profitable films as *Three Men and a Baby* and *Cocktail*, huddled with his assistant Robert L. Burkett, shoulders tight against the invasive crush.

Not far from Eisner, Lear, and Field, director Sydney Pollack (*Tootsie, Out of Africa*) shared anecdotes with Jack Valenti, the diminutive and voluble president of the Motion Picture Association of America. Creative Artists Agency president Michael Ovitz, a talent agent generally considered Hollywood's most powerful man, moved through the crowd, occasionally pausing to receive studio executives and producers, some of whom seemed almost startled to see him in the flesh. Music mogul Irving Azoff, at the time a senior executive at the entertainment conglomerate MCA, Inc., swaggered by with rock star Don Henley. Jeffrey Katzenberg, chairman of The Walt Disney Studios, greeted acquaintances. Sally Field and Goldie Hawn descended the escalator and were immediately surrounded by a small battalion of paparazzi, the uninvited emblems of all A-list movie industry parties.

Only this was not a typical movie industry party. The crowd had not gathered to dispense an award, honor a distinguished achievement, or premiere a hotly awaited new film: it had assembled instead to mark the opening of the 1992 presidential season in Hollywood.

Officially, proceeds from the $1,000 per person dinner were slated for the 1990 reelection campaign of New Jersey Democratic Senator Bill Bradley. But no one at the Century Plaza doubted that this was the first opportunity for the Hollywood elite, California Democratic office-holders, and powers from the Los Angeles business establishment to assess whether the former basketball star had the right stuff for the nation's top job.

Expectations were high—but so, among Bradley's supporters, were anxieties. Though he can be bright and witty in private, the senator's public appearances more often generate adjectives such as "stiff" and "plodding." Hollywood likes flash; throughout his Senate career, Bradley had appeared allergic to it. He had a certain star quality because of his former career as a professional basketball player, but behind a podium he was often as charismatic as old sweatsocks. After Bradley spoke at a smaller fundraiser organized by Michael Eisner in early 1987, the immediate consensus on the Hollywood grapevine was that he had bombed.

It might be more common to think of Hollywood passing judgment on aspiring starlets than on aspiring presidents, but there was nothing unusual about Bradley's visit. Strange as it might seem, the pilgrimage to Hollywood, a community more typically known for the manufacture of fantasy than the shaping of political reality, has become a standard feature of electoral life in virtually every state in the union. On almost any evening you can find a high-ranking politician from outside California in living rooms and corporate offices on the Westside of Los Angeles, wooing Hollywood powers such as Field and Lear and Eisner. In just the forty-eight hours before Bradley arrived, half a dozen other senators had been in Los Angeles, moving purposefully through the beautiful homes on the city's affluent Westside like so many well-dressed locusts.

Most of them come primarily for the same reason Bill Bradley did on this night: money. But they are also drawn by other needs—a desire to recruit stars for campaign appearances, or sometimes merely to share the intoxicating company of the famous and the beautiful, the way John F. Kennedy once did. For all these reasons, and others, few roads in American politics are as well traveled as the one that leads from Washington to Hollywood, from the capital of power to the capital of glamour.

Bradley, for example, has been traveling that road since his first Senate campaign in 1978. Like most Democrats (and many Republicans) with national ambitions, once Bradley arrived in Washington he also learned his way around Hollywood. During that first Senate campaign, he made friends with Michael Eisner, then a young executive at Paramount Pictures. Eisner turned out to be an excellent friend to have. Through Eisner, who ascended to the top job at Disney and led the company's turnaround in the mid-1980s, the senator became friendly with Ovitz. Bradley now had as door-openers the two men generally considered the industry's most influential. Doors opened accordingly. Through their contacts, Bradley met executives at other studios, producers, stars. Meanwhile, the senator established an alliance with a shrewd young investment banker named William M. Wardlaw, who helped to integrate his Hollywood backers with supporters from the other business and political communities of Los Angeles. Later, Bradley developed a close relationship with Pollack, who began to work with the senator, quietly and patiently, to improve his speaking style. As the buzz around Bradley picked up, Field and his assistant Burkett—men who invest as carefully in new political stars as they do in fresh talent on the screen—sought out Bradley and hosted a small fundraiser for him at Field's palatial estate.

All these men now have a deep commitment to Bradley's cause. In a late August meeting in Ovitz's new headquarters, designed by I. M. Pei, while Bradley stood by silently, Eisner told a private meeting of the October dinner's co-chairmen—a who's who of Hollywood liberalism—that he intended to raise enough money to "send a signal to the press and the nation that will create so much pressure that Bill will have to run [for president] in 1992." In the weeks that followed, Eisner and Ovitz—executives that few in Hollywood would risk angering—reached throughout their networks of associates and acquaintances and efficiently squeezed out hundreds of thousands of dollars in contributions. For Eisner in particular, the dinner became a crusade. "As busy as he is, Eisner was calling me three times a day," said one figure in Bradley's entourage. "He does not do anything halfheartedly. He does not let anything go to chance."

Nothing at the Bradley dinner, in fact, was left to chance. Lists were prepared of the top fundraisers in the city and systematically worked by the senator's supporters. Frank Pace, a respected television producer, was brought in to supervise the program, the lighting, and the sound system. On the afternoon of the dinner, Pollack—though deep in the final preparations for his latest film—arrived at the hotel at 5 P.M. to supervise the application of the senator's makeup, and to give him some last-minute coaching for his presentation. "What God didn't give us," said one figure involved in the dinner's preparation, "we will try to compensate for as best we can."

On the evening of the dinner, few of Bradley's supporters seemed sure that would be good enough for this jaded crowd, so accustomed to being courted by the nation's most powerful men and women. While Bradley mingled amiably before the dinner, Pollack bustled as nervously as a producer at a Broadway opening night. But the results of the director's painstaking work were apparent only moments after Bradley came on the stage. Even after Pollack's help, no one would confuse Bradley with William Jennings Bryan. Still, the senator was funny, self-deprecating, and interesting—far more appealing than he had been in his last appearance before the stars. He talked about his own past and the country's future with equal ease; he even kept his composure when the spotlights failed briefly and he was left on the stage in darkness for a moment.

By the time Bradley ceded the stage to comedian Robin Williams for the evening's entertainment ("Good evening and welcome. Free Zsa Zsa!"), it was apparent that a new political star had been born. Bradley left Los Angeles on the red-eye flight back to Washington late that evening with more than $600,000 for his 1990 treasury—a record-setting haul that turned heads in political salons from coast to coast. Michael Eisner had sent up his signal.

If Bill Bradley decides to run for president in 1992, or more likely in 1996, he can expect to collect hundreds of thousands of additional dollars in Hollywood, and at least as much in the wealthy Los Angeles Jewish and business communities that combine with it to form perhaps the richest deposit of political contributors in the nation. He can expect the continued valuable coaching of Pollack. With Eisner and Ovitz making the requests, he can expect to recruit some of the industry's brightest stars to swell crowds for him in Iowa and New Hampshire and other pivotal primary states. In sum, he can expect to become the latest beneficiary of Hollywood's fascination with national elections. As Bill Bradley is learning, for many people in Hollywood, politics is the most engrossing show of all. It is, in fact, the show that never ends.

· · ·

The attraction between Hollywood and politics is often described as a recent phenomenon. Actually, politicians and movie actors have been drawn to each other for as long as there has been a Hollywood. In fact, politicians have found actors useful since antiquity. "Since Rome," wrote Leo Braudy in his encyclopedia history of fame, "politicians had gone to actors to learn oratorical technique." Napoleon, it is said, called on a celebrated actor for advice on how to make small talk. In the United States, World War I provided the first dramatic indication of the potential political value of the new stars of the screen. When Douglas Fairbanks, Charlie Chaplin, and Mary Pickford were deputized to sell war bonds, their appearances nearly generated riots. (The streets around one of their rallies in New York "were a mass of upturned faces, and apparently all who could get the necessary room to free an arm raised it aloft when they were asked to pledge themselves to buy Liberty bonds," the *New York Times* reported.) If stars could sell bonds, why not candidates? Singer Al Jolson, later to star in the first talking picture, led delegations of celebrities into the Republican presidential campaigns of Warren G. Harding in 1920 and Calvin Coolidge four years later. With the pace set by Louis B. Mayer, the guiding force at the Metro-Gold-wyn-Mayer studio, Hollywood was systematically participating in national politics by the late 1920s.

This book explores the abiding mutual fascination between the worlds of show business and politics—two of the most glamorous facets of American life. It considers the political role of other forces in the popular culture, principally popular musicians and television stars, but the main focus is on the movie industry, or what has been commonly described since the 1920s as Hollywood (though much of it was then and is now centered in New York). I set out to examine Hollywood's participation in national politics from that time on, how its role has changed over time, and how those changes illuminate deeper currents in American political life. I have not recounted the intermittent use of political themes in movies, a subject that has been covered with great enthusiasm elsewhere. Instead, I have tried to analyze how Hollywood has come off the backlot and actually joined in national politics—the film community's role in what Franklin D. Roosevelt, in a letter to Orson Welles, described as "the unrehearsed realities of the drama of the American future."

Like the auto industry or the steel industry, or any other economic community, Hollywood alone does not set the tone of our politics; its support, though avidly courted, is rarely decisive. Hollywood's participation in national elections is less important for its influence on who wins than for what it reveals about the mysterious interaction between culture and politics, and how the rise of television as the dominant form of public discourse has transformed American life since World War II.

The relationship between Hollywood and Washington has not remained static over the past seventy years. In fact, it has changed fundamentally. And if a single trend has appeared amid the complex and swirling currents that have connected the two communities over that period, it is the growing sense in Hollywood of its own political legitimacy and a corresponding belief among filmmakers that politicians no longer deserve the respect they once did.

Hollywood has manifested this increasing political assertiveness in two ways. One is through a growing sense of empowerment among Hollywood celebrities. Though stars have long regularly joined in campaigns, they were initially quite passive participants in the political process. With a few notable exceptions, the earliest activists looked at their political engagements largely as an extension of their on-screen duties. When invited to appear with a politician, they did little more than exude glamour and sign autographs; only rarely did they offer their own views on matters of state. In other words, they performed as actors in the world of politics. The idea that fame carried intrinsic power did not develop until quite recently. As late as the mid-1950s, the radical social critic C. Wright Mills, a keen student of celebrity's role in society, saw the intense focus on Hollywood stars as merely a distraction, "a dazzling blind" from the real power of the businessmen, lawyers, militarists, and government officials who shared with them the pinnacle of fame.

In the 1960s, though, as a result of changes in both the film community and the political world, particularly the rise to dominance of television in electoral campaigns, Hollywood figures became increasingly aware of the possibilities fame presented. Since then, the belief that celebrity is a weapon that can be marshaled to attract attention to a distinct political agenda has permeated Hollywood. Stars today are more visible participants in American politics than ever before. This evolving attitude toward the political value of fame, and its implications for the conduct of public debate, is a major theme of this book.

At one level, the growing political aggressiveness of celebrities is a barometer of the extent to which politicians—battered by public disillusion over the Vietnam War, Watergate, and a host of successor scandals—have lost credibility in the past few decades. But celebrities have become far more willing to take public positions not only because politicians seem more fallible, but also because in the era of photo opportunities, sound bites, and manipulative thirty-second campaign commercials, the work of the modern politician does not appear to be very different from that of the actor. "No one politician is trained to make the thousands of decisions politicians are called on to make," said actor Ron Silver, president of a New York organization of politically active celebrities called The Creative Coalition. "When you watch two congressmen debating the nuclear freeze [on television], they are going to be in the same position as Charlton Heston or Richard Dreyfuss or anyone else. The question is not who is going to be more expert, or who has more information, the question is going to be which one is more effective communicating, emotionally."

Such a statement from a Hollywood star, even a politically well-versed one such as Silver, would have been unimaginable thirty years ago. But as television has compelled politicians to behave more like actors—a trend most dramatically symbolized, of course, by Ronald Reagan—actors such as Jane Fonda, Paul Newman, and Charlton Heston have responded by trying to arrogate more of the politician's role: mobilizing constituencies, bringing issues to public attention, and challenging entrenched authority. The intensifying political assertiveness of Hollywood stars—like the rise of Reagan—is a dramatic indication of how the demands of television are blurring the lines between entertainment and politics in what author Neil Postman has called "The Age of Show Business" in our public life. These changes are also followed throughout the book.

If not as dramatically expressed, the increasing sense of empowerment among the Hollywood fundraisers has been no less profound. Like the rise of the Hollywood political activist, this sense of growing power is equally revealing of a disturbing undercurrent in American politics. Through most of the past two decades, money has dominated Hollywood's political participation; just as the representative Hollywood political organizations of the 1930s reflected their times by stressing public outreach and organizing, the signature film industry political group of the 1980s, the Hollywood Women's Political Committee, initially focused all its efforts on fundraising. Hollywood's focus shifted so dramatically to raising money because the rising costs of campaigns have forced politicians to devote an inordinate share of their time to collecting checks, largely to buy television advertisements. The need for money has required politicians—particularly those seeking the presidency—to cultivate the wealthiest members of many communities. At first the attention flattered the moviemakers. But there's no question that over time this obsessive quest for money, in Hollywood at least, has diminished the stature of elected officials.

These changes have dramatically shifted the emotional balance of power between Hollywood and Washington. From the start, each community has been drawn to the other as much from desire as need. Historically, their shared attraction could be reduced to a simple equation: Celebrities looked to politicians to validate them as part of the company of serious men and women; politicians looked to celebrities to validate them as part of the company of the famous. That summary still explains much of the relationship. The association with celebrities certifies politicians as part of what might be called the jet stream—the exclusive and ephemeral community of fame that convenes atop American life, where the most celebrated figures of our society mingle with exaggerated intimacy. As many social critics have observed, fame has supplanted breeding as the ticket into the American aristocracy; our peerage is defined every month on the cover of *Vanity Fair* and *Rolling Stone* and *People.* Washington may have the patent on power, but it is in Hollywood where fame burns most brightly. (Someone once observed that in the capital the most prominent citizens are known by their last name—Bush, Dole, Darman, Baker—while in Hollywood many of the elite require only a first name to be recognized: Warren, Jane, Sly, Arnold, Cher.) Acceptance in Hollywood offers politicians the psychic gratification of being anointed into the fraternity of the famous. Not all politicians share this fascination—Lyndon Johnson, for one, had no interest in celebrities—but enough do to give the relations between the two communities an extraordinary *frisson.*

In Hollywood, the psychological attractions of politics begin with the quest for respect. It seems, paradoxically, to intensify with increased success. Living in a world of fantasy, paid extravagantly, and typically unsure exactly why they have been chosen above all other contenders for such fabulous rewards, movie stars often feel bewildered by and unworthy of the enormous reverence they generate. In no other profession are the most successful practitioners as likely to be quoted belittling the enterprise that has enriched them. "I think a lot of actors feel of their profession that it is a shallow profession, that it is insubstantial," said Robert Redford. "We get paid so much money for just being personalities. Other people are out there digging trenches and working in dangerous jobs . . . that guilt produces some desire for credibility, so they go into campaigns."

The desire for credibility motivates serious and frivolous Hollywood figures alike. It is not surprising that stars known for playing the most vapid roles on screen—Rob Lowe and Morgan Fairchild come to mind— try to demonstrate that undiscovered depths lie beneath an insipid surface by associating with a solemn political or social cause. But the attractions of politics are often just as great for those actors (as well as producers, writers, and directors) who manage to express their beliefs through their work. Though films can deliver serious social commentary, some of the most successful stars speak of feeling intellectually unsatisfied by them; many believe that portraying social ills is not a sufficient response to the problems that concern them. "There's something in the structure of the actor that seems to need to hang on to childhood and there's something in the structure of the actor that requires enormous intelligence," said Warren Beatty, who has written, directed, and produced movies, yet is still drawn to political campaigns as a means of expressing his beliefs. "So you have, in this what I've come to realize is a very noble profession of acting, people who are very intelligent and need at times to express it, and to deal with society seriously. And that's what politics is . . ."

For some Hollywood figures, politics provides only another stage on which to exercise their ego, but in general that seems less a motivating force than this search for validation and the desire among many stars to control their own celebrity. That urge is the final psychological attraction of politics. Much as they crave the attention, stars commonly detest the prosaic demands of fame—interviews with nosy reporters, hordes of paparazzi shadowing them, televised reports on their private lives. Politics affords them the rare chance to use their fame for their own purposes. For some celebrities, that purpose seems to be advancing their careers by keeping their names before the public in a positive light. But in fact politics attracts many stars who have no such need (Meryl Streep and Robert Redford, for example), or who can expect no such benefit (such as some of the young artists who quietly speak about drugs or AIDS before college and high school students). For them—for the majority of socially conscious celebrities—one of the greatest attractions of political activism is the opportunity to shift the blinding and dehumanizing glare of celebrity that follows them onto a worthy cause that might otherwise remain obscure. Susan Sarandon spoke for many when she told one interviewer: "If my privacy is going to be invaded and I'm going to be treated as a commodity, I might as well take advantage of it."

Sarandon's attitude suggests how the growing confidence of the Hollywood political activists has complicated the basic social dynamic between the film community and Washington. Once, the Hollywood elite treated politicians the way everyone else treated the Hollywood elite: as unapproachable, larger-than-life figures. No longer. Today, stars commonly believe their fame and their relationship with their fans gives them as legitimate a role in the public arena as the image-obsessed politicians who compete with them for airtime on the evening news. Similarly, Hollywood executives who raise political funds now seem to earn social status not by demonstrating how friendly they are with politicians but by showing how tough they can be on them. Though both changes reflect the excess of ego in Hollywood, they also offer an important gauge of the diminished stature of politicians in our society.

Practical campaign help and mutual social envy explain much of the attraction between Washington and Hollywood, but not all of it. Somewhere between the hard tangible assistance and the intangible psychic rewards of associating with Hollywood lie the symbolic and cultural connotations of its embrace, and their political implications. This is ground that neither political party has fully explored; but for politicians, associating with celebrities is, consciously or not, part of a search for legitimacy at the most fundamental level.

Establishing such legitimacy is arguably the most delicate task politicians in democratic societies face. In monarchies, the legitimacy of government derives from Heaven or tradition; in dictatorships, power makes the very question moot. But in democratic societies the social basis of governmental authority is constantly shifting, and must be constantly reaffirmed. Democratic leaders are never free of the need to legitimize their rule by grounding themselves in the traditions of their nation.

This has been particularly challenging in the United States, a nation too young to have the unifying traditions of the Old World, and too demographically heterogeneous for the kind of shared cultural experience common to the compact states of Europe. In his 1941 book, *The Hero in America,* Dixon Wecter noted that the vastness of the American continent, too massive to be easily comprehended by any one citizen, created a pressing need for "collective symbols" that "nourish our sense of national continuity." The Founding Fathers were acutely aware of the need to create such symbols, and they did, not only through inanimate artifacts like the Declaration of Independence but through individuals—celebrities, as it were. John Adams noted in a letter to a friend in the early nineteenth century that the revolutionaries had purposefully sought to create in George Washington a symbol of national unity, "a center of union . . . the central stone in the geometrical arch." Distant, stiff, but dignified, Washington perfectly fulfilled that symbolic role. He may not have been the nation's finest president, Adams concluded years later, but "he was the best actor of presidency we have ever had."

Since those days, politicians have tried to bind themselves first to the tradition of the hallowed Founding Fathers, but also to other sources of legitimacy that subsequently evolved. Their task has become more difficult as the most useful source of political tradition and legitimacy that emerged in America—the political parties—has grown less relevant to voters. The causes for the decline of the parties are diverse—rising levels of education, suburbanization, and above all television—but the effect is singular. Once most voters needed to know only what party a candidate belonged to; now, office-seekers have to provide much more information to establish personal credibility and win votes. Though politicians still try to provide voters with an easily accessible summation of their own beliefs by joining with the glorious litany of fallen party heroes ("I stand proudly in the party of Roosevelt and Truman and Kennedy"), they look primarily to other sources to reveal themselves.

Increasingly those sources are cultural. That is not entirely surprising: our shared cultural experiences, particularly those derived from popular culture, are one of the few forms of common currency in this defiantly diverse country. One way that politicians try to establish their identity today is by giving voters a sense of where they stand on the spectrum of cultural values. At the grandest level this involves reverential salutes to the cultural symbols that virtually all Americans cherish: neighborhood, work, and family, for example, which Reagan wielded like symbolic swords during his 1980 nomination acceptance speech. At the more mundane level this process of cultural identification might prompt the president to call the winner of the World Series or the Super Bowl, hoping to share in their aura of success, and also to establish that he is part of the society thrilling to the game, not of the insular minority pondering the latest maneuvers in Congress.

For politicians, Hollywood can be a useful supporting player in this process of establishing legitimacy through association with cultural icons. For as long as there has been a Hollywood, every president has demonstrated that he is aware of it and that it is aware of him, that the celebrated figures of the stage and screen, admired by millions, admire him. It has long been apparent to many elected officials that stars can create deeper emotional bonds with the public than they can. Francis X. Bushman, one of the first silent screen stars, once told an interviewer of riding to Boston for a benefit in a train with Mary Pickford, only to discover that President William Howard Taft was also on board. Taft called Bushman to his seat, and the most powerful man in the United States told the actor that he "envied" him. "He'd watched the demonstration at the station—Mary had had her clothes almost torn off her," Bushman recalled years later, "and I looked like the wrath of God." To the actor, the president said mournfully: "All the people love you and I can't have even the love of half the people."

Taft's lament captured an anomaly that persists to this day: few, if any, politicians generate as much excitement and worship as our most popular entertainers. That does not mean that endorsements from music and screen celebrities can translate directly into large numbers of votes. (There's little evidence that endorsements of any sort, whether from politicians or clergy or stars, can do that.) It does mean that appearances with celebrated figures from the popular culture, in addition to simply attracting attention, can help politicians establish credibility (by signaling that an important segment of the society takes them seriously), and provide voters with shorthand information about their values and preferences. In some cases, stars can become symbols of a candidate's own cultural identity. The televised shots of Ronald Reagan listening to Tammy Wynette at a Florida stock car race on the Fourth of July in 1984 probably told many Southern voters all they needed to know: This man is one of us. Nothing perhaps better illustrated the extent to which Hollywood figures can become icons of transcending cultural power, with real political resonance, than the fact that the Polish union Solidarity, in the last days of its historic 1989 legislative elections, unveiled as its final campaign poster the image of Gary Cooper, as a grimly resolute sheriff, one journalist wrote, "striding toward the viewer, the union's red logo emblazoned on the horizon behind him, a simple caption underneath— 'High Noon.' " All the attributes Cooper symbolized reinforced the powerful message: Solidarity was tough, incorruptible, and coming to dispense justice.

If Hollywood can produce political symbols powerful enough to surmount language and borders, its potential for creating such symbols at home can only be greater. And in fact, in the 1990s both Washington and Hollywood seem increasingly interested in harnessing for political purpose the images generated by our most celebrated figures from the popular culture. Just like the Polish unionists, American political operatives have come to realize that many stars embody desirable attributes—from courage to intelligence—in the popular mind, and that politicians may be able to associate themselves with those qualities by standing with the stars. The 1984 presidential race, when both President Reagan and his Democratic challenger, Walter F. Mondale, sought to legitimize themselves to young people by claiming the affections of rock singer Bruce Springsteen, may be a harbinger of cultural politics to come.

Hollywood's symbolic role in our national life affects politics in one final respect. Hollywood's greatest creation is itself: it has projected a myth of the good life, and of what it means to be famous—primarily that it means to live without the rules of fidelity, responsibility, and sobriety that constrain all other lives. That myth has dazzled generations of politicians, who come to Hollywood not only because they need to but because they are drawn by that vision of the rewards of life among the famous. Two politicians in particular have symbolized this fascination. John F. Kennedy, learning the myth at the knee of his father, Joseph P. Kennedy—who came home from a sojourn in Hollywood with Tom Mix's riding chaps for his sons and Gloria Swanson for himself—was mesmerized by that light; so was another Democratic presidential candidate, who saw himself as a latter-day Kennedy, Gary Hart. Through their experiences, I examine the hold on politicians exercised by the myth of Hollywood, and the danger facing those who succumb to it.

Despite the risks to politicians who become blinded by the glitter, the capital of power and the capital of glamour are inextricably bound. Politicians will always come to Hollywood looking for money. They will always come to the stars looking for help in attracting attention. And many will come just to find out exactly what goes on in those glittering homes high above Los Angeles. As long as Hollywood is part of our cultural life, it will be part of our political life, too.

But its role will undoubtedly continue to evolve. This story begins in the age of the moguls, when Hollywood craved the company of politicians, and concludes in the flickering age of television, when politicians are just one more supplicant pressed up against the Hollywood glass.

PART ONE

THE AGE
OF THE MOGULS

CHAPTER ONE

MAYER, HOOVER, AND HEARST

The Proud Pigeon

One day late in January 1929, Ida R. Koverman, the redoubtable secretary of the Republican County Central Committee of Los Angeles, dispatched to Lawrence Richey, a top aide to newly elected President Herbert Hoover, a plea for rewards for some of her best workers in the campaign just ended. Koverman wanted what loyal party workers everywhere in the country wanted: a chance for the local powers to mingle with the president-to-be in the bright glow of triumph. From all sides Richey faced requests for a moment in the sun for the legions of starched, sober businessmen and burghers who had been the backbone of Hoover's tight-lipped crusade. Koverman's appeal carried more weight than most, for she was more than just a distant local functionary; she was an old friend. Koverman had served as engineer Hoover's private secretary a decade earlier. During the 1920s, when he was off in Washington serving as secretary of commerce, she had been his chief political operative in his home state of California. The amiable familiarity of her letter didn't mask the clear expectation that her requests would be answered.

She needed help in tending to two large egos. The first belonged to Mark L. Requa, an oilman with a long pedigree in California politics. At sixty-three, Requa was now "a gentleman of leisure," Koverman wrote, but "a very nervous individual who is unhappy unless he is extremely busy." Surely Richey could come up with something to occupy him—say, an invitation to the inauguration? The second ego belonged to a new power in local Republican politics, Louis B. Mayer, the vice-president and general manager of the Metro-Goldwyn-Mayer studio. If Requa was winding down, Mayer, like his entire industry, was revving up. In the first two decades of the century, the movie business had been little more than a loose group of questionable characters. But after World War I, the industry relentlessly consolidated. Producers moved into distribution and exhibition to ensure outlets for their films; the major distributors expanded into production to ensure a steady supply of product. The firms grew larger, more stable, and more powerful as America grew more fascinated with movies.

In 1927 Warner Brothers Pictures, Inc., married a sound track to a moving picture, and millions of enthralled Americans heard Al Jolson, on bended knee, singing to his beloved "Mammy." Night after night, families came back for more, transforming Hollywood, and then the entire culture. With the addition of sound, the movie industry had invented a mass entertainment of unparalleled impact. From 1926 through 1930, average weekly attendance rose 45 percent, to 90 million. In just three years, from 1927 through 1930, the industry's total assets more than tripled to $1 billion. Wall Street soon gave it the imprimatur of respectability: Kuhn Loeb & Company allied with Paramount, Lehman Brothers with Loew's Inc., Goldman Sachs & Company with Warner Bros. In this period of breakneck expansion, the studios became huge enterprises whose interests stretched beyond Hollywood to communities in virtually every state. By 1931, five studios alone were aligned with almost 2,400 theaters. The chaotic, slapdash Hollywood of the early years had become a tight core of eight powerful studios, fortified financially by the Eastern investment banks and often allied with huge theater chains.

Less than a decade earlier, the uneducated, avaricious bullies controlling the Hollywood studios had been scorned as vulgar hucksters—despoilers of morals, purveyors of temptation. Now they stood at the pinnacle of American popular culture. Across America, people would learn manner and manners from Hollywood; they would draw their vision of the good life from the screen, and provide a very good life for the men who portrayed it there. Mayer—feisty, self-assured, enormously susceptible to flattery, given to fits of great rage and seizures of droopy bathos—intended to be at the top of the pantheon, recognized not only as the most commanding force in Hollywood, but as a legitimate member of the company of powerful men everywhere.

This Koverman understood. "Re: Louis B. Mayer," she wrote to Lawrence Richey. "Do you remember our talk about making a gesture? Why could we not include a trip to Florida [where Hoover was vacationing] for a couple of days? This is another small boy—new at the game and used to a great deal of attention. I know he would strut around like a proud pigeon."

In 1929 Mayer was new to the game of politics, but an old hand at the young business of filmmaking. He had clawed his way up every step to the lavish executive suite at MGM, a climb as demanding as the reward was exhilarating.

Mayer grew up in the small Canadian town of St. John, New Brunswick, where his family settled after emigrating from a hard Russian life late in the 1880s. In Russia, his father had been a laborer; in the New World he became a junk dealer. Young Louis was conscripted into the business. Stern and severe, his father, wrote one biographer, "sent him across Canada to bid at auctions on salvage, while his mother wept, fearing for his safety." His father drove himself as hard as he did his son, but the family was still left with a life whose boundaries were poverty, grinding work, tradition, and anti-Semitism.

Even as a young man, Mayer yearned for more. Not only materially: more fierce, perhaps, than Mayer's urge to escape poverty was his desire to escape the cultural isolation of the immigrant. That urge ultimately shaped both his aesthetic and his political vision, for in the building of MGM and the courting of politicians such as Hoover, Mayer craved nothing more fervently than acceptance as a full citizen, a genuine American. When Mayer had to declare the date of his birth (no records from Russia being available), he chose as the date the fourth of July.

The choice was symbolic of both his bombastic patriotism and his outsized ambition. Mayer realized early that St. John was no place to satisfy either. He moved to Boston in 1904 to get away from his family and launch his own junk business. Not finding much luck at that, he began his movie career in the fall of 1907 by renting in the gritty blue-collar shoe town of Haverhill, Massachusetts, an old burlesque house which he transformed into a "motion picture theater."

The drive that would take Mayer to the top of Hollywood first became apparent in Haverhill. When he acquired the burlesque house, it was dilapidated. Mayer remodeled it physically and cleaned it up socially, too:

to mark the change from old management to new, the first show he sponsored in the new theater was a religious one, *From the Manger to the Cross*. As one early biographer of Mayer put it, "The best people of the town soon decided that Louis Mayer was an influence for good, and patronized his theater."

By 1911, the first theater had proved profitable enough for him to open a second. Perhaps because of his experience with junk, Mayer had a knack for picking winners among the crude early silent films. From theater ownership he moved into distribution, providing films to theater owners across New England; from there he branched into production as part of Metro Pictures Corp., which opened in January 1915 as a cooperative effort by a group of distributors to ensure more product by financing small producers.

As a young man in a hurry, Mayer was dissatisfied with Metro's pace. While still part of the firm, he repeatedly made side deals to produce and distribute films. He secured the New England rights to D. W. Griffith's *The Birth of a Nation* and made his first fortune. Eventually, Mayer withdrew from the partnership entirely. Luring away popular star Anita Stewart from the Vitagraph Company, he established his own production operation in California. Mayer was through with distribution; he was now a producer.

This was not necessarily a step up. In its formative years, the movie production business had no rules, no roots, and no traditions except larceny. The Los Angeles that welcomed Louis Mayer was a dusty outpost without notable architecture, culture, restaurants, shops or even, in many cases, paved roads. Where bright lights later glittered, orange and lemon trees still grew wild. Coyotes howled. And they provided one of the few diversions. In the first two decades of the century, Los Angeles was dominated by retirees who poured in to escape the harsh Midwest winters. Their smalltown pieties enveloped the city like one of its early summer fogs. Los Angeles boasted of its churches and suppressed saloons, debated the proper length of bathing suits, and shut down at midnight. Just a few years before Mayer arrived, one visitor wrote: "Los Angeles is overrun with militant moralists, connoisseurs of sin, experts of biological purity."

But the area was already emerging as the center of the film business. Los Angeles offered warm weather, diverse surroundings, a civic environment hostile to unions—and, not incidentally, an enormous distance from the attorneys enforcing Thomas Edison's patents on the essential tools of movie-making. Production companies set up on the streets and raced through Westerns, romances, slapstick comedies, morality plays.

They stole one another's stars and schemed to ruin one another's fortunes.

In the bare-knuckled competition, Mayer proved as tough and able as any. From rented production facilities in distant southeast Los Angeles, far from the emerging film center of Hollywood, he turned out more Anita Stewart sagas, and when she could no longer stomach his insistent ways and demanding schedules, he turned to quality directors to assemble "quality films." Still a minor operator, scraping along like many other small producers, he made the move that made his future in February 1923. Mayer lured away Irving G. Thalberg, the precocious young general manager of Universal Film Manufacturing Corp., from "Uncle" Carl Laemmle, who had built the studio and employed Thalberg as his secretary. Just twenty-three, Thalberg became Mayer's vice-president and production assistant with a salary of $600 a week. It was a figure that would soon grow exponentially.

So would Mayer's horizons. His prosperity came from an unlikely source. Metro, the company he abandoned, was subsequently acquired by Loew's, the huge theater chain. Dissatisfied with its operation, Marcus Loew merged it with the equally struggling Goldwyn Company in 1924. (The Goldwyn Company's biggest problem may have been that it lacked any Goldwyns; Samuel Goldwyn, the company's founder, had been forced out in 1922.) Loew didn't think much of either firm's management and sought out Mayer and Thalberg, whom he had met on a trip to Hollywood late the previous year, to assume control of the new studio. Mayer signed on April 10, 1924. He took the title of vice-president and general manager; Thalberg was director of production. Together with attorney J. Robert Rubin, a long-time Mayer associate who operated as liaison to the Loew's management in New York, they made up the so-called Mayer group.

When the new studio opened in nearby Culver City a little over two weeks later, the combination of three minor operators didn't excite much interest in the industry. But Mayer approached the occasion as the major event film historians would later consider it. He assembled a brace of civic and military dignitaries; had flowers dropped from the heavens by a formation of airplanes under the command of Lieutenant C. C. Moseley, and procured telegrams from President Calvin Coolidge and Commerce Secretary Herbert Hoover. In a dignified three-piece suit, behind proper wire spectacles, Mayer beamed like a man who had climbed a very large mountain.

In fact, he had. And he was not alone. The film business, which would become the most glamorous of all, attracted at first only the immigrant and the bounder. Samuel Goldwyn had been a glove salesman. Nicholas M. Schenck, the president of Loew's (and Mayer's nemesis through a long and splenetic association), and his smoother brother Joseph M. Schenck, one of the founders of Twentieth Century-Fox Film Corp., were drugstore owners and later amusement park operators; Eddie Mannix, who became a top Mayer lieutenant, was a bouncer at the Schencks' Palisades Amusement Park in New Jersey. Marcus Loew and Adolph Zukor began as furriers; the Warner brothers, Jack and Harry M. in particular, were butcher's sons. Darryl F. Zanuck, who joined Schenck in launching Twentieth Century, had grown up in Wahoo, Nebraska, and first made his name in Hollywood by writing Rin Tin Tin movies for the Warner brothers. Harry Cohn of Columbia, the son of a tailor, dropped out of school at fourteen. These men were not well educated and they frequently mangled the English language (Goldwyn most famously), but they possessed an elemental instinct that enabled them to grow very rich.

The moguls swaggered through their domains with paternalistic pride, incessantly accumulating: limousines, houses on the beach, money, and an endless parade of pliant young actresses to ease the days. What they didn't have was respectability. It was an itch all their starlets couldn't scratch. "The remarkable point is that Hollywood's elite has no respect for itself," wrote one contemporary. "The businessmen of Hollywood—partly because of their personalities, partly because of their own shortsightedness, more through the snobbery of Los Angeles—are largely ignored in the business-politics of their community. . . . The movie paladins revere, and surely overvalue, the old, the traditional, the accepted. They have no real sense of their own importance; they have no real confidence in their own right to respect. Their hunger for social recognition is pathetic."

Mayer felt this hunger as acutely as any, though he soon outstripped all his rivals in Hollywood. Over time, Mayer's business sense and Thalberg's legendary knack for shaping pictures built MGM into the grandest of the Hollywood studios. The studio chose as its slogan "More stars than there are in heaven," and as Hollywood hyperbole goes, it was accurate enough. Its stable included Clark Gable, Judy Garland, Jean Harlow, Joan Crawford, Greta Garbo, Greer Garson and William Powell. It numbered among its writers William Faulkner, Ben Hecht, F. Scott Fitzgerald, Moss Hart, Anita Loos, Robert Benchley, and Herman Mankiewicz. It turned out lavish spectacles—*Ben Hur, Grand Hotel, Mutiny on the Bounty, The Good Earth*—and towered over Hollywood, immense and serene.

Mayer had a firm hold on the helm. True, Schenck was his superior, and an almost constant irritant. But he was in New York. In Culver City,

Mayer held court behind an intimidating semicircle of desks in a huge, ultramodern office designed by his art director, Cedric Gibbons. Gibbons also designed for Mayer a fabulous twenty-room Spanish-style home on the beach in distant Santa Monica; like Mayer himself, the home suggested both success and solidity, its onyx and marble baths balanced by heavy stucco walls and dark wooden floors. The studio itself was no less magnificent. MGM as it grew was sleek, clean, modern, with a massive white administration building (named for Thalberg) and glimmering white sound stages.

Mayer ruled this domain with indomitable energy. Physically, he was short and stocky, overweight but in a way that suggested not excess but power. He dressed stylishly and groomed himself immaculately; meeting him for the first time, producer Dore Schary, who would later succeed Mayer at MGM, remembered his "well-manicured" fingers. And yet the smoothness was only veneer. Crossed, Mayer was fierce. Even in a three-piece suit, he occasionally used his fists when words appeared insufficient to settle disagreements. His language would have fit comfortably in any shipyard. Schary once watched Mayer dress down an employee so fiercely that when the bombardment had ended Schary, a more sensitive type, stumbled from the room and promptly threw up. "Mayer was a very strong personality," said Doris B. (DoDo) Meyer, the daughter of Universal Studios president Nathan Blumberg, who later grew friendly with Mayer, "and when he spoke people listened, whether they agreed with him or not."

Mayer was imperious, pompous, sensitive about his position—and a ham. After the merger that formed MGM, he took off on a nationwide sales tour, where he "rode on fire engines, visited orphan asylums, shook hands with mayors, and performed any other stunt which would bring headlines," as one contemporary account put it. He took his public appearances seriously, often having writers touch up his remarks; he even took lessons in speaking from actor Conrad Nagel. Mayer became so gifted in his delivery that some on the studio lot suggested that the initials L.B. should stand for Lionel Barrymore. As easily as he pounded the table, he could also summon up tears in negotiations with employees. After he won salary concessions with a misty-eyed performance before a mass meeting of MGM employees during the darkest days of the Depression, one agent who happened on the bizarre scene suggested that Mayer be given the Academy Award "for the best acting of 1933."

Yet there was more than calculation and artifice in Mayer's histrionics, for Mayer genuinely seemed to need to be not only respected, not only feared, but loved, as the stern but wise father is ultimately loved by his children. He paid his employees well, gave them room to work, nurtured their careers, and expected in return loyalty and deference to his counsel.

The lavish office, the luxurious salary, the respect and fear of stars and writers and directors alike all testified to Mayer's position at the pinnacle of Hollywood. And still he wanted more. "He was happy with his arena, he was very prideful of the fact that MGM was number one, that he was the godfather in Hollywood," said Doris Meyer. "He perceived himself as number one in his business and he wanted to be with the number one's of every business. He thought of himself as a world leader, as someone who could talk with the people who made the decisions and tell them how he thought it should be done." When such notables as Winston Churchill or H. G. Wells passed through the film capital, it was typically Mayer who hosted the star-studded luncheons honoring them. Mayer saw in the company of such men a way to distinguish himself from his industry, with its reputation for loose morals and superficial pursuits. Except when absolutely necessary, he minimized his social contacts with other filmmakers; he preferred to court the powerful, the established, the respectable.

It was this nagging urge for status, more than a clearly defined political agenda, that first attracted Mayer and the other moguls to politics. Most of the moguls lacked abiding political convictions of any sort: "They were totally uneducated politically. They knew nothing about how government was run. And they had no real foundation in civics. They reacted purely instinctively to what was going on," said screenwriter and producer Milton Sperling, who worked closely with Zanuck at Twentieth Century and grew to know the rest of the moguls when he married Harry Warner's daughter Betty. It would not be uncommon for a movie executive who hated everything about the New Deal to proudly display a signed photograph of Franklin Roosevelt in his office, or, like Mayer, nonetheless angle for invitations to the White House when he was in Washington.

Generally, the moguls had only the foundations of a political ideology. As entrepreneurs who had scrambled up the hard way, their vague political views were anchored in an apostolic belief in hard work, bootstraps, and the American dream; practically, that translated into the right of those who had scrambled so fiercely to keep what they earned without much government intrusion. Mayer shared all these beliefs, but the forces that shaped his political outlook went deeper. He was the most ideological of the moguls, not because he had any more appetite for theory, but because he had the clearest vision of the nation he thought America ought to be. Mayer was a natural conservative; he believed passionately in the sanctity of order—order in families, order in society. "I worship good women, honorable men, and saintly mothers," he told one MGM writer. He brooked nothing that suggested disrespect for tradition; once when the actor John Gilbert made a disparaging comment about his own mother, Mayer was so offended that he punched him, on principle. He resented his father for his harsh, authoritarian ways, but in his own household he expected to rule without dissent. At home, to his two daughters, Irene and Edith, "Mayer was smothering," wrote Neal Gabler in his history of the Jews who founded Hollywood, "an absolute, un-brookable, strident authority." Even into their twenties, he did not allow his daughters to date without a chaperone. "Mayer," said one of his producers years later, "was a Puritan."

It was ironic that such a man stood atop an industry that would grow into one of the most ruthless enemies of tradition ever unleashed. In time, films helped to shatter local tradition by obliterating the barriers of isolation that sustained them. By showing young people in Indiana and Alabama and Missouri that life could be different elsewhere, the movies made them less willing to accept the life their parents had known. It's unlikely Mayer ever thought about his product in exactly those terms, but if he did the implications would have horrified him, for he recoiled from films that challenged traditional social mores, let alone political convention. (Walter Wanger, a liberal young producer, learned that when he completed *Gabriel over the White House,* an adaptation of a popular British novel that told the story of a carefree American president who has a brush with death and then launches a crusade to lead the country out of the Depression. Mayer considered the movie an insult to Herbert Hoover and tried to prevent its release; ironically, Franklin Roosevelt had concerns about the movie too. Eventually, Wanger mollified both Mayer and the president, and released the film to modest success in 1933.)

With the passion of the outsider, Mayer embraced the values of his adopted land more unreservedly than almost any native. He was, in his own way, an evangelist: he prized above all films that made money, but he believed the studios had a responsibility to use the screen to teach respect for family, patriotism, clean living, smalltown solidarity. Perhaps the MGM films that most reflected his vision of America were the saccharine chronicles of Andy Hardy, the "all-American teen-ager living in an all-American town."

Like the other moguls, though, Mayer could never escape the reminders that many Americans had no room for him in their vision of America. As a Jew, Mayer was barred from the best country clubs and business groups in Los Angeles. The doors to the best private schools were closed to his children. Faced with these silent but impervious barriers, Mayer reacted, not with the bluster he displayed in the studio, but with the religious faith in secular assimilation that had driven him since his youth. In this he was typical of those who founded the great studios. Almost without exception, they downplayed their Jewishness, taking great pains to avoid seeming pushy. "It was more than trying to assimilate," said Sperling. "They were afraid. [Their attitude was] just hide. . . . They knew that this country didn't like Jews. . . . They knew the pendulum could swing very easily in this country." And they knew that even with all the wealth, all the glamour at their command, there remained before them a very long climb to acceptance as part of the American elite.

Contributing to worthy local causes was one way to make that climb. Politics was another. Hollywood's interest in politics predated Mayer's; the film world and the political world had rubbed shoulders since the days of silent movies. In February 1915, *The Birth of a Nation* was screened at the White House—apparently the first film shown there. President Woodrow Wilson agreed to see the movie at the request of an old college chum, author Thomas Dixon, Jr., who had written the novel *(The Clansman)* on which Griffith's classic was based. Dixon thought presidential approval might help the film fend off the attacks it instantly faced from black organizations outraged by its positive portrayal of the Ku Klux Klan. Wilson gave him what he wanted—"It is like writing history with lightning. And my only regret is that it is all so terribly true"—but eventually so much outrage surrounded the film that the president's aides issued a statement improbably insisting that Wilson had never endorsed it.

Despite that rocky start, politicians and entertainers continued to find each other useful. Though screen stars Douglas Fairbanks, Mary Pickford, and Charles Chaplin were deputized with spectacular success to sell bonds during World War I, Washington focused more on Broadway than on Hollywood through the first part of the 1920s. Al Jolson organized Broadway stars for the Republican presidential campaigns in 1920 and 1924. In 1920, Jolson led a delegation of seventy stars from the Harding and Coolidge Theatrical League to serenade Republican candidate Warren G. Harding (with a composition credited to Jolson called "Harding, You're the Man for Us") at his home in Marion, Ohio; Harding repaid them for the visit by declaring agreeably, if vaguely: "There is a great likeness between political life under popular government and many of our most successful productions on the stage. Our American popular government ought not to be a one-lead or a one-star drama of modern civilization."

Four years later, Jolson led another delegation of actors from New

York to the White House for a well-publicized breakfast with Calvin Coolidge, who succeeded to the presidency after Harding's death. Jolson sang a new composition, "Keep Cool with Coolidge," then declared: "The theatrical profession is almost 100 percent for you. Those who are not for you, Mr. President, are those who are not working and there are very few of us in that category." Republicans thought the support of the Broadway stars important enough, testimony in later congressional hearings revealed, to secretly pay all the expenses for the excursion. More money than that may have changed hands before the trip. During the hearings, one supporter of Progressive party candidate Senator Robert M. La Follette of Wisconsin claimed that a press relations agency affiliated with the Shubert Theatrical Companies actually offered to sell La Follette the support of Jolson and the other entertainers for $50,000, and then presumably took their proposition to the Republicans after the La Follette campaign passed on it. The GOP denied the charges and the scandal faded away, but it offered one early indication of how much political strategists valued the endorsement of stars for their candidates.

As the decade progressed, Hollywood began to challenge Broadway as the voice of the entertainment industry in politics. Mayer was the key: he was the first to court national politicians systematically, carving a thin path that would eventually widen into a freeway. In 1924 he volunteered in the Coolidge presidential campaign, an eager, if not particularly significant, neophyte. In that campaign, though, he did meet Koverman, who had much to offer him. A widow with an austere manner, Koverman followed Mayer back to MGM in 1928 as his executive secretary, and later became the studio's public relations director. Through her relationship with Hoover and her involvement in local and state Republican politics, Koverman developed an extensive network of connections. She understood political power. "She helped him a great deal by allowing him to benefit from her political experience, and she knew a lot of the local political figures," said George Murphy, an MGM song-and-dance man who went on to become one of the leading Republican activists in Hollywood and later a U.S. senator from California. "She was an independent political force."

Koverman began to instruct Mayer. Mayer had always been interested in politics; his daughter, Irene Mayer Selznick, remembered him talking about the latest machinations even "when we lived in Massachusetts." Koverman focused his interest. Through her, Mayer became active in the state Republican party and met the local political gentry. Unlike the other studio executives, who blew with the prevailing political winds, Mayer moored himself in the Republican party. "I thought she had a great influence on him," said Mayer's nephew Jack Cummings, who was an MGM producer. "The very fact that she was there gave him a sense of acceptability in the political world. And she opened doors."

The most important door she opened was to Hoover, and Mayer moved through it aggressively. Mayer's courtship of Hoover demonstrated not only the social appeal of politics for the moguls but the growing practical appeal of the moguls for politicians. Through the twenties Mayer wooed Hoover in honeyed tones. After Hoover visited the studio in 1924, Mayer wrote him, expressing "keen enjoyment" over the visit and telling Hoover that the rest of the nation would be privileged to know him as well as Mayer did. Hoover wasn't immune to such flattery, particularly since he recognized in Mayer a man who could assist his higher ambitions. And, as far as he was capable, the dour engineer responded in kind. When Mayer asked to stop in for a visit in Washington on his way to Europe in fall 1924, Hoover cabled back promptly: "Glad to see you any time on twenty-four hours notice." In November 1927, he wrote Mayer brightly: "I haven't much to write about except by way of demonstrating that I have you in mind many times a day."

Mayer swelled with pride about his relationship with such a respected figure as a cabinet secretary who was clearly headed for even grander things. "It meant a great deal to him, as it would to anyone," said Cummings. "He genuinely liked Hoover and Hoover liked him." Mayer's daughter Irene recalled her father "was very proud that Hoover was his friend. . . . It gave him great pride, great pleasure, and Hoover listened to him on certain things." Mayer happily introduced Hoover to his aged father at his home in Santa Monica. He obtained an autographed photo of Hoover and placed it behind his desk in a collection of friendly famous faces that would grow to include New York's Francis Cardinal Spellman and J. Edgar Hoover of the FBI. But Mayer wanted more than pictures. He craved acceptance; but he also understood power. "Mayer, of course, was the shrewdest of the [moguls]," said Sperling. "He was the biggest opportunist of the whole bunch, and he understood better than others how to deal with issues such as relations with the White House."

From the start, Mayer's relations with politicians were based on more than his own need for acceptance. He realized that the visits from notables to the studio were always good publicity. And the regular receptions for senators and congressmen passing through Culver City, wrote one visiting journalist in 1932, "make it easier for M-G-M to borrow a battleship for *Armored Cruiser* or a fleet of Navy planes for *Hell Divers.*"

Mayer's relations with Hoover were no different. His requests to Hoover started small: letters of introduction to ambassadors in London,

Paris, and Rome should his filmmaking projects in Europe need some governmental assistance, help in obtaining introductions from the State Department for Thalberg on an overseas trip; assistance in securing the cooperation of Belgian and British colonial officials for a film company Mayer was sending to Africa to shoot footage for the film *Trader Horn.* Invariably, Hoover's aides responded promptly.

Sometimes Mayer leaned on Hoover more heavily. At the request of press magnate William Randolph Hearst, Mayer sought and received Hoover's help in acquiring "a satisfactory wave length" for a radio station Hearst and Mayer wanted to operate. Later, Mayer sought Hoover's help again in acquiring the preferred wavelength for a Chicago station that Hearst expected would serve as his flagship. After a Hearst aide wired Mayer with yet another request for intervention from his "friend Hoover," Mayer urgently forwarded the request to Koverman, who was in Washington. "Get busy" with Hoover, he instructed her. If Hoover could deliver on this request, Mayer told his shrewd secretary, it would give him "just the ammunition I need" to win Hearst's "support and friendship."

Into the White House

Mayer's prompt response to the powerful Hearst was characteristic. As he built MGM through the twenties, Mayer wooed Hearst even more intently than he wooed Hoover, for Hearst could do more for Mayer than Hoover could. The undisputed lord of the nation's largest press chain, the syndicator of gossip columnist Louella Parsons, Hearst more than any other individual shaped America's view of Hollywood, its stars and its films. His impact on politicians was only slightly more circumscribed. That meant Hearst could also do more for Hoover than Mayer could. As Hoover moved closer to seeking the presidency in 1928, Mayer's principal political function came to be influencing his friend Hearst on behalf of his friend Hoover.

Mayer's relationship with Hearst was grounded firmly in their mutual appreciation of self-interest. It was virtually the only kind of relationship of which either was capable. Ambrose Bierce, one of Hearst's columnists, once wrote that Hearst was "inaccessible to the conception of an unselfish attachment or a disinterested motive." Much the same could be said of Mayer, who couldn't match Hearst's Olympian style (who could?) but gave away nothing in his skill at manipulating people. Self-interest may have inspired the relationship, but it didn't encompass it. Mayer saw Hearst not only as a useful tool but as a Brobdingnagian role model: mogul cubed. In Hearst, Mayer beheld all to which he aspired—power, empire, influence, wealth, culture acquired by the cartload, and an imperial manner more befitting a baron than a businessman—unleashed on a scale he could barely conceive. In a city built on fantasy, Hearst's extravagance outran the imagination.

Mayer ingratiated himself with the press lord through a most unlikely portal: Hearst's heart. The wedge was a young hoofer, Marion Davies, daughter of a minor New York politician. Hearst picked Davies out of a chorus line at Ziegfield's in New York, probably around 1917. He was at the time in his mid-fifties and indifferently married. With characteristic flamboyance, he decided to share his discovery with the nation. He hired tutors in poise, expression, and acting, intending to transform his Brooklyn siren into the brightest film star in the country. He couldn't. The Hearst press canonized Davies, but no one else did, and her movies did poorly at the box office.

Hearst created his own production company, Cosmopolitan Pictures, to produce Davies's films; he distributed the movies through the Goldwyn Company. When Goldwyn was subsumed as part of the merger that created MGM, Mayer doggedly recruited Hearst to transfer his operation to the new enterprise. Mayer pursued the deal not on his faith in Davies—a friendly, good-hearted, reasonably talented comedienne forced by Hearst into shoes far too big—but on his faith in what Hearst could do for him. Mayer agreed to finance Davies's pictures, give Hearst a share of the profits, and pay Davies the huge salary of $10,000 a week. In return, Hearst at least tacitly agreed that his newspapers would look benevolently on Mayer's movies.

After the deal was signed, Hearst began to linger in his native California. He had spent most of the previous thirty years in New York, but he was moving into a new stage of life. After launching his newspaper empire at the close of the nineteenth century, Hearst spent the opening years of the twentieth trying to acquire political power. An arden populist—tweaked for his "socialistic principles" by the *New York Times*—Hearst got himself elected to Congress in 1902, again in 1904, and dreamed of greater success. In 1904, Hearst managed to convince or coerce 263 delegates at the Democratic Convention to support him for the party's presidential nomination, before losing to New York Court of Appeals Judge Alton Brooks Parker. The fire of Hearst's ambition didn't recede for another twenty years, but that second ballot was the high point of his political career. Hearst's ambition was so raw, his power already so vast, that he frightened average voters almost as much as he did party bosses. As a newspaper baron, Hearst was lordly and remote; as a politician, he became almost pathetically persistent. In 1905, he ran for mayor of New York as a third-party candidate and lost. The next year he ran for governor as a Democrat, and lost again. He dreamed of acquiring a Senate seat and yearned for the White House, but never came close to either.

When Hearst stepped off the Twentieth Century Limited in Hollywood with Davies in 1924, it was as if he was closing the book on all that gnawing ambition. Hearst set out to conquer his new territory. With their limousines and mansions, their maids and pools and tennis courts, the moguls thought they understood conspicuous consumption. Hearst's appearance revealed them as amateurs. Soon after his arrival, Hearst built a huge fourteen-room Spanish-style white stucco bungalow for Marion Davies on MGM's Culver City lot. So that Davies's vistas would not be constrained when she left the lot, Hearst built for her in Santa Monica a beach house of 110 rooms. Above these creations towered Hearst's castle in San Simeon, which seemed to have been dragged into the world, full blown and undiluted, from the dank recesses of Hearst's id. Into this castle—actually a complex of buildings topped by a castle—Hearst deposited an astonishing array of artifacts, antiques, and curios from around the world; Hermann Goering pursued the treasures of Europe no more avidly than William Randolph Hearst. Weekends at San Simeon became a prized, if bizarre, experience for the film colony's elite.

Hearst's style stunned even Hollywood. It entranced Mayer. At first skeptical and somewhat overwhelmed, Mayer ultimately was awed. Mayer called Hearst "chief" and Hearst called him "son." (Mayer, like Hoover's other intimates, also called him "chief.") Hearst became a frequent guest at Mayer's home; Mayer's daughter Irene called him "Uncle William." The oddest of couples, Hearst and Mayer found they had much in common. They shared a craving for control and glory. (Hearst frequently wrote front-page editorials, and Mayer, as part of the contract he negotiated with Loew, secured the right to have all of the new studio's films released under his own name, should he so choose.) And as Hearst's populist fervor burned away, their political interests grew more closely aligned as well.

Nurturing elaborate ambitions as a kingmaker, Mayer lobbied Hearst on Hoover's behalf as the 1928 election approached. With Koverman's assistance, Mayer arranged for the candidate and the press lord to meet at Mayer's home during the election year. Hoover dutifully made himself available, for in 1928, Hearst was a prize worth winning. Though his own political dreams had dissolved, Hearst's influence remained enormous.

In 1928, his papers held 10.2 percent of daily national circulation and over 20 percent of total Sunday circulation. No other individual could command as large an audience, and over the next seven years his reach steadily expanded.

It's unlikely Hearst felt he could learn much politically from such a novice as Mayer. Hearst was in no hurry to declare his intentions toward Hoover; he kept Mayer waiting for his decision for months. As the Democrats moved toward nominating Al Smith, an old foe from Hearst's New York days, it seemed inevitable that the publisher would rally to the Republican banner. Distaste for Smith had convinced Hearst to swallow Calvin Coolidge, a gristly bit even for a lapsed populist, four years earlier. But among the Republicans, Hearst had given his heart to Treasury Secretary Andrew W. Mellon. Still, Hearst was a political pragmatist, and when it was clear Mellon couldn't make the race, he turned to Hoover. The endorsement he delivered on June 8, 1928, was less than enthusiastic, but it was an endorsement. In a front-page editorial, Hearst wrote: "Hoover is perhaps more conservative a candidate than the Hearst papers would ordinarily support for the Republican nomination, but the present situation demands conservatism, and Secretary Hoover's conservatism is of the constructive and not the reactionary type."

Mayer was now at high tide. He had allied the two men in public life he admired most, and saw the clear prospect of his old friend—a man who addressed him as "my dear Mayer"—occupying the White House. The petty travails of assembling movies suddenly seemed less compelling. Through the summer and fall of 1928 MGM struggled with the introduction of sound, but Mayer devoted much of his energy to the campaign—annoying his production chief, Thalberg, who considered his problems more pressing than Hoover's.

Mayer arrived at the Republican Convention in Kansas City ten days early to plot strategy with the Hoover forces. After Hoover's nomination, he returned to Washington as part of an inner circle that conferred with the candidate about campaign strategy. Smith's partisans organized an authors', actors', and artists' committee that included George M. Cohan, Irving Berlin, Helen Hayes, George Jessel, Jerome Kern, playwright Marc Connelly, Eddie Cantor, and George Gershwin. Mayer joined the competing Hoover-Curtis Theatrical League, which included Claudette Colbert, Walter Huston, director Fred Niblo, actor Frank Morgan, playwright-director George Abbott, and actress Ethel Clayton. He helped to collect support from the film community, and eventually Hoover received endorsements from Cecil B. DeMille, Joseph M. Schenck, and D. W. Griffith. More important, he received checks: Mayer and Joseph

Schenck each sent $7,000, and DeMille put up $10,000.

Mayer followed each turn of the battle. After a Hoover speech in New Jersey in September, Mayer wired that he was "thrilled" by the candidate's reception. In early October he attended another strategy session with Hoover in Washington. Mayer was so visible in the campaign that New York Mayor Jimmy Walker accused him and Joseph Schenck of attempting to turn over the movie industry to Hoover. With rare modesty, Mayer pleaded powerlessness: "I cannot even induce some of our stars to make personal appearances at a theater showing one of our pictures . . . ," he said indignantly. "This might offer a slight indication of what my chances would be of inducing the entire industry to deliver itself to any party."

As the race moved into its final weeks, Mayer could barely contain his enthusiasm. On October 18, he wired Hoover aide George Akerson that, unable to "resist" any longer, he planned to speak that week before a Beverly Hills group for his friend. When Hoover delivered a nationwide radio address a week later, Mayer dashed off more lavish praise. A few hours later Mayer decided the wire alone couldn't express his enthusiasm. From across the continent, Mayer called Akerson and "bubbled over" with excitement, the aide reported to Hoover. After Hoover was elected, MGM took out a full-page ad in *Variety* to congratulate him and to announce: "The Stars Predict Prosperity!" With his friend in the White House, prosperity seemed destined to settle on Mayer too. Newspaper reports speculated that Hoover was prepared to offer Mayer the ambassadorship to Turkey. One Jewish paper reported that Hoover offered Mayer the job. It is unclear whether the offer was actually made, but Mayer took the reports seriously enough to deny them: "I am not a candidate for any public office of any kind, and even were I a candidate, Mr. Hoover is not yet president, and to discuss such a thing at this time would be decidedly premature," he said in early February 1929. Mayer remained the sultan of Culver City.

He found other rewards. He assumed the lofty position of favored friend to the president. In March, Hoover made Mayer and his wife his first dinner guests at the White House. When the dishes were cleared, Mayer and Hoover relaxed in the president's study and discussed the possibilities of using films for educational purposes. Afterward, Mayer assured the national press, "Business is going to be wonderful under President Hoover's Administration."

Hoover entertained Mayer at the White House again in July and August. His ties with Hoover doubtless helped Mayer win election as vice-president of the California Republican State Central Committee that fall.

When Mayer's daughter Irene passed through Washington with her producer husband, David O. Selznick, on their honeymoon in 1930, the proud father arranged for them to have dinner with the president—over the bridegroom's objections. "My husband was indignant," Irene said, looking back. "He said, 'What has Hoover got to do with our honeymoon? Time is short enough. Why do we have to travel to Washington?' I said, 'My father. It would please him, we haven't done much to please him, so let's do this.' "* Mayer promoted friends for government jobs, and his recommendations were treated seriously. Hoover was perceived as being so close to Mayer that sometimes people anxious to break into the film business wrote to the White House, asking the president to intercede with his powerful friend in California.

Mayer used his connections for larger matters too. After Marcus Loew died, William Fox, another of the industry's pioneers, arranged with Nicholas Schenck in early 1929 to acquire the stock of the Loew family, effectively gaining control of the company, which was MGM's parent. Under pressure from Schenck, who was weighing a counteroffer from Warner Bros., Fox pushed the Justice Department to clear the merger. Fox later told his biographer, Upton Sinclair, that the Coolidge Justice Department verbally approved the deal. In any case, the department didn't object when Fox acquired Mrs. Loew's shares in February 1929, during the closing days of the Coolidge administration. Mayer, on the other hand, objected vociferously. He and the rest of the so-called Mayer group—Thalberg and J. Robert Rubin—felt betrayed by the deal, under which Nicholas Schenck was to realize a multimillion-dollar profit; since they owned no stock, they would not see a cent from the transaction. Mayer met with Fox and pressed his claim for a share of the bounty. Fox told the outraged Mayer he had no grounds for complaint, since he had never demonstrated his faith in the company by purchasing stock.

Mayer was not one to sulk quietly in his tent. While visiting the White House in March for the inauguration—the current practice of inaugurating the president in January did not begin until 1937—the irritated Mayer warned darkly of possible monopoly if the deal was allowed to go through. Fox later told a congressional committee that Mayer bragged of causing the Justice Department to change its view, though Fox himself was dubious; he suspected one of his own financiers had done him in.

But from whatever source, Fox soon found himself with Justice Depart-

---

*The visit pleased Mayer by demonstrating his clout at the White House, but the honeymooners' reactions left him a bit "disappointed," Irene recalled. "We didn't go back and say, 'God, it was so thrilling.' . . . To me the whole thing reflected a kind of pride in me and my husband and his own privilege."

ment resistance. Fox had supported Hoover in 1928, and he hurried to appeal to his friend in the White House. According to Fox, Hoover promised he would intervene with the Justice Department. But apparently Hoover never lifted the phone, and the Justice Department ordered the frantic Fox to divest his Loew's holdings. Even more frantic now, Fox cast about for help. A top Republican National Committee official suggested that the man who might resolve his difficulties was an influential California Republican named Louis B. Mayer—arguably the man in the country least amenable to helping Fox achieve anything. Somewhat stunned, Fox nonetheless bit hard, accepted the inevitable, and brought Mayer East for a meeting. Fox later said he offered Mayer and his group $2 million if the deal was consummated, and the Justice Department's resistance at least temporarily melted away. Mayer insisted that he had never sought to influence the administration, but such reticence seems enormously uncharacteristic. In any case, the merger never occurred; the delay killed it. Fox was immobilized by a car crash in July, then pummeled by the stock market crash in October. Finally, he was hit with a Justice Department suit against the combination and, set upon by his financiers, eventually lost control of his own companies and left the industry. Mayer, who knew power, had repulsed the invader at the gates.

The Dawn of Mogul Politics

When the Depression struck, Mayer never wavered in his support of Hoover. He offered hearty encouragement and bland advice: in February 1931 he sent the president a national survey of business leaders' ideas for reinvigorating the economy. As the campaign year began, Mayer assumed control of the Republican effort in Southern California and tried to reassure defectors in Hollywood. He called Mabel Walker Willebrandt, a Hoover aide (who later came to work at MGM), and told her he needed to bring Joe Schenck to the White House for a pep talk. Schenck, Mayer explained to Willebrandt, "was a rather dominant individual . . . who has been somewhat off the reservation, but has swung back into line." The invitation went out the same day.

Mayer had less luck with Hearst, who had never supported Hoover enthusiastically. By the summer of 1931 he had turned against the president with more emotion than he had ever displayed on his behalf. Hearst was dissatisfied with Hoover's piddling response to the Depression, and he may also have been annoyed by Hoover's failure to protest a few years earlier when France, angered at the Hearst papers' disclosure of secret diplomatic documents, unceremoniously ejected the publisher from the country. As early as January 2, 1932, the old populist came out behind Democratic House Speaker John Nance Garner, an uninspiring Texan, mostly because Hearst (who hardened in his isolationism with each passing year) considered him the least internationalist contender.

Mayer's efforts at mediation failed. Neither Hearst nor Hoover, both stiff and obstinate, had much interest in repairing the breach. In spring 1932, Hoover dismissed Mayer's overtures for a meeting with the publisher. For Mayer, the ultimate ignominy came when Hearst editorially attacked Hoover for failing to deliver on a national program of public works that he promised the publisher when they met at Mayer's home in 1928. Despite all his efforts to mediate between them, Mayer thus became the unwitting instrument of Hearst's final break with Hoover.

Mayer nonetheless threw himself into the 1932 campaign, assuming a much greater role than in 1928. Though box office receipts sagged under the weight of the Depression, Mayer probably spent no more than half his time on studio business that year. With Hoover holed up in the White House, radiating gloom and isolation, the GOP depended largely on surrogate speakers to make his case. As vice-chairman of the California Republican party, Mayer kicked off his campaigning with a statewide radio broadcast in February. "Some of us who are now ruefully and resentfully counting our losses in the stock market and looking around for someone other than ourselves to blame seem not to remember the storm of indignant protest that arose when the President of the United States and his Secretary of Treasury told the country to beware of trouble ahead," Mayer intoned. "Hoover's perceptions are broad. His sympathies are wide and deep. . . . We find even among his political antagonists grudging admission that his leadership is placing the country on a more stable financial footing."

In June, Mayer visited Hoover at the White House and called for the legalization of beer to defuse the controversy over prohibition that was wracking the GOP. From Washington he proceeded to Chicago for a dispirited GOP convention. The candidate stayed behind, and few missed him. The delegates seemed listless, despairing. Mayer tried to cut the tedium and gloom. He stage-managed the half-hour pro-Hoover demonstration on the convention's final day, arranging for sunlamps, balloon drops, and the dramatic appearance of a giant Hoover portrait "out of thin air" once the president was renominated. If the gaiety was mechanical—timed to the moment—it was still a break in the grim foreboding that hung over the convention like a fog.

Mayer arrived home exhilarated, a certified big shot. Reporters sought his assessment of the economy (MGM "sells its products in all parts of the world. We get business reports and we know that America is the white-spot of the world"); the convention's compromise antiprohibition platform plank that called for the states to assume control of liquor within their borders ("Prohibition did eliminate the saloon, but in other ways has brought us to the brink of a national disaster"); and Hoover's fall prospects (he predicted a "triumphant" reelection after a hard fight).

In fact, though, the Hoover campaign faced difficulties in the president's home state that fully suggested the magnitude of the disaster ahead. Mark Requa, who had become California's Republican national committeeman, found many business executives so distressed by the continuing Depression that they closed their wallets to their native son. With campaign money scarce in California and nationally, Requa turned to Mayer, who gave liberally himself and scoured Hollywood for more, offering early testimony to the political potential of the new wealth accumulating under the palms in Southern California. With the money, Requa and Mayer built an energetic political organization that consumed a full floor in an office building. "You will not see any such campaign activity in the country, not even at the national headquarters," wrote one visiting reporter. Mayer added glamour to the grind with a glittering troupe of celebrities: Ethel Barrymore, Lewis Stone, Conrad Nagel, and Wallace Beery all pitched in.

In the campaign's final weeks, the currents all running against Hoover, Mayer swam furiously upstream. As his patron in the White House sank toward repudiation, Mayer reached new political prominence. For his prodigious labors, Mayer was elected chairman of the Republican State Central Committee in September. That position cemented his preeminent political role in Hollywood and made him an even more visible public figure. Mayer increasingly was used as a party ambassador, though his speeches, presumably ghostwritten, were most often smarmy and ponderous. An energetic speaker, he made up with force what he lacked in elegance.

In early October, Mayer launched a series of radio broadcasts by Republican leaders with a fifteen-minute statewide address. Introduced by Beery, Mayer rolled up his sleeves and swatted at the challenger, Franklin D. Roosevelt. The Democrats, Mayer piously warned, offer "an appeal to our prejudices, an appeal to our discontent, an appeal to our passions. I have always found it to be true, whether in politics, business or in personal relations, that the man who seeks to gain his end by arousing suspicions, who would substitute angry feelings for logical reasoning is untrustworthy; that his cause is weak. That is the case with the Democratic opposition." (MGM employees must have wondered if the man counseling dispassionate logic on the radio was the same ham who oscillated between rages and exquisitely timed tears during contract negotiations.) Five days later, Mayer was back on the air, accusing Roosevelt of a campaign of "amiability and meaningless generalities."

None of this mattered. Nor did Hoover's decision to stir himself from his lethargy in September and campaign furiously in the weeks remaining to him. Mayer confidently predicted victory and worked hard for it—as in 1928, he was forced to deny Democratic charges that he was coercing support from his employees. Then he watched helplessly as the deluge swept his friend out of the White House. From then on, when he went to Washington, Mayer would have to sleep in hotels. He would never again be as close to a president.

Hoover's defeat did not diminish Mayer's stature. He remained Hollywood's voice to the outside world. "In politics and public affairs, particularly as they relate to California and the film industry," wrote one observer at the time, "Mayer has no potential rivals at all." Mayer's greatest political disappointment was his inability to reconcile Hearst with Hoover, for whom Mayer still harbored hopes of a comeback. Even as he (inevitably) soured on Roosevelt, Hearst imperially dismissed Mayer's importunings to reconsider the exiled engineer. The disagreements over Hoover added a new edge to relations between the mogul and the press lord, which were already strained by Mayer's increasing skepticism about Marion Davies's abilities. In the fall of 1934, though, Hearst and Mayer managed to find common cause against socialist author Upton Sinclair's bid for the California governorship. Their agreement over the need to fight Sinclair—and the tools needed to do so—influenced the development of Hollywood politics far more than their disagreements about Hoover. The 1934 Sinclair campaign marked a turning point in Hollywood's political participation in almost all respects. It was in the Sinclair campaign that Mayer, Hearst, and the other studio fathers defined what could be called mogul politics. Mogul politics was hard, shrewd, autocratic, and above all, coercive. In sum, it reflected its authors.

The key fact of Hollywood life in the early 1930s was the enormous imbalance of power between the studios and the people who worked for them. Holding even the most glamorous stars to binding contracts, the moguls were committed to controlling their employees off-camera as well as on the lots. Each used different methods. Like the stern but loving parent he saw himself to be, Mayer used charm and misty appeals to family loyalty; Harry Cohn used bluster and intransigence; Darryl Zanuck dangled promises of enriching artistic collaboration. But all resisted any encroachment on their right to shape films and careers and to rule their lots like satraps.

In the 1928 and 1932 presidential races, Democrats had accused Mayer and the other studio heads of strong-arming their employees into the Republican cause. But against Sinclair the moguls leveraged their power much more ruthlessly, and with more dramatic political effect. The 1934 California gubernatorial campaign suggested for the first time how substantial a political force the movie industry could be when mobilized behind a candidate. The national campaigns had only given a taste: in the early 1930s Washington was too distant and uninvolved in the industry for many people in Hollywood to focus on the capital's affairs. Local concerns seemed more relevant—and drew a greater response.

As Sinclair learned. The moguls lined up in horror when Sinclair, who had announced his intention to assess higher taxes on the film industry, won the Democratic gubernatorial nomination in August 1934. So did the rest of California's business community, which had enjoyed three decades of complaisant, virtually unbroken Republican control. Sinclair was the classic insurgent candidate. He had so little money that workers in the campaign's field office had to raise their own funds to buy campaign literature from headquarters. But, in the thick despair of the Depression, Sinclair's powerful promise to end poverty in California (EPIC, which became his campaign slogan) was a vibrant recruiting tool. Sinclair attracted thousands of young people; more than eight hundred EPIC clubs formed statewide.

The business forces arrayed against Sinclair had available virtually unlimited funds, but the most limited of natural resources: Frank F. Merriam, who succeeded to the governorship after the death of James Rolph, Jr., in spring 1934, was hardly a dynamic leading man. So Mayer and Hearst improvised. Exerting political influence more confidently than ever before, the film industry took a leading role in the campaign. Mayer hurried home from a tour of Europe to direct the industry's forces. "As I see it, this is no time to consider either personal or partisan interests," he told reporters cheerfully upon arrival. (The *Los Angeles Examiner* more frankly summarized his message in its headline: "Nonpartisan Attack on Radicals Urged for Public Welfare.") Hearst rushed back from his own grand tour of the Continent to marshal his men.

The generals back in their bunker, the campaign commenced. It was a remarkable display of the moguls' power over their own domains, and through that resource, over the community beyond their gates. First, the producers collected funds for the campaign by pressuring their high-salaried employees to contribute one day's pay to the Merriam cause. Though some resisted—Jean Harlow and James Cagney led an actors' rebellion and several writers enlisted in the California Authors' League for Sinclair—the executives assembled a half-million-dollar war chest. Thus fortified, the industry pressed its campaign against Sinclair on all fronts. Leading executives, such as Twentieth Century's Joseph Schenck, who nominally identified himself as a Democrat, warned that the industry might quit the state if Sinclair triumphed; the Florida legislature responded by passing a bill exempting them from all taxes if they would flee in that direction. Rallies were convened, speakers dispatched. The producers' principal campaign weapon was not words but pictures: fabricated newsreels that warned of calamity if the voters chose Sinclair. Shipped free across the state, the newsreels featured carefully contrasted interviews with California voters about the campaign. The Merriam supporters were unremarkable solid citizens: housewives, service-station attendants, grandmothers, business executives. Sinclair's supporters were shown as shabby, disheveled foreigners with thick accents, threatening vagrants in crowded boxcars rushing toward California to milk Sinclair's socialist paradise. "This interpretation of current events was strangely moving," wrote one observer, "although those with critical eyes wondered why the vagrants were wearing make-up; and some with good memories at once recognized excerpts from the Warner Brothers' previous film fiction 'Wild Boys of the Road.'" Hearst, whose papers controlled nearly half of the state's daily circulation, chipped in with cartoons and editorials that portrayed Sinclair as a foggy mystic with hopelessly unrealistic ideas; for good measure his *Los Angeles Evening Herald* printed a photograph of surly young hobos en route to enlist in Sinclair's cause—which also turned out to have been cannibalized from that Warner Bros. production.

The Sinclair campaign profoundly changed Hollywood's embryonic relationship with politics. In many respects, it represented the political baptism of the moguls. Not that it taught them how to influence elections, for public outcry over the phony newsreels was so great ("Will the nation be warned by California's recent experience?" worried *Harper's*) that the moguls never again undertook so blatant a propaganda campaign. Nor were employees ever shaken down for funds again quite so forcefully. Rather, the Sinclair campaign was pivotal because it taught the moguls the importance of influencing elections. It was the first campaign in which Mayer and the others participated primarily to protect their economic interests. Mayer's early requests of Herbert Hoover suggested that self-interest was always one reason for courting politicians. But the social attractions of politics—the desire to be embraced by powerful men—initially overshadowed the economic ones.

After the Sinclair campaign the two came into closer balance. For the moguls, the social rewards always remained strong. But from 1934 on, these needs were reinforced by economic necessity. With Sinclair, the threat that sparked action was higher state taxes. But new and more complex threats emerged from Washington too: federal investigations of the anticompetitive implications of the studios owning vast theater chains, and the 1935 National Labor Relations (Wagner) Act that provided the legal framework for the industry's creative employees to unionize. Even in Hollywood—a home the filmmakers originally chose in part for its remoteness—the New Deal meant new rules, new arrangements, new problems. "Government invaded their lives for the first time [in the mid-1930s] as it did for all Americans," said Sperling, the Twentieth Century producer. "I don't think they were political at all before those times. Nobody here was. This was pure, raw, private enterprise. . . . They built an industry without rules and regulations. They were brought into politics by legal problems, rules and regulations and so forth. It was a necessity, a business necessity. Events forced it upon them."

For the new challenges, the Sinclair campaign suggested a new attitude. During the 1920s, as one contemporary wrote, the studios' "chief end politically was not to offend." When religious groups accused Hollywood of poisoning the nation's morals in the early 1920s, the studios compliantly brought in Republican Postmaster General Will H. Hays as president of the Motion Picture Producers and Distributors of America and ceded him enormous power, first as political fixer and eventually as censor. That was typical of the moguls' response to outside pressure: as immigrant Jews, Mayer and the other studio fathers always remained uncertain and defensive when pressed by forces from Gentile society. But Mayer's leading role in the Sinclair campaign suggested the moguls had become confident enough of their position to defend their political interests openly—at least when they were perceived as simultaneously defending "American" values.

That last distinction was crucial. No matter how much money he earned, or how many politicians' pictures he displayed on his walls, no matter even that he celebrated his birthday on the nation's, Mayer never lost his immigrants' fear of being labeled un-American. His anxiety was common in the Hollywood executive suites occupied by men who remembered much meaner lives, and it produced a split political personality.

When faced with economic challenges, such as the Sinclair campaign or unionizing efforts within Hollywood, they were fierce adversaries, defiantly upholding the American tradition of free enterprise. But they were far more accommodating to those external critics who subtly or overtly challenged their patriotism by accusing them of harboring Communists—even when that ultimately meant sacrificing skilled craftsmen who enriched them. In both instances the underlying goal was actually the same: to be left alone, to run the studios without interference from anyone—government, unions, the Legion of Decency. Abstractions didn't interest them. ("The executives, most of them came up from the sidewalk; they were promoters, they fell into this wonderful thing where they made a few films, there didn't seem to be much to it and people flocked in, and they made some money," said Roy M. Brewer, a conservative Hollywood union leader who later pressured the moguls to dismiss their Communist employees. "And then they made some more films, and they made some more money. All they understood was that.") Throughout the moguls' long tenures at the studios, the tension between these two powerful urges—the need to protect their economic interests and the desire to affirm their place as respected and patriotic Americans—shaped their approach to politics.

If the Sinclair campaign coalesced the emerging principles of mogul politics, it also, paradoxically, inspired the response. Inevitably the moguls overplayed their hand. By steering his employees into the Merriam campaign, Mayer may have seen himself as the wise father shepherding his flock; but the flock was composed of adults—well-paid, famous, willful adults at that—many of whom chafed at the paternalism that suddenly stretched to matters that had nothing to do with making movies or even avoiding unfavorable publicity. The implied and actual coercion that accompanied the Merriam fundraising ruffled expensive feathers in all the studios. Critics complained of Mayer's "bludgeoning leadership."

The shakedown reinforced the feeling of helplessness among studio employees that had surfaced a year earlier, when the moguls demanded an across-the-board 50 percent pay cut during the banking crisis of March 1933. (It was on this occasion that Mayer gave his teary-eyed performance before the assembled MGM family.) After the unionized electricians and carpenters refused, the producers came back with a second plan: no one under $50 a week would be cut, but those earning more would face cuts of up to 50 percent on a sliding scale. The experience of the unionized technical hands was not lost on the unorganized creative employees. Their only bargaining voice was the Academy of Motion Picture Arts and Sciences, a company union Mayer established in 1927. But after the wage cuts, efforts to organize more representative unions took root. Screenwriters organized the Screen Writers Guild in April 1933 with John Howard Lawson, who would later become Hollywood's most prominent Communist, as president, and settled in for a long bitter fight. The Screen Actors Guild formed that autumn around a less ideological core that included Eddie Cantor and Robert Montgomery.

Unhappiness within the industry over the campaign encouraged not only left-wing union organizing but also liberal political activity. "This aroused a lot of feeling, especially when the studios put the bite on their employees to support the Republicans," said screenwriter Philip Dunne, who became one of the leading voices of discontent. Just a few years after the Sinclair campaign, the desire for unfiltered political expression—and the hunger to declare independence from the studio fathers—inspired a grassroots leftist surge that transformed politics in Hollywood. Mayer and his allies defeated Sinclair, but the cost turned out to be much higher than they ever expected.

Bills came due almost immediately, and from a most unlikely source. In the ultimate indignity, Merriam himself came forth with proposals to tax the industry soon after he settled into office. His tax plan hit the industry on several fronts: a doubling of the corporate franchise tax, a tax on admissions, extension of the sales tax to film, and a state income tax. The case for taxing the film industry was a strong one; a state assemblyman revealed during the debate that the ten largest studios had paid only $13,618 in California state taxes during 1933, and just $3,142 in 1932. Quickly, industry leaders dusted off the threats of exodus they had marshaled just six months earlier on Merriam's behalf. Will Hays rushed West to huddle with his shaken troops. Joseph Schenck went to Florida and announced that the cost of relocation would be offset in only eighteen months by the proffered tax savings. Mayer deplored the trend toward "confiscatory" taxes and echoed Schenck's threats.

Mayer took the case to whoever would listen. Addressing the Los Angeles Breakfast Club, a civic group, he tried the same homey approach he used on his stars. Without a prepared text to anchor him, Mayer was swept by gusts of emotion, and he careened from subject to subject, trying to find the right words to express the depth of his concern for the state, and his simultaneous outrage over Merriam's plans. He announced his willingness to become a Communist if that would ensure security and happiness for the working man. He proclaimed himself willing to accept confiscation of all his money if it would help the nation's parlous state (he quickly added that, in his view, it wouldn't). Finally, like a condemned man making his last appeal against fate, he placed his life in the governor's hands. "My doctors tell me that when I stop working I'll die," Mayer announced to his astonished audience, before adding, helpfully, "I don't want to die. But evidently they want to kill us all—we're all going to stop working."

The industry also managed less emotional appeals. The moguls let it be known that New Jersey was bidding against Florida for the industry's favor. Arizona's name was mentioned. With great fanfare, MGM and Fox inventoried their property, from furniture to film equipment, "to be ready for a hurried exodus," the *Los Angeles Times* reported. Schenck brought the threat to Sacramento, poked into the cubbyholes of the state legislature, and announced upon his return to Los Angeles that "the boys up there" will "take care of things for us."

In fact, the final result was ambiguous. The industry defeated the taxes aimed specifically at it, but watched in helpless horror as its man Merriam stood firm behind the income tax and pushed it through. For the abundantly compensated film executives, the income tax was a financial nightmare. One took it particularly hard: for William Randolph Hearst, Merriam's income tax was the final indignity in a decade of Hollywood disappointments.

Predictably enough, Marion Davies had not done well at the box office; only one of her MGM films turned a profit. Hearst thought his protégé would do better if she could move beyond light comedy, and he had set his sights on weightier parts that Thalberg coveted for his wife, actress Norma Shearer. Through the early 1930s, Mayer reluctantly found himself in the middle of a convoluted domestic dispute between his two resident geniuses. His natural instinct to pacify Hearst was checked by his appreciation of Davies's limits (and perhaps by his irritation over Hearst's treatment of Hoover). Mayer sided with Thalberg and gave to Shearer the plum part of poet Elizabeth Barrett Browning in *The Barretts of Wimpole Street*. Hearst, characteristically, kept pushing. After his summer 1934 tour of Europe, Hearst, fired with enthusiasm for the antiquities of the Continent, convinced himself that the studio's planned film about Marie Antoinette would be a suitable vehicle for Davies. Mayer saw only two problems with this suggestion: the film was already being developed for Shearer; and Davies brought nothing to the role other than her (admittedly rare) experience at living in comparable luxury. Mayer made Hearst an offer he couldn't accept. He told Hearst he could have the property if he paid the cost of the production. Hearst predictably declined, and with the Cosmopolitan contract about to expire, Hearst made overtures to the Warner brothers. In late 1934 they welcomed him, and the famous Marion Davies bungalow was disassembled into three sections and moved crosstown to Burbank and the Warner studios.

But Burbank was only a way station. When Merriam passed the income tax, Hearst could stand no more. His finances strained by publishing losses, Hearst announced that to avoid the new tax's onerous bite, he would have to spend less than six months a year in California. "Heaven knows I do not want to leave California," he wrote in an open letter to *Variety.* "No one does, least of all a native son whose father was a pioneer; but it is ultimately impossible for me to remain here and to occupy a place like San Simeon, on account of the federal and state tax laws." In the final days of October 1935, Hearst left for New York. Mayer warned that others "will be obliged to follow, regardless of their great love of this state."

There was no exodus from Hollywood. The moguls settled in for long reigns at their studios. The industry prospered. Mayer soon became the most highly paid man in America. But Hearst's departure nonetheless marked the end of an era in Hollywood's political education. All around Mayer were the signs of pages turning. His old friend Hoover could not mount a comeback in 1936. That fall, just weeks before Roosevelt's resounding reelection, Thalberg died at thirty-seven. The next year, Hearst shuttered his movie operation after losing as much as $7 million in his quest to convince America that he had chosen the right woman. Hearst was gone; Hoover raised from bitter obscurity only when his political opponents found it profitable to exhume his discredited name. Politically, Mayer was left alone. His day had not passed, but his unchallenged dominance of Hollywood politics had. A very different kind of Hollywood politics—a politics developed in direct counterpoint to the autocratic conservatism of the moguls—was about to remake life in the film community.

CHAPTER TWO

THE COMMUNIST DETOUR

The Political Awakening of Hollywood

Silent through the early 1930s, stifled in the Sinclair campaign, liberal Hollywood awoke to politics in the months that followed as if from a fevered dream. It was a fevered time. Hitler threatened Europe. At home, the Depression resisted Franklin Roosevelt's tinkering. Some of the nation's finest writers declared that democratic capitalism was dead, and that the world now faced the final conflict between communism and fascism.

Such an apocalyptic vision appealed to Hollywood's sense of the dramatic. It was, even then, a place that preferred ringing declarations to careful analysis. Many years later, Joan Didion wrote: "There are no bit players in Hollywood politics: Everyone has an important role, everyone makes things 'happen.'" That was never more true than in the 1930s. When the mass of writers, actors, and directors opened their eyes to politics after the Sinclair campaign in 1934, many rushed directly to the vanguard, arming themselves with ideological intransigence for the coming showdown.

Because it developed under these circumstances, liberal politics in

Hollywood veered immediately toward the fringe. Its initial energy came not from the Democratic party, its logical home, but the Communist party, then at the height of its appeal to American intellectuals. The Communist party was never dominant numerically in Hollywood, and its appeal was greatest for writers, the least powerful members of the creative community. It never attracted many recognizable names. (Those it did attract it could not use to seek public legitimacy because membership was kept secret.) But the Communist party nonetheless dominated liberal politics in Hollywood from the 1930s through the 1950s, first as model, then as target. Its vision of political activism defined Hollywood's vision: grassroots organizing, reaching the public through mass communications and rallies, and above all joining leftist elements—Communists and liberals alike—into one Popular Front against fascism.

In many ways, the Popular Front approach was extraordinarily well suited to Depression-era Hollywood. Its concept of an elite vanguard mobilizing a diverse alliance fit perfectly a community with a few serious activists and many more neophytes suddenly trying to bring into focus the chaotic world beyond the backlots. As late as 1936, liberal screenwriter Morrie Ryskind declared in *The Nation,* "Hollywood is not politically minded. Of current events it knows practically nothing." In the confusion, the Communists seemed to have the most confident and comforting explanations: it was the Communists who wove the bewildering twists and turns of world events into an apparently comprehensible pattern of developments, who saw in the enervating drift a progression, a goal. In Hollywood, as elsewhere during the 1930s, communism seemed to offer not only passion but also order. Its certitude, as much as its fervor, allowed the Communist party to put down deep roots in the film community.

And yet default may have helped it no less. During the first years of the 1930s, politicians in Washington—still more than two days away by train—did not yet fully appreciate how Hollywood's money and celebrity could be harnessed for political causes. Nor was there an effective California Democratic party organization to focus the energy that emerged after the Sinclair campaign. Only the Communist party initially mounted an ongoing effort to organize the film community. The default of the Democratic party, the pitch of the times, and the energy of the Communists sent leftist politics in Hollywood on a tangent from which it did not entirely recover for almost three decades. Through the 1940s, the Communist party had as much influence on Hollywood's internal political life as it did on any community in the country. No major liberal activities took place in Hollywood until the dawn of the Cold War, except for a brief period between 1939 and 1941, without Communists playing an active, and in many instances essential, role.

The Party's powerful position gave progressive politics in Hollywood a unique coloration. It did not prevent Hollywood from becoming an important resource for the Democrats in the 1940s. (That was partly because the Communist party saw the value of alliance with liberals, at least while the United States was allied with the Soviet Union during World War II.) But it unnaturally polarized political debate within the film community. As the *New York Times* later reported: "Talent groups— particularly writers and directors—have broken bonds of friendship, the so-called liberal thinkers grouping at certain tables, the conservatives at others. But in their references to one another, they are 'fascists' or 'communists.' "

Even more important, the Party's prominence directed much of the debate inward. Though Hollywood confronted world issues, California state politics, and finally national politics with great enthusiasm during the 1930s and 1940s, it expended the most energy on internal disputes about the proper role of the Communist party. The alliance that bound the Hollywood Popular Front was always tenuous. For Hollywood's first generation of political activists no issue was more pressing, more intractable, or more wrenching than whether liberals and Communists could speak with a single voice.

In Hollywood, liberal politics began with the word. The coming of sound to motion pictures brought to California actors and especially screenwriters trained in the theater and immersed in the radical traditions of New York leftist politics. Almost without exception, these émigrés found the adjustment wrenching. Escaping penury was pleasant enough, but their new home lacked almost all the qualities they prized in their old one. During the 1920s, the population of Los Angeles more than doubled, from 577,000 to 1.24 million; during the next decade, it increased by nearly another 300,000. Yet with size did not come community. Through the 1930s, Los Angeles remained a city of lonely people who had reluctantly left wherever they were in search of something better, or at least something different. The first refugees from Broadway were in at least this respect typical residents: in 1930 only 20 percent of the people who lived in Los Angeles had been born in California. This degree of transience left a hollow feeling at the city's core. "Life takes on a dreadful vacuity here," the writer James M. Cain complained in 1933. The emptiness incubated so many religious and mystical cults that one writer declared Los Angeles harbored "more sanctified cranks to the acre than . . . any other town in America."

Politics in Southern California displayed the same skew. Without labor unions (which were suppressed by the reactionary business establishment), political machines or strong political parties (which had been shortsightedly repressed by reformers in the Progressive era), Los Angeles had no institutions capable of organizing and moderating political dissent. Rage, despair, fear entered the political process unfiltered, through a succession of fringe political movements that provided momentary meaning for those milling through the city without it. Upton Sinclair found more converts for his EPIC movement in Los Angeles than anywhere else and it was from Long Beach that Dr. Francis Townsend launched his national movement for reviving the economy by providing the elderly with a pension they would be mandated to spend.

From their beautiful homes in Beverly Hills and the Hollywood Hills, the film industry's sheltered elite could look with scorn on the crackpots. In his March 1936 article, Ryskind had accurately caught the prevailing mood: most of the bright and beautiful young men and women growing rich and tan in these golden years were perfectly content to let the world worry about itself. But Hollywood was not immune to the enervating sense of drift that provided L.A.'s political and religious cults with their endless stream of recruits, and for a growing minority within the industry the search for connection with the times grew more urgent.

Most affected were the new screenwriters, men and women such as Lester Cole and John Howard Lawson (both of whom later joined the Communist party), Ryskind and Dorothy Parker. They were, like Ryskind, raised in a tradition of "watching the crowd heckling the Socialist speaker at the corner" and debating the sins of Tammany Hall with anyone who would listen. "The writers' table at the studio [commissary] was a political forum, with very few dissenters," said Milton Sperling. "We were all left-wing." Even at Louis Mayer's MGM, the most conservative of studios, "The writers were naturally more liberal," said Nat Perrin, a successful comedy writer there. "You probably had a hundred writers at Metro who you could count being liberal Democrats and you had your isolated few [on the other side]."

The tradition of political interest and agitation that emigrated West infected not only screenwriters but also such celebrities as Fredric March, James Cagney, and Melvyn Douglas, as well as the occasional producer such as Walter Wanger. Much of Hollywood took the Depression by the pool, with gin, neat. But for the minority who felt moved by the events of the day there was a burning sense of irrelevance that none of the creature comforts could erase. The discontent extended to work. As the Depression lingered, Hollywood slowly turned toward films that reflected at least general social awareness—the romanticized grittiness of the Warner Bros. gangster films, for example; Darryl Zanuck's and John Ford's tough *Grapes of Wrath*; Frank Capra's classic populist odes, *Mr. Deeds Goes to Town* and *Mr. Smith Goes to Washington*. But these inevitably remained exceptions. For writers resolutely raising their consciousness, the obligation to spend their days assembling formula vehicles for Marion Davies or Joan Crawford was numbing. What made it worse was the writers' lack of control over their work—and the corrosive awareness that no one forced them to remain in Hollywood bitching about the studios, lamenting the vacuity of their labors, and struggling to get by on a measly grand or two a week. For many activists the feeling of artistic futility reinforced the reaction against political isolation in the spring of 1936.

Ryskind lambasted Hollywood for being afraid of shadows. But in fact the men running the studios were not entirely blasé about the left-leaning politics incubating on their backlots. In management's eyes, the efforts of Hollywood liberals to organize themselves politically blurred into the attempts to organize labor unions—not an entirely unreasonable conclusion, since the two efforts shared many of the same leaders. The studio heads had little stomach for either. "They didn't want the actors to take a public position," said MGM screenwriter Perrin. "They figured, if you're in a public position and you take a stand you alienate the other side. They didn't care what you did privately, but when you took a public position they felt their investment was being endangered." From the businessman's perspective, Perrin thought, that was a reasonable attitude. But the continuing pressure for silence only quickened the urge for greater political expression.

The Communist party became the first institution to mine that discontent. In part, Hollywood attracted the Party as a potentially powerful vehicle for influencing the culture. "It was part of the general broadening of the Party and trying to reach the cultural life of the country" that led the Party to focus on Hollywood, said Dorothy Healey, a senior official in the Los Angeles County branch of the Communist party from the 1940s through the 1960s. But Hollywood's money transfixed the Communists too: it was one of the few places the Party could find recruits who lived like Republicans and considered themselves proletariat. Though large sums were eventually shipped back East to headquarters, the Party's first efforts to convert Hollywood met with indifference. A handful of radicals, most of them writers transplanted from New York, huddled together as Communists in the early 1930s. But they were few and isolated, gloomy urban anachronisms in the gaudy desert.

The basis for expanding the Party beyond this grim core was established in 1935, when the Soviet Union called on Communists in the West to join with liberals and progressives to form a united or popular front against fascism. Local Communist parties were instructed to moderate their revolutionary rhetoric, climb down from the barricades, reach out to other groups, and focus on practical, short-term goals aimed at strengthening Western resolve to resist Hitler. Each of those tactical shifts made the Party more palatable to left-leaning Americans, especially those—as in Hollywood—whose closest contact with the class struggle was problems with their help. Still, when Paul Jarrico, who had joined the Young Communist League as a college student, arrived at Columbia Pictures as a screenwriter in 1937, the Party's membership in Hollywood numbered "maybe even less than dozens plural. My impression was there were perhaps two dozen [members]."

It was only in the next two years that membership took off, rising in Jarrico's estimate "to a couple of hundred." The numbers were always modest. In their monumental history of the Popular Front in Hollywood, *The Inquisition In Hollywood,* Larry Ceplair and Steven Englund estimate that about three hundred people from the movie industry—most of them probably writers—eventually joined the Communist party. But in a community with so many dilettantes, the Communists' intensity gave them influence well beyond their ranks.

More than any other single factor, the threat of fascism swelled the Party's numbers during the final years of the 1930s. To a growing number of Hollywood writers, actors, and directors, the Communists seemed the most committed to the anti-Nazi cause. That was a powerful selling point, because concern about Hitler became the first political issue to arouse widespread interest in the film industry. The awakening of Hollywood to the anti-Fascist cause proceeded through diverse routes. Many Hollywood Jews, of course, were immediately terrified by Hitler's anti-Semitism. Others in the film community learned of the threat from the European émigrés who washed into Hollywood through the 1930s like treasure from a sunken ship—Ernst Lubitsch, Billy Wilder, Fritz Lang, Otto Preminger, Peter Lorre. For Hollywood, the refugee directors and actors put a face on fascism that the Depression—only a word in Beverly Hills—didn't acquire until much later, when the displaced Okies poured into California. "Their participation was not public," said Milton Sperling, "but the ability to rely on them for clarification of issues was very important."

Concern about Hitler inspired even the most improbable of conversions. None proved more significant than the one experienced by Helen Gahagan Douglas, whose political migration tracked the awakening of liberal Hollywood during the Depression years. Though she would later be accused of excessive sympathy for Communists, Douglas was never attracted to the Party. Rather, she seized the growing opportunities for Hollywood activists within a Democratic party increasingly sensitive to the political value of fame. In time, for Helen Gahagan Douglas, politics became not just a cause, but a career that led her away from the melodrama of Hollywood to the raw emotion of Washington in the first spasms of the Cold War.

Douglas had come to Hollywood by something of a circuitous route in the first place. She was born in Boonton, New Jersey, in 1900 and grew up in Brooklyn. Her father, a civil engineer and a contractor who grew prosperous building railways in the West, dominated her early years. Traditional and authoritarian, he had a bleak view of most women—yet he did not believe his daughter should be shuttled into marriage. "He thought most women were impossible," Helen told a reporter years later. "The only way he could tolerate them was if they had an education." He took that lesson from his mother, Hannah Gahagan, who had attended Antioch College and become one of the first political feminists in Ohio.

That example at first meant little to Helen Douglas, who as a young girl found studies less engaging than the stage. "From the age of five," she wrote in her memoirs, "I had been consumed by dreams" of becoming an actress. Her father, reflecting the common Victorian attitude that for a woman the theater was only a short step above the street, was equally consumed by a passion to prevent her. "Forget about acting," he would thunder to his daughter. "Think!" Eventually, Helen Douglas acquiesced enough to enroll at Barnard College. But even in student productions, it was not long before producers saw her talent and offered her professional parts. When she took the lead in *Dreams for Sale* on Broadway at twenty-two, her course was set. Douglas received rave reviews (Heywood Broun called her "ten of the twelve most beautiful women in America") and despite the coolness of her family, launched her new career.

If Douglas broke with her father by choosing the stage, she was nonetheless shaped by him. She shared his capacity for hard work, his singlemindedness, and eventually his passion for clear and critical thinking. In the 1920s she was a successful Broadway actress before deciding, with a ferocity of commitment that later became her trademark, to undergo two years of serious training for the opera; she turned out to be enormously successful at that too. She met her husband, the actor Melvyn Douglas, when they co-starred in the Broadway play *Tonight or Never* in 1930. One year later, Douglas took his new bride to Hollywood, where he began a career as a wry, sophisticated leading man in light comedy, mostly at MGM. His career bubbled along, but she found Hollywood depressingly tawdry, and preferred the intimate contact of the theater to the posturing for the camera that the movies demanded. Only when faced with a financial crunch did she consent to her single film role, as the luminous star in the original cult classic *She*.

At first, neither of the Douglases concerned themselves much with political affairs; both seemed focused on finding theater opportunities that would liberate them from Hollywood. Melvyn, though, had an unexercised core of basic political beliefs. He had been born in Macon, Georgia, in 1901, the son of a moody and often inscrutable Jewish pianist named Edouard Hesselberg who had emigrated from Russia; his mother was the former Lucy Shakelford, the daughter of a successful Kentucky gentleman. Hesselberg was a distant father. Not unlike Louis Mayer, Hesselberg had an overwhelming need to be accepted in American society; not until Melvyn was a teenager did he learn of his Jewish heritage.

The parents' own strivings often left them little time for their children. By the time Melvyn was ten he was accustomed to coming "home from school to an empty house . . . neither seeing nor hearing any sign of [his parents] until late in the evening, when they returned from whatever social gathering they had been attending." That lonely upbringing seemed to instill in Douglas an independence that he carried through his life; especially in politics, he never worried about standing alone. He left the household early, and enlisted in the army during World War I (he never made it into combat). After the war, he drifted back into the fold, sharing rooms in a Chicago boardinghouse where his parents had settled. Douglas began his search for a career, through jobs as an encyclopedia salesman, gas meter reader, and elevator operator, before drifting into the theater under the tutelage of a Midwest Shakespearean actor named William Owen.

At the same time, Douglas began his political education. Through friends, he was exposed to Chicago's liberal political community; he read Frank Norris, Theodore Dreiser, and Upton Sinclair, learned of Eugene Debs, and met Clarence Darrow. The world of Debs and Darrow attracted the bright young actor, but it paled against the practical necessity of building his career. Melvyn paid his dues in small touring companies, mostly in the Midwest, and finally reached Broadway in January 1928, appearing as a gangster in *A Free Soul*. By then, he had changed his name to Douglas (his mother's grandmother's maiden name) when an agent delicately suggested that Hesselberg was too long to fit on a marquee. With *Tonight or Never* he won a five-year contract in Hollywood from Samuel Goldwyn.

Like his wife, Douglas initially felt uncomfortable with the impersonal demands of filmmaking and uncertain about a Hollywood career. For most of his life, in fact, he appeared unconvinced that making movies was an occupation for a serious person. But the fabulous money in Hollywood pulled him back whenever he strayed to Broadway, and eventually he signed an extended contract at MGM. Through the 1930s, he projected grace and style in such films as *The Gorgeous Hussy* (with Joan Crawford) and *Theodora Goes Wild* (with Irene Dunne) before co-starring with Greta Garbo in *Ninotchka* and earning his laurels as "the man who made Garbo laugh." This all made for a very easy life: the Douglases built themselves a huge home in the Hollywood Hills. But as his success grew, Melvyn's perspective narrowed. Through the first part of the Depression, he worried more about the size of his dressing room at MGM than the state of the nation.

Helen too was largely indifferent to politics in these years. She had grown up in comfortable surroundings—summers in Europe and Vermont, a family chauffeur—that kept all the world's unpleasantness at a distance, and she passively accepted the Republicanism that stretched back four generations in her family. Her first political awakening came when she and Melvyn drove across country to resettle in Hollywood in 1931, when for the first time she saw poverty and suffering. "My eyes were opened," she said years later. "I saw all the young people waiting in stations and piling out of box cars and trucks—the migration from the cities of the young people who couldn't get work."

In the 1932 election, neither Hoover nor Roosevelt seemed to her capable of meeting the needs of the migrants she saw on the road, but the lyrical words of FDR's inaugural speech touched a nerve in her. Soon after the election, she found herself instinctively tensing in anger at a dinner party in Pasadena when the comfortable guests gathered there condemned the New Deal attempts to help the unemployed as socialism. "If the group at that dinner party was representative of Republicans," she recalled later, "it was time I stopped voting Republican." Shocking her family, Douglas joined the Democratic party.

Still, her career remained her driving interest until she traveled through Germany and Eastern Europe for a concert tour in 1937. In Salzburg, she was approached by an Englishman sympathetic to the Nazis to spread the Aryan gospel in America. In Prague, she was warned not to sing the music of German and Austrian composers, so great was the

Czech fear of a Nazi invasion. In Vienna, visiting the elite of the Austrian music world, she was told: "You know the trouble with everything is the Jews, but we are going to send all of them to Madagascar."

The experience changed Helen Douglas's life. Against the great upheavals wracking Europe her passion for her career suddenly seemed shortsighted, insular, selfish. "From my childhood I'd been led to believe it was a nice world. Such a nice world that you just wanted to sing," she recalled later. "But when I saw something of the other side of things, I reacted to that." She returned to the United States committed to finding ways to express herself politically. Her husband, who had seen the same dangerous signs while accompanying her on part of the trip, followed suit. In the years leading to the war, both Douglases would devote as much energy to politics as to the movies, becoming pivotal figures in the struggle between liberals and Communists to define the agenda for the emerging Hollywood left.

Both Melvyn and Helen Douglas became pillars of the film industry's liberal camp. At first neither was overtly hostile to Communists. But none of the events that drove the Douglases to politics—the rise of fascism in Europe, the agony of the Depression at home—shook their basic faith in American institutions. That eventually led them into conflict with the first generation of Hollywood radicals, who, in their exaggerated disaffection, considered such faith naive. MGM screenwriter Donald Ogden Stewart typified that intransigent attitude. Stewart took an even more circuitous route to an even more intense political commitment than either Douglas. Stewart grew up in Columbus, Ohio, at the turn of the century, the son of a staunchly Republican lawyer, and quickly crashed the gates of the Upper Crust. He was burnished at Exeter, certified at Yale (where he was tapped for membership in Skull and Bones), and, after a turn in the navy during World War I and a stint with the American Telephone and Telegraph Company as a clerk, welcomed as a literate satirist at *Vanity Fair*. He was a tall, near-sighted man with thinning hair and an insidious wit—the sort of gaily dissolute yet indomitable character memorialized in F. Scott Fitzgerald's stories. During the 1920s, Stewart traded one-liners at the Algonquin Round Table with Dorothy Parker and Robert Benchley, joined in the expatriate exodus to Europe, effortlessly turned out books of bright social parody, and dabbled in the theater as playwright and actor.

He circled Hollywood too—first as a writer in the silent film days, then as an actor (in a film with Marion Davies entitled *Not So Dumb*); finally, when the rise of the talking picture forced the studios to find writers capable of filling the screen with sly and engaging dialogue, Stewart decamped for MGM in January 1932. His wit and skill transferred easily to the new medium, and over the next several years he enlivened such classic golden age George Cukor comedies as *Holiday* and *The Philadelphia Story* with sophisticated dialogue.

Stewart thrived at MGM. Since his days at Exeter, Stewart, the outsider from a middle-class family in Ohio, had longed for the social approval of the wealthy and well-connected: "I almost pathologically equated High Society with security," he recalled later. In Hollywood, for the first time, he earned enough money to feel he truly belonged in that company. He spent money as stylishly as he earned it. Through the most bitter years of the Depression, he appeared entirely comfortable manufacturing witty scripts for MGM, enjoying the sun at his Bel-Air home, and drinking until he passed out at parties.

The first stirrings of political life in the film community left Stewart unmoved. As one of MGM's highest-paid writers, he had little interest in the attempts to organize a screenwriters' union. When Mayer canvassed MGM employees for a day's pay to stop Upton Sinclair in 1934, Stewart happily subscribed. Nothing in his portfolio of bright, breezy satires suggested a burning interest in anything beyond a well-turned phrase. Visiting Stewart and Dorothy Parker in 1934, Katy Dos Passos, the wife of novelist John Dos Passos, reported back to Edmund Wilson "that the writers had passed out of the phase where they talked about their integrity and said that they wanted a little place in Connecticut to settle down and do something serious—they now said what a wonderful man Thalberg was and how they wanted to try to help him in the new thing that was being done (Technicolor, evidently)."

But the vague unease so common in Depression-era Los Angeles gnawed at Stewart too. Between the parties and the trips to Europe, he fought the nagging sense that his "quest for security through social and financial success had let me up the garden path—a very pleasant path but one which seemed to have come to a dead end." His unease crystallized when he pored over two tracts by Communist popularizer John Strachey as research for a character in a play. Stewart underwent an apparently searing midlife conversion. Like Helen Douglas, he found himself stricken by a need to become part of his time. Unlike Douglas, he lacked the emotional ballast to temper that urge.

For all his gaiety, Stewart was an obsessive character—he did nothing in moderation. (When his wife wilted under the strain of his relentless party-throwing, he organized a nervous breakdown party.) He took to politics with the same passion for extremes. Fired with the convert's fervor, he moved into the orbit of Hollywood's embryonic Communist party—eventually joining it—and found a purpose more compelling, if melodramatic, than winning Thalberg's favor: "to spread this great truth of Socialism so that the upper and middle classes would understand the point of view of the working class."

Even under the spur of his new revelation, Stewart didn't burn his dinner jackets or storm out of MGM in a huff. But he quickly became as earnest as he had been irreverent; he began to pore through the *New Masses.* When he passed a group of carpenters on the MGM lot he smiled at them, secure in the secret knowledge that he was now their "brother." Then he went home to his servants. It was no surprise that John O'Hara, visiting Dorothy Parker in Hollywood during the spring of 1936, thought Stewart quickly progressed beyond earnest to insufferable. "Don Stewart," he wrote to F. Scott Fitzgerald, "who is full of shit, has converted himself to radical thought . . . he is such a horse's ass. . . ."

Even if Stewart, like many of the freshly enlightened in Hollywood, carried his new truths a bit too much like biblical tablets, he was genuinely anxious to express his ideals in action. After some false starts, he found the best vehicle in the anti-Fascist cause. With the same energy he applied to organizing weekends by the pool, Stewart pulled together a public reading of Irwin Shaw's antiwar play *Bury the Dead* at the Hollywood Women's Club in early 1936, just before it opened on Broadway. Stewart was obviously a born organizer, whatever the occasion. For the 1,200 people who assembled, the reading by actor Fredric March, his wife Florence Eldridge, and director John Cromwell provoked a lively discussion not only about fascism and the gloom in Europe but also about working conditions in the industry, the predations of Hearst, and an assortment of pressing domestic political issues. To anyone who attended, it was obvious that an energy previously unseen in the movie colony was gathering.

From there the cause spread quickly. Prince Hubertus zu Lowenstein, exiled leader of the anti-Nazi German Catholic party, passed through Hollywood that spring, met the right people, and was feted at a huge banquet. The prince's visit crystallized the undirected political enthusiasm suddenly swirling through the industry. By June a core group that ranged from Rupert Hughes on the right to Stewart and director Herbert Biberman on the left, with actress Gloria Stuart, Melvyn and Helen Douglas, and Fredric March among those in the middle, came together to form the Hollywood League Against Nazism, soon rechristened the Hollywood Anti-Nazi League for Defense of American Democracy. Stewart was named president.

The success of the Anti-Nazi League created a contagious enthusiasm. From resisting fascism in Germany to fighting fascism in Spain was only a short hop for Hollywood's new band of activists. After Francisco Franco launched his insurrection against Spain's Republican government in 1936, Hollywood enlisted wholeheartedly in the government's cause. The already familiar progressive contingent—Dorothy Parker, freshly returned from a trip to the front, the ubiquitous Stewart, writers Dashiell Hammett and Lester Cole, as well as Melvyn Douglas, Paul Muni, Fredric March, and John Garfield—founded the Motion Picture Artists Committee to Aid Republican Spain, and a Hollywood affiliate of the Joint Anti-Fascist Refugee Committee, a national organization. No other cause so gripped Hollywood during the 1930s. MPAC grew more rapidly than the Anti-Nazi League until membership peaked at 15,000. "For all of us in that period, the Spanish Civil War had tremendous impact," said Alice Hunter, a story editor at Warner Bros. who was active in the anti-Fascist groups. "I don't believe I ever felt as passionately again as I did about the Spanish Civil War—but I think that's true of a whole generation."

Hollywood Communists played pivotal roles in forming both organizations. "The party was the galvanizing force behind the People's Front, the anti-fascist outfits," said Communist screenwriter John Bright, who was active in the groups. The Anti-Nazi League and the committees to aid Spain rippled with glittering names, but the celebrities drifted in and out, many content to appear on a letterhead, others willing to make cameo appearances only at major events. That left effective control of the Popular Front organizations with the much smaller group willing to handle the unglamorous day-to-day operations. Though the Communists lacked the numbers to control the groups outright, "in all these organizations . . . a very small Communist Party played a much bigger part than its numbers because of their willingness to do the work," said screenwriter Philip Dunne, one of the era's leading liberals.

The groups' activities reflected the prevailing wisdom in both liberal and Communist camps during the 1930s about the most effective means of advancing a political agenda. Later Hollywood leaders would attempt to influence political decisions primarily by courting politicians, mostly through campaign contributions. But the Anti-Nazi League and MPAC sought to influence political decisions by changing public opinion. In contrast to the insular and elitist Hollywood political organizations that revolved around private fundraising sessions during the 1980s, the Popular Front groups of the 1930s reached out to the public at every opportunity. The Hollywood groups constantly sponsored grassroots rallies, meetings, and demonstrations—all crowded with stars, directors, writers, and politicians. In just the first two months of 1939, for example, the Anti-Nazi League sponsored a labor rally with Melvyn Douglas at the Los Angeles Coliseum and a Quarantine Hitler rally at the Shrine Auditorium, and joined MPAC for a Save Spain rally at the Hollywood Legion Stadium. The Anti-Nazi League mounted petition drives, held public forums, produced a weekly radio program, published a biweekly newspaper, and picketed the German consulate. It hosted public appearances in Los Angeles for Interior Secretary Harold L. Ickes, black leader W. E. B. Du Bois, author André Malraux, and several local congressmen. On matters of ideology, the Popular Front eventually created enormous problems for the Hollywood liberals. But on matters of political tactics, it was an unsurpassed tutor. Its leaders understood intuitively that in a modern media society, celebrities were most useful as beacons to illuminate a political agenda for the public, not as prizes to dangle privately before politicians.

The vacuum left by the national and state Democratic parties allowed the Communists to assume a large role even in the first Hollywood organization specifically aimed at helping Democratic candidates. The initial impetus for that group came not from the Communists but from screenwriter Philip Dunne. Dunne took to the political world more naturally than most of his colleagues. His father, humorist Finley Peter Dunne, had expressed his own boundless skepticism about politicians through his fictional creation, the inimitable Mr. Dooley. But the elder Dunne had suffered the company of a few representatives of the offending breed, Theodore and Franklin Roosevelt among them; and the impressions they left on his son Philip inclined him toward liberal politics from an early age. Even an expensive boarding-school education capped by a breezy four years at Harvard didn't dilute his ideals; neither did a flowering screenwriting career under Zanuck at Twentieth Century-Fox.

Dunne embodied the liberal virtues: open-minded, curious, empathetic, and dogged. His insight was to see that the causes Hollywood marched behind could be advanced through electoral politics as well as rallies. "I was thinking that the position of the United States depended on what government you had in office," he recalled. "And I said, 'If you really want to help the Allies, reelect Roosevelt.'" With like-minded friends in the anti-Fascist organizations, he floated the idea of creating a Hollywood political organization specifically tied to the Democratic party. Dunne was an enthusiastic proselytizer but by temperament "no organizer." Melvyn Douglas, who understood the need to anchor Hollywood's burgeoning activism within mainstream domestic politics, took up the cause. One night in early 1938 the actor called Dunne, whom he had met through the anti-Fascist groups. "I've been talking to some people about your idea of having a political organization," he said, "and we think we should have a meeting."

Douglas was the organizer Dunne was not. Less charming ("He could be very prickly," Dunne recalled) than persistent, he quickly put flesh on Dunne's sentiment. Soon a group that included Douglas, Dunne, Gloria Stuart, actress Miriam Hopkins, and Dashiell Hammett gathered and decided to form yet another political organization. Douglas sent out a letter to writers, actors, directors, and technicians urging them to join a committee "working within the Democratic party to support and extend the New Deal nationally and, primarily, to bring a new deal to California." Enough signed on that by June 1938, Douglas and the rest were able to organize the Motion Picture Democratic Committee, Hollywood's first explicitly vote-getting organization. Its first test came in the 1938 California gubernatorial race. Against the unremarkable Governor Merriam, the California Democrats put up State Senator Culbert L. Olson. Olson wasn't as controversial or as visionary as Upton Sinclair, but he shared many of the same beliefs; he had been first elected on the EPIC ticket in 1934. Nonetheless, he didn't draw as fevered a reaction as Sinclair from the conservative powers in Hollywood. The moguls didn't like Olson, but he wasn't as terrifying as Sinclair, and Merriam had already disappointed them by approving a state income tax hike.

The Hollywood progressives, in contrast, threw themselves into Olson's campaign. It was a chance not only to elect a governor who supported many of their causes but also to strike a blow at the heavy-handedness of the moguls, who had done so much to foist Merriam on the state four years earlier. In the last campaign, the group complained at its inaugural meeting, "We were forced to help elect a stooge of the reactionaries to the governorship, regardless of what we thought." But in the present campaign, Melvyn Douglas explained in one speech, the group intended "to see that the body of the Motion Picture Industry shall speak for itself and not be made the instrument of any corporation group."

In its first campaign, liberal Hollywood acquitted itself well. No one saw the opportunities more clearly than Melvyn Douglas. While Helen remained in the background, Melvyn became the most identifiable member of the new organization. An accomplished speaker, he barnstormed the state for Olson and drew large crowds. Eventually he was named Olson's Southern California campaign chairman. Other celebrities joined him on the trail, and with earnest amateur energy, the Hollywood group produced a film and radio broadcasts for the challenger. This assistance was a major resource in Olson's underfunded campaign, and when he won, the group was justifiably elated. Suddenly, the Hollywood left had a friend in the statehouse, money in the bank, and an unbounded sense of possibility. Visiting New Dealers—from Eleanor Roosevelt to Frances Perkins—routinely included a stop at the Douglas home on their tours. There was even talk of Melvyn Douglas running for governor. For the activists, it was an exhilarating time. "I worked all day in the studio and all night in the political movement," said Dunne. "And then I'd take a nap in the afternoon and, refreshed, rise and go at it again. It was like that."

In the warm sunshine of success, new groups proliferated. Actor Edward G. Robinson, only slightly more accommodating than most, donated money to well over one hundred political and charitable organizations in 1939, from the Actors' Refugee Committee to the Spanish Child Welfare Association to the Hollywood Committee for Polish Relief. After chronicling in *The Grapes of Wrath* the miserable plight of the Okies, farmers who had abandoned the Dust Bowl for an even more precarious life as migrant workers in California, John Steinbeck formed another committee to provide aid. This became the first vehicle for Helen Gahagan Douglas to express her own political sentiments. The cause she chose was revealing. While her husband had a taste for politics at the highest level—for appearing on platforms with senators and governors, and mixing in Washington with the senior men in the government—Helen Douglas preferred more intimate and tangible, if less glamorous, involvement. She became involved with the Steinbeck committee after Melvyn allowed the group to use their home for a meeting. At first, she consented only to help organize Christmas parties for the children of families living in the federal government's refugee camps. But she lost herself in the depths of the misery. She organized clothing drives, food drives, nursery projects. Looking for contributions, she descended on bakers and butchers amazed to find a Hollywood star in their shops. She persuaded a friend to write a play about the Okies. She became chairman of the group and eventually delivered speeches across the state defending the federal camps against the large growers' intractable opposition. Douglas discovered that her fame as an actress and a singer guaranteed an audience for her talks where there might otherwise have been none. And over the months, addressing audiences friendly and hostile, in halls large and small, she discovered within herself a flair for moving a crowd.

Her experience was not unusual. In the isolation and unreality of Hollywood, politics provided for the growing ranks of activists connection, commitment, satisfaction, and fun. ("It was," Melvyn Douglas wrote in his memoirs, "as exciting a life as one could have desired.") "I think that the overall feeling all that period in the thirties was just one great big party; we were having a wonderful time being useful but also being very social," said actress Gloria Stuart, who joined each new group as soon as it hatched. "There was lots of enthusiasm, and lots of sense of achievement and dedication. But it was enjoyable. It was not traumatic at all. Everybody in it—you've got Dorothy Parker and Robert Benchley and Marc Connelly—were bright, talented people. My husband [Arthur Sheekman] being a writer—he was Groucho Marx's best friend, having written for him—was considered, next to Groucho, the fastest wit in the West, so it was laughing all the way. I don't think members of the [Communist] Party were having as good a time as we were because they were a lot more serious than we were. We gave them a lot of problems."

Stalin, Dies, and the Fall of the Popular Front

Stuart had the equation only half right: both sides in the Popular Front gave each other problems. Strains existed almost from the moment the alliance formed. The same discipline and intensity that attracted some liberals to the Communist party repulsed others. At meetings of the anti-Fascist groups, Party members often used complex and tenacious parliamentary tactics devised in advance at secret "fraction" meetings. Fifty years later, liberals still talk with amazement about Communists who worked to delay votes at meetings until late in the evening, long after most of the bourgeois liberals had repaired to bed and brandy. All this maneuvering for the control of what were, after all, voluntary organizations gradually bred suspicion. Some saw problems emerging early. "Melvyn Douglas very reluctantly accepted support of the Communist Party in the MPDC," said John Bright, a Party member who served on the group's board. "The liberals weren't anxious to cooperate; they were very, very reluctant to work with the Party."

But Douglas had no choice except to work with the Communists. Because the Communist party discovered Hollywood before the Democratic party, put more effort into organizing it, and had a message that appealed to Hollywood's sense of the dramatic, the Communists and their allies on the far left were too numerous, energetic, and integral to the Hollywood political community to ignore. In the mid-1930s the Communists were so entrenched that it was not possible to develop independent, non-Communist liberal institutions in the film community.

That fact shaped the course of Hollywood's political life for the next two decades. The Popular Front accelerated the film community's political engagement; it created an enormously effective means of tapping the latent power of celebrity, and it recruited many Hollywood figures who would otherwise have remained disconnected. Its achievements in calling public attention to the danger of fascism in Europe justified the conclusion of historians Ceplair and Englund that "there is . . . no denying the power and uniqueness of the Front in Hollywood during the . . . years that it flourished."

But for all its successes, the Popular Front route was a detour, one from which liberal Hollywood—pursued by the inquisitors of the right— did not fully recover until the 1960s. As a response to Hitler, the alliance had its own internal logic. But as a tool for influencing American politics on a broad range of issues, it was flawed at the foundation. It was built on a wish, a dream—the belief that in the final struggle with fascism, liberals and Communists had indistinguishable goals. That simply was not true. To a point, liberals and Communists shared common goals. But only to a point. Though they could join to resist fascism abroad and support social reform at home, at some juncture the interests of liberals and Communists in the Popular Front organizations clearly diverged. One organization could not speak for both factions on all issues, and the attempt to find unity, more often than not, only muted the development of an independent liberal voice in Hollywood. Politicians more sophisticated than the Hollywood liberals made the same mistake during the 1930s, but few had more difficulty than the film industry activists in extricating themselves when the alliance turned sour.

At first, the alliance seemed extraordinarily sturdy. In their Popular Front incarnation, the Communists became something like very left-wing Democrats, the first to volunteer to leaflet, to organize Democratic clubs, to knock on doors for liberal candidates. They abandoned millennial change for incremental change and sublimated themselves to the goals of the New Deal. "We were increasingly pro-Roosevelt, pro–New Deal, and the revolutionary stuff was something in the books, but it wasn't something we were working on," said screenwriter Jarrico. "We were working on the elections, we were working on reformist programs—how to get more Social Security or whatever—contemporary, nonrevolutionary causes, including most importantly the United Front against fascism. You don't have a United Front against fascism by talking about overthrowing the [capitalist] system. You underplay that. It may still be something that you someday hope you might turn your attention to, if the conditions are right, but it's not on the agenda. It's not what you are really concerned with."

During the Popular Front years, the Communist party abandoned its revolutionary rhetoric and halted its efforts to build a third party of farmers and workers. But the Party doctrine eventually demanded radical change. Hostility to capitalism remained at the Party's core; it provided the Party's ideological reason for being. The new language was moderation, reform, coexistence; but in the Party's most devout adherents, the old fervor burned. They were in no position to do anything about it, but the most committed Party members dreamed of the economic system's eventual transformation. Without that faith, the Party had no reason to exist.

But revolution was not on the liberals' agenda. Melvyn Douglas might join the Communists in condemning Hitler, but he would not be found waving banners to collectivize the farms and nationalize the banks. Orson Welles might turn up at rallies for civil rights in which Communists also participated, but he did not yearn to undermine the economic system that was rewarding him so lavishly. (As Welles wrote a few years later, "I am an overpaid movie producer with pleasant reasons to rejoice—and I do—in the wholesome practicability of the profit system. I'm all for making money if it means earning it.")

More pressing than the long-term divergence on economic policy were the immediate disputes over foreign policy. Through the late 1930s, liberals found it increasingly difficult to accept the Hollywood Communists' staunch refusal to criticize Joseph Stalin for the same cold repression that motivated the Front to march against Hitler. When the first reports of Stalin's purges drifted in, most Hollywood Party members dismissed them as Western propaganda, in what Stewart called the eagerness to accept "the universal humanity of my socialist dream-country." Hollywood leftists such as Lawson, Dorothy Parker, screenwriter Lester Cole, and Lillian Hellman later signed an open letter defending Stalin's show trials, in which he purged his own government and army. The refusal to find fault with any Soviet action deepened liberal suspicions. As long as the American Communists were committed to defending not only the theory of Marxism but its specific practice under Stalin—as long as the final arbiter of the American party's policies was Moscow's needs— Party members left open the question of whether they owed ultimate loyalty to this country or to the Soviet Union.

Faced with these implacable contradictions between their long-term agenda and that of the liberals—and their own internal contradictions— many Party members preferred not to think about them, and focused instead on the work at hand. The "official point of view," Party member Budd Schulberg recalled, was "that those who were not Communists but were supporting Popular Front organizations . . . were potential material for the Communist membership; they were thought of as being on their way toward having their eyes opened." Party members split on the official prediction's relevance to the real world. Optimists like screenwriter Ring Lardner, Jr., believed that eventually the liberals would be persuaded "of the superiority of socialism and would therefore vote for it; or at least a newer, younger generation of liberals without some of their preconceptions would be able to see that." Pessimists like John Bright feared the Front would eventually fall of its own weight. "There was a great deal of wish thinking involved among the optimists. There were those who took a doomsday view, and there were those who regarded the People's Front as impregnable," he said. "I was a doomsday guy." It was not very long before his worst fears were realized.

Even as the Hollywood Popular Front bustled through 1938, raising money, organizing rallies, and helping to elect a governor, the forces that would expose its contradictions gathered at home and abroad. At home the most visible threat came from the House Un-American Activities Committee, created that spring and placed in the trembling hands of Representative Martin Dies, Democrat of Texas. Impetuous, eager, suspicious of immigrants and intellectuals, hostile to virtually all forms of social change, and inordinately fond of publicity, Dies understood early on that Hollywood was not only fertile but inflammatory territory to investigate. Dies did his best to do so, which wasn't always very good. He never descended on Hollywood as systematically as his successors a decade later, and his approach was no more than scattershot.

But Dies kept firing anyway, and the prevalence of Communists in the thriving Popular Front groups guaranteed him more than an occasional hit. Committee investigator Edward Sullivan toured the West Coast in August 1938, just as the first HUAC hearings opened. He spent most of his time scrutinizing labor leader Harry Bridges. When he returned to Washington, he grimly declared: "All phases of radical and communistic activities are rampant among the studios of Hollywood." Like many of Dies's allegations, Sullivan's sensational charge was absurd in its sweep (nothing but envy and greed was truly "rampant" in Hollywood) but not entirely misdirected. Communists were key members of the Hollywood Popular Front organizations—a point invisibly underlined when Donald Ogden Stewart delivered the Anti-Nazi League's response to Dies's charges.

Dies's accusations weren't news to sophisticated liberals, who under-stood that their colleagues in the Popular Front groups included Commu-nists. But Dies opened eyes anyway, for he provided a chilling warning that the price of alliance with the Communists was rapidly rising. Prag-matic liberals such as Dunne and Melvyn Douglas had operated on the belief that the Communists, as minority members of the organizations, were aiding their causes, rather than the other way around. They had based their participation on that conviction, and it was the line to which they would retreat when pressed. Now Dies served notice that he in-tended to obliterate the line. To the Douglas and Dunne school of liber-als, the real issue was organizational control. To Dies, the issue was no more complicated than association, for anyone who associated with the Communists advanced their cause, willingly or not. He could not imagine a world in which Communists served liberal purposes (admittedly he tended to blur Communist and liberal purposes), and so he conjured in his mind a world in which all liberal purposes abetted by Communists ultimately served Communist ends.

Dies was not the only one to make that strange and politically conve-nient conceptual leap. Once blood was in the water, a legion of successor sleuths—ranging from amateurs and crackpots to those armed with the subpoena power of the state—began splattering outspoken Hollywood liberals with red. With all the patriotic indignation they could muster, the studio heads told anyone who would listen that Communists inspired their labor troubles. Even Melvyn Douglas, whom some Party members considered an outright "red baiter," found himself under attack as a Communist from the Republican speaker of the California State Assem-bly. Douglas eventually secured from Dies, of all people, a telegram indicating that no evidence linked him to the Party.

Douglas was ultimately spared, but the pressure that mounted through 1938 and 1939 was impossible to ignore. For the first time, Hollywood liberals faced the trap that would confront them with increasing fre-quency over the next decade. Inside Hollywood, they could not function politically except in alliance with the Communists; but that alliance greatly complicated their efforts to function in the outside political world. Hollywood liberals were squeezed between the right and the far left—and given little room to maneuver by either. By and large, the liberals did not wish to encourage conservatives who would deny the Communists the right to participate in American politics. But neither did they wish to be manipulated into endorsing the Communist agenda, particularly on poli-cies toward the Soviet Union.

Practical political considerations strengthened that principled urge for independent expression. Many of the Hollywood liberals understood that the alliance with the Communists left all liberal activity vulnerable to attacks from the right. Some liberals attempted to put the Popular Front groups on record as opposing communism as well as fascism, but the mythology of the united front was too strong to overcome. The proposals were voted down. When efforts were made in the Popular Front groups to condemn Stalin as a tyrant rivaling Hitler, the Communists dismissed their sponsors as "fascist lackeys" and "saboteurs."

Each time the Communists demonstrated their effective control of the Popular Front organizations, pressure on liberals to assert their independence increased. When Stalin signed his Non-Aggression Pact with the Nazis on August 24, 1939, he raised that pressure to the breaking point. More than Dies ever could, Stalin forced the components of the Popular Front alliance to declare their ultimate intentions. The morning after the treaty was signed, Dunne bet Melvyn Douglas that the Party's ranks would drain overnight. He was premature. The Hollywood Communists took the news of the pact with stunned disbelief, anger, and finally intransigence. After the initial shock, the Party leadership stabilized shaken Hollywood recruits by arguing that Stalin had acted through shrewd self-interest to buy time to prepare for the eventual conflict with Hitler.

Donald Ogden Stewart's reaction was typical. Like most Hollywood Communists, he was initially horrified by the entente. Eventually he concluded that only Stalin had "the correct Marxist understanding of the situation." Faced with the choice between the Soviet interest in avoiding war and the American interest in maintaining as strong an alliance against Hitler as possible, Stewart realized that his emotional loyalties had tipped. "I was American and my Marxism was American," he remembered years later. "But Russia was the only country of Marxism, and I didn't think I could abandon Stalin without surrendering my life raft." Most Hollywood Communists reached the same conclusion, and the Party held together, with only a few defections.

But the Non-Aggression Pact dissolved the glue that bound the Communists to the Hollywood anti-Fascist coalition—opposition to Hitler. For the mainstream liberal activist, neither attracted to the Party nor appalled by it, cooperation with Party members was based entirely on exigency. Once they aligned themselves behind the pact—once they demonstrated that their support for Stalin was more powerful than their loyalty to any other cause—the Party members no longer shared even short-term goals with Hollywood's anti-Fascist liberals. Nor could they any longer command the respect for intellectual rigor that had smoothed their Hollywood recruitment. Even so sympathetic a liberal as producer

John Houseman thought the gyrations of his Communist friends after the pact made them look "just ridiculous." It was asking too much to maintain respect for those who could reverse their position so agilely overnight. Isolated by his own ideological rigidity, Stewart found himself cut off from old friends. Similar scenes were repeated all over Hollywood.

After a few weeks, the Party compounded the problem by moving beyond its initial explanation for the pact—justifiable self-interest—to demand that the United States remain neutral in the fight against Hitler. In Hollywood, these maneuvers amounted to public suicide. "Because we were stupid enough not to stop with [the argument] that Russia was justified [signing the pact] in its own interest, we then carried it a step further, saying it was an imperialist war on both sides, the Yanks are not coming," said Jarrico. "That just wiped us out as far as our ability to influence anybody or anybody else's desire to remain united with us."

Systematically through the fall of 1939, the Hollywood Communists pressed the new line. The fight centered on the Motion Picture Democratic Committee. There the liberals' worst fears were realized: in an organization ostensibly dedicated to supporting Democratic candidates, the Communists and their allies rejected proposals from Dunne and Douglas to endorse Franklin Roosevelt's toughening stand on Hitler and instead pushed through a neutrality position on the European conflict that mirrored the Communist party's. That resolution left the MPDC liberals in the embarrassing position of standing on record in opposition to their political hero. For the most sophisticated liberals, that uncomfortable and offensive anomaly crystallized the need to escape from the Communists' shadow.

Finally, the group's leading liberals threw down the gauntlet. The group's refusal to condemn Stalin hardened the suspicions of Melvyn Douglas, whose ties to national Democratic leaders gave him a perspective that most of his contemporaries in Hollywood lacked. Perhaps because his own vague ambitions attuned him to the growing opportunities for the Hollywood activists, Douglas understood that the true stakes in acquiescence to the Communist agenda on the war was isolation from national influence. By tainting the Hollywood liberals with radical declarations, he realized, the Communists had become not allies but impediments to the community's political empowerment. That lesson was drilled into Douglas that fall when he conferred with top New Deal officials in Washington. Returning to Hollywood, Douglas told the board in December that the group could not expect to play a role in national Democratic politics unless it distanced itself from "those individuals and organizations" who had suddenly condemned the president's foreign policy. His warnings were dismissed, and Douglas angrily resigned from the group that he had helped to launch. Dunne mounted a final effort to salvage the imploding organization. Before presenting his own proposal to reaffirm support for Roosevelt, Dunne made the real choice even clearer: "The resolution is frankly intended to define our split of purpose and opinion with the Communist Party—since we can get no place until we do state this split."

The split occurred—at least temporarily—though not the way Dunne hoped. When his proposal was resoundingly defeated, the liberals resigned en masse from the MPDC. The same story was repeated in group after group. Its ardor for confronting Hitler gone, the Anti-Nazi League faded away, to be replaced by the American Peace Mobilization, dedicated to opposing U.S. entry into the war. The League of American Writers, which had vociferously denounced fascism, switched to the isolationist line and became the province of true believers.

The MPDC converted most abjectly. Once Dunne's resolution was rejected, it immediately passed, by a unanimous vote, a new statement of policy whose first priority was "Keep America Out of War." Its rhetoric acquired the lifeless stridency of Party tracts. Within weeks, the group attacked Douglas as a reactionary, and—following the hardening Communist party line—excoriated Roosevelt as a warmonger. By May 1940, the MPDC told its dwindled membership that FDR "has jumped into the leadership of this bloody conspiracy . . . to force a peaceful people into slaughter." As fervently as it had pressed for action against the Fascists abroad when Stalin seemed threatened, now the group warned that intervention would lead to fascism at home: "This is what our country faces immediately upon declaration of war: fascism, the mobilization of all industry, labor and society on a ruthless, suppressive military basis in support of a conflict between two imperialisms which become steadily less distinguishable." As the Nazis prepared their final assault on Western Europe in the spring of 1940, the MPDC condemned the "creation of war hysteria" and government efforts "to force the public to regard one belligerent as the 'enemy.' " This debasing surrender to illogic reached its nadir when the group supported an anti-Roosevelt slate of delegates (led by Lieutenant Governor Ellis E. Patterson) in the June 1940 California primary. After the isolationist slate fell, the Hollywood Communists rallied around the presidential candidacy of Party leader Earl Browder, who ran under the slogan "The Yanks Are Not Coming."

The Communists had proved they could impose their will on the Popular Front organizations—but only at the cost of obliterating them. After all the fierce debate and maneuvering, the angry speeches and cries of betrayal, they were left with empty shells—and a growing antipathy among the most politically attuned liberals toward alliance on any issue. Soon after he quit the MPDC, Douglas was talking about creating a liberal organization that would explicitly bar Communists.

No such lasting organization was formed until seven years later, after another attempt to revive the Popular Front. The drift toward global war brought the Communists back into the anti-Fascist fold. When Hitler invaded Russia on June 22, 1941, the interventionists-turned-isolationists reverted. After two years of debilitating and demeaning efforts to defend Stalin's maneuvers, most of the Hollywood Communists took the attack as cause for celebration. Donald Ogden Stewart, distraught over his alienation from old friends because of the pact, "wept with joy" when the news came in.

Though doubts persisted, the Hollywood liberals gradually accepted the embrace of the Communists again. Both sides were initially wary, but the Soviets' heroic fight against Hitler softened suspicions, and eventually the liberals once again came to see the Communists as brothers-in-arms in the new organizations that sprouted during the war. "Some of the liberals were still suspicious of the Communists," said Paul Ziffren, a young Los Angeles attorney in the 1940s who became a major figure in Democratic and Hollywood circles. "And some said, 'What the hell.'"

Given the wartime atmosphere of solidarity, the rapprochement between the Hollywood Democrats and Communists was perhaps inevitable. But alliance was again costly for the liberals. Once the Communists were reestablished in the film community's political structure, all Hollywood activists again faced attacks on their patriotism from increasingly assertive conservatives in Washington, the state house, and Hollywood itself. Those threats confronted even those who were skeptical of the Communists, such as Melvyn and Helen Douglas. As their political careers evolved through the 1940s, neither fully escaped the stigma of the Hollywood liberals' association with the Party. If, in the years surrounding the war, the Douglases dramatized the possibilities for Hollywood activists in Washington, they also paid a price for the community's detour into radicalism. This bill did not come due as long as progressive forces everywhere had the protection of their hero, Franklin Delano Roosevelt. But Roosevelt could not control the White House forever. In FDR's prime, liberal Hollywood first edged onto the national political stage; when he died, it was almost swept from the boards.

CHAPTER THREE

INTO THE MAINSTREAM

Roosevelt and Hollywood

It was not until the end of the 1930s that the two major political parties displayed as much interest in Hollywood as the Communists had. Their motivation was in some ways similar, but in one key respect it was different. Like the Communists, the Democrats and Republicans saw Hollywood as a potential source of funds. But unlike the Communists, who kept their membership secret, the parties increasingly used the stars as public spokespeople and symbols of political beliefs.

Under Franklin Roosevelt, the Democrats exploited the possibilities faster than the Republicans. In Hollywood, as throughout the country, Roosevelt evoked polarizing passions. But from his first bid for the White House in 1932, Roosevelt's side in the film community was always well represented. During the campaign against Herbert Hoover, moguls Jack and Harry Warner organized a huge pageant for Roosevelt at the Los Angeles Coliseum with the help of many top stars and executives.

The event introduced Roosevelt to Los Angeles. But if the Democrats realized quickly enough that stars could be used to draw a crowd in Hollywood, it took them longer to understand how they could be used to communicate with the entire nation. That awareness grew at a time when social scientists concluded that the movies and movie stars were already communicating powerful messages to the 85 million Americans who filed into theaters weekly. Returning to Middletown several years after their classic study of life in the typical (and pseudonymous) Middle American community, Robert S. and Helen Merrell Lynd wrote that adolescents found models for their lives in "the sharp figures of the silver screen which present gay and confident designs for living." Other commentators noticed that "the movie idols have usurped the role of Society in establishing styles." The Gallup Poll discovered that the books people named as their favorites were invariably those the studios had transferred to the screen. In these and other ways, Hollywood and its stars were becoming what one author, writing in 1939, called a "standard of reference" for millions of Americans. Celebrated on screen, in print and over the radio, Hollywood stars inspired more adoration than any figures in the popular culture before them.

Political strategists did not fully understand the political power of that adoration until many years later. But even in the Roosevelt years, the sheer notoriety of the Hollywood heroes—the stories of fans mobbing Edward G. Robinson when he descended from a train in New York while ignoring his fellow passenger Herbert Hoover—made it impossible for politicians to ignore them. And gradually through the 1930s and 1940s more political figures, both in Washington and in Hollywood, came to see how the stars could be used to focus and to amplify political messages.

It was under Roosevelt that the idea of systematically funneling Hollywood into the mainstream of national partisan politics took root. For the first time, the two national parties effectively competed with the Communists for the allegiance of writers, directors, and stars. There was no single guiding intelligence (certainly not FDR himself), nor any coordinated plan. But the expanding aura of celebrity illuminating Hollywood virtually forced closer relations with Washington. The stars were a unique resource in a mass media era: they were not only creatures of mass communication—raised to their exalted status by the enormous attention the new communications technologies made possible—but also tools of mass communication, vehicles for projecting fashions, values, and political messages. Throughout American history each new tool of mass communication had been rapidly fitted for political use. In the 1920s radio was still a novelty, but during the next decade Roosevelt used it to reach the public more effectively than any president before him. The same thing happened with the Hollywood stars. Hollywood's political involvement in the Roosevelt years marked the first uncertain attempts to harness the new mass communication tool—the celluloid celebrity—for partisan electoral purposes.

After the Sinclair backlash, neither the studios nor the parties sought to influence individual campaigns through messages placed directly on the screen (though as World War II neared, the White House may have pressured the studios to muster support for its military buildup). But other weapons for supporting candidates remained at hand in Hollywood. By the late 1930s, the press corps covering Hollywood was exceeded only by those covering New York and Washington. Studio publicists did not want reporters to focus on the stars' political views, but the stars themselves came to realize that their appearances and opinions generated enormous attention. Washington took notice. By 1940, the Democratic National Committee provided money to Hollywood activists to assist them in getting out the word that the stars preferred Roosevelt.

Roosevelt was interested in Hollywood long before it reciprocated. After Warren Harding dispatched the Democratic ticket of James M. Cox and Franklin Roosevelt in 1920, the young politician settled into the life of a New York businessman, practicing law and working as the vice-president of a surety bond company. Through the mid-1920s, he dabbled in investments, fought the polio that had crippled him in 1921, started and discarded a history of the United States—and attempted to write a movie.

Roosevelt composed a twenty-nine-page treatment for a film about John Paul Jones, the Revolutionary War naval hero. Roosevelt's fascination with naval history and the sea was life-long; during his tenure as assistant secretary of the navy in the Wilson administration, he kept a bust of Jones on his mantel. Roosevelt carefully researched his subject: he even considered writing a full-length biography, but knew he lacked the patience to complete it. The research went into his movie.

Roosevelt opened his tale with twelve-year-old John Paul Jones, "a leader of the small boys of the neighborhood" on "The Earl of St. Mary's Isle on the banks of the River Die in Scotland." Over twenty-seven episodes, Roosevelt followed Jones through assorted dramas (including an attempt to capture the Earl of Selkirk, "the man he believes to have been his mother's seducer") that concluded in a dramatic sea battle. At a crucial moment, Roosevelt even introduced "a beautiful young lady . . . with royal blood in her own veins" who helps Jones out of a tight spot in France. His work completed in April 1923, Roosevelt proudly turned over his manuscript to Wells Hawks in the office of the renowned theatrical producer and manager Sam H. Harris. Hawks offered the property to Adolph Zukor at the Famous Players–Lasky Corp. Zukor, understandably intrigued by a submission from such a well-known personality, told Hawks the same day he would be happy to read it. One week later, Zukor's son Eugene wrote Roosevelt to inform him his work had been passed along to a Jane West in the production department. Zukor assured Roosevelt that West was anxious to confer about exactly what he "had in mind"—which might have led Roosevelt to wonder why what he had in his mind wasn't apparent from the manuscript Zukor had in his hand. West conferred with Roosevelt a few days later and arranged a follow-up meeting with Louis Howe, Roosevelt's long-time assistant.

Then, nothing. More than a year later, Roosevelt found himself dispatching the faithful Howe with a pointed note for the Zukors: "Will you be good enough to give Mr. Howe . . . the manuscript on John Paul Jones which I sent you over a year ago. I have need for it immediately." But Roosevelt overcame his disappointment and maintained his interest in the movies. He understood the medium's enormous power and was cautious with it; as president he was sensitive to how, and where, he was portrayed. When newsreel companies offered film footage of FDR for use in such features as Joe E. Brown's *Elmer the Great,* the president's secretary, Stephen T. Early, concerned about maintaining the dignity of the office, asked Will Hays to prevent the studios from using Roosevelt's likeness in movies. ("The President decidedly objects," Early wrote.) Hays passed along the suggestion. For the newsreels themselves, Roosevelt was always accommodating, and he appeared in them roughly every two weeks.

Roosevelt enjoyed movies, and movie people. A dramatic personality himself (Arthur Krock called him "the best showman the White House has ever lodged"), Roosevelt prized colorful dinner-table guests such as Melvyn and Helen Douglas and Douglas Fairbanks, Jr. Delegations of stars attended his inaugurals. The studios went to great lengths to provide any film Roosevelt might wish to see, and Roosevelt was interested enough in their products that the White House obtained its own film operator from the navy. Roosevelt regularly relaxed after dinner with a movie, watching films as often as three or four times a week during the early months of his administration.* The *New York Times* reported that none of Roosevelt's predecessors in the White House "can approach him as a movie enthusiast."

Still, Roosevelt showed no signs of being dazzled by Hollywood glamour. His attitude toward it was entirely utilitarian. He manipulated the stars and the studio fathers the way he manipulated Congress and his own bureaucracy: "It wasn't [the moguls] getting anything out of Roosevelt," said Betty Sheinbaum, Harry Warner's daughter. "It was Roosevelt using Jack and Zanuck and the rest of them." Roosevelt seemed to sense how keenly the moguls craved the social validation of a White House dinner or an autographed photo of the president on their desk—proof that they stood in the company of powerful and serious men, even if they were not allowed into Los Angeles's country clubs. These social benefactions didn't cost Roosevelt much, but they resonated with enormous force in Hollywood's insecure corridors. In exchange for the admiration of men whose cultural influence exceeded even their own understanding, Roosevelt dispensed his favor with regal grace.

Zanuck was invited fairly regularly to the White House. So was Jack Warner, who proved particularly susceptible to the flattery of Roosevelt's mere presence. Though Will Hays was a longstanding GOP stalwart, Roosevelt kept in close touch, often sharing political gossip. When Irving Thalberg died, Roosevelt sent his widow condolences. Even Mayer, a staunch Republican, came by occasionally. Still, Roosevelt did not always enjoy smooth relations with the moguls. As the New Deal unfolded, the government intruded dramatically into the movie industry's previously cloistered affairs, repeatedly challenging its paternalistic, cutthroat approach to business. In 1935, the Wagner Act established the National Labor Relations Board and the framework for organizing unions on a mass scale. That resuscitated the screenwriters' stalled effort to organize. "Until the passage of the Wagner Act," said screenwriter John Bright, "it looked like the cause was lost." Though conservative screenwriters, led by MGM's James K. McGuinness, had worked with Irving Thalberg to form an alternative union called the Screen Playwrights, the militant Screen Writers Guild, with many of the Communist writers among its

*Later, of course, as the demands of World War II engulfed him, Roosevelt had less time to watch films. His aides regularly sent polite letters to Darryl Zanuck, Jack Warner, and the other executives regretfully declining their entreaties for the president to review their latest epic. But nothing apparently dissuaded them. In June 1943, Jack Warner wrote Roosevelt asking him to review the company's *This Is the Army* and offering to deliver the print himself. An exasperated Roosevelt typed to his secretary, General Edwin M. Watson: "Tell Jack Warner I do not have the time to see movies now."

leadership, won an NLRB representation election in 1938. After five years of bitter resistance, the moguls, teeth clenched in rage, were forced to open negotiations with the SWG in September 1938.

For the men in the industry's boardrooms, that constituted more than enough intrusion from the government. But the same year, the Justice Department filed a historic antitrust case accusing the five major studios (as well as Columbia, Universal, and United Artists, less influential players) of conspiring to monopolize the industry in all phases: production, distribution, and exhibition. For twenty years, the government had investigated and intermittently resisted the increasing integration of the industry, accusing individual companies of using their market power to fix prices, freeze out independent competitors, and through a process known as block booking, force exhibitors to accept movies they didn't want as the price of receiving top films. But it had failed to stop the trend toward centralized ownership, and the abuses continued. The 1938 action, which came to be known as the Paramount case, was something else again: a frontal assault on the studios' manner of doing business. The Justice Department proposed a legal remedy the moguls found as chilling as it was sweeping: the government asked the court to sever the largest five studios from any of their exhibition theaters implicated in the restraint of trade.

These conflicts dented Roosevelt's standing with the industry's fathers. As *arrivistes* anxious for social approval, they coveted Roosevelt's favor; as Jews, they applauded his stand against the Nazis. But as conservative businessmen, they recoiled from his domestic policies. Their loyalties fluctuated with their needs. Even Roosevelt's most visible supporters in the boardrooms, the Warner brothers, vacillated. Jack Warner sent Roosevelt fawning letters and then told Philip Dunne: "It looks like our friend Roosevelt is making a horse's ass of himself." Harry Warner was angered when the Justice Department sued the company in a dispute over theaters in St. Louis. Harry was eventually forced to sell the theaters, and he took it as a personal slight from the New Deal. When the 1940 campaign began, none of the Warner brothers appeared on the letterhead of the official Hollywood for Roosevelt group (though Jack's son, Jack Junior, and Harry's son-in-law, Milton Sperling, participated).

But Roosevelt was skillful enough to prevent the moguls from completely abandoning his ship. In November 1940, the studios signed a consent decree that allowed them to keep their theaters, though the agreement required them to cease the anticompetitive practices identified in the suit and submit disputes to a nationally organized arbitration system. At the time, *Variety* reported that the White House, hoping to win from the studios both support for the fall election and more feature films encouraging rearmament, pressured the Justice Department to settle the case. The Justice Department denied receiving any pressure, but there's no question that after the settlement, the movie industry suddenly showed an increased appetite for films dealing with the European conflict and the need for military preparedness. From fall 1940 through the attack on Pearl Harbor, Hollywood obediently churned out three dozen feature films that bolstered Roosevelt's effort to steel the nation for war.

The film industry also enlisted more energetically than before in Roosevelt's second reelection campaign. The Warner brothers' pique* and the defection of the suddenly isolationist Communists were hardly noticed. Charles L. O'Reilly, chairman of the Democratic National Committee's motion picture division, estimated that Roosevelt had the support of "better than eighty-five percent" of the industry in his bid for a third term against Wendell L. Willkie.

With so much star voltage available, the 1940 Roosevelt effort provided the first real suggestion of celebrity's potential value in a national campaign. Democratic leaders gave the first hints of heightened interest in Hollywood when Melvyn Douglas toured Washington and met with the key New Dealers in the fall of 1939. When he returned to Los Angeles, he told the Motion Picture Democratic Committee executive board, "I am convinced . . . there is little doubt in any quarter as to our possible value. . . . I talked to most of the Washington 'glamour boys and girls' . . . and I have their assurances of real cooperation." Though the MPDC collapsed in the dispute over the Hitler-Stalin pact, the liberals reassembled into the Hollywood for Roosevelt group. National Democrats nurtured their progress. "This thing was different than anything before it," said Philip Dunne. "There was complete rapport with the national party. This was big stuff."

The national party used the Hollywood stars more effectively than ever before. As he did in the California governor's race two years earlier, Melvyn Douglas generated large crowds and enormous press attention when he barnstormed the country in October. Endorsement letters from leading actors and actresses provided to the Democratic National Committee were reprinted in major newspapers. Most important, the stars were dispatched in large numbers to deliver radio appeals for the ticket. Radio and the stars functioned synergistically. A star could reach many

---

*Even the Warner brothers hedged their bets, Milton Sperling recalled. "I think Jack went the other way [and supported the GOP] in 1940," he said. "It was a family decision: they wanted to have one foot in each camp."

more people by radio than through personal appearances, and the use of a star could enlarge the audience for a political broadcast. The widespread use of radio dramatically enhanced the political value of celebrity, just as television did later. In the week before the election, the DNC purchased airtime for two national radio broadcasts featuring Douglas Fairbanks, Jr., Humphrey Bogart, Melvyn Douglas, Henry Fonda, Groucho Marx, Lucille Ball, Joan Bennett, and John Garfield. The Democrats' decision to rely so heavily on Hollywood figures to deliver the party's message in the campaign's final hours testified to the growing awareness of their power as messengers.

The same was true elsewhere in the political system. Groups lobbying for American intervention against the Nazis gave Hollywood stars unprecedented prominence in their appeals. The two major groups supporting intervention deployed Melvyn Douglas and Douglas Fairbanks, Jr., to deliver national radio addresses. The government used stars to publicize the need for military strength. Isolationists, who found almost no support in Hollywood, understood how formidable a resource confronted them. During the fall of 1941, isolationist senators held hearings to investigate whether Hollywood's anti-Nazi films were intended to stampede the nation toward war. (With Wendell Willkie, a leading opponent of the isolationists, presenting the case, the moguls aggressively rebuffed the attack.) At the same time other isolationists, increasingly conscious of the stars' capacity to influence the public off-screen as well, complained about the "widely publicized visits of 'stars' to military training camps, their acceptance of military commissions, and appearances on government-sponsored radio broadcasts."

The war itself cemented the use of stars as a bridge between Washington and the public. Obviously the studios, working with the Office of War Information, rushed out battle epics designed to rouse public support for the war effort. Just as important, the war provided the best evidence to date that the stars could influence public opinion through personal appearances and endorsements. Even more than in World War I, the government used the stars as spokespeople to exhort the public for all sorts of worthwhile causes; for one 1942 war bond drive, 337 stars sold almost $850 million in bonds. During one celebrated radio marathon, singer Kate Smith alone sold an incredible $39 million in bonds. At the same time, the stars were extraordinarily effective symbols of the nation's communal purpose and total commitment to the global conflict. Newspapers and movie trailers recounted in great detail the wartime exploits of stars such as Henry Fonda, Clark Gable, and James Stewart, with the attention, as one commentator remembered, reinforcing "our feeling that we were all, the favored and the unfavored, in this thing together, democratically serving and sacrificing." No other figures in American society could make that point so quickly and firmly as the aristocrats of fame, the Hollywood stars.

The war experience appeared to further sensitize political strategists to the stars' ability to reach and move the public. When film community activists gathered to form the Hollywood Democratic Committee (HDC) in 1943, national and local Democrats immediately turned a solicitous eye. The HDC grew out of an ad hoc effort organized in Hollywood for California Governor Culbert Olson in the last days of his unsuccessful 1942 reelection campaign against liberal Republican Earl Warren. Olson's call for help to the Hollywood activists came too late to save his campaign. But for screenwriters Nat Perrin and Sidney Buchman, lyricist E. Y. Harburg, and the other Hollywood partisans who pitched in, it was an exhilarating experience. "What struck me most vividly is that, had we been in this thing weeks earlier, it would have made a total difference," said Perrin. "It disturbed me that we had no organization." After Olson's defeat, Perrin and his allies set out to build one.

When the group went public with its first meeting in January 1943, more than 180 activists signed up. Marc Connelly, screenwriter and veteran of the Algonquin Round Table, was named chairman, mostly for the aura of Eastern respectability he conveyed. "He wore the rimless glasses, he had a very clean, pinkish face and he was well-fed looking," said Perrin. "He looked like Yale, Harvard, Princeton, Ivy League: a Connecticut type of nice Gentile. You couldn't say he was a wild-eyed bomb thrower." The group had its share of those, too: Party members John Howard Lawson, Lester Cole, director Edward Dmytryk, and Paul Jarrico signed on, seeing the need to maintain in the White House a strong supporter of the wartime alliance with the Soviets. The liberals—Perrin, actress Gloria Stuart, and actor Walter Huston among them—filled out the board. With both the radical and liberal camps enthusiastic for their own reasons, the Hollywood Popular Front was reborn. In January 1944, the HDC had almost a thousand members in the fold when California Attorney General Robert W. Kenny, the state's most prominent Democrat, kicked off the election year by telling the group: "The coming elections may determine the course of history for a century to come."

Deep in talented writers and cartoonists and thick with famous names, the HDC quickly emerged as the most sophisticated partisan political organization Hollywood had ever seen: well-funded, fluent in the latest campaign technology, and committed to hardball campaigning. Under the direction of George Pepper, an energetic young violinist whose career was cut short by a hand injury, the HDC functioned as a full-fledged political organization that entered campaigns with decisive force. It systematically identified the most highly paid members of the industry and solicited them for contributions. In a state where the Democratic party was demoralized, the HDC instantly stood out; only six months after it was organized, Kenny told the group it was the only organization working effectively for Democratic aims in California.

In the weeks leading up to the 1944 California primary, the HDC mobilized as if to prove Kenny's assessment. Pepper, ideologically fervent (he was later identified before HUAC as a member of the Communist party) and organizationally gifted, worked himself to exhaustion. In a few weeks, the group raised $35,000 and launched a massive blitz. Its principal target was Democratic Representative John M. Costello of Los Angeles, who had fought the Lend-Lease bill and other administration priorities. Using the grassroots strategy of the first generation Popular Front groups, the HDC flooded his district with 150,000 tabloid newspapers, 50,000 postcards, and a 150,000-piece mailing. The HDC showed media savvy, too. On a broadcast over CBS radio shortly before the primary, Costello was battered by one of his most glamorous constituents, Rita Hayworth: "I don't think I can be blamed for calling him a renegade Democrat," Hayworth cooed, in a voice that brought men closer to the radio. In the final days before the vote, the group pounded Costello with witty radio ads; it even arranged for pickets in front of supermarkets carrying signs that accused him of seeking to raise the price of milk. Costello never knew what hit him. "Workers called at every home," Costello lamented to his colleagues a few weeks after his defeat, "voters were repeatedly telephoned, literature . . . flooded the district, despite the paper shortage, and the radio programs went into full swing along with continual newspaper advertisements."

Each of the HDC's nine endorsed congressional candidates won their primary contests. Among them was Helen Gahagan Douglas, finally taking the step into politics about which others in Hollywood fantasized. The victory capped her remarkable evolution from actress to activist to politician—and her escape from her husband's shadow.

Neither was an easy passage. At first Melvyn appeared poised for the breakthrough into elected office. Through the outbreak of World War II, Melvyn remained the family's big draw on the campaign trail. His conflicts with the Hollywood left over the Hitler-Stalin pact did not diminish his taste for politics, and he remained as eager as anyone in the film industry to assist causes and candidates. His work for Governor Olson in

1938 and Roosevelt in 1940 led Jimmy Roosevelt, the president's son, who had worked for Samuel Goldwyn and knew the film world, to call him Hollywood's "ablest New Deal leader." Governor Olson appointed him to the California State Relief Commission and Social Welfare Board; he regularly received requests to speak before political groups all over the country; and rumors that he would seek office repeatedly percolated into the press.

Douglas never did, but with each passing year he moved more deeply into the political arena. During the fractious 1940 California primary, with the disputes over the Motion Picture Democratic Committee's sudden conversion to neutrality still fresh in his memory, Douglas joined the pro-Roosevelt slate of delegates headed by Olson. When the Roosevelt slate won decisively over both the isolationists and another pledged to former Vice-President John Nance Garner, Douglas became the first actor selected as a delegate to the national convention. The honor affirmed Douglas's position as the star most closely identified with national politics.

But even the enormous spotlight on Melvyn could not entirely obscure Helen Douglas's own formidable skills. Though his greater celebrity guaranteed greater attention to his political activity, her commitment to political action was no less consuming. Excited by her work with the Steinbeck committee, and inspired by the family's friendship with Eleanor Roosevelt, she sought new opportunities. In 1940, she was invited to the convention with Melvyn to sing the national anthem at the opening ceremonies. She welcomed the honor, but was not content to be deployed as glamorous window dressing. When the state delegation offered her the prestigious position of Democratic National Committeewoman from California, she stepped across the line from amateur activist to professional politician; soon after she returned to California, she was appointed the state party's vice-chairman.

In these roles, Helen also threw herself into the 1940 campaign. By her count, she gave 168 speeches for Roosevelt and other Democrats across the country. She was a powerful and eloquent if theatrical speaker who found talking to voters exciting and rewarding. On the campaign trail she felt free from the suffocating cocoon of impersonal adulation that enveloped celebrities, able to reach people not because of who she was but what she said. Attuned to suffering, moved by the response she received, she found the tug of political life increasingly irresistible.

When the war came, Melvyn—his old ambivalence about Hollywood intensified by the great events occurring elsewhere—moved to Washington to direct the arts division of the Office of Civilian Defense, which mobilized artists to support the war effort. Conservatives bitterly attacked the appointment and pummeled him with the old and illogical charge that he was sympathetic to Communists. Douglas bristled but grimly stuck with the job (despite his own doubts about his qualifications) until Columbia Pictures, which refused to release him from his contract, demanded he put aside such trivia as the war effort to make a movie with Joan Crawford. Douglas was no happier in Hollywood than he had been at the outbreak of war, but his difficult experience in Washington seemed to dampen his enthusiasm for politics. He was never again as large a force in Hollywood's political life as he had been up through the early months of the war.

When he finished the Joan Crawford film, rather than returning to government, he enlisted in the army as a private at age forty-one, partly at the advice of Eleanor Roosevelt, who counseled that it would put Douglas "in an impregnable position" to defend his patriotism. After surviving basic training and questions from military intelligence about his association with the Popular Front groups of the 1930s, he was ultimately assigned to direct entertainment for the troops in the China-Burma-India theater—a posting that seemed to symbolize his exile from the center of political life.

Helen, meanwhile, accepted an appointment from Roosevelt in the Southern California civil defense operation, which mobilized with the feverish expectation that a Japanese attack on the West Coast was inevitable. At the same time, she energetically built her women's division of the California Democratic party into a local power base, organizing women around the principle of achieving a greater voice within the male-dominated local party. Helen Douglas did not have her husband's natural instincts for political combat. As Philip Dunne observed, she had the sensibility of the nineteenth-century women reformers: throughout her career she believed the purpose of politics was not to divide spoils but to help the helpless. But she balanced her infectious idealism with a hardheaded pragmatism that anchored her, even if it sometimes made her appear humorless. Within Democratic circles she came to be recognized as someone who took her politics very seriously, and the White House regularly utilized her as a guide through the confusing currents of California politics.

After Melvyn left for the war, Helen's talents stood out more clearly. When Thomas F. Ford, the Democratic representative from Los Angeles's 14th District, decided to retire rather than seek reelection in 1944, he asked her to succeed him. The request shocked her. Congress itself seemed unappealing ("You're asking me to sit and listen to that tedium day after day?" she said to Ford. "I'd go stark raving mad!"), and the possibility of running for office forced her to confront the prospect of surrendering her artistic career entirely. That was the direction her life had been heading for the past seven years, but at first she was uncertain that she could commit herself so unequivocally. Eventually, though, her resistance wore down, and characteristically enthused by the challenge, she entered the primary. The news pleased Roosevelt. He thought Douglas would give the Democrats a counter to Clare Boothe Luce, the elegant playwright and editor elected to Congress as a Republican in 1942. Publicly FDR remained neutral in the primary. But privately he wrote Douglas in early March, "Tom Ford has just told me that you are going to run for Congress in his place. . . . if he has to leave the Congress I can ask nothing better than to have you in his place."

But first she had to get through the primary. Douglas faced six opponents, all men. Her assets in the campaign were her name, her fame, and her energy. But as an affluent actress who didn't live in the district, she faced attack as a carpetbagger. That was a particular problem with the low-income voters in the district's eastern end. Douglas set out to combat her blue-blood image with a grassroots campaign. She organized dozens of meetings in voters' homes and went from house to house, making her case to small groups in living rooms night after night.

Douglas actually had little money and little outside support. Almost immediately the conservative *Los Angeles Times* came out against her. Leftist union leaders, perhaps remembering her husband's conflicts with Communists in Hollywood, also opposed her. But in the campaign she began to find her political voice: passionate, empathetic, populist, and yet grounded in political reality to a degree virtually unique on the Hollywood left. With the help of the Hollywood Democratic Committee and her own indefatigable campaigning, she won the July primary decisively.

Douglas now returned to the 1944 Democratic gathering in Chicago as a candidate. The HDC sent along Gloria Stuart and a staff member to coordinate its fall campaign plans with the top brass of the Democratic National Committee. But Douglas received most of the attention. The Democrats, understanding her symbolic value, consciously focused attention on her. As Roosevelt expected, the press portrayed Douglas as the liberal alternative to Luce. Because Luce had addressed the Republican convention, the Democrats gave Douglas a prominent spot. In her new role as a political diva, Douglas got off to an uncertain start. Cheers greeted her when she rose at the evening session on July 20, but her speech was indifferently received by a convention floor subdued by equal parts of exhaustion and alcohol. That was the least of Douglas's disappointments; far more distressing to her was Roosevelt's decision to allow the delegates to replace liberal Henry A. Wallace as vice-president with centrist Missouri Senator Harry S. Truman. Douglas wept with disappointment when the delegates dumped Wallace.

Among the Hollywood liberals, Helen Douglas's reaction was typical. In Hollywood, Henry Wallace was more popular than any Democrat but Roosevelt; whenever he appeared in the film community, large crowds of stars and producers turned out to see him. This was odd, since Wallace was in most respects an unlikely attraction. Ungainly, mystical, visionary, distracted, the one-time Iowa plant geneticist was no more charismatic than a cornstalk. He was, in fact, among the most unusual men ever to hold national office. The son of a Republican secretary of agriculture, Wallace became a prominent figure in the agricultural discontent of the 1920s as an editor and writer. By the end of the decade, for both political and personal reasons (he believed his father had been badly treated in Warren Harding's cabinet), he converted to the Democratic party. Through Rexford Tugwell, a member of Roosevelt's brain trust, he was brought into contact with Roosevelt, who was impressed with Wallace's passionate idealism.

Passionate idealism was one way of describing Wallace's manner. Other descriptions applied too. Even in the eclectic group gathered around Roosevelt, Wallace stood apart. "At times," wrote one sympathetic historian of the New Deal, "it seemed as if he had a greater sense of intimacy with plants" than with people. Most politicians simply did not know what to make of a man who said such things as "the Biblical record is heavily loaded on the side of the Progressive Independents"; who predicted an impending spiritual reawakening in the United States and in the meantime cavorted with a white Russian mystic named Nicholas Roerich (to whom he wrote letters under the greeting "Dear Guru").

Though Roosevelt wasn't much for gurus, he appeared to like and respect Wallace. In 1940 he plucked Wallace out of the Cabinet, where he had been serving as agriculture secretary, to run with him as vice-president in the race for a third term. Roosevelt reasoned that Wallace, as a native, might soften hostility to the administration in the isolationist Midwest. On that count, he wasn't much help: Wendell Willkie ran strongly all across the Farm Belt. But Wallace found another role, as the president's political lightning rod. With Roosevelt's implicit blessing, Wallace tested public reaction to liberal ideas the president himself found it impolitic to embrace. When Henry Luce piously announced the dawning of "The American Century" in *Life* magazine, it was Wallace who declared the years after World War II would see instead "The Century of the Common Man." His unyielding, undiluted expression of the true faith—cooperation with the Soviets abroad, social justice at home—made Wallace a hero to liberals everywhere, and nowhere more than in Hollywood. Among the Hollywood left, dull, doughy Wallace was widely considered not only Roosevelt's logical successor but the only acceptable choice.

But now his brand of militant Popular Front liberalism—their brand of militant Popular Front liberalism—had become too great a burden for the president to defend. Few in progressive Hollywood could, or would, read the implications. Even as they reached new prominence inside the Democratic ranks, the wind had begun to shift against them.

The Conservative Backlash

That was not the first hint of changing times. The Hollywood left had heard rumbles the previous February when one hundred Hollywood conservatives gathered at the Beverly Wilshire Hotel to launch an organization called the Motion Picture Alliance for the Preservation of American Ideals. The Alliance did not attract as glittering a letterhead as the Popular Front groups, but neither could its names be ignored: Walt Disney and Gary Cooper, directors Sam Wood (who became the group's president), King Vidor, and Clarence Brown, and MGM producer James McGuinness (who took the title of executive committee chairman).

Nor could the Hollywood left miss the menace bristling in the Alliance's strident message: "We refuse to permit the effort of Communist, Fascist, and other totalitarian-minded groups to pervert this powerful medium into an instrument for the dissemination of un-American ideas and beliefs," the group declared in a statement approved at the meeting. "We pledge ourselves to fight, with every means at our organized command, any effort of any group or individual, to divert the loyalty of the screen from the free America that gave it birth."

The manifesto was the latest twist in an old battle. Many of MPA's key supporters—McGuinness, John Lee Mahin, Rupert Hughes—had been stalwarts in the Screen Playwrights, the rival union established in the mid-1930s by conservatives in the Screen Writers Guild. Though the guild won the battle for recognition, the war continued. "The Alliance got started because of the efforts [in the 1930s] to force these guys . . . into the guild by creating a closed shop," said Roy M. Brewer, the representative in Hollywood for the International Alliance of Theatrical Stage Employees, and later the Motion Picture Alliance's president. "They hated the guild because of its Communist origin, and they were resisting it. . . . It was out of the writers' fight that they tried to make this an ideological [fight]."

Both the Screen Playwrights and the Motion Picture Alliance revolved around James McGuinness. McGuinness first came to Hollywood in 1927 to work with producer Winfield Sheehan at the old Fox studio. Like several early screenwriters, he had been in journalism before migrating West—a reporter in Philadelphia, a sports columnist in New York, and one of the original Talk of the Town contributors at the *New Yorker.* From Fox, McGuinness moved to RKO before settling at MGM, where he spent most of his career, first as a writer and then as a producer. His résumé included such films as *A Girl in Every Port* and *Madame X.* One former senior MGM executive said the studio considered McGuinness "a talent but not a great talent. For a certain kind of thing he was quite good—hard-hitting, that kind of thing."

A good drinker, and a beguiling storyteller with a colorful past (one obituary placed him in the U.S. Army's punitive expedition against Pancho Villa in Mexico), McGuinness was in most respects a captivating Irishman. "He was a genial guy—it was the blarney in him," recalled Nat Perrin, the liberal writer who worked closely with him at MGM. "Away from political discussion he was one of the most charming men I ever met." McGuinness married a baroness and lived a comfortable life. But he burned with an ideological antipathy toward Communists. In his single-minded preoccupation, he recalled nothing so much as his prey. Like the Hollywood Communists, McGuinness viewed himself as locked in an apocalyptic struggle with the highest stakes. "He was conscientiously trying to do what he thought was right," said actor George Murphy, a fellow conservative who worked with him at MGM. "He was trying to blunt the efforts of the opposition to take over the industry." His obsession had its elements of *opéra bouffe*; when Ring Lardner, Jr., arrived in Hollywood as a neophyte radical, McGuinness invited him to his home, then took him down into his basement, where he maintained a shooting gallery, and demonstrated his skills with a pistol. "I got the feeling he was telling me these young bastards ought to know we're ready for them," Lardner recalled.

But there was nothing comical about McGuinness's willingness to use words (if not bullets) against his adversaries. Liberals suspected him of naming names to the state committees and HUAC investigators constantly snooping around Hollywood. He made his opposition to Communists abundantly apparent during the persistent struggles for control of the SWG. Like so many ideologues, McGuinness habitually exaggerated both the magnitude of the threat that fixated him and the strength of the other side. He felt constantly on the defensive and worried that his allies lacked the passion and discipline of their opponents.

It was this sense of grudging retreat that sparked the Alliance. Its formation culminated almost a decade of frustration for Hollywood conservatives, who had watched the left grow to dominate the film industry's political scene after the Sinclair campaign. With first the anti-Fascist cause and then Roosevelt sweeping the studios, conservatives felt themselves crowded out of the mainstream of Hollywood life. Their complaints about the Communists in the Popular Front groups during the 1930s were ignored or ridiculed. The Alliance's founders "wanted better public relations established for motion pictures," McGuinness once noted. "They were tired of having their industry represented by Charlie Chaplin . . . and Orson Welles. . . . They resented a succession of organizations using either Hollywood or Motion Pictures in their names and subsequently being disclosed as Communist fronts."

Having boisterously raised their flag with the meeting at the Beverly Wilshire and the publication of the Statement of Principles, the Alliance set off to hunt Communists. They did this primarily by gathering at the American Legion Hall or the Chamber of Commerce to reaffirm the accusation unveiled at their first meeting: that a Communist minority infested Hollywood, spreading insidious anti-American propaganda through the industry product, the movies. This belligerence was undercut by the group's timid refusal, even when taunted by opponents, to name the films or individuals that offended them.

The Alliance's problem was that it lacked any power unless the industry executives backed it, and they were no more than indifferent to its efforts. Senior executives were noticeably absent from its ranks. Though some, particularly at MGM, shared McGuinness's concern about a public backlash against Hollywood Communists, they had no evidence that people were staying away from movies because they thought the studios coddled reds. If anything, many executives thought the Alliance's loud allegations of Communist infiltration only aggravated the public relations problem they claimed to be combatting.

To the hardheaded businessmen in the front office, shifting ideological lines were always subservient to the bottom line. Conservative as they were, the studio heads had no inclination to hurt their operations by forcing out political radicals. Just as important, the executives understood that the Alliance's charges implicated them. The Alliance not only alleged that Communists were present in the studios—that was hardly news—but claimed they were slipping subtle anti-American messages past the executives. At worst, that made the moguls accomplices in the dissemination of Communist propaganda, and at best, too dense to understand how they were being manipulated. Alliance member Lela Rogers, mother of actress Ginger Rogers, told one audience, "The men who head the motion picture industry are politically and socially blind." Understandably, few executives rushed to embrace her conclusions. Rogers's accusation pricked the moguls' undiminished fear that the cossacks of the right would label them un-American. But as long as the charge came only from their own employees—the last group they would take direction from—the moguls did not feel threatened enough to act.

From the outset, McGuinness and the other Alliance leaders understood they could not count on the executives to join their crusade. So they dug in, and awaited reinforcements from Washington.

While they waited, they railed against the New Deal. Their ranks provided a base of support for national Republicans, who followed Roosevelt's lead in trolling more aggressively through Hollywood in the early 1940s. As the 1944 campaign began, Wendell Willkie had the deepest industry roots of any Republican contender. An activist on foreign policy who also embraced many liberal domestic positions, Willkie had been an unusually popular Republican in Hollywood during his first run in 1940. "There had been a big groundswell for him in Hollywood," said Milton Sperling. "A lot of people who previously voted for Roosevelt were talking about Willkie and of course, the third-term precedent was very important to them."

Actor Robert Montgomery discovered Willkie early in the 1940 campaign and touted his virtues to his fellow Hollywood Republicans. Though Mayer and some other conservative purists considered Willkie suspiciously moderate, Montgomery assembled a large group of supporters that included Ginger Rogers, George Murphy, Adolphe Menjou, Irene Dunne, writer Morrie Ryskind, and Ward Bond as well as Gary Cooper, William Powell, Mary Pickford, and gossip columnist Hedda Hopper. Eventually, Mayer came along as well. So did Darryl Zanuck, who seemed particularly taken with Willkie and tried to raise money for him at the studio. After the campaign, Zanuck became Willkie's most dedicated booster in Hollywood. He helped to arrange Willkie's appointment as the industry counsel in the 1941 Senate hearings, and lobbied Willkie to join Twentieth Century-Fox as chairman of the board. Willkie did in April 1942. Zanuck even tried to make a movie from *One World*, the best-selling paean to international cooperation that Willkie wrote after

Roosevelt sent him on an around-the-world goodwill mission in 1942.

With Zanuck and producer Walter Wanger making the introductions, Willkie became a familiar figure in Hollywood. As the 1944 campaign approached, anxious Hollywood Democrats saw Willkie gaining ground. But their fears quickly evaporated. Willkie became more acceptable in Hollywood because he moved steadily to the left between his first and second presidential bids—so far so that he veered outside his party's conservative mainstream. Despite his support in Hollywood and among editorial writers, Willkie never gained a solid footing in the 1944 race. A Gallup Poll in December 1943 found him trailing badly behind New York Governor Thomas E. Dewey. He ran reasonably well in the New Hampshire primary, but not well enough to meet the expectations of a front-runner. Another defeat in Wisconsin finished his presidential hopes.

Willkie's collapse left Dewey with a clear road to the nomination. In Hollywood, few hearts fluttered. Willkie had been "much more popular than Dewey was out there," recalled Herbert Brownell, Dewey's campaign manager. To Dewey, a stiff, officious, somewhat arrogant man, Hollywood was "an alien world." Celebrities made him uncomfortable. He didn't consider them much use in mounting a campaign. "He was aloof with them," Brownell said. "That was of course one of our problems in the management of the Dewey campaign—he wasn't comfortable around the extravaganza type people."

Many of the Motion Picture Alliance stalwarts drifted into the Dewey effort. Other traditional Republicans joined them to give Dewey a respectable base in the industry. But as the general election began, excitement among the Hollywood Republicans was as tightly rationed as gasoline. Gossip columnist Hedda Hopper took a train to the Republican Convention in Chicago with Ida Koverman, Louis Mayer's assistant, and found the scene surprisingly sedate. "It's all over but the shouting," she wrote in her column. "There was precious little of that." Returning home, Hopper wrote Colonel Robert R. McCormick, the Republican publisher of the *Chicago Tribune* (which syndicated her column), that she saw little opportunity for the Republican ticket of Dewey and Ohio Governor John W. Bricker to dent Roosevelt's powerful Hollywood coalition.

Louis Mayer, patriarch of Republican Hollywood, was one of the few executives who pitched in enthusiastically. Mayer and Koverman tried to steer the New York governor through the alien world. Koverman introduced Brownell to local Republican powers, including Kyle Palmer, the influential political editor of the *Los Angeles Times*. In Hollywood, Mayer pointed them to fundraisers and celebrities. "We had no natural connections with the Hollywood industry and he was a good guide to us,"

Brownell said. "So we did listen to him." But as the campaign progressed Mayer faded away, preoccupied with personal problems.

That left director Cecil B. DeMille as Dewey's most prominent Hollywood supporter. DeMille responded with his characteristic brand of exuberant excess. When Dewey came to Los Angeles in late September, DeMille orchestrated a rally that attracted over 93,000 spectators to the Coliseum and exceeded even the Warners' effort for Roosevelt a dozen years earlier. DeMille planned his spectacular to the minute ("6:45 P.M. Mr. DeMille cues Mr. Olson to start band. Band enters, marches to flagpole. . . . Elephants follow behind band, continue around track, doing their stunts and exit"). Besides the elephants and the performing cowboys, and the bands and lights, DeMille gave the crowd a podium packed with stars, from Ginger Rogers to Fred MacMurray, Walt Disney, and David O. Selznick. Each of them delivered heartfelt, if carefully scripted, testimonials. The evening began sliding downhill only at 7:44 P.M., when, according to the script, DeMille cued "Governor Dewey's entrance from tunnel . . ." When Dewey finally arrived on stage (after circling the track in an automobile), he stood dramatically beneath a 52-foot American flag, looked up at the Olympic torch flickering above it, listened to the tumultuous applause roll over him—and then fed the frenetic crowd a soporific treatise on social security and unemployment insurance. In his crowning moment in Hollywood, Dewey laid an egg.

The Roosevelt Maelstrom

Roosevelt had no such problems. His enormous popularity and his aides' increased sensitivity to the Hollywood resource combined to produce a larger role for celebrities in 1944 than even four years earlier. Stars did not play quite as significant a part in the last Roosevelt campaign as they would in campaigns in the television era, but the 1944 effort represented a dramatic step forward not only in the visibility of celebrities but in the national parties' interest in integrating Hollywood into their campaign plans.

With government cooperation vital to the executives' ability to maintain studio operations during the war, the Communists attracted to FDR's alliance with Stalin, and liberals committed to winning a final term for their idol, Roosevelt found eager recruits from boardroom to backlot. The Warner brothers returned to the fold and helped to organize a major fundraiser for the HDC. Quietly, even long-time Republicans signed on. Once Willkie left the race, Zanuck drifted into Roosevelt's camp and raised substantial funds. Spyros Skouras, Zanuck's boss and a man whom Dewey considered a close friend, converted to Roosevelt's cause after the president allowed 500,000 tons of food to be sent as war relief to Greece. Even Sam Goldwyn, who had not previously supported Roosevelt, opened his wallet; by Election Day he had contributed over $56,000 to the Democratic effort.

In its last weeks, the final Roosevelt campaign became a maelstrom that engulfed Hollywood. The excitement was communicable. With many of the old liberal stalwarts off at war or working in the government, new volunteers bubbled up to replace them. Politics entered the industry's consciousness in a way it had not previously; for the first time, many stars expected to play a role in the election. And, for the first time, politics had acquired enough glamour in Hollywood to attract stars for the thrill alone—a phenomenon that would become increasingly common with the passing years. Evelyn Keyes, a beautiful young actress married to director Charles Vidor, heard Rita Hayworth make a speech on the radio and thought: Why not me? "You know we were both these pretty young things married to these great intellectuals," Keyes recalled, "and I remember thinking I was jealous and I wanted to do it too." Keyes went over to see George Pepper and came out of the office chairman of the actors' division at the Hollywood Democratic Committee.

The Democrats' most glittering recruit in the frenzied autumn of 1944 was the nation's newest pop superstar: a skinny young singer and aspiring actor named Frank Sinatra. Sinatra's sympathies were unabashedly liberal; coming from a tough, racially mixed neighborhood in urban New Jersey, Sinatra used his new fame to preach racial tolerance and streetcorner populism. "The thing I like about the President, he's pretty fond of the little man," Sinatra declared during the campaign. "Well, I'm one, even with all of my good fortune." In late September, Sinatra managed to extricate himself from the frantic crowds of bobbysoxers that surrounded his appearances at New York's Paramount Theater long enough to attend an intimate reception for Roosevelt supporters at the White House. Immediately, Republicans complained that Roosevelt had better things to do than swap stories with a mere "crooner." But Roosevelt obviously understood the value of being seen with such a revered popular idol just a few weeks before the election. A few days later, back in New York at the Paramount, Sinatra responded to his critics by dropping a new lyric into the song "Everything Happens to Me."

They asked me down to Washington
To have a cup of tea.
The Republicans started squawking
They're as mad as they can be,
And all I did was say "hello" to a
man named Franklin D.
Everything happens to me.

Roosevelt dazzled Sinatra. Between appearances before the bobbysox-ers, the singer recorded a series of radio spots for the DNC and made a large donation to the Democratic cause. When Dewey was scheduled to appear at the Waldorf-Astoria Hotel in New York, Sinatra stole the crowd simply by appearing there himself. His fans, many of whom were too young to vote, wore buttons that read "Frankie's for F.D.R. and so are we."

If Sinatra, like Melvyn Douglas four years earlier, hinted that an ener-getic star could find a valuable part in a national campaign, Orson Welles settled the question. In the 1944 campaign, Welles assumed the kind of high-profile independent political role that would not become common in Hollywood for another two decades. But that was typical, for Welles was constantly ahead of his time—at least until he finally squandered too much of it.

Born in Wisconsin in 1915 to an inventor with an eye for showgirls and the intellectual musician he improbably married, Orson Welles was a legendary child prodigy. At five, he was performing walk-on parts at the Chicago Opera. At nine, he ran away with a female cousin, intending to support them with streetcorner magic shows. As a teenager, he was a theatrical star in Dublin. By his early twenties, he was a celebrated figure in the New York theater world, cheered for his brilliant collaboration with John Houseman in the Works Progress Administration's Federal Thea-ter. Welles's artistic vision was eclectic, incisive, unsettling; his plays included an acclaimed all-black version of *Macbeth* set in Haiti. At twenty-two, he became a hero of the left when he produced, with Houseman, Marc Blitzstein's leftist "labor opera" called *The Cradle Will Rock* despite attempts from the nervous WPA (already under assault from conserva-tives for coddling subversives in its arts projects) to stop the show. That experience predictably soured Welles on government theater; soon thereafter he and Houseman launched their own Mercury Theater, which they christened with a performance of *Julius Caesar* updated and trans-formed into a parable on fascism.

At that moment, Welles appeared indomitable, the most polymorphously talented showman of his generation. There seemed to be more hours in his day. In 1938, he was twenty-three and the leader of the Mercury Theater, as well as the writer, producer, and star of a series of radio dramas (which included the Halloween night dramatization of H. G. Wells's *War of the Worlds* that convinced thousands of Americans the nation was under siege from invading Martians), when he decided to squeeze Hollywood into his life too. He was lured West by RKO with the offer of complete autonomy to make two movies for a minimum payment of $225,000, with the prospect of greater sums if they proved profitable. Fascinated by film, and perhaps exhausted by the financial difficulties of the Mercury, Welles was, as always, ready for a new challenge. On July 20, 1939, he checked into the Chateau Marmont Hotel in the Hollywood Hills and set out to master his new terrain.

For his first project, he prepared an adaptation of Joseph Conrad's *Heart of Darkness,* but he was forced to abandon the idea when the projected costs topped $1 million. Welles began another film—an adaptation of a nondescript thriller—but that foundered too, and by the time he was to have delivered his first film to RKO he had not even a coherent idea for one. Inspiration finally came in early 1940 when he teamed up with screenwriter Herman Mankiewicz, a former *New Yorker* contributor whose career had been truncated by alcoholism and an irrepressible tendency to alienate his employers. Mankiewicz had one last great idea for a movie—a film about a press tycoon based on William Randolph Hearst that he proposed to call *American.*

Gradually, *American* grew into *Citizen Kane.* Mankiewicz and Welles passed versions of the script back and forth and then feuded over who should get the on-screen credit. They eventually shared the credit after Mankiewicz pressed the issue with the newly formed Screen Writers Guild. That was the most manageable of Welles's problems as he struggled to bring the story of the thinly fictionalized Charles Foster Kane to the screen. Welles, in what would turn out to be a conspicuous exception to his normal habits, finished the film briskly enough. But theater owners afraid of angering the still powerful Hearst refused to book it. Louis Mayer, out of loyalty to his old (if estranged) friend Hearst, or the habit of repressing that of which he disapproved, or fear of the devastation Hearst's papers might visit on the entire industry if the film was released, offered the president of RKO, George J. Schaefer, nearly 850,000 desperately needed dollars if he would withdraw the movie and destroy the negative. Schaefer showed more backbone than Mayer typically did when faced with outside pressure: he not only turned down the offer, but threatened a lawsuit against the major studios for stifling the movie. Finally, in May 1941, the film received its premiere in New York. But many theaters still refused to show it, and the movie that many critics would label the finest American film ever made limped in with meager returns at the box office.

Welles's career in Hollywood wobbled uncertainly after that, with his enormous skills constantly frustrated by his inability to meet deadlines or keep his mind on one project. His chaotic personal life (which included marriage to Rita Hayworth and a constantly shifting array of mistresses) provided one distraction; so did his expanding appetite for politics. His interest in politics was first apparent in his artistic choices, from the filming of *Citizen Kane* to the staging of *The Cradle Will Rock*. Actually, his politics weren't as radical as Blitzstein's, who fervently expected his 1937 opera to usher in the revolution. Intermittently accused of Communist sympathies throughout his career, Welles considered "Marxian dogma [to be] outdated [by] a series of New World conditions." Years later, when he was questioned by investigators from HUAC, Welles insisted, according to his inquisitors' notes, "he was not a Communist, has never been a Communist, does not believe in communism . . . [and] sees no place for it in the United States."

But Welles was an uncompromising, impatient, militant liberal who believed in the Popular Front strategy of alliance with Communists, lamented Roosevelt's "political caution," mourned his decision to drop Henry Wallace from the ticket, and hoped FDR would break with the Southern Democrats to form a truly "liberal party." Welles admired Roosevelt, but he considered Wallace, a man not subservient to the practical political considerations that coarsened the president, "the particular prophet" of his brand of aggressive liberalism. "To me," he once said, "Henry Wallace is the symbol of the righteousness of the progressive idea."

From the moment he emerged in the public eye, Welles lent his name to liberal causes—a group supporting an antilynching bill, another the defense of the civil rights of Mexican-Americans in Los Angeles, even a union attempting to organize department store employees. But he raised his participation to a new level when he joined a liberal international group called the Free World Association in 1943 and placed himself under the tutelage of Louis Dolivet, its charming and enigmatic founder. In the group's magazine Welles wrote tightly argued, if romantically idealistic, editorials calling for a new era of international cooperation. "Giving the world back to its inhabitants is too big a job for the merely practical; too brave a task for pessimism," he wrote. "The architects of an enduring peace must be capable of hope."

With the same unblemished conviction, the man who staged *Macbeth* in Harlem became an early and passionate advocate of civil rights for blacks. "There is no room in the American century for Jim Crow," he declared. In print and behind a podium, Welles's tone was earnest, his bearing impassioned, his rhetoric sometimes self-parodying in its airy grandiloquence. But with the great radio voice that once convinced the nation it was under siege from invading Martians, and the magnetic presence that had not yet begun to slip from him, Welles was an arresting figure, an incalculably valuable political surrogate.

Welles did nothing on a modest scale. When he decided to get involved in politics, he plunged in. For 1944, Welles hatched typically elaborate plans. He went to see George Pepper at the HDC in August and proposed to form a troupe of stars under his direction who would travel through big cities across the country, carrying the Roosevelt message. Pepper was overwhelmed, but though the idea excited the Democratic National Committee, it could not find in its crimped budget the funds to underwrite the project.

Undeterred, Welles simply barnstormed the country himself. No senator's or diplomat's efforts for Roosevelt drew as much attention that fall. Welles appeared in New York City and New Jersey, in Los Angeles, in Florida and West Virginia. He spoke on NBC, CBS, and the Mutual Broadcasting Network. He addressed a luncheon honoring Eleanor Roosevelt and a gathering of servicemen's wives. In September, he introduced Henry Wallace at a huge Madison Square Garden rally in New York. Welles thrilled the crowd with his passionate denunciations of Dewey: "The voice is the voice of Roosevelt," he cried, "but the hands are the hands of Hoover." Welles's speech so stirred the audience that on the way out of the hall he was mobbed by cheering admirers, chanting "Wallace and Welles . . . in '48." In October, Welles carried Roosevelt's banner at the prestigious *New York Herald Tribune* forum, speaking in a session that included Dewey. So passionate, and long-winded, was Welles that he was cut off the air in the middle of his speech, which was threatening to run into the "Scramby Amby" musical quiz show from Hollywood.

Welles campaigned so feverishly for Roosevelt that he collapsed a few days later in New York with a throat infection and a 104-degree temperature. Confined by doctor's orders to his suite at the Waldorf-Astoria, Welles stewed helplessly as the campaign hurtled toward its conclusion. Roosevelt tried to comfort his peripatetic supporter: "I have just learned that you are ill and I hope much you will follow your doctors' orders and take care of yourself," the president wired him on October 23. "The most important thing is for you to get well and be around for the last days of the campaign."

Even with his illness, Welles found it all entrancing. As a campaigner, he could use his gift for language with devastating effect. The more Welles stood in the spotlight, thrashing the Republicans, listening to the cheers, granting audiences to reporters, the more he understood how politics could satisfy even an actor's bottomless craving for approval. To be applauded for reciting the words of others was one thing, but to have crowds hang on your words, your opinions—that was another form of rapture, especially for an artist who believed he was already instructing his audience through his art. John Houseman, his old partner and frequent antagonist, thought Welles hypnotized by the applause. Already disillusioned with Hollywood, restless, driven, and heroically unfocused, Welles at twenty-nine was once again looking for new worlds to conquer. Why not politics? By mid-October, he was telling reporters that he planned to write a political book and privately imagining himself in more of a leading role.

Asked if his new obsession would take him away from the movies, Welles seemed to have already cast his lot. "Pictures? I've done nothing but turn them down. They don't make very good pictures today, I don't think."

Like Welles, stars on both coasts jumped into the campaign with unprecedented fervor. In New York, celebrities flocked to the Independent Voters' Committee of the Arts and Sciences for Roosevelt. Organized in the summer of 1944, the committee coupled Broadway stars and the pipe-smoking Eastern liberal intelligentsia; its letterhead read like the guest list at an especially eclectic Fifth Avenue salon. Among its members it counted such show business personalities as Welles, Fredric March, Bette Davis, and Eddie Cantor. But the real stars were writers, scientists, and literary lights such as Albert Einstein, John Dewey, Bennett Cerf, and Van Wyck Brooks.

Concerned about Roosevelt's prospects in 1944, renowned sculptor Jo Davidson launched the committee with a meeting at his cavernous New York studio. Davidson understood, as he later put it, that "we were mostly virgin voices in things political." To run the group, its founders—more accustomed to debating the distinctions between art and science than between Republicans and Democrats—selected Hannah Dorner, a tough, fiercely leftist ex-newspaperwoman who was as earthbound as they were ethereal. "She was an extremely creative public relations woman," said Alice Hunter, a former Warner Bros. story editor who later worked with the group. "She was one of the most creative people I've ever known."

The committee emerged with a splash by sponsoring the September Madison Square Garden rally at which Henry Wallace and Orson Welles spoke. Buoyed by the initial success, Dorner rushed forward, plotting rallies, broadcasts, speeches. In early October, Roosevelt—again testifying to his awareness of the value of cultural endorsements—received at the White House a delegation from the group bearing a pledge of support from more than a thousand leading artistic and intellectual figures.

The Hollywood Democratic Committee, meanwhile, organized with equal intensity. Democrats brought it into the campaign more intimately than any previous Hollywood organization. As the campaign commenced, California Democrats sought "the closest kind of collaboration" with the group. The national party was no less attentive. Over the summer, the DNC lent the Hollywood activists $8,000 to blanket radio stations with advertisements. Once the group's resources became apparent, George Pepper found himself deluged with requests from all points: state Democratic committees, the DNC, the DNC's advertising agency in New York. The advertising men wanted Olivia de Havilland; the Democrats in Washington State wanted Orson Welles, de Havilland, or Edward G. Robinson; the Independent Voters' Committee wanted Bob Hope; Milwaukee wanted George Jessel to emcee a meeting. From the DNC came a request for Humphrey Bogart to narrate a five-minute radio special in the last week of October; from Tulsa came a plea for any "Hollywood personality." The Kern County Democrats needed celebrities for a rally in Bakersfield, California.

Pepper, juggling orders like a commodities dealer, couldn't meet all these requests, even though he was dealing with almost an embarrassment of riches. To the DNC's Paul Porter, Pepper offered the services of Dalton Trumbo and the rest of the group's "Writers for Roosevelt division." Two days after the DNC requested Bogart, Pepper wired back the actor's approval. On October 12, he dispatched Jimmy Cagney to a "Labor for Roosevelt" broadcast; a week later Pepper sent the sponsors Edward G. Robinson and Paulette Goddard. Copies of the HDC's acerbic radio ads—which could be customized for each campaign—were sent to 162 congressional candidates. Pepper couldn't produce Welles or Robinson for the Democrats in Washington, but on October 12 he convinced Walter Huston and Evelyn Keyes to fly to Seattle to speak beside vice-presidential nominee Harry Truman. That same day, Pepper wired the DNC's advertising agency offering Charles Boyer for a radio spot to dramatize his experiences as a citizen voting for the first time. The next day Pepper wired the DNC, not only offering Boyer again but wondering whether the Democrats could possibly find any use for endorsement advertisements cut by Joan Crawford.

As in 1940, the clearest indication of the parties' heightened interest in the stars came in the final days before the election. Hollywood figures were inescapable in the campaign's last hours. Both sides rushed all their available Hollywood names onto the radio. Ginger Rogers pitched for Dewey, and then the GOP announced that Gary Cooper, Walter Pidgeon, Barbara Stanwyck, and Lionel Barrymore would all deliver final radio appeals. The Democrats countered. In a five-minute speech on CBS, Bogart urged soldiers to use their right to vote. The HDC put on a bare-knuckled half-hour radio show lampooning Dewey with Paul Muni, John Garfield, Gloria Stuart, and Edward G. Robinson. To the tune of the song "Daisy, Daisy," they sang, "Dewey, Dewey/The White House is not for youse/With your hooey/From the New York *Daily News*." In New York, the Independent Voters' Committee joined the CIO to sponsor a raucous Everybody for Roosevelt rally at Madison Square Garden. Welles, recovered from his illness, joined FDR and Frank Sinatra on November 4 for a Saturday night rally in Boston's Fenway Park, Roosevelt's final appearance of the campaign.

The Hollywood Democrats' rousing finish dwarfed all these efforts. The Democratic National Committee approached the HDC to craft the Democrats' final appeal, to run over all four radio networks on the night before the election. At the DNC's request, radio dramatist Norman Corwin wrote the script. Corwin had no previous political experience, but he was, by his own assessment, "a damn good Democrat." And he had a reputation at CBS for producing accessible, even lyrical, programs on such weighty subjects as the Bill of Rights. One friendly critic called him radio's Christopher Marlowe, but he was really more the Frank Capra of the airwaves: the bard of the common man. "My political roots, really were in the earth," he said, "a kind of humanism, an innate sense that something was wrong when blacks were lynched in the South and couldn't get jobs in the North. . . . One could not live and work through the Depression without coming to conclusions about the relationship of the economy to the quality of life."

Given only a few weeks to prepare, Corwin wrote feverishly. "I was under too much pressure," he recalled, "to do anything but think about the logistics and the requirements and the problems." Working through the HDC, he recruited Hollywood's leading liberals: Bogart, perhaps their biggest gun, to narrate; Judy Garland to sing; Cagney and Groucho

Marx to perform satirical sketches; lyricist E. Y. Harburg ("Somewhere Over the Rainbow" and "Brother, Can You Spare a Dime?") to contribute songs. But Corwin sought a tone more immediate than the stars alone, so remote in their fame, could provide. So he interspersed the famous voices with ordinary ones—cutting into his script testimonials from a Tennessee farmer, a brakeman on the New York Central, a Michigan housewife casting her first ballot. From around the country, Corwin assembled his celebrities and ordinary voters into a large CBS studio in Hollywood on Election Eve.

The show was a triumph from the opening notes—the big band rising behind Garland as she sang in a voice infectious with its unclouded enthusiasm, "Here's the way to win the war. . . . You gotta get out and vote." After Garland came Bogart, the voice of uncomplicated common sense: "This is Humphrey Bogart. . . . Personally, I'm voting for Franklin D. Roosevelt because I believe he is one of the world's greatest humanitarians; because he's leading our fight against the enemies of a free world."

Then Garland, sunny and winsome, cut in again; then a sailor, then another, then a soldier, then Garland once more. Corwin artfully weaved together the stars, the ordinary voters, and political leaders. After Garland came an actor imitating Dewey's brand of "doubletalk"; then a Michigan housewife who delivered her pitch with the verve and aplomb of a professional; and then Bogart again, agreeably nervous, stumbling over some of his lines. Then Cagney, Keenan Wynn, and Groucho joyously lampooning that "good old Hoover time."

Soon Bogart was back before the microphone, beckoning listeners to join the "millions and millions of people riding on the Roosevelt special." And with the band and a chorus rumbling behind them in the rhythmic sway of a locomotive, the stars filed past the microphone to deliver rapid-fire endorsements: Tallulah Bankhead and Joan Bennett ("for the champ"); Irving Berlin, Claudette Colbert, Joseph Cotten and John Garfield, Rita Hayworth and George Jessel ("Hello, Mama Jessel. This is Georgie. Vote for Roosevelt."); Danny Kaye, Gene Kelly, Groucho and George Raft, Edward G. Robinson, Lana Turner and Jane Wyman; then on to New York where another dozen celebrities crowded into a studio—Dorothy Parker, Charles Boyer, Milton Berle, Franchot Tone, Frank Sinatra, the names flashing by like freight cars, stretching out endlessly, like Roosevelt himself, encompassing the nation.

For Corwin, for the stars assembled in that Hollywood studio, for Roosevelt in Hyde Park, the broadcast capped a remarkable campaign. From the moment he went off the air, Corwin knew he had a hit. "Usually after one of those big broadcasts one went to Chasen's or Romanoff's and everybody was there," Corwin said. "I think it was Chasen's and I remember the room being abuzz with this program. It was like Sardi's after a Broadway opening." Tallulah Bankhead kissed his hand; Hedda Hopper, bracing for the landslide, passed him in a huff.

The next morning, the voters filed to the polls, reelecting Roosevelt to a fourth term. Democrats gained twenty-one seats in the House; among the new representatives was Helen Gahagan Douglas. For Hollywood, the campaign was a milestone. It announced the film industry's arrival as a force in national partisan politics. Corwin confirmed the power of radio messages to move voters. Welles demonstrated the ability of a celebrity to command public attention for a cause. The HDC showed how energetic Hollywood could be when carefully organized; Jack Warner, Goldwyn, and Zanuck indicated the movie industry's potential as a source of political money. Never had liberal Hollywood performed such an integral part in a national campaign, and never could it share more justifiably in the glow of victory.

Only one discordant note marred the rush to the tape for Roosevelt's Hollywood supporters. Once more, conservatives charged that the Hollywood left was riddled with Communists. Dewey himself set the tone. Desperate for issues that could force Roosevelt to drop his above-the-battle pose, Dewey first raised the specter of Communist party leader Earl Browder (who had, following the serpentine twists of Communist policy, now endorsed FDR for a fourth term) and Sidney Hillman, the leftist CIO leader close to the Roosevelt administration. Then he bore in on his real target. Roosevelt, Dewey charged, "has so weakened and corrupted the Democratic Party that it is readily subject to capture and . . . the forces of Communism are, in fact, now engaged in capturing it."

Conservatives in Washington and Sacramento advanced on the Hollywood left brandishing the same accusations. From Washington, chief HUAC investigator Robert E. Stripling accused the HDC of participating in a plot with the Communist party and the CIO to "purge" anti-Communist members of Congress such as Representative Costello. Three weeks later, at a hearing before California Senator John B. Tenney's Un-American Activities committee, investigator Richard Combs described the HDC as "a Communist-dominated front." On October 13, Tenney summoned Marc Connelly, John Howard Lawson, Albert Maltz, and several other writers to appear at a state legislature hearing investigating Communist influence in the Hollywood Writers' Mobilization.

Six years had passed, but nothing changed: the charges and responses were the same as when Dies first descended on Hollywood in 1938. Communists were, in fact, prominent in all these groups; the conservatives had chosen their targets carefully. But, as in the waning days of the first Popular Front, the conservatives indicted the Hollywood activists for more than mere association with Communists; they charged them with furthering Communist aims, inadvertently or by design. To the right, the assumption remained that any liberal cause which attracted Communist support must ultimately be serving Communist ends.

As Dewey did for the accusers, Roosevelt set the tone for the response. The only president millions of Americans had ever known, the leader of the greatest army democracy had ever assembled, Roosevelt brushed away the charge that Communists controlled the Democratic party as the sulfurous idiocy it was.

The Hollywood liberals fired back no less forcefully. Ignoring the substance of the right's charges, they treated them for what they were—partisan thrusts against the New Deal—and responded with calumnies of their own. Just before the election, producer Walter Wanger, flushed with the fervor of impending victory, told an HDC rally the next night that "the campaign now being waged by the GOP has forever disgraced the men who conduct it. . . . Only once before in modern history has such an election campaign been waged. The time was 1933. The place was Germany."

Once more, the right could not make the Hollywood liberals pay for their reconstituted alliance with the Communists. Defiant, unyielding, as fierce as their foes, the liberals stood secure in the fortress that Roosevelt's impenetrable presence provided. The Hollywood left knew that Martin Dies alone could not scale the walls. And now, in the campaign's final hours, they realized that Dewey would not reach the top either. They saw their political opponents—Dies and Dewey, Hearst and McCormick, Tenney and the Motion Picture Alliance—driven to the fringe of American life, sentenced to frustration and impotence, overmatched by the barriers Roosevelt had erected. But the greater foe was time, and time was inexorably crumbling the walls that protected them.

CHAPTER FOUR

THE STAGE CLEARS

The Last Days of the Popular Front

Time began to run out for the Hollywood Popular Front in April 1945 when President Roosevelt died suddenly from a cerebral hemorrhage. Shaken by the loss of their defender and hero, and unsure of Harry Truman, many activists felt, with Norman Corwin, "terrible forebodings that the era of progressive Democratic government had ended."

Initially, that anxiety only made their independent work behind the progressive agenda seem more pressing. The Hollywood Democratic Committee lengthened its political profile. George Pepper visited Washington and found liberal congressmen not only aware of the group's work but anxious to see it knit more tightly into the national progressive coalition. Back home in Hollywood, the group's leadership heard the same suggestion. Orson Welles and other Hollywood stars well-connected in Eastern literary and artistic circles urged the HDC to join forces with the Independent Citizens Committee of the Arts, Sciences and Professions (ICCASP), the renamed Independent Voters' Committee that had organized writers and artists for Roosevelt in the just-completed campaign. Some HDC members thought the group would be better off steering its own course. But the opportunity to share a letterhead with the Eastern cultural establishment proved irresistible. On June 6, 1945, the Hollywood committee's membership voted to affiliate with ICCASP. The short-lived HDC became the Hollywood Independent Citizens Committee of the Arts, Sciences and Professions or HICCASP, an infelicitous name "pronounced like the cough of a dying man," as one of its board members, Ronald Reagan, later wrote.

Liberal politics had no precedent for the new continent-spanning amalgamation of celebrities and intellectuals. Hollywood and Washington appeared to converge more completely than ever before. Politicians came to Hollywood; Hollywood figures looked to the capital. James Roosevelt, the president's son, was recruited as ICCASP's director of political organization. Former Interior Secretary Harold Ickes joined the national organization as executive director. Producer Milton Sperling weighed and rejected an offer of support for a congressional bid in 1946. Screenwriter Emmet Lavery, president of the Screen Writers Guild, sought the Democratic nomination for a Los Angeles congressional seat, but lost in the primary.

At first, no one symbolized the new attitude in Hollywood more dramatically than Orson Welles. The exhilarating 1944 campaign had raised his interest in politics to the boiling point. After the election, he signed to write a daily political column for the *New York Post* and undertook a lecture tour along the East Coast. He saw himself and his creed standing on the promontory of a new era. "Liberalism is no longer a small voice," he wrote optimistically after the 1944 election. "It is loud and sure. In 1944 it can be heard above all other voices in our nation. . . . We are sure that the next four years are going to be great years . . . difficult, glorious, hazardous, triumphant years. We face those years with the best hopes Americans have ever had the right to hold."

For himself, Welles certainly had great hopes. Fresh from completing his film *The Stranger,* he seriously considered seeking a Senate seat in 1946 before finally backing away. Years later, Welles told his biographer he was convinced not to run by a young California activist named Alan Cranston, a powerful behind-the-scenes figure in state politics. "He told me I couldn't win," Welles said. "He said that I would carry Northern California, but I could never carry Los Angeles because of the strong Communist objections to me." Cranston, now a U.S. senator from California himself, confirms that he counseled Welles against running, but not because of potential Communist opposition to his candidacy. "I just said it was a difficult race to win," Cranston said. "Though I think he could have been a serious candidate." Most likely it was Welles's own chronic disorganization that smothered the idea. That aborted look at the 1946 Senate race turned out to be Welles's last real brush with politics. With his movie career chaotic and the IRS hounding him for back taxes, Welles fled Hollywood not long thereafter for an extended stay in Europe. His youthful promise spectacularly unfulfilled, Welles never again played an important role in Hollywood's political life. He barely reentered its artistic one.

Welles's disintegration and exile deprived the Hollywood left of one of its most articulate and effective spokesmen. But others constantly emerged. In these first confident months after World War II, the Hollywood Popular Front was as strong as it had ever been. But, like the Depression-era Hollywood political groups, it was built on an illusion of unity that could not be sustained. The postwar fall of the second Popular Front eerily echoed the collapse of the first liberal-Communist alliance. In fact, its internal fissures represented the conclusion of the debate interrupted by the war. Under Roosevelt, left-leaning Hollywood had been brought into the Democratic party. But the issue of whether it would find its principal expression through Democratic liberalism or through the independent radicalism of the Popular Front remained unresolved throughout his presidency.

During the war, the question had been muted by the Soviet Union's interest in solidarity with the United States, which transformed the American Communists into Roosevelt's most ardent supporters. But after Hitler fell, the question raised through the 1930s—could Communists and liberals speak with one voice—returned, this time decisively. Through the end of the 1940s it dominated Hollywood political life. With the great centripetal forces of Roosevelt and the war removed, politics in Hollywood hurtled back toward the fringes. Battles between liberals, radicals, and conservatives over the Communist party's proper role in Hollywood's political life were fiercer than any electoral fight. To a considerable extent during this period, politics in Hollywood was about politics in Hollywood. The final act of the Popular Front became the most painful off-screen drama Hollywood had ever endured. The modern era of Hollywood activism began only after the destruction of the dream that inspired its first fledgling steps into politics.

Ironically it was the American Communists, not the liberals, who first understood that the end of hostilities in Europe had shattered comity at home. In the spring of 1945, the Soviets signaled a harder line, repudiating the wartime policy of cooperation with capitalism; in the United States, Party leader Earl Browder was replaced with a veteran hard-line functionary, William Z. Foster. As these policy shifts trickled down through the Party bureaucracy, the Hollywood Communists became as intransigent as they had been accommodating during the war. Once again, they set their own course.

The new Party line manifested itself inside HICCASP through uncompromising denunciations of Truman and his hardening approach toward Stalin. Liberals everywhere grumbled about Truman, the small-town hack, the creature of the bosses, the accidental president, who seemed overwhelmed in his first term both by the job and by Roosevelt's shadow. But reflecting the sharper Party line, Communists in ICCASP moved the organization toward an especially antagonistic position, particularly over Truman's move toward containment of the Soviets. Like its champion, former Vice-President Henry Wallace, ICCASP seemed to value warm relations with the Soviets above all other foreign policy goals and to place principal blame on the United States for the chill. As early as December 1945, at a huge rally in Madison Square Garden, ICCASP endorsed a resolution "denounc[ing]" the Truman administration's "departures from the Roosevelt foreign policy . . . based on the unity of the Big Three." By June 1946, the Hollywood branch declared that on foreign policy Truman was "indistinguishable" from the GOP.

These maneuvers predictably unsettled some of the group's moderates and liberals. "The Communist hard core began to run things openly and to dictate policy," said Milton Sperling, one of the most sympathetic liberals. "They became obnoxious. They really became obnoxious. They said, 'No, we're not going to do it that way, we're going to do it my way, our way.' And the [Communist] Party line became very visible. . . . This offended people. It offended them on a personal level, and it offended them on a political level. They drove out the middle road [members], they drove out the liberals, by hewing to a very straight [Party] line and by organizing everything their own way."

Just as before the war, Hollywood liberals found themselves on record behind positions they did not embrace. "I noticed that when there was a conflict between Russia and the United States, Russia was always assumed to be right, and I thought, 'I can't understand this,' " actress Olivia de Havilland, one of HICCASP's most active members, said later. The same pattern held on domestic policy. In 1946 liberals and moderates urged the group to support for the California Senate nomination former Representative Will Rogers, Jr., an anti-Communist New Dealer and son of the famous humorist. Leftists preferred former Lieutenant Governor Ellis Patterson, who led the anti-Roosevelt isolationist slate in the 1940 Democratic presidential primary. Dore Schary, a liberal producer active in the organization, kept in close touch with Ellenore Hittelman, the group's legislative director, during the fight and warned her that "he was getting all kinds of flak . . . from [the] studios about the fight." Sensing the danger ahead, Schary urged the group to endorse Rogers or stay neutral. But the Los Angeles Communist party, following the new hard line, grimly demanded that its representatives in HICCASP force a vote; the group obediently backed Patterson, who promptly lost the primary to Rogers anyway. But the damage was done. Patterson's endorsement reinforced what Alice Hunter, who became HICCASP's executive director in 1946, described as "The general feeling that the left was in control, was forcing decisions."

The organization's leadership brushed aside such complaints. Principled and idealistic, but also dogmatic and myopic, the Hollywood activists directing HICCASP (and their counterparts in New York) held to the beliefs that animated the Popular Front—cooperation with the Soviets, alliance with domestic Communists—even as the gathering Cold War obliterated their foundations. Against the growing anxiety about Communists in the United States, Hannah Dorner, the national group's executive director, airily declared: "If the ICCASP program is like the Communist line, that is purely coincidental."

For the most sophisticated liberals, the issue could not be dismissed so breezily. While most did not dispute the right of Communists to push their own agenda, they understood that the alliance with Communists restricted their own political expression. With the Party holding effective control over HICCASP, alliance, in fact, virtually neutered the liberals as an independent political force. Not only were the liberals repeatedly placed on record as condemning their own country, but they were tainted with a radical image that diminished their value to the politicians they wished to assist. As its fervor eclipsed its glamour, politicians grew leery of HICCASP and its national parent. "Many a Democratic politician, whose eyes glistened greedily at the sight of ICCASP's shoals of talent, felt . . . hesitant," *Time* reported. "For in some states and cities ICCASP support, because of its vehemence and its leftist tinge, was a handicap."

Like Melvyn Douglas and Philip Dunne seven years earlier, a group of moderates and liberals, including James Roosevelt, Ronald Reagan, Dore Schary, composer Johnny Green, screenwriter Ernest Pascal, and actress Olivia de Havilland, finally forced the issue. In July 1946 they proposed a resolution in HICCASP that rejected communism "as a desirable form of government for the U.S.A." The resolution was a symbolic gesture: it asked the Hollywood activists to choose between the Popular Front vision of independent radicalism and mainstream political participation based on acceptance of the basic American institutions. With the dream of alliance still clouding their vision, the Hollywood activists overwhelmingly chose the former; the resolution failed. Instead, HICCASP subsequently reaffirmed one of the tenets of the Popular Front by declaring itself independent of all political parties—Communist, Democratic, Republican.

As in 1939, the Communists proved they could control the Popular Front, but at a terrible price. At the July 23 meeting, resignations from de Havilland, Joan Fontaine, and two other members were announced. Announced, too, was the resignation of James Roosevelt, who left the group to become chairman of the state Democratic party. One week later, at the group's next meeting, Walter Wanger, actor William Wright, and writer Allen Rivkin resigned. One week after that, John Howard Lawson declared that resignations would no longer be announced.

Resignations from distressed moderates and liberals continued anyway; Reagan withdrew from the group in October and began his long migration to the right. Bette Davis left on the advice of Jules Stein, founder of the powerful talent agency MCA, who warned her the group was seen as Communist-dominated and insisted "you had better get out." Overall membership didn't plummet, but with the departure of these liberals, the group listed sharply left. When Henry Wallace, then serving as commerce secretary, challenged the Truman administration's stiffening policy toward the Soviets in September 1946 (at an ICCASP rally in New York) and was fired by the president, the Hollywood contingent made its final break with Truman. HICCASP passed a resolution supporting "permanent cooperation with the Soviet Union."

These difficult months set a pattern that did not break. The story of the decade's remaining years was the final decoupling of the mainstream liberals from the Communists and the far left. As before the war, a growing (though still relatively small) number of Hollywood liberals came to realize their goals differed from the Communists', even in the short term. Though this pattern of disengagement greatly accelerated after the House Committee on Un-American Activities (HUAC) resumed its Hollywood investigation in late 1947, it was apparent earlier. (The anti-Communist liberals "had come to the conclusion long before" the HUAC hearings that their interests diverged from the Communists', Philip Dunne said. "We felt we had to deal with our country's problems from within and we certainly were not accepting leadership from any organization outside of the country. It was that simple.") HUAC was only a symptom of the Popular Front's fundamental problem as the two superpowers drifted into the Cold War. The inevitable corollary of increased international tension with the Soviets was diminished common ground between liberals and Communists, and less tolerance among conservatives for Communist participation in American life.

By early 1947, long before the first HUAC subpoenas reached Hollywood, the Popular Front began to split into its component parts. Just after Christmas in 1946, representatives of ICCASP and the National Citizens Political Action Committee (NCPAC), another independent progressive organization composed of leftist businessmen, journalists, and politicians, voted to merge into the Progressive Citizens of America (PCA), thereby easing the task of headline writers everywhere. In Hollywood, HICCASP duly voted to affiliate with this latest Popular Front. As the vehicle for a third-party 1948 presidential bid by Henry Wallace, the PCA gave concrete form to the declaration of political independence passed by HICCASP the previous summer; it represented a total break with the Democratic party and conventional liberalism. Still, many of the leading figures in the Hollywood left—including actor Gene Kelly, Norman Corwin, writer Lillian Hellman, and the major film industry Communists—followed Jo Davidson, who became national co-chairman, onto the new letterhead.

One week after the PCA announced its arrival in New York, a prominent group of liberals, among them labor officials and former New Dealers, met in Washington to form Americans for Democratic Action (ADA). On most domestic issues, the ADA and PCA differed little. But they diverged decisively on relations with the Soviets abroad, and even more pointedly, alliance with Communists at home. The PCA welcomed to its membership anyone who supported the group's goals; the ADA, believing liberalism must sever itself from communism, barred Party members. That was the real point of the group, but in Hollywood, it was only a small attraction. There, the arrival of the anti-Communist liberal organization that Melvyn Douglas had talked about in 1940 was received "rather quietly," Philip Dunne recalled. The ADA never grew as large as the Hollywood Popular Front groups. But it provided a home and, for the first time, an independent voice for the industry's small core of anti-Communist liberals, including many of those who bailed out of HICCASP in 1946. Dunne, Melvyn Douglas, Reagan, Allen Rivkin, Olivia de Havilland, Bette Davis, and Will Rogers, Jr. (who lost his Senate bid in the general election) eagerly lent their names.

If the ADA's formation demonstrated that a portion of progressive Hollywood was committed to reconnecting with the mainstream of American politics, the PCA's greater strength in the film community showed how strong the appeal of independent radicalism remained even in the first months of the Cold War. Most Hollywood progressives still believed in unequivocal alliance with the Communists. But with the launching of

ADA, those were no longer the only voices on the left. Just as before the war, internal pressures had once again fractured the Hollywood Popular Front.

External threats to all Hollywood progressives followed soon enough. After Roosevelt's victory in 1944, the Motion Picture Alliance for the Preservation of American Ideals had continued to meet, elect officers, and share grim prophecies—internal exiles whose frustration purified their fervor. After the Republicans gained control of Congress in the 1946 election (in part by linking Democrats to the Communists), the Alliance resurfaced with a massive recruitment drive to "thwart Red domination of the industry." James McGuinness, still the group's guiding force, warned his audience to prepare for "a fight with the most ruthless enemy" they had ever encountered. McGuinness all but distributed C rations for the coming conflict: "To know the nature of your enemy," he told his troops, "you must realize that Communism is a complete conspiratorial movement, dedicated to the overthrow of our form of government for the benefit of a foreign power and an alien ideology."

The studio heads were no more receptive to the Alliance's warnings than in 1944. But as Cold War tensions heightened, reinforcements from Washington finally arrived. Under the chairmanship of Republican Representative J. Parnell Thomas of New Jersey, HUAC finally convened its long-delayed investigation of the Hollywood left in October 1947. Martin Dies had blustered and threatened, but never gone so far. Thomas unveiled a full-scale extravaganza. Over the first week, he led through the spacious hearing room an eccentric parade of "friendly" witnesses whose sympathy for the committee, its methods, and its conclusions, actually varied dramatically. The witnesses broke down into three groups: studio executives led by Jack Warner and Louis B. Mayer, who admitted reds could be found in Hollywood but insisted they had the situation under control and needed no government interference in their affairs ("I have maintained a relentless vigilance against un-American influences," Mayer assured the committee); the union men—Reagan, Robert Montgomery, and George Murphy from the Screen Actors Guild—who essentially repeated the same message; and the Motion Picture Alliance members, led by McGuinness, Ayn Rand, director Sam Wood, and Adolphe Menjou, who (at last) painted for the ravenous congressmen a lurid picture of rampant subversion under the palms. Hollywood, McGuinness warned dramatically, was infested by an "active fifth column—a group of quislings who want to destroy our government in the service of a foreign ideology."

The Alliance's accommodating flourishes alone couldn't salvage the situation. In almost all respects, the committee fell short during the first week of hearings. The Hollywood Communists were slavish apologists for Stalin and, as such, destructive, polarizing, irritating presences in the Hollywood political firmament. But no one seriously suggested they were spies for the Soviet Union or were preparing to launch the revolution by seizing the Thalberg Building at MGM. Thomas and the rest of the committee, including new Republican California Representative Richard M. Nixon, failed miserably at their principal mission of unearthing subversive subtexts in Hollywood's crinkly, translucent fantasies.

The committee was not entirely incorrect in assuming that Hollywood Communists hoped to include progressive material in their movies. But their sights were low: sympathetic treatment of blacks and other minorities, fleeting references to the inability of money to cure all human needs, opaque criticisms of American society's inequities. They sought nothing more from their films than any humanistic liberal, and like the liberals were usually frustrated by the studios. Communist screenwriter Richard Collins, appearing before HUAC years later as a friendly witness, explained: "At one time I think that Communist writers felt that the inclusion of several progressive lines might be a happy thing, but finally it was realized that this didn't mean anything to anybody unless you had a codebook with you that told you what those lines meant, so this policy was dropped and was considered no longer reasonable." Like liberals and conservatives, Communists wrote good movies and bad movies—but few with even a glancing impact on national life.

The first week of the hearings failed also by allowing the Hollywood Communists, whose influence in the film community had already crested, to assume a newly sympathetic role. Inadvertently, HUAC "made the Communists respectable again," said Frank Mankiewicz, son of screenwriter Herman Mankiewicz and a rising figure in the anti-Communist liberal camp. "No matter how anti-Communist you were—and no matter how well you understood that HICCASP and all of these groups were doing the work of the Soviet Union . . . and that they opposed Helen Douglas and FDR . . . and that the CIO was throwing out the Communists—we were of the left; and the idea of making common cause with a J. Parnell Thomas, or a Jack Tenney, who made no distinctions between Communists and socialists and liberals and atheists and the ACLU and all kinds of good people, was inconceivable. So you had to resist them."

And so, almost without exception, Hollywood rallied behind the "unfriendly" witnesses, as the subpoenaed leftists were dubbed. Philip Dunne, actor Alexander Knox, and directors John Huston and William

Wyler organized the Committee for the First Amendment to fight HUAC. Virtually every major Hollywood liberal embraced the effort—Bogart, Katharine Hepburn, Rita Hayworth, Groucho Marx, Garland, Sinatra, Gene Kelly, Orson Welles; when HUAC recessed after its first week of hearings, a large delegation flew to Washington to confront the committee. But the group deflated in the capital. Dunne and the CFA's other organizers tried to explain they were defending the principle of freedom of speech, not the principals in the investigation, about whom many in the delegation had equivocal feelings. That meant the group's members were in Washington, not as character witnesses for the unfriendlies, but as moral support to the industry fathers, who had publicly and privately insisted HUAC could not bully them into a purge of their employees.

When the hearings resumed on Monday, Eric Johnston, who had succeeded Will Hays as head of the producers' association, compromised the liberal delegation's position. Johnston declared himself (and by extension the studios) "heart and soul" for HUAC's mission of exposing Hollywood Communists. Glumly, the celebrity contingent realized they had arrived to fortify a line already breached. Its discomfort deepened as the Hollywood Ten—the ten Hollywood leftists summoned to the stand—truculently dueled with the committee the next week, refusing to take the Fifth Amendment or to say whether they belonged to the Party.

Given the tenor of the times, and the committee's unremitting hostility, the Ten had no good options. But the paradox of their contradictory existence further constrained the Hollywood Communists: the Ten wanted to maintain their credentials as radical critics of American society and their well-paid jobs in the studios. ("We used to say if you want to be a martyr you've got to expect to get your side pierced," Mankiewicz said. "They wanted it both ways: they wanted the glamour of being a martyr and they wanted $5,000 a week for writing trash for the screen.") Those personal considerations complicated the political decisions. Sorting through their limited choices, the Hollywood Ten rejected the strategy of taking the Fifth Amendment before the committee as an implicit agreement that Party membership was criminal (the government prosecutions for membership in the Party did not begin until after they testified); and they rejected candor as politically inopportune and professionally suicidal. Instead, they embraced a strategy based on the First Amendment's protection of freedom of speech. But rather than directly challenging HUAC's interrogations on those grounds, they refused to answer the committee's questions about their Party membership without ever explicitly saying they were not answering.

From a public relations standpoint, they could not have chosen a more disastrous approach. Their serpentine rhetorical twists on the stand led to impossible posturing, rages, and bewildering, self-aggrandizing hysterics ("This is the beginning of the American concentration camp," screenwriter Dalton Trumbo thundered as he was hauled off the stand). More important, their bizarre behavior almost totally eclipsed the underlying First Amendment issues on which their defense supposedly rested. Thomas, hysterical with the gavel himself, seemed to invite vituperation. Each side inspired the other to spit tacks.

This was not the bold statement of principle the delegation of supportive celebrities anticipated. "The behavior of the Ten disenchanted a lot of people," said Dunne, one of the coolest heads in the bunch. "Remember our committee was largely [composed of] innocents." The innocents hardly expected what the Ten gave them. One of the most famous, and (politically) innocent, Judy Garland told Hedda Hopper shortly after the hearings: "It was dreadful when they just [wouldn't] shut up and just say yes or no."

Almost two weeks after they began, the hearings ended inconclusively. The belligerence of the Hollywood Ten helped HUAC gain some ground in the second week, but Thomas could not have been entirely satisfied with the final result. Though the studio heads had welcomed the committee and shown appropriate respect for the gravity of the red threat, they left town without explicitly promising to rid themselves of their talented employees. The committee had not demonstrated any intrinsic threat in keeping the Communists on the payroll and the political threat to the studios was obscure: polls showed no great public support for HUAC's investigation. Even so sympathetic a figure as Reagan considered the hearings an ineffectual "publicity circus."

But the studio heads wavered, and cracked. Once again critics found the moguls' weak spot: the fear of being labeled un-American themselves. This outsider's anxiety amplified each critical remark that followed the hearings. Many mainstream newspapers—from the *New York Times* to the *Detroit Free Press*—condemned HUAC and its methods. But the only sound that penetrated Hollywood executive suites was the drumbeat of outrage from the right. On November 24, Thomas sought contempt citations from the House against the Hollywood Ten; they passed overwhelmingly. One day later the studio chiefs announced they intended to discharge each of the Ten until "such time as he is acquitted or . . . declares under oath that he is not a Communist." No longer would they "knowingly employ a Communist."

Those were bold words, but like many promises from the moguls, empty. From the conclusion of the HUAC hearings in 1947 until early

1950, a rough political truce prevailed in Hollywood. The presidential campaign of 1948 came and went without the fireworks of four years earlier. The defiant Hollywood leftists (including most of the Hollywood Ten, awaiting appeal of their contempt convictions) rallied energetically, if futilely, behind Henry Wallace's third-party bid. Helen Douglas, who was close to Wallace, was the rare Hollywood liberal with the good sense to encourage him not to run. On the backlots, Democrats and Republicans alike displayed little enthusiasm for the principal competitors, Truman and Thomas Dewey. Washington's interest in Hollywood Communists receded. None of the studios systematically identified and dismissed the remaining Party members on their staffs. That rule had prominent exceptions: when MGM called in Donald Ogden Stewart to answer some questions about his past, he read his cue, cleaned out his desk, and settled his contract in 1949. But there was no wholesale purge.*

All this was a false spring. In April 1950 the Supreme Court refused to review the contempt convictions of John Howard Lawson and Dalton Trumbo, who had agreed to serve as test cases for the rest of the Hollywood Ten. The Ten filed off to jail—and another round of red-hunting began in Hollywood. The House Committee on Un-American Activities resumed hearings on Hollywood the following March. The committee had learned from its agreeably stormy but otherwise unsatisfying joust with Hollywood in the 1940s. In 1947, HUAC still felt compelled to attempt to prove the Hollywood Communists threatened America by subtly undermining its values. But after the perjury conviction of Alger Hiss, the outbreak of war in Korea, the conviction of leading Communist party members under the Alien Registration Act (known as the Smith Act), and the arrest of Ethel and Julius Rosenberg on the charge of passing atomic secrets to the Soviets, the danger of domestic Communists no longer needed to be demonstrated; like all articles of faith, it was assumed. Now, merely to identify a Communist was to ostracize him. That greatly simplified HUAC's task. From its friendly and unfriendly

---

*Ironically, the Motion Picture Alliance's Jim McGuinness also left MGM in 1949. To his followers, McGuinness became a martyr in his own revolution. Officially, McGuinness retired after MGM curtailed his authority in a postwar staff reorganization. But some of his confederates insisted that the liberal Dore Schary, who had been brought in as production chief for the flagging studio in 1948, forced him out. Others, like anti-Communist labor leader Roy Brewer, believed Louis Mayer personally gave the order because McGuinness "defied him" by pressing his charges of Communist infiltration so vociferously. MGM formally denied any political motive in McGuinness's dismissal, noting that it still employed such other Alliance stalwarts as director Clarence Brown, actor Robert Taylor, and art director Cedric Gibbons.

witnesses alike, the committee ritualistically demanded the public recita-
tion of names it already knew—the names of present and former Hollywood Communists.

For the former Communists, expiation demanded exposure, the naming of Party colleagues, who would then be summoned to provide yet
more names. The frightened industry fathers promptly blacklisted those
who refused to answer the committee's questions—those who stood behind the Fifth Amendment's protection against self-incrimination—and
those who did not rebut their naming as Communists; by one count, as
many as 250 were barred from the studios. Communists and radicals took
the brunt of the attack, but liberals were not entirely spared. Beyond the
blacklist stood the graylist, a maddeningly amorphous purgatory that
afflicted dozens of other leftists who had not been Communists but were
linked with Popular Front organizations now redefined as Party fronts.
Public and private lists of Hollywood subversives rained on the studios
faster than unsolicited screenplays, and the shaken executives dutifully
bent over like penitents to take their whacks from each new adversary.
After the American Legion in December 1951 accused the studios of still
coddling Communists, panicky studio executives asked the Legion to
forward any information it had on their employees—which turned out to
be mostly listings of old letterheads—and then required all employees
under suspicion to write a letter explaining their earlier involvement in
groups such as HICCASP and the Anti-Nazi League. As the price of
continued employment, dozens of leading Hollywood liberals (from senior MGM executive Dore Schary on down) were forced to write such
demeaning letters.

Those who had prosecuted liberal Hollywood only months earlier now
became its judges. An informal clearance process for the accused
evolved, with "courts" ranging from the American Legion to conservative newspaper columnists such as George E. Sokolsky to the Motion
Picture Alliance (principally in the person of Roy Brewer and his assistant, an ex-Communist named Howard Costigan) assessing their contri-
tion, sincerity, and fitness for employment. Having won the internal civil
war, the Hollywood conservatives piously insisted the Popular Front liberals acknowledge that they had been mistaken all along; that they were
taken in by the Communists when they agitated for a second front during
World War II, fought HUAC, or campaigned for Henry Wallace. That
was more than most liberals could easily bear, and the process of writing
clearance letters became an excruciating exercise in balancing the stubborn demands of conscience against the insistent need to work. Hardly
anyone forced to crawl through the process felt clean at the other end.

Seething in the accumulated frustration of a decade of impotence, the ascendant right would likely have attacked the Hollywood liberals after FDR's death whether or not they allied with the Communists. (Like Martin Dies, many conservatives had difficulty distinguishing between liberal and Communist ends.) To this day, many of the Hollywood radicals maintain that the real aim of HUAC—and the private red-hunters who followed it through Hollywood compiling lists and enforcing the blacklist—was to intimidate the film community's liberals, not oust the relatively few Communists.

That may well be. But there is no doubt that the Hollywood liberals heightened their vulnerability to those attacks by failing to assert their independence from the Communist party's interests. Even after ADA was formed, even after the disputes of 1946, the dream of the Popular Front remained more alluring than mainstream politics for the bulk of the Hollywood left. (That Wallace's hopeless third-party presidential bid attracted far more interest in Hollywood than either Truman or Dewey in 1948 only underlined the point.) In the first years of the Cold War, the pursuit of that dream led the majority of Hollywood progressives toward extremist positions on the fringe of national politics.

Admittedly, more than belief in the Popular Front explained that phenomenon. Some of the forces that led the Hollywood activists toward that fringe had been present in the film industry since its first brush with politics and remain important today. Accustomed to relying more on emotion than analysis, artists tend to take purist positions on political and social matters. The film community's leftist activists constantly find politicians, who deal in the world of the possible, insufficiently liberal. Partly that is because Hollywood figures, like most activists, have the luxury of criticizing without the responsibility of actually making decisions. But the political extremism of the film industry activists also reflects the unique pressures of working in a creative medium that is above all a business. Compelled to compromise constantly in the making of films, Hollywood figures tend to veer toward the other extreme and become purists in politics, as a sort of psychic compensation; people in the industry have always looked to politics as an arena that allows them to demonstrate that they really have deep convictions about something, even if their artistic choices don't display them. Even in the 1940s, all these factors reinforced Hollywood's centrifugal urge in politics. But in retrospect it appears clear that HICCASP's disputes with Truman were driven less by emotional need or differing interpretations of liberalism than by the distinct agenda of the group's Communist contingent—which was, in turn, influenced, if not precisely guided, by the foreign policy agenda of the Soviet Union.

For only a few liberals in 1947 was that manipulation sufficient cause to separate from the Communists. Without the pressure from HUAC and the other hounds of the right, the Communist influence over Hollywood's political life would probably have remained considerable for many years. That prospect did not augur well for Hollywood's political influence, but it hardly justified the blacklist that destroyed so many careers and lives. As writer Murray Kempton has observed, the price paid by the Hollywood Communists greatly exceeded their sins; they were punished for treason when they were guilty only of misplaced belief. They never posed any threat to the nation. No evidence ever suggested that they succeeded at spreading propaganda through the screen or even had a coherent plan to do so. If they had remained at their desks, relations between the United States and the Soviet Union would have unfolded no differently. By the time HUAC arrived, their influence within the film community had already peaked; even without the blacklist, the widening gulf between the United States and the Soviet Union would inexorably have reduced the number of Hollywood liberals willing to ally politically with colleagues who owed their ultimate fealty to Joseph Stalin.

As it was, the 1948 presidential campaign marked the last time Communists played any meaningful role in Hollywood's political life. The issue of whether progressive Hollywood would participate in politics primarily through the Democratic party or the independent Popular Front was finally decided by the destruction of the Popular Front: from that point forward, Hollywood activists found their principal expression within the two major political parties. The corpus of the proud and powerful Hollywood Democratic Committee, which had mutated ever leftward—first into HICCASP, then into PCA, then into a successor organization called NCASP, bewildering acronyms in search of a constituency—drifted away. So too, with the coming of the blacklist, did the Communists themselves—to London, Mexico, New York. The radical exodus deprived the Hollywood left of its most diligent organizers and committed activists, and impeded progressive activity in the film community for at least a decade. From 1936 through 1948, liberal Hollywood almost always supported at least one broad-based political group that provided the infrastructure for sustained involvement in legislative issues and political campaigns. But the Popular Front's demise also ended the era of mass political organization in Hollywood; when NCASP disappeared, it was not replaced. From the late 1940s through the early 1980s—when very different kinds of Hollywood political organizations emerged—political activity in Hollywood would be episodic and atomized, dependent on floating groups of celebrities who attached themselves to a particular cause or candidate. Denied their best organizers, Hollywood progressives gradually forgot the best thing about the Popular Front—its focus on grassroots organizing—and suffered for it.

But in other respects the elimination of the Communist party ultimately strengthened the left in Hollywood—not only by steering it back toward the political mainstream where it could have the most impact, but by branding the right with responsibility for the purge's mean-spirited personal vindictiveness. The inquisition would be a victory from which Hollywood conservatives never quite recovered.

Politics During the Inquisition

That, of course, was hardly the way it appeared in the first years of the blacklist. With conservatives questioning the patriotism of almost anyone who had marched against Hitler or for civil rights in the company of Communists, the Hollywood liberals felt as if a new ice age had descended.

The first wintry gusts toppled Representative Helen Gahagan Douglas, who had thrived in Washington since her election in 1944. She quickly scrubbed off her aura of glamour with hard work and an impenetrable, even grim, seriousness about her job. Friends told reporters she could be charming and witty in private, but few saw that side in public. With Melvyn and her children remaining at home in California, she devoted virtually all her waking hours to work. Douglas understood that as a woman and an actress she would have to be twice as prepared to win respect, and she voraciously consumed books, briefing papers, and government reports. In a Washington still unsure of what to make of a political woman—a beautiful and celebrated one at that—she refused to be baited by reporters hoping to kindle a feud with Clare Boothe Luce, and bridled at questions about her hair or her clothes. She preferred to argue about housing policy, the atom bomb, or, especially, the postwar drift toward confrontation with the Soviet Union.

From the start of her political career, Douglas's Hollywood roots were a beacon for conservatives, who equated the film community with fashionable leftism and vague disloyalty. When Douglas appeared at a UN conference, the *Hollywood Citizen-News* declared: "The people of the United States do not care to have Helen Douglas represent them at the Conference, but they would appreciate it if she would tell them a few things about the aims and purposes of the Russian delegation. Also, the people of the United States would appreciate it if Helen Douglas would tell them what all the Hollywood Communists are . . . up to. . . ."

Those insinuations were unfair. Douglas was not, in any sense, sympathetic to the Communist cause or even the misguided efforts to resuscitate the Popular Front after World War II; she supported the Marshall Plan when the Hollywood leftists opposed it, and opposed her friend Henry Wallace's campaign for the presidency in 1948 when they rallied to it. But in a political environment where all liberal activity seemed suddenly vulnerable, Douglas's Hollywood roots left her more exposed than most.

None of that deterred her from her course. If not a radical, she was a militant liberal, and in her three terms in Congress she accumulated a bold and courageous record. She fought for civilian control of the atom bomb, publicly confronted the racist Mississippi Representative John Rankin, sat in at a coffeeshop that refused to serve blacks, and challenged the excesses of HUAC, one of the few House members to do so. Though occasionally critical of the Soviets, she resisted the trend toward both confrontation abroad and intolerance at home. "The fear of communism in this country is not rational," she declared on the House floor at the moment when that fear was just beginning its postwar assault on civil liberties. "That irrational fear of communism is being deliberately used in many quarters to blind us to our real problems." Among liberals her stature rose so quickly that she was briefly mentioned as a possible running mate for Truman in 1948, an idea about forty years ahead of its time.

In October 1949, Douglas announced her candidacy for the U.S. Senate seat held by Democrat Sheridan Downey. Douglas effectively derided Downey as a tool of big business; a few months later, he sagged into the ropes and withdrew. Manchester Boddy, publisher of the ostensibly liberal *Los Angeles Daily News,* stepped in to challenge Douglas. Boddy had little chance against his better-known opponent, but he rode as far as he could on a shrill red-baiting attack. His paper labeled Douglas "the pink lady," an epithet that stuck. Douglas dispatched Boddy, but the damage was done.

In the general election, Republican candidate Richard M. Nixon merely picked up the publisher's script, calling Douglas "pink right down to her underwear." Later, Nixon distributed a "pink sheet" tracking similarities between the voting records of Douglas and leftist New York Representative Vito Marcantonio, whom many considered a follower of the Communist line. "Nixon and [his campaign manager] Murray Chotiner just used a lot of the Boddy stuff," said attorney Paul Ziffren, Douglas's chief fundraiser in Southern California. The June outbreak of the

Korean War gave their efforts to paint Douglas (at least) pink a suitably grim immediacy.

Nixon tried to use Douglas's Hollywood background against her, occasionally jabbing at actors entering politics. The conservative *Los Angeles Times* joined in, labeling her "the darling of the Hollywood parlor Pinks and Reds." Hollywood became a symbolic weight for Douglas to bear, but it actually provided little practical help for her campaign. Her husband Melvyn—who had difficulty adjusting to a supporting role for his increasingly prominent wife—spent the entire campaign out of state, touring with a play. ("Melvyn had very mixed feelings about her career," said Ziffren. "When Helen and Melvyn were together, Melvyn was the dominant person even when they talked about politics. Helen would be very quiet, which was very unusual for her.") Individual celebrities pitched in behind Douglas (including Ronald Reagan, though some evidence suggests he may have also secretly helped Nixon), but the demoralized progressives were unable to mount any coordinated effort. Hollywood provided hardly any funds for her treasury. It wasn't that Douglas discouraged Hollywood activity for fear of accentuating her show business background. "She would have been delighted to get help," Ziffren said. "She was not running away from Hollywood; Hollywood was running away from her, particularly after the Korean War broke out." More help from Hollywood would not have mattered much anyway: on Election Day, Nixon crushed Douglas by almost 700,000 votes. Inquisitive, empathetic, and indomitable, Douglas had been the brightest star produced by Hollywood's first wave of liberal activism. Now her political career was over.

By 1952, the left's retreat was general across Hollywood. No one was above suspicion; the *Chicago Tribune* accused Darryl Zanuck of "support" for "the Communist party line." For the moguls and their employees alike, the overriding political goal of the early 1950s was to find shelter against the charges of un-Americanism.

That quest irresistibly brought most of them to Dwight D. Eisenhower for the 1952 presidential race. He provided unmatched shelter: there was no better way to affirm your patriotism than to stand beside the man who had won the war against Hitler. That record was a powerful selling point for Jews, too. The combination allowed Eisenhower to appeal across ideological boundaries in Hollywood. As early as 1948, Hollywood activists ranging from Dore Schary and Milton Sperling to Sam Goldwyn and Jack Warner tried to lure Eisenhower into the presidential race, as the candidate for either party. Goldwyn so hoped Eisenhower would run that he insistently told him he had a "duty" to make himself available on either the Democratic or Republican ticket. When Eisenhower finally did decide to seek the Republican nomination four years later, Hollywood poured out for him—probably more energetically than for any Republican candidate ever. "He appealed to the showmen because of the dramatics of the war itself," said Herbert Brownell, who became a key adviser to Eisenhower after managing Thomas Dewey's two presidential bids. "Many of them [had come to know him] because they went themselves or sent representatives to the Allied headquarters in Europe. That was the thing they strove for more than anything else: to get close to Eisenhower. . . . He was the number one dramatic figure in the Western world."

Hollywood's enlistment behind Eisenhower in 1952 was more than a personal triumph. It also represented the apogee of the mogul system of politics. Eisenhower appealed to the moguls on many levels. Not only did he share their basic moderate conservatism and offer protection against the right, but he fit their conception of the American hero: a man of action and few words. His Democratic opponent, Adlai E. Stevenson, seemed the opposite: he reminded the studio chiefs of the fast-talking liberal writers who were constantly wheedling for higher salaries and cracking jokes they didn't understand. "I don't think my father had a political theory about it," said Harry Warner's daughter Betty. "But a Stevenson wasn't something my father felt comfortable with—he wasn't practical, he spoke in phrases nobody could understand. You didn't know what he would do."

As clearly as anything since the Upton Sinclair campaign, the Eisenhower effort showed what the moguls could do for a candidate who moved them. Though power began to diffuse in Hollywood after the Justice Department—reopening the antitrust suit temporarily settled in 1940—won judgments through the late 1940s requiring the studios to sever themselves from their theater chains, the moguls in 1952 remained the industry's dominant force. On Eisenhower's behalf, they leveraged all of their influence. An Eisenhower group coalesced early in the primary season with Darryl Zanuck, Goldwyn, and Warner as co-chairs. Most of the work, though, fell to Frank McCarthy, a bureaucratically adept former army colonel working for Zanuck as a producer. McCarthy, who later produced the film *Patton*, approached the campaign as if he was planning an invasion. Hollywood had never seen a presidential campaign organized so systematically. In March, the Eisenhower forces identified captains at each studio and the major talent agencies. In early April, McCarthy instructed his captains to identify all employees in their organization earning above $500 a week and to determine their presidential preference. To ensure a uniform canvass, McCarthy even prepared a questionnaire that helped his studio captains slot all prospects into one of four categories: Eisenhower supporter; Eisenhower opponent; undecided; and unwilling to state.

Once the prime targets were identified, senior studio officials blanketed them with requests for campaign donations. Zanuck and Warner both sent letters to their employees soliciting money. Zanuck even tried to enlist Howard Hughes, who owned RKO at the time. The three producers organized a well-attended fundraising dinner in April that raised $14,125 and garnered pledges for another $18,910. When the executives returned to business, McCarthy sustained the pressure. He hounded the studio captains for checks, and sent the three co-chairmen almost daily progress reports. "It was an extraordinary effort by these people," said Milton Sperling, Harry Warner's son-in-law, who had by then joined Warner Bros. as a producer. "It was so well organized. They took the studio roll and just said he's giving, he's giving, he's giving. It was like the United Jewish Appeal. It wasn't at all subtle. The implication was always there, if you don't give, you don't belong here; it's disloyal."

The principal obstacles for the Eisenhower steamroller were actually industry conservatives who preferred Senator Robert A. Taft of Ohio, the general's major rival for the GOP nomination. After Taft lost the nomination through intricate last-minute maneuvers at the Republican Convention, his Hollywood supporters returned home sullen and angry. Shortly after the convention, Zanuck attended a dinner of leading Republicans at the home of *Los Angeles Times* political editor Kyle Palmer, the doyen of the California GOP, and found Taft partisans still fuming. When Eisenhower came to Los Angeles for a rally in early August, leading figures in the Motion Picture Alliance stayed away, despite Zanuck's repeated invitations. To Goldwyn, Zanuck expressed concern that such prominent Taft supporters as John Wayne and Cecil B. De-Mille remained unwilling to help Eisenhower. The sniping finally stopped when Zanuck convened a dinner at Fox where vice-presidential nominee Richard Nixon made the case for unity to actors Ward Bond and George Murphy, directors John Ford and Leo McCarey, columnist Hedda Hopper, and other leading conservatives. But it was a measure of the times that Ike's principal problem in Hollywood was the sense among some that he was too moderate.

Hollywood's beleaguered Democrats were no less intent on distancing themselves from even the faintest red tint in 1952. The leadership of the Hollywood effort for Stevenson prominently included men at the forefront of the Communist purge. Foremost among them was union leader

Roy Brewer, the fervent anti-Communist who had supported the congressional investigations of Hollywood, assumed a leading role in the Motion Picture Alliance, and helped to administer the informal clearance process at the heart of the blacklist. A dedicated union man, Brewer was still a staunch lunch-bucket Democrat. But his designation as the Hollywood group's co-chairman, like the naming of HUAC member Representative Clyde Doyle as the group's "honorary chairman," was primarily insurance against accusations that this liberal effort was yet another Communist front. Brewer's assistance came with a stiff, nonnegotiable price. To historian and liberal activist Arthur M. Schlesinger, Jr., a top Stevenson aide, Brewer insisted he would help only if the campaign renounced the assistance of any Hollywood figure who had not "straightened out" accusations of Communist ties. Schlesinger agreed. Stevenson, meanwhile, raised no word of objection to the blacklist.

Though Brewer's prominence in the Democratic campaign symbolized the far left's complete isolation in Hollywood by 1952, Stevenson also had enormous appeal for mainstream liberals revolted by the blacklist. He became the first in a line of Democratic candidates who appealed to the Hollywood liberals' sense of style (his successors included John F. Kennedy and Gary Hart). The Illinois governor was everything the Hollywood progressives imagined themselves to be: witty, worldly, confident, captivating. "He was so charming and so urbane and friendly that you just felt that you really meant something to him," said Philip Dunne. To Bette Davis, he was a "beautiful egghead." Entranced by Stevenson at a party, screenwriter Leonard Spigelgass turned to a Stevenson aide and said, "How can anybody be so charming and not be Jewish?"

Whatever else he was, Stevenson was not that. His roots were Quaker and Presbyterian, and as a young man growing up in Bloomington, Illinois, he shared the common genteel prejudice against blacks and Jews. (Even years later, as a young lawyer, Stevenson joined private clubs that barred Jews.) Stevenson was born with the century in February 1900 to a family of leading Illinois Democrats whose prominence had begun to fray. His grandfather, Adlai Ewing Stevenson, had served as Grover Cleveland's vice-president. But his father, a high-strung, dissatisfied man, had never quite built a career and suffered through a difficult, often unhappy marriage with Stevenson's mother.

The son followed the father's pattern: he suffered through an unhappy marriage of his own and drifted well into middle age without any strong sense of direction. He went to the finest academic institutions—Choate, Princeton, Harvard Law School—but his academic performance was no more than mediocre at any of them; after his second year at Harvard, he flunked out and was forced to finish his law school training at Northwestern University. He found a job at one of Chicago's most prestigious firms, but the law bored him. In the early 1930s he finally found an outlet for his restless energy in the Chicago Council on Foreign Relations, where he became a leading voice against the isolationism dominant in the Midwest. After a brief tour early in the New Deal with the Agricultural Adjustment Administration and more extended service as a special assistant to the navy secretary during World War II, he returned home to Illinois still uncertain what to do with his life. ("Am 47 today—still restless; dissatisfied with myself. What's the matter?" he wrote in his diary on his birthday in 1947.) He planned a race for the Senate in 1948, but was convinced by friends and the local Democratic machine to run instead for governor, and easily defeated the discredited, scandal-plagued Republican incumbent. Four years later, after a successful term in Springfield, he was drafted by the Democratic party as its presidential nominee.

Without any previous background in elected office when he became governor of Illinois, Stevenson was an unusual politician. But he was not nearly so unusual as his admirers claimed. Stevenson was lionized as an intellectual, but he actually much preferred socializing to reading. He had a great flair for language, but little appetite for the solitary life of the mind. He devoted far more energy to cracking the great addresses than the great books. Meeting the right people, moving in the right circles was always a priority. When he embarked on his law career in Chicago, he immediately began to circulate in the upper reaches of exclusive Lake Forest society; his wife, the former Ellen Borden, was the daughter of a woman dubbed one of the "queens of society" in Chicago. Nor was Stevenson as idealistic or liberal as his supporters often suggested: he was a practical, calculating politician who worked well the Chicago Democratic machine while in Illinois, and during the 1952 presidential campaign avoided civil rights initiatives that would alienate the solidly Democratic South. He complained that he was more conservative than his speechwriters made him sound. Because he courted liberal intellectuals, because he flattered them with his attention and dazzled them with his wordplay, they considered him one of them; yet in all these respects he was not.

Still, at a political moment defined by Senator Joseph R. McCarthy's boozy rages, Truman's smalltown vulgarity, and Eisenhower's inarticulate shrugs, Stevenson was an urbane and eloquent voice and liberals flocked to him as a savior. The passion was particularly intense in Hollywood, where political style had always counted as much as substance. Though he didn't know much about show business, Stevenson returned the admiration. He was shrewd enough to realize that help from celebrities could be useful. As early as 1940, he urged the organizers of an Aid the Allies rally he addressed to help boost the crowd by adding Douglas Fairbanks, Jr., to the program. But Stevenson was attracted to Hollywood less for political than for personal reasons. The capital of glamour appealed to his life-long preference for glittering company. And Stevenson, who was divorced from Ellen Borden in 1949, clearly relished the attractions of beautiful women as much as they enjoyed his sparkling wit. (At some level, Stevenson may have also seen public association with women famous for their desirability as a way to squelch occasional whispering campaigns suggesting he was a homosexual.) William McCormick Blair, Jr., Stevenson's traveling aide during the campaign and later ambassador to the Philippines, remembers the candidate persuading author John Gunther to introduce him to Greta Garbo. Gunther set up a meeting in New York. "Stevenson was a fan of hers," Blair said. "And they got on so well. At one point, I remember Stevenson sort of slapping her on the thigh, she was laughing about something. They were talking about their abhorrence of the press being so intrusive and all that. I remember his saying, 'you eccentric you' and he laughed, and she said, 'maybe we're both eccentrics when it comes to that.' I remember when we were leaving he was trying to get her telephone number and she wouldn't give it to him."

Garbo was a rare holdout. Stevenson coyly encouraged the affections of several of Hollywood's leading ladies. Marlene Dietrich, Blair recalled, constantly pushed for time alone with Stevenson; one day she came on the set of *How to Marry a Millionaire* and complained to Lauren Bacall that Stevenson had stopped calling her. After sitting with Stevenson at a luncheon in New York, Tallulah Bankhead gushed to publisher Dorothy Schiff that she hadn't been "so thrilled about a man . . . since she had first met John Barrymore more than 20 years ago." Stevenson affected Myrna Loy the same way.

No one fell harder than Bacall. "I adored Adlai Stevenson," Bacall wrote in her memoirs. "I suppose I even worshipped him. . . . His entrance into my life shook me up completely." Later, she described her feelings as "a combination of hero worship and slight infatuation." To say the least. "She was crazy about Stevenson, almost on a sexual level," said Milton Sperling. "She was insane about him, she just adored him." Mickey Ziffren, the wife of fundraiser Paul Ziffren, remembers Bacall "mooning over" Stevenson at a party, while her husband, Humphrey Bogart, watched "with amusement." Bacall "was closer to him than anybody" in Hollywood, Bill Blair recalled. "I don't think there was anything romantic, as far as I know; but they were very good friends, and she was a very loyal friend, and very helpful. If anyone were to say you shouldn't be supporting Stevenson, she'd really knock them down."

That had always been Betty Bacall's style. In outline her story was familiar to the point of cliché: the young model brought to Hollywood by a powerful older man looking to create a new star. But the story did not have the typical cautionary moral; Bacall was nobody's victim. The director Howard Hawks first discovered her. Or more precisely his wife, a young model herself, saw a face on the cover of *Harper's Bazaar* that she thought might be just the new look that her husband was searching for. The face belonged to eighteen-year-old Betty Bacall, who had been modeling and trying to break into theater in New York. Bacall had virtually no acting experience, but she had an indomitable independence, even insolence, that was aggressive and sexy, intelligent and forthright, and utterly unlike anything else on the screen. Hawks christened her Lauren and cast her opposite Humphrey Bogart in *To Have and Have Not,* his version of the waterlogged Hemingway novel.

Hawks did not maintain control of his creation for long. During the filming she fell in love with her co-star, and he with her. Through 1944, the romance blossomed. Bogart tried to free himself from his third wife, who refused to go quietly. Bogart hesitated, Bacall pined—and the gossip columnists reported the details with the precision of the latest troop movements across Western Europe. When Bogart and Bacall were finally married in 1945, during a break in the filming of *The Big Sleep,* her prospects in Hollywood appeared boundless.

Actually, her career foundered. Away from Hawks, her inexperience came through more clearly. Jack Warner made matters worse by repeatedly casting her in what one critic called "slinky roles" that caricatured her early success with Bogart. Bacall never entirely matched her initial success; nothing she performed on screen equaled the drama and fantasy of her romance with Bogart. But just when she seemed condemned to live out the Hollywood cliché, she revived with a sparkling performance next to Marilyn Monroe in *How to Marry a Millionaire* and then, later in the 1950s, began a successful second career on Broadway.

It was the confidence and independence Bacall projected in her prime that made her so attractive to men, and such a model for women. Those same qualities attracted her to politics. Like Bogart, she was a Democrat. But if he was the voice of calm reason, she was the epitome of passion and outrage. The first fight she flew into was the battle against HUAC in 1947. Bacall joined the Committee for the First Amendment and signed up with Bogart for the ill-fated expedition to Washington to confront the committee. "I became very emotional about it," she recalled years later. "It was my first grown-up exposure to a cause, and my reaction should have clued me in as to how cause-prone I could be."

Like most of liberal Hollywood, Bacall then stewed silently as the blacklist descended over Hollywood. Stevenson's emergence provided the cue for her return to politics. Along with millions of other Americans, Bacall got her first look at Stevenson during the 1952 Democratic Convention, where his acceptance speech impressed her with its wit and erudition. A few weeks later, she met Stevenson on the receiving line at a Hollywood rally; that turned out to be the start of one of the closest relationships in her life. Bacall remained friendly with Stevenson until his death in 1965, corresponded with him regularly, and saw him occasionally over the years.

Stevenson affected Bacall at a personal level, but her political attraction to him was more revealing. Her enlistment in Stevenson's campaign was a declaration of independence—a means of bringing her life in alignment with the resilient characters she played on the screen. When Stevenson emerged on the national stage, Bacall was twenty-eight and one of the most famous women in the country. But she was famous for the glamorous role in which she had been cast by others; like so many stars in Hollywood, before and since, she craved an opportunity to demonstrate there was more to her than what appeared on screen. "I needed to dream," she wrote in her memoirs. "I needed to reach out, to stretch myself, to put my unused energies to use. My choices up to then had been Bogie or work—now they had expanded to political life, to bettering the world and its people, or at least to advancing and being connected with a great man who was capable of doing something about it." Millions of women admired Bacall, even envied her—yet she knew there was something impersonal in her success. The Stevenson campaign offered her a chance to express her belief—and perhaps even to convince herself—that she had something of her own to offer, apart from Howard Hawk's vision of Lauren Bacall, or Bogart's or Jack Warner's. The "campaign . . . disrupted my life completely, " she wrote. "I was flattered to have been included—flattered to have been singled out by Stevenson as someone a bit special." Once she had been accepted in Hollywood, no one in it had the power to make her feel that way any more. To make the star feel like a star, it took a politician.

Though the 1952 campaign didn't unleash quite as much energy in Hollywood as Roosevelt's final race, it returned the movie industry to the front lines of national politics. Both sides looked to Hollywood to provide the same kind of assistance it had provided for Roosevelt.

Hollywood Republicans were so optimistic about ending the Democrats' twenty-year hold on the White House that they formed two campaign groups: the Zanuck-Warner-Goldwyn Independent Volunteer Committee from the primary took responsibility for raising money from potential big donors, while the regular Hollywood Republican Committee led by actor George Murphy aimed at smaller givers. Both camps simultaneously created programs to reach the public. The local Eisenhower organization asked the Zanuck group to target California Democrats, and it conscientiously produced newspaper, radio, and television ads, as well as a nightly radio program during the final days of the campaign. Perhaps still sensitive about slurs on their own patriotism, the group's leaders drew up talking points urging members to stress anti-Communist themes.

Meanwhile, Murphy's Hollywood Republican Committee, whose board included Robert Montgomery, Walt Disney, and Ginger Rogers, dispatched stars to campaign stops across the country and struck many of the same harsh notes, if somewhat more theatrically. Murphy remembers taking a delegation that included John Wayne, Ward Bond, Irene Dunne, and Jeanette MacDonald across Texas. Back in Los Angeles, Hedda Hopper, Ida Koverman, and Irene Dunne organized "A Woman's Brigade for Ike and Dick." For a Los Angeles rally in late September, the group pulled together a twelve-car motorcade. One car carried a box of "taxpayers' money" that was strewn to the winds; another car, filled with extras outfitted in Russian costumes (down to red underwear) requisitioned from Jack Warner and Frank Freeman, represented "Reds in Government."

The Democrats' major resource was Bacall, who reclaimed Bogart from an early attraction to Eisenhower (arranged by Zanuck) and took him out on the road for Stevenson. The couple appeared with Stevenson on a mid-October campaign swing through California, Bacall introducing him before a speech on foreign policy at San Francisco's Cow Palace. "I forgot who wrote the speech," said writer Allen Rivkin, who organized much of the Stevenson effort in Hollywood. "But boy, she was a powerhouse." Then, with Robert Ryan, the two stars joined Stevenson on his final whistle-stop train tour through the Northeast. They quickly proved an enormous asset. "They were what really brought the crowds in more than the candidate," said Stevenson aide Bill Blair, "They would come out and make a few remarks of introduction. But once they went back in, the crowd would keep chanting for them. We'd get ready to introduce the candidate or the local candidates, and the crowd would be chanting all the time 'Bogie and Bacall,' and you'd bring them out again, and then there would be wild cheers." The actors seemed to enjoy their appearances as much as the crowds did. They kept their humor even after a platform collapsed under them in New London, Connecticut. "It was a happy addition," said Schlesinger, one of the governor's speechwriters. "Some stars have a reputation for making special demands all the time. They did not; they were very easy and relaxed. It was a novelty for them, which they were savoring. I think they had a good time." At each stop, Bacall saw Stevenson wave or smile at her. "To my fantasizing mind," she later wrote, "he seemed so vulnerable."

If anything, the addition of Bogart and Bacall worked too well. Their frantic reception at each stop pushed the train more and more behind schedule. Finally, after a few days campaign aides decided to take them off the train and send them on early for a rally in Madison Square Garden. Later that night, Blair was in bed when the phone rang.

"Blair," said the instantly recognizable voice on the other end, colder than the autumn New England night.

"Yes, Betty," Blair said.

"I've got just one question for you: Are you the one who said Bogie and I could not be on the campaign train tomorrow?"

"Well," Blair said weakly, and he launched into an explanation of the delays, and the distraction caused by crowds chanting for her and Bogart while Stevenson tried to speak about Korea or inflation, and the need to have a good rally in New York. Blair tried to make it all seem simple, logical.

"Well, I understand," Bacall said finally. "That's OK."

Bogart and Bacall went on to New York. Blair went back to bed. "But," he said many years later, "I'll never forget that 'Blair, I've got just one question for you.' She was mad."

One week later, Bacall was even more despondent. Bacall and Bogart stayed with Stevenson through the end, joining him in Chicago for his final rally, and after flying back to California to vote, rushing back to Springfield (over Bogart's objections) to spend Election Night with the governor. When they arrived in Illinois, Bogart collapsed into his hotel bed with a virus. Bacall bundled him up and rushed over to the Executive Mansion for what turned out to be a wake. His hero's halo untarnished by the campaign, Eisenhower rolled up a landslide victory. Blair, and many of Stevenson's aides, had felt it coming for weeks. Soaring on her own enthusiasm, Bacall had not. As the states rolled into Eisenhower's column, she sat glumly in front of a television set, her eyes glassy, her heart aching, dazed with disappointment and grief. Though Bacall has remained a Democratic activist to this day, no politician ever touched her as deeply again.

The New Era

The parts played by Bacall and Bogart in the 1952 race—like those assumed by John Wayne and George Murphy—broke no new ground for Hollywood. But the campaign nonetheless marked a fundamental departure in the film community's political participation. The initial Eisenhower-Stevenson race was the first presidential campaign in which television played a major role. Both sides televised their conventions, ran spot advertisements, and bought time for their candidates' speeches. Richard Nixon used television to deliver his famous "Checkers" speech (in which he defended himself from charges of receiving gifts from wealthy supporters partly by insisting he would keep the cocker spaniel—Checkers—given by supporters to his six-year-old daughter Tricia). Television changed everything about American politics; Hollywood's role in the political drama was no exception. Once the television camera's red light went on, nothing was ever the same in Hollywood, or in Washington, or in the relationship between them.

At first, the most important change was television's impact on campaign costs. Between 1920 and 1950 total campaign costs, adjusted for inflation and the electorate's growth, did not increase. But beginning in 1952, television not only displaced other spending but caused overall costs to rise.

Rising costs increased the pressure on fundraisers. In 1952, Hollywood was not the principal source of money for either candidate. (Stevenson depended on wealthy liberals; Eisenhower drew enormous support from the oil industry.) But Hollywood contained one of the nation's largest concentrations of wealthy, politically active people, and both sides expected it to contribute heavily.

From the start, the Hollywood Eisenhower effort focused primarily on fundraising. Frank McCarthy's system of studio captains was aimed at producing checks, not endorsements. So intense was the pressure the studio executives exerted that the Hollywood AFL Film Council demanded the Warners return to their employees money they had "exacted" for the Eisenhower effort; the Warners denied the allegation and kept the checks. Sperling, for example, was a strong Stevenson supporter; but he worked at Warner Bros., was married into the family, and so he wrote a check for Eisenhower too. "I had to give money to Eisenhower because I was being paid by them, because I was a family member," he said. "They just put the tap on people, one after the other. They really should have been arrested for that, forcing people to give money. It was an absolute demand: Give this or else." This made for imperfect labor-management relations but enormously successful fundraising. The Hollywood Eisenhower money piled up steadily through the spring: $19,350 by late March, $55,175 by late April, $73,403 by the convention in July.

But no matter how much the moguls raised, the campaign demanded more, mostly to pay for television. In early June, Howard C. Petersen, Eisenhower's chief fundraiser, anxiously wired Jack Warner for help in collecting funds to buy television time for a Denver rally. Two days later, Warner rushed out letters to potential donors in the studio. Two weeks later, Petersen wired again. This time he needed help in raising $150,000 for a radio and newspaper advertising program to offset Taft's convention expenditures. The pressure remained high through the general election. At the August organizing meeting, GOP leaders told Zanuck they expected the film industry to produce $150,000—twice as much as it apparently collected for Dewey in 1948.

As in the spring, the studio moguls systematically pressured colleagues and employees for money. Warner hectored John Wayne and Gary Cooper. Zanuck engaged in long and argumentative correspondence with Olivia de Havilland. When MCA's Jules Stein refused to give, both Warner and Zanuck upbraided him. Their committee distributed to the studio captains a list of all Republicans, Eisenhower primary supporters, and disgruntled Democrats. The Warners, Goldwyn, and Zanuck kicked in $35,000 through September alone. The committee sent $43,000 to the Southern California Eisenhower committee to help pay for television time.

Still it wasn't enough. Ten days before the election, Zanuck sent Warner and Goldwyn an urgent appeal for more money. In addition to the television costs, he told them, radio and newspaper advertisements demanded more cash—at least $10,000 in the next week. All three reached down for the final push. And on their command, the money poured in—almost $9,300 in the next week, and nearly $4,800 more in the two weeks that followed.

Hollywood frustrated Stevenson's fundraisers as much as it rewarded Ike's. The film community was not a major source of money for Stevenson. "We did not do a very good job of raising money," said the liberal attorney Paul Ziffren, who tried. "We raised just minimal amounts. Anyone who gave $1,000 to Stevenson was a major donor." Stevenson's big collector in Hollywood should have been Dore Schary, who succeeded Louis B. Mayer in the top job at MGM in 1951. (Nick Schenck finally cashiered his old adversary after Mayer theatrically insisted the lot wasn't big enough for both him and Schary.) But Schary was not willing or able to dig out funds either. "Dore Schary as usual was just a big bunch of hot air," insisted Roger Stevens, the theater impresario who assumed the thankless job of raising money for Stevenson. Just before Schary left for an extended vacation in late September, he glumly informed one Democratic official that he was having a "tough time" meeting his financial promises to the party. In mid-October Schary sent out an appeal to eighty-five prospects and received only eight checks, none greater than $250, just $775 in all.

Part of the problem, Roy Brewer thought, was that activists under fire (ironically from Brewer among others) for donating to ostensibly liberal causes in the 1940s hesitated before writing new checks. Stevenson's unwillingness to prostrate himself before fundraisers didn't help. "He hated it," said Bill Blair. "Particularly when you had to have a half-hour before a big affair where you'd meet with the big contributors." Though he might not have agreed, Stevenson actually got off relatively easily: future candidates would face demands from Hollywood fundraisers far more demeaning than anything he endured.

Television changed Hollywood's political role in another important respect. Suddenly, the campaigns scrambled to find advisers who understood how to present people and ideas through the new medium. Years later, a new profession of political media consultant emerged to guide candidates through the maze. But as the new technology surfaced in the 1952 campaign, there were no experts. Campaign aides to Eisenhower and Stevenson—men who grew up on the politics of personal appearance and radio—had no feel for television; most of them barely watched it. And so they reached out to anyone who had experience communicating with the public—to Madison Avenue, to the television networks themselves, and to Hollywood.

Of the Hollywood activists it was Darryl Zanuck who moved most aggressively to insinuate himself into the opening. A small, coiled man with ferocious energy, Zanuck fully believed that he understood how to reach America as well as any man in it. Zanuck had counseled Willkie on his public appearances and campaign message; now he proposed to do the same for Eisenhower. In August, he sent Nixon a sophisticated single-spaced five-page memo warning the vice-presidential nominee that television had created a "new era" in campaigning and offering his services to help Eisenhower cope with it. Zanuck followed up through the fall by producing a newsreel for the campaign called "The Eisenhower Story" and peppering Eisenhower's top advisers with long advisory memos. Zanuck had ideas about almost every strategic and tactical decision facing the campaign: he critiqued ads, warned Sherman Adams, the campaign's chief of staff, to respond more quickly to Stevenson's charges, wrote sample speeches, and urged Adams to focus the general's appeal toward independents and Democrats.

This was classic Zanuck: his approach to any problem was to assault it, as if taking a beach. "He would throw himself at anything," said Jules Buck, his assistant in the late 1940s. "If you looked at Darryl and said, 'You've got a cockroach problem' he would say 'Let's do this and do that.' We used to call him 'Darryl does everything.' . . . He worked the way he fucked. He was very fast." Eisenhower aides didn't know quite what to make of the barrage. "There must of been some public relations fellow on his staff that was doing this," said Herbert Brownell, still incredulous after thirty-five years. "I'm sure that he couldn't personally have done it because he sent us a mass of material, strategy, details of strategy, outlines of strategy." Zanuck, though, almost certainly wrote the memos himself.

George Murphy, who was brought inside the campaign in mid-October to orchestrate logistics and celebrities for Eisenhower's appearances, thought Zanuck's missives had little impact. Brownell agreed that on policy and strategy, Zanuck "had no influence at all." But, Brownell added, "in the line of public relations and [arranging] spectacles, things of that sort, I think his views were very helpful."

No one questioned actor Robert Montgomery's influence on Eisenhower. Murphy brought Montgomery into the campaign after asking one of the Republican National Committee's top public relations men how they intended to improve Eisenhower's disappointing early television appearances.

"I'll handle it," the man told him.

"You don't know anything about it," Murphy replied, "and you won't handle it."

Murphy called the staunchly Republican Montgomery, who agreed to join the campaign sometime after the convention. Eisenhower needed the help; the general took to television like a cat to water. Without his uniform, he seemed to shrink, as if his stars hid shoulder pads. More coach than strategist, Montgomery advised Eisenhower on his gestures, the use of makeup, relaxing for the camera. It was a felicitous match. "He was very effective," said Brownell. "Eisenhower liked him. There was a good chemistry between them. All of us at headquarters were very glad to see him move in there. He started as a volunteer, but they ended up as good personal friends."

Montgomery continued to work with Eisenhower after the campaign, regularly visiting the White House as the president's personal television consultant. Along with Murphy, he was given a major role in the planning of the 1956 Republican Convention. Montgomery consciously downplayed his role, for in those early years of the television age, a president receiving dramatic advice from an actor conjured up images of the ventriloquist's dummy. But in his limited area, Montgomery amassed considerable influence.

Television created the same opportunities for Hollywood Democrats. Shortly after the 1952 convention, writers Allen Rivkin and Leonard Spigelgass traveled to Springfield, Illinois, to confer with Stevenson and his top aides. They saw a succession of bright, witty, energetic men, but no one, including the candidate, who understood anything about television. After they returned to Hollywood, Rivkin and Spigelgass passed suggestions to Springfield for improving Stevenson's television performance. Schary tried to cure Stevenson of his annoying habit of smiling slightly after making a point, even a serious one. Philip Dunne worked with Stevenson and a director in Los Angeles on a series of television commercials.

Four years later, in the Stevenson-Eisenhower rematch, the Democrats assigned even more responsibility to their Hollywood supporters. After suffering through an interminable keynote address from Massachusetts Governor Paul A. Dever in 1952, Democratic National Committee chairman Paul Butler decided the party could not afford to gamble its precious television primetime on an unpredictable single speaker. He decided to split the keynote duties between Tennessee Governor Frank G. Clement and an hour-long film on the legacy of the Democratic party from FDR through Truman. Butler asked Dore Schary to put together the movie. "We felt the Hollywood people would be more creative than a political ad agency," said Paul Ziffren, who worked with Butler on the project.

Excited by the unprecedented responsibility, Schary set to work with Rivkin and Norman Corwin, compiling newsreel film and writing a script. Dashing young Massachusetts Senator John F. Kennedy was chosen as the narrator. When Kennedy flew out to Hollywood to review the script and lay down the narration, Schary held a dinner for Kennedy and Clement to screen the film at his home a few weeks before the convention. The senator left an immediate impression. "After dinner," said Corwin, "he went over the script with me and he had two or three questions about elements appearing on page one, or page five, and when those were answered to his satisfaction, he sort of signaled he felt he was in good hands, and that was it. And then we made arrangements to film it at the Goldwyn studio, and I worked with Kennedy in the filming of it . . . and made a few suggestions on delivery. He was excellent."

For the Hollywood contingent, the keynote film was an extremely satisfying experience because they maintained creative control. Working directly with Stevenson was another matter. Though he enjoyed Holly- wood, probably no candidate more resisted its ministrations. Stevenson stubbornly refused to mold himself to the demands of the television age. "Stevenson had a terrible time with television," said Bill Blair. He fiddled with his scripts until moments before airtime. He refused to shorten his addresses to ensure he would remain within his time limit, and often found himself cut off the air before concluding. And he rebuffed almost all efforts to improve his television performance. Suggestions from Holly- wood (with rare exceptions) were ignored. Even Edward R. Murrow discreetly dropped in to give Stevenson some pointers; they didn't help. "In each state we went into, there were a group of people who were identified with the media . . . [who] thought they were going to 'produce' the candidate, particularly in New York and Los Angeles," said William Wilson, a young CBS producer who joined Stevenson as a television adviser. "And they would always run up against the same thing: the schedule wouldn't permit them to talk to him much, they couldn't get his attention."

Stevenson thought himself principled in holding to his vision of a lofty discourse unsullied by concessions to the new medium. But his failure to realize television's impact was also symptomatic of an intellectual smug- ness that alienated voters. He could not make television disappear by derogating it—nor would his successors hope to. Each generation of candidates who followed Eisenhower and Stevenson accommodated themselves more easily to television's demands for a good show.

Ironically, as political communications grew more to resemble Holly- wood products, Hollywood's role in shaping them diminished. After the 1950s, politicians increasingly turned for communications advice to Mad- ison Avenue and the full-time political consultants who first emerged in the mid-1960s. Though individual Hollywood figures sometimes found roles as vague communication advisers in presidential campaigns—and one, Warren Beatty, found greater opportunities than that—the institu- tional power flowed elsewhere after the initial burst of activity in the

Eisenhower-Stevenson contests. In 1956, the Democrats turned to Hollywood for their convention film. In 1984, the Republicans looked to Madison Avenue; in 1988, the Democrats looked to a political media consultant. Not until the end of the 1980s did a new generation of Hollywood activists systematically try to regain some of that power.

If it didn't increase the strategic role of Hollywood activists, television midwifed the union of Hollywood and politics in a more profound sense. As keenly as good moviemakers, good politicians had always understood the power of symbolism; FDR, among the most substantive of politicians, used symbolism as effectively as anyone in the twentieth century. But television forced politicians, more than ever before, to consciously assume symbolic roles. As an actress, Helen Gahagan Douglas originally found politics exciting because it allowed her to escape her star persona and reach voters as an individual; the television era reversed the equation and reduced most politicians to a persona. To communicate in television's clipped cadences—so uncharitable to complexity or nuanced argument—more and more national politicians did what Stevenson refused to do: they willingly became actors playing a broadly scripted part—virile young hero (John F. Kennedy), ascetic moral leader (Jimmy Carter), benevolent father (Ronald Reagan), read-my-lips tough guy (George Bush). Even though Stevenson's men did not understand the cost of their refusal to adapt to television, they saw this trend emerging. "Sooner or later," predicted George W. Ball, one of Stevenson's top aides and later a prominent diplomat, "Presidential campaigns would have professional actors as candidates who could speak the lines."

This convergence didn't give Hollywood more power over politicians. But it made politicians less intimidating to the industry. Politicians always had a mystique in the movie industry because their world seemed weightier, more substantial than Hollywood's dominion of images. Television diluted that cachet by revealing politicians to be no less subservient to shallow imagery. Once television compelled politicians to primp and posture like actors, it became increasingly common for Hollywood to consider them not so much heroes as ungainly amateurs trying to unlock secrets the stars intuitively knew. As television grew to dominate American public life, that awareness would encourage stars to assume bolder political roles than ever before.

These trends gathered but didn't crest during the Eisenhower years. Instead, while Eisenhower held the White House, the forces that had shaped Hollywood's political life since its inception finally spent themselves.

After more than two decades, the film industry's battle over communism sputtered toward a close. HUAC's visits grew less frequent and less productive for the committee. The Motion Picture Alliance for the Preservation of American Ideals drifted into obscurity. Roy Brewer believed the Alliance faded because Senator Joseph McCarthy's televised rampages discredited the group's militant message. "The McCarthy hearings so confused the American people that there was no way to buck it," Brewer said. "They created the impression you could not isolate the Communist influence without destroying democracy." But the Alliance's larger problem by the mid-1950s was a shortage of targets: the studios had purged their commissaries of Communists and the blacklisted had scattered. After failing to win the international presidency of his union, Brewer himself left Hollywood in 1955 to take a job with Allied Artists in New York.

Eisenhower rallied the moguls more unreservedly than any candidate before him. But the 1952 campaign marked the last triumph for their brand of autocratic politics. Not any political development but economic change undermined their approach. Through the 1950s, power in Hollywood became decentralized. The consent decree severing production from exhibition removed the studios' thumbs from the distribution line and allowed dozens of new independent producers to emerge; by 1957, 165 independent producers were operating in Hollywood, up from just 40 during World War II. Unable to rely on a captive chain of theaters to exhibit as many movies as they could produce, and under increasing competitive pressure from television, the studios found it less profitable to hold stars, writers, and directors under binding contract. Once they achieved their independence, all these craftsmen became less susceptible to the demands through which the studio heads had built their political power. In the wreckage of the old system, a new generation of studio leaders would be forced to find new ways to accumulate political influence.

Age and changed circumstances finally caught up with the moguls, who had, incredibly, ruled Hollywood unchallenged since the 1920s. Darryl Zanuck, his touch slipping, quit Fox in 1956 and went off to produce movies in Europe. The Warner brothers sold their interest to a syndicate headed by a Boston bank; Jack characteristically doublecrossed Harry and held on to his shares and his job. Enraged, Harry suffered a stroke; he died in 1958. Harry Cohn, still holding Columbia firmly in his hands, died that year too. By then, Louis B. Mayer had died as well, after a final attempt to regain control of MGM fell through.

Time swept clear the stage. The first generation of liberal Hollywood activists likewise surrendered the limelight. Helen Gahagan Douglas never played a meaningful political role after her bout with Nixon in 1950; Melvyn receded into the shadows with her. Settling into his new career as a director, Philip Dunne cut back his activities. Bogart, the Democrats' most reliable and popular star for over a decade, died of cancer in 1957. Dore Schary was fired from MGM in 1956, partly because his political activism displeased the new president of Loew's, the corporate parent of MGM.

The regal moguls, radical writers, and besieged liberals who had dominated Hollywood's first thirty years of political engagement were finally gone. As the decade waned, what would replace them as the industry's driving political forces remained unclear; but their departure concluded the first era of Hollywood's relationship with Washington. In the numbing gloom of the blacklist, Hollywood's remaining activists dug in and awaited Act Two.

PART TWO

THE AGE OF TELEVISION

CHAPTER FIVE

JOHN F. KENNEDY AND THE REAWAKENING OF HOLLYWOOD

The New Decade

The curtain went up again with the new decade. With the American Communist party routed and HUAC fading with it, Hollywood slowly climbed down from the barricades. Visible cracks opened in the blacklist. Early in 1960, Otto Preminger publicly hired Dalton Trumbo to write the screenplay for *Exodus*; Kirk Douglas gave Trumbo credit for his clandestine work on the script of the gladiator epic *Spartacus*. Angry mobs did not storm the studios, and their absence stirred a tentative sense of clouds slowly lifting. The charges of un-Americanism had frightened Hollywood into offering mostly bland, conformist fare through the 1950s. Now, as the decade turned, it was *The Apartment,* Billy Wilder's grim, piercing comedy about the dehumanizing climb up the corporate ladder that captured the Oscar as the best picture of 1960. That was the kind of film that inspired the graduates from the inventive early years of live television who poured into Hollywood at the decade's end, a steady flow of young directors and producers hauling grand artistic ambitions behind them like steamer trunks. The film industry remained careful, cautious, and controlled by older men, but pockets of resistance against its culture of artistic comformity now bubbled, unsettled and restive.

With the selection of John F. Kennedy as the Democratic presidential nominee in 1960, the same stirrings crackled through the political system. With his youth, his energy, his ironic detachment (in "Superman Comes to the Supermarket," his celebrated Esquire article published during the 1960 campaign, Norman Mailer likened Kennedy to Marlon Brando with his "remote and private air"), Kennedy personified the yearning to pick up the pace, to press against old ways. Nowhere did that message carry more force than with the artists hoping to shake Hollywood from its torpor. Sydney Pollack, among the most talented of the young directors trying to establish themselves in film, remembers the electric effect of Kennedy's inaugural. "I was watching his inaugural speech in a bungalow exactly like this," he said, sitting in his casual office on the Universal Studios lot, "and it was jam-packed with people on the lot who stopped shooting and were watching this guy with no overcoat on in the cold taking the mantle. And you know that had a big effect on the industry. He was kind of emblematic of this changing of the old guard. It was very much a metaphor for what was happening in Hollywood, with the replacement of the older, more paternal Eisenhower, and this younger, bolder, more liberal kind of guy coming in. That was what was happening in the film marketplace too."

Probably no president but Franklin Roosevelt moved Hollywood as powerfully as Kennedy. As in most aspects of his presidency, Kennedy's impact owed less to his actions, or even his words, than to the hopes and aspirations he unconsciously liberated in his admirers. The connections that Pollack and his contemporaries drew almost certainly never occurred to Kennedy; though Kennedy carefully managed his political image, he showed little interest in his impact as a cultural symbol, in Hollywood or anywhere else. During the campaign, when an aide brought him Mailer's now-legendary article, which forecast that Kennedy would inspire a cultural rebellion against the Eisenhower era's self-satisfied conformity, the candidate dutifully paged through the story, saw nothing likely to bring him many votes, and then said only, "He sure does go on, doesn't he?"

Like his father before him, Kennedy saw Hollywood primarily as a diversion, a retreat from more serious concerns. He didn't care much for "arty" movies; nor did he place much importance on recruiting celebrities as political supporters. "The idea of making a big thing out of a [Arnold] Schwarzenegger type endorsement would have horrified him," said Richard N. Goodwin, who served Kennedy as a top speechwriter in the campaign and the White House. In the film world, the group closest to Kennedy was Frank Sinatra's rowdy "Rat Pack," a lubricious band of comics and singers whose cultural pretensions extended no further than the lounge at the Sands Hotel. The aspect of Hollywood life Kennedy seemed to admire most was Sinatra's ability to produce an apparently numberless supply of beautiful and pliant women. Kennedy seemed to view Hollywood first as a cross between a fraternity and a brothel.

But the attractions of Kennedy the symbol ultimately overwhelmed the limitations of the man. Kennedy fit Hollywood's image of what a president should be. For most of Hollywood, he was a figure of inspiring grace and style, and the enthusiasm he generated spilled over beyond Sinatra and his retainers, beyond Kennedy's own campaign, and finally beyond his lifetime. After the purge and the blacklist, after the gray administrations of Truman and Eisenhower, Kennedy imbued politics with a shimmer and glamour it had lacked for Hollywood since Franklin D. Roosevelt. Though Kennedy's political use of Hollywood was actually quite modest, his friendship with Frank Sinatra, his relationship with Marilyn Monroe, his easy social interaction with the film community's most glittering stars, sent a different message. More than any president before or since, Kennedy testified to the irresistible attraction between power and glamour. Inadvertently perhaps, he thus restored the frayed idea that stars had a legitimate place in the political world.

Kennedy provided a cause that rallied stars just as they were presented with new opportunities to try to convert their fame into influence. At work was more than the end of the blacklist mentality. With the decline of the studios, actors and actresses were freed from the long-term contracts that subtly—and sometimes overtly—discouraged controversial political associations. The concurrent rise to dominance in political life of television, with its insatiable appetite for famous faces, offered a larger platform than ever for those famous faces willing to embrace a candidate or wave a placard. These trends "combined to make people in Hollywood feel they had a forum and some respectability, that they weren't just a piece of fluff," said liberal activist Judith Balaban Quine, the daughter of Paramount president Barney Balaban.

The full force of these changes would not be felt until long after Kennedy's death. But on that frigid day when Kennedy took the oath of office, Quine and Pollack and dozens like them across Hollywood had no doubt that something new had begun. "It was," said Quine, "like we were all shot out of a cannon."

If so, it was a cannon with a very long fuse. Political change, no less than artistic change, came only gradually to Hollywood after the chilling blacklist years. The first political movement to test the new boundaries was the National Committee for a Sane Nuclear Policy, a liberal arms control group that organized a Hollywood chapter in the fall of 1959. After the group's second meeting, which attracted 150 leading directors, actors, and writers, actor Robert Ryan declared: "People in Hollywood are finally ready to speak out for something besides mother love."

At the start, SANE thrived. Under the direction of Ryan, Steve Allen, the erudite talk-show host and comedian, and United Artists vice-president Max E. Youngstein, the group attracted both young stars at the top of the profession and older activists (Norman Corwin, Philip Dunne, Johnny Green) who had been silenced since the collapse of the Popular Front groups a decade earlier. Like George Pepper and Hannah Dorner before them, SANE's organizers bustled with plans to move public opinion with radio shows, concerts, and speaking tours.

If the energy was appreciable, so was the fear lurking just behind it. Even after cracks opened in the blacklist, the old charges of subversion still lingered, fainter perhaps than a decade earlier, but still ominous. For the studio chiefs, it was apparently one thing to allow some blacklisted writers to do publicly what many had been doing privately for the past decade; it was quite another to once again see leading actors identified with groups criticizing the American government. Max Youngstein could track SANE's fortunes by the number of people who refused to lend their name to the letterhead, or who would quietly send in contributions that consisted only of "a cash money order with no signature on the back." Members who had suffered through the purges of the Popular Front groups recoiled as SANE stridently criticized such U.S. policies as the U-2 overflights of the Soviet Union. Eventually, the national parent organization, under attack in Congress, splintered in a wrenching debate over whether to bar Communists from membership; Allen and Ryan sided with those who believed the organization could not afford Communist members. Ryan's assessment of Hollywood's reawakening turned out to be premature; SANE could not withstand these complex pressures. Divided by these disputes and unable to raise sufficient funds, the Hollywood SANE disbanded barely two years after it was born—a testament to the growing urge to activism in Hollywood and to the barriers that still restrained it.

Ultimately, John Kennedy provided the spark that melted the last restraints. That seemed unlikely at first. Kennedy began visiting Hollywood regularly after his sister Pat married actor Peter Lawford in 1954. In 1956 Kennedy met the elder statesmen of studio liberalism when he worked with Dore Schary and Norman Corwin as the narrator for their convention film. Over the next few years, Kennedy turned up in Los Angeles fairly regularly, building up contacts and enjoying himself, as his father, Joseph Kennedy, had before him when he romanced Gloria Swanson in the 1920s. John Kennedy's fondness for Hollywood women dated back to the 1930s, when he visited Los Angeles while spending the summer as a ranchhand in Arizona and had luck with a movie extra he described to a friend as "the best looking thing I have ever seen." On subsequent trips, he romanced starlets Angela Greene, Gene Tierney, and others whose names, so far at least, have been lost to history. His marriage to the former Jacqueline Bouvier did nothing to dim his appreciation for Hollywood's pleasures. "Kennedy was a Hollywood figure before he became president," said producer Milton Sperling. "He used to come out here as a senator to meet girls; he was out here looking for ladies and [agent] Charlie Feldman was finding them for him. There was no big secret."

Many who encountered the young senator on his initial visits found him magnetic and charming. No one fell harder than Frank Sinatra, who met Kennedy through Lawford as early as 1955. Sinatra, at the peak of his popularity as both a singer and an actor, quickly signed on behind Kennedy's presidential aspirations. "Sinatra was a really early Kennedy supporter—very early," said Rosalind Wyman, a Los Angeles city councilwoman at the time and another early recruit. Sinatra turned up regularly at the strategy sessions Kennedy and his men convened for political leaders at Lawford's oceanfront house as the 1960 campaign approached.

But beyond Sinatra, Lawford, and their circle of colleagues and cronies, Kennedy the candidate ignited no brushfires in the film community. "He was just a senator and it didn't amount to a whole lot," said former Florida Senator George A. Smathers, one of Kennedy's closest friends in the Senate. "Nobody [out there] paid too much attention; nobody made too much of it." For much of Hollywood, Kennedy began his presidential bid with two strikes against him. The biggest was his father: the elder Kennedy had a long history in Hollywood, not much of it helpful for his son. After earning his bankroll on Wall Street during the boom years of the Jazz Age, Joseph Kennedy became one of the first Eastern businessmen to understand the movie industry's enormous potential for profit. His subsequent tour through Hollywood left Kennedy remembered for three things: his legendary affair with Swanson, the era's reigning sex star; his acquisitions of both the Film Booking Offices, a production and distribution company, and the Keith-Albee-Orpheum theater chain and their subsequent consolidation into RCA to create the giant Radio-Keith-Orpheum (RKO) holding company; and his anti-Semitism. If the first memory generated amusement and the second wary respect, the third produced only a deep disgust.

Everyone in Hollywood seemed to know at least one story about Joe Kennedy's anti-Semitism. Hollywood legend had enshrined the stormy 1940 meeting where he warned studio executives that they would incite anger against the Jews if they continued producing films hostile to the Nazis. Edwin L. Weisl, the late New York attorney who served on the board of directors at Paramount for decades, had his own favorite example. Apparently, during the Depression Paramount hired Joe Kennedy to propose ways to reverse its sagging fortunes. Kennedy spent several weeks examining the company, and then reported to the board that he had conferred on their problems with President Roosevelt. Roosevelt, Kennedy told the board, explained that he was concerned about the rise of anti-Semitism abroad and at home and convinced that some of the domestic hostility grew from the perception that Jews controlled the movie industry. To reduce the pressure, the financier reported, Roosevelt felt Paramount should sell the company—to Kennedy.

The board was incredulous. Weisl was dubious and, being well-connected politically, decided to check the story with his friend Harry Hopkins. He called Hopkins in the White House, and after posing his question, he could hear Hopkins put down the phone, and then his voice booming across the office—"Hey, chief"—and then Roosevelt's response: "What, Harry?"

"What's this about Joe Kennedy and Paramount?" Hopkins called out.

"What's Paramount?" the president replied.

Hopkins put the phone back to his lips. "There's your answer," he told Weisl.

Soon thereafter, the board sent Weisl to Boston to dismiss Kennedy. As Weisl related the story to his son, attorney Edwin L. Weisl, Jr., Kennedy "in his warm-hearted Irish way" later told a mutual friend, "I'll get that dirty Jew son of a bitch if it's the last thing I do." Those bitter remarks echoed down the decades. Though his son's campaign kept the senior Kennedy under wraps through the election, his absence did not erase the memories. Doris Meyer remembers her father, Universal Studios president Nathan Blumberg, dismissing the young candidate curtly: "I wouldn't vote for him for anything because he is probably a bigot like his father."

Another hurdle slowed the younger Kennedy's progress in Hollywood as the 1960 primaries unfolded: doubts about his liberalism. "At first [the Hollywood liberals] were a little suspicious of him," said California State Supreme Court Justice Stanley Mosk, the state attorney general at the time. "He was a product of wealth, he didn't have a distinguished career in the Senate, and he wasn't known as a liberal." Instead, it was Adlai Stevenson who still stirred the venerable Hollywood liberals. With deposed MGM head Dore Schary in the lead, Hollywood remained among the last strongholds of the quixotic effort to sway the convention to Stevenson at the final hour.

Liberal celebrities did swallow their doubts and move toward Kennedy once he won the nomination—partly out of a lingering distaste for Nixon after his bitter 1950 Senate victory over Helen Gahagan Douglas and his role in the Communist purge. But Hollywood's role remained marginal in Kennedy's campaign. All the myths that have grown around Kennedy's ties to Hollywood obscure an important distinction: his most memorable encounters occurred once he had won the office, not while he was seeking it. There was some help: Henry Fonda and Harry Belafonte appeared in television commercials; Ella Fitzgerald, Gene Kelly, and Milton Berle recorded witty radio ads. The California campaign had a reliable stable of celebrities (and celebrity wives) that it dispatched to various events around the state. Late in the fall, popular star Jeff Chandler and starlet Angie Dickinson joined a delegation of celebrities and intellectuals (including author James A. Michener and historian Arthur M. Schlesinger, Jr.) that barnstormed the nation for the candidate. The New York theater aristocracy gathered for a Broadway rally in mid-October.

But Kennedy and the men around him put no importance on courting celebrities, or working to bring more of them into the campaign. "There was never any feeling at all that having film celebrities appeal for him had any particular merit to it," Goodwin said. Rarely did celebrities appear with Kennedy. (The notable exception was a garment district rally in New York City, where a great crowd saw Kennedy with Melvyn Douglas, Henry Fonda, Janet Leigh, and Tallulah Bankhead.) "They didn't travel with us," recalled Goodwin. "If they would have wanted to travel with him there would have been a desire to keep them away on the grounds that they detracted from the candidate. You had a feeling that people would resent the idea that you felt it necessary to travel around with movie stars. You didn't want to appear frivolous." Early in the year, Kennedy's advisers actually kept Peter Lawford out of Wisconsin after Hubert Humphrey, his chief rival in the primary there, accused Kennedy's "glamorous friends from Hollywood" of trying "to bedazzle the voters."

Kennedy devoted no more attention to wooing the Hollywood fundraisers. By all accounts, the Kennedy campaign raised relatively little money in Hollywood (though Joe Kennedy, for all the hostility he engendered, may have privately tapped old connections). In part because he had the family fortune behind him, Kennedy remained aloof from the fundraising chores. "I don't remember him ever making a phone call to ask for money," said Theodore C. Sorensen, one of his closest advisers. "He would speak at fundraisers. But he was not the type to crawl to anybody." Nor did Kennedy, the first instinctive television performer to seek the presidency, need much advice from Hollywood experts on how to seduce the camera. "If there's anything this President doesn't need," Lawford said a few months into the administration, "it's a TV coach."

Still, the Kennedy campaign, if not the candidate himself, did turn to the entertainment industry once for such coaching. The incident provided a memorable exception to Lawford's dictum. During the preparation for Kennedy's epic debates with Nixon, a mutual friend brought in producer Fred Coe and director Arthur Penn, two leading lights in television and Broadway production, to help the campaign devise technical strategy. Both campaigns were so nervous about these first televised debates that they established painstaking rules to govern the placement of cameras and even the kinds of shots of the candidates allowed on the air. Penn (who went on to success in Hollywood with such films as *Bonnie and Clyde*) and Coe advised the Kennedy team to press for as many close-up shots as possible, reasoning that Kennedy could withstand such scrutiny better than Nixon. The Kennedy men followed their advice, with spectacular results: the indelible image of Nixon, sweaty and shifty-eyed in the first debate, dogged him throughout the campaign and indeed his entire political career.

One Hollywood figure was an integral part of the campaign throughout. Though Frank Sinatra appeared only rarely with Kennedy during the race, his support for the young senator was so well known that he hovered over the campaign anyway. To all appearances, Kennedy and Sinatra genuinely enjoyed each other's company. If more discreet and controlled than the voluble Sinatra—who had a penchant for public brawls and drunken binges—Kennedy nonetheless admired the singer's smirking attitude toward life and shared his hostility to stuffy propriety. David F. Powers and Kenneth P. O'Donnell, two of Kennedy's most loyal aides, later wrote that the president enjoyed Sinatra simply because the singer fed his insatiable appetite for gossip. But George Smathers, the former senator who accompanied Kennedy on some of his most renowned revels, saw an even more direct explanation: "He liked Frank Sinatra because he was fun to be with." Sinatra unquestionably could make life fun for his friends. En route to a campaign appearance in Oregon early in 1960, Kennedy stopped off to visit Sinatra in Las Vegas, where he was filming *Ocean's Eleven* with Lawford, Dean Martin, and Sammy Davis, Jr., the core of his Rat Pack; on Sunday, February 7, 1960, Sinatra introduced Kennedy to an attractive young divorcee named Judith Campbell (now Judith Exner), who had had a brief affair with the singer months earlier. Kennedy began his own affair with her only a few weeks later.

Sinatra performed more public services for Kennedy too. With new lyrics provided by Rat Packer Sammy Cahn, Sinatra recorded a light-hearted version of his hit "High Hopes" ("Oops, there goes the opposition kerplop") that became the campaign's theme song. (During the crucial Wisconsin primary, the campaign shipped 25,000 copies of the record into the state.) On the convention's first night, Sinatra led a group of more than two dozen celebrities through the national anthem. During the general election, Sinatra made himself available whenever he could. He sang on a diving board for a group of Democratic women at Janet Leigh's house, at a Shrine Auditorium rally in Los Angeles, at a Washington fundraiser, and at a huge New Jersey rally, the one event in which the campaign gave the Rat Pack free rein. Sinatra brought fellow Pack members Peter Lawford, Tony Curtis, and Janet Leigh to his home state and produced pandemonium: over 25,000 screaming fans thronged the Sussex Avenue Armory in Newark to hear their favorite son—and, incidentally, Adlai Stevenson.

Though Sinatra spent much of the fall campaign in Hawaii filming *The Devil at 4 O'Clock,* he stayed in touch with Roz Wyman, the Los Angeles city councilwoman who was dispatching celebrities around the state. Whenever Wyman had trouble recruiting fresh bodies, she turned to Sinatra. "Sinatra was the one most able to pick up the phone and get us anybody," Wyman said. "Peter [Lawford] couldn't. Peter didn't have the clout. But Sinatra certainly had an incredible reach. I was always impressed with what Frank could do."

When Kennedy narrowly defeated Nixon that November, Sinatra exulted. In Hawaii, he was led around the *Devil* set on the back of a donkey by director Mervyn LeRoy, a staunch Republican who had bet Sinatra on the election's outcome. ("This will teach him how to vote in '64," Sinatra scrawled on a photo of the event he sent to friends.) No one around him doubted that Sinatra believed he had a real friend in the White House. During the convention, Sinatra had reportedly turned to Lawford and said, "We're on our way to the White House, buddy boy." Now the Oval Office was in sight.

"One of the Gang": The President and the Stars

More than a quarter-century after his death, the men and women in Hollywood who met John Kennedy, however briefly, talk about him with startling clarity and immediacy—as if the tragedy that followed seared him into memory. Their recollections are warm, expansive, detailed— and most revealing for what they omit. Hardly any reminisce about Kennedy's views on civil rights, the arms race, poverty, or the war in Southeast Asia, the business that consumed his days. Instead, they recall, with poignancy and pride, his charm at dinner parties, his witty, casual grace, how they felt at the center of the world when he entered a room. Though his liberalism and energy were appealing, it was not Kennedy's political agenda that made him an arresting figure in Hollywood during his lifetime; it was his social presence.

Hollywood was not a major part of Kennedy's life, certainly not of his presidency; but to his admirers there, it felt that way. Kennedy visited Los Angeles and Palm Springs only a handful of times while in office, but the people who knew him sometimes talk as though he spent every weekend commuting from the White House to the Lawfords' beach house. Through memory, his presence has enlarged. Kennedy's visits left such a vivid impression because he appeared entirely comfortable around celebrities in a way that Eisenhower, or Truman, or even Roosevelt had never been. Writer Leonard Gershe, whose close friendship with Judy Garland brought him into the Lawfords' social circle, thought Kennedy "very gracious with the stars." Janet Leigh recalls him as "very comfort- able among almost any surroundings." For the stars, many of whom considered politics dingy and dull, a civic duty perhaps but hardly a good time, the charismatic Kennedy was a revelation. "They felt he was the first president who had come along who could ever fit in the Hollywood ambience," said Youngstein, the United Artists executive. "They held him in awe. They felt for the first time, 'My god, we've got a show business president who understands us.' "

Kennedy liked movies (his taste ran to adventures), expressed curiosity about the business, and did his homework—he would amaze guests at a small dinner party by quizzing Billy Wilder about his latest film, or asking Janet Leigh about her latest role, or even turning to Joe Naar, a producer friendly with Lawford, and telling him, "I've got an idea for a series." (The president's pitch, unfortunately, has passed into the fog of history. "Apparently it never got to that," Naar said. "Or it was a lousy idea. I can't remember, to tell you the truth.") Kirk Douglas once ran into

Kennedy at a Washington dinner and listened, stunned, for twenty minutes while the nation's chief executive explained to him why the novel *Seven Days in May,* which Douglas was considering adapting to the screen, would make a good movie.

It wasn't only good staff work and feigned interest. Kennedy genuinely enjoyed the Hollywood scene, with all its glamour and artifice, its prickly edges of vanity and insecurity. "He liked the gamesmanship, the show of the thing," said Frederick G. Dutton, a skilled political aide to California Governor Pat Brown, who joined the Kennedy White House. "He had just that much cynicism, detachment: he liked to look at people with their pretense, a bit mockingly, a bit arrogantly. People who played roles—and God knows people in Hollywood and Southern California really play roles—he enjoyed much more than, say, the good gray burghers in Midwestern cities." The president seemed perfectly at ease gabbing about nothing with the world's most famous faces. Years later, Marlon Brando recalled being invited to the president's hotel suite after a Los Angeles fundraiser to find Kennedy in the midst of a large, jubilant, well-lubricated crowd. Before long, Kennedy was needling the actor about his expanding waistline, and Brando was needling him back, and the two men stormed off to find a scale that could settle the matter.

Who could imagine such a scene with Dwight Eisenhower or Richard Nixon or Lyndon Johnson? Above all, to his admirers in Hollywood Kennedy seemed contemporary, approachable, part of their time. "There was sort of an easy social connection between the Kennedys and show business, the Hollywood community, that I had never sensed before," said Steve Allen. "There was something about Jack Kennedy and later Bobby, something about their youthfulness, their idealism, actual or alleged or a mixture, their personal charm: they seemed somehow of our generation, whereas a Lyndon Johnson seemed like some person from a planet called Texas and older than us and not all that hip. They seemed kind of hip and easy to talk to. They just seemed like one of the gang."

Kennedy beguiled the stars even more because he wasn't overly impressed by them. Kennedy never seemed star-struck. Historian and White House aide Arthur M. Schlesinger, Jr., a movie buff occasionally wide-eyed himself at Hollywood gatherings, thought Kennedy stayed so cool because he "had movie stars around the house, so to speak, all his life." To be in a room with the most recognized men and women in the culture—figures of longing and desire for millions across the world—and to know they had all gathered to honor you, even for Kennedy that must have been exhilarating. But Kennedy had his own incandescent celebrity. During the campaign one *Boston Globe* correspondent, observing the candidate's effect on a crowd of women, reported, "It's like watching a crowd of Frank Sinatra fans." Kennedy could meet even the brightest Hollywood stars on their own ground. Who radiated more stardom than the youngest man ever elected president? It seemed entirely appropriate when Warner Bros. announced just two months after his inauguration that it would film *PT 109,* the best-selling account of Kennedy's naval adventures in World War II, and thus make him the first sitting president depicted in a feature film. And that Kennedy wanted himself portrayed by the era's latest sex symbol, Warren Beatty (who rejected the part that eventually went to Cliff Robertson).

No one in Hollywood could match that voltage, except perhaps Sinatra. At the time, no one in Hollywood generated quite as much excitement, attention, and controversy. With enormous talent and energy, Sinatra recorded a series of classic albums for Capitol Records, starred in enjoyable if not quite so memorable films, and took his stage show to Las Vegas and Miami Beach. His Rat Pack fascinated the press and swaggered through the film community, boisterous and arrogant. Sinatra's rages and fits of temper—the way he could savagely denigrate even his closest friends—were repulsive, but his powerful position in the industry could not be denied. In Hollywood he was treated as a force of nature: mercurial, inexplicable, unavoidable. "Frank was the king of the Rat Pack; everybody worshipped at his shrine," Joe Naar said.

Hollywood offered him no higher peaks. During the 1940s, Sinatra had reached the top of his profession as a singer; then, after his recording career tumbled, after his agents at MCA had unceremoniously cut him loose, he had climbed back to the top as an actor, too. When Kennedy emerged as a national figure, Sinatra saw a new mountain ahead. "They were the hottest thing in show business," Naar continued. "Frank was chairman of the board. Jack was president, chairman of the board. The most important guy in the Rat Pack wanted to get next to Jack Kennedy, so you figure it out."

In style and temperament, his affection for James Bond novels, his icy cool, his insouciance, Kennedy personified all that Sinatra envisioned his Rat Pack to be. The Rat Pack was never more than an informal group, exaggerated by press agents, with a membership that expanded and contracted depending on the story. But it was a real enough clique with roots in the group of friends that clustered around Humphrey Bogart and Lauren Bacall in the mid-1950s; by the end of the decade, with Bogart's death, the group included Sinatra, the Lawfords, Dean Martin, Sammy Davis, Jr., Shirley MacLaine, Janet Leigh and Tony Curtis, and at times Judy Garland, Joey Bishop, and Milton

Berle, among others. They gathered for elaborate Christmas parties at Sinatra's, stormed Las Vegas together, gambled and partied and made movies together. They burned brightly, brightly enough to fascinate others in Hollywood, to draw them with hints of freedom, recklessness, danger. Anthony Franciosa, then a young actor on the fringe of the group, remembers: "It always had an aura about it that was very exciting, very much 'wouldn't it be nice if we could all live this way.' Wow. The glitter. It was living on the high wave, really, just taking that high wave and going with it and saying wow, look at this, life was a ball, like they sang about. They were acting it out. . . . That world is very seductive to a young man, because it represents an enormous amount of gratification of the senses, a tremendous amount of it, especially in terms of sex, even though it may not be overtly done. Just the suggestion of it, constantly around you. Even the suggestion of danger: a little bit of dangerous, a little bit of the kids going wild on Saturday night. . . ."

The Rat Pack embodied Hollywood's most elemental myth, its deepest unspoken appeal—that as its final reward, fame offered a life without rules, without the constraints of fidelity, monogamy, sobriety, and the dreary obligation to show up at a job every morning. For Sinatra, for his cronies, life seemed a canvas with no borders. One night Sinatra flew a crowd of friends from Los Angeles to Las Vegas for a glittering black-tie dinner honoring Rosalind Russell's twenty-fifth wedding anniversary; when the champagne and toasts and songs were finished, he hustled them all back in the plane and flew them home. There was an electricity to it: to walk into the Sands Hotel with Sinatra, a phalanx of guards leading the way, heads turning, whispers rolling through the casino like waves, men in tuxedos rushing to greet you, was mesmerizing, almost otherwordly. Just the sheer scent of celebrity at Sinatra's parties was intoxicating. "They charged off each other," remembers Gershe. "The energy in the room was extraordinary."

To this excitement, the association with Kennedy added another synergistic charge. In the popular imagination, the friendship between Sinatra and Kennedy symbolized the union of politics and show business, as if the two men were ambassadors for distinct branches in the American aristocracy of fame. For more than thirty years, the two worlds had flirted with each other; now to the maximum in glamour was married the maximum in power. In the long history of Hollywood's relationship with politics, this was probably the pivotal moment. A bond that could not be broken was forged. It could not be broken because from that point forward the attraction rested not only on such practical considerations as endorsements and fundraising, but also on a legend embedded in the popular culture. The apparently easy and casual association between the glamorous president and the powerful star provided a tangible symbol for the attraction between Hollywood and Washington unequaled before or since. It suggested new rewards at the pinnacle of American life, adding forever to fame's appeal a proximity to power, and to power's allure a proximity to fame; it hinted at the existence of a society where anyone who was famous mingled with everyone else who was famous, where all lines converged. What politician, what star, wouldn't want to be accepted into that company? To be Frank Sinatra, to be on top of Hollywood, the biggest roller in Vegas—what could be better, Leonard Gershe remembers wondering, and then realizing: What could be better than being Frank Sinatra? Being Frank Sinatra walking along with the president.

And what could be better than wielding a president's power? What, if not escaping power's endless obligations, if only briefly, with glamour's limitless freedom? No one had to explain that attraction to John F. Kennedy: he had been reared on it, on the myth of Hollywood as a place where traditional moral restraints did not apply. It was in Hollywood where his father, without sacrificing his home and family in the real world, had courted and won Gloria Swanson, the most desirable woman of her day; it was Hollywood where Joseph Kennedy had gone, as one biographer wrote, in his quest "to have it all, to live beyond the rules in a world of his own making." The myth that dazzled the father—the boundless freedom of fame—transfixed the son; it drew him to Frank Sinatra and his Rat Pack, who seemed to live it more fully than anyone in their time. To a remarkable degree for a politician in the public eye, Kennedy shared the Rat Pack life of parties and beautiful women. During his lifetime, rumors linked him romantically with stars ranging from Angie Dickinson to Marilyn Monroe, to less memorable faces and bodies—stewardesses, secretaries, coat-check girls—that merely passed the time. In the years since his death a small army of authors have made careers exposing (or claiming to) dozens of liaisons—extended, brief, romantic, tawdry. Today, all manner of marginal figures in Hollywood claim to have known the details of Kennedy's amours almost as soon as he hit the pillow.

While he lived, Kennedy's philandering was not nearly as visible as those claims imply; he was not a man to offer his envious friends details of his latest conquest. But neither were Kennedy's habits invisible. Once, Franciosa was shocked to hear a Los Angeles restaurant owner he knew openly sharing an unexpurgated account of a Kennedy party he catered; another local political power told friends of accidentally catching Kennedy in the act with a popular actress. To Naar, Marilyn Monroe's presence at virtually any private event in Los Angeles with the president gave weight to the rumors about her relationship with him: why else would someone so apolitical be there?* Just before the 1960 convention, an anonymous source offered Lyndon B. Johnson's presidential campaign an audiotape allegedly recording an orgy involving Kennedy and some of his Hollywood friends. It was a different time: Johnson's men turned down the tape. Subtle hints—more like code for insiders than tips to the public—even reached the edge of the press. Gossip mogul Walter Winchell laced one of his columns with a potentially incendiary aside: "Judy Campbell of Palm Springs and Bevhills is Topic Number One in Romantic Political Circles."

The rumors did not harm Kennedy in Hollywood. If anything, they reinforced his image among the stars as a regular guy—as someone who shared their sense that the Puritan mores were loosening. When a tipsy Marilyn Monroe appeared in a diaphanous gown—a dress so tight she was literally sewn into it, so skimpy that she described it as "skin and beads"—to sing a sultry and suggestive "Happy Birthday" to the president before a stunned assemblage at a May 1962 Democratic fundraiser in Madison Square Garden, anyone in Hollywood could appreciate the sheer audacity. Kennedy's cool dalliance with Hollywood's most desirable women seemed to confirm the feeling there—more hope, perhaps, than belief—that if you stripped away the tuxedo and the retinue and the boring speeches about taxes and imports and the Cold War, Kennedy was one of them.

Sinatra, in particular, appeared to thrive on that conceit. For all his wealth and notoriety, the proximity to power thrilled him; he wore the relationship with Kennedy, said one friend, "as a man would wear a boutonniere." Sinatra sent JFK his albums, fixed up a guest house for him at his Palm Springs home in anticipation of presidential visits (he even added a heliport), and glowed with pleasure from the most casual interaction. It gave the singer great satisfaction to casually remark at dinner that

---

*To the widespread stories that Robert F. Kennedy had an affair with Marilyn Monroe after his brother broke off whatever relationship he had, Naar offers a dissenting view. The Bobby Kennedy who knew Marilyn Monroe in 1962 was not the charming, empathetic, charismatic leader remembered from his martyred 1968 presidential campaign; he was a hard, driven, pitiless martinet, almost frightening in his intensity. In all, not a particularly attractive package. "I think Bob had a thing for Marilyn, who hated him," Naar said. "Everybody hated him." Naar remembers RFK sitting next to Monroe at dinner one night at the Lawfords, as anxious as a teenager, doting on her, doing his best to be charming; and then, when Kennedy had momentarily looked the other way, Monroe glancing across the table and sticking her finger down her throat, as if she was going to vomit. "All those rumors that Bobbie fucked her is a joke," Naar insists. "She'd fuck you before she would touch him."

the president had called him that day, but "God, I was just too busy to talk." "There was that period when Frank loved to be able to pick up the phone and have a direct line right to the Oval Office," said Gershe—his exaggerated view of Sinatra's access making the real point, that Sinatra had successfuly portrayed himself to his circle as a man at the president's elbow.

Sinatra had long been a loyal Democrat. Now with his friend in the White House, he became an extraordinarily active one. Sinatra wasted no time putting his stamp on the New Frontier. Less than a month after Kennedy's victory, the Democratic National Committee announced that the singer would produce and host an inaugural-eve gala in the Washington National Guard Armory to reduce the party's $4 million debt. Sinatra worked indefatigably over the next six weeks to organize the show. He drafted big names from Las Vegas, Broadway, and Hollywood; so many celebrities flew out from Los Angeles that they had to charter a plane. "He wanted it to be perfect," said Janet Leigh. The only thing Sinatra could not anticipate was a blizzard that kept about half of the paying crowd home; Kennedy didn't make his way through the clogged streets until more than an hour after the scheduled 9 P.M. curtain time. It was nearly 2 A.M. before the show staggered to a close. Still, the event was a success where it counted most: even after expenses, Sinatra reduced the party's debt by $1 million.*

One week after the inaugural gala, Sinatra organized a concert at New York's Carnegie Hall with Dean Martin, Lawford, and Sammy Davis, Jr., to raise funds for Martin Luther King, Jr.; a few months later, he gathered the tribe again for a $100-a-plate California Democratic party fundraiser. "The easiest calls I ever made," said Judy Balaban Quine, who was organizing support in Hollywood for the civil rights movement, "were to Frank, Sammy, and Dean." Sinatra impressed local Democrats as hardworking, dependable, and generous. "When you did an event with Sinatra," said political consultant Joseph R. Cerrell, the state Democratic party executive director at the time, "let me tell you what that meant. I'm telling you he got the other performers, he got the orchestra, he paid the orchestra. He paid the limos. It was rare that you got bills. . . . Or I could call him up and say, 'Hey, we got Senator [Frank E.] Moss of Utah coming

---

*Which is not to say that some expenses didn't irritate the Democratic National Committee. "There were some unhappy experiences with that part of Hollywood at the inaugural," said Samuel C. Brightman, the Democrats' deputy chairman for public affairs at the time. "Matt McCloskey was party treasurer then, and he thought he was getting a great bargain because these guys were working for scale [or free]. But they had a suite open twenty-four hours a day at the Statler, now the Washington Hilton, pouring Chivas for everybody who came. They ran up quite a bill."

in, we want to tour the state for Assembly candidates, legislative candidates. Can I have your plane?' And I'd go out to Burbank, early in the morning, and we'd start a tour: San Bernardino, Palm Springs, East Kern County. Part of the story [when we landed] was Frank Sinatra's jet is coming to Modesto, Fresno. I mean, we didn't pay the gas, much less the food, much less the crew. . . ."

In return, Sinatra asked for nothing, at least none of the favors supporters usually demand. But he craved the impalpable rewards of the president's friendship. Sinatra treated the relationship with uncharacteristic gravity: framing Kennedy's casual notes, even putting a plaque on the door of the room in his home where the candidate had slept. For Sinatra, Kennedy seemed to represent more than just power; despite his own rakish behavior, JFK conveyed a weight and solidity suggestive of Harvard, summers on the Cape, lazy days surrounded and protected by a vivacious family. All that the bright, garish Rat Pack lifestyle—a blue-collar fantasy of what it meant to be rich—eminently lacked. Sinatra understood that and one part of him ached to surmount it; even in Hollywood, he courted the friendship of Bill and Edith Mayer Goetz, whose exclusive dinners marked what stood for high society in the film world. Like his acceptance at the Goetz table, Kennedy's favor gave Sinatra respectability—a reason to be admired, not just feared, by his peers.

How much that mattered to him was apparent literally from the administration's opening hours. On the night of Kennedy's inauguration, Sinatra hosted a private dinner at the Statler Hilton in Washington for the performers in the previous evening's gala. He promised that Kennedy would stop by to deliver his personal thanks. As the evening wore on and Kennedy made his way through the round of inaugural balls, Sinatra sat anxiously in the glittering company "very much on edge, waiting, watching, wondering when [Kennedy] was going to get here—because he had given his word that he would make this dinner, his private dinner," said Gloria Cahn Franks, who was there with her then-husband Sammy Cahn. Dinner began, and proceeded, and eventually people began to check their watches discreetly and murmur: Would the president show? Finally there was a rustle of activity at the door. Peter Lawford bolted from his seat; Sinatra moved to the doorway, Secret Service agents glided into the room, and then "in he came," Franks recalled, "with a roll of newspapers under his arm, and a cigar, a little brown cigar that he used to smoke." Kennedy graciously moved from table to table, greeting the stars, chatting, laughing, while Sinatra sat there "beaming, beaming . . . like the Cheshire cat."

Sinatra had been at center stage for most of his adult life. But in the glow of Kennedy's glory he basked in the world's brightest spotlight. If Sinatra sought no tangible rewards, no honorary appointments, what he needed from Kennedy was, in fact, more demanding, more intimate; he needed the most personal gift of all, the benediction of his presence. It was, as Sinatra would learn, if not the easiest reward for Kennedy to dispense, the easiest for him to withdraw.

For Kennedy, the association with Sinatra was always more casual, its effect equivocal. Despite his infectious charm, Kennedy was a reserved man with very few close friends. "There was a barrier in Kennedy nobody got past; maybe Bobby didn't even get past," said Goodwin. "I don't think it was contrived; that was the man's nature." Kennedy enjoyed Sinatra's company, but those around him never sensed that the brassy singer penetrated the deeper fortifications that turned away so many others; to Arthur Schlesinger, the two men were "celebrity friends" whose relationship generated more sparks in public than private.

Not all those sparks landed where Kennedy's men preferred. Sinatra attracted so much heat that his activities occasionally singed Kennedy. Early in 1960, Sinatra—who had bravely criticized the House Committee on Un-American Activities' investigation of Hollywood Communists in 1947—decided to hire blacklisted screenwriter Albert Maltz to adapt *The Execution of Private Slovik* for his film company. Sinatra hesitated about announcing the deal publicly, fearing it might hurt Kennedy in the Democratic primaries. But Maltz, anxious to punch another hole in the blacklist, urged him forward. Sinatra finally made the announcement in late March. His initial instincts were better. Within days, Sinatra retreated under a hail of criticism led by John Wayne, who publicly wondered "How does Sinatra's friend John F. Kennedy feel about it . . . ?" Sinatra took an ad in the trade papers dismissing such "partisan" attacks, but faced with a mounting furor, he backed off a few days later—some believed at the private insistence of Joseph Kennedy—and dropped Maltz.

If Sinatra could cause Kennedy problems when behaving honorably, he seemed to present limitless possibility for embarrassment in his dark periods. Some observers considered any association with Sinatra and his followers inappropriate for a president. During the campaign, actor Dick Powell, a leading Republican, declared, "If I were working for Kennedy I would try to stay away from the element that is supporting him. I'm good friends with most of them but I think these people hurt Kennedy by their cheap publicity." During the transition, one *New York World Telegram and Sun* columnist breathlessly disclosed, "The spine-tingling worry persists in high places . . . that this unpredictable group of Holly-wood characters may be presumptuous enough to assume they can have the run of the White House for the next four years."

People who didn't like Sinatra—of which there were many—let the White House know. In the weeks after Kennedy's victory, according to the *Wall Street Journal*, "letters deluge[d] Kennedy headquarters urging that Frank Sinatra not get a high federal job." It troubled some Demo-cratic political operatives to see the president portrayed in gossip col-umns, fan magazines, and even a book commemorating the Rat Pack, as part of Sinatra's circle. "There was some concern," said the DNC's Brightman. "It wasn't a big deal. But everybody was a lot more comfort-able when you didn't have them around, when they weren't in the col-umns, when their press agents weren't feeding the columnists about how close they were to the president, and how they did this or that [with him]."

But these political calculations never seriously concerned Kennedy's inner circle. After the inaugural, Sinatra rarely received invitations to the White House—apparently because Jackie Kennedy disliked him—but he visited Kennedy at the family compound in Hyannis Port in September, and two months later sat at the head table when the president appeared at a Los Angeles fundraiser. The president's men faced more important problems than whether Sinatra had really renamed the Rat Pack the Jack Pack to honor his friend in the Oval Office.

That indifference evaporated as evidence accumulated tying Sinatra to leading figures in organized crime. As attorney general, Robert Kennedy put unprecedented priority on prosecuting the mob; one historian later wrote: "Ever since prohibition . . . Attorneys General have been 'declar-ing war' on organized crime, but Robert Kennedy was the first to fight one." In that offensive, the FBI intensified electronic surveillance of suspected mobsters. Among other things, the net brought back new insights about the president's best friend in Hollywood.

Sinatra had maintained public friendships with reputed gangsters since the 1940s. During the 1960 campaign the venerable conservative commentator Westbrook Pegler pointedly questioned why a presidential candidate would associate with a man identified "with the Bugsy Siegel mob in Hollywood" and who "took part in the orgy in the Nacional Hotel in Havana at which Lucky Luciano was the guest of honor [in 1947]."

It was a reasonable inquiry—one that Bobby Kennedy, who knew that world through his work investigating labor racketeering for a Senate committee in the 1950s, should have asked himself—but the president and his men apparently shrugged it off. The FBI wiretaps provided new revelations that could not be ignored. The key information came through the investigation of Momo Salvatore (Sam) Giancana. No gangster more obsessed the Justice Department than Giancana, the reputed chief of the Chicago mob. Giancana was a short, balding killer, with an arrest record that dated back to 1926 and a taste for the high life. He carried on an affair with Phyllis McGuire, the middle sister in the singing group, and counted as one of his friends Frank Sinatra. Among the services Sinatra provided Giancana was an introduction in March 1960 to Judith Campbell Exner, the woman he had set up with President Kennedy the previous month.

Giancana apparently expected heavier lifting from the singer. Through late 1961, wiretaps on Giancana's conversations revealed that the mobster wanted Sinatra to intervene on his behalf with the Justice Department. Even more disturbing was evidence suggesting Sinatra had tried to comply. In December 1961, FBI wiretaps intercepted one of Giancana's lieutenants reporting to the mobster on Sinatra's efforts: "I had a chance to quiz [Sinatra]," the mobster told Giancana. "He says, 'Johnny, I took Sam's name and wrote it down and told Bobby Kennedy, 'this is my buddy. This is my buddy, this is what I want you to know, Bob.' " Sinatra's testimonial brought no relief from the relentless surveillance; within weeks Giancana was complaining that Sinatra "can't get change of a quarter" from the Kennedys.*

From the administration's perspective, the key fact was not that Sinatra's mission failed but that mobsters could apparently compel him to act. Though the FBI generally hoarded its electronic surveillance, that portrait of Sinatra percolated through the top level of the Justice Department and the White House. William G. Hundley, chief of the Justice Department's organized crime and racketeering section, became "well aware of the fact that they were picking up some stuff on Sinatra, and that they considered Sinatra very bad news . . . and to be a tool of these people." In the White House, too, select officials learned that the Giancana wiretaps specifically implicated the singer.

---

*Sinatra's relationship with the Kennedys wasn't Giancana's hole card. While pursued by the Justice Department and shadowed by the FBI, Giancana was simultaneously working with the CIA in their efforts to assassinate Cuban premier Fidel Castro. Giancana—who also claimed to have both directed mob money into Kennedy's cause during the crucial West Virginia primary and helped to engineer vote-stealing in Cook County that gave Kennedy Illinois and his general election victory—expected all these bewildering connections to shelter him. But the investigations continued anyway. Giancana finally faced a federal grand jury in 1965; when he refused to testify, he was cited for contempt and jailed for a year, until the grand jury's term ran out. Justice Department attorneys hoped to subpoena him again, but top officials overruled them, after intervention by the CIA. Giancana was murdered in his home in July 1975, just as aides from a congressional committee investigating the CIA assassination plots arrived in Chicago to arrange for his testimony.

This should not have been a revelation. In Hollywood few people may have fully appreciated the depths of Sinatra's ties to Giancana (though Lawford and others met Giancana in Sinatra's presence), but his long-standing friendships with reputed mobsters were no secret. That did Sinatra no harm: many people in Hollywood befriended mobsters. Mobsters had been integrated into Hollywood financially, socially, and as "fixers" on labor negotiations since the 1930s; the movie men seemed to confuse real-life killers, extortionists, and pimps with the rakish, misunderstood rebels they created on the screen. Bugsy Siegel, another mobster with a taste for bright lights, socialized in Hollywood in the 1940s. Giancana's California confederate John Roselli, who had been convicted in a Hollywood union bribery scandal during the 1940s and labeled by the FBI as "the Capone mob's representative on the West Coast," had worked as a movie extra in his teens. One FBI report said he had worked for Harry Cohn as a bodyguard. By the 1960s, Roselli had become a senior figure in the mob's Los Angeles and Las Vegas operations, and mixed "with the top level of Hollywood society." So did Los Angeles attorney Sidney R. Korshak, who many law enforcement officers considered "the most important link between organized crime and legitimate business."

In a community where such men could put up their feet and loosen their ties, Sinatra's friendship with Giancana raised few eyebrows. In Washington, the attitude was necessarily less nonchalant. Robert Kennedy, always attuned to political danger, sensed that his brother's relationship with Sinatra could be exploited—not only by enemies outside the government but by J. Edgar Hoover, then resisting the attorney general's efforts to bring the FBI under tighter control. In their paper war of memo and directive, the attorney general's weakest flank was his high-living brother in the Oval Office. Hoover watched the president as closely as did the Secret Service, accumulating scraps on JFK's affairs as if they were ordnance. "It reached a point," said Hundley, "where Hoover would send over memos, lots of memos [to Robert Kennedy]. . . . It would be, 'Dear Mr. General, I thought you'd be interested in knowing the President was seen with some bimbo.' . . . If I ran up to the [Attorney General's office on the] fifth floor every time I got a letter from Hoover saying that the President was seeing some young lady, I'd be dead." Against this backdrop of dangerous liaisons, Robert Kennedy came to see the president's friendship with Sinatra as an unacceptable risk.

The attorney general was not the only Kennedy to reach that conclusion. The president had sloughed off the critics who thought it unseemly for him to dignify Sinatra and the Rat Pack with his presence. But the more troubling questions raised by the Giancana taps forced him to reassess the relationship. Though Sinatra would forever blame Robert Kennedy for severing him from JFK, John Kennedy fully shared his conviction, according to White House counsel Myer Feldman. For the president, Feldman insisted, the issue was not that Sinatra might embarrass him politically, but rather that the mob might, in fact, somehow use the singer to impede the government investigation. "It was a question of whether or not it might damage the nation," Feldman said. "The personal damage to him never concerned him so much. But when it became a possible threat to the government [he acted]. The threat was that here the attorney general is prosecuting the mob, and maybe—there was no finding to this effect—maybe there was somebody who was connected to the mob coming to the White House. That we thought we ought to protect against."

That explanation sounds suspiciously selfless, but whatever the motivation, the result was clear. Kennedy dissolved his celebrated friendship with Sinatra. The split came in two stages. First a chill set in, particularly after Sinatra's visit to the family vacation compound in September 1961 drew more press criticism (though the barbs were aimed at Sinatra's swinging image, not his alleged Mafia connections). That fall, Sinatra sent Kennedy several gifts; the return letters were brief and formal, no more expansive than "I am delighted by your very thoughtful gesture." By 1962, the Justice Department had launched a formal investigation of Sinatra's ties to organized crime.

The last act began in the fall of 1961, when FBI wiretaps of Roselli discovered six calls to Judith Campbell Exner, the woman Sinatra had introduced to both Kennedy and Giancana. Even after Kennedy's election, Exner continued to see him regularly, sometimes in the White House; along the way, she had also begun sleeping with Giancana, who was fully aware of her affair with Kennedy. That exposed Kennedy to the extraordinary danger of blackmail.* The tangled skein unraveled as the FBI, following routine practice, checked Exner's phone records after uncovering her contact with Roselli; the agents discovered calls from Exner's phone to the White House.

Even Bobby Kennedy's worst nightmares couldn't match this reality: the president was sharing a mistress with the mobster at the top of the government's hit list, and Hoover had the details in his files. Hoover duly

---

*If one believes Exner's claim that Kennedy also knew of her relationship with Giancana—that, in fact, she arranged meetings between the two men—that multiplied the risk exponentially.

informed the attorney general and the White House of his findings by memo on February 27, 1962. Less than a month later, at 1:10 P.M. on March 22, he met privately at the White House with the president over lunch. No record of their conversation survives. But according to White House files, the last phone contact with Exner occurred a few hours later. The next morning the president flew to California to deliver a speech in Berkeley and then spend the weekend relaxing in Palm Springs; he stayed not with Sinatra but with Bing Crosby, a staunch Republican.

Because the president visited Crosby only one day after his visit from Hoover, most accounts have attributed the break with Sinatra to that meeting. That seems unlikely. In all probability, the decision had been made earlier on the basis of the information from the wiretaps. The discovery of Exner's relationship with Giancana, Feldman maintains, "was another brick in the edifice that would divide him from Sinatra," but not the single decisive factor. "It was a gradual accumulation of information through 1961," he said. Sorensen recalled the same gradual cooling. Circumstantial evidence supports their claims. The decision to stay with Crosby almost certainly must have been made, for logistical reasons alone, before Hoover came to the White House. In fact, as early as January—even before the memo in which Hoover first alerted the White House and the attorney general to his findings about Exner—Kenneth O'Donnell informed a friend of California Governor Pat Brown who wanted to host the president that the housing arrangements had been completed. It was not a single mistake that cost Sinatra Kennedy's friendship, but the associations amassed over a lifetime.

At the time, and even years later, O'Donnell claimed that Kennedy stayed at Crosby's home because its location provided better security than Sinatra's. But that flimsy cover fooled few. The decision's real intent was apparent in both the Justice Department and the White House. "There wasn't much question it just wasn't right for the President to stay with Sinatra by that time," said Ed Guthman, Robert Kennedy's press secretary at the Justice Department. Sinatra understood the decision's intent too. He felt humiliated at the moment he had expected the White House to certify his special status. While Kennedy relaxed at Crosby's, Sinatra stewed in disappointment and rage.

Some prominent California Democrats shared his anger. The decision to stay with Crosby—not only a prominent Republican but a professional rival to Sinatra—struck some as a needless insult to a loyal party worker. "Sinatra had been very good to us and we didn't want to lose [him]," said Rosalind Wyman, who had worked closely with him in 1960. "Sinatra was a great Democrat. Sinatra's instincts were Democratic. He loved Harry

Truman. He loved Roosevelt. Sinatra had performed for us before Kennedy, and we in the party were very grateful. . . . We felt very strongly, and I did quite a few things to make our views known to those people in the White House and to Peter and to Pat [Lawford]. I certainly made Peter know. I certainly let the White House know. Here was a man who had during the campaign done everything we asked him for and more."

The protests achieved nothing. By all accounts, Kennedy did not agonize over the decision to banish Sinatra. "It meant nothing [to him]," said Goodwin. "If Kennedy thought about it in any way, if he thought it would even in the slightest wound his presidency, of course he would cut it off; he would cut off people a lot closer than Sinatra if he had to." Later, Kennedy had a momentary change of heart and thought of inviting Sinatra to a White House function, but the invitation was withdrawn at the last moment.

Ultimately, Kennedy's decision to separate himself from an acquaintance who mingled with mobsters is less surprising than Sinatra's belief that he could balance a relationship with the don and the president. Even many of Sinatra's friends—those whose access to Kennedy depended on his—understood the president's need for caution. Sinatra was not naive; nor was he obtuse. Listening to Giancana's boasts, Sinatra may have believed that the "boys" helped Kennedy during the campaign and that it was hypocritical for the president to turn on them in office. But, valid or not, that point was irrelevant to the decision Sinatra faced: from Bobby Kennedy's actions it was clear that, despite what had happened in the campaign, the administration was committed to full-scale war, and Sinatra could not avoid choosing sides. Perhaps Sinatra never had the option of moving away from Giancana, a man accustomed to ending his friendships emphatically: the FBI wiretaps picked up Giancana and his confederates idly discussing whether to "hit" the singer or his Rat Pack friends for failing to slow down the Justice Department.

But Sinatra showed no sign of trying to break from the mobster. That fall, he performed without charge at a nightclub Giancana opened outside Chicago, and brought along Martin and Davis. Nor, in the weeks after Kennedy's visit to Palm Springs, did Sinatra give any indication of recognizing the president's dilemma; lashing out at the nearest Kennedys available, he furiously cut off all relations with Peter and Pat Lawford. "The man was angry," said one Sinatra friend, "really, really angry." Nursing the hope that others had conspired against him, Sinatra sent the president a floral rocking chair that spring, and received another polite note in response. But he could not mend the rift. By standing next to

Kennedy, Sinatra may have hoped to surmount his past; but he was only stamped with it, more indelibly than ever.

In the end, Sinatra simply misread his man. He knew Kennedy the bon vivant, Kennedy the libertine; that John Kennedy might have winked at an illicit friendship with a mobster. But Sinatra's shock at his exile suggests he didn't understand John Kennedy the politician, who could move coldly and ruthlessly to protect his vital interests. Whatever Sinatra hoped or believed, those never included his revels with the singer. John F. Kennedy was not, finally, one of the gang. In his friendship with the president, Sinatra brought Hollywood to a new intimacy with politics. But the alliance's unhappy end showed only how great a gulf separated the two worlds.

After Kennedy: King, Johnson, and the Reawakening

Though it unnerved the Rat Pack and fueled Hollywood gossip for months, the president's break with Sinatra didn't slow the film community's growing political activity. In part, that was because the Sinatra circle that cared most about the schism had no long-term political interest or commitment; their relationship with Kennedy was social. Among the inner social circle, only Sinatra, and to some extent Sammy Davis, Jr., continued as activists beyond Kennedy's lifetime, and both in erratic courses that eventually led them to the Republicans. For the others, politics ceased to be relevant as soon as Kennedy died. When the sparkling parties dried up, Washington lost its luster. "We had no relationship, any of us, with [Lyndon] Johnson," said Gershe. "It was Camelot; then it turned into San Antonio."

Kennedy had more lasting effect in other quarters. His real impact in Hollywood was to put politics back in the air—to make national events at least as worthy a subject for conversation as Hedda Hopper's latest tidbit. From attention grew interest, and gradually the excitement and energy Kennedy inspired, even in people who never met him, made it easier for other causes to recruit celebrities.

The civil rights movement convulsing the South became the first beneficiary of the new energy. The movement was already accustomed to looking to black singers and actors for help. Black entertainers were a logical source of support for civil rights efforts, and not just because they often had the financial capacity to pay for offices and buses and staff.

More important was their access to the mainstream national media. Through at least the 1950s, blacks were largely invisible in the national press. The exceptions were the handful of entertainment (and to some extent sports) celebrities whose fame transcended color. That fame gave them something no other blacks at the time possessed: a platform to address white America.

From the movement's first real stirrings in the 1950s, no black entertainer used that platform more effectively than Harry Belafonte, a proud and sometimes difficult man acutely conscious of the obligations fame imposed. Belafonte never felt fully comfortable in the role of spokesman for his race, but he understood the unique responsibility of his fame in a nation that offered few outlets to black voices. "A white entertainer can say anything," he once remarked. "No one assumes that he is talking for anybody but himself. But as soon as a Negro celebrity says anything, his words are immediately seized as a statement—not for himself but for his people. Of course, it is not too difficult to understand why this happens. The Negro people have been suppressed for so long and so few Negro voices have been heard in public that no Negro in the public eye can speak without seeming to speak for the larger group of which he is part."

Born in New York City in 1927, Belafonte grew up an angry young man; riding the subways he would scrawl bitter graffiti on ads that seemed to him racist. Even after achieving enormous success—first as a singer with his deep, intoxicating voice, then as an actor—he couldn't escape the realities of black life in the 1950s; once, for instance, a hotel maitre d' angrily attempted to evict him from a club where he was waiting to perform. On screen, he became the first black matinee idol—but when he played Joan Fontaine's love interest in *Island in the Sun*, Darryl Zanuck refused to allow them to kiss, insisting that no scene demanded it.

Belafonte established an early connection with Martin Luther King, Jr., who emerged as a national civil rights leader after spearheading the Montgomery bus boycott in 1956. Belafonte first met King when the young Baptist minister came North to raise funds for the campaign; King struck the prickly, skeptical singer as both determined and grounded. A few months after their first meeting, Belafonte joined King, other civil rights leaders, and several emerging black stars (including Sammy Davis, Jr., and Sidney Poitier) for a Prayer Pilgrimage that gathered 30,000 supporters in Washington. The next year Belafonte was back in Washington with Coretta Scott King and Jackie Robinson for a march in the capital supporting school integration. Belafonte led a group of students to the White House, where they attempted to deliver a petition to President Eisenhower.

From that point on, Belafonte participated, either publicly or behind the scenes, in virtually all of the movement's milestones. Belafonte bolstered King at some of his most difficult moments. He raised money, performed at concerts, acted as a liaison to the Kennedy administration, and helped to craft strategy. When King wanted to mount a voter registration drive in 1961, Belafonte helped him organize it. When King sat in the Birmingham, Alabama, jail, in despair over his inability to provide bail funds for the protesters filling the cells, it was Belafonte who produced $50,000 for bail bonds and relayed to King, through attorney Clarence Jones, the soothing message that he would be there for "whatever else you need." When King and a weary trail of demonstrators completed their triumphant march across Alabama from Selma to Montgomery, Belafonte was there, having organized an all-star show to greet them on the outskirts of town; the stars performed on a stage of coffin crates. He built ties to all segments of the movement, from moderates to radicals, and used his credibility to help mediate the disputes between King and the more militant Student Nonviolent Coordinating Committee. His creativity and commitment provided a textbook on the ways celebrities could meaningfully encourage political change.

White stars inevitably came to the cause more slowly. In Hollywood, the civil rights movement first expanded beyond its limited black base after Kennedy's election. "That was the catalyst," said attorney Jones, who was living in Los Angeles and organizing support for the Southern Christian Leadership Conference at the time. Still, it was slow going through the early 1960s, when the movement won few victories. Sinatra and his friends directed their new enthusiasm into the cause, but the rest of Hollywood remained difficult terrain. For months, King's Hollywood supporters organized small meetings, where they might "pick up ten people who wanted to lick envelopes, or a celebrity who wanted to do something," said Judy Quine, who worked with Allard K. Lowenstein to pry open the locked doors.

The breakthrough in Hollywood, as throughout the nation, came after King's Birmingham campaign in the spring of 1963. The struggle against Birmingham police commissioner Eugene (Bull) Connor, with his dogs and fire hoses, lifted King to a new plane. King brought his old message and his new celebrity to Los Angeles a few weeks after the Birmingham victory. After months of struggling to loosen trickles of support, Quine and the other organizers saw the floodgates open. Liberal Hollywood flocked to King. Appearing at the old Wrigley Field in late May 1963, King addressed a huge interracial crowd that included a large block of celebrities. Paul Newman nervously read to the gathering a list of stars and politicians who had "evinced concern and interest." Later that evening, King addressed a small group of leading entertainers and liberals crowded into Burt Lancaster's Beverly Hills home, spilling over from the living room into the den and the library and the hallway. (Lancaster, filming a movie in France, actually didn't attend; his wife Norma hosted the gathering.) To the hushed group, King quietly told a story of riding in the car with his children past an amusement park, and the pain he felt when he told them they couldn't go inside because they were black. In the capital of plenty, the simple homily of opportunity constrained had its desired effect. Hands reached for wallets. King left Los Angeles at the end of the day with $75,000.

He left behind a new sense of excitement. From the meeting at Lancaster's home, a group coalesced to organize a celebrity delegation to the March on Washington that King had planned for the end of August. To Quine, it seemed as though the resurgent political awareness that had begun to sprout in the late 1950s and had been fertilized by Kennedy "was now blossoming, and mushrooming." In Hollywood, actors Marlon Brando, Charlton Heston, and James Garner emerged as leaders. Working with Belafonte in New York, they assembled probably the most impressive collection of stars gathered to that point for a single political event. From Paris, Burt Lancaster, novelist James Baldwin, and the great expatriate black singer Josephine Baker came bearing a petition of support signed by 1,500 overseas Americans. From New York came Heston, Newman, Joanne Woodward, Poitier, Diahann Carroll, Tony Curtis, and a dozen others. Some ninety industry figures led by Brando and Belafonte took off from Hollywood. Dick Gregory flew in; Ossie Davis, Sammy Davis, Jr., and Lena Horne flew in. Bob Dylan, Joan Baez, Joshua White, Peter, Paul and Mary, all flew in.

On the morning of the march, J. Edgar Hoover had FBI agents call the stars in their hotel rooms, warning them that the day might be violent and urging them not to participate. He dissuaded no one. The stars assembled in Washington had surmounted the real barrier of fear when they climbed on the planes. King's opponents (who included Hoover) claimed his movement was riddled with Communists. For the first time in many years, the red flag did not deter the Hollywood liberals. "It had," Lancaster said, "gone beyond that by then." The response to King in the entertainment industry was so strong that Murray Schumach, the *New York Times* Hollywood correspondent, saw in it the final curtain for the era of anxiety and confusion that began when J. Parnell Thomas came to Los Angeles brandishing subpoenas sixteen years earlier. "This plane trip," he wrote as the celebrities prepared to fly east, "may . . . lift the ceilings of fear." He was right. On the sweltering morning of August 28, 1963, the jubilant contingent of celebrities fell into line with the crowds marching from the Washington Monument to the Lincoln Memorial, and in their company stepped out of the grip of the past.

Hollywood broke from its own racist history more slowly. The civil rights movement drew some of Hollywood's most glamorous celebrities; but Hollywood actually posed one of its most frustrating challenges. If the movement demonstrated that Hollywood stars would again commit themselves to controversial political action, that its executives would again open their wallets to controversial political movements, it also revealed how easily the film community could lend its glamour to causes without being affected by them. "Hollywood per se was not involved in civil rights," said Wendell Franklin, a black stage manager and assistant director. "It was individuals whose names stood out that made the turn in Hollywood, because Hollywood itself hadn't changed that much."

From its inception, the film industry had offered blacks few opportunities. When Sidney Poitier arrived at Twentieth Century-Fox at the end of the 1940s he found it nearly all white, a situation he came to understand was not "untypical" of the studios. Blacks were virtually invisible behind the camera. A *Variety* survey just after King's May 1963 visit found no blacks at all in the local unions representing grips, electrical workers, and soundmen. The Producers Guild also counted no blacks among its members. Only a handful of blacks belonged to the directors' and writers' guilds. "Some of the unions," recalled Franklin, "said they'd cancel the union out before they'd hire a black, especially in camera and in sound." Franklin won his first opportunity to work as a stage manager in television only by approaching a senior network executive at a party where he was working as a bartender.

On-screen opportunities were greater, though not much. Fearful of offending white audiences, particularly in the South, the studios generally assigned black actors roles that reinforced stereotypes. Roles of any kind for black actors were scarce. "Certain stars would not star with blacks," said Maggie Hathaway, a black actress who first came to Hollywood in the mid-1950s. The producers typically defended themselves by maintaining that writers turned in few scripts that called for blacks, but often movies that virtually demanded black performers elaborately contrived to avoid black faces on the screen.

Hollywood's senior management had not heard the rumble of changing times. It began to. Late in 1961, the president of the Los Angeles chapter of the National Association for the Advancement of Colored

People (NAACP) accused the industry of showing blacks only when "they have a crap game." The next summer, the NAACP formed a Hollywood–Beverly Hills chapter to press for greater employment opportunity for blacks in the movie industry, and more accurate on-screen portrayals. Hathaway became its first president. They made little progress with the studio executives. But the explosion of interest in the civil rights cause among industry liberals the following spring framed their cause in a new context; as stars jetted off to join protests in Washington or Mississippi or Alabama, inevitably "people said, 'What about your own backyard?' " recalled Judy Quine.

The NAACP's genteel accusations had not moved the industry. What could? Hathaway managed to squeeze in a brief discussion with King during his trip to Los Angeles. "I asked him what could we do to speed up integration in pictures," she remembered. "We were just about starving to death in those days. . . . We asked him, what could we do to get black people's stories [on screen], black roles for black people? And he said, 'boycott.' That was the only word he used. And so we proposed to boycott."

During the summer of 1963, Hollywood suddenly bristled with confrontation. In late June, Herbert Hill, the NAACP's national labor secretary, came to Hollywood and threatened a massive, coordinated program of legal action and public protest to force open the industry. With the civil rights cause gaining momentum nationally, the studios could not ignore Hill's threats. Instead, they smothered him with attention. Meetings with the producers were convened, negotiations launched; in support of the protesters a group of white stars led by Marlon Brando threatened to boycott the industry themselves unless it offered blacks more opportunities. Throughout the summer of "crisis" (as the *New York Times* labeled it), representatives of the studios made themselves available to the NAACP for long meetings, invariably described as congenial. By the fall, nervous Hollywood executives predicted breakthroughs in casting for blacks.

The breakthroughs never came. Pressure on the studios gradually eased. The white stars who rallied around King never embraced this cause with the same passion. No stars walked away from the set to protest segregation at home. "In a way it was probably easier for James Garner and Burt Lancaster and Charlton Heston to get involved in the March on Washington than to deal with the institutional racism in the industry," said Clarence Jones, the attorney who organized for King among entertainers. "It was easier to participate [in a march] than to go into the studio and say, 'How come, although I'm featured as the star in this picture, there are not any blacks on this lot?' " Black stars didn't display much more interest in confronting their employers.

The studios deflected the protesters with promises. "Every time we decided to boycott Hollywood," Hathaway recalled, her words bitter and distinct, "one studio would say, 'Come on, let's give them everything. They can work as all nationalities.' In about six months we were starving again." Later, the producers proffered cash: a grant to fund the NAACP's annual award honoring those filmmakers who offered the most accurate portrayals of blacks. For many years, there wasn't much to choose from. Aside from the painfully earnest *Guess Who's Coming to Dinner?* in 1967, the studios passed through the 1960s producing few films that dealt with the civil rights movement or the changing dynamics of race relations in America. Blacks did not appear on screen in large numbers until the *Superfly* swarm of exploitation films appeared in the early 1970s.

Even today, blacks have established only a tenuous position in the Hollywood infrastructure. Some progress has been made. The technical unions have opened. Blacks are now regularly featured on television. And there are more black stars on the screen—Eddie Murphy, Bill Cosby, Richard Pryor, Spike Lee. But except in the production operations those stars have established, blacks occupy few important jobs, except for technical ones, off-camera. In the optimistic summer of 1963 this seemed an unlikely outcome. In retrospect, it is not nearly as surprising. Hollywood's encounter with the civil rights movement reaffirmed enduring lessons about its participation in politics. Hollywood is thought of as a liberal place, and in its political expression it tends to be. But its contradictory response to the civil rights movement revealed how mistaken it is to assume that its political liberalism systematically informs the way it does business, or the kinds of films it makes. As an institution, Hollywood resists any agenda—political or social—other than turning a profit. "I think," said one senior studio executive, "movie companies will make a movie with the devil if they think it is going to make money." The inverse of that maxim is that saints without prospects don't get appointments. The replacement of the reactionary first-generation moguls at the top of the studios by men more politically moderate only slightly tempered that fundamental institutional conservatism. As individuals of great wealth, Hollywood's leading powers have always felt free to support controversial causes. But as entertainers and executives appealing to a mass audience they have typically been far more circumspect about systematically integrating those political beliefs into their work.

. . .

If Hollywood's internal politics changed only slowly, its participation in national political events steadily accelerated through the 1960s. The spectacular turnout of stars for the 1963 March on Washington offered the first measure of the political ferment left in Kennedy's wake. But it was not until the next year, with the presidential campaign of 1964, that the full partisan dimensions of Kennedy's impact became apparent. Nothing testified more powerfully to Kennedy's legacy than Hollywood's enthusiastic response to his successor. Kennedy bonded an entire generation of celebrities to the Democratic party. Far more Hollywood figures campaigned for Lyndon B. Johnson in 1964 than for Kennedy four years earlier, though Johnson was as uncomfortable around stars as Kennedy was easy.

When he became president, Johnson had virtually no political relationships in California, much less Hollywood. At the 1960 Democratic Convention in Los Angeles, while politicians from every state careened from party to party as wide-eyed as tourists, Johnson moped. Lloyd N. Hand, a young attorney on the Texas senator's staff, remembers escorting Johnson to a party hosted by Jules Stein, the founder of MCA, Hollywood's most powerful talent agency. In Stein's magnificent home, high above the flickering lights of Los Angeles, Hand entered another world. "I saw more movie stars on one patio balcony than I'd seen in the movies in my lifetime," he recalled. "I was just agog. Joseph Cotten and Audrey Hepburn and this one and that one." Hand was overwhelmed; Johnson was bored. He stamped around the elegant room distractedly for ten minutes, and then turned to Hand and grumbled, "OK, let's go.'"

Johnson "was almost functionally illiterate about who stars were; he didn't know very much about that," said former Johnson White House aide Jack Valenti (who went on to become president of the Motion Picture Association of America, the studios' lobbying organization). Johnson liked Kirk Douglas, Gregory Peck, and John Wayne, and invited them to White House functions; he would call Wayne on his birthday. But he preferred the grittier company of politicians. At first, Johnson held no more attraction for the stars. Nowhere more than in Hollywood—except perhaps Harvard—did the president suffer so much from the stylistic comparison with his predecessor. In Hollywood, he was widely considered crude, unglamorous, parochial—an overgrown hick, a dirt farmer, a man who lifted his dog by the ears. But when Johnson stood for election against Arizona Senator Barry Goldwater, the stars poured out for him. Sinatra receded, but others stepped forward. Max Youngstein, who ran the entertainment division of the California campaign, told one reporter at the time, "There is virtually an unlimited supply of top talent available for the campaign this year." Partly the response reflected grudging respect for Johnson's success at moving a liberal legislative program. But the key to Johnson's Hollywood strength was the overwhelming support for the Democratic party among younger and middle-aged actors and actresses who had either returned to politics under Kennedy or first been exposed through him.

Their enlistment in the Democratic cause established the modern partisan alignment in Hollywood. Through the 1950s, the two major parties had competed on roughly equal terms for Hollywood's allegiance. In the 1940s the Democrats predominated, but the Republicans had a respectable base despite Roosevelt's longevity and popularity. In 1948, with Roosevelt gone, Truman produced no more enthusiasm than Thomas Dewey. In the 1950s, Eisenhower and Adlai Stevenson both had a dependable following in the film industry.

But from the vantage point of 1964, it became apparent that under Kennedy the Democrats had seized an advantage—which they have maintained ever since. In the 1960 campaign, Republican nominee Richard Nixon had little to choose from. For the Democratic Convention, Sinatra mobilized two dozen stars at their profession's peak. But when reliable George Murphy took up the task for the GOP gathering in Chicago, he could manage only William Lundigan, Brian Sullivan, Gene Archer, Patricia Morrison, Louis Sudler—a group that might have trouble securing a reservation at Chasen's—and as his leading men of sorts, Efrem Zimbalist, Jr., and Edgar Bergen the ventriloquist. The *New York Times* did not exaggerate when it declared: "Politics has hit Hollywood, and the Democrats seem to have scored a landslide victory over the Republicans." For the general election, the Republicans attracted bigger names, but they were venerable ones: Irene Dunne and Ginger Rogers, Jimmy Stewart and Dick Powell, John Wayne and Walt Disney. Ronald Reagan, who had been drifting rightward since the late 1940s, finally switched sides and made several appearances for the Republican ticket in his capacity as co-chairman of Southern California Democrats for Nixon. Roughly the same crew turned out to man Goldwater's sinking ship four years later.

All these stars campaigned with energy, conviction, and fading luster. Even Dick Powell acknowledged during the Nixon race that the vice-president's supporters "may not be the most popular at the moment" though, he insisted, "they have dignity and the right image." Dignity alone couldn't ameliorate the effects of age; the GOP was stuck with stars who appealed mostly to people with a personal recollection of the stock market crash. While the Democrats snapped up the hot young names

(Natalie Wood, Steve McQueen, Jack Lemmon, Shirley MacLaine), GOP candidates depended on essentially the same graying idols who had fortified Dewey two decades earlier.

What trapped the GOP in the past? Looking back, no single answer explains the change. One large factor, unquestionably, was Kennedy's enormous appeal, particularly to younger stars. Another was that by the late 1950s, the founding generation of Hollywood moguls, who had provided the backbone of GOP efforts there, were forced from the studios. In 1960, Jack Warner and Sam Goldwyn remained active for Nixon, but Mayer was dead and Zanuck in exile; their successors were less intuitively conservative. With the fall of the moguls, the GOP lost its best Hollywood recruiters.

But those reasons cannot fully explain the phenomenon, because the Hollywood GOP forces began to rely too heavily on familiar faces as early as the 1948 campaign. That timing raises another factor. The GOP's inability to attract new stars after the late 1940s suggests that the hunt for Hollywood Communists may have done as much lasting damage to the political right as it did to the political left. Certainly, for the first generation of Hollywood leftists—liberals and Communists alike—the blacklist was a wrenching, agonizing nightmare. But for the generations that succeeded those maimed by the investigations, it was the inquisitors, not their victims, who bore the shame. As the 1960s progressed and the Vietnam War called into question the entire Cold War edifice, the blacklistees were resurrected in Hollywood as well-meaning progressives hounded for their prescience by the forces of ignorance, reaction, and hysteria. Their ruined careers were raised like bloody shirts as monuments to the danger of reflexive anticommunism. That revisionism was simplistic and overstated—the Party members' careers also offered nothing if not testimony to the intellectual danger of reflexive procommunism—but perhaps for those very reasons the deification of the Hollywood Ten advanced. It reached the point where many people in Hollywood "consider it an honor to have been blacklisted," said writer Paul Jarrico, one of the Party members forced from the industry during the 1950s.

Though Democrats hardly distinguished themselves as civil libertarians during those years, in Hollywood the politicians most prominently associated with the purge were conservative Republicans—J. Parnell Thomas, Joe McCarthy, and above all Nixon, remembered not only for his contributions to HUAC but for his red-baiting 1950 race against Helen Douglas. Their success seeded their party's later frustration. By the 1960s, the GOP's hard-line anticommunism bound it to a policy that in Hollywood increasingly seemed spiteful, mean, and irrational. "The blacklist shamed them," said Milton Sperling, the liberal producer. Ironically, the blacklist's most enduring legacy in Hollywood may have been an implacable skepticism of policies based on the Cold War logic of Communist containment. Mostly this helped Democrats, though not all of them. Johnson, so popular in 1964, came to understand this himself only a few years later.

In the mid-1950s, the Hollywood conservatives' victory over the reviled left seemed total and irreversible. But a decade later—after the powerful surge of younger Hollywood stars into the Democratic camp during the 1960 and 1964 campaigns—the picture looked very different. In their pursuit of the Hollywood Communists and their liberal allies, the conservatives had failed to remember that in American politics no victory is ever complete, and that ideological excess always exacts a price. When the tide rolled back, the right did not face the personal pain that the Communists suffered for their own, earlier, excesses; but the Hollywood conservatives nonetheless paid a tangible political price. Kennedy could claim much of the responsibility for the Democrats' modern advantage in Hollywood, but he shared it with McCarthy and Thomas and Nixon.

CHAPTER SIX

THE GLAMOUR OF MONEY

The New Moguls

The first weekend of February 1960, while visiting Frank Sinatra and Peter Lawford at the Sands Hotel in Las Vegas, Senator John F. Kennedy himself entertained several visitors. He combined business with pleasure. The pleasure was Judith Campbell Exner, whom Frank Sinatra had invited as a distraction from the campaign grind. The business was Los Angeles savings and loan executive Bart Lytton, a former screenwriter, former publicist, and former Hollywood Communist who had improbably re-created himself as one of California's most successful and flamboyant capitalists.

Unlike Exner, Lytton wasn't sure why he was there. He assumed Senator Kennedy had summoned him to get a financial contribution to his presidential campaign. But the candidate only made charming small talk; he never asked for a cent. Exasperated, Lytton finally posed the question himself.

"What's your financial situation?" he asked Kennedy. "How about money?"

"Well, Bart," Kennedy answered, "we're all right through the primary. We don't have any problem through the primary."

Books have commemorated the uninhibited adventures that followed Exner's visit. But history may well record Kennedy's prim response to Lytton as that weekend's most memorable moment. It might have been the last time a presidential candidate told a supporter, any supporter, he didn't need more money. No candidate could ever afford such nonchalance again. Even Kennedy, once he won the White House, was forced to launch an unprecedented fundraising program to eliminate the huge debt his campaign imposed on the Democratic National Committee.

The revolution that began with the first tentative use of television advertising in the contests between Adlai Stevenson and Dwight Eisenhower upended the political world in the two decades that followed. From the early 1950s on, campaigns became increasingly professionalized, relying not only on television advertising but opinion polling, direct mail, jet travel, and expensive efforts to contact and identify supporters. All these sophisticated tools fattened campaign budgets. After adjusting for inflation, the cost of presidential races more than tripled between 1960 and 1972.

As costs increased, so did the centrality of fundraising. For candidates less personally wealthy than Kennedy, it became a consuming compulsion, no more discretionary than breathing. From supporters of every ideological stripe, in every line of enterprise, politicians demanded more financial help. The movie industry was not immune to the pressure. The demands from the Eisenhower campaign on Jack Warner, Darryl Zanuck, and Sam Goldwyn were only an overture. As the exploding costs of campaigns forced more and more politicians to search for funds outside their home states, Hollywood, glittering with affluence, eventually became a regular stop on the national political treasure hunt. Money, acquiring a glamour of its own, became as much a part of Hollywood's political identity as dazzle and glitz.

In the new era of eight-figure national campaigns and then eight-figure state campaigns, new opportunities arose for men and women who could collect money in amounts that would have stunned even Warner and Zanuck. From Hollywood, two men first joined the new fundraising elite. Each showed great facility for the game, not only for the collection of checks but for the cultivation of the politicians who ultimately cashed them. Each achieved more political influence than any of their predecessors at the pinnacle of Hollywood.

Lew R. Wasserman of Beverly Hills and Arthur B. Krim of Manhattan lived a coast apart but were in many ways much alike. It was common in Hollywood to say that if Lew Wasserman wasn't the smartest man in Hollywood, Arthur Krim was. In New York the order might be reversed.

Wasserman at MCA, Inc., an agency that transformed itself into a studio, and Krim at United Artists, a studio that redefined the term, were part of the first generation that succeeded the industry's founding moguls, and among that first generation the only ones who inherited the founders' stubborn durability. They were men dissimilar in background and similar in temperament. Wasserman came from Cleveland and never attended college; Krim grew up in leafy Westchester and was polished by the finest academic institutions. Yet both men were known for intimidating intellect. Both were considered brilliant deal-makers, wizards with numbers, more at home behind an adding machine than in a cutting room. Both expected and gave loyalty; yet both were considered somewhat cold and reserved. Shrewd and farsighted, they understood as quickly as anyone in Hollywood that the rise of television irrevocably altered the movie business.

Both had interests that extended beyond the screen. Like the moguls they supplanted, they coveted the company of powerful men. But they entered that company with a shrewdness and subtlety their predecessors lacked. Both Jews, they built lasting alliances to Gentile centers of power that had rejected their predecessors, or at best only tolerated them.

Wasserman and Krim. They led the men atop Hollywood into a new era of political activism. Both were Democrats, though of different kinds: Wasserman moderate, pragmatic, willing to buck his party when his business interests demanded; Krim more ideological, more dogmatically liberal, less attuned to the industry's political needs. For Wasserman, involvement in politics began as an extension of his responsibilities as an executive; for Krim, it was an escape from them. The pull of Washington never distracted Wasserman from his life mission of building a Hollywood empire; for Krim, no film triumph matched the excitement of sorting through world events with the president.

What they shared was an awareness that the new political era—the era of television and multimillion-dollar campaigns—ran on rules fundamentally different from the old. When the moguls had raised their tribute for politicians, they had squeezed and muscled every dollar out of their own domains, marshaling all their power to force their employees into line. Wasserman and Krim both understood that time had passed by that approach, and not only because its crudeness belonged to an earlier era of brass-knuckled management coercion. Modern campaigns needed so much money that the most successful fundraisers—and thus the most influential men—were those who could reach beyond their own dominion and extract money from other local powers. That required not only clout but also tact, the ability to persuade other proud and wealthy men and women to join their cause. Later, federal campaign finance reforms that limited the size of contributions attached an even higher premium to those skills.

Over time, these changes provided opportunities for other Hollywood players who would rival the influence of Wasserman and Krim. But they would operate in a mold cast—in a style trademarked—by the first of the new moguls.

Lew Wasserman was born in Cleveland in March 1913, the son of Orthodox Jews. The most powerful man in modern Hollywood began his movie career as a theater usher; later he handled promotion for a Cleveland nightclub called the Mayfair Casino. The Mayfair often booked bands from a Chicago-based talent agency called the Music Corporation of America, or MCA. Wasserman impressed MCA's founder, Jules C. Stein, and Stein offered the ambitious young man a job with MCA in Chicago. In December 1936, Wasserman joined the company to which he would devote the rest of his life.

MCA was already a powerful enterprise. It had been formed just over a decade earlier by Stein, an ophthalmologist with an eye for talent, and a piano-playing college friend named William (Billy) Goodheart. They began by booking bands in Chicago during a time when Al Capone, his cohorts and his rivals, controlled most of the city's nightlife. Stein and Goodheart proved as tough as the men they dealt with, established at least a rough peace with them, and expanded rapidly through the Midwest. By the mid-1930s, MCA controlled many of the country's most popular bands, from Tommy Dorsey to Artie Shaw.

From his powerful base in the music industry, Stein took aim at Hollywood. In 1937 he opened a Beverly Hills office under the direction of Taft B. Schreiber, a young agent. But the point man for the invasion became Wasserman, who arrived in California in 1938 and within two years was named vice-president of the company's fledgling motion picture division. Tall, thin, and taciturn, Wasserman fused his life with his company; he was monastic in his dedication to MCA. No one in Hollywood worked harder or schemed more creatively. MCA bid aggressively for famous clients and brought in such names as Bette Davis and Joan Crawford. Even more successful was Wasserman's strategy of obtaining clients by buying other agencies with deeper Hollywood roots; among the first clients MCA acquired that way was Ronald Reagan. (Wasserman initially served as Reagan's personal agent.) The firm's breakthrough came in 1945 when it acquired the prestigious Hayward-Deverich agency headed by Leland Hayward. That brought into the fold more than two hundred clients, including Henry Fonda, Jimmy Stewart, and Billy Wilder. MCA never looked back. It spoke for so much talent, not only in the movie but also in the music business, that it came to be known as the Octopus, its tentacles stretching into every corner of the entertainment industry. In 1946 Stein promoted himself to chairman of the board and rewarded Wasserman for his success by naming him president.

With operating control in his hands, Wasserman expanded MCA even more aggressively than its founder. In an era when Hollywood reeled from the combined onslaughts of television and the anti-Communist purges, when the studios faced the traumatic loss of their theater chains, it was Wasserman who most visibly exuded the unquenchable ambition that had burned in Mayer and Warner and Cohn twenty years earlier.

Wasserman worked nearly all the time, and expected as much from the men around him. Soft-spoken and icily self-controlled in public, he could be ferocious behind closed doors. His temper was legendary; stories percolated through the company of men who fainted under a tongue-lashing from Wasserman, or who rushed from his office, dazed and humiliated, and promptly threw up. Wasserman enraged was fearsome to watch: his voice would rise and, in his agitation, he would begin to lisp and slur his words. As he grew more agitated, his voice would rise again, and the words would cascade from him, louder, more slurred, swept along on waves of fury that tangled his tongue, until finally saliva would start to drip from the corner of his mouth. "He'd reach for his handkerchief, he'd reach to loosen his tie," his former executive assistant Jerry Gershwin recalled, flinching at the memory. "That's when you'd say, 'Look out. Look out!' " Working in his vicinity was like living on the slope of a volcano. But he paid his men well, and inspired them with a sense of mission lacking on the dispirited studio lots.

What set MCA apart was not only its voracity but its ruthlessness and creativity. Wasserman understood that the decay of the studio system after World War II, and then its collapse in the early 1950s, left a vacuum at Hollywood's center. Once the studios could no longer afford to hold large stables of talent under long-term contracts, the top actors, directors, and writers were able to make their own deals. No one dealt more aggressively than Wasserman. In 1949, for a popular Western called *Winchester '73,* he negotiated for Jimmy Stewart the first contract in which a star received a percentage of a film's gross—and set a precedent that eventually provided Hollywood's biggest stars with wealth commensurate with their fame.

Agents as much as stars gained power in the new decentralized Hollywood. Producers could no longer assemble their casts and creative teams by walking through the commissary; they needed agents who could deliver top talent. No one controlled more talent than MCA. Like Stein before him, Wasserman was not content passively to deliver the performers producers demanded; he constantly probed for fresh advantage. During the 1930s, the agency had used its relationships to establish itself as a producer, packaging radio programs featuring acts it represented and selling them to sponsors. Two decades later, Wasserman saw the upheaval racking the studios as an opportunity to emulate that role in Hollywood. "I felt," Wasserman said laconically, many years later, "our organization was capable of earning more than 10 per cent [commissions], and that we could do better on the other side of the table."

The initial opportunity to move across the table—where MCA would buy talent as a producer, not just sell it as an agent—came not in feature films but in the production of television programming, which most of the studios initially derided. MCA moved into the opening. In 1952, the company aggressively lobbied for and won a blanket waiver from the Screen Actors Guild, freeing it from the union's prohibition against agents acting simultaneously as producers. The waiver was arguably the most important event in MCA's history, beginning its metamorphosis from a talent agency to a studio. The agreement also marked a turning point in the fortunes of MCA client Ronald Reagan, whose career had fallen into an apparently fatal tailspin. Because Reagan was SAG president when the union granted the waiver, the agreement instantly aroused suspicion across Hollywood and in the Justice Department, which had been intermittently investigating MCA for possible antitrust violations since the 1940s. Reagan's moribund career was revived after the agreement, as MCA secured for him the job as host and occasional performer in one of its first productions, a weekly television anthology called "General Electric Theater." The Justice Department was never able to establish any criminal quid pro quo, though it later subjected Reagan to extensive questioning before a grand jury investigating MCA.*

Once MCA secured the waiver, Wasserman vigorously employed it. Through the 1950s MCA became the dominant force in television pro-

---

*Whatever Reagan's personal interest in the deal might have been, SAG did not give MCA its waiver without extracting a substantial price. As part of the negotiations, MCA became the first producer to agree to pay actors residuals when television programs in which they performed were rebroadcast. Obtaining such residual payments was the union's highest priority in contract negotiations then simultaneously under way with the producers; once MCA broke the united front of opposition, the remaining producers capitulated. "Every writer, actor and director in this town ought to get down and kiss Ronald Reagan's feet," insists one former MCA agent, "because the man got television residuals. That has paid for most of the houses in the [San Fernando] Valley."

duction. By the late 1950s, MCA's Revue Productions subsidiary had sixteen series on the air and was supplying NBC with a third of its primetime programming.

Flush with cash from its success as a television producer, MCA branched out again. In 1958, to provide a home for its growing operations, MCA paid out nearly $12 million for the 367-acre Universal Pictures lot in the San Fernando Valley. Now the company had room enough to build an empire. On this enormous territory MCA developed not only production facilities and office space but even a studio tour that gave tourists a synthesized glimpse behind the screen. As Hollywood lurched into the 1960s, MCA was still its most powerful talent agency, but to think of it in those terms was anachronistic. Through a series of deft maneuvers, Wasserman had transformed it into a new sort of studio, one that spoke the modern corporate language of diversifying its assets and rationalizing the "manufacture" of its product. "MCA," acknowledged one critic in 1961, "has been the leader in bringing big-business methods to the entertainment industry."

Throughout this period of explosive growth, MCA kept a remarkably low political profile. During the 1952 presidential campaign, Stein (though an ideological conservative) was among the few Hollywood powers who resisted the enormous pressure from Jack Warner, Sam Goldwyn, and Darryl Zanuck to fall in behind Eisenhower. Despite personal pleas from both Zanuck and Warner, Stein insisted that his policy was to stay away from any political activity. Eventually, MCA apparently decided that intransigent defiance of three such powerful men was itself impolitic, and in the general election Wasserman lent his name to the board of directors of the Entertainment Industry Joint Committee for Eisenhower-Nixon. But that was an exception. "Stein was firm on it," said Edd Henry, a long-time MCA vice-president. "I don't know of anyone who talked to a client about politics."

MCA's reluctance to join in political causes fit Stein's and Wasserman's shared conception of the company. As a defense against the agent's historic image as disreputable and pushy—thinly veiled synonyms for Jewish—Stein and Wasserman built MCA around an ideal of Gentile respectability. "Everything was designed to give you the feeling that you were dealing with Ivy League WASPs," said one former agent. Stein furnished the offices from his formidable collection of antiques; Wasserman set an austere dress code—dark suit (preferably black), white shirt, and black tie—and policed it ferociously. Blue suits or even blue blazers with gray slacks might be acceptable, but agents with more sartorial daring risked Wasserman's incendiary temper. Once, when an agent came to a meeting wearing a blazer with a bright red foulard lining, Wasserman turned on him and snapped, "What's the matter with you, you look like a pimp in a whorehouse." Everything about the company was designed to suggest stability, continuity, discretion. MCA agents were expected to keep their names out of the press (Wasserman almost never sat for interviews) and give the company lifetime loyalty. Agents were rarely fired, and rarely quit. "It was like a Jewish Irish Republican Army," said Jere Henshaw, a former executive.

If all this seemed uncharacteristically ascetic for the garish and gaudy playground of Louis Mayer and Jack Warner, that was itself the point. Wasserman saw himself as more than the successor to the original moguls; he seemed to view himself as an improvement over them, as a streamlined and modernized version of the crude and willful studio executives who ruled the Hollywood of his youth. If anything, the key to Wasserman was his singular refusal to do anything as they had done it; his style, his manner, his priorities, all could not have contrasted more with Hollywood's fathers if he had set out to design himself as their inverse.

The moguls were men who understood and relished the parts they played; they were bright, preening, huge in their appetites. Wasserman chose a different role: modern, distant, precise, as hard and inscrutable as the featureless black tower in which he headquartered his empire. His predecessors were mostly Jews who sought desperately to assimilate and betrayed their background by the very tenacity of their attempts to deny it. Without any apparent effort, Wasserman genuinely assimilated: he was even more anonymous in his simple black suit than the Protestant corporate climber in gray flannel. For Wasserman, avoiding political entanglements was just another way of keeping his head down. In 1959 Jack Warner tried to recruit his fellow Eisenhower man for Vice-President Richard Nixon's presidential campaign, but Wasserman passed, reminding Warner that he was a registered Democrat. Wasserman apparently supported Lyndon Johnson's last-minute attempt to win the Democratic nomination. But he played no significant role in the 1960 general election for the Democrats.

MCA's enormous success made Wasserman's reclusiveness increasingly untenable. With the moguls finally gone, someone had to speak for the movie business in its new era. The industry's most powerful man, Wasserman was the logical choice. Inside the industry his profile inexorably became higher. Using his considerable negotiating skills, Wasserman quietly stepped in to craft a compromise that ended a 1960 writers' strike against the television producers. From that point on, he routinely took a leading role in Hollywood labor negotiations. His preeminent position was formalized a few years later when he was named chairman of the Association of Motion Picture and Television Producers, Inc., the producers' collective bargaining organization.

Outside the industry, too, Wasserman's influence grew. Almost imperceptibly, he glided past his contemporaries to emerge as Hollywood's ambassador to outside powers. Dorothy (Buff) Chandler, wife of *Los Angeles Times* publisher Norman Chandler—the core of the downtown business establishment that had scorned and rejected the founding moguls—turned to Wasserman to help her fund the Music Center she hoped would mark Los Angeles's emergence as a cultural force. Her overture wasn't solely a testament to Wasserman's talents; it was a sign that Los Angeles itself was growing more worldly, less provincial, its downtown powers finally realizing they could not transform their dusty community into a world-class city without tapping the creativity and enormous wealth on the Jewish Westside. But it was Wasserman (together with his old friend, Hollywood lawyer Paul Ziffren) who understood the opening and moved through it. More than any of his predecessors, he broke down the barriers that isolated Hollywood from the Los Angeles establishment.

The last barriers to Wasserman's involvement in political affairs came down shortly after Kennedy's election. Internal Hollywood politics set the change in motion. In late 1961, the Screen Actors Guild withdrew the 1952 waiver that allowed MCA to both represent talent and produce programming; MCA could no longer straddle its two worlds. The choice for Wasserman was no choice really. By then, the talent agency provided only a small portion of the company's revenues. In June 1962, MCA declared its intentions by acquiring Decca Records Inc., the parent company of Universal Pictures. With its acquisition of Universal, MCA finalized its reconstitution as a studio; it was now in a position to produce not only for television but also for the screen. Because of the SAG decision, the acquisition meant that the company had to abandon its talent business. It announced plans to spin off the agency to its employees.

But this arrangement failed to satisfy the Justice Department, which had been investigating the company since the waning days of the Eisenhower administration. In July 1962, the Kennedy Justice Department, citing antitrust concerns, filed suit to prevent the Decca merger and the agency divestiture. After weeks of the acrimonious negotiations for which the company was renowned, MCA was allowed to acquire Decca, but the agency—which the government feared would remain under the company's de facto control after the divestiture—was completely dissolved. Its 1,400 clients were set loose.

For Wasserman, the government's intervention was a traumatic event. Years later, he sanctimoniously described it as "the major surprise of my life . . . a useless, unwarranted act." In company legend, it was the act that inspired Wasserman to shed his political passivity and begin acquiring the powerful allies that could prevent a recurrence. "He said," his aide Gershwin recalled, "if you can't beat 'em, you join 'em." Wasserman started to cultivate Democratic friends, while Taft Schreiber built alliances in the Republican party. The bustle of activity from the normally reclusive executives turned heads across Hollywood. Not long after the decision, actor George Murphy ran into Schreiber and asked him about Wasserman's sudden interest in the welfare of Democratic politicians.

"Taft," Murphy said, "last night I had a dream. I dreamed Bobby Kennedy called Lew and said, 'Lew, I've got about twelve or fourteen antitrust suits here against your company, and I think it's about time you became a Democratic fundraiser. . . .' "

"Let me stop you right there," Schreiber said. "It was tougher than that."

In all likelihood, though, by the early 1960s no one had to push Wasserman very hard into the political arena. It was a logical step. With his intervention in labor negotiations, his alliance with the Chandlers, Wasserman was already edging from Hollywood's shadows onto center stage. Once he completed his evolution from agent to studio head, he was ready to take his place at the head of the table. He moved to a nicer home above Sunset Boulevard, turned up at exclusive social events, even granted an occasional interview in which he dispensed oracular dissatisfaction with his colleagues' performance. "Once we took over the studio he was a different kind of person," said Gershwin, who was so close to Wasserman that he inherited his boss's old house when he moved into larger quarters. "He was kind of restricted as an agent, he didn't want the limelight, he felt that all that belonged to the client. As a studio executive he could be more free. He moved from one house to another. He started to display his wealth a little more. . . . And that goes for Mrs. Wasserman as well. They bought a house, they furnished it well, paintings—all of a sudden she became 'Mrs. Wasserman, studio head.' "

From a purely business perspective, the logic for an expanded political role was no less compelling. As a studio, as a diversified entertainment conglomerate, as the public company it became in 1959, MCA simply had more interests affected by the government than it did as a privately owned talent agency. If the Justice Department hadn't sued the company in 1962 and taught Wasserman the importance of powerful friends, something else would have come along to impress the lesson on him. Wasserman had Hollywood wired, but that was no longer enough to protect his interests. His ambitions left him vulnerable to larger forces. "Having a dynamic company he knew he had to get into politics," said Henshaw, the former MCA executive. "He knew he had to get into politics to have juice. They had to have juice."

All this Wasserman understood. So he was more than gracious, more than receptive, when an emissary from the Democratic party flew out to meet with him in early 1963 and suggested it was time for Hollywood's most powerful man to stand up and be counted for the president who had severed his empire.

Physically, the man who called on Lew Wasserman could not have differed more from the MCA chief: Arthur Krim was short and stocky, with a tendency toward roundness. But the two men shared a mental toughness, an unsentimental facility for calmly measuring their options behind eyes that revealed nothing. "There was a great resemblance in the way their brains operated," said Max Youngstein, the former United Artists executive. "It's what I call calculated flexibility."

In contrast to Wasserman's world, Krim grew up comfortably in Mount Vernon, New York; his father owned a prosperous chain of cafeterias. From an early age he was a precocious academic achiever: president of his high school graduating class, Phi Beta Kappa and head of the debating team at Columbia College, top of the class and editor of the *Law Review* at Columbia Law School. Graduating in the Depression year of 1932, Krim joined the New York law firm of Phillips, Nizer—the Nizer being celebrated trial attorney Louis Nizer. There he met another talented young attorney named Robert S. Benjamin, who had worked his way through City College and Fordham Law School and joined the firm one year before Krim. Both men continued their precocious achievements: within a few years each was a partner.

This ascent neither consumed their energies nor sated their ambitions. Phillips, Nizer represented a number of movie companies, and both of the firm's rising young men were drawn to that world. Maintaining his partnership at the law firm, Krim eventually became president of Eagle-Lion Films, Inc., a distinctive but low-budget production company formed by British filmmaker J. Arthur Rank and financier Robert R. Young. Benjamin, meanwhile, became president of the J. Arthur Rank Organization, Inc., general counsel at Eagle-Lion, and apparently still left with time on his hands after adding those responsibilities to the duties of a law-firm partner, a director at Universal.

Krim's first foray into the film business ended unhappily: after constant quarrels with Young, he resigned his post in 1949 and returned to the law firm. He was looking for a new opportunity in the movie industry when a friend suggested an unlikely one: management of United Artists. By 1950, when Krim began examining the prospect, United Artists was one of the industry's most venerable names—and most decrepit studios. Actually, it was an un-studio. The company was formed in 1919 by Charlie Chaplin, Mary Pickford, Douglas Fairbanks, and the legendary director D. W. Griffith—four artists united in their determination to control their own fates. Convinced that the studios were leaching the profits from their films with inflated overhead and distribution fees, they established the company as a no-frills distribution service for the films they intended to make through their own production companies.

Through the 1940s, United Artists attracted an array of talented producers and released some memorable films. But the founders clung to control of the company long after their increasingly rare contributions justified it, and they gradually but inexorably ran it into the ground. By 1951, with Pickford and Chaplin locked in a bitter feud, the company tottered on the edge of bankruptcy. Krim told Pickford as much; he offered her nothing for the corpus. Instead he offered a risky deal: if he and Benjamin could return the company to profitability within three years, they would be given half the stock for a nominal fee. The gamble paid off. The two men showed a profit within a year, and pocketed their half of United Artists. Within a few years they had bought out Chaplin and Pickford, taken the company public, and become very wealthy.

They did so not only by picking good movies but by understanding the changing economics of the business. At a time when the studios were desperately trying to unload fixed assets—from the lots to the stars who swaggered through them—United Artists was, by tradition, free of those encumbrances. It was, in fact, as Krim and Benjamin shrewdly realized, extraordinarily well placed to capitalize on the new dynamics of filmmaking. Like Wasserman at MCA, Krim and Benjamin made the changes that were tearing apart the studios work for them.

All across Hollywood, actors, writers, and producers were now free agents, no longer tethered to the studios or sheltered by them. Krim and Benjamin lured them to United Artists with two formidable attractions: more opportunity to participate in the profit generated by their work, and more freedom to produce it. Eventually all this would become standard in Hollywood, but in its time, it was a revolution. Under Krim and Benjamin, the un-studio, like the old studios in their heyday, made movies that were not only profitable but also artistically rewarding. Its films were topical, intelligent, worldly—Academy Award winners such as *West Side Story, The Apartment,* and *Tom Jones.*

Krim, who took the title of president, and Benjamin, who became chairman of the board, worked together like interchangeable parts. They drew the same salary, often sat for interviews together, and before the other executives rarely, if ever, disagreed. Their personalities were, in fact, quite different—Benjamin warmer, more open to enthusiasms, less abrasive and intense than his fastidious partner—but they had worked together for so long that their thoughts seemed intertwined. Their likemindedness extended to politics. It was Benjamin who first brought Krim into the national arena. An ardent liberal whose heroes were Franklin and Eleanor Roosevelt, Benjamin participated enthusiastically in the 1956 Adlai Stevenson campaign and then plunged into New York reform politics, aligning with Mrs. Roosevelt and Herbert H. Lehman against party boss Carmine G. DeSapio. Krim, whose political views mirrored his partner's, first joined Benjamin during the effort to win a third nomination for Stevenson in 1960. Once Kennedy won the nomination, Benjamin assumed a major role in the nominee's New York State fundraising. Once again, he brought along his partner. Krim, who had previously raised money only for charitable causes, served as chairman for the campaign's final event, an Election Night fundraiser that broke up at 3 A.M. not knowing whether Kennedy had won.

At first, Benjamin was closer to Kennedy's team. But his involvement in the United Nations Association, formed to promote support for the institution, moved him away from partisan politics. That allowed Krim's own talents to emerge. Kennedy's men—who did not have the senior executives of many American companies beseeching them for opportunities to assist the president—realized that Krim too was an unusual asset, and systematically brought him into Kennedy's orbit. Drawn to the larger stage, Krim responded without much prodding. The White House arranged for Krim to attend an Army-Navy football game with Kennedy; that gave the movie executive his first chance to talk privately with the president. Kennedy had his usual effect: Krim went home to New York entranced.

Soon thereafter, using pollster Louis Harris as the intermediary, the White House asked Krim to co-chair a fundraiser for the president the next spring in New York. Krim enthusiastically agreed, and helped to organize a full day of activities built around the president's birthday: a lunch at his beautiful East Side town home for fifty major fundraisers; dinner with nearly four hundred individual $1,000 contributors at the Four Seasons restaurant; and then finally the huge rally at Madison Square Garden, where the president sat puffing a cigar in an overstuffed chair while a thunderstorm lashed the city outside and Marilyn Monroe stunned the crowd with her birthday greeting. Later that evening, the donors, and the president, and the president's men, and the stars who had assembled to honor him all retreated to Krim's home for a party that lasted until the sun rose the next morning. When the receipts from the day's activities were counted, the White House realized that a star was rising too: overall, Krim's labors produced an eye-opening $1 million.

This lucrative success inspired JFK's advisers to grander ambitions. Krim emerged in their eyes as the tool for a larger political purpose—strengthening the president's hand over the unruly assemblage of fiefdoms that characterized the party he ostensibly headed. While recruiting Krim for the New York events, Larry O'Brien, Kenneth O'Donnell, and party fundraiser Richard Maguire explained to him the problem. In 1960, they told Krim, the Kennedy campaign, following tradition, depended largely on local fundraising by Democratic organizations around the country. But much of that money never found its way into their cause. Inevitably, the local organizations, with their own agendas and priorities, used it for their own ends. This too was traditional.

To end that dependence, Kennedy's advisers hoped to establish an independent fundraising operation controlled by the White House that would provide Kennedy with the resources to make contributions to members of Congress who supported his program. The remarkable results in New York convinced them that such an operation could be organized on a national basis, and that the very eager, very talented Arthur Krim was the logical choice to direct it. Krim jumped at the assignment. Thus was born the President's Club.

It was, by intent, an ostentatiously exclusive club. Membership cost $1,000. Details of the club's operations were kept hidden from the press. Its events were closed to the public. For their contributions, members received special briefings from cabinet members, a gold-engraved membership card, an opportunity to meet the president at fundraising dinners, and above all, through those momentary flashes of artificial intimacy with power, a chance to declare themselves part of their community's political elite, to casually drop into conversation at the office what the secretary of state or the president himself had casually told them just the night before.

The club was an immediate success, a pathbreaking innovation. The

President's Club seeded fundamental changes in fundraising, particularly in presidential races. It reflected an explicit awareness that the growing costs of campaigns forced officials to seek out donors throughout their terms, not just in the weeks before Election Day. Its $1,000 givers were often disparaged as fat cats out of place in the party of Jefferson and Jackson, and for the Democrats the pursuit of such contributions did represent a new focus on relatively large donors. But the President's Club's $1,000 men were, in fact, an alternative to dependence on a few very large givers. Even as the parties demanded larger contributions from the well-to-do, the rising cost meant the base had to be spread.

The President's Club also reflected a subtle but pivotal shift in the way political money was collected. Prior to the club, as Kennedy's men explained to Krim, national candidates typically depended on transfers from local party organizations. But the club money went straight to Washington, circumventing the local organization. The President's Club nationalized fundraising. This itself was an epochal shift of political power. But the President's Club circumvented the local organizations in another respect, less tangible though no less telling. Not only was its money collected outside the party structure, it was also raised on the basis of personal loyalty to the president, not necessarily to the party. As far as the club was concerned, the president stood independent of the party. In that sense, the President's Club foreshadowed and reinforced the political atomization—the tendency of voters and donors to measure candidates solely as individuals, not as representatives of competing parties or ideologies—that has come to dominate elections in the television era.

Not all these considerations were on Krim's mind as he set out to build the club. He simply knew that the president's men had asked him to provide a war chest and that he intended to provide it. He began his operations in his home base of New York. Almost immediately, he expanded his efforts to California. For the pillar of his California club, Krim needed someone diligent enough to search out new money and strong enough to work with the contentious local Democratic establishment while maintaining his independence from it. Arthur Krim knew one man in Los Angeles who matched that description, and in Lew Wasserman he found an eager recruit for his new enterprise.

Lew Wasserman emerged as a national political force on the evening of June 7, 1963, when he cosponsored a $1,000-a-plate President's Club dinner for John F. Kennedy at the Beverly Hilton hotel. Wasserman's arrival in turn heralded an even larger political development: the concurrent awakening of Southern California as a major source of money for Democratic causes.

California played only a marginal role in national political fundraising through the 1950s. Despite the state's exploding population and enormous wealth, it exported little money to the national contests between the parties; more often, the parties had to provide infusions of cash to run their California political operations during presidential campaigns. For Democrats, the situation was particularly bleak. At least Eisenhower squeezed some cash out of Republican Hollywood and the downtown Los Angeles business establishment. But almost immediately upon Franklin Roosevelt's death, California reverted into a financial desert for Democrats. To the extent a California Democratic financial organization existed, it was in the north, centered around a group of wealthy San Francisco businessmen. In Southern California, the situation, in the terse summation of Stanley Mosk, then the Democratic attorney general, was "chaos." To serious Democrats—those in the north—Southern California was a lushly appointed playpen, the preserve of undeniably wealthy but fatally idiosyncratic liberals who preferred feuding with one other and fantasizing about an ideal world to the hard business of electing officials. There was money in Southern California, but through the 1950s it was overwhelmingly conservative and Republican, venerable Chandler money, burgeoning aerospace money, musty Pasadena money.

Once Democrat Edmund G. (Pat) Brown won the statehouse in 1958 and Kennedy took the White House two years later, the Democrats felt the first drops at drought's end. Now the California Democrats had something more than promises to offer donors: access to power. What the party still needed was someone who could systematically work that asset. It found the man in 1962 when Brown engineered the election as state Democratic party chairman of a young, relatively unknown Beverly Hills lawyer named Eugene L. Wyman. In Wyman, husband of Democratic activist and Los Angeles City Councilwoman Rosalind Wyman, the state Democrats had an ambitious, ingenious, and dogged fundraiser willing to deal more aggressively than any chairman before him. People always wanted something from the governor: a savings and loan charter, a job, an invitation to the inaugural ball. It was Wyman's genius to transmute those ephemeral desires into spendable political cash. The word on the street was that Wyman never forgot who gave, that a donor could always find a sympathetic ear for his problems in Sacramento; and that, conversely, Wyman never forgot who refused him, and the price of his enmity was high. His approach was later summarized straightforwardly in an internal White House memo as "going to individuals and corporations who had something of interest in the state government." For California Democrats, with their traditions of genteel ineptitude and noble failure, it was a new hardball world.

Wasserman, Hollywood's toughest operator, eased into this rugged environment as though he had been born to it. Krim was a man he could understand, Wyman was a man he could understand. Both Krim and Wyman had strong personal ties to the entertainment industry, but both, in turn, understood their limitations. From Wasserman, each wanted the same thing: access to the riches he could unlock in Hollywood. And from each of them Wasserman sought access, a chance to plug into the currents of political power they had already tapped. These were relationships that could and would endure, for they were built on an understanding deeper than friendship.

The cultivation of Lew Wasserman bore its first full fruit in the 1964 Johnson campaign. Wyman ran the overall California fundraising effort, but Wasserman was the powerful new ingredient. "He was not, in the early 1960s, the principal fundraiser . . . but starting in 1964 Lew became the key guy," said former Johnson aide Lloyd Hand, who had settled in Los Angeles and joined the state campaign's inner circle. Together Wasserman and Wyman collected huge sums, more than California had ever produced for a Democrat. California provided more than five hundred members of the President's Club, more than the president's home state of Texas, and second only to Krim's fecund New York operation. Suddenly, distant California was not only covering its own needs but channeling rivers of money back East; on one day in August 1964, Wasserman's President's Club operation sent a check for $155,000 to the campaign headquarters. Wasserman reached down deeply himself: by Election Day he had personally contributed at least $28,000 to Democratic campaigns—more than Krim, more than Benjamin, more than Bart Lytton, more than all but fourteen other donors to either party. Nor was that all: in the midst of his work for Johnson, Wasserman found time to chair the finance committee for the unsuccessful Democratic senatorial candidate, former White House Press Secretary Pierre Salinger.

This was as splashy a debut as Hollywood had seen since David O. Selznick commandeered downtown Atlanta to unveil *Gone with the Wind.* Still, Johnson's White House didn't realize immediately how useful an ally it had unearthed. At first, Wasserman was hardly an intimate of the president: after he cosponsored a successful June 1964 fundraiser for Johnson, the White House letter of thanks was returned because it was sent to the wrong address. But Wasserman's skill was apparent to the men who worked most closely with him. After the campaign, Hand sought him out for a larger role. Since returning to California in 1961, Hand had functioned as Johnson's unofficial political ambassador, passing on news, representing his interests in local struggles. Now, with the campaign completed, Hand planned to move back to Washington to join the administration. He asked Wasserman to succeed him as Johnson's eyes in California. Wasserman said, "I'd like that," and so the two men flew back to Washington to allow the new president to size up his new ambassador to the coast. Wasserman liked what he saw, and so did Johnson. "He really did then become kind of the key contact," said Hand.

Wasserman actually displayed little interest in the traditional perquisites of such a position. He had relatively little contact with Lyndon Johnson, though White House aides insist Johnson respected him. According to Valenti, Johnson offered Wasserman the position of commerce secretary, not a first-tier job, perhaps, but still a respected place at the Cabinet table; Wasserman preferred to stay at MCA. Political operatives around Johnson saw Wasserman as the rare man who didn't want to ride in the president's limousine—he was satisfied to know that the president recognized his contributions, and he understood that the subtle power that derived from the perception of friendship with the president did not depend on showy public displays of affection.

Everything about Wasserman's relationship with the Johnson White House was carefully calibrated. Wasserman was a source of political intelligence to the White House, particularly Jack Valenti, who courted Wasserman, even as Wasserman courted him. Wasserman corresponded regularly with Valenti, one of Johnson's closest aides, and offered him the use of his home in Palm Springs as early as July 1964. (Two years later, Wasserman, Krim, and Ed Weisl convinced Valenti to leave the White House and become president of the Motion Picture Association of America.) And Wasserman maintained firm control of the President's Club in Southern California, which provided a steady stream of revenue for the national operation. By 1967, an internal White House assessment of the California political scene counted as the major accomplishment of the past several years "the development of a substantial base for political contributions in Southern California." No one except Wyman could claim more of that credit than Wasserman.

In the disorienting maelstrom of California politics, Wasserman kept his balance. Loyal to the president, he played the role Krim intended, both close to the state Democratic establishment and apart from it. Though the press often referred to Wasserman as part of Wyman's fund-raising network, insiders understood that he retained his independence.

"Wasserman was not just [Paul] Ziffren's guy, or later Wyman's guy," said Fred Dutton, the veteran Democratic operative. "Wasserman was always his own guy, from the very beginning." In the lengthy internal White House political assessment of the state prepared in 1967, Wasserman was treated as one of California's few "lone wolves" not controlled by any of the local party's querulous factions.

Politicians came to respect Wasserman as a man who could raise money smoothly and reliably. Unlike Jack Warner, who hectored and commanded, Wasserman didn't pressure his own employees to give— though he certainly made those of like mind aware of impending fund-raisers. He managed the details of fundraising affairs, looking after the food, the entertainment, the program. At a Wasserman event, all the small touches were right. After a large fundraising dinner for Lyndon Johnson in 1967, he wrote the president's daughter Lynda to ensure she knew that the huge floral arrangements from the affair were donated to local hospitals. Wasserman produced what he promised. "If it was supposed to be $200,000 for a fundraiser, you'd show up and it wouldn't be $203,000 or $197,000, it was $200,000," said Washington attorney Robert S. Strauss, former chairman of the Democratic National Committee and now a member of the MCA board. Wasserman's control over events was so complete, his organization so meticulous, that politicians called them "turnkey" affairs. Once when Wasserman was organizing a fundraising dinner for the DNC, party chairman John White came to see him at his home. "What do you want me to do?" White asked. "Just show up," Wasserman said.

Wasserman could not only command money from every cranny of Hollywood, but he could reach beyond the gilded ghetto. That was crucial because Hollywood itself, with such exceptions as the final Franklin Roosevelt race and the 1952 Eisenhower campaign, did not routinely provide very large sums for candidates until the 1970s. (Even as Southern California greatly increased its contributions in 1964, the White House still considered the film business relatively barren terrain; national Republicans through the 1960s looked less to the studios than to the conservative downtown business establishment.) Wasserman had ties everywhere: to the business elite, throughout the Jewish community, to more shadowy powers. Wasserman was, by his own admission, extremely close to attorney Sidney Korshak, a behind-the-scenes Democratic party power and "fixer" in Hollywood labor disputes described in one Justice Department report as perhaps "the most significant link in the relationship between the crime syndicate, politics, labor and management."

Exactly how their relationship began is unclear. But Wasserman was perceived as being so friendly with Korshak that Hugh Hefner once paid the attorney $50,000 merely to arrange a meeting with Wasserman, who had filed a copyright lawsuit against Hefner for reproducing Universal films in his private library. Wasserman denied any knowledge of allegations about Korshak—"I've never seen him with a so-called syndicate member or organization member," he told two *New York Times* reporters researching a series on Korshak's links to organized crime. But in August 1976, just weeks after the *Times* published an exhaustive four-part series on the attorney's connections, Wasserman invited Korshak to an elite dinner he hosted for presidential nominee Jimmy Carter at his home.

Just as Sinatra's relationship with Sam Giancana cost him few friends in Hollywood, so Wasserman's ties with the nebulous Korshak, far from staining his reputation, only enhanced his mystique. It seemed to underline the point that no segment of society exceeded his reach. Each time Wasserman assembled a gathering on behalf of a politician, that conclusion was written in the room. "At a typical fundraiser at Lew's there would be an enormous cross section of powerful Southern Californians: aircraft industry people, retailers, writers, entertainers to be sure . . . heads of other studios, people who had some inherited wealth," said one former MCA executive. "Lew's grasp of who's who in California and his friendships with them are quite extraordinary, quite far-reaching. It was precisely the opposite of the old days, totally, totally the opposite."

In all, Wasserman's work for Lyndon Johnson was a remarkably sophisticated political performance. It put his name on the lips of the men who ran the Democratic party; even more telling was its impact in Hollywood. Wasserman became the political role model for the men and women who succeeded the moguls, and the men and women who succeeded them. Krim demonstrated many of the same political skills. But he was in New York, removed from daily Hollywood life. It was Wasserman, more than any other individual in modern Hollywood, who both established the expectation that movie executives would cultivate friendships with politicians, and demonstrated how to do so.

If Krim did not affect Hollywood as dramatically as Wasserman, the New Yorker moved much closer to the heart of power in Washington. Gradually, Krim achieved a durable friendship with Kennedy. A prodigious reader, a man of diverse interests and experiences, Krim saw himself as more than a fundraiser, but he shouldered without complaint the task the president assigned him. He moved deeply enough into the inner circle to participate in the one meeting Kennedy's advisers convened to launch plans for the 1964 reelection. With each step deeper into Washington, Krim saw a virtually limitless world unfolding before him. Beckoning beyond his immediate responsibilities were opportunities to influence policy on the issues that excited him: civil rights, education, health, Israel. It seemed to him nothing less than the opportunity for a new life.

Then, in a moment, it all vanished. Kennedy's assassination devastated Krim. Disconsolate, and convinced that he could not raise money as effectively for a president he barely knew, he suggested to Bill Moyers that Johnson's old friend Ed Weisl assume control of the President's Club. Weisl thought Krim should stay in the post. He arranged for Krim to meet Johnson at the White House—and thus launched one of the most remarkable relationships in the long interaction between the film world and politics.

Johnson convinced Krim to remain in control of the President's Club. Under Johnson, whose ties to business greatly exceeded Kennedy's, the President's Club grew dramatically. So did Krim's involvement in national affairs. With Johnson, Krim developed the kind of relationship he had hoped to build with Kennedy. More than a fundraiser or political strategist, he became a trusted friend, a sounding board, and counselor on the entire array of concerns facing the president, from personal problems to world affairs. "During the last two years of Johnson's presidency, from 1966 to 1968, there was no single person in or out of the government who had greater influence on Johnson and in whom Johnson reposed greater trust than Krim," said Valenti. "He had a vast and limitless respect for Krim's judgment."

With that ringing declaration, Valenti may have slightly indulged his characteristic bent toward hyperbole. But Krim was, from any angle, unquestionably among the president's most intimate advisers: Krim, who was Jewish, became so close to Johnson that he sometimes attended church with him. To Doris Kearns Goodwin, the historian who worked for Johnson, Krim was "one of the half-dozen closest friends Johnson had at the end of his life." The president offered Krim Cabinet posts, the position as UN ambassador; Krim preferred what amounted to an internal ambassadorship without portfolio. (In the administration's final months, he accepted an honorific appointment as "special consultant" to the president.) Krim's influence transcended his industry; unlike Wasserman's, his political involvement was not fundamentally rooted in his company's needs. In fact, Krim made it a point never to raise industry concerns in the White House; as one White House aide put it, "he didn't carry the brief for the movie industry."

Krim became a familiar figure at the president's side. "I am always cheered," Johnson wrote Krim early in his term, "when there is a Krim around." When he came to Washington, Krim typically spent the night in the White House. With his wife, Mathilde, a cancer researcher, Krim even built a home near Johnson's ranch outside Austin; the two men bought a helicopter together to traverse the hill country. In the last year of Johnson's presidency, Krim saw or spoke with the president on at least 151 different days; he vacationed with him at his ranch in Texas twelve times; he had dinner with him eleven times in just the month before Johnson decided not to seek reelection. Few Cabinet officers had as much contact with their chief executive; for a private citizen to spend so much time with a sitting president is almost unimaginable.

Far more than Kennedy, Johnson also took a personal interest in Krim's fundraising work. Intensely competitive and irremediably insecure, Johnson considered it a personal challenge to break the fundraising records Kennedy set. "That was something he could measure and he liked," said James R. Jones, a top White House aide and later a congressman from Oklahoma. Johnson accordingly gave Krim total support. When Treasury Secretary Henry H. Fowler balked at appearing before a President's Club function because he had been told earlier to stay away from partisan fundraising, Johnson wiped out the instructions with a decisive scrawl. "By all means" tell Fowler to go, he instructed aide Jake Jacobsen—and, the president added, have him "get all of his friends to go."

Above all, Johnson prized Krim's discretion. Johnson favored aides who kept themselves out of the news—"your effectiveness was disproportionate to the amount of press you got," said Jones—and Krim fanatically shielded himself from the spotlight. When the *New York Times* sought him out for a profile, he advised White House Press Secretary George Christian that he planned to duck the reporter, reasoning that "his effectiveness would be destroyed if he ever gets into major stories about his political activities." Given his closeness to the president and his constant presence at the White House, Krim's efforts were surprisingly effective: as Valenti observed, "No inkling of his influential role in the White House ever surfaced."

Even within the government, Krim's discretion was impregnable. In the capital of ego, he was mild, unobtrusive, self-contained. "You would never know from seeing Arthur Krim the amount of wealth he had or power or people that he knew," said Jones. "He was a very self-effacing person. . . . He didn't initiate a whole lot of conversation." Krim was proud of his position, and quick to take offense at any perceived slights. But he rarely tried to assert himself with other officials in the government. On most issues, he kept his views hidden from all but his friend in the

Oval Office. To this day, both former National Security Adviser Walt W. Rostow and former Defense Secretary Clark Clifford are not certain how Krim viewed the war in Vietnam. (Privately, Krim has described himself as an opponent of the war; that would not be surprising, given his views on other issues. But the evidence in the LBJ Library is inconclusive. Krim generally applauded Johnson's efforts in his correspondence with the president, though he also relayed the concerns of staunch Democrats around the country.) "The president wanted Arthur Krim's private judgment," said Clifford—and he kept his judgments private.

That made Krim's influence difficult to assess, even for the president's other advisers. Jones thought Krim appealed to Johnson precisely because he didn't carry "any particular agenda" and, more like a friend than an aide, "sort of sensed where Johnson was going and basically supported it." Rostow considered it not Krim's "style . . . to lobby" the president, even privately. "I would have a guess that Arthur would be rather circumspect and reserved in trying to push his view," he said. But Valenti thought Krim was an important advocate for the Great Society's core domestic agenda—poverty, health, education. Just by virtue of his commitment to those issues and the sheer number of hours he spent with the president, he virtually had to be.

In political matters, Johnson's reliance on Krim was unquestionable. Unnerved by the huge party debt still lingering from the 1964 campaign, Johnson asked Krim to take over the fundraising at the Democratic National Committee in spring 1966; by the end of the year Krim had reduced the debt by two-thirds. Through 1966 and 1967, Krim traveled exhaustively, continuing to build the President's Club and laying the groundwork for what he expected to be Johnson's 1968 reelection campaign.

Although Krim expected another campaign, he wasn't sure. He was actually among the first to know that Johnson might not run again. Johnson told Krim as early as fall 1965 that he did not plan to seek another term; two years later, during a long talk around Thanksgiving, he bluntly repeated the message. And yet, for all his insistence, the president gave Krim every sign that he was running. Just days after his Thanksgiving talk with Krim, he dispatched the movie executive with Democratic operatives Larry O'Brien and James Rowe to organize his supporters in New York against the expected challenge from New York Senator Robert F. Kennedy. Johnson insisted he was stepping down . . . and yet he took great interest in the polls that Krim commissioned in California and in large cities, and in the results that his friend wheedled out of Gallup and Harris. Krim was understandably bewildered. Why would a man leaving office respond as readily as Johnson did when Krim proposed to bring a group of prominent supporters down to his ranch in Texas for a weekend of stroking in April?

Krim read these signs and concluded that Johnson wanted another term, even if he wasn't ready to tell anyone. He plowed ahead. He fastened the bulwarks of his financial operation: Wasserman—a reliable "team man" in Krim's eyes—signed on again to head the California fundraising with Ed Pauley. On January 3, 1968, Krim sent the White House a detailed financial plan for the campaign, proposing seven major fundraising dinners with the president at which he expected to raise between $11 and $12 million. Just over a month later, Jones told Krim the president had approved the schedule.

It was now mid-February, less than a month before the first primary in New Hampshire. When the results from that contest came in on March 12, Johnson, whatever his earlier ambivalence, sensed the final act impending. Minnesota Senator Eugene J. McCarthy, basing his campaign solely on opposition to the Vietnam War, held the president to less than 50 percent of the vote. The signal was unequivocal; blood was in the water. Robert Kennedy entered the hunt a few days later.

Still Krim rushed on; convinced that a sitting president could be bloodied, perhaps, but not dethroned, he gathered ammunition for the protracted fight he thought lay ahead. On March 21, he rallied forty of the faithful at a President's Club luncheon in New York. The next night, over dinner at the White House, Krim briefed Johnson on the political situation in New York. The next night, Krim stayed over at the White House; the day after that he conferred over lunch with the president. Two days later, back in New York, he spoke with the president twice on the phone.

Krim returned to Washington on Saturday, March 30, joining Johnson for dinner with a group of Texans. The next morning, the president greeted his wife and daughter Lynda, and then, before speaking with anyone else, told the White House operator he wanted "to talk to Mr. Krim as soon as she heard from him." To the last hour, Krim was still lining up financial commitments; early that Sunday afternoon he spoke with Bob Strauss about assuming responsibility for fundraising in the Southwest. Then came the call Krim had dreaded for months. By early afternoon he was sitting with Lady Bird, the president's daughter Luci, and her husband, listening to Johnson read the draft of the speech he planned to deliver that evening on national television announcing his withdrawal from the race. Through lunch, with the same group and former aide Horace Busby, who had drafted the text, Krim carried the case against the decision. With the president's family offering silent encouragement, Krim argued that of all the men seeking the office only Johnson had the capacity to complete the programs he had begun. Johnson listened unpersuaded; the decision stood.

Just before 7 P.M., Krim and his wife returned to the Oval Office for another try. Johnson listened to their appeal, then sent the first two pages of the speech to the teleprompter. Still Krim was not through. Finally, while technicians set up the cameras for the 9 P.M. speech and Johnson stood in his bedroom putting on his suit jacket, Krim came to the president one last time. He had no more complex arguments, no more political calculations, only stubborn hope, and little of that. "Your friends outside hope you will reconsider," he told Johnson, his voice heavy and earnest. Johnson looked at his old friend, softly told him the decision was made, and walked into the Oval Office to end his political career.

When Johnson finished, the phones started to ring: Chicago Mayor Richard Daley, Texas Governor John Connally, George Reedy, former press secretary Bill Moyers, Supreme Court Justice Abe Fortas, Nelson Rockefeller. People gathered upstairs. At 11 P.M., Johnson went into the Yellow Room to meet the press, and then a group of friends and family moved back to the West Hall to console each other. Johnson watched the news accounts of his speech. Grimly jovial, as if at a wake, he joked with his long-faced friends. "I may have to learn to drive that helicopter now," he told Krim. As the evening wore into early Monday morning, the crowd drifted away. Clark Clifford left. Jim Jones and George Christian left. At 1 A.M., when the president finally went to bed, everyone had left the White House except his family, and the Krims, who might as well have been.

The Diffusion of Power

In Hollywood political circles, Krim's disappointment was narrowly shared. In anticipation of the campaign, Wyman and Wasserman had rallied most of the Democratic financial establishment behind the president. Few of their big givers defected. But they were no longer the only force in the community. Opposition to the Vietnam War called forth new sources of money that fueled the challenges of McCarthy and Robert F. Kennedy, and in those quarters the news that crushed Krim and surprised Wasserman only lifted hearts.

After Johnson withdrew, most of the party's barons—the local officials, the county chairmen, the old-line fundraisers like Wyman and Wasserman—aligned behind Vice-President Hubert H. Humphrey. Their support was enough to secure him the nomination over the ethereal McCarthy, once an assassin eliminated Kennedy's challenge. Among the faithful, Humphrey's cause stirred great passion—in the final weeks of the unsuccessful fall campaign against Richard M. Nixon, Wasserman loaned Humphrey's campaign almost a quarter of a million dollars that was never repaid. (That was after contributing over $54,000 to Humphrey and other Democratic campaigns that year.)

But in Southern California (as in much of the nation) the insurgents of the McCarthy and Robert Kennedy campaigns joined Humphrey with little enthusiasm, or stayed aloof from him altogether. Calls from Wasserman and Wyman did not move them. They did not aspire to be accepted into the financial establishment the two men had so laboriously erected over the previous decade. Instead, the insurgents gradually formed their own counterestablishment, a loose political confederation that came to be known as the Malibu Mafia.

The Malibu Mafia represented a direct challenge to the orderly Wasserman-Wyman brand of politics that dominated Hollywood and Southern California fundraising through the 1960s. For that wing of the Democratic party, the Malibu Mafia's approach to raising and spending money was both new and threatening. It was not the fuzzy, otherworldly giving— the penance for living so well—that had motivated much of liberal Hollywood since the days of the Popular Front. But neither was it the pragmatic, centrist deal-making that characterized the Wasserman and Wyman approach.

With the polarizing struggle over Vietnam providing the current, the Malibu Mafia instead revived ideology as a fundraising force in Hollywood and the surrounding liberal community. This was their lasting significance. Their politics was aimed not at making friends but at advancing causes. Wasserman, Wyman, and the rest of the liberal Southern California financial establishment erected under Kennedy and Johnson could swallow whatever private doubts they held about the war and support their party's nominee. The Malibu Mafia felt no such fealty. Their gripe was at least as much with the Democratic establishment as with conservatives.

They could afford independence. The Malibu Mafia was an affluent, confident, even glittering group. Several of the pillars came from the entertainment industry; but reflecting the modern mold of Hollywood money politics, they were allied with an equal number of businessmen unconnected to the movies. The group's membership was always a loose matter, but it centered around roughly half a dozen friends, several of whom lived in the exclusive Malibu Colony: economist and philanthropist

Stanley K. Sheinbaum (who was linked to Hollywood through his wife, Betty, the daughter of Harry Warner); producer Norman Lear, father of "All in the Family" and its successors in a line of acerbically contemporary situation comedies; businessman and lawyer Miles L. Rubin; Ted Ashley, chairman of Warner Bros.; industrialists Max Palevsky, who made a fortune selling his computer company to Xerox in 1969 and later dabbled in movie production, Harold Willens, who made his money through textiles and real estate investments, and Leopold S. Wyler, chairman of TRE Corporation, a diversified manufacturer based in Beverly Hills. Around the edges were others: actors Warren Beatty and Paul Newman and businessman Victor H. Palmieri, who made his fortune reviving companies others had wrecked.

The Malibu Mafia was never a tightly organized political machine. It had no form, no chair, no agenda, no scheme, no plan. Friendships within the group varied; Lear, for one, insists he was "never social friends" with any of them except Sheinbaum; Palevsky stormed in and out of alliance with the others. Its members, Willens recalled, "could meet twice a week or not for eighteen months." Ashley's analogy is the most apt: "It was no different than if you had six poker-playing pals and you got together whenever you could, but you didn't have a regular Wednesday night game."

Still, the group shared both goals and perspective. Several of them came into politics through the antiwar movement, and its edge and impatience shaped their approach. A regular speaker on the college teach-in circuit, Sheinbaum ran unsuccessfully for Congress as an antiwar candidate from Santa Barbara in 1966 and 1968. A few years later he made his mark in Los Angeles by spearheading the fundraising for Daniel Ellsberg's defense in the Pentagon Papers case. Willens formed an organization to mobilize businessmen against the Vietnam War and devoted virtually all his time to it for long periods; Palevsky was one of the organization's leading recruits in Southern California. Sheinbaum and Willens both contributed substantially to McCarthy's campaign in 1968 and Sheinbaum served as a McCarthy delegate; Newman campaigned energetically for McCarthy. Palevsky and Palmieri assisted in Robert F. Kennedy's campaign.

The 1968 presidential campaign had hinted at the new financial landscape in liberal Hollywood; the 1972 campaign mapped it. Wyman and the traditionalists rallied around either Senator Edmund S. Muskie or Humphrey. But their efforts were dwarfed by the new Southern California counterestablishment, which proved instrumental in the march of antiwar South Dakota Senator George S. McGovern to the nomination.

"They carried most of the early financial burden," said Frank Mankiewicz, codirector of McGovern's campaign. Palevsky was McGovern's most
important early contributor, making huge gifts and loans that bankrolled
the campaign's successful direct-mail operation; ultimately Palevsky contributed over $319,000 to the campaign, more than all but one other
donor. Rubin, who had not been previously involved in politics, was
another invaluable early recruit. Mankiewicz arranged for him to meet
McGovern at his Malibu home in late 1971. Rubin liked what he saw—
enough to put aside his business and move to New Hampshire for several
weeks to help organize McGovern's phone-canvass operation for the
crucial first primary there.

After the New Hampshire campaign, Rubin agreed to run McGovern's
primary campaign in California. Rubin proposed to build a grassroots
organization across the huge state, much as McGovern had in tiny New
Hampshire. The goal was ambitious, the cost enormous: Rubin calculated that he would have to raise at least $2.5 million. Palevsky came
through with more money, Rubin himself made large contributions, and
Beatty helped by pulling together a rock concert in Los Angeles—part of
a series of concerts he organized for McGovern around the country—that
provided another $300,000 for the treasury.

That wasn't nearly enough. Rubin had to find more money. He asked
Willens, who had raised money for the antiwar effort in Southern California, for names and systematically canvassed them. Throughout Hollywood and the Westside of Los Angeles, the veins of ideological antiwar
money unmined by Wasserman and Wyman were even richer than anyone had suspected. Willens gave a substantial contribution, and found
other big givers. Palmieri put in a large sum. So did Sheinbaum. To Fred
Dutton, a senior adviser in the McGovern campaign, it seemed as if
"Hollywood had turned on the faucets wide open." Rubin met his budget, McGovern toppled Humphrey in the crucial California primary, and
the wealthy Malibu liberals announced themselves as new powers on the
scene.

After the McGovern campaign, the Malibu group continued to work
together—often enough to become the dominant force in left-leaning
Southern California politics through the mid-1970s. Their prickly resistance to being grouped was gradually sanded away. "Once that catchy
phrase was thrust upon us," said Sheinbaum, "I think a self-conscious-
ness did appear where we did work together." Rarely was the entire
assemblage involved in any one project; even during the McGovern campaign, Lear and others had remained aloof. Rather, individuals within the
group informally came together in what Palmieri described as "a network

of shifting alliances." Just after the McGovern campaign, Sheinbaum as chairman and Lear as president revived the moribund American Civil Liberties Union Foundation of Southern California. In 1973, Palevsky took a leading role in Tom Bradley's election as Los Angeles mayor. Two years later, Palevsky, Willens, and Wyler joined forces behind Jimmy Carter. These were glory days: on Labor Day in 1975, Willens invited to his Malibu home Rubin, Sheinbaum, Paul Newman, and Wyler and by the end of the day the five had committed $500,000 to launch the Energy Action Committee, a lobbying organization they intended to use to battle big oil in the legislative wars over energy policy. This was guerrilla politics on a scale that Hollywood and its environs had not seen since the heyday of the Popular Front.

With the emergence of the Malibu Mafia, there was not one liberal financial power center in the entertainment industry but two; and then with the campaign finance reforms imposed after Watergate there were more. The historic amendments to the federal election law approved by Congress in 1974 reinforced the centrifugal trend in political fundraising that began in the 1960s. Rising costs had started it. Because campaign expenses mounted so fast during the 1960s, Krim and Wasserman and the other leading money collectors in both parties had to find many more medium-sized donors, even as they exacted larger contributions from the biggest givers. By itself, that broadening of the base diluted any individual's fundraising power. Then the influence of the Kennedy-Johnson Democratic financial establishment was diminished by the emergence of the insurgent money symbolized in Hollywood by the Malibu Mafia.* That diluted power again. If the leading political financiers were to meet

*Though it didn't affect Hollywood as directly, a parallel process took place in the Republican party during the 1960s. With the rise of Arizona's Barry Goldwater and then Ronald Reagan, there developed a conservative Sunbelt financial infrastructure independent of the moderate Eastern banking and Wall Street money that had long controlled the GOP. By the 1970s, this conservative insurgent money became the dominant financial force in the party. In Hollywood, though, GOP fundraising remained centralized in a few hands. As the Democratic base in Hollywood expanded in the 1970s through the infusion of ideological donors such as the Malibu Mafia, the GOP continued to rely primarily on givers motivated by corporate needs; other business interests in Southern California enlisted in the New Right, but in Hollywood that militantly conservative appeal made few inroads. In the film industry, the GOP continued to depend financially on the more traditional brand of business conservatives heading many of the major companies. In the 1972 campaign, for example, Nixon received six-figure contributions not only from MCA's Jules Stein and Taft Schreiber and from aging Jack Warner, but also from Ted Ashley, who broke from his Malibu Mafia colleagues, hoping to position himself for a possible government appointment with an incumbent who looked like a certain winner. Bob Hope was the lone star to make a major financial contribution to Nixon.

in a smoke-filled room somewhere, they would have needed far more chairs in 1972 than a decade earlier.

The campaign finance reforms accelerated this diffusion of political power with incalculable force. Responding to the huge contributions solicited by Nixon's 1972 reelection campaign (one supporter gave Nixon more than $2 million), Congress tried to cut the legs from under the big donors. It prohibited an individual from donating more than $1,000 to a primary or general election campaign and more than $25,000 annually to all federal candidates; at the same time it established public financing for the presidential general elections. No longer could a single individual carry a campaign, even for a brief time. Instead of a Wasserman making available $300,000 to Humphrey, or Palevsky giving a like amount to McGovern, to achieve equal impact each man would now have to find three hundred friends willing to donate the maximum $1,000. To meet their rising costs, every national campaign now needed thousands, tens of thousands, of donors, more than any had ever found. First dimly apparent in the activities of the President's Club, the new regimen of permanent fundraising was now enshrined in law. Under the new system, candidates were forced to unearth new sources of money constantly, and power shifted away from those who could write great checks toward those who could persuade great numbers of others to write checks. Paradoxically, after the passage of reforms to diminish money's influence, the quest for money increasingly consumed campaigns.

The demands of the new system made Hollywood a more important source of funds. Hollywood's attraction under the old rules had been its unusual concentration of very wealthy people capable of making huge donations; the problem had been that relatively few of them (especially stars) were willing to do so. Under the new system, Hollywood was even more alluringly positioned. In addition to its elite in Ferraris, Hollywood produced an extraordinary number of merely rich agents, writers, producers, and directors who got by with Porsches or BMWs. Wealth in Hollywood dripped into far more hands than in such previously critical money sources as the independent oil business—an industry divided between a few executives whose influence depended on the huge donations now barred and thousands of oil hands who had little to spare for politicians. Hollywood was a deep pool of money built to the demanding specifications of the new law.

The reform made Hollywood more attractive in another respect. Given the strict contribution limits, local supporters alone could no longer meet the steadily rising campaign costs. (The average Senate candidate spent more than six times as much in 1986 as 1974.) One way candidates filled in the gaps was by accepting donations from labor and business political action committees. Another was by intensifying their search for money outside their home states, as presidential candidates had done for decades. Legislators quickly learned that few communities cared enough about distant contests to send checks to them. Hollywood was one, and it had an advantage over almost any other. Unlike contributions from other centers of wealth—the oil patch, Wall Street—Hollywood money generally created no suspicion with voters, an important consideration under the new disclosure requirements. Though an occasional Hollywood contribution—from Jane Fonda, perhaps, or the producers of risqué movies—might send conservatives squawking, no candidates were jumped by Common Cause or Ralph Nader for stuffing their pockets in Brentwood and Bel-Air. It was lucre without odor. "Under disclosure, everybody can surgically remove the oil contributors and make a big deal out of it in the campaign," said veteran Democratic operative William A. Carrick. "Wall Street is a big risk . . . there's a lot more scrutiny from the public. This [Hollywood] money is the cleanest money you can take in politics." Far more than in the 1960s, these considerations made Hollywood an essential stop on the money hunt, particularly for Democrats.

Strangely, no one seized the opportunities created by the new laws more quickly than a group that had been among Hollywood's least politically engaged: rock stars and their managers. Since the law required the candidates to round up large numbers of small donors, several rock impresarios proposed to corral them through concerts. It wasn't an entirely new idea: Sinatra had performed for the Democrats through the 1960s, and Beatty had organized concerts for McGovern in 1972. But for presidential candidates, the reforms offered a new twist: federal matching funds for all contributions of $250 or less in the primaries. Theoretically, that doubled the value of every ticket sold.

That calculation made rock concerts, for a time, appear to be the ticket to financial success in the new era. In the 1976 presidential campaign, the first fought under the new rules, rock stars thundered through the primary states like long-haired cavalry, rescuing financially depleted contenders. Concerts by the Allman Brothers and their Southern rock confederates, the Marshall Tucker Band and Black Oak Arkansas, raised crucial early money for Jimmy Carter at a time when few donors took his campaign seriously. "Those concerts were very important to us when we didn't have any money, when we were desperate," said Patrick H. Caddell, Carter's pollster. "They were critical at that moment."

Much as he liked the money, Carter always looked incongruous stand-ing next to Gregg Allman, as though he was trying to remember to smile. His late-starting competitor for the 1976 nomination, California Gover-nor Edmund G. (Jerry) Brown, Jr., seemed more comfortable around the rock stars he attracted. Though almost fifteen years younger, Brown, a former seminarian, didn't know much more about the music than Carter did. But at some basic level he was more in tune with rock's irreverence; his minimalist, quirky appeal had a vague countercultural edge, a barely concealed smirk, as if his entire campaign, with its warnings against "easy answers" and improvised logistics, was a long "Saturday Night Live" sketch. No one was certain exactly what Brown represented, but it was clear he was not a politician who danced to the usual rhythms. Ascetic, iconoclastic, Delphic, Brown in 1976 was the beatnik as presidential candidate. It wasn't exactly the heart of rock and roll, but it was as close as any presidential contender had ever come. "Jerry was fun," said volu-ble Irving Azoff, at the time the manager for several arena-sized acts, including the Eagles and Dan Fogelberg, and later chairman of MCA's Music Entertainment Group. "You never knew when you were going to get a knock on your door at eleven or twelve at night, and it was Jerry, just wanting to hang. He was just a regular guy in those days. The guy definitely had a fix on life that was not a normal politician's fix on life. He was more our peer, more our age group."

Brown did not enter the 1976 contest until the primary season was almost over. He had no time to build a national fundraising base, so concerts filled much of the gap. Just before he entered the race, Brown met with Azoff and a small group of his clients—Linda Ronstadt, Glenn Frey and Don Henley from the Eagles—and asked them to help. A few days later, Azoff, Jeff Wald, another personal manager for top acts, and radio executive Paul Drew walked into the office of Brown's campaign manager, attorney Michael (Mickey) Kantor, and told him they wanted to put on a concert. Kantor wasn't sure what to make of them—he had never been to a rock concert in his life—but he sensed "there was something there" and told them to go ahead (while reserving the option of pulling the event from Brown's schedule if it didn't come together). Kantor had nothing to worry about. Together with Jackson Browne, Ronstadt and the Eagles put on a sold-out concert in Maryland's Capital Centre a few weeks later that raised more than $165,000; the huge publicity wave from the event helped carry Brown to a primary victory in the state. After that, the rockers put on three more events; in all they provided more than a quarter of Brown's contributions.

Once those grosses hit the front page, candidates with a sudden taste for California rock flooded Azoff's office. Soon he was organizing benefits for senators, congressmen, congressmen who wanted to be senators, and senators who wanted to be president. Brown began dating Linda Ronstadt. Politicians studied album liner notes. Journalists lionized the rock promoters as "the new fat cats." That proved overheated. Concerts became a lasting component of the money hunt, but they did not revolutionize it. Candidates discovered that the events took a lot of planning and were not guaranteed moneymakers. The Federal Election Commission complicated the task of receiving matching funds from concerts by requiring that everyone who bought a ticket fill out a card giving their name and address and certifying that they intended to make a political contribution; not everyone stumbling into an Eagles concert was in shape to provide the information. Not all candidates wanted to be photographed next to a rock star, particularly after Brown's romance with Ronstadt landed him in the tabloids; and not that many rock stars wanted to be photographed next to a politician. More high notes and soaring guitars couldn't keep Brown's second presidential campaign from crashing and burning in 1980. As time went on, the passion for partisan politics waned, and socially conscious rock stars—along with the indifferent friends they dragged with them to the microphone—shifted mostly into gargantuan good works, such as Live Aid and Farm Aid and Hands Across America.

Rock and roll, after all, wasn't the shortcut to filling campaign treasuries in the new system. There was none. As under the old rules, only more so, raising money required the hard work of individuals willing to devote their time and pressure their friends. Not everyone adapted to the new rigors. Denied the huge contributions that gave him voice, Max Palevsky, for one, gradually withdrew. But most of the Malibu Mafia adjusted, though the group never fully congealed into the force it might have been. On issues, the friends remained remarkably in tune. But their deliberations about candidates lacked the same cohesion. They never developed into a Kitchen Cabinet, like the conservative Southern California industrialists who united behind Ronald Reagan a decade earlier and systematically funded his rise to national prominence. Still fundamentally insurgents, many of them shied away from the kingmaker role, which smacked of the backroom traditions they had rebelled against. Alienated from the old establishment, they were ambivalent about forming a new one. "We would have the breakfasts with candidates coming out," looking for endorsements, Miles Rubin remembered, "but that never appealed to me . . . because it was too much like a cabal and we also started to suck in people who were looking for something, whatever that was, whether that was glory or an ambassadorship to some distant land."

Equally inhibiting was their inability to agree on candidates. They increasingly found themselves disappointed by all their options. The demanding ideological tests by which the group's members measured— and often failed—politicians was something new to Hollywood politics. It suggested both a new level of sophistication and critical analysis and a spreading sense of self-righteousness in the Hollywood left. Beneath the Malibu Mafia's selfless fervor for liberal causes rumbled a disturbing undercurrent—an unspoken feeling among several of these extraor- dinarily wealthy and isolated people that they were more reliable defend- ers of the progressive flame than the imperfect politicians who actually fought the fights. As more and more politicians desperate for campaign cash descended on liberal Hollywood through the 1980s, weariness and arrogance alike fertilized that sense of superiority. Eventually it would become as central to Hollywood politics as cocktails by the pool.

Over time, the Malibu Mafia found less common cause. Memories of the war receded, and the lines between the old and the new Democratic establishments in Hollywood blurred; in the 1980 presidential primaries, Carter, Brown, and Edward M. Kennedy all drew liberally from both camps. In 1979 most of the Malibu group united to form an organization called Democrats for Change, which took out newspaper ads urging the Democrats to dump Jimmy Carter in 1980. But they didn't agree on what to do next—Rubin worked hard for Ted Kennedy, Willens less so; Lear and Sheinbaum threw themselves into the third-party candidacy of Illi- nois Republican Representative John Anderson.

That split was revealing. The doyens of the Malibu Mafia remained ideologically compatible friends who occasionally found themselves al- lied, but their interests splintered. Even their luxurious homes held few rooms big enough to contain such combative personalities. "The group," said Willens, "began to move apart." Lear (with significant strategic assistance from Sheinbaum and financial help from several of the others) formed an organization, People For the American Way, to combat the political influence of religious fundamentalists. While slowly withdrawing from electoral fundraising, Sheinbaum continued to devote himself to an ever-lengthening array of liberal causes. Willens lost interest in electoral politics more quickly, and put his money and time into arms control activities. Rubin moved back East and lost touch with the others. So did Ashley, who resigned from Warner Bros. in 1980. Disillusioned, Palevsky, Palmieri, and Wyler drifted back to their business affairs.

The Malibu Mafia's rapid rise and sprawl was emblematic. The intermi- nable demands of the permanent campaign chewed up power brokers, exhausting their capacity or their interest or both. Concerts came into vogue and then suddenly went out; alliances formed and splintered; new fundraisers emerged and, like comets, burned across the sky for a season or two and then disappeared, burned-out and cynical, faded names with unlisted phone numbers. It was a world in which the only constant seemed to be change. But in Hollywood one man absorbed all the changes and bridged the decades.

The Last Mogul

Through it all, Lew Wasserman endured. With Gene Wyman's sudden death from an apparent heart attack in January 1973, Wasserman became Southern California's preeminent fundraiser, the man most prospecting politicians called on first, the leader of the financial establishment. His diversity of acquaintances made him as effective under the new campaign finance rules as his enormous personal wealth had under the old. His shrewdness entrenched his position. With his talent agent's eye, he sorted carefully through the petitioners who pressed against his door like so many aspiring starlets. He built a close relationship with Jerry Brown, who dominated California politics into the early 1980s. In the dim early months of the 1976 presidential campaign, when confusion still cloaked the field, Wasserman invested his prestige behind the obscure contender from Georgia; when Jimmy Carter won the White House, Wasserman's stock among his colleagues soared.*

His roots in the industry were deep enough to withstand changing political tides. Four years later, when the Malibu Mafia and many others in liberal Los Angeles defected, Wasserman put his shoulder behind Carter again (though MCA's Thom Mount worked closely with the Edward M. Kennedy campaign). Despite the enormous dissatisfaction with Carter's performance, it was enough; Wasserman efficiently rounded up checks. Terence R. McAuliffe, a young fundraiser in the Carter campaign, came out to Los Angeles to work with Wasserman and was amazed at the

---

*Even for Wasserman, Carter was actually a long-shot wager. Initially, according to one source, he doubted Carter had the strength of personality to win the White House. "Lew tells the story, or he told it to me, that when he first met Carter, he gave him a little function, a reception at his house," said John White, the DNC chairman under Carter. "Frankly, he just didn't see Carter [as a contender]. Here was this guy, almost shy—he had to move him around the room and introduce him to people. But [Wasserman's] wife said, 'He's going to be president, Lew' . . . and based on his wife's instincts he signed on." He also, typically, hedged his bets early: Wasserman made his first donation to Carter in 1974 but also made larger contributions that year to the nascent presidential campaigns of Senators Henry M. Jackson and Lloyd Bentsen.

impact of the MCA chief's name. "He was the biggest name you could get in fundraising to be helpful for you," McAulliffe remembered. "A lot of times when I would be trying to get other people committed on big events, whenever I said Lew Wasserman was chair it was like curtains opened up. It made a dramatic difference." For McAuliffe, sitting in Wasserman's office day after day was an education in the subtext of power. When Wasserman picked up the phone, there wasn't the cajoling and pressuring and pleading that usually characterizes fundraising calls. It wasn't necessary. "The great thing Lew had going," McAuliffe recalled, "is he had so much clout . . . he didn't have much conversation. He would call up and say, 'It's Lew Wasserman, we have Carter coming out. I want you to do a table, two tables, or some people, five tables.' The person on the other end just said, 'When do you want it?' With Lew it was a very quick call."

The obedient response testified to Wasserman's position within the industry, where he inspired equal parts of envy, admiration, and fear. It also reflected his unofficial status as Hollywood's ambassador to the outside world. Other Hollywood executives and producers, such as Lear and his Malibu Mafia colleagues, spoke to Washington on issues that concerned them; but they spoke as individuals, not for the industry. On matters that affected the business of moviemaking, from the mid-1960s through at least the early 1980s, Wasserman was the industry's unchallenged voice to power. "Lew became somewhat of a motion picture statesman, and in many instances, many instances, others deferred to him," said attorney Frank Rothman, a former law partner of Wyman's who became chairman and chief executive at MGM/UA in 1982. Wasserman assumed a similar role in Hollywood's internal politics. In many Hollywood labor negotiations, "The heads of the other companies just gave him carte blanche," said Michael Franklin, who sat across the table from Wasserman for thirty years as the executive director of first the writers' guild, and then the directors' guild. Other studio heads may have griped about Wasserman's eminence, particularly in labor negotiations, but none had the power to force him out. Nor, deep down, were they confident they could function without him; his ability to break knots made him indispensable. When negotiations collapsed in 1981 between the producers and directors over revenue-sharing on films sold to pay television, it was Wasserman who stepped in and found a deal. "When the silver-haired guy came into the room," said one of the directors' negotiators, "everyone in the room snapped to."

Two factors explained Wasserman's ascent to the very peak of Hollywood. Wasserman was the last of the major studio executives who still owned a significant share of his company; that gave him the freedom to maneuver that Mayer and Warner had enjoyed but that his contemporaries, however well paid, lacked.* With ownership came the second key: staying power. Aside from Arthur Krim, who had little interest in carrying the industry's case to the capital, Wasserman was the only top executive in the modern industry who remained in his chair decade after decade, good years and bad. At a time when constant change defined Hollywood, Wasserman was the rare anchor. His durability alone gave him credibility in Washington. To the senior men in Congress, Wasserman was more than a contemporary; he was a bridge to another era—Ted Kennedy often spoke of Wasserman as a link to the Hollywood his father had known. Once he had carefully and patiently constructed relationships with Washington's most powerful figures, his fellow studio heads, with neither the time nor inclination to learn the capital's rhythms, naturally deferred to his expertise. "In addition to the fact that he was a brilliant guy," said Mike Medavoy, an executive vice-president of Orion Pictures until 1990, when he joined Tri-Star Pictures as chairman, "he had the contacts."

Moreover, he had the interest. Politics never ceased to fascinate him. Wasserman defied the modern trend by remaining involved campaign after campaign. (Krim did too, but he was less visible in Hollywood after Johnson left office and Krim ceded his responsibility as the Democrats' chief fundraiser.)** Wasserman loved to talk about elections, spend time with politicians, measure the men who would succeed his friends Johnson and Carter. "More and more," said Irving Azoff, "that's his fun in life." Age did not diminish his appetite for political intrigue. Wasserman, said Senator Bentsen, "loves" political gossip, "he enjoys it absolutely." Visiting politicians were sometimes amazed at the personal attention he would

---

*Krim, who had enjoyed similar freedom through his substantial ownership of United Artists, arranged the sale of the company to Transamerica Corporation in 1967. Ten years later, unhappy with its management, he proposed to spin off from the conglomerate; when the company rejected the proposal, Krim and four other executives abruptly left United Artists to form Orion Pictures Corporation, a small but generally well-regarded studio. He remains chairman of the board at Orion.

**Krim nonetheless remained a major fundraiser for the Democratic National Committee through the 1970s. But he never again was as close to a national Democrat as he had been to President Johnson. He developed a friendship with Jimmy Carter once he won the presidency, but Krim actually remained neutral in both the 1976 and 1980 Democratic presidential primaries. (Acting as a unifying senior statesman, he did chair a major dinner that raised funds for both President Carter and Edward M. Kennedy after their battle for the nomination was over.) In 1983, Krim organized an early fundraiser in New York City for the presidential campaign of Walter F. Mondale. That was the last time in his remarkable career that Krim took primary responsibility for a political dinner. Though he remains close with many leading Democrats, he has withdrawn from active participation in campaigns.

devote to their concerns. Once a delegation of California congressmen drove out to MCA to recruit Wasserman's help on a ballot initiative. When they reached the entrance at MCA, they were stunned to see the company's chief executive standing in the guard station, awaiting their arrival. Wasserman personally directed them to the parking lot, walking beside their car. Then he led them into a private dining room and, while the company churned on outside the paneled walls, listened for two hours to their appeal, never once bringing in an aide or leaving the room to take a phone call. Wasserman had that rare negotiator's skill, an ability to make people believe he genuinely cared about them, that he sincerely wanted to solve their problems. "He was," said Franklin, the labor executive, "in the best sense of the word, a problem-solver, and he listened and he cared."

The forces that kept Wasserman politically engaged through the years were the same that initially connected him: pride and business, inextricably mixed. "The secret to Lew's life is complete and thorough integration," said one producer who knows him well. "As with everything else, those two ideas were completely integrated. Of course, it was in the best interest of the company [for Lew to be active in politics]. Lew wouldn't think of doing anything that wasn't in the best interest of the company. But the best interest of the company was largely Lew's self-interest as well. He loved being part of the framework of political power in this country."

At some level, he felt obligated to be part of it. With an uncharacteristic *Saturday Evening Post* earnestness, Wasserman sometimes lectured younger executives on the responsibilities that their affluence imposed on them to help the political process function. He took enormous pride in his political relationships. It meant a great deal to Wasserman to be recognized as the industry's de facto leader. Wasserman, who had persevered for decades, who had haggled with Warner and Mayer and Cohn, really had no peers in modern Hollywood, no buddies among the transitory and interchangeable faces that popped up in the executive suites, lasted a few seasons, and then disappeared back into vague independent production deals. His real peers were other power brokers, and he often seemed more relaxed in their company than he ever did at the studio. One young MCA executive saw Wasserman walk through the lot one afternoon with the late New York Senator Jacob K. Javits, laughing, giggling, trading jokes—and suddenly a light went on. "Now I get it," he thought, "there's his equal. That's his peer group."

But Wasserman's political relationships always encompassed more than personal gratification. In this too, Wasserman was very much the modern model: he taught his colleagues political hardball. If the Malibu Mafia and its descendants practiced the politics of ideology, Wasserman perfected the obverse. Under Wasserman's tutelage has emerged a generation of essentially nonideological senior studio executives who give shrewdly and dispassionately to senators and representatives in either party who support their industry's legislative interests. Like Wasserman, they usually let their personal political beliefs guide their participation in presidential politics; but they typically apply more tangible standards to legislators who come seeking help. It is an attitude toward politics typical of any major industry—hardheaded, pragmatic, built around securing influence—and for that reason alone it stands out in a community erected on emotion and fantasy.

As Wasserman led the studios into a more sophisticated era of political investment, senators and congressmen seeking Hollywood's help confronted two very different tests. To raise money from the increasingly ideological Hollywood liberals, a group largely indifferent to industry issues, legislators had to prove their purity on arms control, abortion, the environment, and Central America; to raise money from the increasingly calculating studio executives steeped in Wasserman's tradition, the key was a sympathetic ear and a position on a committee crucial to the industry's fortunes. (Since the fall of the moguls and the Kennedy-era realignment in Hollywood, the third group, of ideological conservatives and loyal Republicans, was much smaller.) The walls were porous; many individuals had ties to both the liberal and studio camps. Occasionally, the two sides united behind candidates—one was Ted Kennedy, an indefatigable defender of both liberal verities and studio interests. But their agendas remained distinct.

As if describing a sovereign nation, the liberals outside it sometimes referred to the studio segment of political Hollywood simply as the "Wasserman wing." It was a fitting term, for in Hollywood Wasserman defined this unsentimental politics. Through the years, Wasserman's ideology remained that of a moderate Democrat. But he never lost sight of his needs. Asked what motivated Wasserman, one U.S. representative who has worked closely with him ranked, in order, "business, personal relationships, and still, a mild tilt to the Democratic side."

From his first steps into politics, Wasserman always ensured that MCA maintained ties across the ideological spectrum. Wasserman generally bolstered the mainstream, establishment Democrats. Senior executive Jennings Lang, a man with a passion for modern art and new ideas, served as the company's ambassador to the left; when Hollywood organized a fundraising party for the defense fund of Daniel Ellsberg in the Pentagon Papers case, a party that drew three of the Beatles, it was in Lang's home that the congregation gathered. Later, Lang's role was inherited by Thom Mount, Sean Daniel, and other young executives. At the same time, Jules Stein and Taft Schreiber built close ties to the Republican party, working closely with Ronald Reagan and later Richard Nixon. No matter who sat behind the desk in the Oval Office, someone in MCA could reach him on the phone. "Wasserman always played things with enormous finesse," said Mount. "Lew would pick a more mainstream candidate that he would back, but he would never neglect the fringe candidates. He would always make them his friend, always keep an open line. There would always be someone close to Lew supporting that candidate."

On legislative matters, Wasserman worked closely with Jack Valenti, who represented the industry's cause in Washington. (Within the industry, it was widely believed that Wasserman disproportionately influenced the industry's chief lobbyist; as one other studio head put it, "the MPAA wagged to Lew's desires.") But Wasserman maintained independent relationships with key senators, including Republicans where necessary. To the industry's lobbying campaigns—its battles with the networks, its struggles with the directors over colorization, and the quiet work of bending tax law to profitable advantage—Wasserman added a valuable touch of class, of seniority and stability. He knew that the best political investments were those that were allowed to mature slowly into genuine friendships. Wasserman didn't spend much time in Washington, but he didn't have to. He didn't spend much time with congressional staff, but he didn't need to. Nor was he compelled to plead for a few minutes of time with a crucial senator. When a movie industry issue came before the Senate, Ted Kennedy, for one, routinely called Wasserman for his assessment.

"It's not a question of Lew coming hat in hand," said one former Democratic Senate aide. Wasserman could visit senior senators like Bentsen, the chairman of the Senate Finance Committee, whom he had known since the Johnson administration, and spend much of his time just socializing and sharing political intelligence; when he did casually raise industry concerns, it was not as a supplicant but as an ally in long-forgotten skirmishes. "He is effective when they have a concern because he has the entrée, he has established the friendships, and he has the confidence of people," said Bentsen. "He is extremely knowledgeable on the subject. He comes in totally without staff. And he doesn't have to go through [congressional] staff; he has relationships personally."

But this comfortable familiarity didn't mean Wasserman was soft; it really meant the opposite. By the 1980s, he had established a depth of relationships that allowed him to push legislators much harder than most lobbyists. "The man has a very tough side to him," said one U.S. representative who has worked closely with Wasserman on industry issues. "There's no doubt about that. I've never seen him blow up. I have, however, seen him express his position with a sense of certitude and firmness and strength and the notion that 'I'm quite serious about this.' . . . Sometimes you talk with people and they go to great pains, if they disagree with you about something, to give some sense that they can understand how you have the other position, though they think it's wrong and you should change it. But with Wasserman, there's that sense that he couldn't conceive of you taking the other position, it's impossible to comprehend [how you could disagree with him]. Most people couldn't get away with that. I think his stature, his bearing, his age, his history in politics, and his accessibility and willingness to help in efforts causes you to sort of accept it from him in situations; it's almost a personal dynamic. It's not putting you down. It's not emasculating. It's not even arrogant. It's just strong. It's more like [he's saying] 'this is something I am serious about. This is something I—the fellow who always takes your phone calls, always helps you out, cares about you, who cares about your political success, who doesn't ask for a lot—care about.' "

No one else could make the movie industry's case as forcefully. During the 1988 presidential campaign, Missouri Democratic Representative Richard A. Gephardt, a moderate, was arguably the Democratic candidate ideologically closest to Wasserman. But when Gephardt, in an ill-advised effort to open fundraising doors in Hollywood, proposed legislation for the directors guild to prevent the producers from colorizing classic black-and-white films, Wasserman chewed out Gephardt's top campaign staff. "What is the smartest young man in Congress running around worrying about who is colorizing films?" Wasserman howled into the phone. "Tell him if he doesn't like colorized films to go to every television in America and take the color knob off."

Wasserman knew his friends, knew who had disappointed him, and especially as he grew older, found fewer reasons to swaddle his judgments. In 1986 Wasserman did little for California's long-time Democratic Senator Alan Cranston; trying to launch a presidential bid in 1984, Cranston had done little for the movie industry the previous year in its bitter legislative battle to prevent the networks from owning more of the programs they broadcast. (Greater ownership would allow the networks to reap more of the lucrative syndication fees producers now receive when programs are sold for reruns.) "Lew basically sat on his hands in the Cranston '86 race," said one senior figure in the campaign, "because there was a very clear perception on the part of the studios that Alan had not been helpful in their fight against the networks. Alan was busy focusing on being president of the United States, and there was an overwhelming sense in that particular circle that he had turned his back on them." It was California's junior senator, freshman Republican Pete Wilson, who carried the fight for the studios, and in 1985 Wasserman rewarded him by holding a fundraiser at his home. Wasserman's assistance helped Wilson raise more money in the industry than any Republican before him—and opened a public fissure between the studio executives and the liberal activists who sided with Wilson's 1988 opponent, Democrat Leo T. McCarthy.

Nothing better demonstrated Wasserman's pragmatism and flexibility than his success at maintaining access to Ronald Reagan's White House. While most of Democratic Hollywood reviled the new president, Wasserman carefully courted him. The work was more difficult than almost anyone in the industry realized. When Reagan succeeded Carter, Wasserman's ties to power were strained by more than ideological differences; there was a knotty personal history to untangle as well. At the moment of Reagan's greatest triumph, Wasserman had known him for forty years. But, though few people were aware of it, the relationship was badly frayed, and Wasserman needed all his skills to rebuild it.

The coolness apparently developed at the tail end of Reagan's acting career. After General Electric pulled the plug on "GE Theater" in 1962, MCA had difficulty finding work for Reagan, who was under contract at its Universal subsidiary. Jere Henshaw, who handled television casting at Universal, remembers that the new directors moving into Hollywood from New York saw Reagan as a B-movie relic whose time had passed. "It was mighty hard to get him jobs," Henshaw said. "People were giving me shit, saying, 'Can't we have a new face?' " Finally, Henshaw proposed to cast Reagan against type as the heavy in a 1964 film called *The Killers*. Reagan uncharacteristically balked, perhaps because he didn't want to carry that unsavory image into his impending second career as a politician. Eventually he took the part (though he didn't relish it; watching the daily footage come in, MCA's Jennings Lang lamented that Reagan was so uncomfortable "he looked constipated"). But Reagan's initial irritation angered Wasserman. "Wasserman didn't like Reagan as a person," said another MCA official. "They bickered over *The Killers*. Reagan didn't want to do the role, he thought it was beneath him. But Lew's attitude was: your career is over, take it and be grateful."

Michael K. Deaver, Reagan's closest personal aide for two decades, confirmed that Reagan's relationship with Wasserman had lapsed by the time he entered the White House. But Deaver said the chill set in even earlier—in the first years of the 1950s, when Wasserman, distracted by his responsibilities as MCA president, turned over Reagan's personal representation to another MCA agent, Arthur Park. Those were some of Reagan's most difficult years in the business: at one point, trying to overcome a long stall in Reagan's career, Park even sent him to Las Vegas to work as master of ceremonies for a variety show. "I don't think they [Reagan and Wasserman] had been on friendly terms, and I don't know if they had even spoken," Deaver said. "Reagan felt that Lew had dropped him when he was down and out and, as he described it to me, [at] the lowest point in his life. I think it was about the time when he had done the Las Vegas stint, and [he felt] Lew, whom he trusted and loved, dropped him. That was devastating to him."

As usual, MCA wasn't completely estranged from its prodigal son. When Reagan first won the California governorship in 1966, Wasserman stood beside the hapless incumbent, Democrat Pat Brown. But both Schreiber and Stein worked energetically in Reagan's cause; Stein was also instrumental in arranging a complex series of land deals that made Reagan personally wealthy for the first time. But Schreiber died in 1976, and Stein just a few weeks into Reagan's first presidential term. MCA's line to its old client lapsed just as its value peaked.

Once Reagan emerged as the Republican nominee for the White House, Wasserman discreetly sought to rebuild his own links. While working publicly for Carter's reelection in 1980, Wasserman also quietly helped the Reagan campaign tap Republican sources in Hollywood, according to one senior MCA executive at the time. "In 1980, Lew hedged his bets; he put a little tentacle out [to Reagan]," the executive said. "And once Reagan was in the White House he repaired the relationship. . . . Lew didn't spend a lot of time in the White House but he did have a lot of respect for the results of the Reagan administration, particularly on foreign policy. . . . In 1984 he was more helpful [to Reagan] than he had been in 1980. It was noticeable inside the company. Remember, Lew is very pragmatic. You'd ask him what to do about politics, and he'd say, 'If you think the train is going to leave the station, be on board.' And this was a very big train." Another executive recalled: "There was no pressure to financially support Reagan. But did Lew give the sense he was doing a good job and convey a sense of affection for him? Yes."

According to Deaver, the real healing began in Reagan's second term, when Wasserman took a leading role in raising funds for his old client's presidential library. After that, Deaver said, Wasserman was once again included in Reagan's circle "as if nothing had ever happened. . . . With Reagan, you know it's always as if nothing had happened in twenty years. It's 'Hi, Lew, how have you been, where have you been?'—that kind of thing." Wasserman repaired his relationship with Reagan to the point where the president and Nancy Reagan contributed a gushing video tribute to a lavish party held at MCA to celebrate the Wassermans' fiftieth wedding anniversary in 1986. When the president left the White House and returned to private life in Los Angeles, the first man he sat down with for lunch was Lew Wasserman.

His friendship with Reagan notwithstanding, Wasserman began to withdraw through the second half of the decade. Aging and slowed by illness (he underwent an operation to remove polyps from his colon in 1987), Wasserman ceded more power within MCA to his designated successor, president Sidney J. Sheinberg. In labor negotiations he has not been a major force since the 1981 directors' talks. In 1990, he began to seriously explore the possibility, arranging the sale of the company to a Japanese concern.

Politically, his style subtly shifted too. As the 1980s progressed, he elevated himself into what another leading Los Angeles fundraiser called "a patriarchal role." After the 1980 presidential campaign, Wasserman passed the point where he personally shouldered the heavy work; like his old colleague Arthur Krim, he no longer took on the prime responsibilities as chairman of a major dinner, or finance chair in a campaign. (When one fundraiser for 1988 Democratic presidential nominee Michael S. Dukakis asked Wasserman to chair a dinner, the MCA chief told him: "You don't need me to do that; you can do it.") Instead, Wasserman helped selected, well-placed senators and representatives, partly by making calls himself as in the old days, but increasingly through the power of his name to induce others to do so.

Wasserman's retrenchment allowed others to emerge. No longer is Wasserman the sole studio executive with ties to Capitol Hill: to varying degrees Sheinberg, Disney's CEO Michael D. Eisner, Fox Inc. chairman Barry Diller, and others have built their own relationships. That was inevitable, and not only because Wasserman gave ground willingly as time went on. It was always unnatural for the proud and imperious men running the studios to yield so much power to one individual. The same was true in labor negotiations. The diffusion of authority among the studio chiefs in the late 1980s was more understandable than its centralization under Wasserman over the previous two decades. (The fact that Universal performed only unevenly as a studio through the 1980s no doubt encouraged executives from other companies to speak more boldly.) But none of the other studio chiefs have yet moved into Wasserman's vacated chair; it may no longer even be possible to aspire to such a position. With the industry so splintered—the studios having been absorbed into conglomerates with directly conflicting interests, one linked to the largest cable network, another building its own television network, another owned by Sony—it is unlikely that any single executive, however skillful, could force and lead consensus as Wasserman did through the 1960s and 1970s.

As his career ebbs, Wasserman's hallmarks remain unchanged: subtlety, discretion, dexterity. To this day, it is difficult to assess exactly how Wasserman uses his clout, or to measure precisely how much clout he actually possesses. Wasserman rarely puts himself before the public, and even more rarely puts down anything on paper. Every night he leaves his desk clean. "Lew Wasserman is a man who never writes memos: if you sue him in an antitrust case and went to get files on that issue, you wouldn't find anything," said Valenti, using a curious example. "He doesn't write anything down. He operates on the phone, he's a taciturn man. He plays his cards close to the vest." Even politicians advocating the industry's cause in Congress and movie lobbyists working with them are not always aware of Wasserman's maneuvers in legislative fights. "I never found him to talk very much in public about what calls or visits he may or may not make," said one veteran industry lobbyist. "Once in a while you might know about it for one reason or another, but he is not a big mouth in that regard. Everybody knew he had the contacts, but he didn't have the need to boast about it as some people do. He didn't say, 'I'm going to call this guy.' It was much more gentlemanly, restrained, like it was nobody's business."

Because his influence was so difficult to trace, it became easy to mythologize. People in Hollywood put nothing past him. In 1983, when Reagan publicly sided with the studios against his own Federal Communications Commission's proposal to allow more network ownership of programming—effectively killing the plan—in Hollywood it was widely believed, without any evidence, that Wasserman nudged the president. (Even Reagan's closest aides aren't sure whether he talked to his former agent on the deal, though it is clear the president discussed Hollywood's side in the dispute with actor Charlton Heston.) When a U.S. attorney who had investigated connections between MCA Records and an alleged New York mobster was fired in 1989, much of Hollywood attributed his dismissal to complaints lodged against him by an MCA attorney at the Justice Department. It's commonly said in the film community that MCA's last line of defense against a hostile takeover is Wasserman's purported ability to jam the deal by pulling strings in Washington.

All that may be within Wasserman's reach. But clearly, his batting average in Washington over the years has been far from perfect. Wasserman has been an essential component of the studios' many legislative victories over the past two decades, particularly the efforts to keep the networks from obtaining more of the huge syndication fees for reruns. But it was Wasserman and Sheinberg who led the industry to its most decisive recent political defeat: the ill-advised legal and then legislative effort to impose royalties on videocassettes to compensate moviemakers for the expected copyright violations from home taping. On matters directly affecting MCA, too, Wasserman's record is mixed. If anything, he had the most difficulty with the administrations of presidents he knew. Under Lyndon Johnson, the Justice Department delayed MCA's proposed merger with Westinghouse in 1968 on antitrust grounds; the two companies finally dropped their plans. Also on antitrust grounds, Carter's Justice Department stopped MCA, three other studios, and the Getty Oil Company from joining to form a cable competitor to HBO. MCA finally broke into the pay-television market by investing in the USA Network ten months later; but the Reagan Justice Department then stopped an effort by MCA (with Paramount) to buy into a merger between Showtime and the Movie Channel, the second and third largest cable networks.

Inside Hollywood, none of that tarnished his luster. To a new Hollywood generation, Wasserman remained as fascinating and mysterious as to the old. Even those liberals who recoiled from his alliances with the GOP marveled at his skill in building them. The quixotic fight against the videocassette—a technology that ultimately crushed MCA's own DiscoVision videodisc alternative—was considered by many of Wasserman's colleagues not an act of folly but "an act of heroism," as one put it. Likewise, the publication of a 1986 book by journalist Dan E. Moldea questioning Wasserman's ties to Sidney Korshak and MCA's links to other alleged organized crime figures left no apparent lasting marks.

Politicians still scrambled for Wasserman's seigneurial blessing. "Wasserman is not a guaranteed stop on the [fundraising] tour," said a leading Los Angeles money collector. "It is one, as a politician, that you hope you can get; not everybody gets it." Each campaign reaffirmed that judgment. As soon as Michael Dukakis won the 1988 Democratic presidential nomination, his aides, using a loophole in the law, drew up plans to canvass wealthy donors for $100,000 contributions. These were the largest sums any campaign had sought since the Watergate reforms, and many of the nominee's fundraisers were unsure whether anyone would even listen to the appeal. In California, the state fundraising chief, a silver-haired transplanted Massachusetts businessman named John L. Battaglino, Sr., was expected to find dozens of such $100,000 contributors. He worried that the goal was unrealistic. He knew that before he could produce dozens of donors, he needed one—someone whose endorsement would legitimize his entire enterprise. So Battaglino went to see the old man at MCA. From his office in Century City, built on land Zanuck once prowled, Battaglino drove out past Beverly Hills, where Goldwyn lived and played, on through Hollywood, near the rented home in which a green Louis Mayer honed his stubborn ambition, and finally out into the Valley, just a few miles from the Burbank lot where Jack and Harry Warner constructed their empire. He was ushered into the office of the last mogul. Anxiously, he made his case. He asked: Was the goal realistic, could it be done? He waited. From across the desk, Lew Wasserman measured Battaglino's purpose, weighed his arguments, and told his visitor to put him down for $100,000. Battaglino had his first check, and the answer to his question.

CHAPTER SEVEN

THE POWER OF GLAMOUR

The New Model

On most political questions, actors Robert Vaughn, the suave star of television's spy spoof "The Man from U.N.C.L.E.," and James Garner, known best for his work in Westerns, found little to divide them. Both were Democrats, liberals, supporters of the civil rights movement. But in November 1967 they walked into a Los Angeles television studio on opposite sides to debate the proper role of movie stars in politics.

To the extent the film community ever seriously discussed anything that couldn't be run through a projector, this was a subject with unusual currency. The currency derived from the context: Ronald Reagan's stunning election as California governor the previous fall. Reagan's election itself followed the surprising victory in the 1964 California Senate race of veteran Republican pitchman George Murphy, the silver-haired former MGM hoofer who learned his politics from Louis B. Mayer. Democrats thought their nominee, former Kennedy press secretary Pierre Salinger, was "a cinch against this faded dancer," Democratic leader Stanley Mosk remembered. They were wrong. Genial, impeccably dressed and charming, if vague, Murphy nimbly ousted Salinger, whose fleshy folds and ever-present cigar recalled Tammany Hall, not Camelot.

Salinger and his supporters derided Murphy as ill-prepared, uninformed, ludicrous; it all rolled off his well-tailored back. "I had this thing researched for months," Murphy said after his campaign. "I wanted to learn if people would accept an actor running for office. And the word was that I had a pretty fair chance. After all, people remember me from all those old movies, and I never played a bad guy—I was always a good guy. It sounds corny, but don't knock it."

After Reagan's victory, Democrats weren't about to. Unlike Murphy, Reagan, at least, had been a visible political figure for years, delivering The Speech, his conservative antigovernment jeremiad (carefully noted on index cards) as a General Electric spokesman and for Republican causes. (He formally switched parties in 1962.) In the waning days of the disastrous Barry Goldwater presidential campaign, the Republicans put Reagan on national television to rouse the disheartened faithful with The Speech. Across the country, conservatives were mesmerized. His appearance couldn't save Goldwater but it launched Reagan's political star, and he declared himself a gubernatorial candidate just over fourteen months later. Still, most Democrats considered Reagan an easy mark, a lightweight washed-up actor with troglodyte values.

This analysis, accurate as far as it went, lacked only relevance. In fact, Reagan wasn't a particularly strong campaigner; he tired easily, made relatively few appearances, and collected misinformation the way most politicians do endorsements. But his mistakes never seemed to hurt him and criticism never tarnished his amiable image. Pat Brown, whose own popularity had been bled by the cuts of eight difficult years, tried first to paint Reagan as an extremist. It seemed difficult for voters to believe that about such a personally reassuring man. Then Brown sent out prominent Democratic celebrities to question the propriety of turning over the top job in the nation's largest state to an actor with no government experience. In one ad, engaging Gene Kelly sat before a microphone and softly, reasonably, lacerated his old colleague: "Hello, I'm Gene Kelly, professional actor. I've played many roles before the camera. I've been a soldier, a gambler and even a major league baseball player. I know I could play the role of a governor, but that I could never really sit in his chair and make decisions affecting the education of millions of children." That gambit had no more success than any of its predecessors; John Forsythe, who cut a similar spot, was inundated with mail chastising him for attacking such a nice man. On election day, Reagan rolled over Brown. When the new governor was inaugurated (at the unusual hour of 12:14 A.M.) on January 3, 1967, he turned to his old friend, now California's junior senator, and said, "Well, George, here we are on the late show again."

To bewildered California Democrats, campaigns suddenly looked just like the late show, the preserve not so much of leaders as leading men—if graying ones. Journalists wondered how dowdy legislators and anonymous city council members would compete with glamorous celebrities who "come with a built-in, though largely fictitious, public image." Many people in Hollywood asked the same question, some with glee, others with apprehension. Conducted through newspaper and magazine articles and television appearances, the debate inside the film industry involved more than the specific question raised by Murphy and Reagan: that is, whether stars should seek elected office. Their success occasioned the first real airing of a more fundamental question: How aggressively should celebrities push their personal political views on their fans?

That was the issue on the table when Garner and Vaughn met in the studios of the local public television station one year after Reagan's victory. Garner took the side of principled reticence. He worried not only about celebrities running for office, but also about celebrities making advertisements for those who did. His view reflected the prevailing attitude in Hollywood's first decades. Through the 1950s, when celebrities joined campaigns it was usually as walking props. Mostly they stood on the stage and waved, or delivered a few vacuous remarks of support for their candidate. This rule was not inviolate: the speeches of Melvyn Douglas and Douglas Fairbanks against the isolationists in the early 1940s were both well crafted and substantive; the same was true of Orson Welles's appearances for FDR in 1944 and Katharine Hepburn's fiery attack on HUAC at a Henry Wallace rally in 1947. But these were eminent exceptions. Celebrities were generally hesitant about imposing themselves on the public as policy experts. Far more typical was the role Lauren Bacall and Humphrey Bogart played for Adlai Stevenson in 1952. "They would be introduced and they would make a pitch for Stevenson and wave," said Bill Blair, Stevenson's assistant. "They didn't have to do anything very much." Likewise, when Frank Sinatra opened his mouth for John F. Kennedy it was to deliver songs, not speeches.

But a combination of forces eroded this modesty through the 1960s and moved the center of the industry closer to Vaughn's position that "it is immoral for an actor to remain silent if he is asked for his public view and is qualified to give it." By the end of the 1960s, celebrities were offering detailed, passionate, and occasionally ill-informed positions on virtually every issue facing the nation. After another two decades, voters faced the spectacle of Meryl Streep addressing Congress on pesticides, Jessica Lange lecturing legislators on the decline of the family farm, and Charlton Heston debating Paul Newman on television about the fine points of nuclear strategy. Rarely any more is there a cause so ragged, a campaign so obscure, that it cannot find at least one Hollywood star aching to unburden himself on its behalf. Just as the modern form of Hollywood financial power evolved in the changed political and entertainment world of the 1960s and 1970s, so the new rules of celebrity activism emerged over the same period.

Many of the same forces were at work. At the root were trends that first appeared in the Kennedy era. The decline of the studios, whose long-term contracts had tended to constrain actors and actresses from offering controversial opinions, and the concurrent fading of the blacklist both struck down entrenched barriers to candor. Kennedy put politics back on Hollywood's agenda, giving the newly liberated stars something to get excited about. Then the electoral success of Reagan and Murphy a few years later inspired even those who disagreed with their views. "It was pretty hard to ignore the fact that Ronald Reagan was elected, George Murphy was elected," said actor-director Warren Beatty. "Ronald Reagan was a very important weathervane of the 1960s [in Hollywood]."

Some took their inspiration literally. Talk-show host, comedian, composer, and author Steve Allen tried to fit another hat on his crowded head with a Democratic congressional nomination in 1965, but ultimately was forced from the field because he was registered as an independent, not a Democrat. In 1968, former child star Shirley Temple Black threw her curls in the ring for a congressional seat, but lost. (She settled for a UN appointment from President Richard Nixon.) Over the next decade, as Reagan's star continued to ascend, political operatives scoured the backlots for the next Hollywood candidate: Vaughn, Forsythe, Gregory Peck, Beatty, Charlton Heston, Robert Redford, and even Garner were all discussed as candidates, often seriously. Some still are mentioned today. (A group of leading California Democrats doggedly sought to recruit Garner for the party's 1990 gubernatorial nomination.) But none of them ever committed themselves to the voters' tender mercies.

Stars like Reagan and Murphy who abandoned Hollywood for politics remained less important than those who balanced the two worlds. The real role models for the new activism came initially out of causes, not electoral campaigns. Harry Belafonte sang for Martin Luther King, Jr.,— but he also delivered speeches and participated in strategy sessions for the movement. Among the white stars, Marlon Brando emerged through the mid-1960s as the most vocal advocate not only for King but for black activists to his left. Always disdainful of the star-making process, and contemptuous not only of mainstream Hollywood but of the very idea of adoration, Brando gradually recognized fame to be a useful political tool.

In tune with the changing times, he exploited it. "For too many years I have neglected the forum which was available to me," he said at one point. "Well, I'm not going to neglect it any more. I'm going to use every means at my disposal to get across what I want to say." Brando made himself available for interviews, rallies, marches, missions to the South, his fame a magnet for cameras and the men and women with notebooks. In 1963, Brando covertly flew into Gadsden, Alabama, with Tony Franciosa, Paul Newman, and Virgil Frye to meet with community leaders and focus press attention on alleged atrocities against blacks in the town, which had successfully kept away reporters for weeks. "There was a lot of fear . . . a lot of paranoia and maybe rightly so," said Franciosa. "I remember Marlon was very relaxed. He was the only one that seemed relaxed."

By 1964, Brando was also appearing at protests for American Indians, whose plight came to consume him. His commitment to using "every means" to advance his cause led him to extraordinary steps by Hollywood standards; in 1973, when he won the Best Actor Academy Award for his portrayal of Vito Corleone, he sent an Indian woman named Sacheen Littlefeather to reject the award, saying he could not accept it "because of the treatment of American Indians in the motion picture industry, on TV, in the movie reruns and the recent happenings at Wounded Knee." Old-line Hollywood—the producers and studio executives and even stars who lived by the old rules—acted as though Brando had desecrated a church, but he appeared satisfied that he had forced his concerns before tens of millions of viewers, if somewhat theatrically and only briefly.

Brando was a crucial figure in Hollywood's changing attitude toward activism because of his enormous professional prestige and the moral intensity he conveyed. But his idiosyncratic causes and enigmatic personality, along with his increasing reclusiveness and fading box office appeal, combined to limit his impact on his colleagues. The polarizing national struggle over the Vietnam War, as it escalated through the late 1960s, provided more accessible examples of the intensifying celebrity activism.

Both sides in the conflict deputized Hollywood stars as spokesmen. John Wayne became a symbol of rugged determination for the war's supporters. Wayne staunchly supported American involvement in Vietnam; he made his controversial 1968 film *The Green Berets* with the express purpose of showing the "world . . . why it is necessary for us to be there," as he explained in a letter to President Lyndon Johnson proposing the film.

But Wayne generally steered clear of direct political entanglements. Though he campaigned some for Nixon, his activities in support of the war—after *The Green Berets,* which many critics considered too simplistic to convert many hearts or minds—mostly consisted of a few gruff one-liners in interviews. He answered the questions reporters asked him, but didn't go looking for microphones. In the progression from the celebrity who came on stage with a smile to the star who hauled to the lectern a footnoted text, Wayne was a transitional figure: he displayed none of the traditional reticence about expressing his views, but little of the new aggressiveness about pushing it on his fans. If anything, he often felt he pushed too hard. "Given the choice," Wayne once lamented, "I find myself talking too much."

Vaughn, who played U.N.C.L.E. agent Napoleon Solo in NBC's takeoff on the James Bond movies, took one large step past Wayne. Vaughn matched the Duke in political ardor, if not fame, but shared none of Wayne's modesty about merchandising his views. In January 1966, Vaughn, a bright, skeptical, ambitious young man often mentioned as a potential political candidate, delivered an antiwar speech in Indianapolis—and was savaged by the conservative local newspaper. The attack drew more attention to his stance, and soon Vaughn was deluged with invitations to repeat the performance at churches, college teach-ins, community gatherings. His growing notoriety created the opportunity for still deeper involvement. Allard Lowenstein, the itinerant organizer of leftist causes, asked Vaughn to assume the national leadership of an antiwar organization dedicated to dumping President Johnson from the Democratic ticket in 1968. Vaughn needed little convincing. He accepted Lowenstein's offer, became chairman of the group called Dissenting Democrats, and "spent the better part of the next eighteen months literally every weekend out on the hustings," he recalled.

Vaughn's eagerness to accept such a polarizing position, and his inexhaustible determination to inject himself into the debate (he appeared for "anyone who was opposed to the war, who could fit me into their schedule"), marked the evolving mores in Hollywood. So did the absence of pressure from producers or sponsors to lower his profile. Even more telling was his willingness to directly and publicly challenge the leader of his party, President Johnson. That attitude, unimaginable only a few years earlier, keenly reflected changing times. It suggested a new stage in the political involvement of Hollywood celebrities, one that accelerated and expanded upon the liberating trends produced by the fall of the studios, and the rise of Kennedy and then Reagan in the early 1960s.

The growing political assertiveness of Hollywood figures toward the end of the decade—particularly in the antiwar movement—was part of a much larger social upheaval: the increasing willingness of Americans of all types, in all communities, to question not only government's decisions but also its truthfulness. The widespread disaffection over the Vietnam War—the growing sense that the White House lied about the war's progress—opened what political analysts later called "the confidence gap" and ended the American tradition of fundamental acquiescence to the decisions of the commander-in-chief. Dismay over the war inspired millions of Americans, for the first time, to resist their government's course directly; their resistance buried the country's unwritten tradition of deference to experts in high places.

This shattering of confidence in government—indeed all authority—was an earthquake whose reverberations still dominate American politics. In Hollywood, the implications were profound. To a great extent, the growing prominence of celebrities in public debate reflected the declining stature of politicians. In the new atmosphere of widespread social skepticism, celebrities, like citizens everywhere, more boldly expressed views that clashed with conventional wisdom. If anything, Hollywood figures, who had probably been even more cautious about expressing dissonant views than the general public through the early 1960s, now pushed to the other extreme. As office-holders lost credibility, many stars came to believe they possessed a tangible political asset that politicians lacked: abiding affection and respect from millions of devoted fans. And as trust plummeted in the symbols of authority—the White House and Congress—an increasing number of stars came to believe those enduring relationships gave them as legitimate a place in public debates as anyone else. Paul Newman captured the emerging creed in an interview with *Playboy* during the 1968 presidential campaign: "I've seen a lot of senators . . . who have a much greater sway than they're entitled to. Who's to say who's an expert? Just because I can sway more people than I have a right to, does that mean that I'm not entitled to my opinions or to voice them? The world situation affects us, as movie people, as much as it does anyone else. . . . The times are too crucial, the priorities too urgent, for anyone to stand aside."

Over time, this became a circular proposition because as more stars volunteered sharply worded, even outrageous political views, the media, particularly television and the huge Hollywood press corps, grew more eager to draw such bright copy from them. The phenomenon of celebrity pundits became, to a significant extent, driven by demand. The willingness of the media to cover even their most uninformed political opinions encouraged celebrities to offer them. With Brando, many stars felt they would be irresponsible not to use the forum constantly presented them. As Richard Dreyfuss became a star in the early 1970s through films such as *American Graffiti* and *Jaws,* he routinely spiced the bland porridge of talk-show interviews with his liberal political views. "No one ever didn't want to talk politics," he remembered. "Sometimes people would [ask] 'What gives you the right?' I'd say, 'He asked me to come on this show, that's what gives me the right. I would be a fool not to take advantage of it.' "

Eventually, the attitude Dreyfuss embodied diffused through Hollywood. But the tensions illuminated in the debate between Garner and Vaughn were never fully resolved. Beginning in the 1960s, the baseline of acceptable political visibility for celebrities steadily increased. From that higher level, though, there remained in Hollywood sharply contrasting attitudes toward the political use of fame. These lingering tensions were played out in the political careers of the prototypical Hollywood "actor-vists" of the late 1960s and 1970s—Paul Newman, Shirley MacLaine, Warren Beatty, Jane Fonda, and Robert Redford. Over the dozen years that began with the challenge to Lyndon Johnson and ended with the election to the White House of Ronald Reagan, these activists built on the experiences of Brando, Belafonte, and the others to open a new era of opportunity and risk for stars in politics. Much as Lew Wasserman and Arthur Krim laid down the revised rules for Hollywood participation in fundraising, they defined the options for celebrities to influence political debate in the television era.

Into the Campaigns

Tony Podesta was organizing Sullivan County, New Hampshire, for the presidential campaign of Senator Eugene McCarthy in the turbulent winter of 1968 when he got his first close look at the political power of fame. It was January 1968, just after McCarthy announced his candidacy. In those dim, uncertain weeks, the senator's campaign consisted of hope, some dedicated antiwar activists, and the first trickles of what eventually became streams of idealistic young students who descended on New Hampshire, "clean for Gene." McCarthy's greatest problem was demonstrating enough credibility to dislodge the immobilizing belief in mainstream Democratic circles that his challenge to President Johnson was suicidal.

On the ground in Sullivan County, that skepticism loomed before Podesta like an invisible wall. The clock ticked off toward the crucial March primary—seven weeks, six weeks—and still, "no one was paying attention to politics," he recalled. Then the campaign sent him one of its few assets: actor Paul Newman. McCarthy had no leading Democratic office-holders willing to spread his message and bolster his prestige; none dared break with the White House for such an unpromising insurgency. Newman was bolder. An early and vocal opponent of the Vietnam War, a veteran of protests from the civil rights movement, he joined the campaign at a point when McCarthy "stood alone," the actor later recalled. "He had no machine. He had himself, his wife, their daughter Mary and one public-relations guy."

In the frigid New England winter, Newman tramped through the New Hampshire woods. He hit the shivering small towns like early spring. Podesta remembers the day Newman came to Sullivan County: "We scheduled him to do a walking tour of Main Street in Claremont, the county seat. We picked him up at the airport; they had scheduled him to come in at nine in the morning. I go out to the airport to meet him and come into town, we come around the corner into Main Street—and there is a crowd of 700 people in a town of maybe 10,000. It was the biggest political event in the history of the town. We were unable to get out of the car."

Newman was not the only one to put his fame behind McCarthy. Opposition to the war drew many stars to the cause. Though much of Democratic Hollywood yearned for Senator Robert F. Kennedy, his delay in entering the race allowed the Minnesota senator to take an early edge in the celebrity sweepstakes. Ultimately, McCarthy's forces paraded through New Hampshire such stars as Newman, Robert Vaughn, Robert Ryan, Myrna Loy, Tony Randall, and Leonard Nimoy. "I remember being in supermarkets, never sleeping, eating hamburgers in cars, and going, going, going," said Randall. "You never really stopped." For McCarthy's beleaguered supporters, these glamorous reinforcements offered encouraging evidence that his uphill crusade had credibility in at least one highly visible segment of society. "They meant a kind of stamp of approval from an institution that was recognized as central to our culture," said Blair Clark, a former CBS vice-president who served as McCarthy's campaign manager. "The actor-star is somebody who represents people's dreams and hopes, because they are rich and successful and they have embodied various characters that people wish they were like. It is sort of a transferrable charisma. And I don't sneer at it at all, even in a serious, intellectually snobbish way. It's legitimate. Why isn't that as good a stamp of approval as some guy who has been elected lieutenant governor three times?"

The glitter brigade that reinforced McCarthy opened a new front in

Hollywood's political engagement. Stars, of course, had adorned presidential campaigns since the 1920s. But typically they waited until the parties settled on their nominees to bestow their endorsements. And in a presidential general election—a race that involved tens of millions of voters and constituted a referendum on the nation's direction—a celebrity, no matter how beloved, was inevitably only one of many voices. McCarthy's experience in New Hampshire heralded a somewhat weightier role for stars in presidential politics. In part the change reflected the growing political confidence of stars evident in the antiwar and civil rights movements. But it was principally changes in the political system that created the new opportunities. Most important was a trend McCarthy himself best exemplified. The 1968 campaign marked the last time the presidential nominee in either party was chosen through the private caucuses of party leaders; from that point forward, the major force in the nomination became voters themselves, casting ballots in primaries and caucuses.

Under the old system, celebrities had no real place in the battles for the presidential nomination: glamour helped candidates little when their target audience was a handful of party leaders who responded to hard calculations of prospects and power. But the stars' value ascended once the candidates were forced to sell themselves directly through primaries to the public, whose affections were more malleable. And in contrast to the presidential general elections, the growing importance of primaries—particularly the critical early primaries in small states, where less than 100,000 people might vote—created a field small enough for the stars to play on meaningfully.

The opening of the nomination process, which accelerated with internal party-rule changes through the 1970s, elevated celebrity endorsements in a second respect. The reforms allowed more marginal political figures—relatively obscure senators and governors and even U.S. representatives who could never have dreamed of taking home a nomination decided in the back room—to bid for the presidency. With smaller figures now contesting the nomination, stars could play a larger role. For the first time, it became routine for serious presidential candidates to be surrounded by celebrities who were better-known national figures. In January 1968, Paul Newman and several of the other stars who descended on New Hampshire were unquestionably more familiar than the man they campaigned for. That didn't mean they could have shown better at the polls. Nor did their fame necessarily transfer to McCarthy, and there's no evidence that their fans voted for McCarthy directly because of their endorsements (certainly McCarthy would reject that proposition).

Clearly, unhappiness with Johnson, not the blessing of Felix Unger and Mr. Spock, was the most important factor in McCarthy's dramatic showing. Randall, for one, doubted that "we ever influenced one human being's vote."

But Randall was overly modest. The emerging dynamic of presidential nominations provided Randall, Newman, and the rest of McCarthy's stars with, if not a pivotal role, at least a significantly more purposeful one than their predecessors. For McCarthy, attracting notice (along with raising the money that could buy attention through ads) was the most pressing priority. The presence of Newman and the others in small New Hampshire towns undeniably allowed McCarthy to receive attention from voters and the media that he would not have otherwise. That attention bolstered his prospects. Randall's modesty notwithstanding, that was tangible, if not decisive, assistance; it was, in any case, tangible enough that presidential candidates reflexively sought it in the primary campaigns that followed.

By these changed rules, stars were most useful to candidates with the least visibility. When he finally entered the race, Robert F. Kennedy attracted enormous support from Hollywood. But he never needed it: his own fame drew crowds and cameras. Stars provided more useful service to McCarthy, a distant, chilly figure who rarely lit up a meeting hall and always remained enigmatic to the public. Newman in particular stayed on the trail long after New Hampshire, devoting most weekends through the spring to the crusade. For the Wisconsin primary, Newman hung around Polish pool halls in Milwaukee demonstrating the form he displayed in *The Hustler*. In urban Indiana, his reception was even more impassioned than in rural New Hampshire. "Once we figured out what was going on here, we began to advance him harder than we advanced the candidate," said Podesta. "He came to Lake County, Indiana—that's Gary-Hammond . . . working-class, steelworkers. We got in there on a Wednesday morning. He got into the airport at 8:30 [A.M.]; he did nine stops before lunch. We picked him up in a station wagon with a flap-down back, and had four guys, plus a driver, riding in the backup car who were all real big, real strong. We'd pull up to a street corner in Gary, wherever. The four guys would come out of the car, lock arms around the car, flip the back down and he'd get up and give a little talk. There'd be four hundred people there, five hundred people there, at 10 A.M. in the middle of downtown Gary. . . . There wasn't anybody who had the kind of electricity Newman did. We didn't get those kinds of crowds for McCarthy."

For all the help it received, McCarthy's was a transitional campaign in the political application of glamour. The increasing visibility of the stars on the campaign trail still threatened a backlash. In New Hampshire, Johnson's supporters complained that McCarthy's campaign was "trying to turn the serious business of a presidential primary into a carnival by importing movie stars into the state to tout their candidate." Even Newman, despite his bold remarks to *Playboy* that summer, wondered whether he belonged on the midway. He was uncomfortable with the mechanics of campaigning, delivering speeches, shaking hands, moving through crowds, keeping his tongue with reporters asking the same questions day after day, city after city. He understood the absurdity of trying to discuss the war or anything else amid the Beatlesque riots of young women who surrounded his car, screamed during his speeches, and swooned when he took off his coat; in Indiana, a group of women fought over a box of Kentucky Fried Chicken bones he left in a staff car at the airport.

And yet for all his hesitation, Newman dragged himself to Wisconsin and Oregon and Indiana. On the screen he was renowned for fashioning alienated antiheroes. But ultimately, his off-screen message to his peers was not only of engagement but responsibility. To one crowd in Indiana, he declared: "I don't want it written on my gravestone, 'He was not part of his times.' " For the socially conscious star, that was again a creed.

After the 1968 campaign, another powerful change in the political system hardened that conviction. Through the first decade or so of the television era, politicians generally kept a curtain over their use of Madison Avenue advertising techniques, fearing the charge that they were being sold to the voters like soap. But in the 1968 presidential campaign the curtain was finally pulled back (Joe McGinniss wrote *The Selling of the President* that year), and reporters began openly reporting how the demands of television on campaigns were blurring the distinction between entertainment and politics.

That realization broke down another barrier to the political use of fame. As politics came to be seen as more packaged, slicker, more like acting, many stars felt less anxiety about using their celebrity as a political tool. Since politicians were openly, willingly, embracing the actor's tools—artifice, image, fame—the star activists were less hesitant to apply the same assets to their own causes. Shirley MacLaine said as much to a *New York Times* reporter in 1971: "What I'm most interested in these days is manipulating the system. And today the communications are more important than the politics. They have become the new politics. And maybe the communicators are the new politicians. . . . I will unabashedly use my celebrity to try to influence people. I think this is a proper use of power. I mean, what good does my turquoise swimming pool in California do anybody else?"

MacLaine, who first came to fame fifteen years earlier playing long-legged free spirits and serving as the designated mascot for Sinatra's Rat Pack, brought the same uncomplicated attitude to politics. Unlike Newman, she displayed no doubts about her legitimacy: if people were willing to listen to her, she seemed to believe, that gave her the right to speak to them. Armed with that belief, she became a significant presence in the contest for the 1972 Democratic presidential nomination. Her work for George McGovern was so extensive that it eventually landed her on the cover of *Newsweek*. MacLaine first met McGovern at the 1968 Democratic Convention, where the South Dakota senator mounted a last-minute candidacy as a stand-in for the late Robert Kennedy. That quickly collapsed, but MacLaine was impressed with McGovern's performance in a debate with Humphrey and McCarthy. That fall she campaigned for McGovern's Senate reelection in South Dakota.

As soon as McGovern hinted he might be interested in seeking the nomination four years later, MacLaine was off and running. In 1969 she invited the senator to her Encino home to meet the liberal Hollywood elite. "She invited the top stars in Hollywood who had some liberal inclinations, antiwar or environmental interests, and interests in women's activities or civil rights," McGovern recalled. "It was a liberal crowd, but people that hadn't been too deeply involved in a partisan campaign before. . . . I thought the reaction of the crowd was pretty good, and I aroused their curiosity. They were puzzled as to how a guy from a little state like South Dakota and a freshman senator could seriously think he could run for president, and yet they were intrigued by it, and somewhat puzzled as to why Shirley thought it was important to be doing this in 1969. As always, Shirley was deadly earnest about it, and probably considerably ahead of where everybody else was in terms of emotional and political commitment."

Initially, McGovern himself wasn't certain why a man who hoped to be president needed to be in Shirley MacLaine's living room. But he quickly reassessed. More than any of his competitors, McGovern recognized the potential value of Hollywood under the new campaign rules; he saw the film community as both a tangible and intangible asset—a way to attract money and media attention and also a source of legitimacy for an outsider who began the race scraping the bottom in the polls. "Rather soon after that dinner, I began to visualize what they could do," he said, "particularly on the fundraising end, but also in lending a certain amount of appeal or charisma and interest in the campaign. I had seen John Kennedy do a little of that, and Adlai Stevenson, but it occurred to me that with the antiwar sentiment running as strong as it was in the country, and with electric personalities such as John and Robert Kennedy and Martin Luther King gone, and with Teddy [Kennedy] probably out of the race because of his difficulties at Chappaquiddick, they were probably up for grabs with someone who would take a clear antiwar, liberal position. And so they became, I wouldn't say an all-important aspect of my thinking, but one of the factors I was very aware of early in the campaign . . . to lend credibility to the campaign."

McGovern saw the lesson implicit in Newman's formidable assistance to McCarthy four years earlier. That experience suggested a star might, in some circumstances, invest a campaign with credibility. This was a historic switch. Perpetually insecure, actors and actresses had always seen friendships with politicians as a way to enhance *their* credibility as serious people. But the McCarthy experience showed that for a little-known candidate, the reverse might be possible. McGovern certainly believed so. With no support in the Democratic establishment, McGovern saw liberal Hollywood as one of the few sympathetic power centers whose support might cause voters to take him more seriously. "If stars of the entertainment world that people respected and loved were standing with me, I thought that would answer some of the skepticism about [my prospects]," he said. "There was a lot of talk in those days that I was a nice guy, but [I did not have] much chance. . . . So publicly having a guy like Burt Lancaster or Warren Beatty or Jack Nicholson, Dennis Weaver, Leonard Nimoy, people like that, [stand with me] tended to, I thought, send a signal out across the country: He can't be all bad, he can't be a complete zero."

Not only those stars but dozens of others eventually joined his crusade. McGovern was able to attract such widespread Hollywood help largely through the remarkable efforts of MacLaine and her brother, actor Warren Beatty. Moved mostly by opposition to the Vietnam War, both put their careers on hold to devote themselves full time to his campaign from 1971 on. "Other celebrities came and went," said Patrick H. Caddell, McGovern's young pollster, "but those two were always there." Of the two, MacLaine was more visible to the public. Warm, gregarious, approachable, MacLaine carried McGovern's message into more than two dozen states and hundreds of communities. From the first primary in New Hampshire through the campaign's dispiriting climax, she appeared in living rooms, at fundraisers, before unions, at suburban ladies' clubs, and on college campuses. No audience was too small for her witty jabs against "a bunch of overgrown boys playing war games."

Her marathon campaign days tested even her dancer's legs. "She was effective because she could talk to anybody about anything," said Judith L. Oldham, who ran McGovern's speaker's bureau. "You could send her anywhere and she could just walk in and start talking." Her views sometimes veered off in strange directions: at the National Democratic Club she called on her party to take a stand for increased male sterilization as a solution to overpopulation—a political proposition that seemed calculated to invert Lyndon Johnson's dictum that once you had a man by the balls, his heart and mind would duly follow. And occasionally she spoke a bit overenthusiastically (McGovern once walked in on the tail end of a speech in which she promised he could cut the defense budget by a sum that exceeded its total). But she hadn't yet wandered into New Age mysticism—she was, on balance, a sturdy, dependable surrogate. McGovern was utterly amazed by the amount of time she gave, and finally told her he was overwhelmed by her generosity. "It's really not all that generous," she told him. "This country is so screwed up I don't think we're going to produce any great films until we're out of Vietnam and get this country straightened out."

With her inextinguishable energy and perseverance, MacLaine took Newman's model of weekend commitment and expanded it into a seven-day-a-week, red-eyed compulsion. She took another new step for a star by shouldering official responsibilities within the campaign structure. A McGovern delegate, she took a central role in the convention debate over the abortion plank of the platform. With Bella S. Abzug, she was named co-chair of McGovern's "women's advisory committee" in the general election. And she was the campaign's most articulate defender of the right of celebrities to participate in national politics. After newscaster Harry Reasoner took a jab at actors endorsing candidates, MacLaine fired off an op-ed piece to the *New York Times*. "Large numbers of Americans seem to understand now . . . that it is the responsibility of everyone, including artists, to search for humane solutions to society's problems," she wrote. "Somehow they sense that artists can be both companions and prophets of social change because they are so inextricably involved with the full range of human life. . . . Politics that are void of the insight of art—its compassion, humor and laughter—are doomed to sterility and abstractions." If the language was high-flown, her sentiment was genuine, and it revealed the spreading conviction in Hollywood that stars belonged next to the candidate on the platform.

Still, that conviction was not universal. One prominent, intensely political star who didn't feel comfortable on that platform was MacLaine's brother, Warren Beatty. Their differing approaches to politics grew from much deeper differences between them. From the outset of his career, with his precocious success in Elia Kazan's teen romance *Splendor in the Grass,* Beatty was as veiled and reticent, on-screen as well as off, as MacLaine was direct. As a star, then a producer, then a writer and a director, he has been a presence in Hollywood for thirty years, but often a maddeningly immaterial one. Pinning down Beatty is like trying to corral smoke. Just finding him, physically, is a challenge: he is perpetually en route. His thoughts can be as elusive. He is easy to talk to, engaging, often charming, and he speaks with precision and intelligence on many subjects, but occasionally it seems as if he is responding to a different question that only he can hear. Critics have often cited the same quality in his work. His characters frequently display a disconnectedness, a vague restlessness, that words cannot fully express nor actions entirely erase. For all his renown as the premier Hollywood Casanova of his generation, there is some of that same solitariness in Beatty himself. He is a careful, bright, guarded man, extremely reluctant to expose himself to situations outside his control. In the era of videotape, he knows that missteps follow you to the grave. In a community prone to willful disbelief and reckless enthusiasms, he has always seemed wary—of typecasting, expectations, entanglements, the media, fame itself. "When a person, whether he wants it or not, scares up a lot of publicity, then he's going to go down the tubes very quickly if he is a dummy," he said. "I mean, you just know those times in your life, when you've been famous for a long time, when you're going to attract too much attention. You just know it. You smell it. You know when you are going to walk out of a restaurant and people are going to be taking pictures of you. It is just something you smell."

A man so resistant to indiscriminate illumination did not belong on the campaign trail, whatever his political passions. Still, Beatty tried it. In 1968, riding the wave from his previous year's star turn in *Bonnie and Clyde,* he campaigned for Robert Kennedy in the presidential race. After Kennedy's assassination, he spoke on behalf of gun control legislation pending in Congress. (Some thought that ironic given his movie's orgiastic glamorization of violence; Beatty responded that the film showed violence's bloody reality.) The bill's supporters sent him to speak before groups likely to oppose the legislation, hoping the sparks would attract cameras from the evening news. Beatty gamely provided tinder before a Giants game at Candlestick Park in San Francisco and at a Sonny Liston heavyweight fight in the Cow Palace. "I got in some very comedic situations with these things," he says now. "People started throwing bottles at me."

Three years later, he put himself in front of the bottles again for George McGovern. Like his sister, he met McGovern at the 1968 convention and enlisted early behind his dark-horse 1972 candidacy. Beatty traveled with the candidate, introduced him, knocked on doors, and spoke in living rooms, union halls, and college campuses in the early primary states of New Hampshire and Florida. He could be a compelling public speaker, but to many in the campaign he looked in these situations like a man whose shoes were too tight. In Wisconsin, a group of rowdy students at his speech unnerved him and caused him to question the traditional public role he had assumed. His sister could walk into a room of suburban housewives in Ohio and have them slapping their knees and welcoming her as a long-lost relative with a few off-color jokes; for Beatty, those situations were both difficult and unfulfilling. "Not only was it not enough, it embarrassed me," Beatty recalled. "I felt that the advertising aspect of the participation made me feel silly. It just wasn't very interesting to me. . . ." Nor did he consider it much help to the candidate. "I think the public is innately suspicious of the self-forwarding, publicity-seeking, capricious artist who would like to attach some mood of seriousness to his persona by participating in public affairs," Beatty said. "I have a high level of cynicism myself. . . . I guess it was hard for me to risk that kind of criticism."

That didn't mean he wanted to remove himself from the campaign. Beatty had been tugged toward politics since his youth; as a child, like any "good, red-blooded American boy" he fantasized a life as a leader—governor, president. His mature interest traced back to the early 1960s, when John F. Kennedy, through Pierre Salinger, asked him to portray the young president-to-be in *PT-109*. (After reading the script, Beatty not only turned down the part but told the White House he didn't think the film should be made. Much later, according to Beatty, when he finally met Kennedy, the president smiled and whispered, "Well, you were sure right about that.") Through the late 1960s, he found himself increasingly uncertain that commenting on the culture through films, however incisively, was a sufficient response to the times.

This was not an anxiety unique to Beatty. It confronted all those in the artistic world who lent their prestige to political causes, and all those who decided not to. Was the artist better served by participating in events or by remaining aloof from them? This was the flip side of the question argued by Garner and Vaughn. They debated: Was the public better served when artists engaged in politics? Beatty, like many before him, wondered: Was the artist better served by engaging in politics? Could you tell the truth only with detachment and distance? Or was art an insufficient response to the Vietnam War, the turmoil in the inner cities? Paul Newman dragged himself through small towns and frigid mornings and mobs of screaming girls in 1968 because he didn't want to be remembered as not part of his time; his implicit conclusion was that it was not enough to embody American alienation on the screen, to reveal it—that the actor was not immune to the responsibility to wrestle with the thing itself, not just its celluloid shadow.

Beatty turned over the same question, and ultimately reached the same place. "There's no reason why the artist isn't part of his times," he said, looking back. "The artist simply says in an uncompromising way what the truth is. The politician says, 'That may be the truth but we've got to improve things, we've got to cooperate, you can't have everything you want in your expression of the truth, I can't have everything I want— maybe we can work something out.' Something had to be worked out in 1968 and 1972. People were dying in Vietnam, and the immediacy of that problem, and the racial problems that were underneath it, these were very immediate things. And you had the sexual revolution of the 1960s. This was a very immediate thing. And all of the ancillary fallout from these things was very immediate, and, really, making movies next to the participation in the societal interaction of that was boring. Boring."

To his own mind, Beatty found exceptions: his films *Bonnie and Clyde*, *Shampoo*, *Reds*. But these were increasingly punctuated by long silences, long absences from the screen. There were many reasons Beatty made films less frequently as his career progressed, but in the early 1970s, at least, one was that he found the off-screen dramas more compelling. "I found myself turning down movies that were very commercially viable and some very good movies," he continued. "At the time I just couldn't get interested in those. Also I came into the movies at such an early age . . . so I became what you'd call a movie star much earlier than those other guys, and I just couldn't continue to make movies all the time. I just couldn't do it. I guess it was a matter of just too much compromise in the making of movies, and I thought if I'm going to compromise . . . I'm going to compromise on the immediate issues of the day. I want to know what's happening. It was very hard in 1968 to go into a sound stage and find that more interesting than what was happening outside. That also applied to 1972."

So as the 1972 presidential campaign progressed Beatty was ready to venture out of the sound stage, even if, after Wisconsin, he didn't want to venture too far out, at least not where the crowd could reach him. His preferred audience was narrower—the McGovern campaign team itself. To them, Beatty presented himself not as a campaigner but as a political strategist, as a source of ideas on how to reach the public. "What I was very interested in was the amazingly accessible tools to power in this country, particularly at the time," he said. "So I was always more interested in bizarre ideas that would utilize what I felt was a very flexible mass of public opinion, a very changeable, dangerously changeable, mass of public opinion. . . . [My interest was] campaigning ideas, the presentation of things. I was full of kind of theatrical, bizarre notions of what should be done."

Beatty amassed more influence inside the McGovern campaign than any Hollywood figure had ever accumulated in a presidential campaign. Even MacLaine, despite her titles, never found a voice inside the campaign commensurate with her commitment. Her role remained the public one, albeit expanded greatly. With his reluctance to play that part, Beatty took the evolution of star power another step, creating an unprecedented private role: the star as strategist. Just Darryl Zanuck had aspired to anything like it, and he only from afar, with volleys of memos. (Robert Montgomery, the only other analogue, had been more a technican in his dealings with Eisenhower.) Beatty operated at the heart of the campaign, a ghost in the machine.

In the free-form chaos of the McGovern operation, he struck most of the candidate's political advisers as serious, thoughtful, quiet, and easy to deal with, if a perfectionist on his own projects. Beatty kept a light touch in the swirl of events. During the Wisconsin primary, Frank Mankiewicz, a senior manager in the campaign, checked into a hotel and found a message from Beatty waiting for him. "You know, when you got messages in those days, they asked you to call a particular long distance operator," Mankiewicz remembered. "They'd say call operator six in Los Angeles; it was just a way of getting a call." Mankiewicz called the operator, the operator found Beatty, and then, while Mankiewicz waited on the line, she asked, to specify payment for the call: 'Mr. Beatty, what is your special billing?' 'Well,' he said, deadpan, 'always above the title, in a size of type no smaller than that of the director.'

Beatty's informal nature fit the campaign's. His youth was not conspicuous in an organization with a twenty-two-year-old pollster and a campaign manager only in his mid-thirties. Beatty established a particular rapport with that young campaign manager, a former Colorado attorney named Gary Hart. "They were very simpatico," remembered Oldham. "They went out together. They were both interested in each other. Gary was always drawn to Warren's star quality, and Warren was interested in Gary's cerebral qualities. Gary had enormous charisma in that campaign. I think they just sort of fed off each other." They even looked vaguely similar—tall, thin, with modish long hair. Campaign workers joked that when Hollywood made the movie about McGovern's rise, Beatty would be the natural choice to play Hart. "People would get them mixed up," said Oldham. Once, she recalled, Hart was eating lunch with MacLaine when a group of campaign interns descended on the table, convinced they could snare an autograph from Warren Beatty.

Beatty's ties, though, weren't only with Hart. He built relationships with Mankiewicz, Miles Rubin, Caddell, and the candidate himself.* The actor wasn't routinely included in campaign strategy meetings, but when he was around headquarters in Washington, he was welcome to sit in. "Warren was a real adviser, political advice, ideas, strategy," recalled Caddell. "He wasn't in the loop per se, but he was in the loop floating in and out. He would show up [at meetings] and he would be there, and he would not sit there passively. He would be an active participant and would be expected to be an active participant. Warren, of course, was on the phone with everybody every day, too. He really played a fairly significant role." His strength inside the campaign was his very lack of political experience. Mankiewicz thought he "had fresh ideas" because he "didn't carry any baggage. He didn't know what you couldn't do; he didn't have all the political lore. He didn't know you couldn't do this, or you couldn't do that. He was always coming up with quite interesting ideas."

Beatty's most interesting idea came to him during the Florida primary. With the campaign strapped for money, Beatty proposed to raise funds with a series of coast-to-coast rock concerts. At the time, no electric guitars had yet been fired up for a candidate. Beatty himself didn't know much about rock and roll, but once he decided to become an impresario, he tracked down several of the industry's top stars. Keeping the operation closely under his control, Beatty eventually organized five concerts, beginning in Los Angeles in April and concluding two months later in New York. He targeted the performers conservatively; on his stage there were no high-decibel rebels to frighten away the middle class. As it turned out, there were more acoustic guitars than electric. In California, he convinced Barbra Streisand, James Taylor, and Carole King—the latter two

---

*Hart, in fact, was not his major ally inside the campaign. Responsible for organizing the details of the campaign structure, such as it was, Hart had less time than Caddell and some others for Beatty's iconoclastic suggestions on how to sell McGovern and his message. "Gary," said Beatty, "thought my ideas were funny." Hart recalled thinking many of Beatty's suggestions were "wacky."

at the peak of their popularity, and both extremely hesitant about linking themselves to a politician—to sing for McGovern, and persuaded Gene Hackman, Jack Nicholson, Julie Christie, and Sally Kellerman to serve as celebrity ushers to direct big givers to their seats. For the climactic fifth concert in New York's Madison Square Garden, Beatty reunited Simon and Garfunkel, Mike Nichols and Elaine May, and Peter, Paul and Mary. The concerts produced at least $1 million for the cash-starved campaign; characteristically, Beatty stayed off-stage throughout, orchestrating the events from the wings.

The Hollywood legions Beatty assembled set a tone for the campaign; it was said in 1972 that one of the easiest ways to understand the differences between McGovern and President Nixon was to look at the stars gathered around them. Nixon had enthusiastic and widespread support in old Hollywood; he commanded the allegiance of the venerable icons, now lined and craggy—John Wayne and Jimmy Stewart, Charlton Heston, Bing Crosby, Rosalind Russell, even Frank Sinatra, who had grown close to Vice-President Spiro T. Agnew (who shared his hatred for the Eastern elite and the media) and completed the disaffection from the Democratic party that began a decade earlier when he was exiled from the Kennedy White House. For one huge party during the campaign at Nixon's Western White House in San Clemente, the president's men attracted some four hundred Hollywood supporters. Henry Kissinger came to the bash with actress Jill St. John on his arm, but, with a few other exceptions, that was about as close to contemporary as the gathering came: mostly the president mingled stiffly with stars who could have gathered just as easily for Dwight Eisenhower—Wayne, Jack Benny, Eddie Fisher, Sinatra, Lawrence Welk, Connie Francis, George Jessel, Art Linkletter, Jack Warner. That was, in a way, the point: Nixon's party assembled the heroes of voters who probably wished the 1960s never happened. At a time when many older Americans feared the collapse of traditional morality and recoiled from the sex, drugs, and violence that suddenly permeated so many films, Nixon's supporters almost all stood for normalcy, propriety, the way things used to be—or at least the way they were imagined on-screen. Through their company, Nixon affirmed the modest values of their fans. If there was a mustiness to Nixon's celebrity entourage (one guest at the San Clemente party called it "The Hollywood Wax Museum"), there was an undeniable solidity, too.

Beatty understood that appeal—he liked Wayne, and enjoyed his company, he even enjoyed the company of Ronald Reagan—but he searched for a contrasting note. The entertainers around McGovern were predominantly young, hip, irreverent. Their presence provided McGovern with an aura that Beatty hoped would enhance his political appeal to the young voters presumably least cemented into Nixon's silent majority of John Wayne and Jimmy Stewart fans. Like it or not, Beatty argued at the Madison Square Garden show, "A great deal of the leadership of this [younger] generation comes from music and film people." With the concerts, he aimed to provide a "stamp of approval" for McGovern from those cultural heroes whose audience might otherwise never listen to a politician.

That was a reasonable idea given the premise, which had considerable currency in the McGovern campaign, that the Democrats might win the election by activating a huge block of voters currently alienated from the political system. But the premise itself was flawed. If that block did exist in a form that could be mobilized—it remains debatable—the soft-spoken, uncharismatic McGovern was not the candidate to awaken it, no matter how many rock stars Beatty arrayed around him. And if McGovern ever had any chance of doing so, he undermined them at the Democratic Convention by selecting as his running mate Missouri Senator Thomas F. Eagleton, and then dropping him after learning that he had been treated for mental illness.

The Eagleton fiasco produced Beatty's boldest campaign gambit. He looked at the disaster as an opportunity to solve one of McGovern's deepest problems. Throughout his race to the nomination, and in his search for a vice-president, McGovern had been consistently rebuffed by the party leadership. Beatty thought he should publicly challenge the party elders to come to his aid by convening the Democratic National Committee and calling on it to find the new vice-presidential nominee. Presumably, the DNC would turn to one of the senior Democrats avoiding McGovern—Edmund Muskie, Hubert Humphrey, Ted Kennedy— who would be harder pressed to reject a public summons from their own party. Beatty's preferred choice was Humphrey. He went to see the former vice-president and after four hours artfully backed Humphrey into the corner he had avoided since McGovern bested him for the nomination. Humphrey finally acknowledged to Beatty that if the DNC publicly called on him to accept the nomination for the vice-presidency, he couldn't turn away from the offer.

Beatty rushed back to McGovern and reported the news. McGovern was suitably impressed. But too gentle a man to box Humphrey into the same corner, he instead asked him directly whether he would accept the vice-presidency nomination. That gave Humphrey the wiggle-room Beatty's formulation didn't; he said no, McGovern settled on Sargent Shriver, and the two of them went down to a record-setting defeat. It's

Hollywood's role in national politics began with the friendship between MGM's Louis B. Mayer and President Herbert Hoover (above). Mayer's greatest goal was to enlist his friend, press lord and producer William Randolph Hearst (below), into Hoover's cause.

*The heavy-handed conservative politics of the movie moguls along
with the hard times inspired a leftist Hollywood backlash during the
Depression. Among the leaders were actors Melvyn and Helen Douglas
(above), seen with their son Peter in 1933, and Orson Welles (below),
surrounded by reporters after his "War of the Worlds" broadcast shocked
the nation in 1938.*

*Both national political parties first seriously mined Hollywood
during the 1940s. A star himself, Franklin Roosevelt (above, with son
Elliott and Katharine Hepburn during the 1940 campaign) drew enormous
support. But Republican Wendell Willkie also had a dependable following,
led by studio executive Darryl F. Zanuck, in the striped suit (below).*

When the blacklist descended, liberals found little to cheer about. In 1948, gruff Harry S. Truman (above) inspired only a few stalwarts, including Ronald Reagan and Lauren Bacall, who joined him at a rally in Los Angeles. But four years later, elegant Adlai Stevenson (below, with MGM chief Dore Schary) became the first in a line of Democrats who appealed to the Hollywood liberals' sense of style.

The myth crystallized: the attraction between John F. Kennedy and Frank Sinatra (above, at JFK's inauguration) irrevocably joined politics and show business, suggesting limitless rewards at the pinnacle of American life. No one pursued the new political opportunities for stars more aggressively—or at greater cost—than Jane Fonda (below, being taken into custody at Ford Hood in Texas in 1970), whose ardent opposition to the Vietnam War made her a symbol for conservatives of a trendy radicalism.

With the moguls finally cleared from the stage, two of their successors brought Hollywood into the modern era of big-dollar political influence. MCA's chief executive, Lew R. Wasserman (above), able to raise huge sums for favored politicians, became the most powerful man in Hollywood; and in Washington United Artists' Arthur B. Krim (below) emerged as one of the most trusted advisers to President Lyndon Johnson.

In the 1980s, celebrities became an ineradicable feature of modern media politics, fulfilling many roles. Robert Redford stepped in front of the microphones with Michael Dukakis (above); and Warren Beatty (below) counseled Gary Hart offstage.

By the end of the 1980s,
Hollywood had become so
embedded in American politics
that no scene was too strange to
imagine. Ronald and Nancy
Reagan hosted Michael Jackson
at the White House (left)...

...President George Bush talked
fitness with "The Terminator,"
Arnold Schwarzenegger
(above), and former radical
Tom Hayden (left, comparing
notes with actor Rob Lowe)
joined his wife, Jane Fonda, to
organize the Brat Pack into a
new power base.

not likely Humphrey's presence on the ticket would have made much difference.

The outcome of the Humphrey maneuver typified Beatty's experience in the campaign. The freshness that made him intriguing to many on the staff ultimately constrained his influence. He had virtually unlimited access to the candidate and the senior staff and a fertile political imagination, but most of his ideas, now lost in the fog of campaign history, were too audacious or impractical for McGovern's men. "He was always a bold-stroke guy and he couldn't understand why you couldn't do those things," said Hart. "He was always for . . . spending all the campaign money to get him on primetime television for half an hour—or something bizarre like that."

Quiet, and actually somewhat shy, Beatty lacked skill at the in-fighting necessary to translate his ideas into action. ("He's not a challenger," said Mankiewicz, "he's an answerer.") Still, he was taken seriously throughout; he was never dismissed as a meddling actor. In the end, Beatty was left characteristically ambivalent about his role. "I felt that I had made somewhat of a contribution," he said, "but that it was hard for me to function in the confines of a national campaign that wouldn't do what I said." He laughed at how absurd that sounded, but the laughter didn't hide his belief that the McGovern campaign didn't fully appreciate how to take advantage of a star who wanted to do more than wave.

If disappointing in some respects, Beatty found the experience far from disillusioning. He liked politics and stayed close to it. Through the 1970s, as his stardom and stature within the industry grew from critically acclaimed hits such as *Shampoo* and *Heaven Can Wait,* he was often mentioned as a possible candidate for office. He usually dismissed the speculation by joking that if he ran, people would only find out how unsuited he was for public office.

But Beatty actually considered the prospect much more seriously. In his infrequent interviews, he dwelled with unusual intensity on the conflict between politics and the arts—between the politician and the artist in the same person, one building his career around compromise, the other pretending or believing himself to be immune from it. Later, he even made a film, *Reds,* that examined this conflict through the career of the idealistic author John Reed, who gave up his career as a journalist to work as a functionary in the new Soviet state. The film was ambivalent on whether Reed made the right choice, just as Beatty still presents himself as ambivalent about his own contrasting decision to stick to his craft.

In the years since the McGovern campaign, Beatty has had ample opportunities to make the jump. As Reagan left the State House in 1974, a private poll measuring the Democratic prospects to succeed him as California's governor put Beatty at the top of the list. Beatty found the news "mildly titillating." He was confident he could function in the political arena; after fifteen years in Hollywood, he figured the media had unearthed all the scandal it was going to find on him. But he remained at the gate, drawn to movies he wanted to make and unconvinced that the public would be interested in what he wanted to say. "I believe I ran out of gas [on the idea of running], at a time when it seemed that the country was, in certain areas, in decline and that the people didn't want to accept that," he said. "And [as a result] the leader who tried to force the people to accept that would not only be unpopular by bringing bad news, but as the messenger of the bad news he would be dismissed or worse. . . . I never wanted to play Don Quixote, particularly, and you know, that is the primary thing that concerned me."

Two years later, a group of Hubert Humphrey supporters approached Beatty about entering several presidential primaries as a stand-in for the former vice-president. The idea intrigued Humphrey, and Beatty rolled it around long enough to present it to a *New York Times* reporter "as somewhat of an expression of resistance to the primary system itself, and as an expression of frustration at the fact that the leadership of the Democratic Party . . . are not participating [running] in the primaries." But the plan never progressed beyond speculation. Beatty insists he "never took it too seriously, because I thought the fun of doing something like that would be saying what I thought, rather than saying what I thought somebody else thought."

As other opportunities appeared, Beatty let them pass, perhaps waiting in vain for a summons that never arrived. ("I think," said McGovern, "that he would have liked to have had some groundswell develop.") Only fifty-three, he still refuses to close off the possibility of following Reed and Reagan into a political career. If issues sharpen, if the political pulse quickens, perhaps then, Beatty says distantly, "one would want to rise to the occasion." But that would be surprising. He may someday seek office, but it would be a striking deviation from five decades of behavior for Beatty to subject himself to so much direct public scrutiny in a situation over which he could exert so little control. His preferred political métier is offstage. As famous as anyone in Hollywood, Beatty defined a new backstage role for celebrity activists. He has found his greatest political expression, not in front of a microphone, but on the telephone, often late at night, whispering advice to George McGovern, and then a decade later to McGovern's former campaign manager, when Gary Hart sought the Democratic presidential nomination for himself.

A Woman on the Edge

As Beatty pursued a muffled, private approach to power, Jane Fonda roared directly down the highway. Though convinced that artists had a place in politics, Beatty believed they must be careful in publicly pushing causes. In Fonda, passion buried care. More than Marlon Brando or Paul Newman, more than Shirley MacLaine, more than anyone who came before her, Fonda unabashedly sharpened fame into a political weapon. In her, all the liberalizing trends that loosened stars' inhibitions through the previous decade reached their peak. She pushed everything to extremes. She exposed herself to greater risk, professionally, and even physically, than any of the other celebrity activists. More pointedly than anyone in Hollywood, she used her fame to challenge government's credibility. She embraced causes more radical than almost any of her colleagues. And more than anyone else before or since, she demonstrated the power of celebrities to influence political debate in the mass media era, and the potential dangers of allowing them to do so. For three years of intense political activity in the early 1970s, she was a woman constantly on the edge, powered by a combustible mixture of media savvy and political naiveté.

After watching Fonda's strong performance in the 1969 film *They Shoot Horses, Don't They?* critic Pauline Kael wrote that the actress "stands a good chance of personifying American tensions and dominating our movies in the seventies as Bette Davis did in the thirties." In fact, through the decade's first years, she performed that function even more dramatically off-screen. The melodramatic radical declarations that Fonda sprayed across the news pages like so much shrapnel did not misrepresent the various leftist movements with which she aligned herself; that was the problem. What Fonda did was publicize, both through her own words and as a symbol, the tensions in the New Left and the antiwar movement. From the movement's point of view, many of the things Fonda said on the evening news were better left unsaid. She stood bravely with many worthwhile and difficult causes, but the blinding light of her celebrity magnified their contradictions. She became the test case, not likely to be equaled, of how a star with unlimited access to the media can rip through a cause like a hurricane, too fast and furious for anyone's control—eventually, even her own.

The daughter of film star Henry Fonda, Jane Fonda did not grow up planning a film career. She drifted into Hollywood after studying indifferently at Vassar, modeling, and taking classes at New York's famous Actors Studio. Her first film, *Tall Story,* was released in 1960, and Fonda spent the next several years commuting back and forth between Hollywood and Broadway. After several moderately successful screen performances, Fonda met French director Roger Vadim, who had earlier discovered and romanced Brigitte Bardot and Catherine Deneuve. Fonda eventually moved to France and married Vadim, who transformed the lithe young actress into his latest sex star and sent her skittering across the galaxy in search of the ultimate pleasures in his sly film version of the celebrated French cartoon *Barbarella.*

Through the middle years of the 1960s, Fonda returned regularly to Hollywood to work. But she spent most of her time in France, immersed in the growing excitement (and anti-Americanism) of the French left. It was in that company that Fonda was first systematically exposed to criticism of the U.S. role in Vietnam. Surrounded by the intoxicating revolutionary fervor of Paris in 1968, Fonda watched, with keen interest and a vague ache, the changes roiling her own country: protest marches on the Pentagon, riots in the black ghettos, and the chaos at the Chicago Democratic convention. Later that year, she returned to the United States to film *They Shoot Horses;* the next year, her marriage dissolving, her career seemingly beckoning, she returned to do publicity on the film. This time, anxious to "find some way that I could be part of what was going on," she stayed.

Many people in the Hollywood to which Fonda returned were similarly searching. Though much of the industry's leadership structure—the studio executives, producers, and agents who controlled the levers—remained indifferent to the political passions building in American society, others were drawn to that energy, particularly on the left. Partisan politics attracted the liberals who marched with McCarthy and Kennedy, and then organized around Beatty and MacLaine for McGovern. Others, following the early example of Robert Vaughn's Dissenting Democrats, enlisted in the antiwar movement.

Politics more radical than that also found a narrow foothold. After the enormous success of *Easy Rider* in 1969, studios scrambled for ways to merchandise alienation to the young. That gave a certain cachet to a radical subculture centered around Bert Schneider, the tall, thin, somewhat mysterious producer of *Easy Rider* and later the Academy Award–winning documentary on the Vietnam War, *Hearts and Minds.* Schneider was a passionate advocate of leftist causes, particularly the Black Panthers, who were welcomed into some of the Westside's finest living rooms like veterans from the front. The romance of revolution produced scenes too bizarre to satirize: at one point, Donald Sutherland's wife, who was holding a meeting for the Black Panthers, locked the actor out of their home because he was a security risk. "It was fervent, and a lot of people did good things," said Jeremy Larner, a former speechwriter for Gene McCarthy who moved to Hollywood when Schneider's company produced his novel *Drive, He Said.* "I felt that it wasn't deep because nothing about these people was deep. There wasn't any real political thought involved; there was just a kind of feeling of superiority, a feeling that they were consuming the more advanced products in the culture: Huey Newton is in my living room. There was a very excited and feverish romanticism."

Fonda wanted something more pungent; she had already experienced cocktail-party revolution in the salons of Paris, raising a clenched fist while the maid cleared the hors d'oeuvres. It wasn't enough, she said later, to go "to parties with all the other rich liberals. . . . It seemed so inadequate. It always seemed [to be] tokenism." To Fonda, growing increasingly radicalized by the week, if not the hour, the times demanded a grittier response. Within months of her return to California, she became a full-time political activist. There was no question of her using politics to advance her career: she put her career on hold. She went for long periods without working or producing any income. At one point, her finances were so strained that she had to hock jewelry to pay her expenses. "She had courage beyond courage," said Stephen Jaffe, her press agent at the time. "She had the philosophy of, 'Let the chips fall where they may, I don't care if I'm going to lose everything I've got.' "

Fonda was a comet. Intense and apparently humorless, her wardrobe simple, her hair hanging low over her forehead, her thin frame braced and guarded, she raced back and forth across the country, marching, picketing, rallying. Causes cascaded on one another: she fasted for peace with Dr. Benjamin Spock in Denver, lobbied against the war in Washington, raised money for the Black Panthers in Hollywood, toured the alternative GI coffeehouses outside military bases around the country. She organized the FTA show (its initials alternately translated, depending on the audience, as Free the Army, or Fuck the Army) with Donald Sutherland and, with a supporting cast that included Peter Boyle, Dick Gregory, and Ben Vereen, led the troupe across the United States and Asia, entertaining and proselytizing to soldiers as a counterculture response to Bob Hope. She marched with welfare mothers in Las Vegas, visited Angela Davis in prison, and sat sympathetically with returned veterans in Detroit as they recounted atrocities for the antiwar Winter Soldier investigation in 1971. To one audience in New York she declared, "Can any of you say, 'But I am safe, I have done nothing,' when the prisons of this country are overflowing with people who may be executed because of who they are, not because of what they have done. . . . This is not America in 1970, it is Berlin in 1936 and we are all Jews." She declared herself "a revolutionary, a revolutionary woman."

All of this left her somewhat out of place at the typical Brentwood soirée. Socially, Hollywood was "not at all" part of her life then, said Paula Weinstein, a former student activist who worked for Fonda reading scripts and later became her agent. "On occasion she would go someplace she was asked. But it was not at all her life." Her professional interaction was also minimal. Though she won the Best Actress Academy Award in 1972 for her riveting performance as a call girl in *Klute,* she didn't release another mainstream Hollywood movie until 1977. As her political activities grew more controversial, her agent at the time, Mike Medavoy, thought the studios displayed a marked coolness toward her; one Warner Bros. executive, Medavoy recalled, told him that some exhibitors said they couldn't show her pictures, "which obviously made it difficult to sign her."*

If the studios were cool toward Fonda, the feeling was reciprocal. "She was seriously thinking about quitting acting altogether," said Bruce Gilbert, who worked closely with Fonda in the antiwar movement and later produced many of her most successful films. "She felt . . . she had the possibility of affecting real historical change for the good, and she felt like the movies, at least the movies that she had been doing, were, like, who cares? They don't make a difference, they are just, at best, some kind of entertainment, they're not what I want to do with my life." For all that insistence, Tom Hayden, the antiwar activist who married Fonda in 1973,

---

*It's not clear whether this coolness actually cost Fonda any parts. Weinstein, who succeeded Medavoy as her agent a few years later, also found some studio executives hesitant about signing Fonda—but never so hesitant that they didn't ink the deals. The *New York Times* reported in a 1974 profile of Fonda that she had turned down roles in *The Exorcist, Oklahoma Crude,* and *Chinatown.* Fonda herself told journalist Craig Unger in 1989, "We glibly say I was gray listed, but whether or not it was a combination of the fact that I was pregnant, not able to work or too busy to work, not sure I wanted a career, combined with hesitation on the part of the studios, it was definitely not the fifties. When I decided I did want a career, it came out full-blown."

three years after her divorce from Vadim, saw anxiety rustling beneath her bravado. "On the surface she said, 'So be it, I'm trying to end this war,'" he recalled. "[But] she must have been coping with a very great fear that her career was being destroyed. . . . I don't know if she thought her career was dead. I know she contemplated that it was dead."

Her efforts to connect her old and new lives disappointed her. In March 1971, she tried to reach out, working with Donald Sutherland to organize an antiwar group called The Entertainment Industry for Peace and Justice. It announced itself with a bang: twelve hundred Hollywood figures came to a meeting at the Beverly Hilton. Fonda buttonholed the industry's top stars and executives to lend their names. An office was opened on Sunset Boulevard; plans were launched for a huge rally at the Hollywood Bowl. Nothing came of it. The organization collapsed after only a few meetings, strangled by sectarian debate. It seemed, at the time, a fitting commentary on her distance from the industry.

Fonda's relations were most strained with the Hollywood icon closest to her: her father, Henry Fonda. Fonda was a reliable liberal (he had campaigned for Stevenson and Kennedy), but he was reluctant to challenge the government over Vietnam; he came back from a 1967 trip to the front convinced that the media were undermining morale by ignoring the army's progress. Eventually he grew more skeptical about the war, but his daughter's flamboyant outspokenness still frightened and irritated him. Father and daughter traded barbs in print, reconciled, broke again. When Jane Fonda went to New York to film *Klute,* she had to rent an apartment because her father would not let her stay in his elegant townhouse. "I remember we went over to the house because she had some stuff there. . . . She just took her clothing and left," recalled Mark Lane, a leftist attorney who became her closest political adviser in the early 1970s. "She was really shaken by it."

More than differences in political approach separated the two famous Fondas; the public shouting match fed on the private silences between father and daughter and the insecurities each wrestled with. To some extent, friends thought, Jane Fonda's political rebellion was an extension of her personal rebellion against her emotionally crimped upbringing. Henry Fonda's unhappiness with his daughter's radicalism, in turn, reflected his own fears. "First of all, [Henry] was a very strange fellow in many ways, because he thought once he got finished with a job that he was never going to work again," said actor John Forsythe, who had known Henry Fonda since replacing him on Broadway in *Mr. Roberts* during the 1950s. "He was very work-oriented. And he thought that Jane was hurting his career. He had no consideration at all about her career." One night at a party in Malibu Henry Fonda brought up his complaint again, and Forsythe jumped on him.

"Jesus Christ, Hank, I don't understand your attitude," Forsythe said. "If she was my daughter, I can't tell you how proud [I'd be]. She puts her life, her career, her family, everything on the line, and you can't ask for more than that."

"Goddamn it," Fonda snapped back, "she's costing me work."

"In what sense?"

"People think I'm on the same wavelength as her," said Jane Fonda's father with disgust.

For all her alienation from the film business, Jane Fonda understood it was her Hollywood past that opened the door to her future. Much as she regretted the kittenish roles that brought her fame, she took an ironic pleasure in turning celebrity on its head. As her awakening progressed, she increasingly disapproved of the publicity machine and its profitable stirring of desire in ordinary people to replicate the unreachable lives portrayed on the screen. During the FTA tour she agonized about whether to give autographs to soldiers, fearing they would think she was putting herself above them; eventually she agreed to sign autographs as long as the person requesting it gave her one too. But she came to understand her celebrity as her principal political tool; she applied a sort of moral jujitsu, using her fame to work against the tenets of the society that revered it. "She felt it was, in fact, the responsibility of her fame to use that platform [provided by celebrity]," said Jaffe. "She just happened to be the daughter of a famous actor, she just happened to be a famous actress herself, yet far and away more important than working was to use everything she could, in terms of the fame, to end the war."

Sometimes, her visibility worked against her. One predictable result of frantic motion was mistakes. Fonda learned her politics with a microphone six inches from her lips; it was an expensive tutorial. Her knowledge of American history and politics was about what might be expected of a wealthy suburbanite who dropped out of college in her teens. At the beginning, said Lane, "her level [of knowledge] was zero." She tried to get by on zeal, and couldn't always. She quickly earned a reputation for misstatements. In an appearance on the Dick Cavett television show, trying to support her argument that the United States should stay out of Vietnam, she declared that America, after all, had received no help from foreigners in its Revolutionary War. Later that night, with Jaffe and Lane, she watched a tape of the show and sat in crushed disappointment. It was not an infrequent occurrence: so confident and strident on stage, Fonda often agonized looking back. "She got depressed about a lot of the things she said," said Lane.

Her errors deepened her credibility problems, which was considerable to begin with. Fonda suffered because her movie image had been so insubstantial: light comedies such as *Cat Ballou* and sex farces like *Barbarella*. John Wayne had no more inherent moral authority to speak about the war than Fonda, but he had an easier time pushing his views because he had played war heroes for so long that many Americans confused him with the genuine article. His cinema image provided a credibility that hers did not. Wayne was known for winning the West and storming Normandy; Fonda was best remembered for stripping in zero gravity. Many reporters treated her conversion to weightier pursuits with skepticism that bordered on scorn.

Her response was to prepare for their inquisitions. "She began to study with the fervor of a lawyer who had two weeks to pass the bar and hadn't gone to law school," said Jaffe. Or an actress cramming for a part. Her long hours of self-education helped; Fonda was bright, a quick study. She grew smoother in her presentation, more assured in her command of facts, if a bit self-conscious about reciting them. With Jaffe, she strategized for hours about how to approach the media and gradually she became more comfortable around reporters, though her guard never entirely dropped.

Fonda learned her lines well enough. The deeper problem was that she had no anchoring beliefs to guide her whenever she was forced beyond the script. In those first frantic years of the 1970s, she was extraordinarily malleable, committed to a leftism that was as vague as it was passionate. In one interview, she defined herself as a "socialist" but one "without a theory, without an ideology." Lane wasn't sure she even understood the concepts. Her views changed monthly, weekly, sometimes hourly. Once, at a speech in Detroit when a group of students asked what they could do to protest the war, she told them to write to Congress. A few months later, she turned to Lane, as distraught as if she had told them to enlist: "Oh, my God, I said write to Congress. That was so naive!" During the preparation for the Winter Soldier hearings, which aimed to present a wide spectrum of GIs talking about atrocities in Vietnam, she met with a union leader and came away convinced that the program had to focus on working-class veterans. The next day she met with a local black leader and decided that the sessions had to highlight the experience of minorities in Vietnam. It was potluck politics: everything on the counter got swept into the stew. "If the movement took five years to get from point 'a' to point 'b,' Jane did it in ten minutes," said Lane. "Her political concepts were changing all the time."

Fonda underwent so many epiphanies principally because she had so little confidence in her own views. Since childhood, largely because of her father's remoteness, she had grown up deeply insecure. Fame did not fill the hole. She disguised her insecurity in public with a hard, self-confident façade. But what many people around her observed was a tendency to find a male mentor and subjugate herself to his point of view. In her acting career, that Svengali role was played first by a shadowy Greek director named Andreas Voutsinas, and then Vadim; when she launched her second career as an activist, she attached herself first to Fred Gardner, the father of the GI coffeehouse movement, then to Lane, and finally to Hayden.

To her artistic mentors, Fonda struggled to prove herself an actress; to her political mentors, she struggled to demonstrate herself a committed radical. Into the 1970s, as the movement factionalized, fractured, and grew more strident, Fonda fought constantly to remain at the vanguard. She felt herself always on trial from the left, not the right, on the unspoken charge of being a rich dilettante on a day trip. As she subsequently realized, her "self-loathing and contempt" for her background and her insatiable need to prove herself "sincere" led Fonda to assume the most radical positions in any debate. Her audience was less the public she was ostensibly trying to reach than the cadres she hoped to impress. She ran through militant declarations ("I didn't even know what the words really meant," she said later) as if trying to find the secret password to a new club.

And so, all the ingredients for an explosion had been assembled: an actress with extreme visibility who had sat out most of the 1960s and been shaped instead by the most exaggerated forces of the decade's end, when, to a portion of the left, actual revolt seemed imminent; who was in such a hurry and so fervent that she rushed into statements, making errors of fact and judgment; who had no grounding in her own experience or viewpoint to filter the passions that raged through the movement; and who was insecure and desperate to prove her purity. The question was not whether Jane Fonda would explode, but when.

Years after the explosion finally came, years after the trip to Hanoi, where she posed smiling atop the anti-aircraft gun aimed at American planes and delivered broadcasts telling American pilots that their actions made them war criminals, Jane Fonda would be driven to retrace her steps, again and again, like a survivor in a car wreck, trying to isolate just where she lost control. How did you get to the gun? Why did you make the broadcasts? Interviewers would pick at the wound, and she would reach back through the years, as if recalling the slick on the road, the squeal of the tires, and try to explain, or remember, or understand herself, why she didn't veer away, why she never saw the danger ahead. Where did she turn onto the road that led her to that moment? Could she even remember? Did she understand even then?

How did she get to North Vietnam? There were legitimate, immediate explanations. It was the summer of 1972. Throughout the spring, North Vietnam invited delegations of antiwar Americans to visit the country, to document the havoc Nixon's bombing was causing in civilian areas, to underline their charge that the administration planned to drown and starve the country by systematically bombing the dikes that protected its growing areas from flooding. In July 1972, leaving from Paris, Fonda flew to North Vietnam to see for herself.

But those facts offered only a partial explanation. Fonda had been moving toward her trip to North Vietnam ever since she returned from Paris almost three years earlier. Her journey since her return had been one not of homecoming but of alienation. Her travels took her to so many dark corners of America, so many monuments to the society's inequities, that all she could see in her own country was failure and corruption. She needed some model, some example to hold above the muck she waded through, and she found it in the North Vietnamese and Vietcong fighting "the encroachment of the American cancer." There were practical reasons why she flew to Hanoi at just that moment, but beneath them was the need to move beyond marching on army bases, or on Congress, or in the black ghetto, and to stand where the struggle against U.S. injustice was hottest; there was, as Hayden remembered, "a certain romantic wish to associate yourself with the supposed enemy and stand in solidarity with them."

Two notes dominated her trip, the same ones that defined her political activity at home. There was the genuine empathy she felt for suffering, and the cartoonish shrillness of her response to it. It was the horror of the civilian devastation she saw, the ruined hospitals and schools and houses, that drove Fonda, angry and anguished, to the radio to appeal to U.S. pilots. On many of the broadcasts, Fonda's unfiltered shame at her country's complicity in such indiscriminate destruction came through as pained and moving. "In the area where I went yesterday," she lamented in one broadcast to pilots, "it was easy to see that there are no military targets, there is no important highway, there is no communication network, there is no heavy industry. These are peasants. They grow rice and they rear pigs."

But the confused romanticism that initially set her on the road to North Vietnam ultimately betrayed her. What came across most clearly in Fonda's tour was not her instinctive anguish at the bombing, but her studied disaffection from her own country and her simplistic glorification of the North, all delivered in mock-revolutionary rhetoric that could have been lifted from a 1937 copy of *New Masses*. In the horror of the quagmire the Vietnam War had become, she could see only American perfidy and evil. With its "selfish principles," she told the Vietnamese in one broadcast, "U.S. society is not an answer to those who seek happiness. . . . I am also convinced that the unhappiness the American people are suffering physically and spiritually will not happen to the Vietnamese people, and we thank you for bringing us this hope."

Years later, Fonda would tell an interviewer that she regretted allowing herself to be photographed on the gun because it seemed to suggest she was "siding with them [the North Vietnamese] militarily. . . . Nothing could be further from the truth." That unqualified declaration doesn't square with the broadcasts she made over her two-week trip: they reveal instead a woman whose loyalties had become so confused, whose rage at her own country was so great that she felt thrilled to be among people who were taking up arms against the projection of its power. The impression left from her extensive broadcasts in North Vietnam, most of them aimed at U.S. servicemen, is that Fonda felt more emotional kinship with the North Vietnamese soldiers and civilians manning the anti-aircraft guns than with the U.S. airmen trying to destroy them, that her opposition to U.S. participation in the war had blurred into support of the North Vietnamese cause. "We . . . support the Vietnamese people's struggle," she declared in a broadcast on July 23. "We understand that you and we have a common enemy—U.S. imperialism. You and we have engaged in the same struggle, and your victory will also be that of the American people and of all peace-loving peoples throughout the world."

Fonda did not precisely ask U.S. servicemen to disobey their orders. But that was not an unreasonable implication for a listening airman to draw from her assertion that "the men who are ordering you to use these weapons are war criminals according to international law, and in the past, in Germany and in Japan, men who were guilty of these kinds of crimes were tried and executed." Or that "the use of these bombs or the condoning the use of these bombs makes one a war criminal."

Like Donald Ogden Stewart during the Stalin era, Fonda was mesmerized by her "socialist dream country." For Fonda, it was insufficient to find the United States at fault; North Vietnam had to be above reproach. "Never in my life have I been in a country of people that are so loving, and so nonalienated," she told U.S. servicemen in one broadcast. "They are truly at peace with their land and with each other. What do you see in the streets? You see people holding hands, arms around each other, helping each other, talking to each other, hugging each other, working together in the fields." Even the American prisoners of war, she said in one broadcast, would return from their exposure to this culture "better citizens then when they left." In an interview just after her return, Fonda made the captivity sound like a consciousness-raising group under the "humane" tutelage of the North Vietnamese: the prisoners, she said, "paint, they teach each other classes; they were very strong, interested, intellectual men who were thinking a lot of new kinds of thoughts because of the books they'd been reading."

Fonda returned from North Vietnam to ripples of controversy, not waves. The reaction grew over time. Her broadcasts were covered on the evening news, in the *New York Times,* the *Washington Post,* and the other major newspapers, but they weren't front-page events. Her trip generated much fulmination from the right, but no concrete action. The House Internal Security Committee, successor to the House Un-American Activities Committee that once summoned the Hollywood Ten, threatened to subpoena her but backed off when they realized she would welcome the forum.

In Hollywood, Raymond P. Caldiero, a businessman in charge of organizing celebrity support for President Nixon, remembered "outrage" among Hollywood conservatives about the trip. But that was narrowly felt. "It wasn't like it was a catastrophic event on which everybody started remarking," said Medavoy, Fonda's agent at the time. "Because you have to remember at this point, most people, certainly in this community, were against the war. And the fact was I don't think . . . anybody really understood what this trip was about." The reaction to the trip, in any case, was not strong enough to knock Fonda off stride. That fall, she and Hayden crisscrossed the country for the Indochina Peace Campaign, a grassroots organization they formed to focus an antiwar message on the states with the most electoral votes in the November presidential election. They opened an office in Washington, and on Labor Day in 1972 took to the road to encourage a large antiwar vote. Though they didn't specifically endorse McGovern (whose campaign was not too anxious for their embrace anyway), they indicated they would personally vote for him, and urged their audiences, whatever their feelings about the Democrats, to register their displeasure with the war by voting against Nixon.

The trip was another testament to Fonda's extraordinary power to force her views into the public eye. Armed only with Hayden's strategy and Fonda's fame, the couple produced virtually a shadow presidential campaign—without any of the accompanying amenities—just Hayden, Fonda, singer Holly Near, an antiwar former POW and an occasional guest speaker rushing by bus, car, and plane to county fairs, churches, colleges, synagogues. "It was . . . five 45-minute speeches a day, not to mention short appearances and press conferences, so it was like ten or fifteen appearances a day," Hayden remembered. Occasionally they faced threats of violence, but the dominant response both felt was one of homecoming. "The overwhelming experience was the feeling that middle Americans were coming around to our corner and we were connecting," Hayden said. "It was very, very liberating and exciting."

It was also very premature. Fonda generated more outrage the next spring when she declared, as the first POWs returned home from Vietnam, that prisoners who claimed they had been to tortured by the North Vietnamese were "liars and hypocrites." That bilious outburst reflected not only Fonda's alienation but Hayden's own lingering anger; as he later recalled, he may have offered the comment first. Not that anyone was fighting for authorship: Fonda's comments generated legitimate and widespread outrage. She was condemned far more violently than the previous summer. Fred Branfman, who ran the IPC operation in Washington, remembers watching the television and thinking, "Ouch. That, I thought, was stupid." The South Carolina state legislature approved a resolution asking state theaters not to show her films, protesters hanged her in effigy when she appeared at the University of Southern California; Indiana's state senate passed a resolution demanding she apologize; and Maryland legislators discussed whether to remove her tongue or execute her.

Fonda reconsidered a little bit in the subsequent firestorm, but not much. She had gone too far to back away from her idealized vision of North Vietnam. In the midst of the dispute, she told *Newsweek,* "There was most probably torture of POWs. Guys who misbehaved and treated their guards in a racist fashion or tried to escape were tortured. . . . But to say that torture was systematic and a policy of the North Vietnamese government is a lie. And the guys are hypocrites. They're trying to make themselves look self-righteous, but they are war criminals according to law." Even given several months to think about it, she backed down only half a step in a letter to the *Los Angeles Times,* acknowledging that she "was not there" and thus unable to refute all charges of brutality; but she repeated her assertion that the POWs were "hypocrites" and "pawns" of the Nixon administration and "lying" about systematic torture. Her monumental callousness overwhelmed the kernel of truth in her complaint that the Nixon administration was highlighting the POWs to divert attention from the disabled and disillusioned veterans disgusted with the war.

That curious and dispiriting episode symbolized Fonda's ambiguous career as a radical activist. Time and again, she demonstrated that a Hollywood star could produce unlimited publicity. But she left open the larger question of that publicity's impact. Did her trip to Hanoi, her marches and press conferences, help end the war sooner or only solidify hostility in Middle America against the protesters? Did it save lives, cost them, or have no discernible effect?

In the end, it is impossible to measure Fonda's impact on the antiwar movement. In the totality of the national debate, she was, of course, only a minor factor. But that says more about the enormity of the issue than the intensity of her efforts. No celebrity had ever maintained more presence, over a sustained period, in a serious national debate. She stoked passions on both sides. For the antiwar activists, especially as the fervor of the late 1960s corroded into despair, she rallied the troops; to Branfman she was no less than "Joan of Arc." Many protesters found her an inspirational symbol of the extent to which antiwar feeling had permeated the society. Clearly, the Nixon administration worried that Fonda was an effective force: the FBI, Secret Service, CIA, and State Department kept dossiers on her, monitored her bank transactions, opened her mail.

At the same time, she became a rallying point for the war's supporters. Particularly after the trip to Hanoi and her fusillade on the returning POWs, she embodied the aspects of the antiwar movement that it was better off suppressing: that portions of the movement believed the POWs to be war criminals, that some were more sympathetic to the men shooting at American soldiers than to those soldiers themselves. These were the accusations the right leveled at the war's opponents, and for those working in the mainstream Fonda seemed to prove their contentions. On balance, said George McGovern, a senator at the time, the antiwar forces in Congress "thought she was making it harder. I think they didn't condemn her and they knew it was well motivated, but I think they felt that [she] complicated the antiwar stance."

Other allies were more charitable. Edward F. Snyder, who worked with Fonda as co-chairman of the Coalition to Stop Funding the War, thought that while she symbolized for the war's supporters "the worst of the peace movement because she was fraternizing with the 'enemy' [and] giving them aid and comfort," her overall impact was equivocal. When she came with Hayden to lobby against funding for the war on Capitol Hill, Snyder found her surprisingly effective, able to obtain audiences even with members "who were inclined to be critical of her position." He remembers thinking that her trip to Hanoi would repel wavering members of Congress; but despite the revulsion the trip generated, Snyder believed it may have advanced the cause because it showed the intensity of opposition. If nothing else, Snyder and others thought, Fonda's radicalism provided cover for less incendiary dissent.

No calculus finally sorts it out. The answer may be that Fonda's lack of dexterity and her ideological shrillness essentially neutralized her extraordinary energy and commitment. Fonda understood the war was wrong, but in her eagerness to certify her radicalism, failed to learn a grammar that effectively made that case to Middle America. She succeeded in proving her conviction to the committed, and all impartial observers had to admire her courage for pressing her views at all cost. But to those who supported the administration, and even to many uncertain about the war, she became a symbol of coddled insensitivity and confused loyalties. It's not difficult to understand why men held in captivity, listening to her calls for their jailers to remain firm in the struggle, would hold grudges for decades.

Fonda captured the fundamental absurdity of the enticing and dangerous situation confronting Hollywood activists in the new era of media politics. At the heart of her difficulties was the fact that her fame allowed her to be irresponsible without losing her platform. Because her influence was based on her celebrity, not her acumen, because the media were willing to report anything she said, not just the remarks she could support, she never faced the prospect of being silenced if she did not think through her message. Instead, the press continued to hand Fonda shovels, and she continued to dig herself into holes.

It was a problem increasingly common in Hollywood as the internal restraints against public assertiveness melted away. The heightened willingness of the press to transmit the stars' political views did not by itself make those views more coherent. If anything, the more outrageous the remarks, the more likely they were to be covered. "These people have such a very difficult time thinking," thought screenwriter Jeremy Larner, "because no matter how fatuous what they say is, it gets taken very seriously."

Because she was a celebrity, Fonda was spared the rigors of serious thinking. But she was not spared the political price for her lack of it. Her enormous presence in the debate over the war showed her colleagues how sharp a weapon could be fashioned from fame. Her scars taught them that the blade could cut both ways.

Slowly Fonda appeared to learn these lessons herself. As the war wound down, she backed away from the front. Gradually, she reconnected with Hollywood, starring in a series of successful movies through the late 1970s, highlighted by her Vietnam War drama, *Coming Home.* Hayden launched a political career of his own, unsuccessfully challenging Democratic U.S. Senator John V. Tunney in a 1976 primary. Fonda increasingly ceded to him the leading role, particularly after she caused a major flap in the 1976 contest by accusing Tunney of dating teenagers. Hayden was forced to apologize and, according to campaign aides, was furious at Fonda. That was not a singular occurrence. His dismay at her missteps deepened her insecurities and strengthened her desire to lower her political profile through the mid-1970s, according to many friends. "At that point," said one close friend, "she felt herself to be an intellectually limited person, and that to a large extent was Tom's attraction. He completely intimidated her. That's been the ruling dynamic of their relationship from the beginning. She thought she had to subject herself to ever more intense study under Tom's leadership. She would just flagellate herself for making these mistakes."

The wounds from her radical moment never fully healed: the California state legislature rejected her nomination to the state arts council in 1979, citing her trip to Hanoi; and conservative and veterans' groups regularly protested her appearances. But time tamped the passions. Fonda enjoyed a wildly successful second career as a hyper-fit exercise maven, earning a fortune through workout salons, books, and videotapes. Hayden built a grassroots political organization with the proceeds and eventually won election to the California State Assembly in 1982. Through films such as *The China Syndrome* and *On Golden Pond,* Fonda once again became a top star. She campaigned against nuclear power and toxic wastes, and for "economic democracy," but more decorously. Eventually, in 1988, under pressure from local veterans' groups in Connecticut, where she was filming a movie, she apologized to veterans and POWs on national television for her remarks seventeen years earlier.

By then, few people in Hollywood remembered exactly what she had said or done or believed. It is not a community with much regard for the nuances of history, or for stories with morals that cannot be summarized the way television critics summarize new films: thumbs up, or thumbs down. In the 1980s, the ironies and complexities of her experience lost to time, Fonda would be elevated to political inspiration and role model by a generation of younger Hollywood actors and actresses, most of whom had not entered elementary school when she took to the microphone in Hanoi. They could not see the scars, only the survivor standing despite them.

After the Fire: Robert Redford

For Hollywood generally, the late 1970s were a time of political retrenchment. Passions stoked by the war were banked as the last Americans left Vietnam. No politician generated the following of McGovern, or even Nixon, except perhaps for California Governor Jerry Brown, whose appeal owed as much to curiosity as inspiration. Jimmy Carter actively avoided Hollywood. "He was totally uninterested," said Pat Caddell, who polled for the president. "I mean, totally unaffected by celebrities; just couldn't care less. . . . He just didn't see where it added anything." Hollywood felt much the same way about Carter. "He was really a foreigner here," said Mike Medavoy.

As emotions cooled nationally, the pendulum in the industry swung back toward greater political discretion. Once again notes of restraint sounded among Hollywood's activists. Both in substance and style, no one reflected the shift better than Robert Redford. As it evolved, his political career captured the more measured approach to the application of fame that predominated as the nation's political temperature lowered. Though he kept himself apart from Hollywood, living in rural Utah, visiting the film capital as infrequently as possible, he was as much a barometer of changing attitudes among the star activists in the late 1970s as Fonda was in the first part of the decade.

Like many actors, Redford was drawn to politics only after establishing himself on the screen. Concentrating on his career, he sat out the social movements of the 1960s. But when he achieved more success at the decade's end (particularly with his breakthrough role as Paul Newman's sidekick in the hit Western *Butch Cassidy and the Sundance Kid*), he picked up his head. Redford began to feel that a film career wasn't substantive enough for a thinking person. "Frankly," he told one interviewer, "it bothers me sometimes because I find it boring. . . . I don't feel it's enough."

The issue that first attracted Redford was not a front-page national dispute but an obscure local one. In 1970, he joined with several small environmental groups to stop the Utah highway department from building a six-lane freeway through a canyon near his home. That success inspired Redford to take more interest in politics, and political activists to take more interest in him. International celebrities with a bent for current events never have difficulty finding tutors, or supplicants. Once his interest in environmental issues became known, others concerned with the cause made their way to Utah. At first, Redford's involvement mostly took the form of assistance for independent filmmakers "who were trying to make films to demonstrate the injustices to the Indians or the environment," he recalled. "I helped by helping to edit or narrate their films." Those activities sent out more ripples, and soon national environmental groups petitioned him for help as a fundraiser and speaker. The process fed on itself. "At the same time I was being educated, I was getting angrier," Redford said. "The angrier I got the more I spoke out. It all came together, and it had its own momentum . . . the more I did it the more I was asked to do it."

His concerns—energy and the environment—were less combustible than Jane Fonda's, but at first his anger was comparable. "[Initially], my involvement in politics was quite radical and very singular," he said. "Those were the Nixon years, they were years of deception and deceit. It was the beginning of this condition that is now very prevalent in our society where people confuse not getting caught in a lie to be the equivalent of honesty. . . . I felt there was every reason to go out as an individual, because there was such a lack of awareness in the early 1970s. . . . My role, if I was going to contribute, seemed to be in the area of raising awareness, calling attention to something."

Even so, from the start, Redford approached the use of his fame more guardedly than Fonda or MacLaine, or even Newman. As in his films, he only opened up so much. He worked primarily on anonymous local issues, generally avoiding the splashy national debates and campaigns that drew the spotlight. That reflected his passion for privacy, which probably exceeded even Beatty's, but also his belief that he could exert the greatest influence at the lowest level. At one point, Redford accepted an appointment as chairman of the Provo Canyon Sewer District Committee.

If Redford did not commit nearly as much of his life to activism as, say, Fonda, he also avoided the vanguardism that got her into so much trouble; he often issued his manifestos in interviews with *Ladies' Home Journal,* the quintessential forum for reaching Middle America. He did not pretend to be an expert on all problems facing the nation; he stuck closely to the intertwined problems of environmental protection and energy conservation. He moved cautiously, and typically only after considerable study; it often seemed he would rather say nothing than make a mistake. "Redford is a different breed of cat, politically or any other way," said Jeremy Larner, who worked with him on the classic 1972 film *The Candidate*. "He is very controlled about what he does. And he doesn't want to get in situations where he is used by other people."

Redford could be irritatingly condescending in his blanket denunciations of politicians, but the edge was softened by his modesty about his own role; it was almost as if he felt he was a guest in another man's home, rather than a terrorist determined to burn it down. He displayed an instinctive political modesty that recalled Beatty's doubts, and Garner's before him, about the willingness of the public to hear the political views of their celluloid heroes. "I think by instinct I knew in 1969 and 1970 that it was going to be a double-edged sword with me, with anyone in my business," Redford said. "The fact that you have a built-in platform because of your visibility doesn't mean it is easily convertible into votes or persuasion. Because you have the platform . . . doesn't mean you are going to win a point. People are curious. They come out to a shopping mall to see what you look like, but not necessarily to vote [or listen] to you."

Redford's skepticism about the political process reinforced his caution. Over the years, he spent many hours lobbying in Washington on environmental and energy conservation causes (his tutor was Joan Claybrook, the head of Ralph Nader's Public Citizen organization), and observing the press corps for his role as *Washington Post* reporter Bob Woodward in *All the President's Men*. Claybrook thought the actor had a gift for working Capitol Hill. "He was terrific, he was just a natural at doing it," she recalled. "He knew his stuff. When he went to see a senator he was really well-briefed. . . . And he could see everyone he wanted."

But about three days in the capital was all Redford could take before fleeing back to the mountains. "You get caught up in a kind of false energy," he said. "There is this pace there, of things getting done, particularly on [Capitol] Hill, everybody keeping to a schedule, everybody dresses up. And that has its own energy. There is this big energy going on, and not all that much happening. But it is extremely attractive because you come away from it thinking that you've really done something. Well, you've just been a lot of places on time."

He was no more eager for the company of politicians on the campaign trail. Once he became known as an activist, candidates routinely sought his crowd-enlarging presence. Mostly he recoiled. Redford's dim view of politicians was accurately summarized by his work in *The Candidate*. Written by Larner, the movie portrayed an idealistic lawyer who wins election only by sacrificing his dearest principles at the urging of manipulative campaign advisers. (Fittingly, according to some friends, the film inspired the political aspirations of young Dan Quayle, whose supporters then sold him—in a considerable physiognomic stretch—as a Robert Redford look-alike.) "That film reflected a lot of my feelings about the political system," Redford said. "I developed this attitude about politics that was pretty cynical pretty early on just based on what I came to learn about our system and how we got people elected." If anything, the film reflected a softening of his attitude; studying politicians for the role gave him somewhat more empathy for their problems. "Making that film settled me into a position of about as much reason as I was going to have on the subject. . . . I went into it more blind with my anger and my negative feelings," Redford said. "Coming out of it, I understood more."

Still, his cynicism remained pungent. More than anything in the movie, a publicity stunt for its release may have best symbolized his views. Just before the 1972 political conventions, Redford, in a parody of the campaign, went on a mock whistle-stop tour through Florida. He would pull into a town and draw a huge crowd, larger than the presidential candidates had earlier that spring in the Florida primary, and then stride to the back of the train, tousled and dramatic, and declare: "I appreciate your coming out. I only ask you to think of this, my friends: I have absolutely nothing to say." And then the train would pull away.

That caustic stunt reflected his jaundiced assessment of politicians, but also suggested his sustained doubts about his own legitimacy as a spokesman. It wasn't only that Redford was uncertain that people were listening to him. It was that he was unsure whether they should. During the height of the McGovern campaign, when Beatty had collared virtually every liberal in Hollywood, Redford publicly demurred. He told journalist Richard Reeves, "I don't believe anyone cares what I have to say. Something funny happens to actors. As soon as people know you, you have some kind of power. As soon as people want to see you, you begin to think you really have something to say." He worried about imposing himself not only on his fans but also on what he called "the trenchmen," the scientists and attorneys actually grappling with the issues in the trenches. Redford understood how frustrating it could be for those underpaid, unpublicized people to work on a problem for years, to devote their lives to it, and then watch a movie star, filling time between films, breeze into town and attract half a dozen cameras for his casual assessment.

In all, Redford's experiences as a visible activist for environmental causes through the early 1970s deepened his initial doubts. His anxieties never reached the point where he didn't want to affect the debate; in that sense he remained very much the modern star activist. But he wasn't certain that his approach—the public leveraging of fame that had become increasingly common in Hollywood—actually achieved that goal.

For Redford, these conflicts peaked in the 1976 fight against the Kaiparowits power project—a huge coal-mining and power-plant complex planned by a consortium of utility companies for the desert in southern Utah, near five national parks and monuments. Redford asked the Environmental Defense Fund, a Washington-based group he had helped over the years, to open an office in Salt Lake City to focus on the project and the sharpening resource wars in the West. They pleaded poverty; Redford raised the money himself. For a year, Redford studied the plan, arming himself for conflict. Then, because opponents were unable to attract the media, he assumed a major public role in the campaign against the project. "That was the highlight of my single activism," he said.

Using his celebrity as the lure, Redford attracted a critical light that seared the project. He called a producer at "60 Minutes" who agreed to air a spot on the controversy, as long as Redford appeared for his side. Redford agreed (provided, he said, that the producers also sought out the project's top supporters, including the Utah governor) and led CBS through the site, the dramatic physical beauty underlining his words with silent intensity. "It was," Redford recalled, "a tremendously effective show." Ultimately, with the actor's considerable assistance, the opponents raised enough dust that one of the principal partners, Southern California Edison, pulled out and the project collapsed.

It was a great victory, but one that brought Redford's doubts about his methods to a head. The fight produced more intensity of feeling than he was willing to endure. Local residents who wanted the jobs the plant represented even burned Redford in effigy. "It got pretty redneck rough for a while," he recalled. "There were threats to my family and me that went on. I decided at that time that it was time to shift to a new role, and that for all the speaking out I was doing, it was probably being canceled out by the opposition to me speaking out and the resentment. And the threat to my family: I felt it wasn't fair to them, they weren't asking for this."

So Redford, like Beatty before him, sought a role with less visibility and potentially more access to power. He took on the singularly unglamorous task of encouraging greater environmental sensitivity among midlevel corporate managers. That was a long way from the picket line or rambles with "60 Minutes," but his run-ins with corporate executives had convinced him that many companies lacked the expertise to assess environmental issues even when they wished to. Redford, perhaps somewhat grandiosely, thought he could help fill the gap. He formed an organization called the Institute for Resource Management and through it raised the funds to design a model university course that would teach the principles of balanced resource use. But the project foundered. Its focus was too diffuse—it was difficult to see, even if universities picked up the model, how it would shift corporate behavior. Redford didn't want to finance it himself ("it would look bad, like my own toy") and, at the time at least, it was not a subject sufficiently flashy to loosen checkbooks at Hollywood cocktail parties.

When Reagan was elected president in 1980, Redford cut his losses and moved on. Though he abandoned his hopes of merchandising the course, he held to his conviction that building institutions made more sense than fighting for headlines. He redirected his institute to a new mission. With Reagan turning over the Interior Department to James G. Watt and the Environmental Protection Agency to Anne M. Gorsuch, Redford saw that "it was going to be really a rough time" for environmental causes. But rather than launching confrontational attacks on the administration and business, he decided to try to bring together environmentalists with the industry groups whose voices carried the most weight in Reagan's Washington. "It seemed that a mechanism that could bring the two groups together, to try to understand the way to go forward together, would be more radical than anything I could do," he said. "I thought that I would submerge my own involvement to a lower-key role, behind the scenes more, because I was known as an extreme environmentalist at that time. If you could get to industry and show them that you could make gains by working with environmental groups, that was the best thing you could do."

In effect, Redford turned his fame, his fundraising power, and his credibility away from the public and toward a precise and narrow audience. Through the 1980s, he organized, under the auspices of his Institute for Resource Management, a series of private conferences that allowed environmentalists and industry leaders to debate and reach greater consensus on the issues that divided them.

For the first conference, Redford brought environmentalists and utility executives to his Sundance Institute in Utah to examine the future of the electric power industry. For the next conference, he convened natural resource companies, environmentalists, and Indian leaders to discuss the treatment of Indian lands. Then he convinced senior oil company executives to sit down with top environmentalists to discuss offshore oil drilling in Alaska. Both sides usually went home impressed with the meetings—

and the host. Redford's old adversary from the Kaiparowits fight, Southern California Edison chairman and chief executive officer Howard Allen, came away from the first conference impressed enough to accept Redford's request to serve as the institute's chairman of the board.

"The door-opener is that it is Robert Redford the actor, who is a celebrity," said Allen. "But if he didn't have substance and an intellectual approach, it wouldn't have lasted. And you can't help but sit there and hear him really ad lib the opening of these conferences—or some cases where he has participated the whole time—and come away with anything but an impression of the substantiveness of the man. His business is communications, and he has to be a quick study. But to translate that into clean air and global warming and natural resources and all the other issues takes some pretty basic brainpower and sincerity, and he has both."

From Allen's perspective, the conferences have been "a positive force in achieving a dialogue and better understanding among government, industry, environmental groups, wildlife groups, Native Americans, regulators, and about anyone who has a self-interest to advocate or protect." In the conference on offshore oil, the two sides actually reached a formal agreement on their differences. "It was a beautiful thing the way the process evolved," Redford said. "It took about eighteen months [after the conference] to put together an agreed-upon accord, from both groups, but we did. They signed a resolution, and we took it to [Interior Secretary Donald P.] Hodel in Washington, all of us, we went together. We said, 'Here is a process that will work and we accept.' He thanked us very much, put it on the shelf and buried it."

That was a disappointment, but the conferences have both pleased and changed Redford. The long hours of informal exposure to business leaders softened the anger that Redford often displayed in the 1970s. He lashed out less, took more moderate positions. "He really is a hell of a lot more balanced," said Allen. "In the earlier days, I felt he was only looking at one part of the broad issue. Today, I think, through experience he realized that Native Americans are not going to better their standard of living if they don't develop some of their resources, or you're not going to have the experience of driving on our highways at reasonable cost if we can't develop some offshore oil."*

---

*In his newly conciliatory role, Redford, by the late 1980s, finally agreed to support a revised plan to build a modern highway through Provo Canyon, near his home. But his conversion—which came after public hearings indicated extensive support in the community for improvement on the winding old road that currently traverses the canyon—came too late for many in the conservative Utah towns that surround his Sundance homestead. Redford is "probably the most hated man in this county," a reporter for the local weekly told the *Wall Street Journal* in late 1989.

If Redford had sanded some of his edges, he nonetheless remained on the front line of emerging environmental concerns. During a 1988 trip to the Soviet Union for an exhibition of his films, Redford met with officials at the Soviet Academy of Sciences and invited them back to Utah for a private superpower summit on global warming and the greenhouse effect. They agreed, and for three days in August 1989, Redford hosted many of the top environmental scientists from both countries. "The idea," Redford said at the time, "was to find what we could agree on and act on that." That was a fitting summary for his political work over the previous decade.

But even as his private mediating efforts took root, Redford was drawn again toward the public role. By the late 1980s, environmental issues had suddenly exploded into vogue. He felt himself nearing another turning point. "There are three stages [to my involvement]," Redford said. "An individual, more radical, outspoken approach . . . in the early 1970s. Then there was the formation of the IRM for the 1980s, where I took a more submerged role. Now we are moving into a new era. I think everything is accelerating so rapidly. The environment is no longer a dirty word. We are beginning to use the word 'planet.' Everybody is recognizing the fact that we have to start working together. So it is now a time of action . . . and I would rather be freed up personally to be available to that, rather than completely spending all my time in a mechanism that brings people together."

The first indication of his changed attitude came in 1988 as he campaigned across the country for Democratic presidential nominee Michael Dukakis. Redford appeared with Dukakis in New Jersey (his speech was marred by persistent hecklers), and then set off on his own through half a dozen states. Though he opened his first appearance with a gibe at Dan Quayle, his political doppelganger, Redford tried to stick to the high road. "I campaigned for the environment," he said afterward, "never really for Dukakis." In the end, he was disappointed at his reception: "It got not a lot of attention because the media had decided at that time . . . that he was a loser."

But the trip revealed cracks in his earlier conviction that it did little good to burnish a candidate with his fame. His attitude toward campaigning "is changing," Redford said. "It might be shifting in this sense. . . . [In national elections] I [still] don't think it matters. There is a huge roster of celebrities on both sides and they cancel each other out. I just honestly don't believe that one individual celebrity does that much for a candidate. I think you can make a difference in a congressional race when you go into a district: for a [Representative] Phil Sharp or a [Senator] Tom Harkin in Indiana and Iowa, when you stand there in a room and say, 'I am here because I see a side of this person you may not get to see, I see the hard work he does outside for you.' That's one way to help." If New Jersey Senator Bill Bradley seeks the 1992 Democratic presidential nomination, Redford said, he could even imagine a more visible role in that campaign. "Bradley is possibly a different matter," he said. "He is a friend and I've supported him through two elections. He is a real student. I like his approach, and his process [for making decisions]."

Redford's return to the national spotlight illuminated an underlying truth. After the enormous changes that have swept through Hollywood and national politics in the past three decades, there is no reverting to the days when stars kept their opinions to themselves. There remain individual voices in Hollywood (and Washington) who counsel prudence, and individual stars behave with varying degrees of restraint. But the demands from politicians and causes on celebrities are so insistent, and the media platform so enticing, that exceedingly few stars with an interest in public life mute themselves entirely. When Redford decided to make himself available for an interview with CBS on the occasion of his global warming conference, the network virtually turned over to him its entire morning news show for discussion of the issue. Given his passion about the problem, it's not surprising Redford accepted the offer, despite his ambivalence about the propriety of stars proselytizing to their fans.

It's likely that over time there will be more such episodes. Few politically interested stars are as reticent as Redford about using the opportunities presented by fame to influence the public. Quite the opposite: many celebrities have concluded that because their lives are so publicly displayed, they influence their fans whether they consciously choose to or not. For Michael Stipe, lead singer of the popular rock band R.E.M., that awareness was crystallized when two young fans approached a friend of the band in tears, devastated and disillusioned because they had heard unfounded rumors that one of the band members was addicted to heroin. That incident quickened Stipe's already gestating desire to use his implicit platform. Now, during the band's concerts and in interviews, he regularly urges fans to become involved in environmental and other social causes. Not all celebrities are given such dramatic demonstrations of their impact on their audience, but many more than ever now share with Stipe the conviction that stardom is "a megaphone."

With that belief widespread in Hollywood, it is no more possible to imagine a campaign season without celebrities than it is a return to the days when candidates sat on the front porch, waiting for voters to come to them. None of the recent trends that have encouraged stars to greater activism—the decentralization of power in Hollywood, the rise of television politics, the loss of esteem of politicians—are likely to be reversed. Nor are we as a society likely to end our habit of reducing complex issues and social movements to contests between competing individuals—a phenomenon that makes stars, our most recognizable individuals, logical spokepeople for those movements. At least since the rise of the big city newspapers after the Civil War, American journalism has been marked by the "tendency to translate every situation into the terms of personal will and conflict," as one historian wrote. With its need for recognizable spokesmen and its insistence that all debate be compressed into easily digestible fifteen-second "sound bites," television has exponentially advanced that process. The result, as author Richard Schickel has observed, is that we constantly create political celebrities to simplify and apprehend complex issues. In the shorthand of modern politics, Ralph Nader is consumerism, Jerry Falwell is religious fundamentalism, North Carolina Republican Senator Jesse A. Helms is conservatism, and Ted Kennedy is liberalism. Because most Americans do not pay much attention to the details of public debate, they use these symbolic individuals as touchstones to orient themselves, to provide a quick gauge of how they feel about ideas, or issues, or candidates.

The expanding mobilization of Hollywood figures for political purposes has to be seen in that modern context of simplified debate, political celebrities, and minute public attention spans. National politicians have, with growing shrewdness, exploited the potential political value of fame since the days of Franklin Roosevelt. But, as the experiences of Newman, MacLaine, Fonda, and Redford suggest, stars have become much more relevant to politics in the past three decades—a period during which the public (with the notable exception of the Vietnam War era) has generally come to see politics as less relevant to their lives.

That is not a coincidence. The glamorous rise of the celebrity activist marks nothing so much as the dreary anesthetizing of American politics. Celebrities have not caused the public to lose interest in politics; but their heightened political use is an understandable response to an uninterested public. Political campaigns and Washington's decisions occupy such a marginal place in American life today that it is not unreasonable for political strategists to believe they must bribe the public to pay attention by occasionally adorning obscure debates with famous faces. At a time when public debate revolves around personalities who stand as political symbols, it is inevitable that causes will deploy as spokespeople stars who are themselves symbols—of intelligence, empathy, bravery, compassion, desire. It may be irrational for our public dialogues and presidential elections to be reduced to blips of choreographed symbolism on the evening news. But it is hardly irrational for causes and candidates to fight for their fleeting moment by enticing the camera with a star.

In that sense, the routine enlistment of celebrities as political spokespeople stands as the logical result of sound-bite politics. The overriding rules of political communication in the television age—keep it short, keep it visual, keep it dramatic—are rules that Hollywood understands. Actors and actresses may have enormous knowledge about a subject or they may have none. But few politicians are as skilled as Hollywood's top stars at staring into a camera and sounding as if they know what they're talking about, at least for their fifteen seconds on the local news. "The more the forum—television—proliferates," says Warren Beatty, "the more it is going to fall to people who can express themselves clearly and dramatically to sway public opinion, to coalesce public opinion. . . . Reagan was not an accident." That doesn't mean the Senate will eventually be filled with fading actors (if for no other reason than that few would subject themselves to the public rigors of campaigning). But it does mean that for better or worse, the star with a cause and a microphone—like negative commercials, focus groups, instant analysis, and the message of the day—has become a permanent feature of modern media politics.

CHAPTER EIGHT

THE REAGAN BACKLASH AND BEYOND

Star Wars

To many of those on both sides of the divide, nothing better symbolized the steady blurring of the lines between entertainment and
politics than the methodical rise of Ronald Reagan as a national
conservative leader. Throughout his career as California governor, in his
unsuccessful attempt to wrest from Gerald R. Ford the GOP's presidential nomination in 1976, and finally in his capture of the nomination four
years later, Reagan pointedly demonstrated the enormous practical value
of an actor's training in an era when television dominated politics. As if
by flicking a switch, Reagan could convey sincerity, conviction, anger,
humility, sadness, pride. Other politicians withered under the camera's
insistent eye; Reagan reveled in it. Richard B. Wirthlin, the pollster in all
Reagan's national campaigns, remembers being stunned at Reagan's
ability "to take a line and repeat it 110 times, and sound just as fresh and
just as new the 110th time as the first time he used it." For a politician
it was indeed remarkable; but Reagan's "gift" was nothing more than the
hard-won skill of an actor who had spent years manufacturing sincerity
on command, take after wearying take, on the Warner Bros. lot.

His years in those surroundings prepared him for his new life in other respects. Without a script Reagan was always subject to political pratfalls; but with one, he was Fred Astaire. Adlai Stevenson, the most literary presidential nominee in the television era, had been renowned for his inability to compress his words into the unforgiving deadlines of televised commercials; Reagan, the Hollywood journeyman, consistently hit his marks to the second. "I remember being with the governor in early 1980, with Pete Dailey, who was doing his ads," Wirthlin recalled, "and we were using the governor to speak directly to the camera. Pete would say, 'We have about 16, 17 seconds of direct copy, give the governor his cues.' And he would deliver 16, 17 seconds. Pete said he never met anyone who could time so perfectly his comments." Reagan had perfect timing in another sense, too. He had a sharp instinct for the defining dramatic moment—the lifting of an old movie line ("I am paying for this microphone") to separate himself from the rest of the Republican candidates at a pivotal 1980 debate in New Hampshire, the resonant question to the electorate ("Are you better off than you were four years ago?") that rang like a concluding cannon burst in his only debate with President Carter that fall.

Still, as the 1980 race took shape, the Carter campaign assumed that Reagan's Hollywood roots would hobble him. In a memo that summer outlining the campaign's advertising strategy, Gerald M. Rafshoon, Carter's media adviser, listed a series of contrasts he intended to draw between the incumbent and his challenger: "Young/old . . . vigorous/old . . . smart/dumb . . . engineer/actor." The Carter team hoped to offer Reagan's acting career as evidence that he was not up to the nation's top job.

Each of Rafshoon's comparisons had merit: Reagan was old, far less vigorous physically or mentally than Carter, and shaped in his reactive approach toward administration by long years of dutifully taking direction in Hollywood. (His political advisers often described him as the most agreeable candidate they had ever worked with.) Still, from the start there were reasons to be dubious of the attempt to paint Reagan into that corner: California Governor Pat Brown had had little success with the same arguments fourteen years earlier, when Reagan lacked any government experience at all. Nonetheless, Rafshoon's memo reflected political reality in at least one respect: Reagan's history as an actor did remain an important part of his public persona long after his two terms as chief executive of the nation's largest state. In one of his initial surveys for the 1976 challenge to President Ford, Wirthlin asked voters the first thing that came to mind when they heard Reagan's name: slightly more said movie actor than governor of California. Four years later, after the race against Ford, more people perceived Reagan as a significant political figure. But even in the 1980 campaign, almost one in ten voters saw him principally as an actor.

With Democrats hoping to strengthen that perception (Carter declared hopefully in one speech that when the campaign was over Reagan would be "right back . . . in Hollywood as a movie actor"), Reagan's men took a careful approach toward their candidate's years in the service of Jack Warner and Lew Wasserman. They did not put it on the marquee. On the campaign trail, Reagan was rarely surrounded by celebrities; when he was, they were mostly old friends—Jimmy Stewart, Charlton Heston, Bob Hope, and the leading GOP convert of the previous decade, Frank Sinatra. And Reagan's Hollywood years were hardly highlighted in the long biographical spot that anchored his advertising campaign. "We surely didn't play to it," said Wirthlin. "It didn't serve the strategic imperative of the campaign at that time, which was to position Ronald Reagan as a strong, effective leader. . . ."

But neither did the campaign run away from Reagan's background on the backlot. Hollywood figures were funneled into the limited roles the campaign deemed useful. In his soothing voice, Jimmy Stewart taped radio ads; Sinatra, Dean Martin, and Wayne Newton performed at fundraising concerts. For the crucial passage in his nationally televised speech on Election Eve, Reagan invoked the late John Wayne. To challenge Carter's claim that a malaise had sapped the will of the American people, Reagan summoned, not the words of a former president or statesman, but the Duke's vision of a mythical, simpler and stronger America. "Last year I lost a friend who was more than a symbol of the Hollywood dream industry," Reagan declared. "To millions he was a symbol of our country itself. Duke Wayne did not believe our country was ready for the dustbin of history. Just before his death, he said in his own blunt way, 'Just give the American people a good cause and there's nothing they can't lick.' " Those were hardly the words of a man afraid to draw attention to his Hollywood roots.

Reagan's confidence was well placed. As the Democrats unhappily learned, the charge that Reagan was "only" and actor carried weight only with the converted. Voters who didn't like Reagan's ideology wrote him off as an uninformed actor, but others did not reject him when reminded of his background. The same pattern held in office. The denigration of the president as an actor who relied on advisers to script even his most basic movements and remarks always shadowed Reagan, but it never engulfed him. Inevitably, as he settled into the presidency, negotiated with Congress, and mingled with international leaders, Americans were increasingly less likely to think of him as an actor at all. By 1982, Wirthlin was no longer measuring the association: it had become politically meaningless.

Except in one particular, highly politicized community. The last place that forgave Ronald Reagan for being an actor was Hollywood. From the moment of his first political success in Sacramento, the Hollywood left took Reagan's rise as a personal insult. After his election as governor, liberal director William Wyler said ruefully to Charlton Heston, "You know, if we had given Reagan a couple of good parts, he'd never be in Sacramento now." The hostility deepened as Reagan ascended the political ladder. Early in the 1980 campaign, when young Morgan Mason, son of actor James Mason and a Reagan campaign aide, sent out roughly two thousand letters seeking support in the movie, television, and publishing industries, he received only a hundred responses, "about ninety of them hate letters." That was another reason Reagan was surrounded only by old friends from Hollywood in the last days of the campaign.

Reagan's landslide election in 1980 alternately horrified, stunned, and amazed Hollywood liberals. The idea that his conservatism spoke to emerging currents of public opinion dismayed by the drift of the Carter years was never seriously considered. It was widely assumed that Reagan had mesmerized the public with cheap stagecraft. In the salons of the Westside, the communal cry was that if the public wanted to elect an actor, why couldn't it at least have chosen a good one? "It had sort of the same impact of a movie everyone knows is terrible getting great reviews and having great audiences," said actor Robert Foxworth, who starred on CBS's "Falcon Crest." "It is kind of sickening when you know there is so much better work being done. It was like, 'How did he make it?' " Perplexed, the liberals wondered: Why did the public buy an act we could see through so easily? Almost without exception, the Hollywood left was convinced that its own understanding of the actor's tools provided unique abilities to penetrate Reagan's façade and expose the shallowness it saw behind it. "What we were seeing was Frankenstein's monster in a sense; we were seeing this media product . . . and we knew! We knew who this guy really was!" said actor Mike Farrell, who is as liberal in real life as B. J. Hunnicutt, the kind-hearted doctor he portrayed on "M*A*S*H."

That deepening sense of the camera's enormous power in presidential campaigns grew out of partisan dismay at Reagan's victory, but its implication for Hollywood's political role was in one crucial respect nonpartisan. Reagan's success reinforced the belief that the growing use of entertainment techniques in elections diminished any legitimate objection to the participation of stars in politics. In the long-simmering internal debate over Hollywood's proper role, Reagan at last provided the irrefutable example for those who counseled more aggressive engagement. "At a time when we have a former actor as President of the United States, I don't see how anyone can ask that question," Jane Fonda told one interviewer who asked whether it was proper for stars to use their fame for political causes. Even many conservatives felt the same way. Gradually the Republican voices that had been muted, at least since Watergate, resurfaced. "Never before did so many conservatives make their views known," said Charlton Heston, the conservative who made his views known more clearly than any other.

Over time, though, the conservative voices would be obscured by the chorus raised in Hollywood against Reagan. Though he emboldened Republicans and encouraged political activity on both sides, Reagan's lasting impact was to reinvigorate the Hollywood left after the torpor of the Carter administration. In their eagerness to combat Reagan, to "expose" him, the Hollywood liberals launched a wave of organization building more vigorous than anything seen since the 1940s, when Reagan himself trooped to meetings of the Hollywood Democratic Committee. What had once inspired him, Reagan now inspired to opposition.

Opposition to Reagan's agenda bubbled up from Hollywood even before he took the oath of office. First off the line was producer Norman Lear, the father of Archie Bunker, Maude, and Mary Hartman. In 1980, while researching a satirical movie about evangelism, Lear screened dozens of episodes of Jerry Falwell's television program, an experience he found anything but amusing. Rather, he saw Falwell and the other fundamentalist preachers congregating around Reagan as terrifying. "It was the relentless political message that got to me," Lear recalled afterward. "Hour after hour they were telling people, 'You are a good Christian or a bad Christian, depending on your view of the Supreme Court, or capital punishment." The rise of the fundamentalists became a burning concern for Lear, who had a somewhat idiosyncratic response to issues that troubled him: he bought advertisements to share his feelings. When he fell for Illinois Representative John B. Anderson, who was seeking the GOP presidential nomination that spring, Lear simply took out full-page ads in the *Boston Globe* on the eve of the Massachusetts primary. When he finished screening Falwell's fulminations, he decided—the way another man might dispatch a letter to the editor of the local newspaper—to write a television commercial denouncing the intolerance of the fundamentalists.

Lear was smart enough to understand that he made an imperfect foil for Falwell. "I was not a credible foe," he said later. "I was Jewish, a member of the Hollywood community. So I sought to get help from the mainline church leaders." While Reagan marched toward the White House with Falwell in tow, Lear flew around the country vetting his ideas with mainstream religious leaders; eventually, like a Jewish pope, he assembled his own ecclesiastical advisory council. Lear ran half a dozen ideas for television commercials by them; half they rejected as offensive, the others they blessed. Lear then put on his first advertisement—a hard-hat sitting on a forklift complaining about preachers meddling in poli-tics—in October 1980, a few weeks before the Reagan landslide.

While writing the commerical, Lear had given little thought to how, or even whether, to follow his initial salvo. But others convinced him to tack onto the ad's conclusion a toll-free number to solicit donations toward the airtime cost. (Lear had financed the commercial's production him-self.) Not long after the ad was broadcast, Lear unexpectedly had in his possession the names of nearly ten thousand people sympathetic to his message. His conversations with religious leaders revealed that no other group intended to monitor and challenge the religious right. The elec-tion results made clear that Falwell would not be returned to obscurity. So Lear suddenly had the means to build an organization, and the need, too: in early 1981, he provided the seed money for a group called People For the American Way.* "I didn't sit down to start an organization," Lear would often say. "For me, that was an act of spontaneous combustion."

Exactly what the new organization would do remained unsettled for some time. Different visions contended. Lear's approach to politics was sweeping. He thought less in terms of legislative thrust and parry than of the grand sweep of cultural history; he saw himself as more Toynbee than Tip O'Neill. Unlike his Malibu Mafia friends—Stanley Sheinbaum, for example, or Max Palevsky—Lear preferred expounding on the crisis of the American character to scheming about how the Democrats could retake the Senate. "Palevsky and Stanley, say, have substantive agendas; Norman really doesn't," said Anthony Podesta, the former organizer for Eugene McCarthy who became the first president of People For the American Way. "If you asked Stanley what three things he'd want the president to do, he'd have a list; if you asked Norman, he'd talk about the national spirit."

The national spirit was precisely Lear's original target for the new

---

*The group actually incorporated under the name Citizens for Constitutional Concerns, but went by People For the American Way from the beginning; several years later, it reincorporated under its common name.

group. Lear figured enough organizations were filing lawsuits and monitoring Congress; he wanted to insinuate ideas into the culture. His goal was to appeal as broadly as possible by phrasing the issue as broadly as possible, as a choice between tolerance (the American way) and intolerance (the fundamentalist way). That vision shaped the group's character. To launch the organization, Lear found important support and early funds from several of his old allies in the Malibu Mafia, most prominently Ted Ashley and Sheinbaum, and other Hollywood figures such as Martin Sheen and Burt Lancaster. But Lear carefully limited their participation; his fears of identifying the fundamentalist opposition with left-wing, bohemian, and, not incidentally, Jewish Hollywood remained strong, and he weighted the board of directors with establishment corporate and religious figures.

The same approach, simultaneously cautious and cosmic, determined the group's initial activities. Lear recruited the skilled and quirky director Jonathan Demme *(Melvin and Howard, Married to the Mob)* to cut a series of ads showing ordinary people and celebrities talking about the different ways they liked their eggs, their music, and their sports. "Freedom of thought," the ads concluded, "that's the American way."

Lear saw this as an exquisitely subtle plea for tolerance, which it may have been, but its connection to, say, the censorship of textbooks seemed unduly obscure to Podesta and others in the group. Instead of defending omelets, they preferred that the organization take a stand, for example, against the school prayer amendment. Lear initially recoiled from that idea. "He thought it was too controversial," Podesta recalled. "Norman was not remotely political. It was all whitebread mid-America: [he thought] we've got to stand for things no one can disagree with."

These divergent perspectives gave the organization a schizophrenic character in its first months. From Washington, it would appeal for new members by promising a brass-knuckled fight against the religious right; then Lear would produce a red-white-and-blue primetime television special showing Barry Goldwater introducing marching bands and John Wayne (on tape) saluting Jane Fonda's right to say whatever she wanted. At one level, the show was brilliant symbolism, an attempt to reclaim the flag and patriotic values from conservatives; at another, it was a mystifying reaffirmation of the obvious to members of the group anxious to rumble with creationists. "Norman had a unique ability to see how the public consciousness should be pricked," said one early board member, "but he did not see how that change in consciousness could be plugged into political goals." It was as if Lear sometimes couldn't see the trees for the forest.

Gradually, Podesta (with assistance from Sheinbaum and other board members) steered the organization toward a more traditional lobbying and organizing role. Lear didn't quarrel with success, and his imprint on the organization remained strong. Because of his continued involvement, the group maintained its sophisticated approach to transmitting its message through television. And it raised significant funds from Lear's Hollywood associates. But once the group plunged into legislative fights, the center of its activities shifted from Lear's office in Los Angeles to Washington. As it grew through the 1980s into one of the capital's most powerful liberal lobbying organizations—a key player, for example, in the 1987 fight to deny a Supreme Court seat to Appellate Judge Robert H. Bork—the group simultaneously diminished as a force in Hollywood's political life. In Hollywood itself, the response to Reagan shifted to other issues.

Initially, the most powerful of these was the administration's belligerent approach in Central America. Within months of Reagan's inaugural, dozens of Hollywood figures placed an angry advertisement in a Los Angeles alternative newspaper demanding "non-intervention in El Salvador." Of those who signed the plea, none became more prominent in opposition to Reagan's Central American policy than Mike Farrell.

Farrell offered a telling example of how image informed reality in modern Hollywood politics. Though he inherited liberal instincts—his father had been a blue-collar Democrat—Farrell became involved in Central American concerns largely because the character he played on M*A*S*H "was seen as a compassionate soul," he recalled. Assuming that B.J.'s gentle humanism reflected Farrell's own attitudes, a refugee organization called CONCERN asked him to join their cause. The assumption was accurate. Farrell viewed a film the group had produced on refugee children in Asia, was moved, and eventually signed on as the organization's North American spokesman. About the time Reagan ousted Carter, Farrell traveled with the group to visit refugee camps in Southeast Asia. The misery overwhelmed him, and so did something else: the bizarre experience of being recognized "even in these little hole-in-the-wall camps. . . . I continue to be stupefied by that."

The experience convinced Farrell of the enormity of his fame and solidified his urge to direct it purposefully. "I felt a responsibility, opportunity too, but a responsibility is what I felt most," he said. "It is a kind of an ombudsman role: people who don't have the voice can say something to me, and I can go out and translate it to a crowd and it has some effect. And they feel they are noticed if I pay some attention. I feel like it is my job, my duty almost, to see that that attention is paid because I have access to the media."

When CONCERN organized another trip to refugee camps early in 1982, this time in Honduras, on the El Salvador border, Farrell signed on again. The experience shook him even more than the first. "It was the same brutality, the same horror, the same wounded souls, the same scars, all this stuff that is so difficult for any human being to take in and relate to," he said. "But the difference was, when I came back from Cambodia and talked about it, people said, 'Well, those people are Communists.' . . . When I came back from Central America, the guys doing that dirty stuff are American-trained, American-armed, American-funded, and in some cases Americans themselves. Paid for by me. My tax dollars. It was infuriating." Farrell came back angry and vocal, and almost instantly groups fighting the administration's policies in the region swarmed over him. Soon, he was appearing on television and in the press warning of "another Vietnam."

Among those traveling with Farrell through the refugee camps in early 1982 was Margery Tabankin, a veteran liberal organizer and former Carter administration official newly installed as the executive director of the liberal Arca Foundation in Washington. Like Farrell, Tabankin came back from the tour committed to fighting Reagan's Central American policies. She convinced the foundation to finance trips through the region for notables in business, politics, and entertainment. Over the next few years, liberal Hollywood celebrities, from Robert Foxworth to Mandy Patinkin, trooped through Central America under Arca's direction. Others, such as Richard Gere, were recruited to the cause through Dr. Charles Clements, author of the book *Witness to War* and an early opponent of the Reagan program.

Almost invariably the stars came back sympathetic to the Sandinista government in Nicaragua and repelled by the American-backed forces in El Salvador. "The depth of the madness surprised me," said Richard Gere. "El Salvador especially is the most tense place I've been in my life. . . . It's a horrendous experience being there. And this is our show-place in Central America. Everyone is terrified, constantly. When we flew into Managua, as soon as you get down there, everything is okay, people are smiling, things are functioning properly. You immediately feel like you can talk openly, which you couldn't in El Salvador." The newly energized stars provided a steady stream of recruits for groups opposing aid to the contras and the Salvadoran government. Eventually the Hollywood figures coalesced into their own organization, the Committee of Concern for Central America, which sent lobbyists to Washington, brought Nicaraguan leader Daniel Ortega to speak in Los Angeles, and launched a national series of celebrity-studded town meetings to mobilize opposition to the administration's policies.

To some extent, the distant war in Central America appealed to the Hollywood left because it was more immediate for them than for most people: through local organizations, those active in the cause were regularly exposed to the refugees streaming into Southern California. But the interest also drew on the powerful ideological hunger in various corners of the film industry for an issue around which to resist the conservative ascendancy symbolized by Reagan.

"The civil rights movement had moved into the antiwar movement [during the 1960s] but once the war was over there was a kind of loss of balance," said Farrell. "Some of [that energy] translated into the various rights movements: Chicano rights, gay rights, continuation of black rights, women's rights. But it was kind of disparate movements banging into each other. . . . I don't want to make it sound premeditated but it was kind of like there was this roiling resentment [at the country's direction] and people knew things were wrong, and suddenly [with El Salvador and Nicaragua] there was this real thing they could get their hands on, instead of these vague ephemeral issues that weren't satisfying, that you couldn't get your teeth into. This was a real one, and people's response to it seemed to have been very personal and passionate."

The same hunger drew dozens of Hollywood figures into the campaign for a nuclear freeze that erupted in 1982 as a grassroots protest against Reagan's military buildup and hostility toward arms control. Suddenly, dinner parties and story conferences were interrupted for earnest discussions of megatonnage and EMP; fear of nuclear winter settled over the land of perennial sunshine. Stars and executives cast around for ways to do something about what more than one called, with the insularity of those thoroughly removed from ordinary cares, "the only issue that really mattered."

Businessman and veteran antiwar activist Harold Willens, late of the Malibu Mafia, focused the sudden outpouring of energy by pushing a November 1982 ballot initiative to place the state of California on record behind a nuclear freeze. Hollywood flocked to his side, more enthusiastically than it had to any cause since the early 1970s. Defiantly unexpert, the stars felt comfortable with the movement's general aura, which stressed the importance of the public taking back control of the issue from the obscurantist nuclear theorists. Soon so many people were buzzing through Hollywood carrying freeze banners that even the most cautious felt safety in numbers.

To this general appeal was added some hardnosed political organizing. Early on, freeze supporters shrewdly enlisted a coterie of well-placed publicists and managers and through that network reached an extraordinary number of top stars. Paul Newman became the leading spokesman for the cause. Sally Field hosted fundraisers. Dozens of stars listened earnestly and glamorously at fundraising concerts and brunches and cocktail parties; even Lew Wasserman lent his name. In one of the strangest media events of the decade, Paul Newman and freeze opponent Charlton Heston haltingly attempted to debate the issues on ABC's late-night news program "The Last Word," whose early demise was apparently not related to their bizarre appearance, though it probably should have been.

That strange event left many observers temporarily wondering whether the trend toward the use of stars as mouthpieces for complex issues had gone too far. ("See what happens when we elect an actor President?" one critic wrote after the dreary spectacle. "We get nuclear policy debated on TV by Moses and Butch Cassidy.") But the moment of introspection passed, and the debate roared on. Stars were essential for both raising money and attracting attention. "When I ran the nuclear freeze PR in 1982," said Hollywood public relations consultant Josh Baran, "we did a news conference with Harold Willens. . . . I got one person. KPFK [a local public radio station] showed up. Not good for my image as a mega-PR muffin. So I called Paul Newman. He said he would help. . . . We did another news conference, with Willens and him and one other person there. I had 150 press there, twelve camera crews. . . . That's when I learned you have to have circus acts, you have to have celebrities."

Narrowly, and with the significant help of Hollywood, the freeze initiative passed in California that fall. And then, just as quickly, the freeze movement collapsed, in Hollywood as everywhere else. The movement could claim credit for stirring the Reagan administration to more serious negotiations, but it was also a reminder that Hollywood experienced sudden and fierce fevers of concern that lasted as long as the average new situation comedy.

Yet, in shifting forms, the desire to stand against Reagan remained strong in the Hollywood left. Perhaps inevitably, in an industry built on the power of personality, the ideological dispute over Reagan eventually distilled into a single ongoing battle between two immediately recognizable stars playing broadly scripted parts: the liberal and the conservative. Under the avid eye of the Hollywood media, liberal Edward Asner and conservative Charlton Heston spent much of Reagan's first term at each other's throats in a battle that amply justified the label almost instantly applied to it, Star Wars.

. . .

They were unlikely combatants. Asner, short and stocky, grew up in Kansas City, the son of an immigrant scrap-metal dealer who spoke no English; he knocked around Broadway and Hollywood for years before landing the role of Lou Grant on "The Mary Tyler Moore Show." As the gruff, acerbic, and endearing Grant, Asner blossomed, collecting a shelf of Emmy Awards. He came as slowly to political activism as to stardom: though he considered himself a liberal, he joined in none of the causes of the 1960s. But as his fame grew—he became the headliner in his own show when CBS spun off "Lou Grant" as a dramatic series following the last episode of "Mary Tyler Moore"—his earlier silence gnawed at him. "I was totally opposed to the Vietnam War, I signed whatever I could, but I never put myself on the street to be arrested," he recalled. "I was never asked. . . . Most of the time, I was of the feeling that much bigger names were doing it, and they didn't need me. And yet, I felt I had been cautious, and it bothered me."

His growing celebrity—"the fact that each year built up more avuncular effect from Lou Grant"—gave Asner a rising sense of possibility, and he gradually emerged as a dependable ally for liberal candidates, with a shrewd sense of the political power of fame. "If I attract attention in terms of my efforts and causes, it is the way I can do good," he said. "I am the equivalent of so many column inches in the newspaper. . . . If every issue that needed it were given sufficient coverage, if there was a campaign law that said the incumbent would receive no more press than the challenger, I could sit home and take my shoes off."

Heston's road to fame was smoother, his political evolution more turbulent. Born in Illinois, he gravitated toward acting in high school after a lonely childhood in rural Michigan, where his father operated a lumber mill, and later a Chicago suburb. He made his Broadway debut in *Antony and Cleopatra* in 1947, and was working regularly in Hollywood just three years later. Tall and handsome, he grew into an international star through his portrayal of epic figures in 1950s epics: Moses in *The Ten Commandments,* Ben-Hur, for which he won an Academy Award in the film of the same name. He was known for booming bromides and wearing togas in the company of thousands of extras, but he worked skillfully in smaller settings too, such as his role as a Mexican detective in Orson Welles's dark *Touch of Evil.*

Like Welles himself, Heston grew up a "classic Roosevelt liberal"; he cast his first vote for Franklin Roosevelt and supported Adlai Stevenson and John F. Kennedy. He played a key role in organizing Hollywood behind Martin Luther King, Jr., and stood at the head of the celebrity contingent that joined King's March on Washington in 1963. Heston's disaffection from the Democratic party began as he campaigned for Kennedy's successor, Lyndon Johnson. "I suppose that was specifically my apotheosis on the road to Damascus," he said, sounding dangerously like one of his own biblical characters. "I was shooting a film on location up in Northern California . . . and every day I drove to location early in the morning along a deserted highway that had a big billboard on it for Barry Goldwater. And it had simply a portrait of Senator Goldwater and the text in big letters: 'In your heart, you know he's right.' I kept driving by that, and finally I thought, 'Son of a bitch, that's true. He is right.'"

Heston still voted for Johnson, but his migration had begun. Like many defectors from youthful liberalism, he often said, "I did not shift . . . it was the Democrats who shifted"; but in fact, Heston gravitated toward leaders far more conservative than any of his boyhood idols. He supported Richard Nixon and campaigned for Ronald Reagan; by the time of Reagan's election he was the first star conservatives called when they needed a flash of glamour. "I guess, I'm sort of the official conservative spokesman," Heston said. "I didn't seek it out, but there it is."

For all their differences, both men shared one prominent characteristic: their off-screen credibility derived largely from their fictional personas. Building on the perception of Lou Grant as a tough but sensitive realist, the cynic with a heart of gold, Asner had a unique capacity to make liberalism gritty and realistic. Even he, though, couldn't match for symbolic credibility Heston, who had behind his words decades of playing authority figures—by his count "three presidents, three saints, and two geniuses." At the top of the list was Moses, who spoke in stentorian tones the undiluted word of God, something few contemporary politicians could be accused of. It was, after all, only a movie (and a pompous one at that), but the association of Heston with Moses remained incredibly strong three decades after he parted the Red Sea for Cecil B. De-Mille. Mark Mellman, a prominent Democratic pollster, has worked in races where the Republicans called in Heston as a spokesman. "We've heard people in focus groups talk about the fact that Charlton Heston says something on television and you believe it because it's Charlton Heston," he said. "That clearly seems to have an impact on people. They recognize it shouldn't be there . . . but they can't help but have that feeling. . . . People say, 'If he's saying it, it must be true.' It's Moses, God. That's the thing that people really latch onto. Maybe fifteen years, twenty years from now, when no one is around who's seen that movie, he'll be less effective."

Ronald Reagan's victory put Moses and Lou Grant on their collision

course. As Heston rose in prominence among the Hollywood conservatives, Asner surged to the lead of the liberals. He emerged as a force
within the Screen Actors Guild during a bitter 1980 strike, when he
walked the picket line with the rank and file and was thrust forward as a
spokesman for their unhappiness with the negotiations. He came out of
the strike talking about "saving the people of the United States from the
conservatives," and people spoke about running him for political office.
Instead, in November 1981, he sought the presidency of SAG, the same
job once held by both Reagan and Heston, and won.

His election gave Asner an even larger platform, which he eagerly
employed. Asner had a straightforward view of politics: he thought one of
liberalism's greatest problems was its abiding image of weakness, wimpi-
ness, unmanly equivocation. ("One of the grossest, stupidest mistakes of
the American left has been the failure to find out how best to present their
balls and go out clanging them as loudly and as frostily as possible," he
huffed. "They could have created a credo, a manifesto of giving liberalism
an erection.") No one was going to call Edward Asner a wimp. As president
of one of the AFL's most visible unions, he took after Reagan in language
unfiltered by diplomacy, fear, or experience. In an interview published just
after his election, he said of his distant predecessor, "I think he's doing
some of the best acting he's ever done. But by the time he's finished, I
don't think the country's going to be too willing to let another actor run for
office. He's a hard man to hate. But many of the policies coming from him
are hateful." At every opportunity, he particularly denounced Reagan's
policies in El Salvador, which he considered inexcusable interference with
the "justified wars" of the rebels.

Asner's pugilistic liberalism immediately ruffled conservatives, who
had been a strong presence in the union since its founding. His problems
began with internal SAG issues. Asner's union philosophy was as different from Heston's (and Reagan's, for that matter) as his political attitudes. Asner wanted to mold the union into a militant force on labor and
public policy issues, aligned closely with the national AFL-CIO and other
unions (during his campaign for the presidency he marched with the
striking air traffic controllers dismissed by Reagan). He envisioned SAG
branching out to include extras, represented separately by the Screen
Extras Guild, and perhaps eventually growing into an industrywide
union, the larger the better—one that "protects everybody—actors, directors, writers, musicians, secretaries."

That muscular view of blue-collar solidarity alienated the substantial
portion of actors who had always preferred to think of themselves as
independent professionals rather than huddled masses, members of a

guild, not a union. Those members, mostly politically conservative as well, envisioned a minimalist union, one that provided its members with basic services but carried no economic or political brief. The conservatives recoiled from Asner's plans for greater ties with the AFL, and even more pointedly opposed his efforts to merge SAG with the less prestigious extras' guild as the first step toward wider affiliations.

But the dispute that flamed through the early 1980s extended beyond internal SAG affairs, and was ultimately fanned by the high emotions in Hollywood over the industry's alumnus in the White House. "Inevitably," said Heston, "this being the first time a member of the film community was in the White House, there would be strong allegiances and strong hostilities." For the conservatives watching the Hollywood left march and rally against their old colleague, the Asner administration at SAG seemed to provide an opportunity to make a stand. Many participants on both sides came to see the battle over Asner as a proxy for the war simmering over Reagan. "There were lines being drawn, there were people saying, 'If you believe in unionism, if you believe in progressive principles, you've got to be on the line for it,'" said Mike Farrell, one of Asner's staunchest allies. "It was a way of saying we're not going to lay down here and be a launching pad for Ronald Reagan and be quiet about it. . . . And Heston and his acolytes began to pick up their cudgels from their side, and it began to be a real smash and bash contest."

What ensued was internal political debate more vicious than anything Hollywood had seen since HUAC descended on Los Angeles. (Even Jane Fonda's radical phase inspired far more discussion outside Hollywood than inside.) The fireworks began in November 1981, when, at its first meeting following Asner's election, the SAG board voted to send a $5,000 contribution to the air traffic controllers. The gesture was clearly a symbolic dig at Reagan, but opponents chose other grounds to contest it: Heston argued it was irrational for a union suffering huge unemployment to send the dues "of unemployed actors to the striking air controllers when the average wage of a striking air controller is $50,000 a year."

That put off the real issue for only a short time. The board's overt disapproval of Reagan became clear just a few weeks later. Noisily, in late November the board withdrew a lifetime achievement award that a SAG committee had recommended for Reagan. To honor Reagan while he was at war with the air traffic controllers, the union's public affairs officer declared, "would be a blatant slap in the face to the rest of the labor movement." Heston immediately denounced the decision as "a grievous error" that would split the union.

As president, Asnwer did not vote in either decision, but there was no question he approved of them. Asner, in fact, did nothing to hide his views, and the rising tensions inside SAG next focused directly on Asner's personal hostility to Reagan's agenda. In February 1982, appearing outside the State Department with a Hollywood delegation that included Lee Grant, Howard Hesseman, and Bert Schneider, Asner presented a check for $25,000 to a group called Medical Aid for El Salvador, which provided medical supplies for the leftist rebels fighting the U.S.-backed government there. That appearance escalated hostilities in Hollywood. Asner's actions enraged conservatives who were already uneasy about the votes rebuffing Reagan and supporting the air traffic controllers. Charging that Asner had failed to indicate clearly that he was speaking only for himself and not the union in his support for the rebels, some conservatives even launched a short-lived petition drive to recall him. Reagan weighed into the dispute by declaring that Asner's actions left him "very disturbed." In a "state of shock over what I had walked into," Asner suddenly came "to realize that my ideas of right were not necessarily in agreement with other people's, to the extent some of those other people thought me a traitor."

Almost seventy liberals fired back with an ad in the *Hollywood Reporter* that declared, "Ed Asner: You're Not Alone." While the board defended Asner from charges that he improperly used his position, angry conservatives picketed outside the union hall. Hate mail poured into SAG's office; Asner received a death threat. He survived, but his show didn't: with sponsors nervous about the controversy surrounding the star, CBS in May canceled "Lou Grant," whose ratings had slipped. Just days later, SAG's members dealt Asner another blow by narrowly rejecting his proposed merger with the extras' guild.

Controversy did not slow Asner down. His militant image frightened away some moderate and centrist Democrats, but left-leaning candidates and organizations still eagerly sought his appearances. Even after the demise of "Lou Grant," he showed no signs of fear: in the mid-1980s, he became one of the loudest internal dissenters from the AFL-CIO's support of the administration's hard-line anti-Communist position in Central America.

Heston meanwhile maintained a high profile defending Reagan and criticizing Asner (at one point, he accused Asner of using the union for his personal political agenda "like some Mafia don"). The SAG conservatives, whose ranks grew to include Clint Eastwood, Jimmy Stewart, Burt Reynolds, Frank Sinatra, Bob Hope, and Barbara Stanwyck, formed a rump group called Actors Working for an Actors Guild that ran candidates for the SAG board and regularly provided the media with stinging critiques of Asner's stewardship.

As the criticism intensified, Asner denounced Heston as "Reagan's stooge." To this day, Heston insists the White House neither encouraged nor directed his staunch defense of the president. "I was at great pains never to discuss it with the president," Heston said. "It came up once or twice talking to Nancy. That's just sort of a private pal kind of conversation. But I was determined to be able to always say I've not discussed this with the president, and I never did." White House aides also maintain that they did not spur Heston. ("There were other things going on; I don't remember that being a major concern," said one top aide drily.) But there's no doubt that Reagan's public remarks indicated his unhappiness with the chorus of condemnation rising from his old community. Heston surely could never have believed that his old colleague now in the Oval Office disapproved of his efforts.

The battle between Asner and Heston smoldered for years. "I was too emotional to even dream of [an attempt at reconciliation]," Asner said. "And I believed objectively that the man is a megalomaniac, more so than I am, and he would stop at nothing to gain the publicity." Actually, as the months passed, both contestants seemed increasingly weary of the fight. But the absurd enormity of the media coverage, the constant presence of microphones in their faces, encouraged them to sustain the combat. Asner never missed an opportunity to deliver a punch ("I realized each time that it was a challenge to my balls if I couldn't get out there with him"), nor Heston a chance to display elaborate moral outrage. (He brooded sanctimoniously for years because Asner called him a "cocksucker" within range of some microphones.)

Both men treasured their ability to focus the media on their causes. ("I can get on 'The Tonight Show' or 'Good Morning America' more easily than half the senators in the country; three-quarters of the senators," Heston said. "That isn't fair, but I'm a citizen, I get to shoot my mouth off and I do.") But their increasingly ritualistic duel underlined the danger of that attention. To meet the expectations of the media, Asner and Heston willingly transformed themselves into caricatures and abandoned any pretense of dialogue, or even debate. Their conflict took on more the coloration of a play, with each new escalation in the war of words staged entirely for public effect. Over time, these two men so proud of their skill at manipulating the media appeared trapped in the roles they had scripted for themselves.

For the most sophisticated Hollywood observers, the Asner-Heston struggle became a frightening parable of how the reduction of people into symbols—the very process that at a fundamental level provided stars with their political platform—exaggerated and polarized political conflict. "Lines are more sharply drawn now than they ever were," lamented actor John Forsythe, a political supporter of Asner and friend of Heston. "With the heightened visibility of everybody, there comes a heightened antagonism in confrontations. The Asner-Heston thing was a perfect example of it. God, they abused each other terribly."

Finally, the abuse slowed and trickled away. After four years in office, Asner decided not to seek a third term as SAG president in 1985; Heston consciously withdrew from internal SAG struggles, concentrating his energy on national conservative causes. The affair left Heston philosophical and Asner bitter. Heston's career, slowing somewhat anyway in its later stages, suffered no apparent damage; but Asner remained convinced that the controversy contributed to the demise of "Lou Grant." Except for a few stalwarts who stood beside him, Asner came away considering the overall commitment in Hollywood to serious politics "very thin."

Those feelings are understandable but myopic. Asner's personal misfortunes can obscure the larger picture: the events surrounding his SAG presidency actually demonstrated the strength of the liberal cause in Hollywood during the early 1980s. What was most striking about the affair was that it was Heston—already dueling with Paul Newman on the nuclear freeze and defending Reagan on Central America—who had to stand against Asner, too. Though Heston was an effective spokesman, his prominence on issue after issue—from gun control to Republican efforts to redraw congressional lines in California that they maintained favored Democrats—underlined the lack of stars willing to publicly embrace conservative causes. That reflected not only caution but also the community's political imbalance. When Asner ran for reelection at SAG during the height of the dispute in 1983, he was overwhelmingly reelected. Despite all the controversy, it was a reminder that even in Reagan's shadow, Hollywood's political instincts remained firmly liberal. "The Hollywood community is probably as liberal as any community outside the university faculty," Heston said. "I certainly wasn't able to change that. Nor did I imagine it was a doable thing."

The Reorganization of Hollywood

That became still more apparent as Reagan prepared for his reelection campaign in 1984. His opponent, former Vice-President Walter F. Mondale, generated little more enthusiasm among the stars than Reagan did.

A gray establishment Midwesterner, Mondale always looked out of place in the bright sparkle of Los Angeles, as if he was constantly searching for a factory gate he could never find.

But the national Democratic committees recognized the depth of anti-Reagan feeling among the Hollywood liberals, and in the months before the election sent out to Los Angeles Andy Spahn, a young organizer who had formerly worked for Tom Hayden, to recruit celebrities to aid the party's efforts. Working with funds provided by the Democratic National Committee, the Democratic Senatorial Campaign Committee, and the Democratic Congressional Campaign Committee, Spahn organized a short-lived but effective group called the Democratic Entertainment Industry Project. Mondale's conspicuous lack of magnetism did not discourage him. "With Ronald Reagan in the White House spurring all kinds of political activity," Spahn recalled, "it seemed like the opportunity was there."

It was. Hayden and Jane Fonda sponsored a well-attended recruitment meeting in the backyard of their Santa Monica home that produced for Spahn a list of celebrities willing to campaign. At the same time, Spahn cultivated and moved into the Democratic fundraising orbit a previously untapped group of Hollywood women, principally studio executives, producers, and attorneys, who had become active that spring in funding women's voter registration activities.

Hollywood's help did nothing to stem the avalanche that descended on Mondale that fall. But the Democratic organizing effort nonetheless provided lasting benefit. From that singular root flowered two distinct organizations that came to symbolize Hollywood's political roles in the 1980s. Both were distinctly liberal. ("Conservatives tend to say I can do it myself, while there is a kind of a group bonding urge with the liberal left," said Heston. "In fact, they're right: that's the way to do it. But conservatives tend to sit off by themselves and write letters to the editor and go on the talk shows and make their points.") Both testified to the community's rising political interest—and to the enormous changes in the film industry and national politics since the last Hollywood political organizations flourished during the prime of the Popular Front, almost half a century earlier. Unlike the original Hollywood organizations, neither of the groups that developed from the 1984 campaign had any significant grassroots presence. Instead of organizing and public outreach, the lifeblood of politics in the 1930s, they were built around media and money, the muscle and sinew of politics in the 1980s.

· · ·

Media, not money, was the strength of Network, the group that traced its roots to the June 1984 meeting in the backyard of Fonda and Hayden. Reagan's landslide, particularly his surprising success among young voters, provided the group's immediate impetus. When pollster Patrick Caddell spoke at a Hayden fundraiser the following spring, he stressed the dangers of that demographic trend to the Democrats. His warning left a strong impression on Patrick Lippert, an engaging young aide to Hayden who had a keen interest in the movie business. At a time when teenagers had improbably become the most fervent fans of a conservative septuagenarian president, Lippert thought that the young Hollywood stars then emerging as the "Brat Pack" might be organized into an alternative political role model.

The idea appealed to Hayden, and particularly to Fonda, who saw in it reminders of her own youthful indoctrination into Hollywood politics. "I was remembering back to 1964 or '65 when I was a starlet and the civil rights movement was raging in the South," she told one interviewer. "And I got an invitation to an event that [Marlon] Brando was hosting, and I remembered how much that meant to me. First of all, that I'd been asked: it meant that people took me seriously. And I was given all this information, and it really turned me on." With that memory in mind, Fonda and Hayden invited several dozen young stars to their home one September evening in 1985 to see if they couldn't convert the Breakfast Club into the Hollywood equivalent of an Americans for Democratic Action chapter.

Lippert and Havi Scheindlin, at the time director of Hayden's political committee, both remember Fonda nervously wondering whether the young stars would consent to come to her home, whether they would consider her experience relevant to their own. For moral support, Fonda invited role models to describe their own political activities: Sally Field, Mike Farrell, and Robert Walden, who had starred with Asner in "Lou Grant." As it turned out, Fonda had nothing to worry about. The cream of young Hollywood showed up—Tom Cruise, Rob Lowe, Judd Nelson, Eric Stoltz, Daphne Zuniga, Rosanna Arquette—nearly fifty in all, and they spent almost three hours in her living room, just as excited to be asked for their views as Fonda had been twenty years earlier. From that meeting emerged Network, an informal organization that channeled the young stars into campaigns and causes. With Lippert's energetic direction, the group quickly justified its name, developing a vibrant network of young stars who showed up at dinners, rallies, and other events.

Their function was precisely focused. The group raised no money: its

members had precociously absorbed the venerable Hollywood maxim—
stars don't pay. Efforts to build fundraisers around the young stars were
consistently disappointing; the people who flocked to their movies typically had little money to spend. Their principal purpose was to attract
crowds and cameras to causes and candidates with their budding fame.
In 1986, after several months of organizing, Hayden and Fonda road-
tested their crew by sending busloads of celebrities around the state
behind Proposition 65, a clean-water ballot initiative they had sponsored.
The enormous publicity surrounding the caravan helped the initiative
overcome large expenditures against it by the oil and chemical industries
and register a solid victory in November. "We never would have gotten
the attention without them," said Tom Epstein, a Los Angeles political
organizer who ran the campaign. "What they did was help us break
through the clutter and raise our profile above everything else."

That victory stirred the young stars to enlist for more. One group went
to the Soviet Union to promote arms control under the auspices of SANE.
Alexandra Paul, a young actress active in Network, went with Martin
Sheen to protest nuclear weapons testing in Nevada and was arrested.
Meg Ryan and Rob Lowe campaigned with Hayden against a nuclear
power plant in Sacramento. A delegation composed of Lowe and actresses Sarah Jessica Parker, Marlee Matlin, and Mary Stuart Masterson
presented California Republican Senator Pete Wilson with petitions and
a huge postcard signed by hundreds of young people opposing Robert
Bork's nomination to the Supreme Court. A large group traveled with
Hayden to the Democratic National Convention in July 1988, and many
of them then rejoined him on a campaign swing for the Democratic ticket
that fall.

Most of the Network members understood and welcomed their role as
bait for the media. In that sense, they epitomized the modern Hollywood
mores: having grown up in the era of sound-bite politics, "Entertainment
Tonight," and *People* magazine, they had no hesitation about applying
fame as a political weapon. The internal Hollywood debates of the 1960s
over the appropriateness of foisting political views on fans seemed ana-
chronistic to them. Many, in fact, seemed most excited by the prospect
of bending the fame that shadowed them toward their own interests.
"There are people in the world who think that every time your picture
is taken you lose part of your soul," said Rob Lowe, the young actor who
was probably the group's top draw. "I used to laugh about that. Not any
more. It happens to very few people, and whenever it doesn't happen I'll
be in trouble. But when you walk out and get blasted by photographers,

like the hundreds of them at the Academy Awards, you literally feel like you're being shot at. . . . Somehow it is a little less painful when it's for a reason, a good cause."

The young stars' instinct to channel their fame was easy to understand. More perplexing was the group's liberal orientation. At a time when young people were voting as Republican as the wealthy, these young and extremely wealthy people enthusiastically lined up behind aggressive liberal politics. Some young actors and actresses, such as Scott Baio from television's "Happy Days" and Susan Howard from "Dallas," joined the Republican camp under Reagan. But they were far fewer than might be expected given Reagan's popularity among young voters. "I didn't think Reagan did anything as far as increasing the Republican strength in the Hollywood community," said one high-ranking industry Republican glumly. "Reagan is looked upon favorably by the old Hollywood community. I think he is rejected by the contemporary Hollywood community." Most of the ascending stars flocked not to Reagan but to Network.

It is difficult to explain exactly why; few of the young stars themselves had many ideas why their peers veered left at a time when most of their age group careened right. Part of the explanation could be found in the same cultural forces that tended to push most Hollywood actors left: the instinctive desire among artists to view themselves as outsiders and social critics, the need to develop empathy with a diverse assortment of characters as part of their craft. Having achieved lucrative success so early, some also felt particularly keenly the guilt over their lavish rewards common to Hollywood liberals.

Other factors peculiar to the young stars reinforced those leanings. Many of the young recruits were raised by parents who had been immersed in the same tides that thrust Hayden and Fonda to prominence in the 1960s. The father of actress Daphne Zuniga (*The Sure Thing, Space-balls*) was a left-wing Guatemalan who migrated to Berkeley and participated in the Free Speech Movement. Rob Lowe sold Kool-Aid for the McGovern campaign in 1972. Some of the young stars seemed to envy their parents for living through more turbulent times; Judd Nelson once told an interviewer, "You were incredibly lucky living through the 1960s." At political meetings in Hayden and Fonda's home, many of the young actresses wore earrings in the shape of the peace symbol; others wore tie-dyed T-shirts that might have come from John Sebastian's personal collection. With his graying hair, conservative suits, and button-down collars, Hayden, the symbol of sixties rebellion, looked more like he belonged in this decade than they did.

The most important factor in the young stars' political awakening, though, was their enormous admiration for Fonda. When Andy Spahn organized for the Democrats in 1984, he found that some established Hollywood figures, remembering her misadventures in the 1970s, shied away from associating with the actress. But to the young stars, Fonda was an untainted heroine. When Zuniga set off for Los Angeles and a film career, her father told her: "If you are going to Hollywood with all those phony people, at least be like Jane Fonda, because you know she says what she thinks and has a brain." Almost without exception, the young stars agreed. "She is a symbol, especially to a lot of the young actors, of how you can become socially responsible with the power you have as a celebrity," said Neil Meron, a young producer active in Network.

When Fonda and Hayden reached out to the young stars, they accelerated the Brat Pack's lurch to the left. By exposing young Hollywood to politics through their prism, they focused what might have remained undirected interest. "What they've done, for a lot of people, is they've awakened their political sides," said Rob Lowe. "People who never really ever considered it, they had brought them into that kind of a world."

No comparable group on the right sought to recruit the young stars; in fact, with the exception of Heston and the handful of other conservatives defending Reagan, the right was virtually invisible in Hollywood as the Brat Pack awakened to politics. Their enlistment in the liberal camp showed how the political realignment that shook the community in John F. Kennedy's day perpetuated itself. By the time Rob Lowe and Meg Ryan sought political guidance, almost all of the activist role models in the community were liberals—not only Fonda, but figures such as Mike Farrell, Warren Beatty, Robert Redford, and Ed Asner. The liberal attitudes of the young stars reflected, above all, the extent to which liberalism dominated the Hollywood artistic community. Much as young people elsewhere, having come to political maturity under Reagan, adopted the dominant values of their surroundings by voting conservative, these young stars gravitated to the competing values of their own idiosyncratic community. Other than through television, no conservative ideas ever reached them. Asked if he personally knew any conservatives in Hollywood, Rob Lowe said, "I can't think of one example." That was typical.

Network's attractions were not only ideological. Some of the Network members seemed to view the group's events as just another chance to hear their own voice. Almost every event offered testimony that other Brat Packers saw campaigning as a means to a more substantial image, much the way several of them took to wearing clear glasses when they wanted to look serious.

But at the organization's core were about a dozen young people with mixed success in the industry who took their politics very seriously. In place of the dense revolutionary ideology Fonda had absorbed at their age, they had a vague but insistent desire to do good. At the same time Network coalesced, many of the young stars organized a parallel group called Young Artists United, which avoided partisan politics and instead sent speakers directly into high schools and colleges to talk about sex and drugs and AIDS. The young activists worried about accepting roles in movies that violated their beliefs; Zuniga, reading unsuccessfully for a part in the hit movie *Top Gun*, tried to convince star Tom Cruise to alter the script so his heroic young airman eventually questions his militaristic ways. ("I tried," she sighed later, "but 'Top Gun' was 'Top Gun.' ") They worried about being informed, and dutifully turned up for meetings with not only candidates but drab policy experts who couldn't pack a room in Washington. They fretted about being proper role models. Alexandra Paul, one of the founders of Young Artists United, worried that using celebrities to adorn causes might make young people expect too much fun in their politics: "How do you make people care enough to do it even if it is not fun? If you wean them on concerts they're not going to want to do anything more boring. The point is, it is very serious business."

Certainly the core group in Network took it that way. One evening, on a bus ride back from an outing to the California State Democratic Convention arranged by Network, a handful of young women in the group earnestly discussed whether to expel Rob Lowe from the movement for the sin of dating Fawn Hall, Oliver North's secretary.

"The guy's been here making movies since he was, what, seventeen?" said one, finally, in Lowe's defense. "He doesn't know anything."

"Well," the other said, "I could never take him seriously again."

"How could you ever take him seriously?" said Lowe's defender.

Perhaps that was the group's greatest appeal for the young stars: as the invitation from Brando had for Fonda, participation in Network gave them a sense that others in the community took them seriously. To be in Network was to be certified by the first family of leftist Hollywood politics. Most of the young actors and actresses sought primarily the favor of Fonda who, as a major star with complete control over her career, had achieved exactly what they hoped to inside Hollywood as well as in politics; but Hayden, as the political analyst and strategist who guided their operations, also played a substantial role in bestowing that approval.

It troubled some other political operatives that they had to go through Hayden to secure help from the young activists, and not only because of the political problems that association with Hayden and Fonda could still present. Many simply disliked working with Hayden. Since his election to the State Assembly in 1982, Hayden had done everything he could to present himself as a mainstream politician. His moves toward the center annoyed some Hollywood liberals who did not, or could not, understand the impracticality of trying to function in the state capital as a purist. As a symbol of 1960s idealism, Hayden was often held to ideological standards irrelevant to the 1980s. But the objections to allying with Hayden were as much personal as political. Much of the Hollywood liberal community saw him as a cynical manipulator, obsessed with maneuvering each situation to his own long-term political advantage. "There is a feeling," said one fellow Hollywood liberal, "that no matter who you are, no matter what you do with him, you are a pawn in Tom's long-term agenda. Hundreds of people in the community feel that way." Another liberal Hollywood activist said, "The problem with Hayden and Fonda is that they are creating disciples."

None of those doubts seemed to penetrate the Network. Almost without exception, the group treated Hayden's political advice as gospel—so much so that it became common for other Hollywood politicos to describe the young women in the organization as the "Haydenettes." For his part, Hayden seemed acutely conscious of his influence over his troops and, in contrast to the criticism leveled against him, quite careful about using it. Like Fonda, he had a benevolent, almost paternal attitude toward the young stars. He often said, "These people are so young, they're like my kids."

Hayden steered the group, but gently, and generally toward mainstream Democratic politics. His role was especially great during the 1988 campaign, when Fonda was away for months at a time making films. On the night of the Super Tuesday primaries in March, Hayden welcomed a crowd of younger stars, including Meg Ryan, Bruce Willis, and Sarah Jessica Parker, into the couple's home. He patiently answered their questions ("What can be done to make people aware of the influence of the big defense contractors?" Bruce Willis asked in a surprisingly soft voice), and smoothly moved them toward Michael Dukakis, who emerged from the day's voting as the clear Democratic front-runner. It was a strange sight: the firebrand who had gone to Newark to rouse the black ghetto twenty years earlier now organizing a group of young millionaires, many barely out of their teens. If it seemed to some a commentary on the way progressive politics had mutated in the United States, or a statement on the changes in Hayden's own life, he gave no sign of sharing those ironies. To his young charges he never condescended, and he defended their sincerity against all questions, public or private.

This was not always easy. Even with the best of intentions, the group's activities sometimes generated images of exquisite incongruity.

When Hayden gathered more than two dozen celebrities to campaign for the Democratic ticket and register voters on a swing through the West Coast in October 1988, it often appeared that the audience was composed mostly of *Tiger Beat* readers. Leaving rallies, frantic teenage girls trying to get a last glimpse of Rob Lowe or Robert Downey, Jr., typically surrounded the buses. ("I've seen it worse," Lowe said laconically one night when the bus was imobilized by a horde of teenagers pulsing with pubescent lust. "It was worse during Proposition 65 [in 1986].") Even that could not match for sheer weirdness watching Justine Bateman—whose portrayal of Michael J. Fox's dizzy sister on "Family Ties" seemed drawn entirely from personal experience—offering political advice to a crowd of young voters.* "What do you think of the eighteen-to-twenty-four year-old age group?" she remarked at one outing. "Pretty bitchen', huh?"

The posing by the young stars could be insufferable. When the group landed in Seattle during their 1988 campaign swing through the Northwest, inside a dimly lit plane enshrouded in fog on the airport runway, Lowe, actress Elizabeth Perkins (from *Big*), Downey, and Katie Wagner—the party-girl daughter of actor Robert Wagner, whose sole purpose on the trip seemed to test the proposition that celebrity could be inherited—sat wearing their sunglasses in the gloom. After a few hours of this, reporters traveling with the group began wearing their sunglasses too. But none of the stars seemed to understand they were being ribbed, which only showed how difficult it was to make fun of people too self-absorbed to notice anyone else. It would not be unusual at events where the young stars were the advertised draw to find them mingling solely with each other, protecting themselves from the assembled public with the impenetrable aura of superiority that people in the movie industry seem to perfect as soon as they acquire an agent.

Their political posing could be just as embarrassing. Occassionally the Network stars gave the impression of trying to replicate the steely radicalism they imagined Fonda had once espoused. One morning on the campaign trip for Dukakis, Perkins hectored a blue-collar, largely Hispanic

---

*Until a videotape of Rob Lowe's sexual antics came out following the Democratic Convention, the most memorable performance of the gathering came from Justine Bateman, who pestered a visiting senator at a breakfast organized by Hayden to explain why she had to pay so much in taxes. Can't we pass a law or something? she asked.

audience in Stockton about the assault of the wealthy on the middle class under the Reagan administration. It was like watching a Beverly Hills staging of *Waiting for Lefty*: here was a group of rich young people trying to incite into class warfare what appeared to be an assemblage of enormously content middle-class families looking for a mild Sunday morning outing. (When she gave the speech again the next day before a group of college students in San Diego, someone from the audience finally yelled out the obvious: "But you're rich!")

Even some of the people around Hayden who were leading this troupe into politics wondered whether more good or ill would come from sending out into the world as political role models Lowe and Moon Unit Zappa, the somewhat unpredictable daughter of rock star Frank Zappa. On one campaign outing with the group, Fonda's press secretary spent much of the trip trying to discourage reporters from talking to young Zappa, who actually had an interesting, if somewhat angular, perspective on her generation. "[Jon] Bon Jovi I feel is another great role model for kids," she said. "He makes you have so much fun, and when you're having the most fun he says, 'Register to vote.' "

In fact, twin realities limited the group's political usefulness: few people over twenty-five had heard of any of them (at least until the videotape of Lowe's sexual escapades became an instant late-night cable classic); and several of the most politically interested, including Lowe and Nelson, had careers that were either stalled or skidding. When Hayden took the group to Seattle during the 1988 campaign, one local reporter climbed on the bus at the airport, scanned the list of "celebrities" in mystification, and then finally exclaimed, "Who's Donovan Leitch? Who are these people?"

For all this strangeness, though, there were also many moments when the group produced intimate connections with their audiences. When they stopped posturing and reached into their own experiences, some of them were capable of unaffectedly articulating the doubts and aspirations of their young fans. One night at a campaign rally in Sacramento, Rob Lowe, with evident sincerity, told a huge and squealing crowd, "I think you and I take a real bad rap, that we're apathetic, we don't care, that we're the yuppie generation. I hate that as much as the Brat Pack. I'm here to tell you I'm no Brat Packer, and you're no yuppie. We care about each other." Did he mean it? The audience, at least, thought so, and it was hard to disagree. There was no question of sincerity a few days later when Daphne Zuniga, speaking to a group of mostly low-income Hispanic students at an East Los Angeles college, spoke about her own experience attending college on student loans. "There should be room in America for your dream," she told the small group that had gathered. "There's room for all of us and all of our dreams."

That was an unmanufactured moment of genuine poignancy, something exceedingly rare in contemporary politics. The silliness and pretension of the young stars often grated, but such moments were a reminder that not just ego gratification fueled their participation. It was hard to imagine that all these young people dragged themselves to so many events only because they wanted to be taken seriously. ("People who get involved here don't have anything to gain," said Alexandra Paul. "It's extracurricular stuff and they have to care because a lot of the time it's a drag.") There was more at work, and many of them had the flavor of being committed for the long run to political activism, not only as expiation for their precocious success but out of acute awareness of their influence over thousands of impressionable fans. "I sort of felt the power of the voice," is the way actress Mary Stuart Masterson, a young veteran of the John Hughes cycle of teen angst films, explained her attraction to political causes. "I was seeing that Brat Pack image, that it was cool to be a bad boy, that it was cool to have an attitude . . . to not take things seriously. The big thing these kids miss is taking themselves seriously, and I felt very responsible . . . with the new weight of my position to help them do that."

So did many of her friends, in large part because Hayden and Fonda awakened them to the implicit power of their fame. By the mid-1980s, it was apparent that despite Reagan's enormous appeal to young people, Hayden and Fonda had locked in the next generation of Hollywood stars to an assertive and vocal liberalism.

Still, the prototypical Hollywood political organization of the decade was not the Brat Pack's Network but the Hollywood Women's Political Committee (HWPC). Like Network, it also grew out of the anti-Reagan sentiment organized for the 1984 campaign. But unlike the Hayden-Fonda group, whose strength rested in the ephemeral attractions of young celebrities, HWPC built its influence on hard, spendable cash—the signature of Hollywood's political involvement in the 1980s. Network aimed at moving the public through the media; HWPC, by contrast, showed almost no public face. It aimed to influence politics by cultivating in backrooms and closed ballrooms the powerful legislators who came to them desperate for campaign money. The group's glittering fundraising dinners were for large donors and typically locked out the press, not to mention the public. Even within Hollywood it was self-consciously exclusive: membership in the PAC (which cost $2,500 annually at first) was carefully rationed. One young actress, among the industry's most active, waited three years for an invitation and became so disgusted she turned it down when it arrived. "What were they trying to say?" she wondered, looking back. "That I wasn't serious enough?"

No one patronized the HWPC itself. None of the deference that marked Hollywood's first decades of interaction with the political world survived in its approach. For politicians, negotiations with the organization could resemble strategic arms talks. Depending on the viewer's perspective, the group symbolized Hollywood's power and idealism, or its arrogance and insularity. In fact, it symbolized all that. As a group, the Hollywood Women embodied all the schizophrenia of modern Hollywood politics, encapsulating its self-righteous selflessness in a hard shell of soft hearts. Much as Network reflected the widespread belief among celebrities that their political opinions deserved a public audience, HWPC operated on the explicit conviction that politicians could learn from listening to their Hollywood donors.

Suspicious of the press, skeptical of elected officials, sensitive about their prerogatives, and defiantly committed to their ideals, the Hollywood Women confronted the political world with shoulders squared, ready for combat. They could be fearless: when Democratic Senator Bill Bradley came to Los Angeles for a major fundraiser in 1987, they boldly purchased a full-page advertisement in the trade papers challenging his vote in favor of contra aid. And they could be foolhardy: in 1988, angered that Michael Dukakis was forced to cancel his appearance at a fundraiser it organized for the ticket, the group petulantly withheld some of the proceeds from the campaign until virtually the eve of the election. "I think you're dealing with a group of people who feel their power," said one woman Democratic operative who has worked closely with them. "They want people to cater to them. Some of them individually are okay. But together you can get some very difficult people. And they just want everybody to know they are in charge."

Money galvanized the group from the start. Its roots went back to spring 1984, when a group of entertainment industry women, including songwriter Marilyn Bergman, then–Columbia Pictures Television president Barbara Corday, and producers Barbara Boyle and Paula Weinstein, a dozen in all, met at Boyle's house to form a nonprofit group called the Hollywood Women's Coalition. Aligning them was a shared desire to prevent Reagan from claiming that his old community supported him. To make the point, they held a fundraiser at the Hollywood Palladium that collected voter registration funds for the National Organization for

Women. That event only whetted their appetites. It convinced the women that raising money was their best opportunity to influence the campaign. But several of them felt that collecting voter registration funds left them on the periphery. Once the Democrats named as their vice-presidential nominee New York Representative Geraldine A. Ferraro, the first woman on a national ticket, the Hollywood Women were ready for a leading role.

Andy Spahn, the young Democratic party aide organizing Hollywood for the campaign, was in a position to channel the women's excitement over Ferraro's nomination, and they did not disappoint him. When he brought them in to work on a major Democratic fundraising dinner planned for Los Angeles that fall, they seized the opportunity. The network of liberal women combed through Hollywood for checks "relentlessly," in the words of one Democratic operative who worked with them. Every week a leadership group gathered at the Columbia conference room to chart their progress. Before long they began to sense the synergistic possibilities of lasting association. Shortly after the Democratic National Convention they formed a political action committee, the Hollywood Women's Political Committee, to participate directly in partisan campaigns. The Hollywood Women's Coalition, the remnant of a more decorous political vision, soon disappeared.

No one missed it. The fall fundraising dinner for Mondale and Ferraro became the hugely successful highlight of the dreary campaign in Hollywood. Though Mondale's prospects had already evaporated, the women raised over $300,000 for the dinner—roughly half of the total collected that night. Walter Mondale was on a rocket to obscurity, but in Hollywood a new player had arrived.

The group seemed to emerge overnight, but its appearance actually reflected two long-term Hollywood trends. One was the determination of women, steadily rising through the Hollywood power structure, to establish themselves as forces within the industry; the HWPC made as strong a statement in Hollywood as in Washington. For women who had made the difficult climb to Hollywood influence, the group offered political independence from "the boys" who typically introduced senators and presidential hopefuls. "Basically," said one member, "these are women who had finally achieved power in the industry and had been giving money for these individual fundraisers because Jack Valenti asked them or Michael Eisner asked them, and these women finally said, 'I think we want to decide where to give it now, and we don't want to give it just because of how they vote on copyright or source licensing.' These women . . . decided they wanted to play with Jack Valenti and Lew Wasserman and all those guys."

And like Network, the group was also an echo of the baby boom. Network connected to politics the children of the baby boomers; HWPC reactivated the baby boomers themselves. In the early 1970s, after the remarkable success of *Easy Rider,* the graying men running the studios rushed to install in corner offices young executives they expected to fashion more hits out of the alienation of their peers. Those "baby moguls" had since moved up the ladder in Hollywood, losing their own alienation, acquiring in its place influence and enormous wealth, enough to make some of them wonder if they had become the people they used to ridicule. Anxiety that strong could produce action. "There is a whole generation of people who were active in the '60s, have a political consciousness, have achieved a point in life where they are successful, where they don't have to spend all of their time worrying about their careers," said producer Paula Weinstein, one of the HWPC's founders, "and they are really ready now to put their money down."

Weinstein herself personified both forces that fed the HWPC. So ardent a leftist was her mother, Hannah Dorner, the fiery organizer of HICCASP in the 1940s, that she was remembered largely by the nickname "Red Hannah." In college Weinstein plunged into civil rights and antiwar causes. She entered the industry in 1973 as a script reader for Jane Fonda, who knew her mother; from there she found a job in a talent agency; then as Fonda's agent; then as a studio executive at Warner Bros., the Ladd Company, and United Artists, where she was named president of the motion picture division. In 1983, she became an independent producer; by the decade's end she had been associated with such well-regarded films as *A Dry White Season* and *The Fabulous Baker Boys.* She was determined and intense, and surprised to find how much she enjoyed the wealth and power that accompanied her success. "I don't think any of us knew we were driven," she said of the generation that rose through Hollywood with her, "until they gave us these jobs." In her steady, determined climb, she avoided politics, except for a minor role in Tom Hayden's 1976 Senate campaign. In 1980, she still remained largely aloof, but the barrier cracked, and even "if it didn't translate into any real activism," she watched the election closely. Like most of the Hollywood left, she saw Reagan's election as "a trauma"; his victory left her wondering if her generation, through its preoccupation with success, had "hand[ed] over our time" to Reagan and the right.

The HWPC was an antidote to those feelings. It drew on the same psychic needs that had powered liberal fundraising in Hollywood for generations: it allowed its members to reaffirm their militant ideology without repudiating their comfortable lives. For such satisfaction, $2,500 a year (later reduced to $1,500) was a small price. Through 1985, selectively recruiting women who shared its political sentiments, HWPC grew steadily. Success itself broadened its appeal. As the group became more prominent, it could attract not only women drawn to its ideology but those who wanted to move into the inner political circle, or merely to network with other powerful women. Recruitment lunches sponsored by Bergman and Weinstein were sellouts: Membership grew from 12 to 35 in September 1985, and to 70 the next spring. The group held a fundraiser at Spago, the hip Sunset Boulevard restaurant, for the Democratic Senatorial Campaign Committee, and then spent weeks hammering out a statement of principles.

The statement disclosed much not only about the specific group of women who adopted it, but also about the reaction across the liberal community to Reagan's sustained popularity. At a time when many in the Democratic party, shocked by Reagan's landslide reelection, were groping for a new formula, HWPC unabashedly reaffirmed the liberal verities of the 1960s. Like most of the Hollywood fundraisers, they considered the lesson of 1984 to be that, if anything, Mondale had been insufficiently liberal in his challenge. No one could accuse them of moderation. In its statement, HWPC declared: "We are committed to the belief that the ultimate defense of the United States of America lies in the immediate dismantling of the global nuclear war machine. . . . It is time to expose and penalize as criminals those who knowingly destroy the balance of nature. . . . We are committed to an economic policy based on every citizen's full participation in our country's economic wealth." Those were not just pieties: the group said it would back only those candidates who shared those views, who passed its tests; the rest could fend for themselves. "We are not consensus Democrats," Weinstein proudly told one reporter, "and are never going to be."

That vision was simultaneously the group's strength and its weakness. Ideological purity gave the organization an elite sense of purpose and commitment that attracted members. It inspired members with the belief that while the Democratic party was bending to expediency in its desperation to regain the White House, they stood firm for principle. And it meant they did not ask office-holders for the demeaning legislative favors—help on a tax bill, defense against regulators—that marked so much fundraising, even in Hollywood.

For politicians, the problem was that the group carried its convictions to excess. In its dealings with elected officials, HWPC operated in the gray area where commitment and idealism blurred into intransigence and arrogance. Part of the difficulty was personal style. ("In meetings I've seen them in, it's not that the questions they raise are stupid, far from it, it's that their insecurity shows in the abrasive way they ask the questions," said one woman Democrat. "They think that's the way you show you are serious. And some of the bad rap they get is men getting angry about a group of women grilling them.") But ideological abrasiveness also marked the organization. It distilled into noxious purity the feeling in Hollywood, common since the late 1970s, that the wealthy liberals of Bel-Air and Brentwood were more committed to progressive causes than the politicians who beseeched them for checks.

Nothing better demonstrated that attitude than a meeting HWPC held with Senator Edward M. Kennedy in the autumn of 1986. An old friend of Marilyn Bergman, Kennedy agreed to meet with the women at Bergman's house. The unbowed champion of liberal causes for the past twenty years, Kennedy settled into an overstuffed chair ready for a gentle evening of exhortation and congratulation. The first question came at him like a right cross. One of the women cited several recent speeches Kennedy had made calling for a reassessment of liberal dogma and then pounced: was it true that he was leading the party in a retreat from liberalism? Stunned, Kennedy bleated indignation: "How dare you question my credentials?" The evening went downhill from there. Throughout the session, facing what sounded like an "interrogation," Kennedy "was notching up, notching up, notching up," recalled one participant. Finally, when one of the group members said it could not support such moderate-to-conservative Southern Democratic Senate candidates as Representative John B. Breaux (running in Louisiana) and Governor Robert Graham (in Florida), Kennedy exploded.

"What do you know about John Breaux and Bob Graham?" he roared. "What do you know about being a congressman from the Louisiana backwoods and representing that district? Here's a young man who's stood up for civil rights, been active on the floor, taken his lumps in one of the worst, most conservative Southern districts in the country, and you people have the nerve to cast judgment on him?"

When he finished on Breaux, he started on Graham, still roaring, while the women blanched. And when he had finished defending Graham, he still had more to get off his chest.

"You know what, if it means Bob Graham and John Breaux get elected to the Senate, and they're going to be with me only 50 percent of the time, 60 percent of the time, 70 percent, I don't give a damn because it means I'm going to be chairman of the Senate Labor and Human Resources Committee, and that's what this election is all about. This election is not about people in West Los Angeles applying litmus-test standards to people who live in another part of the country you don't understand. If this means you want to hold your nose and not give money to people, I'm not going to worry about whether the contra war is ended. You can worry about it."

It seemed to one observer that Marilyn Bergman had neglected to breathe during this entire outburst. Soon, several of the women jumped in to apologize. And in fact many of them felt bad about the way they had phrased their questions. (Apparently they healed the wounds, because Kennedy later appeared at HWPC events.) But the women remained defiant on the two key points Kennedy raised: they did not plan to accept any politician's commitment to liberal ideals on faith alone, and they did not intend to help candidates who would move the party away from those ideals, as they interpreted them. "From Kennedy's point of view, he has to look at it that way on candidates like Breaux and Graham," said one of the group's senior members. "From our point of view, we don't."

That attitude virtually guaranteed conflict with politicians and political operatives. Visitors from Washington often felt the group was both personally overbearing and politically naive in establishing inviolate ideological tests for its support, and then recoiling in elaborate disappointment when the politicians they helped elect failed to meet all their expectations. "In some ways, I'm sympathetic to their dilemma," said one of the Democrats' leading political strategists, who has made the trip to court HWPC more than once. "They've done all these things, they've made this extraordinary commitment in some ways, and it hasn't had any impact. Whose fault is that? We can find fault with the party, but their expectation is way too high. You just don't get in and things change, like that. You spend your lifetime doing this stuff and things still don't change, or they change marginally. That impatience makes them angry at the process, makes them hold the candidates to unattainable standards; it puts them in artificial adversarial relationships as their impatience makes them want to apply more scrutiny to the people they help. It is just a vicious circle."

From the politicians' perspective, those complaints are entirely reasonable; self-righteousness rises from liberal Los Angeles like fog from the shore. But politics is not primarily about getting along. It is about advancing ideas, passing legislation, electing candidates. In a broad sense, as Kennedy argued in Marilyn Bergman's living room, HWPC may, in fact, hinder its agenda by rejecting Democrats who share only part of it. But even the sharpest critic could not deny that the group has generated enormous resources for liberal causes. More than any organization since the 1940s, HWPC marshaled Hollywood's vast wealth behind a coherent and consistent political agenda. It demonstrated what the

Malibu Mafia had only hinted at in the 1970s: in the modern era of decentralized political fundraising, Hollywood could be as valuable a resource for liberals as any community in the country. For that kind of performance, most Democrats were more than willing to accept a little ideological hazing. The same purity that drove candidates to distraction also inspired financial efforts that left them groping for superlatives.

The breakthrough for HWPC came in 1986—and not in Hollywood but thousands of miles away in Chernobyl. When the Soviet nuclear power plant exploded in April, it crystallized a growing anxiety over the environment and the arms race in one unusually powerful Hollywood woman, Barbra Streisand. Streisand had been politically dormant since the early 1970s when she sang for the McGovern campaign. But in spring 1986 she joined the Hollywood women's group, largely through the influence of Marilyn Bergman (who had, with her husband Alan Bergman, written the lyrics for Streisand's hit song "The Way We Were"). Once the singer's political interest revived, there ensured a process that might be called The Education of Barbra Streisand. When it was completed, HWPC had put itself on the national map with one of the most spectacular fundraising events in American political history.

As though nurturing a fragile bud, HWPC tenderly nourished the political reawakening of Streisand, a brilliant but reclusive artist skittish about public appearances. One day shortly after the Chernobyl accident, Marilyn Bergman had lunch with Stanley Sheinbaum, the long-time liberal activist, and told him that Streisand wanted to learn more about nuclear issues. Sheinbaum agreed to help. Dinners where Streisand could meet policy experts were convened at his home and the singer's. Leading analysts such as Marvin L. Goldberger, at the time president of the California Institute of Technology, and physicist Sidney Drell, from Stanford, were drafted as tutors, much the way they might be for a politician planning a new arms control initiative. "I found myself providing her literature, books, articles, [Robert] Scheer's book [on the Reagan administration's nuclear policies]," Sheinbaum recalled. Streisand drank it up. "She started with very little knowledge and a great deal of suddenly awakened concern," Goldberger said. "What we were trying to do was help Barbra find an appropriate vehicle for making a contribution toward a set of issues about which she had very recently become deeply concerned. . . . I had two roles: one was that of someone who knows a great deal about nuclear power, nuclear reactors, and has also spent an awful lot of time worrying about strategic weapons and international security. So in a sense I was a resource person that tried, when necessary, to separate fact from fiction. Secondly, both I and my wife tried to think about what was the appropriate vehicle for her to make the maximum contribution in this area about which she was greatly concerned."

That issue concerned many more people than the Goldberger family. As soon as Streisand demonstrated her interest, HWPC hoped to have her appear on their behalf. Word of the Hollywood Women's fundraising prowess had raced through Washington following the 1984 campaign, and almost daily senators and their aides washed up like jet-lagged orphans on the doorstep of the group's executive director, Marlene Saritzky, a former aide to a Democratic congressman. Rather than diluting their efforts through many small events for the individual senators who besieged them, the group decided instead to organize a single large fundraiser and divide the proceeds among many beneficiaries. In the back of almost everyone's mind percolated the large hope that Streisand, who had not sung in public for five years, would be the headliner.

So the education of Barbra Streisand entered a second stage: finding the most effective means for her to express her concerns. In that process, the key force was Marilyn Bergman. Bergman was the HWPC member closest to Streisand and with the longest track record in Los Angeles liberal politics. Passionate herself about the idea, Bergman focused Streisand's concern on an immediate goal—regaining the Senate for the Democrats in the November election. "Marilyn realized the way Barbra Streisand can help them [win back the Senate] is to raise money," recalled attorney Bonnie Reiss, the group's treasurer, "and the way she could do that is to sing."

Once Streisand crossed that large threshold, there remained the issue of exactly where and when to appear. Ideas gradually came into focus. In midsummer, with the election only three months away, Streisand gave final approval to the event. Rather than renting a large and impersonal hall, Streisand decided to hold the affair in the intimate setting of her own secluded Malibu home—though that necessitated carving out an amphitheater from a flat lawn in a matter of weeks. Logistical difficulties paled beside the extraordinary appeal of being able to offer not only Streisand performing, but Streisand performing in her own home. For such an unusual opportunity, the ticket price of $5,000 a couple might not seem excessive. To underscore the event's personal nature, Streisand recorded on audio cassette hundreds of individual invitations, which landed on the desks of Hollywood's most powerful men and women like a summons.

From Washington, the Democratic Senatorial Campaign Committee (DSCC), which stood to be the event's principal beneficiary, looked at the

Streisand dinner both skeptically and avidly. Officially it doubted that HWPC could meet its target of $1 million; on the other hand, when Marilyn Bergman came to Washington to brief Senator George J. Mitchell, at that time the DSCC chairman, he proposed they turn over all the proceeds to the committee as the most efficient way of helping to recapture the Senate. Bergman balked on both fronts: she was confident the combination of Streisand's appeal and the group's reach could produce extraordinary results, and insistent that HWPC control the proceeds to ensure that its money did not go to Democrats whose views it did not approve. Instead, HWPC negotiated a complicated arrangement to split the funds among its own political action committee, the DSCC (with the private understanding that the money would go to California Democratic Senator Alan Cranston, facing a tough reelection that fall), four liberal Democratic challengers, and one incumbent, Senator Patrick J. Leahy of Vermont.

The event had so much appeal that the DSCC arranged junkets for groups of big donors from Miami and Cleveland and other cities. But the vast majority of tables were gobbled up in Hollywood itself. Inside the studios, the Streisand dinner became the most unlikely of political events: a hot ticket. Suddenly the $1 million estimate for the dinner seemed low. Projections were revised as executives and producers fought for tickets. Incredibly, the women ultimately had to turn away about thirty couples—or $150,000—who wanted to attend. The event, on a Saturday night in early September, turned out to be a paparazzi's paradise, a convocation of all the swells of the Southern California political and entertainment world. From Jack Nicholson to Chevy Chase to Sydney Pollack, Goldie Hawn, and Bette Midler, the Streisand dinner attracted almost as many stars as the Academy Awards. And it was a better show. Luminescent and powerful, Streisand sang seventeen songs, jabbed at the GOP (with satiric verses written by the Bergmans), and left her very jaded crowd close to speechless.

When HWPC finished collecting the checks, the bottom line had the same effect in Washington. The Streisand dinner raised $1.5 million, far above expectations, and just as relevant to the sponsors, more than Reagan raised at a fundraising appearance in Los Angeles the next night. The evening undeniably helped the Democrats regain the Senate (only one of the six senators who received funds did not win), instantly became a symbol of liberal Hollywood's financial power, and remains the most potent expression of the Hollywood left's ferocious decade-long desire to repudiate its prodigal son in the White House.

• • •

And yet even at this triumphant pinnacle, discordant notes intruded. The glow of Streisand's enormous success obscured them at the time, but they offered important insights into the problems facing both the Hollywood Women and the liberal community around them as they pursued greater political influence.

One was the absence of one of the senators slated as a beneficiary, Pat Leahy, who decided to stay home in Vermont. "The feeling," said one Leahy aide, "was we don't need to. . . . Why take the risk of being seen as too glitzy six weeks before the election?"

His hesitation was a pointed reminder that association with the glamour of Hollywood could sting candidates. Stars brought crowds, they brought attention, they could invest a candidate with credibility. But even many of the celebrity activists realized that some voters looked skeptically on their participation in campaigns, that the mixed feelings Americans harbor about Hollywood stars—the envy and resentment their privileged lives evoke—could splash onto the candidates they endorse.

"In a lot of communities in this country, it works against you, it works against your candidate to have you identified with the entertainment business," said Robert Foxworth, one of the most active Hollywood liberals. "I think a lot of people hate us. A lot of people have this sort of grinding distaste for people who make a lot of money playing games essentially." Leahy's fear reflected an awareness that candidates who spent too much time with celebrities could be portrayed as unduly dazzled by the bright lights. "The point is who is rushing to whom," said Democratic pollster Peter Hart. "It is one thing for the candidate to be pursued by the stars; it is another thing for the candidate to pursue the stars. The candidate who says, 'Look, it's the greatest thrill in my life to be able to meet you,' that's not I think where we want that person coming from."

Leahy's decision to stay home was a disappointment. More so was the absence of Harriett Woods, the Democratic Senate nominee from Missouri. Woods remained at home for a more disturbing reason than Leahy: she feared that association with Hollywood's ideologically belligerent liberals could be used to intimate that she was out of touch with the moderate values of her Midwest state. Though she was a favorite of the Hollywood women's group, had accepted a financial contribution from them in her primary, and had invited Sally Field, Mike Farrell, Lily Tomlin, and Morgan Fairchild into the state to campaign for her, Woods went a step farther than Leahy: she not only refused to attend the Streisand dinner, she also refused the group's offer of money from the event. For

Woods, whose GOP opponent ultimately outspent her by $1 million, the opportunity to pick up roughly $100,000 on a single evening was enormously attractive. But the political risks of a weekend in Malibu were more daunting—largely because it would have brought Woods into contact with one of the HWPC's most prominent members.

Early in the campaign, Jane Fonda sent Woods a personal contribution of $2,000. Almost immediately conservatives, and some veterans, still smarting over Fonda's trip to Hanoi almost fifteen years earlier, demanded that Woods return the money. The contribution, one veteran declared at a press conference, "was a slap in the face of every Vietnam veteran in Missouri." Woods and her supporters argued quite reasonably that she could not be blamed for the views of all her supporters. But the controversy became a flashpoint in the campaign, creating a far more liberal image of Woods than she preferred. Her opponents successfully equated Woods with her prominent, still enormously controversial supporter. It was not a subtle argument. Avoiding urban areas where perceptions of Fonda might be more favorable, opponents ran ads targeted at rural communities showing Fonda on the anti-aircraft gun in North Vietnam and then lambasting "Hanoi Harriett" for associating with her.

Like a hammer blow, the assault was no less effective for its bluntness. Woods remembered: "The use of Jane Fonda was not just Jane Fonda. It was to make me seem an extremist and therefore to try to tie me to [her views]: I'm a woman, she's a woman; I'm a liberal, she's viewed as having been a disloyal liberal. So if you can kind of transfer the disloyal or extremist aspect over to me, then that pushes me beyond the mainstream liberal bounds, which in my case was totally inaccurate." Woods offered to transfer Fonda's contribution to charity, or to a veterans' group. She said what Fonda "had done in North Vietnam was wrong and dumb." But the issue smoldered on, a dangerous distraction in a tight campaign. The charge put Woods off-balance from the outset, and "helped to keep me from mainstreaming myself," she said.

Democratic South Dakota Representative Thomas A. Daschle, also seeking a Senate seat that fall, faced a similar, if not quite so vitriolic, situation. Republican incumbent Senator James Abdnor, a dreary campaigner battered by the weak farm economy, ran ads attacking Daschle for inviting Fonda, rather than a South Dakotan, to testify at a House Agriculture Committee hearing. The ads jabbed Daschle at several levels: not only was he cavorting with Hollywood but with diet-and-exercise maven Fonda, who the ads flamboyantly but inaccurately accused of opposing the consumption of red meat—something of a red-meat issue itself in a cattle-producing state such as South Dakota. The ads did not specifically raise Fonda's antiwar history. But Abdnor's advisers assumed that just the mention of Fonda's name would trigger the associations—and push Daschle to the left. "Jane comes with instant baggage, and you don't need to explain to voters who she is," said Larry McCarthy, Abdnor's media consultant.

Facing a politically weak but well-founded incumbent, Daschle figured he could risk the backlash and flew out to Los Angeles for the Streisand dinner; Woods stayed home. When Woods turned down the offer, HWPC was stunned and offended. "Most of us thought she was stupid," said one of the group's members. "Once you're on the defensive, you're in a losing situation. We thought she should have fought it through." Woods herself was not happy rejecting the offer. "But," she said, "we knew we had to balance off the advantage of the money with the use of that [event by my opponents]: the argument that 'Aha, you see, that is the crowd she prefers to the people of Missouri.' "*

When Daschle returned home from Malibu, he faced exactly that charge. Abdnor ran an ad specifically attacking him on the Streisand dinner, using the glittering gathering to underline his argument that Daschle fit in better with the slick operators of Hollywood and New York than the plain folks of South Dakota. "Does Tom Daschle really think the way South Dakotans do?" an announcer asked in one Abdnor ad after the screen flashed with a news article about the Streisand dinner. "Or is he the liberal all his Hollywood . . . supporters say he is?" With little else to work with, the Republicans slammed away at that theme. Campaigning for Abdnor in South Dakota a few weeks after the Streisand event, President Reagan brought the association back into the headlines: "I was out in California and I couldn't help but notice that the chic of Hollywood had gathered at one posh Malibu home to raise huge sums of money for left-leaning Senate candidates."

On Election Day, Woods was swept away, the victim of many forces beyond her association with Fonda; Daschle weathered the storm. But Abdnor's advisers came away convinced that the attacks on Hollywood in general and Fonda in particular did more damage than any of their other charges. "Fonda was our single best negative," said McCarthy. In the context of GOP efforts to portray Daschle as too slick for the state, the association with Hollywood "didn't help," agreed Mark Mellman, Daschle's pollster. Still, Daschle survived, which suggested the limits of Hollywood-bashing as a campaign strategy. In 1988, a Republican Senate

---

*In late October, HWPC quietly sent Woods a $5,000 contribution that did not have to be reported until after Election Day.

candidate in New Jersey tried to tie his opponent to Hayden and Fonda, and also failed (partly because it was revealed the Republican was personally friendly with Hayden). In a society so infatuated with Hollywood, it is not surprising that most voters didn't begrudge Daschle some glamour and glitter. "I think the attack doesn't work some places," concluded Woods, looking back, "but if you get just the right situation it can hurt you."

The possibility of falling into just that sort of situation, though, remains in many candidates' minds as they ponder the riches HWPC controls. "I can think of an awful lot of meetings I've sat in on in Democratic campaigns where they say, 'We want to go to the Hollywood Women's Political Committee because it's money and good contacts, and we want to be there, but what is our opponent going to do with an organization that Jane Fonda is associated with?'" said Democratic pollster Geoff Garin. "They are really conflicted over that." During the 1990 campaign, Republicans employed that line of attack more aggressively than ever, with candidates in several states, accusing their opponents of insulting veterans by accepting contributions from an organization associated with Fonda. In most cases, the charge quickly passed, but it lingered in the Texas gubernatorial race, where the state GOP ran radio ads linking Democratic nominee Ann W. Richards to Fonda, as well as other liberal groups. The HWPC and its Hollywood supporters condemned these tactics as red-baiting. But GOP strategists saw them as a way of intimidating Democratic candidates from mining Hollywood for support.

The need for money almost always overcomes the fear of Fonda, or of being seared by the bright lights. But the caution is nonetheless well placed. What Woods painfully learned is that as political debate continues to be compressed into bites of manipulated imagery, stars—with their sharply defined images—can become a shorthand symbol of the values of the candidates they illuminate. As the 1980s progressed, the politics of cultural association would loom increasingly large in Hollywood's relationship with Washington.

CHAPTER NINE

GARY AND WARREN: THE LIMITS OF FREEDOM

The Fatal Attraction

No politician learned the risks of associating with Hollywood more dramatically than Gary Hart. No candidate benefitted more tangibly from the rising tide of Hollywood activism in the 1980s. Hollywood money helped launch his 1984 bid for the presidency, and Hollywood glitter gilded his image as something fresh and different. From the start of his political career, stars surrounded and certified Hart, their company burnishing this cerebral and often withdrawn man with an unlikely sheen of glamour.

Like John F. Kennedy a generation earlier, Hart fit Hollywood's vision of a president: young, handsome, future-oriented, vaguely anti-establishment, artistic (he wrote novels), interested in their work, pleased by their company. "To the people out here he was something very fresh," said producer John Davis, the son of billionaire investor Marvin Davis. "He didn't campaign like an Eastern politician, he didn't sound like an Eastern politician; he sounded like a fresh choice." Hart's appeal was great enough to attract into politics many stars and movie executives who never before had had time for campaigns. In Hollywood, at least, Hart truly was the choice of a new generation.

No candidate did Hollywood more wish to help, no candidate did Hollywood work more diligently for—and yet, in many ways, no candidate did Hollywood hurt more than Gary Hart. At a practical level, Hollywood offered great assistance. At a symbolic level, Hart's association with Hollywood reinforced his greatest political problem: the sense among political insiders, eventually transmitted to the public, that there was something not quite solid about him. Hart was anything but a trivial man—he diverted himself on the campaign by reading Tolstoy and Kierkegaard. But in his two bids for the presidency he constantly battled charges that he lacked depth and gravity: first on policy, then on morals. His ease in Hollywood—a community that to the world symbolizes freedom from limiting morality—and his close friendship with Warren Beatty, Hollywood's most celebrated Casanova, provided his critics with an insidious metaphor for their doubts about his judgment and values.

After a religiously stern upbringing in small-town Kansas, Hart simply appeared to enjoy the gaudy Hollywood life too much. "He was excited by being with celebrities, that gave him a thrill, a kick, and he wanted to emulate their lifestyle as far as drinking and nightlife and women and all the rest," said Theodore Sorensen, the former Kennedy aide who served as co-chairman of Hart's 1984 presidential campaign. Others close to Hart insist he was not starstruck or impressed by famous names. Nor did Hart—a man with an inexhaustible appetite for even the most abstruse public policy debates—literally crave a Hollywood life of poolside story meetings. But he appeared riveted by the myth that Hollywood embodies in American life—the myth that celebrity offers exaggerated personal freedom. Throughout his political career, rumors regularly linked Hart romantically with women other than his wife; even after those rumors reached the public in the first days of his 1988 presidential campaign, Hart defiantly pursued a relationship with a model and occasional actress named Donna Rice. Even when it threatened all he aspired to, Gary Hart remained mesmerized by the vision of a life without conventional rules.

The myth had also dazzled Hart's idol, John Kennedy, a man who seemed to dance lightly over the same ground where Hart grimly burrowed for pleasure. Kennedy's friendship with Frank Sinatra and dalliance with Marilyn Monroe chiseled into the culture the assumption that power's rewards included access to the iridescent life of the famous, with its code of license barred to ordinary men and women. Like Kennedy, Hart had just enough of the artist's imagination to envision all those possibilities. Perhaps more than any intervening politician, Hart seemed to match Kennedy's reverence for the Hollywood myth of manhood: that to live fully one must, as Norman Mailer wrote, "fight well . . . love well and love many, be cool, be daring, be dashing, be wild, be wily, be resourceful, be a brave gun."

In the end, as with Kennedy, the other modern politician most intimate with Hollywood, Hart's experience only demonstrated how great a gulf separated the two worlds. Actors and politicians shared a common celebrity, and mutual affinities. But they lived by different rules, a fact with teeth for politicians who forgot it. Hollywood helped to launch Hart's national career, and yet it is difficult to disagree with Robert Redford when he calls the fascination between the austere candidate and the capital of glamour a "fatal attraction."

At first there were no symbols in Hart's Hollywood connections, just friends and allies. Hart's ties to the film world went back to his tenure as McGovern's campaign manager in 1972, when he struck up friendships with Warren Beatty and Jack Nicholson and other stars who flocked to the senator from South Dakota. Those ties proved useful when Hart sought his own political career. Nicholson and Beatty campaigned for Hart when he was elected to the Senate from Colorado in 1974. Over the years, Redford also made appearances for him. In 1980, Redford introduced Hart to Mike Medavoy, the former agent for Jane Fonda who was then a senior executive at Orion Pictures. Medavoy arranged a fundraiser for Hart's reelection that year. When the senator decided to run for president, Hart sought out Medavoy again.

"Why are you coming to me?" Medavoy asked Hart. "Go to Lew Wasserman or Arthur Krim."

"Those people are going to be tired," Hart assured him. "This is their last hurrah." It was time, he told Medavoy, for a new generation to assert itself in Hollywood.

Medavoy needed little encouragement to assert himself. Intense by nature, sometimes brusque, he was eager to rise with the senator from Colorado. His early support was essential to establish Hart's credibility in the entertainment industry and, through it, the other veins of money that cut through Los Angeles like gold threading a hillside.

Hart's presidential campaign burst on Los Angeles in November 1982 with a flashy banquet on the Twentieth Century-Fox lot organized by Medavoy and Marvin Davis, who owned the studio at the time. It was a glamorous affair—Beatty introduced the candidate—and at $500 a head raised $100,000 for Hart, substantial numbers for a candidate down with the asterisks in the polls. But as Hart performed poorly in the rounds of straw polls that confronted the Democratic presidential hopefuls in 1983, the big givers pulled back. During the dim months when his campaign often appeared to be foundering, Hart's California fundraising moved a step downscale into a network centered on a young attorney named John B. Emerson.

As affable as he was ambitious, Emerson was strategically placed in the influential Los Angeles law firm of Manatt, Phelps, Rothenberg, and Tunney, whose name partners included Charles T. Manatt, former chairman of the Democratic National Committee, and former Senator John Tunney. Emerson's parents, a Presbyterian minister and a social worker, had both been active in liberal causes, and after the Democratic debacle of 1980 he decided to organize a group of similarly minded young professionals who wanted to network their way into politics. He named the organization the Lexington Group, and its driven achievers in their Hondas and BMWs represented generational politics in the embryonic state; they were yuppies just waiting for classic rock and Reeboks. And, as it turned out, Gary Hart.

"We started with people we knew, young lawyers, and we moved from there to their clients, young guys in business," Emerson recalled. "Then we discovered the California entrepreneurs. One of our first events was hosted by David Stein and Barry Brief [two wealthy young Orange County developers] at Brief's house. The people we were going after are people who were active in the civil rights movement, the antiwar movement, and are now successful." Hart's nascent campaign was running along the same tracks, and Emerson became intrigued early on. He first helped Hart assemble an event with young people in San Francisco in May 1982, and soon was arranging the candidate's visits to the state. Eventually he became Hart's state chairman in California.

When Hart stumbled in 1983 and the big givers withdrew, it was largely to Emerson's young professionals that his California fundraisers turned for the crucial early funds. Their transfusions helped sustain Hart through his surprise victory over front-runner Walter Mondale in the 1984 New Hampshire primary, after which money rained onto Hart's Hollywood backers. "After New Hampshire," said Medavoy. "I couldn't answer the phone fast enough [from the donors]: they all wanted to get on." On the day after Hart's stunning upset, Emerson had seven television cameras in his office and almost a thousand phone calls inundating his law firm. The switchboard collapsed under the pressure. Unsolicited checks for Hart poured into Emerson's office at the rate of nearly $5,000 a day.

Celebrities rushed to the ascending political star as well. In early 1984, the campaign sent to Los Angeles Patricia Duff, who had worked in Congress and for Democratic consultants in Washington, to nurture

Hart's core of entertainment industry contacts. Some entertainment industry figures were involved with Emerson's Lexington Group and became early Hart supporters. But moving beyond that group and Hart's few old friends proved difficult. When Duff first arrived, potential recruits typically said, "Who's Gary Hart? Give us a break." As the campaign progressed and Hart broke from obscurity, his intriguing image produced an extraordinary outpouring. Not since McGovern had so many stars—particularly so many who had never previously campaigned—congregated around a candidate. Steve Martin hosted one event; Robin Williams and Rob Lowe appeared at a fundraiser; John Forsythe and Penny Marshall spoke; Debra Winger campaigned in Ohio; Kenny Loggins performed in San Francisco; Jack Nicholson and Donna Mills barnstormed Texas.

Like McGovern, Hart understood the value of being introduced to the public in the company of admired and trusted cultural figures. "It's a little bit like [the stars] are going to people in the country and saying, 'You know who I am, and I want to tell you about my friend George [McGovern] or Gary, and I want you to support him.' It's almost a transfer," Hart said. "They've developed a relationship with the audience and they're trying to move the audience toward the candidate. I think it can carry over in terms of entertainers."

Eventually Duff had more stars than she could use, for as the first questions about Hart's solidity arose—with revelations that he had misstated his age and changed his name—Hart's Hollywood popularity suddenly carried delicate connotations. As the campaign progressed, the glamour that initially created excitement around Hart threatened to underscore Mondale's charge that the senator lacked substance, that only flash, and no "beef," stood behind his claim to new ideas. "Too much glitter is not good for the candidate," Duff said. "Especially after the question about his age and whether Gary was more style over substance we couldn't use our celebrities as much as I wanted to. We had to be very careful."

Those doubts hobbled Hart just enough for Mondale to outlast him for the 1984 Democratic nomination. Hart returned to the Senate after the campaign and began plotting his 1988 bid. He buried the concern that he lacked policy substance with a series of detailed addresses laying out his proposals. As his campaign aides prepared for the second attempt at the nomination, they remained cautious about projecting too glamorous an image; when an invitation came into the campaign for Hart to attend the Academy Awards, the staff quickly scuttled it. But in Los Angeles Patricia Duff, who married Mike Medavoy after the 1984 campaign, continued to recruit in Hollywood. One event at the Medavoy home in early 1987 targeted black celebrities, who were virtually invisible in the 1984 effort. Tom Hayden and Jane Fonda signed on, and most people around them expected their legion of young celebrities from Network to follow. Patricia Medavoy also assembled a Media Advisory Group that brought together communications experts from both Hollywood and the political world, among them former *Newsweek* editor William Broyles, Jr., who had become a television producer; Lorne Michaels, the producer of "Saturday Night Live"; Larry Smith, Hart's former administrative assistant; and Danny Goldberg, a young manager of rock acts (such as Bonnie Raitt and Belinda Carlisle) with a zest for politics. Goldberg had first come to prominence in the Hollywood political world a few years earlier by skillfully organizing the music industry's resistance to Tipper Gore and the other Washington wives agitating for a rating system on rock records. Together with other young impresarios, Goldberg was also ready to serve as a cornerstone of the campaign to recruit support for Hart in the record industry.

In all, as he prepared to launch his second bid for the Democratic presidential nomination, Gary Hart had assembled more Hollywood resources than any candidate in memory.

Hart's most significant Hollywood resource kept himself almost entirely apart from the rest of the senator's supporters there. Warren Beatty did not attend many events, campaign with other stars, recruit them, or participate in the Media Advisory Group. He had as little to do with Hollywood as possible. But he was a persistent, if shadowy, presence in both Hart campaigns. Often, he manifested himself only over the phone, keeping tabs, checking the staff's views on the latest twists in the race, assessing Hart's morale, funneling information from the staff to Hart, from Hart to the staff. He was always difficult to find, yet somehow always around. (Hart, who prided himself on his own capacity for surprise and secrecy, called Beatty The Phantom.) "He was disruptive to my sleep," said Kathy Bushkin, Hart's long-time press secretary and his chief press spokesperson in the 1984 campaign. "He was the kind of person who called you at three in the morning and just wanted to know what was going on."

Beatty himself describes his role in the Hart races vaguely. "I don't think of myself as having done much," he said. "I tried to be a good friend and I tried to help in any way that I could. There was a part of me that always . . . I don't know. I did whatever I could." That included much more than Beatty's modesty implies. In the McGovern campaign Beatty established the backstage role for the star; in the Hart campaigns he perfected it. "Warren always hoped," said Bushkin, "to make this the greatest movie he ever directed or produced."

As in the McGovern campaign, Beatty meant that, to a considerable extent, literally. Though he took no title, Beatty actively tried to shape the media strategy and message for both Hart campaigns. His influence derived initially from Hart's respect for his communication skills. "I think he is clearly very smart about public mood and opinion," Hart said, "very smart. He cannot always translate that into politics any more than my instincts in the same regard can be translated into what are the movies you ought to make. But I always liked to talk to him to get a sense of public mood, and cultural currents and how they might influence visceral feelings about politics, about leaders, about issues."

In 1984 and again four years later, others came to share Hart's assessment. As in 1972, Beatty saw his role mostly as challenging the limits of conventional wisdom. "Warren deals in a world of big ideas because he is trying to get big audiences to watch his products," said Mark Green, a speechwriter for Hart in 1984. "So in meetings he would sometimes come up with ideas you could call 'Hail Mary' passes, some of which were great and some of which were a little far out."*

Hart shared Green's feelings. "I always thought a lot of [Warren's] tactical ideas didn't make any sense, the bold-stroke stuff," Hart recalled. "Warren was one of those people, like many who don't understand the nomination process, who get very frustrated in the early stages and want a breakthrough before New Hampshire. I must have spent hours saying, 'Warren, there is nothing I can do to jump from two per cent [in the polls before the first primaries].' In November, December, January [1984], he would say, 'Take all the money you've got, go on television, and if you don't jump ten points get out of the race.' That's the sort of thing he would advise. And I would say, 'Warren, you don't understand, it's Iowa and New Hampshire, you narrow down the field and it's going to be me and Mondale.' . . . But, see, Warren's style has always been to come off the wall with crazy things." And some of them hit home.

Consistently and effectively, Beatty urged Hart to strain from his lan-

*When Green won the Democratic nomination to challenge Republican Senator Alfonse M. D'Amato in New York in 1986, Beatty gave him "Hail Mary" advice too. "He would constantly call me about the D'Amato race: strategy, try this, try that, very reasonable," Green recalled. "The only unreasonable thing he said was kind of a high-concept approach. He said, 'Mark, you are now the only nominee in America to refuse all money from political action committees. In order to distinguish yourself from Al D'Amato, go the next step and refuse all money completely so the contrast couldn't be clearer.' I said, 'Hmm, well, who would pay for this phone call?' . . . But he was on to something."

guage the bureaucratic garble that masquerades as oratory in Washington. He pressed the candidate to talk less about policy abstractions and more about the realities voters face. "His biggest role was that he talked to Gary, as a non-inside-the-beltway thinker, about what he thought was going on," Bushkin remembered. "His judgment is obviously as skewed as everyone else's is by their own experiences, and God knows Warren doesn't live a lunchbucket kind of life—but if Gary was using language in a speech or a debate that was too lawyerlike or Washington-oriented Warren could remind him that couldn't sell. He was trying to get Gary focused on . . . making his points in graphic, effective ways."

Beatty's less-is-more view of publicity colored Hart's. Hart often cited Beatty's refusal to give interviews when resisting his press staff's routine requests to talk with reporters. On the other hand, in 1987 Hart relied largely on Beatty's advice in accepting from his staff an unusual strategy for the first stage of the campaign: a heavy burst of publicity around the announcement, and then several months of low visibility, writing, giving speeches to small audiences, staying out of the headlines. Hart's thinking was, "You don't want to become old news," he recalled. "I think I learned from him [the importance of managing publicity] as much by example as anything else." Hart took the precedent a long step further than even Beatty thought wise. Hart believed Beatty's refusal to reveal his personal life created a mystique that deepened interest in the actor, and often cited that to rebut the staff's argument that Hart needed to talk more about himself to voters. But to the staff's relief, Beatty argued to Hart that, in this respect, their situations were not comparable—that while Hart might need less overall exposure, people needed to know him more intimately. "Warren was always talking to Gary about ways to show things about himself, which he wasn't comfortable doing," said William H. Shore, Hart's longtime aide. That advice helped erode, if not break down, Hart's stubborn insistence that voters cared more about candidates' position papers than their personalities.*

Because of his long relationship with Hart, Beatty also functioned in an entirely different sphere, as counselor and confidant to the candidate. On many tense occasions the staff looked to Beatty, who seemed unruffled by any situation, to compose the tightly wired candidate. "He could absolutely get Gary to calm down," said Bushkin. "If Gary was obsessed

---

*Hart remembers Beatty's advice more equivocally than his aides. "Warren as a participant in that debate does not jump out as a unique figure," he said. "Even he was ambivalent about that. At one time he would say, 'I think you ought to do something like that.' At another time he wouldn't. So he would go back and forth, as we all would." Beatty would not discuss specific advice he gave Hart during the campaigns.

about some problem, he could absolutely get his mind off of it." During the final stages of the 1984 campaign, Beatty typically was the last man in the room with Hart before the debates between the candidates, relaxing him and focusing him on the confrontation ahead. In the maelstrom of the Democratic Convention that summer, he did the same.

His friendship with Hart also allowed Beatty finally to exercise his ideas on a campaign's fundamental shape and direction. In the early months of the 1984 race, Beatty had little presence. But as the campaign fell into confusion following Hart's loss to Mondale in the Illinois primary, Beatty threw himself physically into the operation. When the campaign shifted to New York, Raymond D. Strother, Hart's media consultant, Pat Caddell, his pollster, and Beatty convinced the candidate to give a half-hour televised speech as a way of reviving his flagging effort. It was the sort of bold stroke that appealed to both Beatty and Caddell. But on the evening it was to be recorded a snowstorm immobilized the East Coast. Hart arrived at the studio late; Caddell, who had the only copy of the speech, arrived even later. The speech, after Caddell's rewrite, came in roughly twice as long as the half-hour the campaign had purchased. With airtime pressing against them, Beatty joined Strother and Caddell in frantically revising and cutting. It was more like triage than surgery; Caddell and Beatty scribbled changes even as Hart recorded the first pages. Hart was tired and looked it, the preparation was rushed and sounded it, and the speech bombed. But Strother came out of the debacle impressed by Beatty's steadiness amid the chaos. "Beatty was a stable influence in the room, very calm, very stable," recalled Strother, "not what I expected from a high-profile Hollywood person. He let everyone express themselves first and then jumped in, actually kind of timidly nosed himself in. . . . Beatty always seemed to be tuned into the larger picture."

Over the next few weeks, through the New York primary and especially in its dispiriting aftermath, Beatty was a pivotal figure in the campaign, perhaps in some ways the pivotal figure. "He was, at one time in the campaign," said Caddell, "the only person the candidate would talk to. This was around New York, Pennsylvania. It's a very strange period in the campaign. He's a very close friend of the candidate, therefore Gary was comfortable being with him, trusted him. He wasn't [comfortable] with any of us, and therefore Beatty was a refuge for him."

That may slightly overstate Beatty's primacy. But there's no question he assumed a key role in trying to rebuild the campaign's chaotic internal structure after Hart stumbled following his initial breakthrough. Beatty's first job was to reconcile Caddell and Hart, whose relationship had collapsed in an outburst of competing strategic visions, personality clashes, and ego competition. Much the way Caddell once thought he could convince Beatty to marry Diane Keaton, Beatty thought he alone could bring together the willful candidate and his mercurial pollster. "I will solve this," he told Caddell, as he packed his bags for New York. "I am coming to solve this."

Beatty tried. Caddell had physically removed himself from the campaign; he was staying in a separate hotel, in his own words, sulking "like Achilles in his tent." Beatty coaxed him out, arranging dinners after the long campaign days where he, Caddell, and Hart would talk about anything but the race itself. That kept Caddell in the campaign orbit but did not resolve the dispute, which, beyond the personal friction, boiled down to Hart's resistance to Caddell's strategy of challenging Mondale more directly. While the campaign careened through New York, Beatty continued his effort to bring both men to a common ground that would point the campaign on a clear strategic path. Finally, on the evening after Mondale won a solid victory in New York, when the senator's advisers had convened in the hotel room of campaign manager Oliver (Pudge) Henkel to assess their options, Beatty watched Caddell remain self-consciously silent and decided the time for stroking was past. After an hour, when Caddell had still not spoken a word, merely paced and glowered, Beatty took him outside and dressed him down. It was, he told Caddell, no time to brood. Though Beatty could be so soft-spoken as to be nearly inaudible, this was not one of those occasions. "He just really ripped the shit out of me about it and made me go back in there," Caddell recalled. And in fact, once he entered the debate with the other advisers, Caddell carried it with his contention that Hart needed to sharpen his differences with Mondale.

Soon enough that decision slipped again. The confusion over message symbolized the campaign's overall lack of direction. Hart and his team limped into Pennsylvania for the next primary, bewildered, divided, adrift. As clearly as anyone in Hart's demoralized assemblage, Beatty saw the need for internal restructuring and helped to arrange it. In an elevator at the campaign's headquarters hotel in Pittsburgh, Beatty cornered John T. McEvoy, a veteran Washington political operative who had been a consultant for the campaign and who had come to assist in the preparation for the next debate.

"You've got to come into this campaign," Beatty said. "You've got to run this campaign."

"That's very flattering," McEvoy said. "But we've never met, so why exactly do you think that?"

Beatty told McEvoy the campaign desperately needed a change, and that others had spoken highly of him. McEvoy told him he could not leave his law practice to work full-time for Hart; Beatty said, "We've got to talk some more." They did, in Beatty's suite at the hotel, where Hart and his staff were preparing for the debate, largely under Beatty's direction. (Caddell had walked out again in another dispute with the candidate. "It's your campaign," he said to Beatty, "you take care of it.") McEvoy eventually agreed to come in as senior counsel. For the next several weeks he ran the campaign, helping Hart to a series of late primary victories, until Henkel, the original campaign manager, reasserted his authority. "Beatty was as instrumental in my coming to the campaign as anyone," McEvoy said.

In the hectic, depressing weeks of early spring, while Hart struggled to recover from his missteps in the industrial states, Beatty felt mostly the lost opportunity of his earlier distance from the operation. Riding in from an airport during the Texas primary with Hart aide Bill Shore, Beatty slammed his fist into his palm and exclaimed, "How could I have waited so long?"

Though Beatty retreated from his hands-on role once the reorganization was in place, he remained a strong presence through the campaign's last weeks, especially for the final contest in California. More confident than a decade earlier, Beatty pressed his views more doggedly, but he accepted defeat graciously. He did not demand special treatment or limousines; he would jump on the bus with the rest of the staff. (In New York, after the tense editing session for Hart's disastrous half-hour broadcast, Beatty went to sleep on the floor of the editing room.) Most people in the national campaign agreed with media consultant Ray Strother that Beatty "had Hart's best interest in mind at all times. He wasn't using him for publicity." That was rare enough, but Beatty was rare in another sense: after he had lobbied Hart on some point, small or large, senior staff members who disagreed with the decision could reopen the issue with Beatty, and if they could convince him he was wrong, he would call Hart and say so.

"What he did was play the role of cardinal, of senior close friend, with an aplomb and effectiveness I've not seen in other presidential campaigns, and I've been in four of them," said McEvoy. "The senior friend is usually an officious guy, however well-meaning, who ham-handedly sticks his head in where it doesn't belong, and you wind up having to coddle him and move around him. But Beatty never was like that. He was always a welcome figure . . . because he had a positive influence on what happened without in any way displacing the people who had personal responsibilities for things. When things would start coming unglued, he wouldn't necessarily rush to glue them back together at that moment, but you got the sense he would speak to Hart later. You might describe him as glue in a very loosely jointed operation."

In the aborted 1988 campaign Beatty did not assume as great an operational responsibility, but he once again insinuated ideas into the mix through his regular phone conversations not only with Hart but also with Shore and campaign manager William P. Dixon. Mostly he kept his counsel for Hart. Aides who proposed an idea to Hart grew accustomed to him saying, a day or two later, that he had checked it with Beatty.

Beatty's relationship with Hart ran deeper than with any of the staff members; as Caddell put it, he was not another "prince" vying with Hart for history's benediction as the architect of his success. Hart saw Beatty in a different light. An old friend with a sympathetic ear, a record of accomplishment Hart respected, and no stake in the endless internal struggles, Beatty could raise issues with Hart that the staff could not. Hart did not hesitate to tell Beatty when he disliked his proposals; but Hart could also take criticism from Beatty he might reject from aides, who he sometimes perceived as trying to make their reputations at the expense of his own.

Still, Hart's complex relationship with Beatty was not completely free from competition. From the first days of the McGovern campaign, people observing Hart and Beatty found them intrigued by each other's accomplishments. With his own vague political ambitions, it could not always have been easy for Beatty to watch his friend reach for the grand prize. When Hart first decided to run for president, it was apparent to him that Beatty found it difficult to accept the fact that *he* was not the candidate. On the other hand, Beatty's artistic accomplishments excited similar yearnings in Hart. "Whenever I would hear Hart talk about Warren with awestruck tones, it had to do with Warren's ability to communicate through film, not that Warren had a gorgeous woman at dinner," said Shore. Beatty himself felt Hart envied his freedom to express himself without a politician's fear of offending some portion of the public. "I think Gary would have liked to have made a movie like *Reds*," Beatty said, "and I think that he would like to have the freedom to . . . say exactly what he thinks the truth is." (Hart obviously had a rare artistic bent for an American politician, but he saw his admiration for Beatty's work in less heroic terms. "*Reds* was brilliant, brilliant, brilliant," he said. "I'm fascinated by that. But the fascination is not that I can tell a truth that I can't tell in politics; it's just, 'What a creative thing to do.' ")

To whatever degree, Beatty's artistic accomplishment was one attraction for Hart. But many around the candidate had no doubt he also found the freedom of Beatty's affluent, glamorous, indulgent life of personal and sexual freedom—the Hollywood myth distilled—extremely attractive. With steely defiance, Hart insists it had no appeal for him at all—something that is difficult to believe could be true for anyone outside a monastery. "I've been three years now out of politics. If I envied his life I would be out here [Los Angeles] doing something, practicing law in Los Angeles, asking [Mike] Medavoy to get me a job in the industry," he said firmly. "I live in Colorado. . . . This was always a good place for me to escape for a couple of days, come out here, give a speech, take a couple of days off, stay at Warren's place, relax. . . . But I wouldn't live like that."

Others close to Hart saw the relationship in different terms. "Beatty didn't need Gary Hart the way movie stars frequently need politicians for validation," said McEvoy. "He was Warren Beatty, he was terribly successful, he had all the women he could ever handle, he was very rich and he didn't seem to need it; he was doing it for a friend. . . . On the other hand, as everything that has happened has shown, Hart had this big hole in the middle, and I think he needed Beatty: this kid from Kansas needed a movie star. Beatty took him into a world of power, in terms of hard power, and sexual power, where there was license for things that were forbidden in Ottawa, Kansas. . . . The difference was Beatty was a single [unmarried] movie star, and his reputation was in fact enhanced by it, and Hart was playing with fire at all times. To me it was clear that Hart needed Beatty far more than Beatty needed Hart."

These complex strands of envy and affinity have often been woven into a neat ball: the conclusion that Hart wanted to be Beatty and Beatty wanted to be Hart. That judgment, although it has an alluring symmetry, is ultimately too neat. Both men did see things they admired in the other. But it is unlikely either would have been happy in the other's shoes. Hart didn't crave the adoration of fans so much as the reverence of voters—he wanted, as Caddell suggests, "political adulation," not silver-screen celebrity, to be "Jack Kennedy, not a movie star." ("It presumes neither one of us knows who we are," Hart said of the argument that he wanted to be Beatty. "I don't want to be a movie star, never did. To say that a person who has been in public life for fifteen or twenty years and is very deeply motivated by issues and ideas . . . is sort of confused about what he wanted to do in life is nonsense.") And Beatty, for all his attraction to the political world, all his hopes of achieving office, understood that a political career would entail sacrifices he might not easily endure.

Their jostle and envy were, in fact, normal for two accomplished men of nearly the same age. They were more complementary than competitive: what drew them together was less the fantasy of transformation than the reality that each enriched the other's life. Joined, they created possibilities neither could have produced alone. Each enabled the other's aspirations: through Hart, Beatty could operate at the highest level of national politics; through Beatty, Hart could touch the quintessence of the Hollywood myth. Their friendship, which both men counted among their deepest, ultimately thrived on synergy, much like John F. Kennedy's friendship with Frank Sinatra. They saw in each other similar temperaments in dissimilar circumstances. "They weren't in competition," said Patricia Medavoy. "They were like two bookends; they were like yin and yang. They were alter egos."

Beyond his tangible assistance as counselor and adviser to Hart, Beatty affected his friend's campaigns on a completely different level: as a symbol. Not since Kennedy's friendship with Sinatra had a Washington-Hollywood relationship carried such symbolic power or inspired so many rumors. If not necessarily to the public at large, certainly to political insiders the combination of Beatty and Hart created powerful and dangerous symbolic associations. Around other politicians, Beatty projected intelligence, grace, sophistication; but when placed against the background of Gary Hart all that bled away, and only Beatty's reputation as a hedonist and ladykiller survived. That simplification caricatured their relationship: thoughtful and creative, Beatty obviously offered Hart more than proximity to beautiful women. But for many politicians, Beatty's luxurious lifestyle (or at least their vision of Beatty's lifestyle) provided an accessible outline of what they believed Hart craved: the unlimited freedom to pursue casual sexual liaisons. It can be argued that John Kennedy's combination of institutional power and personal freedom more precisely encapsulated Hart's discordant ambitions. But Kennedy was a distant model, whose heroic political legacy blurred the comparison; Beatty was close at hand. It was as if Beatty provided a finished picture that allowed critics to connect the confusing dots of Hart's behavior. Even some close friends of Hart thought, as one put it, that Beatty "embodied the kind of freedom that Hart psychologically wished for himself."

No one but Beatty and Hart knows exactly what they did together on those weekends through the 1970s and 1980s when Hart regularly visited the actor in Los Angeles. But many politicians and campaign operatives, including some around Hart, assumed the worst. No one thought Beatty led Hart astray. But they worried that Beatty made it too easy, probably by overt action, at least by example, for Hart to indulge his worst instincts.

As time passed, whatever they actually did became virtually irrelevant. Beatty's myth was so strong, and so perfectly blended with what many politicians believed about Hart anyway, that in the absence of compelling contrary evidence, their mere association was raised as supporting proof of the rumors of extramarital affairs buzzing around Hart. In that sense, the cliché that Hart wished he was Beatty (while Beatty wished he was Hart) took on a life of its own, free of the subtle nuances that shaped their relationship. As compatible as they were in practice, the two men were more incompatible at the level of symbol. Much the same way that opponents changed perceptions of Harriett Woods in her 1986 Senate race by melding her image with Jane Fonda's, whispers in Washington blended Beatty and Hart into an imaginary amalgam that combined the least attractive aspects of both.

For the campaign, these symbolic concerns manifested themselves mostly in discussions about whether Hart should stay at Beatty's house, as he preferred to do on his campaign trips to Los Angeles, and also when taking a few days off from the trail. Because Beatty generally kept a low profile in the campaign, Hart's visits to his home were the most visible aspects of the actor's participation. Ironically, when Hart stayed at Beatty's house, at least in the later years, Beatty often was out of town. But the association remained powerful: if Hart was not illicitly pursuing women, the argument went, why was he secluding himself in such impregnable and fabled surroundings?

Fully aware of that belief, Hart's staff frequently tried to persuade him to stay elsewhere in Los Angeles. The Medavoys offered to let the candidate stay at their home; even better, Marvin Davis offered him use of the Beverly Hills Hotel at the time he owned it. Sometimes, for logistical reasons, Hart would stay somewhere other than Beatty's. But he never conceded the point that staying there meant danger, and he always drifted back to the actor's aerie. When Patricia Medavoy told Hart that with all the rumors circulating, staying at Beatty's was reckless, he angrily rejected the idea. C. Richard (Rick) Allen, a young attorney who had succeeded John Emerson as the California coordinator in the 1988 campaign, received the same cold response when he raised the issue with Hart. So did others, in Los Angeles and in Denver. Hart would set his jaw, insist he did nothing improper while at Beatty's—"You've been there," he would challenge, "what did you see?"—and say that he wouldn't change just because others might draw the wrong conclusions. Beatty's house was quiet and removed, a refuge where he could think and write, Hart insisted. "In this campaign," he would say, his voice rising, "are we going to be so bent around perception that we can't do something that is innocent?"

Years later, Hart still grows animated remembering the internal debates over his visits to Beatty. "We had that discussion. I said, 'Nonsense. Nonsense.' . . . If women had been running around up there and all that, I wouldn't have stayed there. But they weren't. Warren has friends and sometimes they stay there, but that is his business and not mine. . . . There was only one person on earth who legitimately could be concerned about me staying with Warren and that's my wife, and she was never concerned. And if she wasn't concerned it is nobody else's business. . . . Warren is a friend. I obviously think of him as a movie star; but I think of him as a guy, a friend. We are within six months of age of each other, grew up in much the same kind of family, talked about it a lot—he has been a friend that I have related to. And you don't have many of those in life, in anybody's life, particularly in politics. And I value that; and I was not about to dump on that to accommodate some critics. If people want to say there are orgies going on up there, and I was chasing young starlets, there was nothing I could do about that."

To defend a friend was admirable. But what Hart strangely refused to understand, even as the evidence accumulated around him, was that in matters of ethics, perception is crucial. What made Hart's intransigence even more baffling was that he clearly recognized that the public took cues about politicians from the cultural figures they associated with. Beatty understood that too, and his last intent was to damage his friend's prospects. It's difficult to believe he would have objected if Hart had stayed elsewhere to help his campaign. But Hart raised the decision to a matter of principle: it became as symbolic to him as it was to his critics. To turn away from Beatty would be to admit that he could not run for president by his own rules. "To me you have to draw the line," he said, "and if I was going to say I'm not going to stay at Warren's any more, then it would be something else. Once you start down that track . . . there is no end to it."

The Fall of Gary Hart

But the track Hart was on led him along a rough road. As the 1988 campaign approached, the rumors about Hart's personal life obscured his prospects among political insiders in many communities, Hollywood prominent among them. As early as 1984, Robert Redford, who had campaigned for Hart earlier, minimized his participation in the campaign out of concern about Hart's personal behavior. "I had supported him through two senatorial races, but I did not feel he should run for national office, so I didn't do it," Redford recalled. "I didn't think it was a good idea; I did not think he was qualified for national office." (Redford later told one interviewer, "The worst thing that ever happened to Gary Hart was getting into 'The Hollywood Set.' . . . Gary ended up thinking he was invisible.") When the whispers audibly deepened on the eve of the 1988 race, more potential supporters came to share that view. "Everybody knew Gary had that propensity for excitement of the flesh, and people warned him," said producer John Davis, a Hart backer. "Everybody heard the whispers. . . . He had been warned, he had been warned a lot."

Hart's decision to continue staying at Beatty's—if for no other reason than that it demonstrated questionable political judgment—fed those flames in Hollywood, particularly among women. When Patricia Medavoy tried to recruit actress Morgan Fairchild to the campaign, she hesitated, and then explained why: "I keep hearing these stories about Warren Beatty's house, wild parties, women." Medavoy tried to defuse her concern: "Did he ever come on to you?" she asked, and Fairchild had to say no. But in Hollywood the issue of Hart's behavior, and Beatty's influence over him, continually resurfaced.

This anxiety limited Hart's support in the film community. Though he was by far the strongest of the Democratic candidates heading into 1988, his position was not as impregnable as might have been expected after 1984. His initial fundraiser in January 1987 raised only $100,000. That was more than the other candidates could have collected at that point, but quarrying the money was more difficult than Hart's supporters expected. It was, in fact, no more than Hart had raised four years earlier at the Twentieth Century-Fox event when few people knew him. The take was not large enough to discourage any of his competitors from digging in Hollywood, nor did it give the impression of great momentum.

Hart himself was strangely hesitant about the race. One week before he was due to announce his candidacy, he thought seriously about not running, according to several sources in the campaign. Out loud he wondered whether he was up to the job if he won, and if he could endure the demands of a presidential race—the relentless schedule, the loss of "privacy." Beatty was one of the people with whom he examined the decision most carefully. Exactly what Beatty told Hart isn't known. "Presumably Beatty was listening and kicking things back with him," said one senior aide in the campaign. "If lifestyle was an aspect of the decision,

Beatty was one of the few people he could talk about it with."

Whatever Beatty told him, Hart decided not to derail the train and announced his candidacy on April 13, 1987. Within days he might have been reconsidering. By the time Hart arrived for his first swing through Los Angeles for an evening of fundraising, just two days after his announcement, the rumors about alleged affairs had already leaked into the national press. For his first event, Hart visited the home of Marvin Davis, where John Davis and Patricia Medavoy had assembled (at $1,000 a head) a substantial chunk of Hollywood's elite, from senior studio executives Frank G. Wells (of Disney) and Frank G. Mancuso (of Paramount) to Sally Field and Goldie Hawn. But the event turned out to be a nightmare when federal marshals, operating on a request from a debtor still unpaid from Hart's 1984 campaign, stormed into Davis's home demanding the receipts. When the marshals arrived, Marvin Davis, an imposing man even without a billion dollars in the bank, told them, "You will wait in the kitchen," and they cooled their heels while Hart entertained the crowd. But they left with the checks.

As the marshals loitered in Davis's kitchen, a similar scene unfolded at the site of Hart's second fundraiser of the day, the Palace nightclub, where the candidate was scheduled to speak after he finished at Davis's home. Only this time, the marshals demanding the proceeds were not in the quiet of a rich man's house but on a main street in Hollywood, blustering at Hart's staff only a few feet away from the huge press corps assembling for the star-studded party. At one point, the marshals threatened to lock out on the sidewalk anyone who could not pay cash for tickets, which ranged in price from $50 to $1,000. Only through frantic last-minute negotiations were the doors opened and disaster avoided.

The sudden eruption of the debt crisis put Hart in a sour enough mood. Then on the way into the Palace, one of the television reporters bellowed at him and his wife: "Any comment on the womanizer rumors, Gary?" The sense of impending doom only accentuated the event's over-frenetic feel. Outside the Palace, crowds of curious tourists bustled like extras from *The Day of the Locust.* Like so many arbitrageurs, the paparazzi enforced the pitiless free market of fame. No one with a camera looked up when Tom Bradley, the mayor of Los Angeles, walked by, stiff and solemn. But when actress Melanie Griffith walked in—Melanie Griffith with the spiked punky hairdo, the once and future wife of Don Johnson, the kinky seductress from *Something Wild*—that was a different story. She set off a bank of strobes when she passed between the rows of photographers and television cameras bracketing the club's entrance behind velvet ropes. Inside, she encountered a wave of photographers near the front door, and when she made her way upstairs to the crowded VIP lounge behind the bar, another wave descended on her, snapping, snapping, snapping until, blinking furiously, she finally said, "Okay, okay, okay, thank you, thank you."

Actors John Forsythe, Elliott Gould, and Robert Walden and actresses Rosanna Arquette, Jane Fonda, and Donna Mills all received the same treatment: "Entertainment Tonight" microphones were shoved in their faces and bursts of flashbulbs exploded around them like gunfire. Actress Morgan Fairchild almost set off a riot among the paparazzi, who took one look at her tight red dress and saw green. When she vamped down the line, tossed her blond hair, arched her back, and thrust her breasts toward the exploding flashbulbs, the paparazzi hooted and hollered and chanted, "Mor-gan, Mor-gan." The velvet ropes barely held. And when she walked through the front door, the paparazzi massed and fired again, nearly blinding a man in a wheelchair who was trying to make his way into the hall just a few feet ahead of her.

Upstairs, in the VIP lounge, Hart chatted with the stars, the big givers who still had some party left in them after the fete at Davis's home, and anyone else who had managed to talk their way past the layers of security designed to keep out the common folk. After a few minutes of crowded mingling, the candidate made his way downstairs, where he stood like Patton before a huge flag (actually the one used in the movie) on a stark stage, and gave a shortened version of his spare announcement speech from earlier in the week. When he finished, the sound system kicked in with a teeth-rattling tape of "Born to Run" and the crowd chanted "Gary, Gary" and the sparkling globe sprinkled light like rain over the swaying young women in dungaree jackets who pressed against the young men in the Italian silks of the upwardly mobile. The cameramen rushed the stage in pursuit of Hart, but he was already gone. He drove himself off into the night in a Mercedes that belonged to Beatty.

Within a few weeks, it was all moot. On the weekend of May 1, the *Miami Herald,* acting on a tip, trailed Hart and discovered his relationship with Donna Rice, the aspiring model he had met at a New Year's Day party in Aspen at the home of rock star Don Henley (Hart was attending as a guest of the Medavoys). Soon Hart's earlier cruise aboard a yacht to Bimini with Rice, attorney William C. (Billy) Broadhurst, and another woman was revealed; and then, with the dam finally cracked, stories of other liaisons percolated toward print. Only days after the first reports, Hart retreated to Denver to pull the plug on his faltering campaign.

For many in Hollywood the disaster confirmed their worst suspicions about Hart's behavior and judgment. Many were furious at the candidate. John Davis thought the disaster showed only how important it was that candidates now faced greater scrutiny and a long screening process. "I was relieved that we found out something about him early enough to do something about it," he said. "If the guy wasn't cut out to be president of the United States, better we find out now. He didn't have the character to be president, he didn't have the judgment to be president: the system worked." Across Hollywood, in the studio suites and in the living rooms where the Westside liberals congregated, friends of Hart and foes of Hart echoed Davis's views.

Warren Beatty did not.

Distraught, furious at the press ("I thought the news media were manipulated throughout the presidential campaign," he would say later, "from before that until the end of it."), "angry at everything" as one friend recalled, Beatty desperately tried to prevent Gary Hart from withdrawing. Any anger he felt at Hart, any doubts he held about his friend's judgment, all his understanding about the price of private indiscretion publicly revealed, were put aside. As Hart flew back to Denver on Thursday, May 7, to ponder his fate, Beatty became the strongest voice urging him to remain in the race.

On that afternoon, Caddell was meeting with Fox chairman Barry Diller and facing strange rumors that he had somehow orchestrated not only Hart's meeting with Rice but the disclosure of their relationship. ("I didn't know whether to laugh or cry," he said later, "[at] the sense that you are so powerful versus the sense that you are that base a person.") Caddell called Beatty to check in on the day's events, and Beatty, stewing with undirected rage, told the pollster that maybe he should "look for cover" now that Hart was falling out of the race. Caddell, whose temper ordinarily measured on the Richter scale and who was, understandably, especially sensitive that afternoon, instantly exploded, one of the few times he lashed out at Beatty. Within moments, Beatty realized he had pushed too far and reached to make amends. "Come to the house," he said. "I insist you come to the house. Come up here right now."

When Caddell reached the house, he found actor Sean Penn there talking with Beatty's current girlfriend, and Beatty on the phone with Hart. Eventually, Penn drifted off, and Caddell, with Beatty's girlfriend, drove down to Beverly Hills for dinner while Beatty remained locked on the phone to Denver. Beatty didn't arrive at the restaurant until they had finished eating. He sat down and, in his circuitous manner, trolled for Caddell's thoughts.

"What do you think of the campaign people?" Beatty asked, nervous and intent.

"I know what you're asking," Caddell said. "I know what is going on in Denver. They are in the middle of the eye of the storm. Everyone is telling them to get out of the race."

"What would you do?" Beatty said.

"I wouldn't get out of the race," Caddell answered.

What then? Beatty asked.

Turn it around, Caddell said, and then he explained: Hart would probably be forced out eventually, but he had to leave the race on his own terms. To go out the next morning, with the press snapping at his heels, would be to "go down in history as Donna Rice's playmate, and his intellectual self will not be able to absorb that."

True, said Beatty, gently coaxing Caddell—who was actually at that moment an adviser to Delaware Senator Joseph R. Biden, Jr., another of the Democratic hopefuls—but what's the alternative?

"This great moment has been built up for him," Caddell said. "He can get up there and say . . . 'I came to announce my withdrawal from the race, but last night I went to bed and I couldn't sleep and I got up this morning and looked in the mirror and said, "Hell no . . . you're not going to drive me out of the race. Let he who is without sin cast the first stone." ' " Caddell paused. "You know, make them eat their microphones. The country will go crazy."

Beatty listened to Caddell's scenario with evident interest, encouraging, arguing, probing, looking for the holes in the idea. It appealed not only to his will to keep Hart in the race but also to his dramatic instincts, his love of the political long bomb. This was the ultimate "Hail Mary" pass—a stroke bold enough to refurbish Hart's image or completely fry it. "Warren understood in an instant," Caddell said later. "That was his great political gift: he understood drama, because he could understand being dramatic. When do you get served up a moment like this?"

When dinner was over and they had rushed back up the hill to Beatty's house, the actor disappeared into another room to make Caddell's case to Hart over the phone. Beatty cajoled and tugged at Hart until early Friday morning. Caddell drifted off to sleep. Beatty kept at it. Finally, at about 1:30 A.M. in Denver, Beatty called Hart's aide Bill Shore, who had just collapsed into sleep after the chaotic day. "I've just gotten off the phone with Gary," Beatty told Shore, who was too groggy to be stunned at finding Beatty on the other end of his phone at that hour. "The only way I can help is to fly out to Denver and convince him not to pull out." Beatty told Shore that Hart thought the actor should fly out and talk to the staff one last time; but Shore was too exhausted to have any meaningful conversation with Beatty, even about whether further conversation made sense.

"Look, Warren," he said, "I'm so tired I can't have this conversation. We have to talk later. I'll call you at five." Shore woke up John Emerson, the deputy campaign manager, and enlisted him to join in the call. Then he fell into oblivion for a few hours. At 5 A.M. Denver time, just hours before Hart was scheduled to meet the press, they rang Beatty, who had fallen asleep himself. Beatty roused himself for one last push. Weary but determined, he spun his version of Caddell's scenario again. "What Gary should do," he told the two exhausted young aides, "is admit he is an adulterer and then refuse to answer any more questions about his personal life." The issue will die, Beatty insisted. Emerson and Shore respected the intent, but neither was moved: the field was being rolled up, it was too late to throw a bomb. After disclosure of the trip to Bimini, Hart's support had hemorrhaged. "Warren, it's raining concrete," Emerson finally told him. There was nothing left to say. Beatty put down the phone and went back to sleep.

The next morning Caddell, who had spent the night at Beatty's, turned on the television for Hart's press conference. For a moment, listening to his defiant first words, Caddell thought Hart would follow the advice Beatty had transmitted; then he looked at the candidate's eyes and saw that he would not. A few seconds later it was clear Hart was leaving the race. Beatty did not wake up to watch the press conference; he knew the result before he went to bed. Whatever the words, whatever the gestures, he knew he had failed to convince Hart to renew the long march that once promised to bring them both to the seat of power.

Seven months later, on the advice of Beatty among others, Hart reentered the race. The gesture was futile. Hart stalked the other candidates like a ghost, searching for redemption along with votes in the snow of Iowa and New Hampshire. But after the first primaries his support evaporated, and he was gone again, suddenly, like an old tune fallen out of memory. Hart withdrew to his home in Troublesome Gulch, where the press had camped in the desperate hours of May, but which was now secluded from prying eyes by 135 acres of surrounding land he bought with a quarter-million-dollar loan from Warren Beatty.

After Gary Hart so recklessly threw away a commanding opportunity to win the presidency, pop psychologists declared open season on his psyche. Explanations for his bewildering behavior split roughly in half: Hart either harbored a self-destructive urge (as Caddell publicly suggested) and wanted to be caught, or believed he could live beyond the rules, a viewpoint summarized by the assertion that Hart really wished to be Beatty, a man whose life seemingly had no limits.

Hart, not surprisingly, accepted neither explanation. He argued at the time, and months later, that his "lifestyle" was not the real issue in his demise; rather, it was his refusal to meet the expectations of the political establishment—the party bosses and consultants, the press—about how to run for president. In Hart's vision of the campaign, he is the political equivalent of a James Dean character: destroyed for the sin of being different.

In the long months after Hart's fall, Beatty kept his own counsel about the events. Even those closest to both men are uncertain how Beatty felt about the rumors and ripples that surrounded his friendship with Hart or the stories about Hart's alleged affairs themselves. "He knows Gary, he knew the problems," said Caddell. "But he thought they could be dealt with and Gary could win. . . . He was very sympathetic to Gary's belief that he had a private life, and people should be able to have a life, and much more complex things I'm not going to get into."

One senior figure in the 1988 campaign believes that however Beatty might have caroused with Hart earlier, by the mid-1980s the actor tried to suggest to his friend that he could no longer live that way. "In many small ways, that's what Beatty was saying," said the official. "My sense is Beatty realized that was no longer tenable. He was a very dependable, solid voice of reason as to what had to be done in that period of American history to be elected president." Beatty's own attitudes toward scandal offer some supporting evidence for that contention. So skilled at the manipulation of public image, Beatty recognized the limits of control; that's why he carefully avoided not only interviews, but also placing himself in situations capable of creating attention he could not control. That same sophisticated perspective guided his interaction with politicians: the political operatives who knew him best almost universally considered Beatty too shrewd and careful to ever place an elected official in a situation that could compromise them both. "Nobody ever got a bad story about Hart with Beatty," said McEvoy, and except for the vague rumors, he's right.

Even with time and distance, Beatty still spoke about Hart's fall carefully, guardedly, and with evident anguish. But in conversation, Beatty gave tantalizing hints that he was disappointed in the way Hart displayed himself on his trip to Bimini early in 1988 (where he allowed himself to be photographed with Donna Rice on his lap), even while calling the actual controversy over his relationship with Rice "a ridiculous matter."

"I can, [but] I won't address myself to the lack of carefulness in his private [life]," Beatty said. "Well, let me put it another way. I won't address myself to his assumption that the public and the media would overlook certain things in their politicians simply because they had in the past." At another point, Beatty said, "professional politicians" who had "hitched" themselves to Hart could justifiably say to the candidate, "You're a very intelligent man, you know the media has gone completely crazy here, if you were going to accept this job of running for office, then you should have listened to your own intelligence and [realized] you cannot do what so many previous presidents did. Things are different now." But on the most basic question, whether Beatty directly gave Hart that advice himself, the actor is not talking. "That's none of your business," he said firmly, though without rancor.

At first he was equally remote when asked whether he thought Hart wanted to be Beatty.

"Well," he said, and paused, "I think that Gary Hart has more the mentality and soul of an artist than he does of a politician. And the thing you speak about, that you've heard said a number of times. . . . I don't know specifically what you are referring to. . . . I don't know specifically what is meant. It sort of ripples off the tongue of some wiseacre easily. I think that there are very few politicians that I know in Washington who, after putting up with what they have to put up with, wouldn't look at certain aspects of being a movie star and think that they were attractive."

Mostly, it is suggested, the ability to retreat behind a gate, like the one outside Beatty's home?

"It's not only the ability to go behind a gate somewhere—which, by the way, a movie star doesn't have much more than a politician because the movie star is hounded as much—but the results of the hounding have a different interpretation for the movie star. The movie star is allowed to live the way that you live. The politician is not. The politician is held to the higher standard; I won't say a higher standard, a different standard. I think we have to be very careful about what context we're talking in. The movie actor has the freedom to say what he wants to say and he will not lose the 'election' if 49 percent of the electorate agrees with him. In fact, the movie actor can do very, very well if 10 percent of the electorate agrees with him. So I think it is very hard for a politician who has the capacity to perceive the truth, and who has the artistic soul to want to speak the truth, not to have the opportunity to do it.

"And so, it makes me so impatient when the study of these poor people who have to run for public office is so superficial that they [the public] really don't know their positions on public issues, but they do know their positions in these ridiculous social-sexual or superficial areas. . . . I think that the sad truth is that the important public positions on public issues and events are difficult to dramatize, and even if they are dramatized, the huge proliferation of simplistic media is going to get into that more accessible soap-opera level of crap."

Beatty sits back in his chair, suddenly distant, as though lost in memory or private thoughts he wishes to keep from his lips. Conversation moves on but winds back around. Did Hart covet Beatty's life, did he believe that what was acceptable behavior for Beatty should be acceptable for him?

"I still don't know what you mean," Beatty said, "and I don't think you know what you mean."

Fine, then, no fencing: Did Hart envy Beatty's history of dating beautiful, famous women? Did he wish, though he was married, to emulate Beatty's single life?

"After some time, you are getting down to less superficial stuff," Beatty said, leaning forward, as though he had found an opening in a trap. "You are saying he's married and I'm not. Now I don't know whether there is a part of Gary Hart that would like to be unmarried and have the freedom and mobility that I've had. I can tell you there is a significant part of me that would like to have children like Gary Hart has and have a long [relationship]; Gary Hart has been with the same woman for thirty-five years. And there is a part of me that envies that. . . . So I think it is just superficial to go in and say . . ." Beatty let the thought drift off. "I know the man very well," he said defiantly. "I have tremendous respect for him. . . . The thinking on Gary has been so shallow."

That may be, but the events that led to Hart's downfall had an undeniable complexity about them. It was, after all, a friend, Caddell, who said that Hart had a self-destructive urge.

"You could say," Beatty responded after some time, "that he had a self-destructive urge if you say that to attain public office is the point of life. You could also say that what a man has to do to obtain public office is to destroy himself."

It's easy to understand why Beatty, with his vaulting artistic and political ambitions, cleaved to Hart. In many ways, Hart was a visionary and iconoclastic politician, with keen insight into the underlying rhythms of national mood and the intersection between politics and culture. His understanding evolved over time. He began his national political career, in his own words, as "a conventional" campaign manager whose vision of a successful campaign derived from Theodore White's account of the steely Irish legions who carried John F. Kennedy to victory in 1960. But by 1987 he was listening intently to ethereal discussions in his Media Advisory Group about the role of myth and symbol in presidential politics. One member of the group, an academic named Sara Hankins, presented the case that a presidential campaign is not unlike the cultural process of building a myth—creating in the candidate a symbol that taps into the common experiences and aspirations that unify the nation. The most successful presidents, Hankins and others argued to Hart, either consciously or unconsciously presented themselves as the embodiment of one of the basic heroic types revered by the culture: the warrior known for his enemies (Teddy Roosevelt), the wise father (Dwight Eisenhower), or blends of the above (Ronald Reagan and Franklin Roosevelt). In very preliminary discussions, the group debated how Hart could align his appeal with one of those archetypes.

Michael Dukakis or George Bush would probably fidget or snore through such a discussion. But Hart found it an intriguing window on the fundamental political problem of recent years: making elections relevant to the tens of millions of voters disaffected by them. Hart intuitively understood that at a time when politics has grown increasingly disconnected from the organic life of the nation, the historic challenge in a democracy—of establishing social legitimacy for political acts—is deepened and complicated. By 1987 Hart realized that a campaign could not bridge those gaps merely by issuing position papers, that in the broadest sense a candidate had to establish himself as part of the culture. "Campaigns are myths, are myth-creating; I had occasion to learn this in the last few years," Hart said. "I hadn't really thought about it. But it was sort of put to me that way [by Hankins]. And I began to think about politics as myth. When you think about it, it makes some sense. You are creating a hero; a candidate is really trying to become hero so he can become leader, and it may be in our culture you have to become a hero before you can become a leader. . . . It's not bad: as Joseph Campbell has showed, myth has had a lot to do with culture throughout history."

But Hart's understanding of the mythic and cultural underpinnings of politics had an enormous blind spot. Hart apparently believed he could, as Beatty did, separate his "private" life from the persona he offered the public. To this day, Hart insists the public did not need more personal information about him, and the only "people who wanted to know more about me were reporters." In effect, he argued that the heroic myth of the candidate could be constructed entirely from the material of his public life: that what he chose to display is all that should be displayed. That is a view of celebrity common in Hollywood. As an actor, Beatty could build a divide between his private and public selves: he could re-create himself as often as he wished—the lover in *Shampoo*, the idealist in *Heaven Can Wait*, the revolutionary intellectual in *Reds*; he could retreat into silence and shadow when the lights became too bright and owe nothing more to his fans than another movie.

In that sense, Beatty was Hart's model. But the model did not translate: it was another Hollywood convention that was dangerous when applied to politics. In the modern political era, when politicians sell themselves not as heirs to an ideological or partisan tradition but as individuals, no clear divide separates private and public life. For Hart, who stood fundamentally alone, with few politicians or friends around him, whose appeal called for sundering tradition, this was especially true. In the era of news from nowhere, he was the candidate from nowhere. When Hart's judgment in "private" affairs publicly lapsed—when he displayed his utter disdain for the rules of ordinary propriety in a presidential campaign—all his position papers could not plug the hole in the public's willingness to accept him as a serious man.

For all the congruence between the tasks of an actor and a politician, all the similarities in their psyches, their craving for acclaim, their skill at defining roles, here was a fundamental difference. An actor could put behind him his personal life each time he stepped before the camera; a candidate could not. In that sense, Hart could not be Beatty. Though critical of the press for probing into Hart's affairs, Beatty seemed to understand this distinction—imperfectly, but more than his friend the politician. (The master of reticence, Beatty had, after all, urged his reluctant friend to show more of himself to the public.) "Gary Hart realized that in order to change this country . . . the public had to passionately endorse him," Beatty said. "Right away, he was in trouble [after his relationship with Rice was exposed]. Because when he destroyed that passionate endorsement of him, he destroyed his candidacy."

That was as close as Warren Beatty ever came to blaming Hart for the events that ended his political career. But Beatty's ferocious efforts to keep Hart in the race, his encouragement of Hart's quixotic hopes of resurrection, and his refusal to accept political reality as it accumulated before him—something of which he had never been previously accused—suggest how deeply the lost opportunity cut him. Beatty believed Hart should be president, but he may have also seen in Hart's demise his own final chance for lasting political influence slipping away.

With all the elements of farce, Hart's last campaign looks, in reflection, more like tragedy. Hart could not choose his myth: he hoped to portray himself as a thoughtful man unburdened by political convention; instead, it was the celebrity's frivolous freedom from moral convention that ultimately defined him. His best friend suffered much the same fate. No one was more loyal to Hart than Beatty, nor more committed to his cause. But, like Hollywood itself, Beatty at once smoothed his path and snarled it. He did all he could to help Hart, but he could not control the image he had created. With all his skill, Beatty still could not remake his myth of limitless indulgence. It was the myth of Hollywood crystallized, and in each generation it fell to one man to personify it: in John F. Kennedy's day, Sinatra had carried the torch; now it was Beatty's. He could not shed it. And no more than Sinatra could he prevent it from searing his patron or consuming his own ambitions. Even in the life of Warren Beatty there were limits after all.

CHAPTER TEN

HOLLYWOOD NOW

The Carnival of Money

With roughly half a billion dollars to his venerable name, Frederick W. (Ted) Field, heir to the Marshall Field department store fortune, investor, movie producer, and former racecar driver, qualifies as one of the nation's richest men.

His assistant for public affairs, a shrewd, balding, often abrasive attorney named Robert L. Burkett, qualifies as one of the most tenacious.

One bright spring morning in 1987, Burkett was entertaining a visitor and, as usual, simultaneously talking on the phone. Brilliant sunshine poured through his fourteenth-story window. Below, traffic hummed up and down Wilshire Boulevard. On the corner of his desk, a long row of magazines, from *The Nation* to *American Film*, were stacked neatly. Around the office were photos of Field and Burkett with various politicians. Burkett was leaning back in his chair, looking out the window toward Westwood and the Santa Monica Mountains and cradling the phone under his ear. Into the receiver he said firmly, "I am not going to have Michael Eisner [the chairman of the Walt Disney Company] waiting fifteen minutes for food, I can tell you that right now." The person on the other end said something, and Burkett said good-bye. Then he looked across his desk, focused on his guest, and rattled off facts as though reading from a prompter on the far wall.

"The breakfast will raise $450,000. Two hundred [thousand], me. One hundred twenty-five, [Carl] Rheuban [a savings and loan executive]. Fifty [David] Pollock [a stockbroker]. Fifty, [Lisa] Specht [a Westside attorney]. It will have French champagne, imported caviar, poached salmon, Florentine turkey, omelets. In all, a very schmaltzy buffet."

The phone rang again. Burkett glanced at a small monitor behind his desk that allows his secretary to tell him who's calling. A name flashed by in green letters. Burkett picked up the phone, exchanged brief pleasantries, listened for a moment, and then, suddenly stern, said, "If one word gets whispered in the wrong ear, kid, it's over."

He put down the phone, swiveled his chair, and resumed: "Field was born in Chicago. His family was divorced. His mother, Katherine Fanning, edits the *Christian Science Monitor.* * He moved to Newport Beach in his late teens and got involved in sponsoring a racing team in the international Grand Prix circuit. He became a racecar driver. He raced internationally in Grand Prix races. He is no longer involved in the racing business.

"He moved to Los Angeles in the early 1980s. At that time, Field Enterprises was liquidated." This fact deserves more elaboration than Burkett offered. Field Enterprises, Inc., whose assets included the *Chicago Sun-Times,* assorted real estate, and several television stations, was liquidated in 1983 because Field and his half-brother Marshall Field V could not agree on how to run it. The sale left the reclusive Ted Field with a grubstake for his new life in Hollywood of roughly $260 million. Field managed to make something of it. He dabbled in real estate, bought and sold (at a healthy profit) Panavision, Inc., a movie camera company, and produced such movies as *Cocktail* and *Three Men and a Baby.* He did all of this very well. His net worth soared. When *Three Men and a Baby* rose to the top of the box office reports, a common refrain was, "Just what Ted Field needs, another $100 million."

Along the way Field acquired an interest in Democratic politics. He was too shy to imagine himself a candidate, or even an appointee. But he had strong political beliefs, and he had the resources to support organizations that expressed those beliefs; he understood one of money's great rewards—that it allows you to expose others to ideas you believe they should be exposed to. Field's political agenda was somewhat eclectic but generally quite progressive. As Burkett explained, "Ted is not a liberal.

---

*She no longer does.

Ted in another age would probably have been a Jacob Javits Republican. He is very conservative fiscally, he is certainly anti-Communist. It all sort of fits the profile. Progressive on social issues, very, very much concerned with civil rights, separation of church and state, and personally committed to arms control.

"He wasn't doing any politics in the late 1970s. In 1982, he began in a very quiet way to give to People For the American Way. I was working for People For, only half-time at that point, and I was going through a printout of small donations. I called him cold, and he responded. In the 1984 presidential race he wasn't involved. But he began to give to some peace organizations."

Though he avoided public attention the way a vampire does sunlight—he never talks to the press, and is often invisible, even at events at his own home—Field's generous contributions to liberal causes inevitably caught the attention of politicians. In 1985, California Senator Alan Cranston, an indefatigable fundraiser, made contact with Field; so did then–Democratic National Committee Chairman Paul G. Kirk, Jr. Their attention was rewarded with a six-figure gift to the DNC.

By then, Burkett was working full-time for People For the American Way founder Norman Lear as a political assistant, meeting candidates, organizing fundraising events, funneling Lear's money into worthy causes. In January 1986, as Lear's emissary, he attended a meeting of the DNC business council in Florida. Field was also there. On the first evening, they listened to Senator Joseph R. Biden, Jr., of Delaware give the keynote address, a rousing call for the members of the baby boom generation to reassert themselves politically. After the speech, both impressed by the senator, Burkett and Field sat and talked. Field told Burkett he wanted to find someone who could help guide his political activities the way Burkett did Lear's. Burkett said, "There aren't many people who do what I do." Field said, "How about you?" A few months later Burkett went to work for Field.

Through the 1986 campaign, with Burkett's guidance, Field emerged as one of the most important sources of funds for Democratic candidates in the country. In addition to his six-figure contribution to the DNC and direct fundraising for several Democratic hopefuls, Field contributed roughly $200,000 to state parties and other citizen action organizations indirectly supporting the Democratic Senate candidates, as well as an equal amount to liberal lobbying groups. And when Biden began to organize his presidential campaign, Ted Field and Bob Burkett were staunchly in his corner.

That long road had brought Field and Burkett to the "schmaltzy buffet" Burkett had been discussing on the phone all morning. It was to be the first major fundraising event in Los Angeles for Biden's presidential campaign. The $1,000-a-plate brunch was also the first political event Field was hosting at the magnificent old Harold Lloyd estate he had purchased the previous year. It was, in many respects, as much a coming-out party for Field as for Biden, and Burkett took no chances that the results might embarrass his boss.

Burkett came to fundraising late, after a quiet career as a lawyer, but he had a natural gift for it. The gift was that his skin seemed to be coated with asbestos. He learned the value of such insulation when he was raising funds as a volunteer for a Jewish television network in Los Angeles during the early 1980s. (A chance encounter with Stanley Sheinbaum, who functioned as a one-man referral agency for California progressive causes, had led Burkett, who was looking for new direction, into the operation.) One day, while working for the network, Burkett met Stanley Hirsch, a major power in the Los Angeles Jewish community. Hirsch came over to the table where Burkett was having lunch with another man, they spoke about the project, and Hirsch told Burkett if he ever needed money to call him. When the network faced bankruptcy, Burkett called Hirsch. He told him he needed $25,000. Hirsch said, 'I'll get back to you." Burkett waited about four days, and when Hirsch had not gotten back to him, he called his office. Hirsch was unavailable. Burkett called again. Hirsch was in a meeting. Burkett refused to take the hint. He called Hirsch every day, three times a day. After about three days of the barrage, Burkett got lucky, or so he momentarily believed: he called during lunch while the secretary was out, and Hirsch picked up the phone. "Mr. Hirsch," he said, 'it's Bob Burkett." He did not get out another word before Hirsch exploded into the receiver, "Listen, you have been a pain in the ass, I never want to talk to you again; you're ruined, you're finished." Burkett hung up the phone, waited twenty-four hours, and called Hirsch again, as if nothing had happened. Hirsch, who understood the value of *chutzpah* for a man with Burkett's avocation, gave him $10,000. A friendship, and a fundraiser, was born.

This was the genteel approach Burkett applied to his efforts on behalf of Biden. "For this event," he said, leaning back and idly stretching his legs onto his desk, "I got on the phone March 7 and got off the phone March 31. I called every single person in the Rolodex who had the means to do it. Every person Ted gave money to for some cause, I called every one. That was about a quarter of it. Entertainment people: They were about 15 percent. [Studio executives] Eisner, Frank Wells, Lee Rich, Sean Daniel, [agents] Mike Marcus, Jeff Berg, everyone we had connections with. Then about five percent were people we had other business relationships with. The rest was my own personal network, and people who've met Biden. Carl Rheuban did primarily Jewish; Lisa Specht did her network; David Pollock did his."

Not everyone in political Hollywood liked to work with Burkett. He could be brusque and peremptory, and he sometimes gave the impression of forgetting that he only worked for a man worth $500 million. But even his critics acknowledged that his aggressiveness made him extremely effective as a money collector. When Biden arrived in Los Angeles a few days later, the proof was displayed at Field's huge home in a canyon high above Beverly Hills. It was a perfect Southern California morning: the sunshine was crystalline, the caviar imported, and the carefully manicured lawns as green as money. The receipts at the door were not shabby either. Biden took in only slightly less than Burkett expected, $435,000 in all—a figure still so striking (it was far more than frontrunner Gary Hart had raised in Los Angeles only a few days earlier) that the campaign released a list of contributors to verify its claim. "I don't know about California standards," Biden told the crowd as they sipped champagne on the great lawn, "but back East where I come from, anybody who raises [this much money] at a single sitting, it's a pretty big deal."

It was the hope of just such a rich strike that drew politicians to Los Angeles week after week, month after month. At times, it seemed as though the next stop on the Washington Metro after Capitol Hill was Bel-Air. (The attraction extended beyond national borders: it has become routine for international leaders—from Nelson Mandela to representatives of Czechoslovakia's Civic Forum—to replenish their treasuries in Hollywood.) During the height of a campaign season, Los Angeles had the feel of a political carnival, a carnival of money, with fundraising events strung through the hills like booths on a midway. These events were constructed, like martinis, with three essential ingredients: people with lots of money, recognizable faces from the movie screen, and politicians. The possible combinations were uncountable. For one week during the 1986 campaign season, the datebook of Marlene Saritzky, executive director of the Hollywood Women's Political Committee, looked like this: Sunday afternoon brunch (at $10 a plate) at Stanley Sheinbaum's house with Mike Farrell to raise money for the "heroes in the Sanctuary movement" who were convicted of violating immigration law by ferrying Central American refugees into the United States; Monday evening meeting at the powerful law firm of Manatt, Phelps, Rothenberg, and Tunney with

The Lexington Group ($500 annually to join), the organization of politically connected young professionals, to hear a state supreme court justice talk about the conservative campaign to unseat state Chief Justice Rose Bird; Tuesday night black-tie dinner ($300 a ticket) of the American Jewish Congress with Norman Lear, Ed Asner, and Senator Biden to honor Sheinbaum; Wednesday night $250-per-person cocktail party for Harriett Woods at Lear's home with Barbra Streisand, rock star Don Henley, and Alan and Marilyn Bergman; Thursday night $100-a-ticket "Voters for Choice" party at the home of Barbara Corday with Cybill Shepherd and Donna Mills; and, finally, the following Monday, a $250-a-head blowout at the Hard Rock Café for the Hayden-Fonda clean-water initiative with Streisand, Henley, Rosanna Arquette, Whoopi Goldberg, Eddie Van Halen, and Kareem Abdul-Jabbar.

There was something dazzling, even intoxicating, about this convergence of glamour and money and power. Politics in Los Angeles had a sheen it lacked elsewhere. It was the only city in which the people attending political events were better known than the politicians on the invitation. In Washington, the dreary fundraising receptions of the real estate brokers and the car dealers were a kind of currency, attendance a straight business transaction—money for access. There was no flash, no jazz. In Los Angeles, political fundraising was as much spectacle as business. Candidates eagerly anticipated their prospecting trips to the coast, not only because they expected a lucrative payoff but because they enjoyed the carnival atmosphere—the beautiful homes and beautiful women, the magnificent views from high in the hills, the mingling with movie stars and movie moguls and imagining themselves the next John Kennedy, celebrated by the elite of both coasts. For an evening, a senator from South Dakota or a representative from Missouri could also be a star.

For the Los Angeles fundraisers, the carnival offered the dazzling illusion of intimacy. Almost every night they could pick and choose among the nation's political elite. Sean Daniel, a young studio executive, summed up his options during one particularly frenetic week in 1987: "I am going to see Senator Paul Simon at the home of Stanley Sheinbaum," he said. "The next night I can see him at Donna Mill's house. I am choosing Sheinbaum rather than Mills to see Simon. Tonight is Mike Dukakis at Sally Field's. I will be there. On Monday I happened to be at Morton's, which is kind of an industry watering hole, and I'm sitting there and there goes Dukakis and Gloria Steinem. Then Whoopi Goldberg rolls in. Where is she going? She is going to Michael Dukakis's table. You have to keep up."

Sitting in their secluded mansions in Brentwood or Bel-Air, a continent away from the capital, their days primarily consumed by the manu-facture of celluloid fantasies, it was easy for the Los Angeles fundraisers to nonetheless believe they were at the center of things. The most power-ful men and women in Washington—rising stars in the Senate, crusty committee chairs in the House—called them, charmed them, asked them to dinner or breakfast, invited them to Washington to observe a hearing, to drop by and meet the wife. If you raised money in Los Angeles, these men could land on your doorstep, it seemed, at almost any time; soon after he went to work collecting checks for Norman Lear, Bob Burkett, in the midst of a garage sale, found on his front lawn Representative Tom Daschle, who wished to become Senator Tom Daschle. A precise if infor-mal social quid pro quo evolved: The greater the needs of the politician, the more lush the offer of ego-flattering intimacy. "A typical congressman comes in and he says, 'I'm in a tough race, I've been targeted by the Republicans, can you raise me $10,000?'" said one young Los Angeles fundraiser. "On the other hand, a guy who is thinking about running for president in four, eight, twelve years, calls you up and says, 'You want to go camping?'" To be a prominent political fundraiser in Los Angeles, to be seen as a key to the golden door of Hollywood or the other communi-ties of wealth that spun around it like satellites, was to be invited behind the carnival midway, to a continuous party with the most interesting and powerful people in the world—not only Lloyd Bentsen and Bob Dole and George Bush, but Warren Beatty and Barbra Streisand and Charlton Heston.

And yet it was a party that ultimately exhausted almost everyone who joined it.

For agents or producers or studio executives, the first time a senator called was exciting; the second time too; and perhaps even the third. But eventually the routinized offer of intimacy, with its implied price of find-ing five friends to give $1,000, or ten friends to give $500, lost its dazzle. "It's like when a guy asks you out and it's flattering and he asks you out every night and you wonder [doesn't he have anything better to do?]," said producer Paula Weinstein. "At the beginning, it was extremely flat-tering. This one wants to call me. Oh, that senator wants to have dinner with us. Suddenly, you're saying, 'Don't you want to be home with your wife? Your community?'"

And it was rarely just one senator who called. Once a new fundraiser emerged, the name whistled back to Washington, and soon there were others, offering the same friendship, the same intimate peek behind the political curtain, in return for just some time and, oh, maybe a few phone calls to close friends. Sydney Pollack, the director, lent his name to one event and soon it seemed to him that his phone number had been scribbled on the bathroom wall at the Senate Democratic caucus. "I won't even go down the list of calls the last three days that have come in," he said wearily one afternoon. "The senators. The Senate season is coming like crazy and every one of them calls and says, 'I'm going to be in California, Sydney; I'd love to have a little lunch with you; I'd love to have a little talk with you; I'd love to have a little meeting with you.'"

For the established fundraisers, the calls were not always so gentle and ingratiating; there was an edge, too—an impatience that hinted at the desperation that gripped candidates. Some senators needed to raise $10,000 a day during an election year, and they would sit at the phone in Washington dialing, dialing, dialing against the clock until in the darkness of early evening they came to the names of their friends in California. I need your help, the typical senator would say, and those who understood the subterranean language of politics understood it was more than a request. I need your help, they would say, not I want your help. Some requests came even more unvarnished: when Burkett worked for Lear, he would receive calls from the aides of senators or sometimes the senators themselves who had supported the liberal causes Lear supports and now were counting on him to support them. "You owe me," they would tell Burkett, "and fuck you if you don't produce."

Almost every Democrat in the Senate (and many Republicans) expected Los Angeles to deliver $75,000, $100,000, $200,000, sometimes more. Eventually, even the most ambitious fundraisers began to wonder how many pockets there were to pick. There was always another candidate at the door, another invitation on their desk. Everyone worked off the same lists, and the circle was not that large. At times the multiplying demands felt like a crossfire. "Somebody is a friend of Bob Dole's or somebody is a friend of [GOP Senator] Alan Simpson's or somebody is a friend of somebody," said producer Jerry Weintraub, whose intimate friendship with George Bush made him a visible figure in Republican circles. "They come in here, and you try to support them. But it becomes a little overwhelming after a while."

By the winter of 1986, it was apparent in Los Angeles that the fundraising season had no clear end; election day marked barely a pause. One afternoon early in 1987, a few days after Senator Bill Bradley of New Jersey had passed through on a fundraising mission for his 1990 reelection, Betsy Kenny, who had replaced Burkett as Lear's political assistant, said, "I thought we were going to have a breather, but there is no breather." The rising costs of campaigns forced candidates to begin their fundraising earlier and earlier; the calls that once came in June and July of an off-year now came in January and February. Stanley Sheinbaum began to talk of the candidates as "obsessed people," and though he still opened his living room to those he supported, and though his allies still opened their homes, many of them began to feel trapped. There was just no end to it: as soon as the Senate candidates left Los Angeles in the fall of 1986, the presidential hopefuls of 1988 followed on their heels. "I'm going to be in Los Angeles next week," they would say into the phone, as if they were casually dropping in to catch some sun. "Would you like to have lunch?"

Excess bred excess in response. To their dismay, the 1988 candidates, particularly on the Democratic side, learned that familiarity had peeled away the awe from presidential politics in Los Angeles. When Gary Hart, Hollywood's early favorite, was forced from the race just days after Field's brunch for Biden, the film community appeared to be wide open for the remaining contenders. But in fact the road to contributions and endorsements remained maddeningly circuitous. Through the early months of 1987, hardly anyone in Hollywood seemed particularly anxious to meet a presidential candidate, or to side with any of them. "The fact that we were all unknown meant that most of the time you had no chance at all of asking directly for money," said former Arizona Governor Bruce E. Babbitt, one of the Democratic contenders. "Round one was making your pitch and getting their attention and becoming known—all the while burning up enormous amounts of time."

Both worn out and pumped up by all the attention, Hollywood's liberal donors took the audition process to a new stage for 1988 by formalizing it. Rather than waiting for the candidates to come to him, Lear convened in his Brentwood home a series of dinners at which the cream of liberal Los Angeles could review the presidential candidates one by one through several hours of private questioning. To these dinners, which became in their own circle a prized invitation, Lear gathered a revolving group of A-list entertainment industry figures, such as Barry Diller, chairman of Fox, Inc.; Field and Burkett; rock star Don Henley; songwriters Marilyn and Alan Bergman; rock musician manager Danny Goldberg; producer Gary David Goldberg ("Family Ties"); Paula Weinstein and her producer husband, Mark Rosenberg; and other political operatives involved with People For the American Way. Then Lear invited the candidates. From Babbitt in January 1986 through Senator Paul Simon the following September, all of the Democratic candidates accepted, knowing they would receive no money, but only an audience with people who might, if moved, later help them raise some.

The sessions followed a pattern. After an elegant meal and a short speech, the presidential hopefuls moved into Lear's screening room for a confidential discussion with the group. Fireworks often followed. Jesse Jackson was both defensive and pugnacious when pressed at wearying length about his views on Israel and Jews. (For his part, Jackson set the tone by acting as though he was addressing a Jewish organization—which, in precise fact, he was not.) Biden was alternatively charming and combative, condescending and compelling, when challenged about his views on abortion and opposition to school busing. Dukakis was brisk, comfortable, and confident—maybe a bit too confident in the view of one attendee who detected "kind of a snake-oil quality about him."

The Republican front-runners in the 1988 campaign, Vice-President George Bush and Senate Majority Leader Robert Dole, had the stature to avoid such demands for inspection. Both focused their California fundraising on corporate leaders and businessmen, maintained only limited contact with Hollywood, and efficiently collected checks with a minimal loss of time. While most of the Democrats were still banging on the doors in Los Angeles, Vice-President Bush collected almost $600,000 at the Century Plaza Hotel in June 1987. A few months later Dole collected roughly twice as much in one evening with the help of Harry Evans Sloane, the co-chairman of New World Pictures.

Meanwhile, the Democrats treaded water. Once Lear set the precedent, other Hollywood powers also sought private time to grill the candidates. The Hollywood Women's Political Committee set up its own screening sessions and told each of the candidates it expected several hours. Eventually the Hollywood survivors of the Hart shipwreck assembled themselves and announced they too were ready to review the candidates. (By the end of the campaign they had gathered themselves into a new political organization called the Show Coalition.)

Most of the candidates saw the sessions with HWPC and Hart activists as similar to what they did everywhere: appeasing specific interest groups who spoke for an identifiable constituency. "HWPC was more like meeting with the UAW . . . a group that has a particular agenda," said Edward E. (Ted) Kaufman, Biden's chief of staff. "I think we ended up meeting with them as much for political as financial reasons." The Lear dinners had no other attraction but money.

Nothing was more revealing about the dinners than the fact that none of the Democratic presidential contenders felt they could afford to ignore the summons. In fact, once the dinners became known, several eagerly sought the audience. Still, in private, some of the candidates and their advisers were offended by the idea of a small, affluent group passing judgment on their fitness to speak for the dispossessed. Walking out of Lear's house after Biden's stormy encounter with the group, Ted Kaufman turned to the senator and said, "We have just participated in the greatest demonstration for public finance I have ever seen." After Hart left the race, he spoke angrily of the arrogance implicit in the invitations. "My uncle would like to meet all the presidential candidates too," he roared at dinner one evening. "Who the hell do these people think they are?" Looking back after the campaign, Babbitt said: "The problem with the Southern California fundraising community is it is a very trendy crowd. They want a leading man. It was an unbelievable experience this last time around. They had fallen for Hart, Hart was their leading man. . . . After that it was kind of endless discussion and indecision and groping for a group decision and a revelation that would make people feel good. There were these curious kinds of hints, preoccupation with peripheral issues. I've never had more exhilarating discussions of the front-line states in South Africa or that kind of thing, but very little concern with the large, direct, here-today issues."

While in the race, none of the candidates voiced these concerns publicly. They could not afford to. With fundraising consuming, in some cases, up to two-thirds of their time, any opportunity to connect with a potentially significant money collector could not be ignored. Alternately the candidates saw the Lear dinners as an opportunity ("You are looking for multipliers," said former Representative Bob Edgar, chief fundraiser for Senator Paul Simon. "There is that possibility that one or two people in the room can raise $100,000") or a responsibility. ("If we snub Norman Lear it has implications," said one Dukakis fundraiser. "We can't say Norman Lear is not going to raise anything. It's something you have to do. You have to court the establishment even if they don't raise any money.")

Lear and his friends understood how badly the candidates needed their assistance. That awareness inspired the dinners; it also gave them their tone. The dinners rested on a hard foundation of theatrical skepticism: the sense that the politicians were small, manipulative, obsessed with money, flaky and unpredictable. "It was quite hostile," said Tony Podesta, who participated in the dinners through his position at People For the American Way. "It was largely demeaning to the candidates." Small groups of voters in Iowa and New Hampshire often imposed equally demeaning demands on the candidates. But the Lear dinners were somehow more offensive because they allowed the candidates to be tested, not by ordinary voters, but by an affluent, self-anointed handful of gatekeepers. If a similar screening session had been organized by conservative corporate leaders, many of the same people attending Lear's sessions would probably have condemned them as a plutocratic plot.

Seen through the perspective of history, the dinners presented a very mixed picture of the state of liberalism in the film world. On one hand, they demonstrated how eager the Hollywood liberals were to find a candidate who could win the presidency. On the other, they showed how Hollywood liberalism had mutated since its rebirth in the 1960s. During the Depression, when progressive causes everywhere expanded from the bottom up, the founding generation of Hollywood liberals reached out to the public through rallies and town meetings. In these contemporary encounters, the opposite impulse reigned: the idea was to spirit the candidates away from the public and local grassroots activists as quickly as possible and display them in a private living room, where presumably they would reveal themselves in a way they had not in dozens of speeches, interviews, and campaign appearances. In some respects the point of the sessions was arguably to prove that the candidates could be required to appear in a private living room. None of Hollywood's wealthy donors asked the candidates, over whom they had much leverage, to make themselves publicly available to groups who did not have the power to compel their appearance; the Hollywood Women, for example, never rented an auditorium and invited the women of Los Angeles to address the candidates with their concerns, which might have differed considerably from those of the comfortable few dozen who gathered under their banner. Quite the opposite: Norman Lear thought it would have been inappropriate and unfair to the candidates to invite anyone but wealthy people to his sessions. "I think it is a terrific idea," he said, shortly before the last dinner. "But in all fairness, these people [the candidates] have a limited amount of time, and the name of the game is raising that word of mouth and money. Maybe I should reverse the order."

Those remarks revealed more perhaps than Lear realized. The Lear dinners' exclusionary ethos bothered some of the people attending ("It is a serious problem," said one. "These people have never been down in the street, they don't know what it is all about, and they are not thinking that way"), but Lear was not one of them. For all his commitment to progressive ideals, Lear had an enormous blind spot: he was fully comfortable with the thought that he and a few like-minded friends should give direction to the candidates and, for that matter, the nation. Asked why he had organized the dinners, Lear said airily, "I decided to do it because I am going to vote in this election as I do in all elections, and I wanted to know as much as I could about each of these people who are courting this vote." Lear was so oblivious to the elitism in his political approach that it seemed almost innocent. But such an extraordinary statement could only come from someone who thought his own stature made it entirely reasonable that the men who might sit in the Oval Office should first pass muster in his living room.

Lear's screening sessions did not solve the candidates' immediate problems in Hollywood. Some of the people around the table eventually gave significant help: Barry Diller to Dukakis, Field to Biden. But most of the valuable connections were made elsewhere, and the core of the dinners, Lear and Sheinbaum, were left vaguely disappointed with all the contenders. None matched Lear's vision of the spiritual leader he believed the nation needed. "My personal impression of the candidates is kind of the same impression I had as I watched the dozens of hours of Iran-contra hearings," Lear said shortly after the last dinner in fall 1987. "I wish somewhere there was a little less cool and little more personal passion. They project a little more interest in which way the winds are blowing and a little less desire to say, 'You may disagree with me, but this is the way I wish to take you.'" Eventually, Sheinbaum signed on to assist Jesse Jackson. But Lear, though he personally contributed some funds and hosted a session for Dukakis to meet the stars, raised no money for the Democratic ticket through the general election, despite requests from the nominee's campaign to do so.

The producer's lack of enthusiasm was a fitting symbol of Hollywood's expanding political ego, one that ought to remind future candidates of the questionable value of indulging it. And yet Lear's dinners were also a logical response from the donors to a system that had spun out of control. Both sides were victimized by a campaign finance regime that compelled candidates to spend such an enormous amount of time looking for money. For the candidates, the price was wasting precious time— time that could have been spent with ordinary voters—listening to the idiosyncratic concerns of a wealthy and isolated elite that pushed them toward the most militant liberal positions on social and foreign policy issues. For the donors, the price was a dehumanizing demand for money, and the realization that the closeness they enjoyed with the candidates was as genuine as in most other intimate encounters where cash changed hands. "Perhaps [the candidates] are sincere that they want to hear what is on other people's minds," Lear said, after the last dinner, "but it has not been my observation, from Ted Kennedy to Walter Mondale or any of the current crop, that they walk away with something that they are going to call you about three weeks later and say, 'You know that thought you mentioned?'"

There are worse sins than arrogance and insularity: none of the people at Norman Lear's table asked the visiting politicians to protect their collapsing savings-and-loan or arrange a defense contract. All believed they were pointing the candidates toward the true path. But the Lear dinners testified as to how the preoccupation with raising money had twisted Hollywood's priorities and hardened its approach, diminished the politicians who besieged it, and left both sides too busy chasing and writing checks to focus their energies on the tangible problems that ostensibly attracted them to politics in the first place.

Small Victories

The first Democrat who broke from the treadmill of meeting-and-greeting in Los Angeles was Biden. With Field and Rheuban as his anchors, a long record of support for Israel providing entrée to the Jewish community, and Kaufman creatively searching out new blood, he showed early and diverse financial strength beyond any of his competitors. Biden's supporters optimistically faced the fall of 1987, with its traditional quickening of the campaign pace. Leaning back from his desk one afternoon in August, Burkett sketched out the coming months in glowing terms: "We will definitely raise over $1 million in Southern California. By the end of the year we will be at $700,000. It is getting harder but the money just keeps coming in. I've got a steady stream of money coming in."

One month later, Biden was suddenly out of the race, the victim of disclosures that he had plagiarized a speech and exaggerated his law school record. Biden's fall revived the sour feeling left by Hart's demise. In a year when donors were already uncertain which of the Democrats had the right stuff, the spate of scandals provided both reason and excuse to hold off from commitments: How could you ask friends for funds if you didn't know whether the candidate would survive long enough to cash the check? Through the waning weeks of 1987, the candidates could generate nothing more than brief boomlets among the Hollywood Democrats: Sally Field committed to Michael Dukakis and held a well-attended party for him to meet the stars; Barry Diller held a somewhat more sparsely attended fundraiser for the governor. When Democratic Representative Patricia Schroeder flirted with a candidacy that fall, many women rushed to her, but Schroeder decided it was too late to enter the race. Schroeder, at least, left Los Angeles heartened by her reception; that was more than most of the other Democrats could say. "There is absolute frustration," said an aide to one of the Democratic candidates over lunch that fall. "All of the campaigns are frustrated with the pace of giving. The candidates keep asking, 'Where are the checks? Where are the checks?'"

Even the primary voting did not bring an answer to their plea. Unlike what happened in 1984, when Hollywood money surged toward Gary Hart after his emergence in Iowa and New Hampshire, there was no corresponding rush toward either Richard Gephardt or Michael Dukakis after they won those contests in 1988. Gephardt's victory in Iowa—after he spent months camping out in the state—neither surprised nor impressed the Los Angeles liberals. "The phones are not ringing off the hook," a Gephardt aide said the day after Iowa. "We have been ringing them off the hook. The money is coming. But it is not coming as fast as we want. We are not Gary Hart." One week later, on the morning after the New Hampshire primary, Nikolas Patsaouras, a perceptive and intense Greek businessman who served as Dukakis's lead fundraiser for Southern California, skillfully lined up financial support for the governor in Los Angeles's Asian and Hispanic communities, among Jews, and from small businessmen. But none of his new commitments that day came from Hollywood.

The reason became clear a few days later on a hazy February afternoon when a well-connected Hollywood agent sat down amid the chic bustle of Harry's Bar and American Grill in Century City to talk about the campaign. Occasionally looking around the room to keep track of the competition cutting deals over linguine, the agent spoke about the race in tones he might use to explain a highly touted film that had inexplicably flopped. "I am cooling it on the campaign," he said wearily. "I was for Hart and then that became a joke. Then I was for Biden." He laughed harshly and sipped his water.

All of the candidates, or at least their emissaries, had made passes at him since, he said. None set his pulse racing. "It's a man in search of a candidate. If it came down to it, I would vote for Dukakis. Would I vote for Gore or Gephardt? It depends who the Republican is. Would I vote for Simon? Probably quicker than Gore or Gephardt. But am I excited about any of those guys? Would I want to work for any of them? No. Michael Dukakis does not strike me as a major leader of this country."

This was clearly a man with an eye for talent.

"I had dinner one night with Gephardt," the agent continued. "He's just not that interesting. I don't particularly like his trade ideas. Gore, I do hold this thing with his wife [Tipper, who supported proposals to require record albums to be rated, like films, for obscenity] against him. Also, on a general basis, he's too conservative for me."

A delicate pasta was brought to the table. More Pellegrino water was ordered. How much interest is there in the campaign? the agent was asked. "I hear about it," he said, as though reporting the rumor of a distant event. "I get calls from people trying to recruit me. They call and say, 'What about so and so?' After I say I'm not interested, they drop the issue. There isn't a lot of pushing. I don't get a real lot of emotional energy from people who have sold me hard in the past." Maybe everyone is waiting for New York Governor Mario M. Cuomo, he said. Then again, maybe no one is interested. He speared a forkful of pasta and leaned across the small table. "Look, we in the industry are a bunch of people who are all salesmen," he said. "We want to get excited about what we are selling. We want to get excited about the product. Once we get excited we jump in full force. But first we have to get excited." He chewed and talked, and then said, with an air of finality, "But none of the candidates are either exciting or saying anything that is exciting."

As it turned out, none of the Democratic contenders ever excited the mainstream Hollywood-liberal axis. The HWPC, for example, after reviewing all the candidates at length, decided to help none of them. That was typical. The candidates who did best in Los Angeles were those least tied to the traditional Democratic establishment: Dukakis, who raised far more money among people wearing polyester than Armani; and Jackson, who worked through the black entertainment industry, the black middle class, and the most liberal elements on the fringes of the white Westside.

In many respects, Jackson was the most logical draw in Hollywood. He appealed not only to the pride of black entertainers and executives but also to the extremely liberal instincts of many white stars. On issues such as Central America and arms control, Jackson was closer to the Hollywood mainstream than any of his competitors (which said as much about the Hollywood mainstream as about Jackson). Alone among the Democrats he also radiated stardom; and, as a man who seemed spurred above all by the quest for respect, he genuinely enjoyed—even coveted—the intimate friendship of stars as another indication he had reached the heights of American society. Like Adlai Stevenson or Gary Hart, he brightened up noticeably when surrounded by beautiful and famous women; but his acceptance by powerful and revered cultural figures such as Bill Cosby and Quincy Jones also nourished his sense of arrival. Having the most celebrated blacks in the nation clustered around him silently testified to his preeminent place in American black life. At the same time, their presence offered another sign that his campaign was as legitimate as any white candidate's. "In modern days, all these candidates for president have a cadre of celebrities around them," said Gerald Austin, Jackson's campaign manager in 1988. "Jesse had his too. It was another way of saying: I am a viable candidate."

Jackson faced some resistance among Hollywood executives because of the lingering allegations of anti-Semitism, but his relations with Jews in Los Angeles never reached the acrimonious depths they had in New York. Some influential Jewish figures, such as Sheinbaum, actively supported him. And, unlike the other Democrats, he could work another vein in Hollywood: the black entertainment industry executives who had leveraged their relationships with black artists into positions of authority and power. Jackson found much important support from such figures as producer Berry Gordy and attorney Larkin Arnold, a former senior executive at CBS Records.

In 1984, Jackson had failed to exploit his intrinsic appeal to Hollywood; in 1988, he was more attuned to it. So was Chris Hammond, the young aide who ran the California campaign for Jackson. Initially, they looked almost entirely to black entertainers. In October 1987, Jackson turned out an impressive entertainment industry delegation for a fundraising birthday party at a Hollywood hotel. The stars were almost all black: Cicely Tyson and Quincy Jones (who hosted the evening), singers Marilyn McCoo and Freda Payne, and actress Marla Gibbs. It was black artists Jackson had in mind when he exhorted his crowd at evening's end: "Figure out what to do. Bill Cosby's on board, Roberta's on board [Roberta Flack]. . . . Why can't we have a mega-affair in L.A. and New York? We can. We have the talent. There is nothing we cannot produce that will not appeal to everybody in America."

But Jackson's political appeal extended well beyond the black community in 1988, and eventually his Hollywood roster reflected his wider audience. Though the most grandiose schemes never came through (plans for huge fundraising concerts by Stevie Wonder and Whitney Houston, among others, ran aground in the fog that habitually enveloped Jackson's campaigns),* Jackson's entertainment industry support grew remarkably as he surged into serious contention through early 1988.

In the end, Jackson attracted a more eclectic (and probably larger) group of entertainers than any of the other Democrats, from punk rockers to country-and-western artists, from screen stars such as Martin Sheen

---

*Other potential sources of significant help balked. The most important was Eddie Murphy, who quietly turned up sometimes at the Los Angeles–area dance clubs where Hammond regularly organized small fundraising and voter registration events. But Murphy refused to allow the campaign to publicize his presence, and he refused to make his support more visible. "We tried to get Murphy and Arsenio [Hall] to do more, but they wouldn't," said Hammond. "Eddie was like most of the athletes: he had gotten to this crossover [white] market and he couldn't be frontline."

and Tony Franciosa to radio personality Casey Kasem, from folk singer Holly Near to Roberta Flack. In Hollywood, the rainbow was real. Spike Lee, the talented young black filmmaker, directed an artsy campaign commercial (whose airing actually had to be reduced because its stark and menacing portrayal of Jackson confronting drugs in Harlem frightened viewers). Actress Margot Kidder traveled with the campaign like a mascot. Cosby performed at a fundraising concert in Iowa, appeared in a television commercial, and occasionally counseled the candidate. Kris Kristofferson wrote a song about Jackson and appeared with Willie Nelson, as well as Sheen, Natalie Cole, Bonnie Raitt, and two dozen other racially diverse celebrities at a fundraising rally just before the California primary that vividly symbolized the breadth of Jackson's following. Other appearances underlined the same point. Jermaine Jackson showed up at parties.* Two underground rock bands, the Red Hot Chili Peppers and Thelonious Monster, headlined a fundraiser for an almost entirely white audience. Hammond assembled black television stars for fundraising events that appealed to the black middle-class donors who watched their shows. Rappers performed in get-out-the-vote ads just before the California primary. Even within the Hollywood Women's Political Committee, some members fantasized about moving the group toward an endorsement of Jackson. That never happened, but by the end of the race Jackson had built in Hollywood a deep and diverse base of support that should serve all his future political ambitions well.

Dukakis never energized Hollywood the same way. But as the primaries progressed, he acquired for many Hollywood executives the charisma that only winners possess. His appeal in Hollywood was summarized shortly after the New York primary by Irving Azoff, the former rock manager, then working as an executive at MCA: "I've had a lot of exposure to Jesse Jackson over the years and I think I've seen the real Jesse Jackson and he's not the one out there campaigning. I thought Gore was disgusting. You don't have Bill Bradley and you don't have [Senator] Sam Nunn and you don't have Cuomo. I'm right in Dukakis's corner. By process of elimination, I'm a big Dukakis fan." Inevitably, as he moved to the head of the field, Dukakis picked up a number of the glittering names. Ted Field and Bob Burkett, after measuring offers from all the candidates, came on the day before Super Tuesday. Frank Wells, the politically ambitious Disney president, cosponsored a breakfast in March.

---

*For an event at Arnold's home in May, Hammond thought he had a commitment from Janet Jackson. But the event took place around the time that the sixteenth-century French mystic Nostradamus had allegedly predicted an earthquake for California.

But the careful moguls who drifted slowly toward Dukakis were not, in any sense, the key to his financial success in California during the primaries. John L. Battaglino, Sr., the Massachusetts businessman who moved to California to run the overall Dukakis fundraising effort there, took an almost populist glee in collecting funds without the help of the Westside establishment. Battaglino combed through neighborhoods that candidates usually saw only from the windows of planes: the San Fernando Valley, Sacramento, even tiny San Martin. In Los Angeles, the Dukakis campaign ventured beyond the traditional Democratic enclaves of the liberal Westside and Hollywood to raise substantial sums in the Hispanic and Asian communities, as well as among Greeks who flocked to their native son. Only four of Dukakis's more than forty fundraising events during the primaries drew principally from the movie world.

When all the primary receipts were tallied, Dukakis had raised over $2.2 million in California, more than anywhere but Massachusetts and New York. It was an enormous financial success, and to several of Dukakis's fundraisers, nothing was more satisfying than doing it without the help of the gatekeepers who had demanded the candidates first sing for their supper. "When it comes to money Dukakis proved Hollywood is not an absolute, maybe a necessary, but not an absolute ingredient," said Nick Patsaouras, the Greek businessman who raised substantial funds for Dukakis. "We got where we are without that help." It was a fittingly ironic valediction for a campaign season that began with Hollywood drunk on its own financial power. After brusquely demanding that all the candidates acknowledge their centrality, the Hollywood liberals ended up with a nominee who owned them nothing.

Meanwhile, George Bush also marched to the nomination without spending much time in Hollywood. Through the spring, he quietly raised $2.6 million in California, more than anywhere but Texas and New York. Bush's experience with the new moguls was limited, though; the wealthy downtown business establishment in Los Angeles offered an alternative unavailable to Democrats, and Hollywood remained relatively hardscrabble ground for the GOP throughout 1988. That, however, did not mean the vice-president's limited interaction with the film industry was not occasionally as bizarre as the Democrats'.

For the first fundraising event to fill the Presidential Trust, a multimillion-dollar fund the national parties are allowed to spend on their nominees' behalf in the general election, Bush flew in early June to the Beverly Hills home of producer Jerry Weintraub (*The Karate Kid*), a former manager of rock musicians who had recently launched his own ministudio, The Weintraub Entertainment Group. Weintraub had a vacation home

in Kennebunkport, Maine, and, as is his manner, Bush had made lasting
friends with his neighbor. When his friend Bush won the Republican
presidential nomination, Weintraub wanted to do something to help. The
something the Bush campaign came up with was a $10,000-a-couple
dinner that collected $1.1 million. (Actually, most of the money came not
from Hollywood, or even Weintraub, but from corporate sources tapped
by businessmen Donald L. Bren of the Irvine Company and Lodwrick M.
Cook, chairman and chief executive officer of ARCO.)

The receipts were satisfying enough, but in all other respects Weintraub's party for his friend was, from beginning to end, the sort of evening that gives Hollywood its reputation in Washington. Weintraub's
house, invariably described in news reports as a mansion, was far too
small for the huge crowd, many of whom came to know each other as
intimately as straphangers in a subway rush hour; the costs of the lavish
presentation were immense; and the entertainment was mostly inadvertent. Weintraub had lined up Frank Sinatra for the after-dinner show. But
Sinatra never sang; according to one well-placed Republican, he threatened until the last minute not even to attend. At the dinner, Sinatra
inexplicably brooded, flashing surly displeasure at anyone who tried to
engage him. One Hollywood Republican was called over to talk to Barbara Bush for twenty minutes because Sinatra, sitting beside her,
wouldn't talk to her. "Sinatra sat there with his back turned the whole
time," the Republican said. "He is a very strange man."

When the meal had been cleared, Weintraub took to the microphone
in the front of the tent he had pitched on his lawn, looked out on the sea
of contented industrialists in their gray pinstripes and blue blazers, and
said to audible disappointment that Sinatra's doctor had ordered him not
to sing because of a sore throat. "But he insisted on being here anyway,"
Weintraub continued gamely, "because when he's with you, he's with you
all the way."

With that, Weintraub called to the microphone "Francis Albert Sinatra." Sinatra shuffled to the stage like a prizefighter who had taken one
too many hits to the head. He leaned over the microphone and said, "I
wish I was Dean Martin because then I'd be bombed." It appeared he had
accomplished the feat entirely well in his own skin. Sinatra rambled for
a few minutes, wandering from subject to subject the way a drunk driver
drifts from lane to lane, stuffing his hands into the pockets of his suit
jacket, which he had buttoned closed, as though trying to keep warm. The
jacket looked as if it might burst. Sinatra looked lost. Then he said,
"Somebody tell me who the hell I'm supposed to introduce." Voices from
the audience called out "Jane Weintraub." Weintraub's wife, who had

sung professionally in the 1950s under the name Jane Morgan, had agreed to stand in for Sinatra as the entertainment, but Sinatra appeared puzzled. "Janie?" he said hesitantly. "Janie don't need no introduction." He looked out at the crowd blankly, muttered something about the drinks at his table being very strong, and finally, just as the confused buzz from the elegant tables became vaguely noticeable, ceded the floor to Jane Weintraub. At that moment, Camelot seemed a very long time ago.

The Politics of Culture

After the spring's elaborate courting rituals, the fall general election was almost anticlimactic in Hollywood.

Fundraising again dominated. That, by itself, was incongruous. On paper, the federal election laws prevent the presidential nominees, who each receive more than $46 million in public financing, from soliciting additional funds during the general election. But by 1988 ingenious lawyers had shredded those laws; fundraising continued from the primaries to the general election without even a figleaf of intermission. The search for cash actually accelerated during the general election, as both Dukakis and Bush frantically collected millions of dollars through a loophole Congress opened after the 1976 campaign.

Like many legal loopholes, this one was opened with the best of intentions. In that 1976 campaign, the first conducted after the major 1974 amendments to the election law, the state political parties were allowed to spend only $1,000 promoting the presidential tickets. Because President Gerald Ford and his challenger, Jimmy Carter, spent most of their money on television advertisements, no funds were left for bumper stickers and the other paraphernalia that traditionally adorned presidential elections at the local level. Commentators wailed about the death of grassroots campaigning. In 1979, Congress responded by amending the law to allow the state parties to spend an unlimited amount during the presidential election on such "party-building" local activities, which included not only printing bumper stickers but also organizing more substantive voter registration and get-out-the-vote campaigns.

That attempt to bring back the grassroots volunteer reopened the door instead for the fat-cat contributor. Since those "party-building" activities theoretically assist all candidates on the ballot, only the portion of the expenditures that helps federal candidates had to be funded with "hard money"—that is, contributions subject to the strict limits and disclosure requirements governing federal elections. (Individuals, for example, cannot give more than $5,000 in hard money to a state party.) The remaining portion of the party-building expenditures—the share that assists state and local candidates—can be funded with so-called soft money, which is not subject to the federal limits. Claiming (disingenuously) that most of the party-building expenditures during the general election benefit local candidates, the two parties now routinely fund enormous voter registration and get-out-the-vote drives in the presidential campaign through soft money, freeing their public grant for television purchases and allowing large contributors again to subsidize their operations.

That pattern was set in 1980, but in 1988 the contenders took it to new heights. First the Dukakis campaign, and then Bush, systematically solicited $100,000 contributions (most of it in soft money) from the wealthiest men and women in the country. Los Angeles became a principal target for both sides. In the general election, the Dukakis campaign brought in the Westside financial elite it had worked around in the primary. Just one day after the last primaries, Dukakis's chief fundraiser, Robert A. Farmer, flew out to Los Angeles and, with his California aides in tow, pocketed $100,000 contributions from six major Los Angeles powers, including Lew Wasserman, Ted Field, and Barry Diller of Fox. By the end of an election supposedly insulated from private money, the Dukakis campaign claimed 130 "trustees" across the country who gave or raised $100,000, while the Bush campaign, with its larger universe of affluent supporters, found 267.

The Democrats launched their program with almost messianic glee. In 1980 and 1984, the Republicans had raised substantially more soft money than the Democrats; many wealthy Democrats saw Farmer's program for eliminating that advantage as a sign of the party's commitment to retake the White House in 1988. "The notion was, let's fight this battle on an even field for the first time," said Burkett one morning in late summer. "Let's give whoever the candidate is an opportunity to be on a level playing field with the Republican candidate." But by October the bloom had faded, and not only because Dukakis's prospects had too. In Hollywood, the relentless pressure for money—the $100,000 solicitations were followed by requests for hard money for the state Dukakis and Bush efforts, last-minute wails for assistance from embattled senators, and a major fundraising push by the HWPC—grated on nerves already strained by the 1986 campaign. Dismay ripened into disgust. "I'm angry about it, because I think that it is simply not right," said Barry Diller, expressing a view that had permeated both parties by Election Day. "It is not right for our entire political sensibility to be mostly governed by the level of checks that we write, and it is terribly wrong for the candidates to be in that kind of endless position of looking for money. And I don't mean this just in terms of presidential: I mean this at every level. For senators and congressmen from out of state to be forced to spend time flying around the U.S.—and I'm not talking about those with national ambitions—to raise money, when they should be doing other things, it breeds nothing good. There is not a good thing to be said about the amount of money that's spent as well as the money gathering that it necessitates. It's rotten. Rotten to the core."

Celebrities felt less pressure than the fundraisers during the general election. Neither side gave high priority to luring stars onto the campaign trail. But the celebrity appearances that were made offered intriguing hints about the continuing attempts to think about Hollywood figures in terms of their cultural symbolism.

From the 1920s, Hollywood has always had one clear symbolic role in politics. Because Hollywood is a powerful cultural force in its own right, its embrace subtly helps to ground political leaders in the culture. Deference from stars who are themselves revered symbolically affirms the national political leadership's primacy in the society.

That is a useful brick in the social foundation of government—a reminder that the same rules govern all of us. But it operates at the level of the zeitgeist: it is too ethereal to help any individual candidate facing election. Most candidates think the zeitgeist can take care of itself. In terms of assistance a politician can actually touch, Hollywood's political role remains limited mostly to raising money, attracting crowds and the media (through appearances by celebrities), and occasionally offering some technical assistance (such as the radio broadcast Norman Corwin wrote for Franklin Roosevelt in 1944 or the campaign commercials directors Sydney Pollack and Tony Bill produced for Dukakis in 1988). But as campaigns continue to move toward contests between symbols that encapsulate competing values, and visual images displace words as the dominant vocabulary of political communication, Hollywood's symbolic power is likely to be seen increasingly as a tangible political weapon, too.

This manipulation of Hollywood symbolism involves the calculated deployment of icons in the pop culture to make political points. That means not just deputizing a conveniently available star to build a crowd, but rather orchestrating the association with individual celebrities (or Hollywood itself) to suggest the cultural values of the candidates.

The importance of cultural values in determining voter decisions has not been carefully studied, but they are a visibly growing part of many campaigns. Despite what Gary Hart or editorial writers want to believe, issues are not the only, and not necessarily always the dominant, criteria voters use to assess candidates. After the 1988 presidential campaign it would be difficult to deny that assessments of a candidate's cultural values—everything from a politician's attitude toward family or religion to the kind of food* and music he or she likes—are also extremely important to voters. "Any little bit of information that connects [candidates] culturally makes them more interesting to voters and gives voters a better insight," said Robert M. Teeter, President Bush's pollster. "They want to see the home they live in, the kind of car they drive, what kind of music they like, whether they play tennis or go fishing." This is not surprising or even distressing. More than intellect is involved in creating trust. Since at least the early nineteenth century, presidential candidates have tried to convince voters that they come from the same soil and were shaped by the same experiences:† in the campaign of 1840, when supporters of President Martin Van Buren ridiculed the qualifications of challenger William Henry Harrison by saying he would be content to live in a log cabin with a jug of cider, the wealthy Harrison appropriated those symbols of rural life, used them to successfully identify with the farmers pioneering the wilderness, and ousted Van Buren.

Such symbols of cultural compatibility have become even more important to campaigns over the past forty years with the dramatic decline in allegiance to the two major parties. Once the parties provided the uniform standard voters used to measure a candidate's values against their own; but in this era of split-ticket voting, fewer people now conclude that a candidate shares their values simply because they share the same party label. Today, most voters look for other cues. In the television era, the battle over the symbols that illuminate cultural values extends widely—to the flag, family, and neighborhood; the last campaign saw Dukakis wielding a rusting snowblower in support of his claim to flinty fiscal prudence and Bush wrapping himself in Old Glory. Since the 1988 campaign, the politics of cultural symbolism have moved to the center of the struggle between the two parties. For months in 1990—while the budget deficit festered and the foundations of the Cold War world eroded—Congress

---

*It was surely not accidental that the White House widely publicized George Bush's distaste for broccoli.

†Examples of the attempts by candidates to create that impression could fill another book. But as one indication of the importance of passing that test, it is worth recalling that when it was revealed that some of the younger 1988 Democratic presidential candidates had smoked marijuana while in college, the question many baby boomers asked was why the others had not.

debated no issue with more passion than whether to amend the Constitution to ban flag burning, except perhaps how to restrict grants from the National Endowment for the Arts. These elaborately choreographed disputes each displayed the primacy politicians now place on projecting mainstream cultural attitudes. It is within this larger struggle to project sympathetic cultural values to the electorate that celebrities—some of whom have public images so sharply defined that they represent a kind of cultural shorthand—are finding their new supporting political roles, sometimes inadvertently.

The use of celebrities as one tool for signaling the values of candidates has been slowly growing in recent years. In 1972, George McGovern and Warren Beatty used rock stars to suggest to disaffected young voters that the candidate was not a typical politician. The final hours of the 1980 campaign saw Carter and Reagan both surrounding themselves with competing myths drawn from popular culture: on Election Eve, while Ronald Reagan cited John Wayne as the antithesis of Carter's vision of American malaise, the Carter campaign countered with Henry Fonda, the venerable voice of Middle American common sense, as the spokesman for its last appeal. Later in the decade, the damage caused to Democrats Harriett Woods and Tom Daschle from association with Fonda's daughter Jane, and the strains caused Hart by his friendship with Beatty, showed that the images associated with famous figures could be used just as easily to tar politicians.

These maneuvers represent a further refinement of the political application of fame—one that builds on the shifts in political tactics and Hollywood attitudes during the Vietnam War era that allowed Jane Fonda, Paul Newman, and their contemporaries to take larger political roles than any of their predecessors. What galvanized those stars was the slowly spreading awareness that in a society which relentlessly personifies issues—a trend greatly accelerated by the demands of television for pictures that simplify ideas—their fame was a concrete political tool. They gradually realized that fame allowed them to attract cameras—the political ante in the television age—and that they could use that media attention to push a political agenda. It also became apparent that Moses spoke with a louder voice than Barbarella—that the stars' personal credibility depended heavily on their on-screen image. But it has taken longer to understand how the specific image a star projects can color the candidates and causes he or she stands beside.

Not all stars, of course, send out such distinct cultural messages: What exactly comes to mind when the name Robert De Niro is mentioned? But a significant number of entertainers are symbols of affinity for easily defined groups: the Brat Pack with young people, sixties rock stars with baby boomers, country-and-western artists with Southerners, the Jimmy Stewart generation of film stars with senior citizens. For their fans, these entertainers embody memories, lifestyles, places and times, shared experiences. They can suggest a way of looking at the world, symbolizing not only experiences but also values: you can often tell a lot about someone by how they feel about John Wayne or Sylvester Stallone, or whether they prefer Bob Dylan to Elvis Presley. They are all part of the code people use to recognize others like themselves.

It is no different with politicians. To these distinct audiences, politicians can declare their own cultural preferences and personal values by the kinds of celebrities they associate with. They can try to place themselves within those webs of shared experience—or at least demonstrate their respect for them—by linking with a figure who symbolizes them. Sharing an appreciation for a kind of music or a film star is one way a politician can create an initial connection, just as new acquaintances often feel more comfortable if they discover they like the same bands or the same movies. "It does communicate something about you," said Teeter, the pollster for President Bush, "about shared values, about what you like."

For politicians the risk in associating with celebrities has always been of sending out another cultural message—of appearing too attracted to Hollywood's indulgent lifestyle. That's roughly what happened to Hart, at least among political insiders. There are other risks in employing stars as symbolic character references. When it becomes too overt or calculated, this kind of cultural positioning undermines itself by reinforcing the voters' suspicion that most politicians are manipulative and insincere. If a candidate sends cultural messages discordant with his political ones (a family-values Republican, say, who campaigns with heavy metal bands), that doesn't help much either.

But used carefully, these cultural messages can help politicians make themselves more three-dimensional, particularly to the many voters who pay little attention to elections. "Both politicians and products are judged in part by the company they keep," said Democratic pollster Geoff Garin. "In 1976, when Jimmy Carter quoted Bob Dylan in his presidential campaign, it said more to a generation of voters than hours of commercials could say. It said this guy doesn't ignore the way our generation thinks, he is more open-minded than the traditional politician. Jimmy Carter quoting Bob Dylan made Jimmy Carter a lot more interesting to a hell of a lot of baby boomers."

To play these cultural roles, stars need not be personally credible messengers on public policy, the way they must to push individual causes; what matters instead is how their image affects the way voters see a politician who associates with them. In some cases, celebrities can be among the most efficient ways for campaigns to provide clues to voters about a candidate's deepest beliefs. By talking about Dylan, for example, Carter did more than link himself with a popular figure: symbolically he suggested a respect for the 1960s criticism of American society the singer embodied. "It's not measurable as something that would be decisive in a campaign," said Garin. "But if after an election is over you quizzed voters on what they remember about the campaign and the candidate, in an awful lot of cases their use of cultural symbols would probably be a lot more memorable than their positions on issues. A lot of rock-and-roll-age voters remember more about who owned Bruce Springsteen in the 1984 campaign than they do about the two candidates' proposals on the deficits. Voters insist on judging politics on their own terms, and their own terms very often don't have anything to do with position papers."

As Garin suggests, sometimes a cultural figure generates symbolism so powerful that both sides covet it. The 1984 campaign offered the strange spectacle of the president of the United States and his Democratic challenger falling over each other to embrace Springsteen, then at the pinnacle of his "Born in the U.S.A." popularity. Both candidates—or at least their advisers—understood that Springsteen tapped into genuine emotions at a level politicians almost never can. To the public that summer, Springsteen suggested many different things—class conflict, rocker with a heart (he gave large donations to food banks in most of the cities on that concert tour), American hero—but there was no doubt that to almost anyone paying attention his message was one of integrity, of convictions deeply felt and passionately portrayed.

Reagan's team made the first pass at Springsteen. After a George Will column about a late-summer Springsteen concert at Washington's Capital Centre brought the singer to the White House's attention, Reagan's staff asked Springsteen to appear with the president in New Jersey at a mid-September campaign stop. When Springsteen refused, the president simply summoned him in his speech: "America's future rests in a thousand dreams inside your hearts; it rests in the message of hope in songs so many young Americans admire: New Jersey's own Bruce Springsteen." During a concert in Pittsburgh a few days later, Springsteen, whose songs crackle with intuitive blue-collar populism, repudiated the president (if somewhat indirectly). Walter Mondale then happily declared to a press conference, "Bruce Springsteen may have been born to run, but he wasn't born yesterday."

Each party projected a different Springsteen: the Democrats a working-class hero, the bard of those left behind by Reaganism; the Republicans a man who showed hard work could achieve any dream, Horatio Alger with a backbeat. For Reagan, Springsteen also fit into what senior White House strategist Richard G. Darman called in a June 1984 memo the attempt to "Paint RR as the personification of all that is right with or heroized by America." In reality, the message of Springsteen's *Born in the U.S.A.* album was quite different: it actually explored the unmet promises in the American dream. But the booming beat and red-white-and-blue motif at his concerts were frequently misinterpreted as a hymn to American resurgence, power-driven theme music for Reagan's "Morning Again in America" commercials. No matter what Springsteen actually intended, insisted John Buckley, press secretary in the 1984 Reagan campaign, "for the vast majority of Americans that summer there was no irony in 'Born in the U.S.A.' 'Born in the U.S.A.' was a refrain that neatly dovetailed with our success in the Olympics that year and with the campaign's theme that America is back, prouder, stronger, better." In effect, the singer's image became so powerful that even he lost control over it.

Not entirely, though. By recoiling from the president's embrace, Springsteen minimized his value to the White House and illustrated another important point: politicians often stumble when reaching into the popular culture because so many of them are completely, unimaginably obtuse about it. Some are fans, and many enjoy the excitement of associating with celebrities; but they are often oblivious to artists' work, or how that work might reveal trends in the nation. Only someone who had never listened to the words in a Springsteen album could have expected the singer to allow Reagan to appropriate his name.

Their isolation ensures that the national leadership of neither party thinks consistently about how cultural associations might influence votes. But the Republicans have taken more of a stab at it than the Democrats, at least since John Kennedy caroused with Sinatra and Carter confessed his affection for Dylan and the Allman Brothers. Paradoxically Hart, who failed to recognize the dangerous symbolism of his association with Beatty, was the one Democrat in recent times who showed signs of thinking about the broader questions; he explored the role of myth in politics through his Media Advisory Group. But the compulsive pursuit of his own myths forced him from the race before those ideas could germinate.

As a product of the pop culture himself, Reagan instinctively understood how to create connections through cultural associations. If anything, he often seemed to confuse fiction with reality, usually preferring the former to the latter in a crunch. Throughout his political career, he wove dialogue from movies into his speeches to highlight points insufficiently illustrated by mere facts. He appropriated as his own nickname "The Gipper," the label applied to doomed Notre Dame football star George Gipp whom Reagan portrayed in the 1940 film *Knute Rockne—All American*. His political image, of a patriotic and benevolent optimist, a kindly father stern when provoked, seemed made entirely from celluloid—equal parts John Wayne, Andy Hardy, and "Father Knows Best." As the accessible and yet distant embodiment of a simpler and stronger America, Reagan was a vast screen on which values could be projected.

Still, Reagan as president initially offered cultural messages that affirmed the worst stereotypes of the party he led. His first inaugural, a nouveau riche orgy, provided matchless symbols of ersatz royalty and uninhibited wealth, with businessmen in tuxedos stepping over the homeless into limousines. It was the worst of Beverly Hills affectation joined with the heights of corporate indifference. Those notes were never silenced—the Reagans kept spending the holidays with rich friends in Palm Springs; Nancy never entirely undid the damage done by her china, designer dresses, and imperial arrogance.

But other cultural messages gradually emerged too, of a different, more sophisticated tone. Under Reagan, the GOP cultural message went out over two channels. Over one Reagan reached back to the past; over the other he leaned into the future. In the first pose, Reagan pined for a simpler time, when proprieties were more decorously observed, in the popular culture as everywhere else. His lament against sexual explicitness and obscenity in movies and magazines opened up into a critique now common in the GOP of the freedom in modern arts and letters. From former Education Secretary William J. Bennett's criticism of American education to author Allan Bloom's condemnation of rock and roll, to North Carolina Senator Jesse A. Helms's battles with the National Endowment for the Arts, the theme is consistent: against experimentation, against art that jars middle-class sensibility or challenges traditional authority (either secular or in the hereafter). Reagan and his acolytes personified a cultural fundamentalism that reassured conservatives, particularly religious conservatives, that the Republicans shared their dismay over the shifts in the nation's mores reflected by these changing artistic styles. That had been Reagan's cultural agenda since the dawn of his political career; even after he left the White House, he restated it when he visited Tokyo and told his Japanese hosts he thought Sony's acquisition of Columbia Pictures Entertainment, Inc., might help clean up Hollywood.

As president, though, that stern, hopelessly uncool moralism was not

Reagan's only cultural message. While the cultural critique went out through one speaker, to one audience, through the other blasted a contrary message—what one aide in the reelection campaign called "the ongoing attempt to show Reagan's affinity for pop culture." The effect was not dissonance but stereo: or, as the aide put it, "There was text and subtext."

Within the White House, there developed something akin to a pop culture cabal composed of several young speechwriters and youthful political assistants Morgan Mason, the son of actor James Mason, and Lee Atwater, a Southern political operative with an inveterate taste for hard-ball politics, B-movies, and rhythm and blues. In the reelection campaign they were joined enthusiastically by press secretary Buckley, nephew of William Buckley and erstwhile rock critic of his uncle's *National Review*. All were committed to giving Reagan a more contemporary image, not to mention aligning Republicanism with the cultural forces they danced to. Not everyone around Reagan thought the semaphores they choreographed had much merit; pollster Richard Wirthlin for example, saw little use in the references. But imagist-in-chief Michael Deaver looked benignly on their efforts, as did Darman, himself a keen student of popular culture.

The driving force was Atwater. Atwater had been fascinated with the role of culture in politics since he emerged as a star practitioner of brass-knuckled campaigning in the South Carolina Republican party of Senator Strom Thurmond in the mid-1970s. "I started thinking about it and observing it in the late 1970s and . . . I became very infatuated with the notion of American culture and how it connected to politics," Atwater said. "And I came to the conclusion by the late 1970s or early 1980s that, in many respects, if you could analyze voters' values and their lifestyles, and provide symbols that they could identify with from the standpoint of their values and lifestyles, that you could connect with them at least as well as you could by simply discussing typical ideology and issue types of questions."

Atwater and the other culturally attuned White House aides created these symbols for Reagan in two ways: by bringing figures from the popular culture to the White House for well-publicized visits and by salting Reagan's speeches with references to contemporary trends, particularly movies. The overriding goal in both cases was to portray Reagan as in tune with his times.

Reagan regularly drew on current films and television programs for his public remarks (citing everything from *Rambo* to Vanna White to Clint Eastwood), including one State of the Union address, where he quoted the concluding line of dialogue from *Back to the Future,* a movie that had gently spoofed him. This was not the inadvertent mingling of fact and movie script that characterized Reagan's earlier speeches, but a systematic attempt to loot from the popular culture. The effort spread beyond movie dialogue: one aide drew up a plan to ensure that the president interacted with the championship teams in all sports; others arranged to have him photographed weightlifting when bodybuilding became popular, attending the Firecracker 400 stock car race in Florida on the Fourth of July, saluting Roy Acuff at the Grand Ole Opry in Nashville, and, of course, celebrating Bruce Springsteen in New Jersey. In the summer of his reelection campaign, Reagan officially opened the Olympic Games in Los Angeles, and during the fall, spoke about the U.S. team so often it might as well have been on the ballot with him. It seemed, in the summer of 1984, that all roads in American popular culture converged on Ronald Reagan.

The associations Atwater and his colleagues engineered unquestionably exaggerated Reagan's connection with the everyday culture, and occasionally they got caught: the Springsteen debacle showed the danger of pushing credibility too far. (After Reagan referred to Springsteen, reporters pointedly asked Buckley which record was the president's favorite.) But most of the time, their efforts seemed plausible. That was not only because it was easy to imagine Reagan actually watching Vanna White spin letters on "Wheel of Fortune." It was also because Reagan appeared to be constructed of so many diverse bits of Americana that hardly anyone questioned the addition of a few new ones. If they were synthetically bonded to him, that was no matter: for Reagan it was genuine to be synthetic.

In fact, the most synthetic associations—the ones that tied the oldest president to rock figures and other icons of the youth culture—were probably the most useful. Association with pop culture figures was seen as one way for "[Reagan] to reassure young people he wasn't trapped in the past," in John Buckley's words. This effort to absorb the youth culture was a major shift from the 1960s, when Reagan came to power largely by standing in outraged opposition to the counterculture blooming on campuses across California. Some of the Californians in his entourage now felt Reagan had been excessively hostile to young people as governor. With the sons and daughters of Reagan's 1960s antagonists already trending Republican, these advisers hoped to send out a more sympathetic message from the White House.

They went to considerable lengths to do this. They briefly discussed obtaining singer John Cougar Mellencamp's "Pink Houses"—an upbeat

ode to contentment with the simple life—as a campaign song. When that
failed, they reached out for Springsteen; Atwater looked at buying ads on
MTV and generated favorable publicity from just the thought. During
1980, the actors who campaigned with Reagan had all been eligible for
Social Security; once in office, the White House worked to surround the
president with younger, hipper entertainers.

His aides were not able to win many endorsements from young stars,
but as president of all the people, he could at least host fresher faces.
Visits from celebrities were easy to sell because they passed the cardinal
rule of policy in Reagan's administration: they made good pictures.
Mason arranged for Elton John to meet the president (after dutifully
typing up a 3 $\times$ 5 index card to brief Reagan on his last album); Michael
Jackson moonwalked through the White House; Lee Atwater brought in
James Brown, who had not yet set up residence in the South Carolina
State Park Correctional Center. (Brown, apparently a fan of James
Mason, surprised the actor's son by convincingly imitating the father,
while Atwater beamed at his elbow.) Sylvester Stallone premiered his
instantly forgotten movie *Victory*. Even Warren Beatty was brought by for
a screening of *Reds*. Though conservatives fulminated, the story circulated that the president got along famously with his Democratic guest.*

All this flowed into the same stream. "I think that some of us may have
tried to be more careful to get the younger Hollywood types. . . . It was
the future and youth and that sort of thing that we were concerned
about," said Deaver. There were limits to this strategy; clearly a celebrity
association that began with Frank Sinatra was not the cutting edge. But
Reagan blended all these disparate references into an engaging collage:
rock stars and country stars, aging matinee idols and freshly scrubbed
Olympic heroes, all the associations contributed to the whole. Reagan,
unlike most politicians, gave the sense he knew what was going on outside
the world of politics, that he understood the cultural trends that mattered
more to most people than whether the reconciliation bill came in on time.
He was president of the America that tuned to "Entertainment Tonight"
before "MacNeil-Lehrer"—which was about forty-nine states' worth.

In the 1988 George Bush campaign, the use of popular culture was not
as contrived as in the Reagan White House. But with Atwater, who had
been only deputy campaign manager in the 1984 Reagan campaign,
installed in the top job, the Bush effort stressed from the outset the

---

*"Yeah," that's true, Beatty said. "Every time I saw him—I can remember dinners that go
back through the years—I always liked him. I always felt that he said what he meant and
he had convictions . . . and he was not a pretentious man. He doesn't pretend to be
something other than what he is."

importance of cultural symbols in guiding votes. The most effective, and controversial, of the symbols Atwater used to define the two candidates had nothing to do with celebrities: Atwater manipulated such symbols as the flag, Dukakis's membership in the American Civil Liberties Union, gun control, and above all, furloughed black Massachusetts convict Willie Horton to question the Democrat's patriotism, to suggest his values were too liberal for ordinary Americans, and to hint he would be too pliant to the political demands of blacks. Atwater pushed to the edge of propriety, and in some cases beyond, but generally he had his fingers on the right buttons—the ones that triggered the voters' deepest anxieties about the Democrats' values.

Atwater used references to popular culture and selected campaign appearances by celebrities to reinforce these basic themes. Some of this was haphazard. The Bush campaign actually did not put much emphasis on recruiting celebrities: the man in charge of finding stars and athletes to endorse the vice-president had no access to the senior staff. But the Bush forces made more from their little pool of star supporters than the Democrats did from their much larger group by understanding that celebrities could be used to send cultural signals.

Bush's advisers deployed their share of meaningless has-beens to wave to indifferent crowds. But the best Bush appearances with stars had a point to them. These almost invariably involved country-and-western stars. During the campaign, Bush had around him almost as many country artists as Secret Service—from Chet Atkins to Lee Greenwood to the Gatlin Brothers; in all, the campaign lined up three dozen country acts as supporters. Bush's most memorable encounter with Nashville actually came on a bus trip across central Illinois with singers Loretta Lynn, Crystal Gayle, and Peggy Sue that generated invaluable shots on the evening news of the down-home veep strumming the guitar with the singers. At one stop, to underline the point of who was a real American and who was not, Lynn, her drawl thickened theatrically, said Dukakis was not her kind of politician: "Why," she declared in words that brought one of the subterranean Bush messages dangerously close to the light, "I can't even pronounce his name!"

All these appearances helped Bush combat his preppie Ivy League image. The company of the country artists highlighted Bush's pork-rinds side; each round of "Stand by Your Man" pushed into the background the blue-blood son of a senator, the privileged effete, that the Democrats had so successfully painted at their convention. Atwater understood that traveling with Gayle and Lynn—in a bus!—carried Bush deep into the heartland; their company, like the battle over the Pledge of Allegiance, was another way of indicating that Bush shared the preferences and pastimes of ordinary Americans.

"I certainly thought there was value [in appearing with country artists] because I did not think the American people knew what kind of music he likes," Atwater said. "That's one of the first things I ask someone: What kind of music do you like? It is something I ask just for political reasons. When he told me the artists that he liked—the Oak Ridge Boys, Loretta Lynn, Crystal Gayle—I was very surprised and I felt it should be highlighted. It was natural, it was authentic, and I think there are a lot of people in this country who like to know what kind of music somebody listens to, particularly from my generation. . . . I must say that if the Vice-President told me that his favorite type of music was chamber music, I don't know what my feeling would have been from a campaign sense."*

Other stars also provided Bush with resonant symbols. In particular, Bush regularly shared stages with such stoic cinema loners as Chuck Norris and Arnold Schwarzenegger. To Atwater, they served the same function that rock stars did for George McGovern: they brought the candidate to the attention of an audience that might otherwise have never tuned into the campaign—in this case, mostly less-educated and working-class young men with minimal interest in politics. "People like Chuck Norris and Arnold Schwarzenegger have followings that transcend the typical political crowd," Atwater said. "When I traveled one day with Bush, we campaigned up in the [Central] Valley in California, and we were in a mobile home, a van. And we had Chuck Norris with us. Everywhere we went there were scores of people with Chuck Norris sweatshirts on. I talked to them. They didn't care about politics. Some of them never voted. But they were going to vote. A man like Norris, a man like Schwarzenegger, can bring in people from their own followings that are not typically prone to care about politics one way or the other."

Some Dukakis aides thought that surrounding Bush with celluloid tough guys also reinforced the Republicans' attempt to portray the vice-president as strong and his challenger as weak. Who better to sniff out weakness than the indestructible Terminator? In a well-reported Midwest swing with Bush just days before the election, Schwarzenegger thundered that the Democrats had left America with "an economy that looked like Pee-wee Herman, a pipsqueak defense, and a foreign policy with training wheels on it." These endorsements from strong, silent types—archetypes of the American belief that a big stick is better than a slick mouth—

---

*Not surprisingly, it turns out the Yale-educated president also has a fondness for classical music, if not orchestral accompaniment on the campaign trail.

strengthened too what Peggy Noonan, the vice-president's ace script-writer, called her attempt to craft Bush in the mold of a modern Gary Cooper, an occasionally inarticulate individualist who could draw on hidden reserves of quiet strength. And if the campaign suggested Bush was the choice of manly, macho, patriotic Hollywood—the sort of men who shot first and worried about the ACLU later—at the same time it tied Dukakis to the most pungent symbol of the inverse. In one California appearance, the vice-president declared it would not surprise him if Dukakis "thinks a naval exercise is something you find in the 'Jane Fonda Workout Book' "—a construction that managed to question Dukakis's manliness and his patriotism in a single sentence.

All of this wroked so well because it never appeared as forced as some of the Reagan references. (The Springsteen debacle taught Atwater the value of sticking to associations with intrinsic credibility.) And stars were not visible enough in the Bush effort to create the impression that he had "gone Hollywood"; they were effective supporting players in an overall cultural offensive that overwhelmed Dukakis's early lead. It was months before the Dukakis campaign understood how the symbols Bush employed—everything from Willie Horton to Chuck Norris—had reshaped the race, and when they did it was too late to do anything but complain that Bush was obscuring the real issues (a questionable proposition given the importance of cultural values to voters)—and privately marvel at the skill of the Republicans' performance. "This was well thought out," said John Sasso, the Dukakis campaign's vice-chairman and the candidate's closest adviser. "They understand the symbols of the country, not just flag, not just patriotism, not just war heroes—all of those things—but the symbols that relate to figures in popular culture and what that says about a candidate, a president."

For the buttoned-down Dukakis campaign, the politics of culture merited barely an afterthought. Dukakis himself had no interest in the potential political value of figures who might turn up on the cover of *People*. At the fundraiser Barry Diller sponsored in 1987, Nick Patsaouras found the governor at the bar with Beatty and Jack Nicholson; after only a few minutes Dukakis rolled his eyes at Patsaouras as if to say: Get me out of here.* That wasn't an entirely unreasonable response—though Beatty, at

---

*The disenchantment was mutual. When Dukakis appeared in mid-September at Norman Lear's home before two hundred of Hollywood's finest to encourage more celebrities to campaign, he gave a tepid performance that actually dampened interest in Hollywood. (It didn't help that Lear burdened Dukakis with an overelaborate introduction virtually impossible to live up to.) But that pattern was fairly typical. Patrick Lippert, the young Tom Hayden aide, signed on with the Dukakis campaign in California to help recruit celebrities. But he found that many of them came back from appearances with Dukakis with diminished

least, might have had interesting ideas to offer—but it revealed a deeper complacency. Dukakis and his aides never sifted through the mass media stream for nuggets that could have been useful. "Perhaps he could have more easily brought more people into the fold," said producer Fred Zollo (*Mississippi Burning*), who had known and supported Dukakis since attending college in Massachusetts in the 1970s. "I think there was, not a slight fear or distaste, but a slight suspicion of those people. It is important to realize a presidential campaign is a media experience and there are film people, directors, producers, actors, writers, who believe in their work intensely, and believe in issues, who could have . . . been used." By mid-September, Irving Azoff glumly declared, "There has never been a Democratic candidate for president at this stage of the election to have less contact with the Westside entertainment and liberal Jewish communities."

For the Democrats, the idea of illuminating aspects of Dukakis's personality through associations with the popular culture started and ended at the convention, when Olympia Dukakis talked about his snowblower in a film used to introduce him. She worked in that role not only because she was his cousin but because she carried from her performance in *Moonstruck* the image of the wise, earthy mother—sensible, grounded, practical, the same things the convention film tried to project about the chilly and cerebral Dukakis.*

The campaign did effectively reinforce its son-of-immigrants theme through the repeated use of Neil Diamond's anthem "America." But their creativity extended no further. Aides gave fleeting thought to using famous Democrats (Meryl Streep, Robert Redford) in endorsement ads, but that idea was dropped out of the conviction that Dukakis's problems had advanced too far to be remedied by testimonials. A small group of Hollywood screenwriters supplied the speechwriters with well-turned sound bites. ("For a while it was hit the theme of the week," said screenwriter Gary Ross, who organized the group at the campaign's request, "but once they fell behind it was just like, bail water.") On the campaign

---

interest. "Dukakis was aloof," Lippert said, and even worse, didn't know who many of the stars were.

*The difference between Olympia's assured performance in the convention film and her halting delivery on the podium was a reminder of how difficult it is for many stars to face an electoral audience. Backstage, recalled one Dukakis aide, "we could not get her to go out. She had absolute stage fright." Even the film had mixed effect: though it successfully portrayed Dukakis as a regular guy, it hammered home his ordinariness so relentlessly that some viewers thought it diminished the stature he had acquired through his late-spring series of primary victories over Jesse Jackson.

trail itself, stars were used mostly to entertain the press; the goal was to divert reporters who might have otherwise amused themselves by picking the wings off the candidate. Redford did campaign but, after one well-publicized appearance with Dukakis, separately from the candidate.

In part, the campaign's problem was that its shifting messages repeatedly ran into walls of resistance—even the immigrant theme played poorly in Middle America, campaign pollster Tom Kiley found—and so it was never quite clear what themes Dukakis might have used cultural associations to reinforce. Nor were popular figures readily available who could symbolically rebut the charges Bush hurled. "Who would our great cultural points have been?" asked political consultant Francis O'Brien, a former Paramount Pictures executive who served as a senior adviser in the campaign. "One of the weaknesses of the Democratic party is we are considered un-American. We needed a John Wayne. The closest thing is Gregory Peck, but he is almost too old. Paul Newman was only minimally active this year. With Dukakis there was no one you could match him up with who [helped] where his problems were."

But that wasn't all. Within the Dukakis campaign, the use of cultural symbols and associations to project values seemed to be viewed as a Hollywood affectation or cynical media manipulation, in either case irrelevant to the real business of grinding out position papers. That myopia ironically allowed cultural contrasts to become an unusually decisive factor in the 1988 campaign.

"We did a terrible job of that," said Sasso. "It is one of the things the Republicans understand better than we do. When you have Loretta Lynn singing to George Bush on a bus going through the heartland, when you have Bush deliver a line saying the only naval exercise Dukakis understands is in Jane Fonda's workout book, it is important. It is key because . . . you are going to be in people's living rooms every night. They want to know you relate to the same things they relate to and it's not just the budget and education, it's the same things they relate to every day: it's entertainment and culture. We don't get it. If we do get it, we don't use it. We don't put the time and appreciation into it that it requires."

One incident epitomized that failure. Over the summer, Danny Goldberg, the rock manager who had supported Hart, proposed a cultural assault on Dukakis's Harvard Yard–liberal image, using country-and-western artists such as Rosanne Cash and Rodney Crowell to hold a fundraising concert with the candidate in Nashville. To Goldberg, the money was tangential: the concert really offered an opportunity to soften Southern and rural perceptions of the quintessentially Northeastern and academic Dukakis—the man who had once told Iowa farmers to grow endive. Together with a former associate who had moved to Nashville, Goldberg arranged for the performers, the date, the hall—all the campaign had to do was provide the candidate. He contacted everyone he knew in the California and national operations. "I must have had twenty different conversations," he said. In one memo to the campaign, he passionately and convincingly laid out the case for the concert: "This event will raise a considerable amount of money but it would do something far more important: it's a one-in-a-million media photo-op that can't be ignored. It gives Michael Dukakis a breakthrough in every media source; an opportunity to embrace REAGAN-DEMOCRATS and be seen with the music they love, the musicians they love, the politicians they love and in the city they not only love but which stands at the core of their cultural identity, dissolving the barriers between 'Northern Liberals' and 'Southern Conservatives.' Remember: George Bush had Country Stars at the Republican Convention singing the National Anthem!! Everything except the candidate's commitment is ready."

All his fervor failed to catch any attention. Goldberg could not interest the Dukakis campaign in the idea. "It is killing me, killing me," he lamented one day during the campaign. "I can't get them to take it seriously. They treat me like I'm speaking Swahili." He offered to organize the event for vice-presidential nominee Lloyd Bentsen if Dukakis wasn't available. That didn't help. Gradually he began to feel merely patronized, and the proposal died. "I think they had a blind spot about the culture," Goldberg said after the campaign. "I think the people around Michael Dukakis, George Mitchell, Richard Gephardt are not listening to talk radio, are not watching primetime television, are not going to see the top movies, and someone around Lee Atwater is. Democrats had 90 percent of the [celebrity] fish this year and they [the Republicans] did better with their 10 percent."

As if to prove Goldberg's point, Atwater celebrated Bush's victory by organizing a symbolic counter-inauguration bash. He invited a long list of legendary rhythm-and-blues artists, and picked up a guitar himself. The wailing guitars and harmonica solos all rang out the same subliminal point: that the Republican party was no longer limited to aging suburbanites who spent Saturday night curled up with Lawrence Welk reruns. It was possible to be in step and in the GOP at the same time—something that was not true before Atwater and a handful of other Republican strategists began manipulating cultural symbols a decade earlier.

. . .

Frustrated with the Democrats, some of the most intent and sophisticated of the Hollywood liberals came out of the 1988 campaign talking about waging cultural politics themselves. That impulse was actually apparent as early as 1980, with the decision by Norman Lear—who understood the link between culture and politics as keenly as anyone in the film community—to create People For the American Way and battle the religious right on the cultural terrain. People For used images, advertisements, and symbols to try to recapture for the left such basic values as patriotism and tolerance. Through the 1980s, the group did so brilliantly, but mostly from Washington; it didn't really set a tone in Hollywood. Money still defined Hollywood's political participation through most of the decade. By 1988, an uneasiness with that role set in and stirred some new thinking.

One spur was the awareness that candidates were more eager to take home money than ideas from Hollywood. In part, that realization inspired renewed interest in recapturing some of the institutional authority to shape the advertising in political campaigns lost by Hollywood to Madison Avenue and political consultants at the dawn of the television era. But it also prompted discussion of a far more ambitious agenda: the systematic transmission of the Hollywood liberals' own political messages through the mass media. If candidates wouldn't listen to their thoughts on how to sell liberalism, some of the Hollywood figures thought, why not implement those ideas themselves?

Disappointed with the Dukakis campaign, Danny Goldberg became the first Hollywood liberal since Lear to move down that path. In October 1987, through the machinations of the ubiquitous Stanley Sheinbaum, the American Civil Liberties Union Foundation of Southern California named Goldberg chairman. When Bush attacked the organization in 1988 and Dukakis proved incapable of defending it, Goldberg responded with television commercials using Burt Lancaster and cast members from the hit NBC show "L.A. Law." It was, incredibly, the first time the ACLU had ever sold itself through television advertisements. Goldberg approached the task of defending the ACLU, not as if he was preparing for a final exam at Harvard Law School—roughly the Dukakis campaign approach—but on the same gut level that the Bush campaign aimed its attacks. "In thirty seconds you can't make a lot of substantive arguments," he said at the time, "but you can evoke some emotions." Which the ads did, focusing tightly on the venerable figure of Lancaster as he turned the Bush campaign's taunt into an affirmation: "I'm Burt Lancaster and I have a confession to make," he said. "I'm a card-carrying member of the ACLU."

After the campaign, the interest in shaping political messages quickened in Hollywood. Politics is like anything else: when you observe a phenomenon, you change it. The more that was written about Hollywood's preoccupation with fundraising, the more people there looked to demonstrate they were more than just wallets. Many leading fundraisers, such as HWPC, joined in efforts to reform the campaign finance laws that had driven legislators to camp out in Brentwood and Malibu. "The last election where these candidates spent more time here than in their home states made everybody crazy. Crazy!" said Paula Weinstein, the producer and Hollywood Women's Political Committee leader. "After this process through the last year, most of the people I know here—in all phases, not just HWPC—are talking about how we take a community that is clearly interested, wanting to be active and make it active, beyond going to the dinners and raising the money."

The extent of this conversion can easily be overstated: it was confined to a handful of independent but like-thinking individuals. In that small group, though, the disappointment of 1988 encouraged renewed organizing. In New York, celebrities gathered into an organization called the Creative Coalition out of a sense that as symbols they had "potential power, whether we deserve to or not," said actor Ron Silver *(Enemies, A Love Story),* one of the group's founders. "The culture works in sound bites. We don't have discourse; we have bumper stickers. If that's the way it is going to be functioning politically, you look for icons, images that can get the message across as quickly as possible, as effectively as possible. Nobody [is] better in the world than celebrities."

In Hollywood, the growing urge to shape political messages was first manifested in the decision by HWPC to find other ways to express itself than writing checks. After the election, HWPC hired as executive director Margery Tabankin, the veteran liberal political organizer who had sent celebrities through Central America in the early 1980s. To Tabankin, the women indicated that without diminishing their commitment to fundraising (when Nelson Mandela came to Los Angeles in 1990, they spearheaded a dinner that raised $1.2 million), they wanted to find other ways to push their political agenda. In the spring of 1989, they gave one indication of their commitment by creating a nonprofit auxiliary to absorb the Network organization and its director, Patrick Lippert, after Tom Hayden and Jane Fonda ended their marriage and the group foundered. Through that new organization, the Hollywood Policy Center, HWPC escalated its efforts to join celebrities with causes.

The rising controversy over abortion in the spring of 1989 gave the women their first opportunity to test the new machinery. In April, HWPC dispatched a delegation of about sixty celebrities (including several, such as Glenn Close, not ordinarily associated with political causes) to a march in Washington supporting abortion rights—and sent them with specific guidance to stress the theme of personal choice when discussing the issue, rather than engaging in when-does-life-begin debates. That instruction grew out of meetings within the group, and sessions with Democratic strategists in Washington, which measured the appeal of various potential messages. HWPC was not the only organization that came to the choice theme as the centerpiece of the abortion rights case, but their participation in the deliberations represented a new degree of sophistication in controlling and directing the messages celebrities project.

Since then, the organization has convened creative and marketing executives from studios, as well as local advertising firms, to craft television commercials for an independent expenditure campaign on the abortion issue. But its main focus remains directing a cohesive choice message through celebrities, ensuring that they reinforce the symbolism feminist and abortion rights groups are using. Through 1990, the group functioned as a clearinghouse, trying to match celebrities with the pro-choice rallies in regions where they might have the most appeal. "We always try to pair the celebrities with grassroots leaders," said Tabankin. "We are trying to be the supporting cast—we will never be the centerpiece. . . . But [the stars] have validity when they talk from the heart on this."

Hollywood's awakening in 1989 to environmental issues even more dramatically displayed the community's eagerness to find new ways to influence political debate. The sudden greening of Hollywood—which acquired the intensity of a revival—drew on the general social concern fanned by fears of the greenhouse effect and depletion of the ozone layer that moved environmentalism to the top of the nation's agenda after the 1988 election. In the film community, what coalesced that diffuse interest was the disenchantment another Hollywood activist felt with a political career built on muscling friends for checks.

By fall 1988, attorney Bonnie Reiss, former treasurer of HWPC, was looking for a way to express her political ideals more directly. At the suggestion of Tabankin, a neighbor in her Santa Monica condominium, she attended a conference in Washington, D.C., on global warming. After listening for three days to the dire predictions of rising oceans and wheatfields reduced to deserts, all delivered by eminent scientists to eminent scientists, Reiss rose from her chair and said, "This is all very disturbing and impressive, but wouldn't one mention of the problem on 'The Cosby Show' reach more people than all your books and papers?"

It was a suggestion that reflected the emerging mindset in Hollywood—and one that instantly struck a chord with some of the audience in Washington. Among the people at the conference intrigued by Reiss's suggestion was veteran liberal gadfly Jeremy Rifkin, who has made a career out of popularizing issues at the most distant junctions of science and politics. Inspired by her own vision of Bill Cosby spreading the green revolution, Reiss arranged for Rifkin to visit Hollywood a few weeks later, hoping to use the trip as the springboard to "a mass attempt at organizing the industry for a mass public-education campaign."

Rifkin flew out in December and briefed a diverse assortment of industry leaders on enviromental problems through a series of dinners, from the Brat Packers at Meg Ryan's house to music industry figures at the home of Morgan Mason and his wife, rock singer Belinda Carlisle. One of the dinners was hosted by Lear and his wife Lyn, a psychotherapist, and a few weeks later, Reiss presented to the Lears her idea for an industrywide organization to insinuate environmental messages into television programs and movies. Norman Lear agreed to provide seed money, and Reiss set off to organize the group.

By January, Reiss was "going like gangbusters," recruiting stars, attorneys, publicists. But she soon ran into a wall. Reiss envisioned a large and diverse organization with hundreds of members across the industry; that was not Lear's vision. As is his manner, Lear preferred to organize a small, elite group of senior executives to green the rest of the industry; at the same time, his wife Lyn wanted to ensure there was room in that narrow circle for the wives of other Hollywood figures, who had suddenly awakened to the cause. The Lears' vision was incompatible with Reiss's. Rather than accept their approach, Reiss went off to pursue her own idea, christening the group the Earth Communications Office. Reiss quickly recruited dozens of industry figures, of varying stature and fame, to her organization. Meanwhile the Lears went ahead and formed their own group, the Environmental Media Association (EMA), whose board included only a handful of industry heavyweights—and some very well-placed wives.

Though they represented different philosophies of political organization, the two groups shared a common approach to political communications. Each was built on the belief that, through its dominant position in the culture, Hollywood can change political attitudes and personal behavior. As the Lears' organization argued in a message to supporters, "Films, television programs and music have a unique ability to infuse the popular culture with a particular message."

EMA worked with production companies and studios to insert environmental messages directly into scripts and to encourage filmmakers to tackle environmental subjects. Reiss's approach was more eclectic: it included working with producers, but also encouraging stars to shoot environmental public service announcements, and urging recording artists to include environmental messages on their album liner notes. By late 1989, it was almost impossible to avoid the messages: Candice Bergen was recycling bottles and car pooling on "Murphy Brown"; Barbara Streisand and Belinda Carlisle, among others, had inserted pitches for the environment in their latest albums; and characters on "thirtysomething" were volunteering to combat the construction of a local incinerator. On Earth Day in April 1990, Hollywood stars were inescapable at rallies across the country.

If sustained, this new burst of Hollywood activity is bound to have at least some influence on politics and personal behavior. Tremendous communications skill is concentrated within Hollywood, and all these activities—from the environmental groups to the HWPC choice campaign to People For the American Way—represent the most serious effort ever to focus that resource on a political agenda. Given the power of television and films in the society, and the way that celebrities can set models for behavior, there is enormous potential in the attempt, particularly in efforts to suggest alternatives in daily behavior, such as car pooling and recycling.

And yet there are grounds for caution, too. One reason is that the portion of the Hollywood environmentalists' effort that uses the public airwaves to proselytize for a private political agenda creates a precedent that must be carefully examined. To the extent that the effort involves the equivalent of inserting noncontroversial public service announcements into the body of television shows, there's little to quarrel with; the "disease-of-the-week" television movies already do the same. But if the effort moves beyond that to support an environmental vision of the proper energy path, or strategies to combat the greenhouse effect, or specific legislation, it could involve the networks in the public transmission of private propaganda disguised as entertainment.

Obviously television sends out messages of all sorts all the time. But even those sympathetic to the environmental cause need to consider whether they want to see the networks systematically employed as the tools of competing ideological groups. Would the Hollywood activists feel so comfortable if conservative writers and producers gathered to infuse television programs with the subliminal message that Mikhail Gorbachev is a fraud and the Cold War is not over? Or if the auto manufacturers and electric utilities gathered to insert into programs the argument that the threat from the greenhouse effect has been exaggerated?

On its own terms, too, the Hollywood left's effort to assume a more direct role in broadcasting political messages may in some respects become counterproductive. Even some of the most prominent Hollywood activists see the need to proceed carefully. "We're so arrogant if we think we can foist our ideas on the American people," said Patricia Medavoy. "We can fall flat on our faces unless we think it through."

Two concerns leap out. One is the same problem candidates face when trying to appeal here: Hollywood lives so differently from ordinary America that its perceptions of the political mainstream are often skewed. The early messages the Hollywood activists sent on the environmental and abortion issues found that vital center—but there remains the danger to liberals that the Hollywood communicators, as they grow more confident, will burden them with unpopular vanguard appeals on social and foreign policy issues. For all Hollywood's conviction that it has its fingers on America's pulse, selling movies is not really comparable to selling political messages. (As Warren Beatty observed, a moviemaker can do just fine appealing to only 10 percent of the public; the politician has to worry about 50.1.) And many Hollywood activists simply have no contact at all with the vast rolling blur of flyover states between Los Angeles and New York. Once, Representative Lee H. Hamilton, the stolid, crew-cut Democrat from Indiana and former chairman of the House Intelligence Committee, addressed a group of about sixty-five Westside and Hollywood liberals at the home of Stanley Sheinbaum. After taking questions for half an hour, Hamilton noted their direction, and posed one of his own: How many people here have been to Indiana? he asked. Two or three hands rose sheepishly in response. Hamilton paused a second, and then, with the slightest hint of a twinkle in his impassive eyes, asked: How many people here have been to Nicaragua? Instantly he faced a forest of upraised palms.

A second reason liberals might be cautious about a more visible political role for the film community is that Hollywood's lifestyle leaves it open to charges of hypocrisy when pushing some of liberalism's core messages: restraint and self-denial for the public good (on the environment, for example) or social fairness (in economic policy, say). Without major changes in personal behavior, the Hollywood environmental activists, among others, run the risk of embodying one of liberalism's most damaging stereotypes: the wealthy do-gooder who tells everyone else to tighten belts for the common good. "Look at the individual lifestyles," said Bob Hattoy, the Southern California regional director of the Sierra Club, and a skeptic of the Hollywood role. "It's consumptive to the point of greed and avarice. L.A. represents the worst of the consumer society, and these people are the worst symbols of that. Individuals may help, but I don't think with the industry of Hollywood we [the environmentalists] are in good hands."

His fear is well placed: causes, no less than candidates, can be dismissed as trendy when too much Hollywood glitter surrounds them. It's conceivable that too close an identification with Hollywood could reinforce the idea that environmental concerns are something only rich people can afford to act upon (rather than just fret about). Early focus-group testing by Reiss's organization found enormous resistance to celebrities delivering environmental advice, except where they could tie it directly into their own lives. Reiss is sensitive to this: she understands that before her group can sent out stars to preach conservation, she will have to convince some of them to surrender their Porsches and BMWs.

Maybe she will be able to, but more likely she won't. Hollywood is a community with an extraordinary lack of self-awareness. Without a tradition of serious press scrutiny, it has never developed an ability to see itself clearly or critically. It is generally too self-absorbed to recognize even the most blatant hypocrisy. At the first meeting of the Lears' EMA—an organization dedicated to guiding Americans toward a more environmentally sensitive life—the sensitive, energy-conscious Hollywood moguls showed up in gas-guzzling luxury cars and stretch limousines. No screenwriter would dare such a caricature of limousine liberals: it would be too ludicrous to imagine if it wasn't true. Another example: when the Southern California ACLU held a conference on cultural censorship in 1989, the assembled Hollywood liberals gleefully took the cudgels to the New Right philistines trying to censor obscenity on rock records or sex on television. But no one questioned the alleged attempts by powerful agent Michael Ovitz and actor Dan Aykroyd to prevent distribution of the film *Wired*, about the death of John Belushi because they disapproved of its portrayal of Hollywood in general and Belushi in particular. That was different. That was Hollywood.

After any sustained exposure to the Hollywood politicos, such examples make it difficult not to conclude that for some people in the film community, political "beliefs" are nothing more than another consumer good; that political activities, like a good psychiatrist, are just another means of boosting self-esteem—a way of saying, "I'm rich, I'm powerful, I'm important, and you know what, I'm a good person too. If I wasn't, I wouldn't have Ted Kennedy in my living room." This sort of public therapy is not, by any means, the only consideration that drives people from Hollywood into political activism—seventy years of interaction have demonstrated that an enormous assortment of psychological, ideological, and even business considerations bring together the capitals of glamour and power. But there's no denying Hollywood is a community rank with the self-satisfaction money breeds.

Despite all that—in some ways because of all that—the film community's growing interest in direct political action is no surprise. It merely extends the pattern that has guided the relationship between Hollywood and politics since the dawn of the television age: the solidifying consensus among many stars and moguls alike that they are more committed to a liberal agenda than the flightly, undependable politicians. On one hand, that attitude reached its zenith in the demeaning way Hollywood treated the Democratic presidential candidates during the fundraising auditions of 1987; that behavior was so extreme, it is unlikely to be repeated. New Jersey Senator Bill Bradley, a possible future presidential candidate, for example, has already collected huge sums in Hollywood without suffering the same indignities as his predecessors.

On the other hand, the belief is still growing in Hollywood that the communications skills required to win elections have eliminated the distance between politics and show business. That conviction is likely to see further expression on two fronts. One will be an increased willingness of stars to speak out politically; politicians are convinced it helps, and in Hollywood doubts about the propriety of using fame as a political weapon have evaporated. That belief will also be expressed through attempts to marshal stars and Hollywood creative talent in efforts, such as the two environmental organizations and People For the American Way, to alter the cultural images of political causes. ("There are one hundred Michael Deavers in the movie business, in the record business," said Danny Goldberg. "If this sort of thing is going to affect the next generation, we should be involved.") Though Hollywood's participation is likely to remain overwhelmingly liberal for some time, it would not be surprising if Hollywood Republicans eventually attempted to join that conflict with their own organizations. As the 1988 presidential campaign and the struggle over the constitutional amendment to ban flag burning demonstrated, cultural values are becoming a crucial political battleground, and Hollywood activists of all ideological persuasions believe, perhaps too confidently, that they know the terrain as well as anyone.

In time even those advances are bound to retrench at least somewhat, as they fail to produce immediate results. That cycle of enthusiastic engagement and rapid disappointment has marked Hollywood's political involvement from the start. But for the foreseeable future Hollywood is unlikely to again be as quiet as it was in the 1950s or even the late 1970s.

One reason is that the new Hollywood political institutions, just like the Communist party and Popular Front half a century ago, have a stake in encouraging activism that might otherwise not occur; as Edward Asner put it, politics in Hollywood has become "big business." Even in Hollywood the basic principles of bureaucracy apply: as long as these groups are churning out newsletters and holding recruitment meetings, they will find activities for their members.

Even more important, the continued compression of political dialogue into sound bites and visual symbols guarantees that causes and candidates will routinely seek out celebrities who can attract cameras and flash cultural signals to the public. At the same time, as a walk past any newsstand attests, the media's tendency to personify issues in individuals, and the public's hunger for news about famous people, show no signs of abating. These trends have combined to make fame a very tangible form of social power in America. To be famous is to have a public voice. And in any society, to have a public voice is to have influence.

When evaluating whether Hollywood figures deserve that influence or "belong" in politics, it makes more sense to discuss these basic trends than the propriety of ill-informed actors mouthing off about issues they do not understand. When that occurs, it is lamentable. But politicians often do the same thing. The real problem is that political debate is being reduced to symbols and sound bites, not that Hollywood figures are increasingly being used to supply them. The improbable credence given to many Hollywood figures as political spokespeople is merely a reflection of a more unsettling truth: that, as author Neil Postman has observed, in the television age credibility derives as much from "the impression of sincerity, authenticity, vulnerability or attractiveness" as from experience or knowledge. Hollywood activists are not even the best (worst?) examples of that phenomenon: Ronald Reagan demonstrated its validity far more as president than he ever did as an actor campaigning for Barry Goldwater or Harry Truman.

Hollywood stars are an ineradicable part of the political world we have made; but they did not make that world, and they should not be blamed for it. It's easy to overstate their impact: in all but very rare cases, they are only supporting political players. If stars could transfer their appeal directly into votes, as pollster Peter Hart notes, "we would just look at Q-scores [a star's favorability rating] and Roseanne Barr, Bill Cosby, or Harry Reasoner would choose our next president." Stars do not choose our presidents. They do not establish our political trends. They only respond to them. Their growing political prominence merely illuminates the other, less visible, changes that have remade our politics under television's unblinking eye. Put another way, Hollywood has not trivialized American politics; politicians, their consultants, the disengaged public, and the inexorable demands of television for abbreviated debate have trivialized American politics. We have all lowered the level of discussion to a point where stars can more easily participate.

That may be unfortunate, but it is irreversible. To say that Americans would make better political choices if they did not receive most of their information from television is like saying they would better understand the politics of France if more of them spoke French. It's true, but irrelevant. Television is the dominant medium of debate in American politics, and its requirements will continue to shape the form of political communications. The challenge for politicians is to find ways to communicate complex ideas and sympathetic values effectively under those rules, not to condemn the rules—or to the Hollywood figures who have found meaningful if limited roles to play within them.

In the end, it is difficult to blame the stars for exploiting those opportunities. For all the posturing and self-indulgence, all the hypocrisy and inanity that sometimes mark Hollywood's political activities, Hollywood is too deeply embedded in America's culture to be isolated from its politics. The film community is crowded with people who confuse having money with having something to say. But for many others in Hollywood—probably, in fact, most of those who work with causes—participation in politics represents nothing more than an opportunity to give something back to a society that has rewarded them beyond their wildest dreams. When they speak genuinely, and from their own experience, stars can move the public as effectively as any politician—sometimes even more effectively because they speak from a place politicians almost never approach—that is, the inside of their audience's imagination. And from that privileged and intimate position the most sincere and skilled can invest expressions of belief with not only glamour but dignity.

On the last day of the caravan Tom Hayden organized for the Democratic presidential ticket in 1988, the buses carrying the group pulled in for their final stop at East Los Angeles College, a small, weathered, largely Hispanic institution far from the city's wealthy Westside. The caravan had already traveled by plane and bus to Seattle, Portland, and Sacramento; Stockton, Oakland, and San Francisco; Long Beach and San Diego. It was late in the afternoon. Only a small crowd of students were there to greet them. Everyone was tired. Most of the reporters had already gone home. After the long weekend, the stars were anxious to do the same. They gave their speeches, signed some autographs, and piled back into the buses.

Actor Danny Glover, best known as Mel Gibson's co-star in the *Lethal Weapon* films and for his portrayal of Nelson Mandela in an HBO drama, remained behind. Since joining the tour the previous day, Glover had been a singular presence. While other stars used their time on stage to talk about the Supreme Court or the environment or to flay George Bush with clever one-liners, Glover spoke about drug problems in the neighborhood where he lived and his fears for his young daughter. Earlier in the afternoon, Glover had read to the students a Langston Hughes poem with such intensity that his voice trembled and cracked. While the rest of the stars sat in the buses, celebrating the end of the tour, Glover stood on the deserted stage with Julie Carmen, a young Hispanic actress. Glover had agreed to assume from Carmen the fast she had conducted the previous three days for the United Farm Workers. Cesar Chavez, the UFW leader, had begun the fast in July to protest the use of certain pesticides on grapes; in late August, after thirty-six days, he passed on the fast to Jesse Jackson. After three days, Jackson passed it on to the Reverend Joseph E. Lowery of the Southern Christian Leadership Conference. Lowery passed it on to Martin Sheen, who passed it on to actor Edward James Olmos, who passed it on to Sheen's son, actor Emilio Estevez. Eleven others had assumed the fast before it came to Julie Carmen. Now she was about to transfer the cross that symbolized the vigil to Glover in the empty courtyard of East Los Angeles College.

From the buses where the stars waited to return to Los Angeles, nothing she said was audible. All that could be seen were students milling, Carmen speaking, and Glover standing silently with a sign that said, "Boycott Grapes." Then the young actress Daphne Zuniga walked out of the bus and back into the courtyard. Morgan Fairchild followed. Then actress Alfre Woodward and actor Michael Gross. Soon the bus had emptied, and the entire troupe had returned to the stage. They stood quietly behind Glover and Carmen. There were no cameras present, no reporters, no publicists; only a handful of students remained. Carmen said a few words in Spanish. Then she took off the cross and held it out for Glover. The late afternoon sun dipped behind the downtown Los Angeles skyline. Glover stepped into the fading light and placed the cross around his neck.

AFTERWORD
TO THE VINTAGE EDITION

One evening last November I found myself standing with roughly a dozen television cameramen, assorted photographers, and a handful of other reporters outside a soundstage on a movie lot in Culver City. We were staring, with great earnestness, at a plate of rice on a table. Next to the plate of rice was another plate of rice, though this plate also had on it beans and tortillas. And next to that plate was another, more colorful setting: shrimp salad and mixed greens, breast of chicken stuffed with sun-dried tomatoes and mozzarella cheese, angel hair pasta with pesto, and an intriguing almond truffle, filled with pastries, fresh fruit, and homemade candy.

Standing behind the rice, and the rice and beans, and the shrimp salad and chicken and pesto was a tall thin man with glasses. He was talking about "the unequal distribution of food in the world," a disparity symbolized by the plates arrayed on the table in front of him. His name was John Hammock, and he was executive director of an organization called Oxfam America, which tries to fight world hunger. Hammock explained that one of the ways Oxfam raises money and awareness is through something called a Hunger Banquet, a bit of culinary agitprop in which those attending draw lots to see if they will eat like the 15 percent of the world in the rich countries (pesto and truffles and fine wines), the 25 percent in the middle (rice and beans), or the 60 percent barely subsisting (plain rice). As best I could tell, none of the three dozen cameramen and reporters assembled in front of Hammock had ever heard of him before or had even the slightest interest in anything he was saying.

It wasn't the lecture on world hunger that brought out the microphones from Fox and CNN and ABC Radio on this chilly evening. It was the incongruous fact that this Hunger Banquet would feature the participation of some of the most affluent, well-fed people on the planet: Hollywood stars like Cybill Shepherd and Mike Farrell, Ed Harris and Amy Madigan, Esai Morales and Lou Diamond Phillips, and, most of all, Mel Gibson and Danny Glover—who, in the end, decided at the last minute they couldn't be spared from the set of *Lethal Weapon 3* and instead sent video messages of support.

The absence of Gibson and Glover considerably dimmed the assembled star power, but the paparazzi and the television reporters appeared satisfied. They arrayed themselves outside the soundstage in a long thin line reminiscent of the troop deployments in the Civil War and hunkered down, waiting for the stars to arrive. Then, as the limousines and BMWs discharged their famous cargo, the reporters fired salvos of questions— Why are you here? Have you ever been hungry? Do you feel a little ridiculous?—and the photographers lunged and fired at the stars, just as they do almost every night somewhere on the west side of Los Angeles, at events not unlike this one.

Well, maybe not exactly like this one. Inside, Oxfam had transformed the soundstage into an elaborate set. On the far wall was a backdrop of a city at night; underneath it were tables covered with linen and set with china and crystal, Pellegrino water and white wine. The rich countries. On the other side of velvet ropes were picnic benches and plastic chairs arrayed under a bleak desert scene: the middle-class. And toward the back of the room was a large area that contained nothing but straw (or a good movie facsimile), crates, garbage cans, and some *faux* rocks from the prop department.

Soon the room was buzzing with activity. Videos of Danny Glover extolling Oxfam's work played incessantly on monitors around the room. Ed Harris and Amy Madigan served rice to the people milling around on the straw. Waiters in tuxedos circulated behind the velvet ropes, pouring wine for the privileged few, who looked appropriately uncomfortable. Women, dressed in black from head to toe, mingled exuberantly with men in suits, their high heels kicking up the straw as they passed. The television reporters, infuriating the young men and women assigned to tend them, broke out of their enclosure and swarmed into the crowd to get better shots of the stars playing peasant for a night. When I left, the last thing I saw was Cybill Shepherd, in a stunning red pantsuit, sitting on a plastic rock surrounded by photographers, eating a plate of rice with her hands.

As I drove home that evening, I wondered about the moral of this strange episode. There was no question that using pampered Hollywood celebrities to dramatize world hunger was so illogical as to be offensive. In its staggering lack of self-awareness, the event reminded me of a newsletter I had received some months earlier from the Environmental Media Association, which lamented the ecological damage caused by the greedy and selfish industrialized nations under a banner headline that declared: Too Many Rich Folks. I understand how living in Los Angeles can make you feel that way; but still it seemed a strange message from an organization founded by an affluent and exceedingly comfortable circle of Hollywood wives to teach the rest of us how to trespass less intrusively upon the earth.

But if Oxfam's celebrity Hunger Banquet embodied the insularity and arrogance of so much Hollywood activism, it also reminded me of the emotional and political logic that draws together stars and causes. Ego is unquestionably part of the attraction. On the way into the event, some celebrities, such as Esai Morales, unburdened themselves of puffed-up ideological diatribes on the offenses of the West against the Third World. But far more of the stars spoke quietly and modestly of their own limited ability to empathize with true privation and their un-complicated desire to help an organization whose cause seemed to them just. And as the reporters probed the stars for hypocrisy, some of the stars, quite fairly, turned the question around. "Obviously all of you wouldn't have been here if stars weren't here," said actor Lou Diamond Phillips, when asked if he found the entire event a bit strange. "Obviously we're all going to get in our limos and go home at the end of the evening. [But] it takes this kind of endorsement to get attention focused on the cause."

Just so. In that exchange, Phillips captured why so much of Hollywood politics is infuriating, but also why it continues to flourish. It is infuriating because stars often take purist positions glaringly in contrast with the reality of their cossetted lives. And it flourishes because the press turns on its strobe lights whenever they do take those positions—the more extreme the better. Add to the mix an apparently irreversible decline in the stature of political leaders, and you have the ingredients for undiminishing involvement by celebrities in the political world.

In the past months, the institutionalization of Hollywood political life has continued to accelerate. The Environmental Media Association, which could be the emblematic Hollywood organization of the 1990s in the way that the Hollywood Women's Political Committee dominated the 1980s with its focus on fundraising, congratulated itself one night in September 1991 with a huge awards banquet that demonstrated the group's reach, attracting dozens of stars and executives. (Few of whom, incidentally, could tear themselves away from their limousines and luxury cars long enough to follow the invitation's request to car pool.) The HWPC itself continued to aggressively raise money for candidates and causes. In New York a group called the Creative Coalition effectively mobilized celebrities against restrictions on funding for the National Endowment for the Arts. A fourth major organization, the Show Coalition, organized for its members an energetic schedule of lectures and panel discussions featuring senators, academics, and activists; the group even demonstrated an unusual degree of self-awareness by sponsoring a daylong seminar that examined the impact of movie violence on a violent society—the kind of intimate subject liberal Hollywood activists have avoided for generations.

In a different way, the film community's reaction to the Gulf War also hinted at a deepening level of self-awareness among the Hollywood stars about their political involvements. Though, by most accounts, opposition to the war was proportionately much greater in Hollywood than among the public at large, few of the stars rushed forward with inflammatory statements. (Actress Margot Kidder was perhaps the most prominent exception.) Undoubtedly, some celebrities—perhaps with Jane Fonda's experiences of twenty years earlier in mind—were reluctant to get on the wrong side of an overwhelming public consensus behind the war, especially once the fighting had begun. But their caution may have owed more to another Vietnam memory: many stars seemed genuinely eager to avoid actions that conveyed the impression to the troops that the public at home did not support them.

This outburst of thoughtfulness could have been temporary. The past year produced its usual quantity of impulsive, ill-informed, and often offensive celebrity declarations on the usual assortment of subjects. (Actor Alec Baldwin appears especially prone to ridiculous remarks.) And there were the inevitable examples of stars being manipulated into positions they seemed not to fully understand; actress Angela Lansbury—displaying far less perspicacity than J. B. Fletcher, the mystery writer she plays on "Murder, She Wrote"—appeared in Democratic ads opposing a term-limit ballot initiative in California in 1990, and then withdrew after the ads were criticized as misleading. (Her son, presumably trying to be helpful, explained that his mother "doesn't really read newspapers.")

But Hollywood's reaction to the initial maneuvering in the 1992 presidential race also pointed to a new caution. Though reigning box office champ Arnold Schwarzenegger was firmly planted behind President Bush—and so flamboyantly visible in his political activities that one national magazine speculated he might follow the lead of another prominent Republican actor and eventually seek the state's governorship—few stars had publicly aligned themselves with any of the Democratic contenders in the weeks leading up to the first primary.

Inevitably, though, the less flamboyant and more lucrative work of fundraising commenced across West Los Angeles as soon as the race began. Nebraska Senator Bob Kerrey, a handsome Vietnam War hero who once dated Debra Winger, quickly emerged as Hollywood's favorite candidate. Kerrey tapped as his national finance chairman one of Los Angeles's most effective fundraisers, Robert L. Burkett, the political adviser to film producer and businessman Ted Field.

Burkett was smart enough to know that a national financial base could not be built on Hollywood alone (or Los Angeles itself, for that matter). But Hollywood clearly represented one of the major financial assets available to Kerrey, a little-known figure on the national stage whose own state is better known for exporting beef than cash. In November, Kerrey held a successful fundraiser at the home of Fox's Barry Diller; the impressive guest list—which included record mogul David Geffen; top agents Jeff Berg, Ron Meyer, and Jim Wiatt; producers Sherry Lansing and Rosalie Swedlin; influential lawyers Ken Ziffren and Skip Brittenham; as well as actress Sally Field and her powerful publicist, Pat Kingsley—eloquently suggested that if Kerrey's campaign takes flight, he may find considerably more fuel in the film world.

Iowa Senator Tom Harkin also found friends among some of the industry's leading liberals, such as songwriters Marilyn and Alan Bergman and rock manager Danny Goldberg, as well as Iowa native Roseanne Barr. But, surprisingly, Kerrey's most spirited competition for Hollywood dollars came from the most moderate contender in the Democratic field: Arkansas Governor Bill Clinton. With his cerebral message and insistence that the party must reexamine many traditional liberal verities, Clinton is a much more unusual Hollywood favorite than the stylish Kerrey or the doctrinaire Harkin. But he has clearly found a niche, attracting the help of Tri-Star Pictures chairman Mike Medavoy, former Columbia Pictures chief Dawn Steel, and television producers Linda Bloodworth-Thomason and Harry Thomason, the creators of the hit show "Designing Women." In the time-honored tradition of waiting for the box office results before getting too friendly with anyone, some in Hollywood appeared to be hedging their bets between Clinton and Kerrey: Diller, for example, committed to raise funds for both men.

As this book goes to press, many other liberals in the film community are awaiting a final word from New York's inscrutable governor, Mario M. Cuomo, before committing to any of the candidates. But, with or without Cuomo elbowing at the trough, the contenders are likely to be disappointed by their final take in Hollywood. As the 1992 campaign commences, Hollywood is in the grip of a recession as deep as any it has known in twenty years; it appears likely that the industry, after giddily allowing salaries and expenses to soar during the euphoric 1980s, is heading for an extended period of consolidation.

How long that retrenchment lasts, and how much it constricts the film community's ability to fund campaigns, is one of the major unanswered questions about Hollywood's political role in the 1990s. Another is whether Creative Artists Agency chairman Michael Ovitz, whose ever-ascending influence within the industry was symbolized by his brokering the sale of Lew R. Wasserman's MCA to the giant Japanese firm of Matsushita Electric Industrial Co., will attempt to assume Wasserman's mantle as the film community's preeminent voice in Washington. A third question is who will be the next Hollywood figure to follow Reagan into the political world. It might be Schwarzenegger—though he would probably find it difficult to convince voters to see him as something more than Conan or the Terminator. In the meantime, former singer Sonny Bono— as unlikely a possibility as could be imagined—has organized a surprisingly accomplished campaign team to back his bid for a Republican U.S. Senate nomination in California.

Other questions will inevitably arise behind these as Hollywood's relationship with Washington continues to evolve. But as Oxfam America's Hunger Banquet so keenly demonstrated, some things about the interaction between the political and film worlds will never change. As long as they can attract the press, the stars of the 1990s—like the stars of the 1930s and the 1960s—will find the lure of political combat irresistible. With placards and bromides, they will always be there on the evening news: earnest, committed, and, oftentimes, more than a bit silly.

—Ronald Brownstein,

Los Angeles, December 1991

NOTES

Unless otherwise indicated in the notes, all quotations in the text are taken directly from interviews with the person quoted. The following abbreviations are used in the notes:

ALLEN: Steve Allen papers, private collection
AMPAS: Academy of Motion Picture Arts and Sciences Library
DDEL: Dwight D. Eisenhower Presidential Library
FDRL: Franklin D. Roosevelt Presidential Library
HHL: Herbert Hoover Presidential Library
JFKL: John F. Kennedy Presidential Library
LBJL: Lyndon B. Johnson Presidential Library
LL: Lilly Library, Indiana University
UCLA: Special collections library, University of California (Los Angeles)
USC: University of Southern California Cinema-Television Library and Archives of Performing Arts; also, Warner Brothers Archives (USC)
WSHS: Wisconsin State Historical Society Library

INTRODUCTION: THE CAPITAL OF GLAMOUR AND THE CAPITAL OF POWER

PAGE 4. Half a dozen other senators: Valenti interview.

PAGE 7. Politicians had gone to actors: Leo Braudy. *The Frenzy of Renown: Fame and Its History* (New York: Oxford University Press, 1986), p. 568.
Napoleon . . . small talk: Ibid., p. 403.
Buy Liberty bonds: *New York Times,* 4/9/18.
Unrehearsed realities: Roosevelt to Welles, 11/25/44, FDRL.

PAGE 8. A dazzling blind: C. Wright Mills, *The Power Elite* (New York: Oxford University Press, 1956), p. 345.

PAGE 11. Might as well take advantage: *Mother Jones,* 2–3/89.

PAGE 12. Nourish our sense: Dixon Wecter, *The Hero in America: A Chronicle of Hero Worship,* (New York: Scribner, 1941), p. 3.
A center of union: John A. Schutz and Douglass Adair, eds., *The Spur of Fame: Dialogues of John Adams and Benjamin Rush, 1805–1813* (San Marino, Calif.: Huntington Library, 1966), p. 212.
The best actor: Ibid., p. 181.

PAGE 14. Half the people: *P/M,* 9/24/44.
High Noon: *New Yorker,* 11/13/89.

CHAPTER ONE: MAYER, HOOVER, AND HEARST

PAGE 19. Hoover's private secretary: *Los Angeles Times,* 11/25/54.

PAGE 20. More stable and more powerful: Howard T. Lewis, *The Motion Picture Industry* (New York: Van Nostrand, 1933), pp. 13–15.
Rose 45 percent: Alice Goldfarb Marquis, *Hopes and Ashes: The Birth of Modern Times* (New York: Free Press, 1986), p. 55.
More than tripled: Lewis, p. 24.
Wall Street . . . imprimatur: Ibid., p. 79.

PAGE 21. Like a proud pigeon: Koverman to Richey, 1/28/29, HHL.
Fearing for his safety: Neal Gabler, *An Empire of Their Own: How the Jews Invented Hollywood* (New York: Crown, 1988), p. 83.
Moved to Boston: Bosley Crowther, *Hollywood Rajah: The Life and Times of Louis B. Mayer* (New York: Holt, Rinehart and Winston, 1960), p. 21.

PAGE 22. The first show he sponsored: *New Yorker,* 3/28/36.
An influence for good: Ibid.
Theater owners across New England: Crowther, *Rajah,* p. 41.
Financing small producers: Ibid., p. 44.
Coyotes howled. Gabler, p. 105.
Shut down at midnight: Carey McWilliams, *Southern California: An Island on the Land* (Salt Lake City: Peregrine Smith Books, 1983), p. 158.
Biological purity: Ibid.

PAGE 23. Employed Thalberg as his secretary: Crowther, *Rajah,* p. 88.
$600 a week: Bosley Crowther, *The Lion's Share: The Story of an Entertainment Empire* (New York: Dutton, 1957), p. 77.
Flowers dropped: *Los Angeles Times,* 4/27/24.
Procured telegrams: Crowther, *Rajah,* p. 118.

PAGE 24. Was a bouncer: Ibid., p. 115.

Butcher's sons: Leo C. Rosten, *Hollywood: The Movie Colony, the Movie Makers* (New York: Harcourt, Brace, 1941), p. 177.

Hunger for social recognition: Ibid, p. 70.

PAGE 25. Dark wooden floors: *Architectural Digest*, 4/90.

Well-manicured fingers: Dore Schary, *Heyday: An Autobiography* (Boston: Little, Brown, 1979), p. 114.

Promptly threw up: Ibid., p. 125.

Which would bring headlines: *New Yorker*, 3/28/36.

Took lessons in speaking: Samuel Marx, *Mayer and Thalberg: The Make-Believe Saints* (New York: Random House, 1975), p. 52.

Could also summon tears: *New Yorker*, 3/28/36.

Best acting of 1933; Ibid.

PAGE 26. Mayer hosted: Ibid.

Angle for invitations: Phone message from J. F. T. O'Connor, 5/8/39 FDRL.

I worship: Gabler, p. 119.

PAGE 27. Punched him on principle: Ibid., p. 88.

Strident authority: Ibid., p. 81.

Without a chaperone: Ibid., p. 107.

Mayer was a Puritan: Marx, p. 226.

Saccharine chronicles: Gabler, p. 215.

PAGE 28. Apparently the first film: Richard Schickel, *D. W. Griffith: An American Life* (New York, Simon and Schuster, 1984), p. 269.

Wilson had never endorsed it: Ibid., pp. 270, 298.

Harding repaid them: *New York Times*, 8/26/20.

Jolson led: *New York Times*, 10/18/24.

PAGE 29. Secretly pay all the expenses: *New York Times*, 10/30/24.

In 1924 he volunteered: Crowther, *Rajah*, p. 118.

Koverman . . . later became: *Los Angeles Times*, 11/25/54.

PAGE 30. Would be privileged to know: Mayer to Hoover, 9/2/24, HHL.

Glad to see you: Hoover to Mayer, 9/8/24.

Have you in mind: Hoover to Mayer 11/28/27.

Introduced Hoover to his father: Cummings interview.

Collection of faces: Schary, p. 114.

Make it easier for MGM: *Fortune*, 12/32.

PAGE 31. Should his filmmaking projects: Unnamed aide to Hoover, 9/23/24, HHL.

Cooperation of Belgian and British officials: Record of telephone call, 1/28/29, HHL.

Satisfactory wave length: Hoover to Mayer, 1/2/26, HHL.

Just the ammunition: Mayer to Koverman, 12/2/27, HHL.

Ambrose Bierce . . . once wrote: W. A. Swanberg, *Citizen Hearst* (New York: Scribner, 1961), p. 287.

PAGE 32. Hearst picked Davies: Ibid., p. 305.

He hired tutors: Ibid., p. 322.

Movies did poorly: Ibid., p. 365.

Hearst created his own: Crowther, *Rajah*, p. 122.

PAGE 32. Pay Davies the huge salary: Swanberg, p. 376.
Hearst at least tacitly agreed: Crowther, *Rajah*, p. 123.
263 delegates: Swanberg, p. 222.

PAGE 33. Dreamed . . . and yearned: Ibid., p. 369.
Mayer called Hearst: Marx, p. 55.
Called him Uncle William: Irene Mayer Selznick, *A Private View* (New York: Knopf, 1983), p. 83.
Secured the right: Crowther, *Rajah*, p. 95.
Mayer arranged: Rodney P. Carlisle, *Hearst and the New Deal: The Progressive as Reactionary* (New York and London: Garland Publishing, 1979), p. 68.

PAGE 34. His papers held: Ibid., p. 9.
His reach steadily expanded: Ibid.
In a front-page editorial: Ibid., p. 33.
Thalberg considered his problems: Crowther, *Rajah*, p. 137.
Mayer arrived: *Washington Herald*, 3/12/29.
Conferred with the candidate: *Los Angeles Times*, 6/16/28.
Smith's partisans organized: *Variety*, 9/26/28.
Which included Colbert . . . and Clayton: *Variety*, 10/31/28.
He received checks: *Los Angeles Times*, 10/27/28.

PAGE 35. Thrilled by the reception: Mayer to Hoover, 9/19/28, HHL.
He attended another: Mayer to Hoover, 10/9/28, HHL.
I cannot even induce: *Los Angeles Times*, 7/11/28.
MGM took out: *Variety*, 11/7/28.
One Jewish paper reported: *Los Angeles Times*, 2/1/29.
I am not a candidate: *Los Angeles Times*, 2/2/29.
His first dinner guests: *Washington Herald*, 3/12/29.
Business is going to be wonderful: Ibid.
Hoover entertained Mayer: Letter from Dale C. Mayer, HHL, 3/16/88.

PAGE 36. Fox pushed the Justice Department: Upton Sinclair, *Upton Sinclair Presents William Fox* (New York: Arno Press, 1970), p. 84.
Verbally approved the deal: Ibid., p. 86.
Would not see a cent: Crowther, *Rajah*, p. 143.
Fox told the outraged Mayer: Sinclair, p. 90.
Mayer warned darkly: Crowther, *Rajah*, p. 147.
He suspected one of his own: *New York Times*, 11/24/33.

PAGE 37. He hurried to appeal: Sinclair, p. 88.
A top Republican official: Ibid., p. 89.
Fox later said: Ibid., pp. 91–92.
Hit with a Justice Department suit: Crowther, *Lion's*, p. 161.
Lost control and left: Crowther, *Rajah*, p. 148.
Mayer assumed control: *Los Angeles Times*, 1/22/32.
Mayer explained to Willebrandt: Notes on call, 8/19/32, HHL.
He turned against the president: Carlisle, p. 49.
May have also been annoyed: Swanberg, p. 419.

PAGE 38. Came out behind Garner: Carlisle, p. 55.

PAGE 38   Hoover dismissed Mayer's overtures: Richard Norton Smith, *An Uncommon Man: The Triumph of Herbert Hoover* (New York: Simon and Schuster, 1984), p. 137.
Hearst editorially attacked: Carlisle, p. 68.
No more than half his time: *Fortune*, 12/32.
Some of us who are ruefully: *Los Angeles Times*, 2/22/32.
In June, Mayer visited: *Los Angeles Herald*, 6/2/32.
A giant Hoover portrait: *Illustrated News*, 6/17/32.

PAGE 39.   Reporters sought his assessment: *Los Angeles Herald*, 6/21/32, *Los Angeles Examiner*, 6/22/32.
You will not see: *Chicago Tribune*, 10/7/32.
Mayer was elected: *Los Angeles Times*, 9/23/32.
The Democrats, Mayer warned: *Los Angeles Times*, 10/6/32.

PAGE 40.   Mayer was back on the air: *Los Angeles Times*, 10/11/32.
Was forced to deny: *Los Angeles Examiner*, 10/28/32.
Mayer has no rivals: *New Yorker*, 4/4/36.
Hearst imperially dismissed: Crowther, *Rajah*, p. 197.

PAGE 41.   More than eight hundred EPIC clubs: McWilliams, p. 298.
This is no time to consider: *Los Angeles Examiner*, 10/8/34.

PAGE 42.   The producers collected funds: Rosten, p. 136.
Though some resisted: Ibid.
The Florida legislature responded: Ibid., p. 135.
Rallies were convened: *New Yorker*, 4/4/36.
This interpretation of current events: *Harper's*, 3/35.
Portrayed Sinclair as a foggy mystic: Carlisle, p. 87.
Printed a photograph of young hobos: Rosten, p. 137.

PAGE 43.   Chief end was not to offend: *Harper's*, 3/35.

PAGE 44.   Critics complained of Mayer's: Ibid.

PAGE 45.   The Screen Actors Guild formed: Nancy Lynn Schwartz, *The Hollywood Writers' Wars* (New York: Knopf, 1982), p. 29.
The ten largest studios had paid only: *Los Angeles Times*, 4/6/35.
Will Hays rushed West: *New York Times*, 4/7/35.
Joseph Schenck went to Florida: Ibid.
Mayer deplored: *Los Angeles Times*, 3/14/35.
Mayer proclaimed himself willing: *New Theater*, 9/35.

PAGE 46.   My doctors tell me: *New Yorker*, 4/4/36.
MGM and Fox inventoried: *Los Angeles Times*, 3/14/35.
The boys . . . will take care of things: *Los Angeles Times*, 4/6/35.
Merriam stood firm: *New York Times*, 10/23/35.
Davies had not done well: Swanberg, p. 410.
Mayer sided with Thalberg: Crowther, *Rajah*, p. 185.

PAGE 47.   Moved crosstown to Burbank: Ibid., p. 201.
Heaven knows I do not: *Variety*, 10/23/35.
Hearst left for New York: Ibid.
Mayer warned that others: *New York Times*, 10/23/35.
Hearst shuttered his movie operation: Swanberg, p. 486.

CHAPTER TWO: THE COMMUNIST DETOUR

PAGE 48. There are no bit players: *Saturday Evening Post,* 7/27/68.

PAGE 49. Morrie Ryskind declared: *The Nation,* 3/4/36.

PAGE 50. They are fascists or communists: *New York Times,* 4/23/44.
The population of Los Angeles: McWilliams, p. 14.
Only 20 percent of the people: Ibid., p. 165.
James M. Cain complained: Ibid., p. 237.

PAGE 51. More sanctified cranks: Ibid., p. 249.
Sinclair found more converts: Ibid., p. 297.
Watching the crowd heckling: *The Nation,* 3/4/36.

PAGE 52. Hollywood attracted the Party: Dorothy Healey interview.

PAGE 53. About three hundred people from the movie industry: Larry Ceplair and Steven Englund, *The Inquisition in Hollywood: Politics in the Film Community 1930–1960* (Berkeley: University of California Press, 1983), p. 65.

PAGE 54. From the age of five: Helen Gahagan Douglas, *A Full Life* (Garden City, N.Y.: Doubleday, 1982), p. 3.
Forget about acting: Ibid., p. 7.

PAGE 55. Her single film role: Ibid., p. 119.
Not until Melvyn was a teenager: Melvyn Douglas and Tom Arthur, *See You at the Movies: The Autobiography of Melvyn Douglas* (Lanham, Md.: University Press of America, 1986), p. 8.
He was accustomed: Ibid., p. 7.
He was exposed to Chicago's: Ibid., p. 9.

PAGE 56. An agent delicately suggested: Ibid., p. 62.
The size of his dressing room: Ibid., p. 110.
Passively accepted the Republicanism: Helen Douglas, p. 102.
My eyes were opened: *New York Times,* undated.
Douglas joined the Democratic: Helen Douglas, p. 103.

PAGE 57. In Vienna . . . she was told: *New York Times,* undated.
Suddenly seemed shortsighted: Helen Douglas, University of California (Berkeley) oral history, p. 49, UCLA.
Her husband . . . followed suit: Melvyn Douglas, p. 111.

PAGE 58. Stewart decamped for MGM: Donald Ogden Stewart, *By a Stroke of Luck! An Autobiography* (New York and London: Paddington Press, 1975), p. 194.
Almost pathologically equated: Ibid., p. 84.
He appeared entirely comfortable: Ibid., p. 205.
He had little interest in attempts: Ibid., p. 203.
Stewart happily subscribed: Ibid., p. 208.
Katy Dos Passos reported: Edmund Wilson, *The Thirties* (New York: Farrar, Straus, 1980), p. 488.
Have come to a dead end: Stewart, p. 213.
His unease crystallized: Ibid.

PAGE 59. To spread this great truth: Ibid., p. 217.

PAGE 59. Secure in the secret knowledge: Ibid., p. 221.

He is such a horse's ass: Marion Meade, *Dorothy Parker: What Fresh Hell Is This?* (New York: Villard Books, 1988), p. 252.

Stewart pulled together: Stewart, p. 223.

For the 1,200 people who assembled: *The Nation,* 5/13/36.

A core group . . . came together to form: *Hollywood Now,* 1/26/38.

Stewart was named: Stewart, p. 231.

PAGE 60. MPAC grew more rapidly: Ceplair and Englund, pp. 113–17.

PAGE 61. The Anti-Nazi League mounted: *Hollywood Now,* 6/25/38.

But the elder Dunne had suffered: Philip Dunne, *Take Two: A Life in Movies and Politics* (New York: McGraw-Hill, 1980), pp. 10–11.

PAGE 62. Douglas sent out a letter: Rosten, p. 138.

The group complained: *Hollywood Now,* 6/11/38.

Melvyn Douglas explained in one speech: Shrine Auditorium speech, undated 1938, Melvyn Douglas papers, WSHS.

Eventually he was named: Helen Douglas, p. 137.

PAGE 63. The Hollywood group produced: Ceplair and Englund, p. 119.

Douglas discovered that her fame: Helen Douglas oral history, p. 54.

PAGE 64. As exciting a life: Melvyn Douglas, p. 112.

PAGE 65. There is . . . no denying: Ceplair and Englund, p. 128.

PAGE 66. The Communist party abandoned: Irving Howe and Lewis Coser, *The American Communist Party: A Critical History, 1919–1957* (Boston: Beacon Press, 1957), p. 331.

The old fervor burned: Ibid., p. 339.

An overpaid movie producer: *Free World,* 10/43.

The universal humanity: Stewart, p. 237.

Hollywood leftists . . . signed: *New Masses,* 5/3/38.

Many Party members preferred: Jarrico interview.

PAGE 67. When he returned to Washington: *Los Angeles Times,* 8/15/38.

PAGE 68. Even Melvyn Douglas . . . found himself: Melvyn Douglas, p. 115.

PAGE 69. The proposals were voted down: Rosten, p. 141.

Dunne bet Melvyn Douglas: Dunne, p. 114.

The correct Marxist understanding: Stewart, p. 249.

I didn't think I could abandon Stalin: Ibid., p. 247.

Only a few defections: Jarrico interview.

PAGE 70. Stewart . . . found himself cut off: Stewart, p. 249.

Those individuals and organizations: Melvyn Douglas to MPDC Executive Board, 12/18/39, Melvyn Douglas papers, WSHS.

PAGE 71. The resolution is frankly intended: MPDC Minutes, 12/22/39, Melvyn Douglas papers, WSHS.

The Anti-Nazi League faded away: Schwartz, p. 150.

Switched to the isolationist line: Ibid., p. 163.

This bloody conspiracy: *MPDC Newsletter* 5/22/40, Melvyn Douglas papers, WSHS.

This is what our country faces: Ibid., 5/22/40.

An anti-Roosevelt slate: Ibid., 5/2/40.

PAGE 72. Douglas was talking about creating: Melvyn Douglas to Humphrey Cobb, Melvyn Douglas papers, WSHS, 6/10/40.
Wept with joy: Stewart, p. 257.

CHAPTER THREE: INTO THE MAINSTREAM

PAGE 74. Adolescents found models for their lives: Rosten, p. 367.
The movie idols have usurped: Ibid., p. 316.
A standard of reference: Margaret Farrand Thorpe, *America at the Movies* (New Haven, Conn.: Yale University Press, 1939), p. 113.

PAGE 75. The press corps covering Hollywood: Rosten, p. 7.
He even considered writing: Frank Freidel, *Franklin D. Roosevelt: The Ordeal* (Boston: Little, Brown, 1954), p. 191.
Roosevelt composed: Jones treatment, FDRL.

PAGE 76. Hawks offered the property: Hawks to Zukor, 4/24/23, FDRL.
Zukor assured Roosevelt: Zukor to Roosevelt, 5/2/23, FDRL.
West conferred: West to Roosevelt, 5/8/23, FDRL.
More than a year later: Roosevelt to Adolph Zukor, Jr., 7/22/24, FDRL.
Early . . . asked Hays: Early to Hays, 4/24/33, FDRL.
Hays passed along the suggestion: Hays to Early 5/5/33, FDRL.
Roughly every two weeks: *New York Times*, 1/31/37.
Three or four times a week: Early memo 5/6/33, FDRL.

PAGE 77. None of Roosevelt's predecessors: *New York Times*, 1/31/37.

PAGE 78. Were forced to open negotiations: Ceplair and Englund, pp. 38–45.
The Justice Department filed: Michael Conant, *Antitrust in the Motion Picture Industry* (Berkeley: University of California Press, 1966), p. 36.
The Justice Department proposed: Ibid., p. 95.
Jack Warner . . . told Philip Dunne: Dunne interview.
Harry Warner was angered: *Fortune*, 12/37; Sperling interview.
The studios signed a consent decree: Conant, p. 95.

PAGE 79. The Justice Department denied: Richard W. Steele, *Propaganda in an Open Society: The Roosevelt Administration and the Media, 1933–1941* (Westport, Conn.: Greenwood Press, 1985), p. 157.
Hollywood obediently churned out: Ibid., p. 161.
Better than eighty-five percent: Charles O'Reilly to Roosevelt, 11/20/40, FDRL.
I am convinced: Douglas to MPDC, 12/18/39, Melvyn Douglas papers, WSHS.
Endorsement letters from leading actors: Ralph Block to Marguerite LeHand, 11/16/40 FDRL.

PAGE 80. Two national radio broadcasts: Ibid.
The widely publicized visits of stars: Steele, p. 164.
Almost $850 million in bonds. Richard R. Lingeman, *Don't You Know There's A War On? The American Home Front, 1941–1945* (New York: Perigee Books, 1980), p. 175.

PAGE 81. Democratically serving and sacrificing: Richard Schickel, *Intimate*

Strangers: The Culture of Celebrity (Garden City, N.Y.: Doubleday, 1985), p. 79.

PAGE 81. Filled out the board: Responses to *Time* magazine, 1946, HDC papers, WSHS.

PAGE 82. It systematically identified: Executive board minutes, 3/21/44, HDC papers, WSHS.

Kenny told the group: Board meeting, 6/1/43, HDC paper's, WSHS.

Pepper . . . worked himself to exhaustion: *P/M*, 10/6/44.

The group raised $35,000: HDC accomplishments, 10/44, HDC papers, WSHS.

The HDC flooded: *Target for Today*, 5/44, HDC papers, WSHS.

A renegade Democrat: Hollywood Town Meeting, 5/11/44, transcript in HDC papers, WSHS.

Raise the price of milk: Costello statement in *Congressional Record*, 6/23/44.

Workers called at every home: Ibid.

PAGE 83. Ablest New Deal leader: *Fortune*, 3/40.

To sing the national anthem: Helen Douglas, p. 158.

She gave 168 speeches: Ibid., p. 167.

On the campaign trail she felt free: Ibid.

PAGE 84. Eleanor Roosevelt . . . counseled: Melvyn Douglas, p. 123.

You're asking me to sit: Helen Douglas, p. 186.

PAGE 85. Privately he wrote Douglas: Roosevelt to Helen Douglas, 3/2/44, FDRL.

The *Los Angeles Times* came out against: Helen Douglas, p. 190.

She began to find her voice: Alvin P. Meyers, University of California (Berkeley) oral history, p. 212, UCLA.

PAGE 86. Greater . . . intimacy with plants: Arthur M. Schlesinger, *The Coming of the New Deal* (Boston: Houghton Mifflin, 1959), p. 34.

Most politicians simply: Ibid., pp. 30–31.

PAGE 87. We refuse to permit: *Hollywood Reporter*, 2/7/44.

PAGE 88. He had been in journalism . . .: *Los Angeles Times*, 12/5/50.

Liberals suspected: Mary McCall to McGuinness 11/1/43, Westbrook Pegler papers, HHL.

PAGE 89. The Alliance's founders wanted: James McGuinness, "Double Cross in Hollywood," July 1944, Westbrook Pegler papers, HHL.

PAGE 90. Are politically and socially blind: *Los Angeles Daily News*, 6/6/44.

Montgomery assembled: Rosten, p. 160; George Murphy with Victor Lasky, *Say . . . Didn't You Used to Be George Murphy?* (New York: Bartholomew House, 1970), p. 264.

Willkie did in April: *New York Times*, 4/10/42.

PAGE 91. It's all over but the shouting: Hopper column, 6/30/44, Hedda Hopper papers, AMPAS.

She saw little opportunity: Hopper to McCormick, 7/19/44, Hedda Hopper papers, AMPAS.

Koverman introduced Brownell: Brownell interview.

PAGE 92. DeMille planned his spectacular: *P/M*, 9/25/44.

PAGE 92   A podium packed with stars: *Los Angeles Times,* 9/23/44.

A soporific treatise: Richard Norton Smith, *Thomas E. Dewey and His Times* (New York: Touchstone, 1984), p. 419.

PAGE 93.   Zanuck . . . raised substantial funds: Robert E. Hannegan to Grace G. Tully, 10/26/44, FDRL.

Spyros Skouras . . . converted: Charles P. Skouras to Hannegan 11/2/44; Spyros Skouras to Roosevelt, 6/3/44, FDRL.

Even Sam Goldwyn: Edwin Pauley to Roosevelt, 11/5/44, FDRL.

The thing I like: *P/M,* 10/2/44.

Immediately, Republicans complained: E. J. Kahn, Jr., *The Voice: The Story of an American Phenomenon* (New York and London: Harper and Brothers, 1947), p. 30.

Sinatra responded to his critics: *Los Angeles Times,* 10/12/44.

PAGE 94.   His fans . . . wore buttons: Kahn, p. 57.

At five he was performing: Barbara Leaming, *Orson Welles: A Biography* (New York: Penguin Books, 1986), p. 13.

At nine he ran away: *Current Biography,* 1941.

PAGE 95.   On July 20, 1939: Leaming, p. 205.

Schaefer . . . turned down the offer: Otto Friedrich, *City of Nets: A Portrait of Hollywood in the 1940s* (New York: Harper and Row, 1986).

PAGE 96.   Limped in with meager returns: Leaming, pp. 262–65.

Blitzstein fervently expected: Ibid., p. 160.

Welles considered Marxian dogma: "Orson Wells [*sic*] Asks Liberals To Be Radical," undated, Orson Welles papers, LL.

Years later, when he was questioned: Internal HUAC report on Welles interview 9/9/47, Westbrook Pegler papers, HHL.

Hoped FDR would break: *Free World,* 9/44.

Welles . . . considered Wallace: Ibid.

Wallace is the symbol: *P/M,* 9/20/44.

Even a union: *Los Angeles Times,* 5/10/44.

Giving the world back: *Free World,* 10/43.

PAGE 97.   No room . . . for Jim Crow: *Free World,* 7/44.

Could not find in its . . . budget: Milton Biow to John Hamm 8/28/44, HDC papers, WSHS.

The voice is the voice of Roosevelt: *P/M,* 9/22/44.

Welles's speech so stirred: Leaming, p. 357.

So . . . long-winded was Welles: *P/M,* 10/19/44.

He collapsed a few days later: *Los Angeles Times,* 10/24/44.

I have just learned: Roosevelt to Welles, 10/23/44, FDRL.

PAGE 98.   Privately imagining himself: Leaming, p. 358.

I've done nothing but turn them down: *P/M,* 10/20/44.

Davidson understood: *Time,* 9/9/46.

PAGE 99.   In early October: White House memo, 10/5/44, FDRL.

California Democrats sought: Executive board minutes, 8/18/44, HDC papers, WSHS.

The DNC lent: Pauley to Pepper, 10/12/44, HDC papers, WSHS.

Pepper offered . . . Dalton Trumbo: Pepper to Porter, 10/10/44, HDC papers, WSHS.

PAGE 99   He dispatched Jimmy Cagney: "Report of Campaign Activities," 10/27/44, HDC papers, WSHS.

PAGE 100. The GOP announced: *Los Angeles Times*, 10/31/44.

A raucous . . . rally: *P/M*, 11/3/44.

Radio's Christopher Marlowe: Eric Barnouw, *The Golden Web: A History of Broadcasting in the United States.*, vol. 2, *1933–1953* (New York: Oxford University Press, 1968), p. 213.

PAGE 101. Here's the way to win the war: All quotes from the broadcast are taken from the transcript in the HDC papers, WSHS.

PAGE 102. Hopper . . . passed him in a huff: Schwartz, p. 215.

Desperate for issues: Smith, *Dewey*, p. 433.

Weakened and corrupted the Democratic Party: *Los Angeles Times*, 11/2/44.

HUAC investigator . . . accused: *Los Angeles Herald Examiner*, 9/13/44.

Combs described the HDC: Jack Tenney oral history, p. 1142, UCLA.

Tenney summoned: *Los Angeles Times*, 10/14/44.

PAGE 103. Wanger . . . told an HDC rally: *Los Angeles Daily News*, 11/6/44.

CHAPTER FOUR: THE STAGE CLEARS

PAGE 104. George Pepper visited: Board minutes, 2/28/45, HDC papers, WSHS.

PAGE 105. On June 6: HICCASP internal history, p. 37, HDC papers, WSHS.

Pronounced like the cough: Ronald Reagan with Richard G. Hubler, *Where's the Rest of Me?* (New York: Duell, Sloan and Pearce, 1965), p. 166.

Harold Ickes joined: Alonzo L. Hamby, *Beyond the New Deal: Harry S. Truman and American Liberalism* (New York and London: Columbia University Press, 1973), p. 72.

Producer Milton Sperling: Sperling interview.

Liberalism is no longer: *Free World*, 12/44.

He seriously considered seeking: Leaming, p. 386.

He told me I couldn't win: Ibid.

Could have been a serious candidate: Cranston interview.

PAGE 106. Browder was replaced: Hugh Thomas, *Armed Truce: The Beginnings of the Cold War, 1945–1946* (New York: Atheneum, 1987), p. 162.

PAGE 107. Based on the unity of the Big Three: Crisis meeting, HDC papers, WSHS.

Truman was indistinguishable: *Hollywood Independent*, 6/15/46, HDC papers, WSHS.

When there was a conflict: *Los Angeles Evening Herald Express*, 9/5/58.

PAGE 108. Schary urged the group: Hittelman interview.

The group obediently backed Patterson: Ceplair and Englund, p. 238.

That is purely coincidental: *Time*, 9/9/46.

Many a Democratic politician: Ibid.

PAGE 109. Resignations are noted in minutes of 7/30/46 and 8/6/46 HICCASP board meetings, HDC papers, WSHS.

PAGE 109   On the advice of Jules Stein: Davis interview.
             HICCASP passed a resolution: Membership meeting, 10/2/46, HDC
             papers, WSHS.

PAGE 110.   Many . . . followed . . . onto the new letterhead: Richard J. Walton,
             Henry Wallace, Harry Truman, and the Cold War (New York: Viking,
             1976), p. 160.
             The PCA welcomed: Ibid., p. 133.

PAGE 111.   To know the nature of your enemy: *Beverly Hills Bulletin*, 2/27/47.
             I have maintained . . . vigilance: *New York Times*, 10/21/47.
             McGuinness warned dramatically: *New York Tribune*, 10/23/47.

PAGE 113.   Organized the Committee for the First Amendment: Gordon Kahn,
             Hollywood on Trial: The Story of the Ten Who Were Indicted (New York:
             Boni and Gaer, 1948), p. 135.
             Johnston declared himself: Friedrich, p. 325.
             Rather than directly challenging: Ceplair and Englund, pp. 261–71.

PAGE 114.   It was dreadful: Undated notes of phone conversation between Gar-
             land and Hopper, Hedda Hopper papers, AMPAS.
             Polls showed no great support: William L. O'Neill, *A Better World: The
             Great Schism: Stalinism and the American Intellectuals* (New York: Touch-
             stone, 1982), p. 223.
             Many mainstream newspapers: Walter Goodman, *The Committee: The
             Extraordinary Career of the House Committee on Un-American Activities* (New
             York: Farrar, Straus, 1968), p. 231.
             Thomas sought contempt citations: Kahn, p. 175.
             The studio chiefs announced: *New York Times*, 11/26/47.

PAGE 115.   MGM called in . . . Stewart: Ceplair and Englund, p. 363.
             MGM formally denied: Undated MGM statement, Dore Schary
             papers, WSHS.
             The Supreme Court refused: David Caute, *The Great Fear: The Anti-
             Communist Purge under Truman and Eisenhower* (New York: Simon and
             Schuster, 1978), p. 498.

PAGE 116.   250 were barred: Ibid., p. 515.
             After the American Legion: John Cogley, *Report on Blacklisting*, vol.
             1, *Movies* (New York: Fund for the Republic, 1956), p. 127.

PAGE 119.   The *Hollywood Citizen-News* declared: *Hollywood Citizen-News*, 5/9/45.

PAGE 120.   That irrational fear of communism: Helen Douglas, p. 232.
             She was briefly mentioned: Ibid., p. 274.
             His paper labeled Douglas: Ibid., p. 301.
             Pink right down to her underwear: Stephen E. Ambrose, *Nixon: The
             Education of a Politician, 1913–1962* (New York: Simon and Schuster,
             1987), p. 218.

PAGE 121.   Nixon tried to use: Ibid.
             The *Los Angeles Times* joined in: Ibid.
             Melvyn . . . spent the entire campaign: Helen Douglas, p. 324.
             The *Chicago Tribune* accused . . . Zanuck: *Chicago Tribune*, 7/3/52.
             Goldwyn . . . insistently told him: Goldwyn to Eisenhower, 4/15/48,
             DDEL.

PAGE 122. In March, the Eisenhower forces: McCarthy to Zanuck, Warner, Goldwyn (ZWG), 3/28/52, Warner papers, USC.

McCarthy instructed: McCarthy to studio captains, 4/10/52, Warner papers, USC.

PAGE 123. Zanuck even tried to enlist: McCarthy to ZWG, 3/28/52, Warner papers, USC.

The three producers . . . raised $14,125: McCarthy to Howard Petersen, 5/1/52, Warner papers, USC.

Zanuck attended a dinner: Zanuck to Goldwyn, 8/6/52, Warner papers, USC.

Leading figures in the . . . Alliance stayed away: Ibid.

Zanuck expressed concern: Ibid.

The sniping finally stopped: Ibid.

PAGE 124. His designation as the . . . co-chairman: Allen Rivkin memo, 8/1/52, Dore Schary papers, WSHS.

Schlesinger agreed. Brewer and Schlesinger interviews.

Spiegelgass turned to a Stevenson aide: Bill Blair interview.

Stevenson joined private clubs: John Bartlow Martin, *Adlai Stevenson of Illinois: The Life of Adlai E. Stevenson* (Garden City, N.Y.: Doubleday, 1976), p. 117.

PAGE 125. He wrote in his diary: Ibid., p. 260.

One of the "queens of society": Ibid., p. 86.

More conservative than his speechwriters: Ibid., p. 637.

PAGE 126. By adding Douglas Fairbanks, Jr.: Ibid., p. 175.

Tallulah Bankhead gushed: Ibid., p. 656.

Affected Myrna Loy: Myrna Loy and James Kotsilibas-Davis, *Myrna Loy: Being And Becoming* (New York: Donald I. Fine, 1988), p. 278.

I adored Adlai Stevenson: Lauren Bacall, *Lauren Bacall By Myself* (New York: Knopf, 1979), p. 202.

A combination of hero worship: Ibid., p. 204.

PAGE 128. I became very emotional: Ibid., p. 159.

I needed to dream: Ibid., p. 204.

The campaign . . . disrupted: Ibid.

PAGE 129. Stress anti-Communist themes: Entertainment Industry Joint Committee talking points, undated, Warner papers, USC.

Murphy remembers: Murphy interview.

Requisitioned from Jack Warner: Memo to Warner 10/6/52, Warner papers, USC; *Los Angeles Times*, 10/1/52.

The two stars joined Stevenson: *New York Times*, 10/25/52.

PAGE 130. Even after a platform collapsed: *New York Times*, 10/28/52.

To my fantasizing mind: Bacall, p. 200.

She was mad: Blair interview.

PAGE 131. Dazed with disappointment: Bacall, pp. 203–5.

Caused overall costs to rise: Alexander Heard, *The Costs of Democracy* (Chapel Hill: University of North Carolina Press, 1960), p. 403.

AFL Film Council demanded: *Variety*, 9/17/52.

PAGE 132. Petersen . . . anxiously wired Jack Warner: Petersen to Warner, 6/18/52, Warner papers, USC.

GOP leaders told Zanuck: Zanuck to Warner, 8/15/52, Warner papers, USC.

Their committee distributed: EIJC memo, undated, Warner papers, USC.

Kicked in $35,000: Zanuck to Murphy, 9/27/52, Warner papers, USC.

The committee sent $43,000: Zanuck to Goldwyn and Warner, 10/25/52, Warner papers, USC.

At least $10,000: Ibid.

The film community was not a major source: Roger Stevens interview.

PAGE 133. Having a tough time: Schary to Senator Blair Moody, 9/22/52, Schary Papers, WSHS.

Just $775 in all: Schary papers, WSHS.

PAGE 134. Offering his services: Zanuck to Nixon, 8/7/52, Warner papers, USC.

You won't handle it: Murphy interview.

Montgomery advised Eisenhower: Brownell interview.

PAGE 135. Along with Murphy he was given: Murphy, p. 351; Martin Mayer, *Madison Avenue: U.S.A.* (New York: Harper and Brothers, 1958), p. 299.

They saw a succession: Minutes of Hollywood Stevenson group meeting, 8/17/52, Schary papers, WSHS.

Schary tried to cure: Schary, p. 252.

Butler asked Dore Schary: Ibid., p. 301.

PAGE 137. Professional actors as candidates: George W. Ball, *The Past Has Another Pattern: Memoirs* (New York and London: Norton, 1982), p. 143.

PAGE 138. Brewer himself left Hollywood: Cogley, p. 158.

165 independent producers: Conant, p. 113.

PAGE 139. Partly because his political activism displeased: Schary, p. 5.

CHAPTER FIVE: JOHN F. KENNEDY AND THE REAWAKENING OF HOLLYWOOD

PAGE 144. He sure does go on: Richard Goodwin interview.

PAGE 146. People in Hollywood . . . are ready: *New York Times*, 10/20/59.

Members . . . recoiled as SANE criticized: Johnny Greene to Steve Allen and Robert Ryan, 6/16/60, Allen papers.

Allen and Ryan sided: Allen to Ed Meyerding, 9/26/60, Allen papers.

PAGE 147. The best-looking thing: Peter Collier and David Horowitz, *The Kennedys: An American Drama* (New York: Warner Books, 1984), p. 68.

Sinatra turned up regularly: Thomas M. Rees oral history, p. 8, JFKL.

PAGE 148. I'll get that dirty Jew: Ed Weisl, Jr., interview.

PAGE 149. California campaign had a reliable stable: Roz Wyman interview.

The New York theater aristocracy: *Boston Globe*, 10/18/60.

The notable exception: *Boston Globe*, 10/27/60.

Kennedy's advisers . . . kept Peter Lawford out: *Hollywood Citizen-News*, 7/11/60.

PAGE 150. If there's anything this President: *Newsweek*, 3/6/61.

The Kennedy men followed: Sorensen, Penn interviews.

The president enjoyed Sinatra: Kenneth P. O'Donnell and David F. Powers with Joe McCarthy, *Johnny, We Hardly Knew Ye* (Boston and Toronto: Little, Brown, 1970), p. 18.

PAGE 151. Sinatra introduced Kennedy to . . . Judith Campbell: Judith Exner with Ovid Demaris, *My Story* (New York: Grove Press, 1977), p. 86.

Kennedy began his own affair: Ibid., p. 99.

During the crucial Wisconsin primary: Stephen Smith to Pat Lawford, 2/23/60, JFKL.

At a Shrine Auditorium rally: *Boston Globe*, 9/10/60.

At a Washington fundraiser: DNC press release 9/19/60, JFKL.

The one event in which the campaign: *New York Mirror*, 1/12/61.

Though Sinatra spent much of the fall campaign: Kitty Kelley, *His Way* (New York and Toronto: Bantam Books, 1987), p. 304.

We're on our way: Ibid., p. 303.

PAGE 152. Kirk Douglas once ran into Kennedy: Kirk Douglas, *The Ragman's Son* (New York: Simon and Schuster, 1988), p. 349.

PAGE 153. Before long, Kennedy was needling: *Playboy*, 1/79.

PAGE 154. It's like watching a crowd: *Boston Globe*, 9/28/60.

And that Kennedy wanted himself portrayed: Warner Brothers production memo, 2/13/61, Jack Warner papers, USC.

PAGE 155. To walk into the Sands Hotel: Joe Naar interview.

PAGE 156. It was Hollywood where Joseph Kennedy: Doris Kearns Goodwin, *The Fitzgeralds and The Kennedys: An American Saga* (New York: Simon and Schuster, 1987), p. 391.

He was not a man: Smathers, Sorensen interviews.

PAGE 157. Johnson's men turned down the tape: Ed Weisl, Jr., interview.

Gossip mogul Walter Winchell: *Los Angeles Herald*, 5/9/62.

To sing a sultry and suggestive "Happy Birthday": *New York Times*, 5/20/62.

Sinatra . . . fixed up a guest house: Kelley, p. 307.

It gave the singer great satisfaction: Gershe interview.

PAGE 158. The Democratic National Committee announced: *Variety*, 12/2/60.

They had to charter a plane: Janet Leigh, *There Really Was a Hollywood* (Garden City, N.Y.: Doubleday, 1964), p. 267.

Reduced the debt by $1 million: Herbert E. Alexander, *Financing the 1960 Election* (Princeton, N.J.: Citizens' Research Foundation, 1962), p. 80.

Sinatra organized a concert at Carnegie Hall: Taylor Branch, *Parting the Waters: America in the King Years, 1954–1963* (New York: Simon and Schuster, 1988), p. 385.

California Democratic party fund-raiser: *Los Angeles Times*, 5/15/61.

PAGE 159. He courted the friendship of Bill Goetz: Gershe interview.

PAGE 160. Maltz . . . urged Sinatra: Maltz oral history, pp. 953–54, UCLA.

John Wayne . . . publicly wondered: *Los Angeles Herald and Express*, 3/22/60.

Sinatra . . . backed off: *New York Times*, 4/10/60.

PAGE 160.   Dick Powell . . . declared: *Los Angeles Times*, 10/22/60.

The spine-tingling worry: *New York World Telegram & Sun*, 12/13/60.

PAGE 161.   Letters deluged Kennedy headquarters: *Wall Street Journal*, 12/30/60.

Never seriously concerned Kennedy's inner circle: Sorensen interview.

Sinatra sat at the head table: *New York Times*, 11/19/61.

Robert Kennedy was the first: Victor S. Navasky, *Kennedy Justice* (New York: Atheneum, 1977), p. 46.

Pegler pointedly questioned: Pegler column, undated 1960, Pegler papers, HHL.

PAGE 162.   He carried on an affair: Clyde Tolson to J. Edgar Hoover, 7/13/60, Giancana file, FBI.

Among the services Sinatra provided: Exner, p. 116.

FBI wiretaps intercepted: G. Robert Blakey and Richard N. Billings, *The Plot to Kill the President* (New York: Times Books, 1981), p. 383.

Giancana was murdered: Ibid., pp. 390–91.

Select officials learned: Myer Feldman interview.

PAGE 163.   His long-standing friendships . . . were no secret: Naar interview; Kelley, p. 288.

He had worked for Harry Cohn: Hoover to Attorney General, 9/16/47, Roselli file, FBI.

Mixed with the top level: Michael Selsman interview.

The most important link: *New York Times*, 6/27/76.

The president had sloughed off: Feldman interview.

PAGE 164.   I am delighted: Kennedy to Sinatra, 10/23/61, JFKL.

The Justice Department had launched: Hank Messick, *The Beauties and the Beasts: The Mob in Show Business* (New York: David McKay, 1973), p. 183.

FBI wiretaps of Roselli: Blakey and Billings, p. 379.

Exner's claim that Kennedy also knew: *People*, 2/29/88.

PAGE 165.   The last phone contact with Exner: Blakey and Billings, p. 380.

O'Donnell informed a friend: O'Donnell to Leo Freedman, 1/29/62, JFKL.

PAGE 166.   The invitation was withdrawn: Arthur M. Schlesinger, Jr., *Robert Kennedy and His Times* (New York: Ballantine Books, 1978), p. 534.

Even many of Sinatra's friends: Naar, Gershe interviews.

The FBI wiretaps picked up Giancana: *Rolling Stone*, 3/19/81.

PAGE 168.   A white entertainer can say anything: Arnold Shaw, *Belafonte* (Philadelphia and New York: Chilton, 1960), p. 193.

He would scrawl bitter graffiti: Ibid., p. 45.

Attempted to evict him: Ibid., p. 149.

Darryl Zanuck refused: Ibid., pp. 241–43.

Belafonte first met King: Branch, p. 185.

Belafonte joined King: Ibid., p. 218.

The next year Belafonte was back: *New York Times*, 10/26/58.

PAGE 169.   When King wanted to mount: Branch, p. 388.

Whatever else you need: Ibid., p. 735.

PAGE 169   The stars performed on a stage of coffin crates: *New York Times*, 3/25/65.

King quietly told a story: Franciosa interview.

Used his credibility: Branch, p. 578; *New York Times*, 5/1/65.

Paul Newman nervously read: Branch, p. 804.

PAGE 170.   Lancaster . . . actually didn't attend: Lancaster interview.

King quietly told a story: Franciosa interview.

King left Los Angeles: *Jet*, 6/13/63.

A petition of support: Thomas Gentile, *March on Washington: August 28, 1963* (Washington, D.C.: New Day Publications, 1983), p. 222.

From New York came Heston: *Variety*, 9/4/63.

Led by Brando and Belafonte: *Los Angeles Herald*, 8/28/63.

Bob Dylan, Joan Baez . . .: *Variety*, 9/4/63.

Hoover had FBI agents: Gentile, p. 212.

This plane trip: *New York Times*, 8/25/63.

PAGE 171.   When Sidney Poitier arrived: Sidney Poitier, *This Life* (New York: Knopf, 1980), p. 131.

Only a handful of blacks: *Variety*, 6/6/63.

PAGE 172.   Only when they have a crap game: *New York Times*, 11/29/61.

Herbert Hill . . . came to Hollywood: *New York Times*, 6/26/63.

White stars . . . threatened: *Hollywood Citizen-News*, 7/13/63.

The summer of crisis: *New York Times*, 6/30/63.

Executives . . . predicted breakthroughs: *Wall Street Journal*, 9/24/63.

PAGE 173.   Black stars didn't display: Hathaway interview.

Blacks occupy few important jobs. *Premiere*, 3/89.

PAGE 174.   Johnson had . . . no political relationships: Hand interview.

He would call Wayne: Valenti interview.

PAGE 175.   Virtually an unlimited supply: *New York Times*, 10/13/64.

He could manage only Lundigan: Murphy, p. 367.

Politics has hit Hollywood: *New York Times*, 4/17/60.

In his capacity as co-chairman: *Los Angeles Times*, 10/2/60.

Even Dick Powell acknowledged: *Los Angeles Times*, 10/22/60.

CHAPTER SIX: THE GLAMOUR OF MONEY

PAGE 178.   We're all right through the primary: Bart Lytton oral history, p. 7, JFKL.

PAGE 181.   The son of Orthodox Jews: *Los Angeles Times*, 1/30/78.

Wasserman impressed MCA's founder: *Time*, 1/1/65.

MCA controlled: Dan E. Moldea, *Dark Victory: Ronald Reagan, MCA, and the Mob* (New York: Viking, 1986), p. 17.

Was named vice-president: Michael Pye, *Moguls: Inside the Business of Show Business* (New York: Holt, Rinehart and Winston, 1980), p. 47.

MCA bid aggressively: Moldea, p. 30.

Among the first clients: Ibid., p. 168.

The firm's breakthrough came: *Fortune*, 7/60.

PAGE 182.   He negotiated for Jimmy Stewart: Pye, p. 45.

PAGE 183.   I felt . . . we could do better: *New York Times*, 10/20/85.

PAGE 183   Once MCA broke the united front: David F. Prindle, *The Politics of Glamour: Ideology and Democracy in the Screen Actors Guild* (Madison: University of Wisconsin Press, 1988), p. 80.

PAGE 184.   MCA's Revue Productions subsidiary: *Fortune,* 7/60.
MCA paid out nearly $12 million: *The Reporter,* 11/23/61.
MCA has been the leader: Ibid.
Stein insisted that his policy: Stein to Warner, 10/4/52, Jack Warner papers, USC.

PAGE 185.   Wasserman apparently supported: Walter Jenkins to Wasserman, 3/31/64, LBJL.

PAGE 186.   Dorothy Chandler . . . turned to Wasserman: David Halbertstam, *The Powers That Be* (New York: Knopf, 1979), p. 274.
It announced plans to spin off: Moldea, pp. 162–63.

PAGE 187.   Its 1,400 clients were set loose: Ibid., p. 211.
The major surprise: *W,* 10/8/82.
It was tougher than that: Murphy interview.
Even granted an occasional interview: *New York Times,* 5/8/62.

PAGE 188.   He was a precocious . . . achiever: *Harper's,* 2/58.
Within a few years each was a partner: Ibid.
Benjamin meanwhile: *New York Times,* 7/22/62.

PAGE 189.   When a friend suggested: *Harper's,* 2/58.
The two men showed a profit: Ibid.

PAGE 190.   They drew the same salary: *Wall Street Journal,* 5/9/66; Youngstein interview.
An ardent liberal: United Nations Association of the United States, *Robert S. Benjamin: A Citizen's Citizen* (New York: United Nations Association, 1980), p. 83.
Moved him away from partisan politics: Ibid., p. 84.
A full day of activities: *New York Times,* 5/20/62.

PAGE 191.   Krim's labors produced: Herbert E. Alexander, *Responsibility in Party Finance* (Princeton, N.J.: Citizen's Research Foundation, 1963), p. 16.

PAGE 192.   Almost immediately, he expanded: *New York Times,* 4/29/66.

PAGE 193.   It exported little money: Theodore H. White, *The Making of the President, 1972* (New York: Atheneum, 1973), p. 124.
Lawyer named Eugene L. Wyman: *Los Angeles Times,* 8/27/62.
His approach was later summarized: Bill Connell to Marvin Watson, 5/9/67, LBJL.

PAGE 194.   California provided: Herbert E. Alexander, *Financing the 1964 Election* (Princeton, N.J.: Citizens' Research Foundation, 1966), p. 137.
Wasserman reached down: Congressional Quarterly, "1964 Campaign Contributions and Expenditures," *CQ,* 1966.
Wasserman found time: *Newsweek,* 4/27/64.
The White House letter . . . was returned: Valenti to Wasserman, 6/22/64.

PAGE 195.   Johnson offered Wasserman: Valenti interview.
The development of a substantial base: Connell to Watson, 5/9/67, LBJL.

PAGE 196.   One of California's few lone wolves: Ibid.

PAGE 196   He wrote the president's daughter: Wasserman to Lynda Johnson, 6/26/67, LBJL.
　　　　　Politicians called them turnkey affairs: Strauss, Charles Manatt interviews.
　　　　　Just show up: White interview.
　　　　　The most significant link: *New York Times*, 6/27/76.

PAGE 197.   Hefner once paid: Moldea, p. 338.
　　　　　I've never seen him: Wasserman interview with Seymour Hersh, 3/3/76.
　　　　　Wasserman invited Korshak: *Los Angeles Times*, 8/23/76.
　　　　　The one meeting Kennedy's advisers convened: Sorensen interview.

PAGE 198.   He sometimes attended church: James Jones interview.
　　　　　I am always cheered: Johnson to Krim, 8/25/65, LBJL.

PAGE 199.   The two men bought a helicopter: Jones interview.
　　　　　In the last year: Johnson diary cards, LBJL.
　　　　　By all means: Jacobsen to Johnson, 5/21/66, LBJL.
　　　　　His effectiveness would be destroyed: Christian to Johnson, 12/5/67, LBJL.
　　　　　No inkling of his influential role: Jack Valenti, *A Very Human President* (New York: Norton, 1975), pp. 367–68.

PAGE 200.   Krim had reduced the debt: John Criswell to Watson, 12/5/66, LBJL.
　　　　　Johnson told Krim: Lyndon B. Johnson, *The Vantage Point: Perspectives of the Presidency, 1963–69* (New York: Holt, Rinehart and Winston, 1971), p. 427.
　　　　　The polls that Krim commissioned: Watson to Johnson, 10/30/67 and 11/21/67, LBJL.

PAGE 201.   Respond as readily as Johnson: Watson to Jones, 1/31/68, LBJL.
　　　　　A reliable team man: Memo of Krim call 2/6/68, LBJL.
　　　　　A detailed financial plan: Krim to Watson, 1/3/68, LBJL.
　　　　　The president had approved: Jones to Watson, 2/13/68.
　　　　　He rallied forty of the faithful: *New York Times*, 3/22/68.
　　　　　Krim briefed Johnson: White House daily diary, 3/22/68, LBJL.
　　　　　The president . . . told the White House operator: White House daily diary, 3/31/68, LBJL.
　　　　　He spoke with Bob Strauss: Strauss interview.
　　　　　By early afternoon, he was sitting: White House daily diary, 3/31/68, LBJL.

PAGE 202.   Krim argued . . . that only Johnson: Johnson, p. 434.
　　　　　Krim and his wife returned: White House daily diary, 3/31/68.
　　　　　Johnson . . . softly told him: Johnson, p. 434.
　　　　　Everyone had left the White House: White House daily diary, 3/31/68.

PAGE 203.   Wasserman loaned Humphrey's campaign: Herbert E. Alexander, *Financing the 1972 Election* (Lexington, Mass.: Lexington Books, 1976), p. 154.
　　　　　That was after contributing over $54,000: Ibid.

PAGE 204.   Palevsky and Palmieri assisted: *Los Angeles Times*, 2/4/73; Palmieri interview.

PAGE 205. Palevsky contributed over $319,000: Alexander, *1972*, p. 377.

Rubin liked what he saw: Rubin interview.

Provided another $300,000: Alexander, *1972*, p. 125.

PAGE 206. Looked like a certain winner: *New York*, 6/24/74.

Bob Hope was the lone star: *Variety*, 10/2/73.

PAGE 209. Brown didn't know much more about music: Azoff interview.

They provided more than a quarter: Herbert E. Alexander, *Financing the 1976 Election* (Washington, D.C.: Congressional Quarterly, 1979), p. 227.

PAGE 210. The Federal Election Commission complicated: Fred Eiland interview.

PAGE 211. Most of the Malibu group united: Willens interview.

Rubin worked hard for . . . Kennedy: Herbert E. Alexander, *Financing the 1980 Election* (Lexington, Mass.: Lexington Books, 1983), p. 231.

So did Ashley: Ashley interview

PAGE 212. Hedged his bets: Alexander, *1976*, pp. 827–29.

PAGE 213. Rothman . . . who became chairman: *Los Angeles Times*, 2/9/82.

PAGE 217. It was in Lang's home: *Rolling Stone*, 5/10/73.

PAGE 220. Park even sent him to Las Vegas: Bill Boyarsky, *Ronald Reagan* (New York: Random House, 1981), p. 77.

PAGE 221. A gushing video tribute: *Los Angeles Times*, 7/15/86.

PAGE 222. The President discussed . . . with . . . Heston: *Washington Post*, 11/3/83.

Complaints lodged against him: *Los Angeles Times*, 4/4/89.

PAGE 223. The Justice Department delayed: *Los Angeles Times*, 11/1/68.

The two companies . . . dropped: *New York Times*, 4/25/69.

Carter's Justice Department stopped MCA: *New York Times*, 10/16/81; *Washington Post*, 1/1/81.

To buy into a merger: *Washington Post*, 1/1/84.

CHAPTER SEVEN: THE POWER OF GLAMOUR

PAGE 226. I was always a good guy: *Coronet*, 9/66.

In one ad . . . Gene Kelly: *Time*, 10/7/66.

Forsythe . . . was inundated: Forsythe interview.

Well, George, here we are: Lou Cannon, *Ronnie and Jesse: A Political Odyssey* (Garden City, N.Y.: Doubleday, 1969), p. 131.

PAGE 227. Journalists wondered: *Coronet*, 9/66.

It is immoral for an actor: *Los Angeles Times*, 11/21/67.

PAGE 228. Ultimately was forced: Allen interview.

PAGE 229. I have neglected the forum: Bob Thomas, *Marlon: Portrait of the Rebel as an Artist* (New York: Random House, 1973), p. 184.

He sent an Indian woman: *Los Angeles Times*, 3/28/73.

With the . . . purpose of showing the world: John Wayne to Lyndon Johnson, 12/28/65, LBJL.

PAGE 230. I find myself talking: Emanuel Levy, *John Wayne: Prophet of the American Way of Life* (London: Scarecrow Press, 1988), p. 278.

PAGE 231.   Paul Newman captured: *Playboy,* 7/68.
PAGE 233.   When McCarthy stood alone: Ibid.
PAGE 235.   Polish pool halls: *Newsweek,* 4/8/68.
PAGE 236.   Johnson's supporters complained: *Variety,* 3/20/68.
            He was uncomfortable: *Rolling Stone,* 7/5/73.
            Fought over a box: Podesta interview.
            He was not part of his times: *New York Times,* 4/22/68.
            What I'm most interested in: *New York Times,* 8/8/71.
PAGE 237.   That fall she campaigned: McGovern interview.
            McGovern recognized the potential value: Ibid.
PAGE 238.   MacLaine carried McGovern's message: *Newsweek,* 9/25/72.
            From the first primary: Ibid.
PAGE 239.   A bunch of overgrown boys: Ibid.
            Increased male sterilization: *Los Angeles Herald Examiner,* 6/15/71.
            It's really not all that generous: McGovern interview.
            She took a central role: *New York Times,* 6/28/72.
            She was named co-chair: *Los Angeles Times,* 8/26/72.
            Large numbers of Americans: *New York Times,* 5/18/72.
PAGE 241.   In Wisconsin a group of rowdy students: Hart interview.
PAGE 244.   Campaign workers joked: Caddell interview.
            He tracked down . . . top stars: *Los Angeles Times,* 4/11/72; McGovern
            interview.
            In California, he convinced: *New York Times,* 4/17/72.
PAGE 245.   For the climactic . . . concert: *New York Times,* 6/15/72.
            Produced at least $1 million: Alexander, *1972,* p. 125.
            The president mingled: *Los Angeles Times,* 8/28/72.
            Hollywood Wax Museum: *Life,* 9/8/72.
PAGE 246.   Stamp of approval . . . for McGovern: *New York Times,* 6/15/72; Beatty
            interview.
PAGE 248.   A private poll: *New Times,* 10/19/73.
            An expression of resistance: *New York Times,* 2/28/76.
PAGE 250.   Find some way: *Washington Post,* 7/29/73.
PAGE 251.   It seemed so inadequate: Peter N. Carroll, *Famous in America: The
            Passion to Succeed* (New York: Dutton, 1985), p. 96.
            She had to hock jewelry: Stephen Jaffe interview.
PAGE 252.   Visited Angela Davis: Carroll, p. 157.
            Can any of you say: *Show,* 3/71.
            A revolutionary woman: *New York Times,* 2/3/74.
            Fonda . . . had turned down roles: Ibid.
PAGE 253.   Twelve hundred Hollywood figures: *Los Angeles Herald Examiner,*
            3/6/71.
            Fonda buttonholed . . . top stars: Jaffe interview.
            Plans were launched: *Esquire,* 2/77.
            Strangled by sectarian debate: Jaffe interview.
            A 1967 trip to the front: *Variety,* 5/10/67.
PAGE 254.   On the same wavelength: Forsythe interview.
            Who dropped out . . . in her teens: Thomas Kiernan, *Jane Fonda:
            Heroine for Our Time* (New York: Delilah Books, 1982), pp. 63–65.

PAGE 255.   She defined herself as a socialist: Carroll, p. 156.
            That was so naive: Lane interview.

PAGE 256.   I didn't even know: Barbara Zheutlin and David Talbot, *Creative Differences: Profiles of Hollywood Dissidents* (Boston: South End Press, 1978), p. 140.

PAGE 257.   The encroachment of the American cancer: U.S. Foreign Broadcast Information Service (FBIS), Asia and Pacific Daily Report, 7/27/72 p. K-32.
            It was the horror: Fonda appearance on Phil Donahue, 9/6/72.
            There are no military targets: FBIS, 7/17/72, p. K-27.

PAGE 258.   U.S. society is not: FBIS, 7/25/72, p. K-14.
            Nothing could be further from the truth: *Vanity Fair*, 11/88.
            We . . . support the Vietnamese people's struggle: FBIS, 7/25/72, p. K-14.
            Makes one a war criminal: FBIS, 7/18/72, p. K-20.

PAGE 259.   Never in my life: FBIS, 7/18/72, p. K-20.
            Better citizens: FBIS, 7/24/72, p. K-24.
            The humane tutelage: Donahue, 9/6/72.
            She would welcome the forum: *Washington Post*, 8/26/72; Steve Rivers interview.

PAGE 260.   He may have offered: Tom Hayden, *Reunion: A Memoir* (New York: Random House, 1988), p. 455.
            The South Carolina state legislature: *Hollywood Reporter*, 4/23/73.
            Protesters hanged her in effigy: *Los Angeles Times*, 4/13/73.
            Indiana's state Senate: *Newsweek*, 4/16/73.
            Whether to remove her tongue: *New York Times*, 2/3/74.
            There was most probably torture: *Newsweek*, 4/16/73.
            Letter to the *Los Angeles Times*: *Los Angeles Times*, 6/9/73.

PAGE 261.   The Nixon administration worried: *Washington Post*, 2/18/75.

PAGE 264.   He sat out the social movements: *Playgirl*, 8/76.
            I find it boring: Ibid.

PAGE 265.   Redford accepted an appointment: *Time*, 2/2/76.

PAGE 267.   He would pull into a town: *Los Angeles Herald Examiner*, 4/29/84.
            I don't believe anyone cares: *Saturday Review*, 7/8/72.

PAGE 270.   Probably the most hated man: *Wall Street Journal*, 9/28/89.

PAGE 272.   Stardom is a megaphone: Stipe interview.

PAGE 273.   Tendency to translate: Braudy, p. 508.

CHAPTER EIGHT: THE REAGAN BACKLASH AND BEYOND

PAGE 276.   Rafshoon . . . listed a series of contrasts: Kathleen Hall Jamieson, *Packaging the Presidency: A History and Criticism of Presidential Campaign Advertising* (New York: Oxford University Press, 1984), p. 404.

PAGE 277.   Saw him principally as an actor: Wirthlin interview.
            They were mostly old friends: *Los Angeles Times*, 11/3/80.
            Sinatra, Dean Martin, and Wayne Newton performed: *US*, 1/22/80.
            Last year I lost a friend: Jamieson, p. 444.

PAGE 277   Voters who didn't like: Caddell, Wirthlin, Peter Hart interviews.
PAGE 278.   Wyler said ruefully: Heston interview.
            Only a hundred responses: Mason interview.
PAGE 279.   At a time when we have a former actor: *U.S. News and World Report*, 4/26/82.
            The relentless political message: *Los Angeles Times*, 11/29/86.
PAGE 280.   Half they rejected as offensive: Tony Podesta interview.
            Nearly ten thousand people: *Washington Post*, 2/3/86.
PAGE 281.   Lear found important support: Podesta interview.
PAGE 282.   Hollywood figures placed an angry advertisement: *LA Weekly*, 8/7/81.
PAGE 283.   The depth of the madness: Gere interview with Nina Easton.
PAGE 285.   Even Lew Wasserman: *LA Weekly*, 10/15/82.
            Newman . . . and Heston . . . attempted to debate: *Los Angeles Herald Examiner*, 10/30/82.
            One critic wrote: *Los Angeles Times*, 11/2/82.
PAGE 286.   Asner . . . grew up in Kansas City: *New York*, 3/15/82.
            He came . . . slowly to political activism: *Newsweek*, 3/22/82.
PAGE 288.   Saving the people . . . from the conservatives: *TV Guide*, 4/11/81.
            In an interview . . . just after: *Hollywood Reporter*, 11/25/81.
            The justified wars: Ibid.
            Marched with the striking air traffic controllers: *Los Angeles Herald Examiner*, 9/15/81.
            He envisioned SAG: *TV Guide*, 4/11/81.
PAGE 289.   A $5,000 contribution: Prindle, p. 138.
            Heston argued it was irrational: Heston interview.
            Heston immediately denounced: *Variety*, 12/21/81.
            But there was no question: Asner interview.
PAGE 290.   Asner presented a check: *Los Angeles Herald Examiner*, 2/16/82.
            Reagan weighed into the dispute: *Variety*, 2/22/82.
            Liberals fired back with an ad: *Hollywood Reporter*, 3/26/82.
            Angry conservatives picketed: *Variety*, 2/26/82.
            Like some mafia don: *Newsweek*, 3/22/82.
            A rump group: Prindle, p. 151.
PAGE 291.   Reagan's stooge: *Los Angeles Herald Examiner*, 5/18/82.
PAGE 294.   I was remembering back to 1964: Fonda interview with Craig Unger.
PAGE 296.   Judd Nelson once told: Nelson interview with Craig Unger.
PAGE 298.   Top Gun was Top Gun: Zuniga interview with Craig Unger.
PAGE 304.   To participate directly in partisan: Bonnie Reiss interview.
            Roughly half of the total: Andy Spahn interview.
PAGE 306.   We are not consensus Democrats: *Los Angeles Times*, 3/9/87.
PAGE 311.   Bergman balked on both fronts: DSCC source interview.
            The HWPC negotiated: Reiss interview.
            Turn away about thirty couples: Ibid.
            Streisand sang seventeen songs: *Los Angeles Times*, 9/8/86.
PAGE 313.   A slap in the face: *St. Louis Post-Dispatch*, 6/6/86.
            Avoiding urban areas: Woods interview.

PAGE 314. Does Tom Daschle really think: *National Journal,* 11/1/86.
I was out in California: *Washington Post,* 10/21/86.

CHAPTER NINE: GARY AND WARREN: THE LIMITS OF FREEDOM

PAGE 317. Fight well, love well: Norman Mailer, *Some Honorable Men* (Boston and Toronto: Little, Brown, 1966), p. 16.
PAGE 318. Those people are going to be tired: Mike Medavoy interview.
PAGE 319. Eventually he became: Emerson interview.
Unsolicited checks for Hart: Ibid.
PAGE 324. Whose relationship had collapsed: Caddell interview.
PAGE 325. I will solve this: Ibid.
Beatty coaxed him out: Ibid.
You've got to come into this campaign: McEvoy interview.
PAGE 326. Beatty went to sleep: Strother interview.
PAGE 327. Beatty could raise issues: Bushkin interview.
PAGE 328. A political career would entail sacrifices: Beatty interview.
PAGE 330. Beatty was often out of town: Shore, Emerson interviews.
PAGE 332. The worst thing that ever happened: *Esquire,* 3/88.
I keep hearing these stories: Patricia Medavoy interview.
PAGE 333. You will wait in the kitchen: John Davis interview.
PAGE 334. In a Mercedes that belonged to Beatty: Tom Epstein interview.
At a New Year's Day party: *Los Angeles Times,* 5/6/87.
As a guest of the Medavoys: Ibid.
PAGE 336. Beatty listened . . . with evident interest: Caddell interview.
PAGE 337. Beatty . . . had fallen asleep: Shore interview.
Beatty put down the phone: Shore, Emerson interviews.
135 acres of surrounding land: *New York Times,* 12/20/87.

CHAPTER TEN: HOLLYWOOD NOW

PAGE 345. Roughly $260 million: *Wall Street Journal,* 8/24/89.
PAGE 346. Field said, How about you?: Burkett interview.
PAGE 353. Dole collected roughly twice: *New York Times,* 10/30/87.
PAGE 356. Lear . . . raised no money: Confidential interviews, Dukakis aides.
PAGE 361. Hammond thought he had: Hammond interview.
PAGE 362. Over $2.2 million in California: Herbert E. Alexander, "Financing the Presidential Elections, 1988." Paper presented at the Institute for Political Studies in Japan, September 1989, p. 12.
PAGE 365. By the end of an election: Ibid., p. 27.
PAGE 367. Supporters of . . . Van Buren ridiculed: Jamieson, p. 9.
PAGE 368. The Carter campaign countered: Ibid., p. 413.
PAGE 370. The president simply summoned: David Marsh, *Glory Days: Bruce Springsteen in the 1980s* (New York: Pantheon Books, 1987), pp. 254–60.
PAGE 375. His aides were not able: Mason interview.

PAGE 376. Lined up three dozen country acts: "Final Report of the Celebrity Division, Bush Quayle/'88," 11/5/88.

Lynn . . . said Dukakis: *New York Times*, 9/29/88.

PAGE 377. Schwarzenegger thundered: *Los Angeles Times*, 11/4/88.

Not surprisingly, it turns out: *New York Times*, 5/1/90.

PAGE 378. A modern Gary Cooper: *Village Voice*, 1/3/89.

Dukakis thinks a naval exercise: *New York Times*, 9/6/88.

Get me out of here: Patsaouras interview.

PAGE 379. Even the film had mixed effect: Tom Kiley interview.

That idea was dropped: Sasso, Francis O'Brien interviews.

PAGE 381. In one memo to the campaign: Goldberg to Patrick Lippert, undated, fall 1988.

PAGE 382. The first time the ACLU: *New York Times*, 9/28/88.

I'm Burt Lancaster: Commercial transcript, 9/88.

PAGE 390. The impression of sincerity: Neil Postman, *Amusing Ourselves to Death: Public Discourse in the Age of Show Business* (New York: Viking, 1985), p. 102.

BIBLIOGRAPHY

Adair, Douglass. *Fame and the Founding Fathers.* New York: Norton, 1974.

Alexander, Herbert E. *Financing the 1960 Election.* Princeton, N.J.: Citizens' Research Foundation, 1962.

———. *Responsibility in Party Finance.* Princeton, N.J.: Citizens' Research Foundation, 1963.

———. *Financing the 1964 Election.* Princeton, N.J.: Citizens' Research Foundation, 1966.

———. *Financing the 1968 Election.* Lexington, Mass.: Lexington Books, 1971.

———. *Financing the 1972 Election.* Lexington, Mass.: Lexington Books, 1976.

———. *Financing the 1976 Election.* Washington, D.C.: Congressional Quarterly, 1979.

———. *Financing the 1980 Election.* Lexington, Mass.: Lexington Books, 1983.

———. "Financing the Presidential Elections, 1988." Paper presented at the Institute for Political Studies in Japan, September 1989.

———, and Brian A. Haggerty. *Financing the 1984 Election.* Lexington, Mass.: Lexington Books, 1987.

Ambrose, Stephen E. *Eisenhower: Volume One.* New York: Touchstone, 1985.

————. *Nixon: The Education of a Politician, 1913–1962.* New York: Simon and Schuster, 1987.

Bacall, Lauren. *Lauren Bacall By Myself.* New York: Knopf, 1979.

Ball, George W. *The Past Has Another Pattern: Memoirs.* New York and London: Norton, 1982.

Barnouw, Eric. *The Golden Web: A History of Broadcasting in the United States.* Vol. II, *1933–1953.* New York: Oxford University Press, 1968.

Beard, Charles A., and Mary R. Beard. *America in Midpassage.* New York: Macmillan, 1939.

Bentley, Eric, ed. *Thirty Years of Treason: Excepts from Hearings Before the House Committee on Un-American Activities.* New York: Viking, 1971.

Bishop, Jim. *FDR's Last Year.* New York: William Morrow, 1974.

Bisnow, Mark. *Diary of a Dark Horse: The 1980 Anderson Presidential Campaign.* Carbondale, Ill.: Southern Illinois University Press, 1983.

Blair, Joan, and Clay Blair Jr. *The Search for JFK.* New York: Berkley, 1976.

Blakey, G. Robert, and Richard N. Billings. *The Plot to Kill the President.* New York: Times Books, 1981.

Blum, John Morton. *V Was for Victory: Politics and American Culture during World War II.* New York and London: Harcourt Brace Jovanovich, 1976.

————. *The Price of Vision: The Diary of Henry A. Wallace, 1942–46.* Boston: Houghton Mifflin, 1973.

Blumenthal, Sidney. *Our Long National Daydream: A Political Pageant of the Reagan Era.* New York: Harper and Row, 1988.

Boyarsky, Bill. *Ronald Reagan.* New York: Random House, 1981.

Bradlee, Benjamin C. *Conversations with Kennedy.* New York: Norton, 1975.

Branch, Taylor. *Parting the Waters: America in the King Years, 1954–1963.* New York: Simon and Schuster, 1988.

Branden, Barbara. *The Passion of Ayn Rand.* Garden City, N.Y.: Anchor Books, 1987.

Braudy, Leo. *The Frenzy of Renown: Fame and Its History.* New York: Oxford University Press, 1986.

Cannon, Lou. *Ronnie and Jesse: A Political Odyssey.* Garden City, N.Y,: Doubleday, 1969.

Carlisle, Rodney P. *Hearst and the New Deal: The Progressive as Reactionary.* New York and London: Garland Publishing, 1979.

Carroll, Peter N. *Famous in America: The Passion to Succeed.* New York: Dutton, 1985.

Caute, David. *The Great Fear: The Anti-Communist Purge under Truman and Eisenhower.* New York: Simon and Schuster, 1978.

Ceplair, Larry, and Steven Englund. *The Inquisition in Hollywood: Politics in the Film Community 1930–1960.* Berkeley: University of California Press, 1983.

Christensen, Terry. *Reel Politics: American Political Movies from Birth of a Nation to Platoon.* New York: Basil Blackwell, 1987.

Clurman, Harold. *The Fervent Years: The Story of the Group Theater and the*

Thirties. New York: Harcourt Brace Jovanovich, 1975.

Cogley, John. *Report on Blacklisting.* Vol. 1, *Movies.* New York: Fund for the Republic, 1956.

Cole, Lester. *Hollywood Red.* Palo Alto, Calif.: Ramparts Press, 1981.

Collier, Peter, and David Horowitz. *The Kennedys: An American Drama.* New York: Warner Books, 1984.

Committee on Un-American Activities, House of Representatives. *Citations by Official Government Agencies of Organizations and Publications Found to Be Communist or Communist Fronts.* Washington, D.C.: 1948.

Conant, Michael. *Antitrust in the Motion Picture Industry.* Berkeley: University of California Press, 1966.

Craven, Wesley Frank. *The Legend of the Founding Fathers.* New York: New York University Press, 1956.

Crowther, Bosley. *Hollywood Rajah: The Life and Times of Louis B. Mayer.* New York: Holt, Rinehart and Winston, 1960.

————. *The Lion's Share: The Story of an Entertainment Empire.* New York: Dutton, 1957.

Douglas, Helen Gahagan. *A Full Life.* Garden City, N.Y.: Doubleday, 1982.

Douglas, Kirk. *The Ragman's Son.* New York: Simon and Schuster, 1988.

Douglas, Melvyn, and Tom Arthur. *See You at the Movies: The Autobiography of Melvyn Douglas.* Lanham, Md.: University Press of America, 1986.

Dunne, Philip. *Take Two: A Life in Movies and Politics.* New York: McGraw-Hill, 1980.

Edwards, Anne. *Early Reagan.* New York: William Morrow, 1987.

Erickson, Paul D. *Reagan Speaks: The Making of an American Myth.* New York and London: New York University Press, 1985.

Ewen, Stuart. *All Consuming Images.* New York: Basic Books, 1988.

Exner, Judith, with Ovid Demaris. *My Story.* New York: Grove Press, 1977.

Fairbanks, Douglas, Jr., *The Salad Days.* Garden City, N.Y.: Doubleday, 1988.

Freedland, Michael. *The Warner Brothers.* New York: St. Martin's Press, 1983.

Freidel, Frank. *Franklin D. Roosevelt: The Ordeal.* Boston: Little, Brown, 1954.

————. *Franklin D. Roosevelt: Launching the New Deal.* Boston: Little, Brown, 1973.

Friedrich, Otto. *City of Nets: A Portrait of Hollywood in the 1940s.* New York: Harper and Row, 1986.

Gabler, Neal. *An Empire of Their Own: How the Jews Invented Hollywood.* New York: Crown, 1988.

Gage, Nicholas. *The Mafia Is Not an Equal Opportunity Employer.* New York: McGraw-Hill, 1971.

Geist, Kenneth L. *Pictures Will Talk: The Life and Films of Joseph L. Mankiewicz.* New York: Scribner, 1978.

Gentile, Thomas. *March on Washington: August 28, 1963.* Washington, D.C.: New Day Publications, 1983.

Germond, Jack, and Jules Witcover. *Wake Us When It's Over: Presidential Politics of 1984.* New York: Macmillan, 1985.

Goodman, Walter. *The Committee: The Extraordinary Career of the House Committee on Un-American Activities.* New York: Farrar, Straus, 1968.

Goodwin, Doris Kearns. *The Fitzgeralds and the Kennedys: An American Saga.* New York: Simon and Schuster, 1987.

Gussow, Mel. *Darryl F. Zanuck: Don't Say Yes Until I Finish Talking.* New York: Da Capo Press, 1980.

Halberstam, David. *The Powers That Be.* New York: Knopf, 1979.

Hamby, Alonzo L. *Beyond the New Deal: Harry S. Truman and American Liberalism.* New York and London: Columbia University Press, 1973.

Hayden, Tom. *Reunion: A Memoir.* New York: Random House, 1988.

Heard, Alexander. *The Costs of Democracy.* Chapel Hill: University of North Carolina Press, 1960.

Hellman, Lillian. *Scoundrel Time.* Boston and Toronto: Little, Brown, 1976.

Hopper, Hedda, and James Brough. *The Whole Truth and Nothing But.* Garden City, N.Y.: Doubleday, 1963.

Houseman, John. *Front and Center.* New York: Touchstone, 1979.

Howe, Irving, and Lewis Coser. *The American Communist Party: A Critical History, 1919–1957.* Boston: Beacon Press, 1957.

Isserman, Maurice. *Which Side Were You On?* Middletown, Conn.: Wesleyan University Press, 1982.

Jamieson, Kathleen Hall. *Packaging the Presidency: A History and Criticism of Presidential Campaign Advertising.* New York: Oxford University Press, 1984.

Johnson, Lyndon B. *The Vantage Point: Perspectives of the Presidency.* New York: Holt, Rinehart and Winston, 1971.

Kahn, E.J., Jr. *The Voice: The Story of an American Phenomenon.* New York and London: Harper and Brothers, 1947.

Kahn, Gordon. *Hollywood on Trial: The Story of the Ten Who Were Indicted.* New York: Boni and Gaer, 1948.

Kanfer, Stefan. *A Journal of the Plague Years.* New York: Atheneum, 1973.

Kelley, Kitty. *His Way.* New York and Toronto: Bantam Books, 1987.
———. *Jackie Oh!* Secaucus, N.J.: Lyle Stuart, 1978.

Kempton, Murray. *Part of Our Time.* New York: Simon and Schuster, 1955.

Keyes, Evelyn. *Scarlett O'Hara's Younger Sister.* Secaucus, N.J.: Lyle Stuart, 1977.

Kiernan, Thomas. *Jane Fonda: Heroine for Our Time.* New York: Delilah Books, 1982.

Klapp, Orrin E. *Symbolic Leaders: Public Dramas and Public Men.* Chicago: Aldine, 1964.

Kotkin, Joel, and Paul Grabowicz. *California Inc.* New York: Rawson, Wade, 1982.

Lardner, James. *Fast Forward: Hollywood, the Japanese, and the Onslaught of the VCR.* New York: Norton, 1987.

Leaming, Barbara. *Orson Welles: A Biography.* New York: Penguin Books, 1986.

Leigh, Janet. *There Really Was a Hollywood.* Garden City, N.Y.: Doubleday, 1964.

Levy, Emanuel. *John Wayne: Prophet of the American Way of Life.* London: Scarecrow Press, 1988.

Lewis, Howard T. *The Motion Picture Industry.* New York: Van Nostrand, 1933.

Lingeman, Richard R. *Don't You Know There's a War On? The American Home Front, 1941–1945.* New York: Perigee Books, 1980.

Loy, Myrna, and James Kotsilibas-Davis. *Myrna Loy: Being and Becoming.* New York: Donald I. Fine, 1988.

Mailer, Norman. *Some Honorable Men.* Boston and Toronto: Little, Brown, 1966.

Marquis, Alice Goldfarb. *Hopes and Ashes: The Birth of Modern Times.* New York: Free Press, 1986.

Marsh, David. *Glory Days: Bruce Springsteen in the 1980s.* New York: Pantheon Books, 1987.

Martin, John Bartlow. *Adlai Stevenson of Illinois: The Life of Adlai E. Stevenson.* Garden City, N.Y.: Doubleday, 1976.

Marx, Arthur. *Goldwyn: A Biography of the Man Behind the Myth.* New York: Norton, 1976.

Marx, Samuel. *Mayer and Thalberg: The Make-Believe Saints.* New York: Random House, 1975.

Mayer, Martin. *Madison Avenue: U.S.A.* New York: Harper and Brothers, 1958.

McCarthy, Eugene J. *The Year of the People.* Garden City, N.Y.: Doubleday, 1969.

McWilliams, Carey. *Southern California: An Island on the Land.* Salt Lake City: Peregrine Smith Books, 1983.

Meade, Marion. *Dorothy Parker: What Fresh Hell Is This?* New York: Villard Books, 1988.

Mencken, H. L. *Making a President.* New York: Knopf, 1932.

Messick, Hank. *The Beauties and the Beasts: The Mob in Show Business.* New York: David McKay, 1973.

Michener, James A. *Report of the County Chairman.* New York: Random House, 1961.

Mills, C. Wright. *The Power Elite.* New York: Oxford University Press, 1956.

Moldea, Dan E. *Dark Victory: Ronald Reagan, MCA, and the Mob.* New York: Viking, 1986.

Murphy, George, with Victor Lasky. *Say . . . Didn't You Used to Be George Murphy?* New York: Bartholomew House, 1970.

Navasky, Victor S. *Kennedy Justice.* New York: Atheneum, 1977.

———. *Naming Names.* New York: Penguin Books, 1981.

Neal, Steve. *Dark Horse: A Biography of Wendell Willkie*. Garden City, N.Y.: Doubleday, 1984.

O'Brien, Lawrence F. *No Final Victories*. Garden City, N.Y.: Doubleday, 1974.

O'Donnell, Kenneth P., and David F. Powers with Joe McCarthy. *Johnny, We Hardly Knew Ye*. Boston and Toronto: Little, Brown, 1970.

O'Neill, William L. *A Better World: The Great Schism: Stalinism and the American Intellectuals*. New York: Touchstone, 1982.

Parmet, Herbert S. *JFK: The Presidency of John F. Kennedy*. New York: Dial Press, 1983.

Pells, Richard H. *The Liberal Mind in a Conservative Age: American Intellectuals in the 1940s and 1950s*. New York: Harper and Row, 1985.

————. *Radical Visions and American Dreams: Culture and Social Thought in the Depression Years*. Middletown, Conn.: Wesleyan University Press, 1984.

Perkins, Frances. *The Roosevelt I Knew*. New York: Viking, 1946.

Petersen, William (ed.). *American Social Patterns*. Garden City, N.Y.: Doubleday, 1956.

Poitier, Sidney. *This Life*. New York: Knopf, 1980.

Postman, Neil. *Amusing Ourselves to Death: Public Discourse in the Age of Show Business*. New York: Viking, 1985.

Powdermaker, Hortense. *Hollywood: The Dream Factory*. Boston: Little, Brown, 1951.

Powers, Richard Gid. *Secrecy and Power: The Life of J. Edgar Hoover*. New York: Free Press, 1987.

Prindle, David F. *The Politics of Glamour: Ideology and Democracy in the Screen Actors Guild*. Madison: University of Wisconsin Press, 1988.

Pye, Michael. *Moguls: Inside the Business of Show Business*. New York: Holt, Rinehart and Winston, 1980.

Ramsaye, Terry (ed.). *International Motion Picture Almanac, 1949–50*. New York: Quigley Publications, 1949.

Reagan, Ronald, with Richard G. Hubler. *Where's the Rest of Me?* New York: Duell, Sloan and Pearce, 1965.

Rhode, Eric. *A History of the Cinema: From Its Origins to 1970*. New York: Da Capo Press, 1976.

Rivkin, Allen, and Laura Kerr. *Hello Hollywood*. Garden City, N.Y.: Doubleday, 1962.

Robinson, David. *Chaplin: His Life and Art*. New York: McGraw-Hill, 1985.

Roosevelt, James, with Bill Libby. *My Parents*. Chicago: Playboy Press, 1976.

Rosten, Leo C. *Hollywood: The Movie Colony, the Movie Makers*. New York: Harcourt, Brace, 1941.

Sayre, Nora. *Running Time: Films of the Cold War*. New York: Dial Press, 1982.

Schary, Dore. *Heyday: An Autobiography*. Boston: Little, Brown, 1979.

Schickel, Richard. *Intimate Strangers: The Culture of Celebrity*. Garden City, N.Y.: Doubleday, 1985.

―――. *D. W. Griffith: An American Life.* New York: Simon and Schuster, 1984.

Schlesinger, Arthur M., Jr. *The Coming of the New Deal.* Boston: Houghton Mifflin, 1959.

―――. *Robert Kennedy and His Times.* New York: Ballantine Books, 1978.

Schutz, John A., and Douglass Adair, eds.. *The Spur of Fame: Dialogues of John Adams and Benjamin Rush, 1805–1813.* San Marino, Calif.: Huntington Library, 1966.

Schwartz, Nancy Lynn. *The Hollywood Writers' War.* New York: Knopf, 1982.

Selznick, Irene Mayer. *A Private View.* New York: Knopf, 1983.

Shannon, David A. *The Decline of American Communism: A History of the Communist Party of the United States since 1945.* New York: Harcourt Brace Jovanovich, 1959.

Shaw, Arnold. *Belafonte.* Philadelphia and New York: Chilton, 1960.

Sinclair, Upton. *Upton Sinclair Presents William Fox.* New York: Arno Press, 1970.

Smith, Richard Norton. *An Uncommon Man: The Triumph of Herbert Hoover.* New York: Simon and Schuster, 1984.

―――. *Thomas E. Dewey and His Times.* New York: Touchstone, 1984.

Sorensen, Theodore C. *Kennedy.* New York: Harper and Row, 1965.

Steele, Richard W. *Propaganda in an Open Society: The Roosevelt Administration and the Media, 1933–1941.* Westport, Conn.: Greenwood Press, 1985.

Stewart, Donald Ogden. *By a Stroke of Luck! An Autobiography.* New York and London: Paddington Press, 1975.

Summers, Anthony. *Goddess: The Secret Lives of Marilyn Monroe.* New York: Macmillan, 1985.

Swanberg, W. A. *Citizen Hearst.* New York: Scribner, 1961.

Taylor, John Russell. *Strangers in Paradise: The Hollywood Emigrés, 1933–1950.* New York: Holt, Rinehart and Winston, 1983.

Thomas, Bob. *King Cohn: The Life and Times of Harry Cohn.* London: Barrie and Rockliff, 1967.

―――. *Marlon: Portrait of the Rebel as an Artist.* New York: Random House, 1973.

Thomas, Hugh. *Armed Truce: The Beginnings of the Cold War, 1945–1946.* New York: Atheneum, 1987.

Thorp, Margaret Farrand. *America at the Movies.* New Haven, Conn.: Yale University Press, 1939.

Tully, Grace. *FDR: My Boss.* New York: Scribner, 1949.

United Nations Association of the United States. *Robert S. Benjamin: A Citizen's Citizen.* New York: United Nations Association, 1980.

Valenti, Jack. *A Very Human President.* New York: Norton, 1975.

Viertel, Salka. *The Kindness of Strangers.* New York: Holt, Rinehart and Winston, 1969.

Walton, Richard J. *Henry Wallace, Harry Truman, and the Cold War.* New York: Viking, 1976.

Warner, Jack, with Dean Jennings. *My First Hundred Years in Hollywood.* New York: Random House, 1964.

Wecter, Dixon. *The Hero in America: A Chronicle of Hero Worship.* New York: Scribner, 1941.

White, Theodore H. *The Making of the President, 1968.* New York: Atheneum, 1969.

————. *The Making of the President, 1972.* New York: Atheneum, 1973.

Wills, Garry. *Reagan's America: Innocents at Home.* Garden City, N.Y.: Doubleday, 1987.

Wilson, Edmund. *The Thirties.* New York: Farrar, Straus, 1980.

Winkler, John K. *William Randolph Hearst: A New Appraisal.* New York: Hastings House, 1955.

Wofford, Harris. *Of Kennedys and Kings: Making Sense of the Sixties.* New York: Farrar, Straus, 1980.

Wright, William. *Lillian Hellman: The Image, The Woman.* New York: Ballantine Books, 1986.

Zanuck, Darryl. *Tunis Expedition.* New York: Random House, 1943.

Zheutlin, Barbara, and David Talbot. *Creative Differences: Profiles of Hollywood Dissidents.* Boston: South End Press, 1978.

Zierold, Norman. *The Moguls.* New York: Avon Books, 1969.

INDEX